GENERATIVE PERSPECTIVES ON LANGUAGE ACQUISITION

LANGUAGE ACQUISITION & LANGUAGE DISORDERS

EDITORS

Harald Clahsen
University of Essex

William Rutherford
University of Southern California

Volume 14

Harald Clahsen (ed.)

Generative Perspectives on Language Acquisition
Empirical findings, theoretical considerations and crosslinguistic comparisons

GENERATIVE PERSPECTIVES ON LANGUAGE ACQUISITION

EMPIRICAL FINDINGS,
THEORETICAL CONSIDERATIONS AND
CROSSLINGUISTIC COMPARISONS

Edited by

HARALD CLAHSEN

JOHN BENJAMINS PUBLISHING COMPANY
AMSTERDAM/PHILADELPHIA

1896

TM The paper used in this publication meets the minimum requirements of American National Standard for Information Sciences — Permanence of Paper for Printed Library Materials, ANSI Z39.48-1984.

Library of Congress Cataloging-in-Publication Data

Generative perspectives on language acquisition : empirical findings, theoretical considerations, and cross-linguistic comparisons / edited by Harald Clahsen.
  p.   cm. -- (Language acquisition & language disorders : ISSN 0925-0123; v. 14)
  Chiefly based on papers presented at a workshop held Mar. 18-20, 1994, University of Essex.
  Includes bibliographical references and index.
  Contents: The optional-infinitive stage in child English / Tony Harris & Ken Wexler -- Towards a structure-building model of acquisition / Andrew Radford -- The underspecification of functional categories in early grammar / Nina Hyams -- Lexical learning in early syntactic development / Harald Clahsen, Sonja Eisenbeiss & Martina Penke -- Strong continuity, parameter setting, and the trigger hierarchy : on the acquisition of the DP in Bernese Swiss German and High German / Zvi Penner & Jürgen Weissenborn -- Subject-verb and object-verb agreement in early Basque / Jürgen M. Meisel & Maria-Jose Ezeizabarrena -- Acquisition of Italian interrogatives / Maria Teresa Guasti -- Root infinitives, clitics, and truncated structures / Liliane Haegeman -- On the acquisition of subject and object clitics in French / Cornelia Hamann, Luigi Rizzi & Uli H. Frauenfelder -- Clitics in L2 French / Lydia White -- The initial hypothesis of syntax : a minimalist perspective on language acquisition and attrition / Christer Platzack -- The role of merger theory and formal features in acquisition / Thomas Roeper -- Now, hang on a minute : some reflections on emerging orthodoxies / Martin Atkinson.
  1. Language acquisition--Congresses. 2. Generative grammar--Congresses. I. Clahsen, Harald. II. Series.
  P118.G36   1996
  401'.93--dc20   96-22417
  ISBN 90 272 2480 3 (Eur.) / 1-55619-777-2 (US) (alk. paper)   CIP

John Benjamins Publishing Co. • P.O.Box 75577 • 1070 AN Amsterdam • The Netherlands
John Benjamins North America • P.O.Box 27519 • Philadelphia PA 19118-0519 • USA

Contents

Tables and Figures

Tables

Abbreviations

Object language is italicized throughout, with a translation in English following in single quotation marks. Additionaly, italics are used for emphasis. Parts of examples may be highlighted by underscoring.

An overscore must be read as negating the overscored (e.g., A vs. $\overline{A}$), whereas a prime indicates a projection level (e.g., X'). The word *case* begins with capital C when it refers to grammatical Case.

Technical terms are set in small capitals. Grammatical categories are printed in full capitals, usually abbreviated; features are represented between angled brackets. Indications of children's ages have the format (years;months.days).

Abbreviations

θ	theta (= thematic)	HMC	head movement constraint
Φ	phi (= person, number, and gender features)	IHS	initial hypothesis of syntax
		I(NFL)	inflection
ADJ	adjunct	IO	indirect object
ADV	adverb	L1	first language (acquisition)
AGR	agreement	L2	second language (acquisition)
ASL	American Sign Language	LF	logical form
AUX	auxiliary	LLH	lexical learning hypothesis
C(OMP)	complementizer	MLP	minimal lexical projection
D(ET)	determiner	MLU	mean length utterance
DO	direct object	MMC	Mad Magazine clause
ECP	empty category principle	MPP	minimal projection principle
FCH	full clause hypothesis	N	noun
FP	functional projection	nc	null constant

NEG	negation	UBH	universal base hypothesis
NUM	number	UG	universal grammar
PF	phonological form	V	verb
SCH	small clause hypothesis	V2	verb second
Spec	specifier	XP	X phrase (X=N, V, A, D, etc.)
t	trace		

Abbreviations used in interlinear glosses

A, ABS	absolutive	INF	infinitive
ACC	accusative	INTR	intransitive
ADV	adverb	MASC	masculine
AFF	affirmative	NEUT	neuter
CL	clitic	NEG	negation
COMP	complementizer	OBJ	object
DAT, Ø	dative	OBL	oblique
DO	direct object	PERF	perfective
E, ERG	ergative	PL	plural
FEM	feminine	PRES	present
fiN	finite	Q	question
FUT	future	SUBJ	subject
GEN	genitive	SG	singular
IO	indirect object	TRANS	transitive
IMPERF	imperfective		

Contributors

Martin Atkinson
Department of Language & Linguistics
University of Essex
Colchester CO4 3SQ, UK
matkin@essex.ac.uk

Harald Clahsen
Department of Language & Linguistics
University of Essex
Colchester CO4 3SQ, UK
harald@essex.ac.uk

Sonja Eisenbeiss
Department of Linguistics
University of Düsseldorf
40225 Düsseldorf, Germany
eisenbei@ling.sapir.uni-duesseldorf.de

Maria-Jose Ezeizabarrena
Department of Romance Languages
University of Hamburg
Von-Melle-Park 6
20146 Hamburg, Germany

Uli Frauenfelder
Laboratory of Experimental Psycholinguistics
University of Geneva
1211 Geneva, Switzerland

Maria Teresa Guasti
Department of Cognitive Science
San Raffaele Hospital
via Olgettina 581
20134 Milano, Italy
guastim@dibit.hsr.it

Liliane Haegeman
Department of English
University of Geneva
22 Boulevard des Philosophes
1205 Geneva, Switzerland
haegeman@uni2a.unige.ch

Cornelia Hamann
Department of General Linguistics
University of Geneva
22 Boulevard des Philosophes
1205 Geneva, Switzerland
hamann@uni2a.unige.ch

Toni Harris
Department of Brain & Cognitive Sciences
Massachusetts Institute of Technology, E10-020
Cambridge, MA 02139, USA
harris@psyche.mit.edu

Andrew Radford
Department of Language & Linguistic
University of Essex
Colchester CO4 3SQ, UK
radford@essex.ac.uk

Nina Hyams
Department of Linguistics
University of California, Los Angeles
Los Angeles, CA 90024, USA
iyg2nmh@mvs.oac.ucla.edu

Luigi Rizzi
Department of General Linguistics
University of Geneva
22 Boulevard des Philosophes
1205 Geneva, Switzerland
rizzi@uni2a.unige.ch

Jürgen Meisel
Department of Romance Languages
University of Hamburg
Von-Melle-Park 6
20146 Hamburg, Germany
jmm@rrz.uni-hamburg.de

Tom Roeper
Department of Linguistics
University of Massachusetts
Amherst, MA 01003, USA
roeper@cs.umass.edu

Martina Penke
Department of Linguistics
University of Düsseldorf
40225 Düsseldorf, Germany
penke@ling.sapir.uni-duesseldorf.de

Jürgen Weissenborn
Department of Linguistics
University of Potsdam
Gutenbergstr.67
14415 Potsdam, Germany
weissenb@rz.uni-potsdam.de

Zvika Penner
Department of Linguistics
University of Berne
Gesellschaftsstr. 6
3012 Bern, Switzerland
penner@isw.unibe.ch

Ken Wexler
Department of Brain & Cognitive Scie
Massachusetts Institute of Technology, E1(
Cambridge, MA 02139, USA
wexler@psyche.mit.edu

Christer Platzack
Department of Scandinavian Linguistics
Lund University
Helgonabacken 14
223 62 Lund, Sweden
platzack@nordlund.lu.se

Lydia White
Department of Linguistics
McGill University
1001 Sherbrooke Street West
Montreal, QUE H3A 1G5, Canada
lwhite@langs.lan.mcgill.ca

Introduction

Harald Clahsen

University of Essex

Twenty years ago, the field of language acquisition research appeared to be relatively clearly demarcated and easy to access. Simplifying somewhat, we might say that researchers could, typically, be assigned to one of the following three schools of thought. One group, the so-called nativists, believed in a strong innate component for language acquisition. The second group — known as interactionists — focused on the role of caretaker-child communication for acquiring language, while the third group, the cognitivists, believed that language acquisition is driven by the same mechanisms as a person's general cognitive development.

Today, however, it is far from clear whether there still exists a field called "language acquisition" like before. The specialization of research questions and topics of empirical investigation has gone so far that we can now identify several subdisciplines of what used to be called the field of language acquisition research. Within each subdiscipline, new and highly specific controversial issues have arisen, competing theoretical approaches are being discussed, and each area has its own conferences, workshops, etc. Consider, for instance, one of the major international get-togethers for language acquisition researchers, the annual Boston University Conference on Language Development. During the last few years, there have been separate sections for "syntax & linguistic theory" and "morphology & words" (to take only two of a number of subdisciplines that have emerged over the last years.) The participants in these two sections of the BU conference are virtually in complementary distribution. That is, in the morphology section, you will typically find yourself surrounded by psychologists, whereas in the syntax section you are likely to be sitting among a group of theoretical linguists — but not *vice versa*. The methods of investigation that are typically used within each group are different: whereas experiments with children and computer simulations are used in morphology research, the analysis of speech corpora is the predominant method in studies on the acquisition of syntax. The issues, too, are different, even though they may not necessarily be specific to either syntax or morphology, such as the connectionist-vs.-symbolist debate in morphology, or notions like "parameter setting" and "continuity" in syntax. Note that these issues are equally pertinent to the acquisition of sentence structure and the acquisition of word structure, but for some reason a somewhat arbitrary division of issues has taken place. What happens at the BU conference is, I think, indicative of a general trend towards greater specialization in language acquisition studies. Casual inspection of some major scientific journals would also corroborate this picture. Just count the number of papers on morphology that appeared in the journal "Language Acquisition" and compare it with the number of syntax acquisition papers in "Cognition" — you will find that both figures are close to zero! The reason for this is obvious: whereas "Language Acquisition" seems to have specialized in syntax, "Cognition" seems to prefer papers on the acquisition of morphology. Some acquisition researchers are rather worried about the splitting up of what used to be the field of language acquisition into several more or less autonomous subdisciplines. To prevent the field from disintegrating even further, conferences and workshops are organized at which participants are invited to "cross boundaries", and organizers strive to provide acquisition researchers with a "unified account", or an "integrated perspective" on language acquisition. In my experience, these attempts usually remain quite fruitless, and they have certainly not helped the field to become more coherent, or led to greater integration.

One might indeed regret the fact that it is increasingly difficult to oversee the various subdisciplines of language acquisition research. However, disintegration of the field is only one part of the story. The other part is quite the opposite, namely the integration of previously unconnected, or only loosely connected, fields of research. Consider, for example, the study of the acquisition of syntax. Some years ago, an experienced and highly respected colleague warned me to be cautious whenever theoretical syntacticians tampered with language acquisition issues. "They only use your findings if they suit their theories", he told me, "and they won't get their fingers dirty by analyzing or even quantifying language acquisition data." However, all this has now changed, and the collection of papers in the present volume provides a clear testimony of this change. Syntacticians now analyze and sometimes even quantify child language data, and they use this kind of evidence along with the traditional adult data to test their theories. Acquisition researchers, in turn, use insights from syntactic theory to make sense of their data. The days when at acquisition conferences, syntacticians would contribute by telling you amusing anecdotes about their own children seem to be over. In short, the subdiscipline of syntax acquisition research has developed closer links with theoretical linguistics, and this has led to greater integration of previously separate fields of research. For some reason, syntax acquisition research seems to be the driving force here. Other subdisciplines, such as the acquisition of morphology, have not yet developed similarly close links to theoretical linguistics.

The major aim of this book is to enhance the existing but still somewhat fragile links between language acquisition research and theoretical linguistics. With regard to previous research, this seems to be a most promising avenue for the study of syntax, and this is why the book focusses on the acquisition of syntax and on syntactic theory, specifically on Chomskyan Generative Grammar.

The theme of this book is generative perspectives on language acquisition, and this notion covers some of the basic assumptions and research questions shared by the authors of this volume. Let me just focus here on two basic characteristics of the generative research program in language acquisition; more comprehensive accounts can be found, e.g., in Goodluck (1991) and Atkinson (1992). The first one is that the child is seen as the major protagonist in language acquisition, and that the acquisition of language structure is explicable in terms of mechanisms inherent to the child. Though no generative acquisition researcher would seriously question the fact that children learn something from their parents' speech, they still maintain that children end up knowing more about language structure than was contained within the information they found in the environment. One example would be the ability to reject ungrammatical sentences for which direct information was not available from the input. This view contrasts with a popular line of thought — represented for example in the works of C. Snow, M. Halliday and their collaborators — according to which language acquisition is seen as an interactive process in which caretakers and children mutually accommodate. Generative acquisition researchers make the specific assumption that children do not have access to information about which strings of words are ungrammatical, i.e., to what is called negative evidence about the particular language they are acquiring. There are several reasons why this might be a plausible assumption. First, children cannot always trust their parents: even if parents sometimes correct their children's ungrammatical sentences, children do not receive feedback from their parents for all the ungrammatical sentences they produce. Second, caretakers differ in terms of the kinds of feedback they provide: yet their children are similar in what they acquire about the structure of a particular language. Third, parents' corrections are not uniquely marked as corrections; it is therefore hard for the child to know what to count as a correction (cf. Marcus 1993 for more arguments and some empirical findings on this). The conclusion that generative acquisition researchers, including the ones represented in this book, have drawn is that children's development of language structure should be accounted for without relying on specific environmental requirements such as negative evidence, or specific features of caretaker behavior.

The second characteristic of the generative research program in language acquisition is the claim that with respect to knowledge of language structure, young children and their parents are not so different as one might think. This means that even though two-year olds talk differently from their parents, the system underlying their knowledge of language structure is said to be basically the same as that of their parents. Two-year olds and their parents are both claimed to represent their knowledge of language in the form of grammars, and the architecture as well as the categories and contents of these grammars are largely identical. This view contrasts with other approaches to language acquisition in which developmental mechanisms are postulated that hold for children but not for adults, or for specific well-defined developmental stages but not for the steady final state of language acquisition (cf. for example Slobin's 1985 operating principles or some of Clark 's (1993) principles of lexical development). Generative acquisition researchers strive to do without such developmental principles; instead, many subscribe to what Pinker (1984) called the continuity assumption, which states that the child's learning device does not change over time and does not generate developmental patterns that are impossible in the adult language; cf., however, Atkinson (this volume) for an opposing view. The continuity assumption provides an external constraint, or guideline, for analyses of child language: all the sentences children use throughout all stages should be analyzed in terms of the same constraints that are assumed for the adult grammar, i.e., in terms of a limited set of X-bar principles and other elements of UG. Advocates of continuity would want to avoid positing specific principles or properties that hold for child but not for adult language and assuming radical changes in the child's learning device, unless they are forced to do so by empirical evidence.

The continuity assumption might be useful as a guideline for analyzing child language data, but it does not solve the developmental problem of language acquisition. Clearly, the speech of young children is different from that of adults, some constructions develop earlier than others, and there are identifiable developmental sequences in the acquisition of language structure which hold across different individuals, some even across different languages. How can we explain development if the learning device is assumed not to change over time? The answers to this question are controversial among generative acquisition researchers. Here are three popular scenarios:

Full competence plus external developments
The first approach claims that young children when they begin to produce sentences already have full grammatical competence of the particular language they are exposed to, and that differences between sentences children produce and adults' sentences should be attributed to external factors, i.e. to developments in domains other than grammatical competence. Consider, as an illustration, Weissenborn's (1992) analysis of early null subjects. According to Weissenborn, young children leave out many subjects that are required in the adult language because they have not yet acquired the appropriate pragmatic constraints that hold for null versus overt subjects in the adult language. The grammatical constraints and parameter settings, however, are said to be the same for child and adult language. Thus, the child's grammatical knowledge is identical to that of adults, but the sentences children use differ from those of their parents due to developmental delays in other domains. In the present book, the paper by Hyams represents this view most clearly.

Full competence plus maturation
The second approach assumes that UG principles and most of the grammatical categories are operative when the child starts to produce sentences. Differences between the sentences of young children and those of adults are explained in terms of maturation. The claim is made that there are UG-external learning constraints which restrict the availability of grammatical categories to the child up to a certain stage and are then successively lost due to maturation. Consider, for example, Wexler (1994) who argued that the feature TENSE matures at around the age of 2;5, and Rizzi (1993) who suggested that the constraint which requires all root clauses to be headed by CP in adult language is not yet operative in young children, but that it matures at the age of approximately 2;5. With these maturational hypotheses, Wexler and Rizzi tried to derive a set of observed differences between children's and adults' sentences from a single source. The maturation hypothesis is represented in several contributions to the present book. Rizzi's account is adopted in the study by Haegeman. A matura-

tional hypothesis is also assumed by Harris & Wexler. The theoretical issues involved are explicitly discussed in Atkinson.

Gradual structure-building plus lexical learning
The third approach shares with the two other views the assumption that all UG principles are available to the child from the onset of acquisition. However, the grammar of the particular language the child is acquiring is claimed to develop gradually, through the interaction of available abstract knowledge, e.g. about X-bar principles, and the child's learning of the lexicon. This view does not violate the continuity assumption as the child's learning device does not change over time. Rather, grammatical development under this view results from an increase in the child's lexicon, i.e., in the set of lexical and morphological items which the child has acquired. Three studies in the present book argue in favour of this approach: Radford, Meisel & Ezeizabarrena and Clahsen, Eisenbeiss & Penke.

All the papers in the present book consider child language development, and the focus is on monolingual children; only the paper by White explicitly addresses issues of bilingual language acquisition. The volume attempts to provide a cross-linguistic perspective on the issues under consideration. Chapters 1 to 10 present new evidence from the acquisition of six different languages (in order of appearance): English, German, Basque, Italian, Dutch, and French. Chapters 11 and 12 (Platzack, Roeper) are mainly theoretical contributions which rely on existing evidence, (in Platzack's paper taken from Swedish and in Roeper's from different Germanic languages). The final chapter (Atkinson) provides an overall commentary focussing on the issue of continuity in grammatical development.

Child English
Harris & Wexler argue, on the basis of spontaneous speech data and an elicited production experiment, that English-speaking children go through a stage at which the finite inflection on verbs, in particular the third person singular present tense, is optionally used. They also found that in negative sentences, *do*-support is optional, and that in sentences without *do* the main verb is likely not to be marked for TENSE, i.e., sentences such as *he not goes* are extremely rare. In previous work, Wexler (1994) argued that children acquiring French, German, Dutch, and Mainland Scandinavian go through a stage at which both finite and nonfinite verbs appear in the root clause, but in different word orders: finite verbs raise to some higher functional projection and non-finite verbs do

not raise. Wexler explained this pattern in terms of maturation: the TENSE projection has not yet become obligatory in every root representation, and thus infinitival verbs are possible in such circumstances. The purpose of the present paper is to demonstrate that English-speaking children also go through the optional infinitive stage.

Radford suggests a three-stage VP > IP > CP model in which functional architecture is gradually created through lexical learning or, to use his term, minimal lexical projection: the acquisition of a new type of lexical or morphological item will lead to the projection of a new phrase. Like Harris & Wexler, Radford postulates a stage of early English at which functional categories such as IP are optionally projected, but in contrast to Harris & Wexler, Radford argues that this is preceded by a stage at which the child's grammar does not generate any kind of functional categories, but only lexical projections. This is an extension of the small clause hypothesis Radford originally proposed in his (1990) book. In the present paper, he provides an analysis of Case marking of subjects as well as of early negative and interrogative sentences in the small-clause stage, and he argues that the small clause stage seems to exist in the acquisition of languages other than English (Mauritian Creole, Spanish, Welsh).

Hyams offers a new treatment of null subjects in early English, and she reports some new findings on the development of DPs in child Dutch. She proposes to maintain the full competence hypothesis of syntactic development, and to explain child/adult differences in terms of an underdeveloped pragmatic component. Specifically, the claim is made that young children do not have a pragmatic principle of Tense/Definiteness interpretation (= Rule T, by analogy with Rule I of Reinhart 1983) which would force them not to use infinitives in contexts in which adults would use finite (i.e. tense-marked) verbs and which would disallow indeterminate NPs in contexts in which adults would use definite NPs. Instead, as long as the pragmatic principle has not been acquired, children's grammars are said to generate underspecified inflectional categories, such as INFL without tense features and Det without definiteness features. In this way, she accounts for the major characteristics of early root infinitives and early DPs.

Child German
Clahsen, Eisenbeiss & Penke investigate phrase-structure development in terms of the lexical learning hypothesis and the notion of underspecification. Three theoretical claims are made and tested on longitudinal data from five monolingual children. First, early child grammars may generate underspecified phrase-

structure positions, i.e. positions with fewer features or feature specifications than the corresponding positions in the adult grammar. This accounts for subtle differences between child and adult German with respect to verb placement. Second, new features and feature specifications are added to existing syntactic positions as a result of the child's learning of lexical and morphological items. This explains developmental correlations between lexical acquisitions, e.g. inflectional paradigms, and syntactic properties, e.g. verb and subject raising. Third, functional categories gradually emerge based on X-bar Theory and lexical/morphological evidence from the input. This accounts for developmental dissociations in the creation of functional categories.

Penner & Weissenborn argue that there is evidence for a complete DP structure in German from the very first stages of acquisition. This evidence, they argue, supports the full competence (= strong continuity) assumption. They present a detailed analysis of the subtle differences in the DP-system of adults between Standard German and Bernese Swiss German and argue that differences in the order of acquisition of these systems can be explained by assuming that some kinds of input data are more easily accessible to children than others. Specifically they claim that syntactic parameters which involve a root/non-root distinction can be set relatively early, because the input data that is required to set these parameters is highly salient, whereas paradigmatically encoded information, e.g. concerning inflection, is less easily accessible from the input. This leads to the expectation that possessor raising to Spec-DP should emerge early in development in both varieties of German, because, with respect to possessor DPs, there is a root/non-root contrast in the input which is said to be easily accessible. The acquisition of the Standard German possessive marker, however, should be delayed due to its morphological defectiveness. The authors present longitudinal data from two children to demonstrate that these expectations are actually borne out.

Child Basque

Meisel & Ezeizabarrena's study is based on longitudinal data from two bilingual children (Spanish/Basque) and one monolingual Basque child. They present several findings on the acquisition of subject–verb agreement and object–verb agreement which they interpret in terms of gradual structure-building plus lexical learning. In the earliest phase represented in their data, Meisel & Ezeizabarrena did not find any evidence for AGR-projections; the children use default forms of finite verbs, there is no agreement paradigm of distinct affixes and no verb raising across negation. This system has changed in what they call phase 3. At this point in development, children have acquired the subject–verb-agreement paradigm, and they raise finite verbs across negation, indicating that AGRS-P has become syntactically active. Meisel & Ezeizabarrena also found that subject agreement emerges before object agreement, and they point to Georgopoulos (1991) for a similar claim about the typology of agreement systems. They rely on the Extended Projection Principle, a principle of UG that makes explicit reference to subjects, but not to objects, to explain why subject agreement emerges earlier than object agreement.

Child Dutch

Haegeman investigates the development of early clause structure in Dutch, based on longitudinal data from one child, Hein, between 2;4 and 3;1. Haegeman shows that the sentences with non-finite verbs that Hein uses do not contain *wh*-phrases, subject or object clitics and hardly any negatives. She derives these properties from Rizzi's (1993) maturational hypothesis, according to which root infinitives are truncated structures that do not project a CP-layer, and she argues that alternative approaches that treat root infinitives as full CPs (cf. e.g. Boser *et al.* 1992 for German) fail to account for the observed characteristics of early root infinitives.

Child Italian

Guasti takes a striking fact about early English and develops this into a cross-linguistic investigation. In a previous study, Guasti, Thornton & Wexler (1995) found that English-speaking children produce adult-like affirmative questions, while at the same time negative questions contained many errors, e.g. no subject–aux inversion, double auxiliaries, etc. For the present paper, Guasti has replicated this study on early Italian, with different results: Italian children produce adult-like affirmative and negative questions from the beginning. Elaborating on Rizzi (1992), she assumes that adult Italian differs from adult English with respect to the features specified in the Comp-position: ⟨+Infl⟩ in English, and ⟨+Infl, +V⟩ in Italian. With respect to child language, Guasti assumes a default strategy of placing negation inside the projection containing the ⟨+V⟩ feature. In Italian, this can easily be achieved in questions since both IP and CP contain the feature ⟨+V⟩, and thus children perform like adults in Italian questions. In English negative questions, the clitic negation *n't* which is attached to the auxiliary needs to be raised to Comp. This, however, violates the default strategy as Comp does not have any ⟨+V⟩ features in English. This

xxiv HARALD CLAHSEN

conflict is claimed to be the reason for the errors English-speaking children produce in such cases.

Child French
Hamann, Rizzi & Frauenfelder examine subject and object clitics in the speech of one monolingual child between 2;0 and 2;10. Their data demonstrate that this child shows mastery of the correct positioning of clitic forms from the beginning of data collection. The authors also found that this child acquires subject clitics prior to object clitics. Finally, subject clitics appear to be restricted to tensed clauses, rarely occurring in root infinitives. The paper discusses the implications of these findings for Rizzi's (1993) truncation hypothesis and for the linguistic analysis of Romance clitics.

White investigates the acquisition of French clitics by two five-year old children in a bilingual setting with English as their first language. Her empirical findings are largely parallel to those of Hamann, Rizzi & Frauenfelder: clitics are placed in the appropriate clitic positions, subject clitics appear adjacent to finite verbs, and subject clitics are acquired before object clitics. White adopts Sportiche's (1992) idea that clitic pronouns head their own projections. This implies that French has clitic projections, whereas English has not. The early acquisition of (subject) clitics in her bilingual children, however, and the parallels with monolingual French children suggest that the children's knowledge of English did not have any negative effects on their acquisition of French clitics. The paper discusses the implications of this finding for approaches to second language development.

The two subsequent papers, by Platzack and by Roeper use previous empirical findings and reanalyze them from the perspective of the Minimalist program of Chomsky (1995).

Platzack relies on findings from a wide range of subjects - monolingual children, aphasics, bilingual adults and language-impaired children - all with reference to Swedish data. Platzack infers a markedness hypothesis from Chomsky's theory: overt movement is more costly and thus more marked than invisible or covert movement. Assuming a universal Spec–Head–Complement order for all phrases (cf. Kayne 1994), he predicts that because it is unmarked and does not involve any overt movement, the various groups of subjects he is concerned with will fall back on this basic word order and will have difficulty acquiring other orders. In this way, Platzack explains delays in the acquisition of verb second, the use of verb–object orders in the acquisition of SOV languages, the use of preverbal negation in the acquisition of Swedish, etc.

Roeper focusses on another aspect of Chomsky's theory, namely the idea of feature-based projections, and applies it to acquisition. According to Chomsky (1995), UG no longer contains a fixed set of categories NP, VP, PP, etc., but instead makes use of a so-called merger operation which, in principle allows for an infinite set of possible phrase markers to be generated, corresponding to the features associated with individual lexical items. Roeper argues that Chomsky's theory allows us to represent the underspecified functional categories that children develop in the course of acquisition, as well as micro-steps in phrase-structure development in which children create syntactic positions with lexically-specific subcategorizations.

In the final chapter, **Atkinson** critically discusses some central issues of generative studies of children's syntactic development focussing on the particular variant of the Full Competence Hypothesis argued for by Ken Wexler and his collaborators (Poeppel & Wexler 1993; Wexler 1994; Harris & Wexler, this volume). Atkinson argues that methodological arguments supposed to support the FCH ("Assume full competence from day zero, and you will not have to explain development") are in fact dubious. Atkinson also claims that the empirical evidence for the FCH is not as sound as Wexler makes us believe and that the "optional infinitive" stage is preceded by an earlier stage at which there is no evidence for any functional categories in the child's grammar. Furthermore, Atkinson criticizes structure-building models, particularly Radford (this volume) and Clahsen, Eisenbeiss & Penke (this volume), for not making explicit enough the developmental mechanisms that lead the child from one stage to the next. Atkinson himself feels that the maturation of functional categories remains an interesting option which has not been discounted.

Most of the chapters in this book have grown out of a research workshop held at the University of Essex, 18-20 March 1994. The main purpose of this workshop was to bring together researchers studying language acquisition from a generative perspective and to discuss their latest findings. In addition, the participants of the workshop discussed future perspectives for cross-linguistic acquisition research specifically in the European context, and, as a result, they have launched an initiative for setting up collaborative research projects on language acquisition in Europe.

The workshop and this initiative would not have been possible without financial support from the Research Promotion Fund of the University of Essex and an additional grant provided by the British Academy. Thanks are also due to my colleagues in the Department of Language and Linguistics at Essex, particularly to Roger Hawkins, Andrew Radford and Martin Atkinson, for their support and encouragement in the preparation of the workshop. Special thanks to Claudia Felser for helping with the important details of organizing the workshop.

Each paper in this book was externally (and of course internally) reviewed, and I am grateful to the following colleagues for participating in the reviewing process: Sergej Avrutin, Masha Babyonyshev, Katherine Demuth, Marcel den Dikken, Nigel Duffield, Lynn Eubank, Helen Goodluck, Teresa Guasti, Teun Hoekstra, Nina Hyams, Colin Philipps, Amy Pierce, David Poeppel, Susan Powers, Bernhard Rohrbacher, Jeannette Schaeffer, Neil Smith, William Snyder, Margaret Thomas, Rozz Thornton, Alessandra Tomaselli, Anne Vainikka, and Helmut Zobl.

Final thanks go to the participants themselves for their contributions to the workshop and to the book. Due to their unusually short reaction times for providing me with their manuscripts and revised versions it was possible to keep publication latency to a minimum. I also gratefully acknowledge the fact that several participants made use of their own funds and grant money to join the workshop at Essex.

References

Atkinson, M. 1992. *Children's Syntax: An introduction to principles and paramters theory.* Oxford: Basil Blackwell.

Boser, K., B. Lust, L. Santelmann & J. Whitman 1992. "The Syntax of CP and V2 in Early Child German: The Strong Continuity Hypothesis. *Proceedings of NELS 22,* ed. by B.K. Broderick, 51–65. Amherst, Mass.: Graduate Linguistic Student Association.

Chomsky, N. 1995. *The Minimalist Program.* Cambridge, Mass.: MIT Press.

Clark, E. 1993. *The Lexicon in Acquisition.* Cambridge: Cambridge University Press.

Georgopoulos, C. 1991. "On A- and A'-agreement." *Lingua* 85.135–169.

Goodluck, H. 1991. *Language Acquisition: A linguistic introduction.* Oxford: Basil Blackwell.

Guasti, M.T., R. Thornton & K. Wexler 1995. "Negation in Children's Questions: The case of English." *Proceedings of the 19th Annual Boston University Conference on Language Development,* ed. by D. McLaughlin and S. McEwen, 228–239. Somerville, Mass.: Cascadilla Press.

Kayne, R. 1994. *The Antisymmetry of Syntax.* Cambridge, Mass.: MIT Press.

Marcus, G. 1993. "Negative Evidence in Language Acquisition." *Cognition* 46.53-85.

Pinker, S. 1984. *Language Learnability and Language Development*. Cambridge, Mass.: Harvard University Press.

Poeppel, D. & K. Wexler 1993. "The Full Competence Hypothesis of Clause Structure in Early German." *Language* 69.1–33.

Radford, A. 1990. *Syntactic Theory and the Acquisition of English Syntax: The nature of early child grammars of English*. Oxford: Basil Blackwell.

Reinhart, T. 1983. *Anaphora and Semantic Interpretation*. London: Croom Helm.

Rizzi, L. 1992. "Speculations on Verb Second." *Grammar in Progress,* ed. by J. Mascaró & M. Nespor, 375–386. Dordrecht: Foris.

Rizzi, L. 1993. "Some Notes on Linguistic Theory and Language Development: The case of root infinitives." *Language Acquisition* 3.371–394.

Slobin, D. 1985. *The Cross-Linguistic Study of Language Acquisition*. Vol. 1. Hillsdale, N.J.: Lawrence Erlbaum.

Sportiche, D. 1992. "Clitic Constructions." Ms., University of California at Los Angeles.

Weissenborn, J. 1992. "Null Subjects in Early Grammars: Implications for parameter-setting theories." *Theoretical Issues in Language Acquisition: Continuity and change in development,* ed. by J. Weissenborn, H. Goodluck & T. Roeper, 269–299. Hillsdale, N.J.: Lawrence Erlbaum.

Wexler, K. 1994. "Optional Infinitives, Head Movement and the Economy of Derivations in Child Grammar." *Verb Movement,* ed. by D. Lightfoot & N. Hornstein, 305–350. Cambridge: Cambridge University Press.

The Optional-Infinitive Stage in Child English
Evidence from Negation

Tony Harris   Ken Wexler
Massachusetts Institute of Technology

1. Introduction

For more than 30 years, extensive research has gone into the documentation of characteristics of early inflectional and clausal development in the grammar of English-speaking children. From this research we have learned much about particular characteristics of children's productions. It seems fair to say, however, that a general picture of English grammar at this stage has eluded the field of developmental psycholinguistics.

The purpose of this paper is to show that a general picture of the distinctive characteristics of early grammar has recently been built up under the name of the OPTIONAL-INFINITIVE STAGE (Wexler 1990, 1992, 1994) which also applies to English. The optional-infinitive stage is one in which the child's grammar accepts root infinitives as grammatical, for example, *she go*, while at the same time it accepts tensed forms as grammatical, e.g., *she goes*. Between the ages of approximately 1;10–2;7,[1] both forms occur.

We maintain that the child knows the grammatical distinctions between finite (e.g., marked *-ed*, *-s*) and nonfinite forms (appearing as bare stems in English). In particular, we will show that the tensed form *goes* is not allowed by the child's grammar after the negative *not*. We will show that this result and some further results follow from the optional-infinitive stage. We will also show that other possible hypotheses about the tenseless forms of the verb do not predict the observed data.

Most of the evidence came from languages other than English, languages, in which the stage was directly observable. Wexler argued that the optional-infinitive analysis also applied to early English, and provided some predictions that the theory made, along with some preliminary data. This paper provides much more detailed evidence concerning those predictions, evidence both from natural production and from an elicited production experiment. We will conclude that, in fact, the predictions are borne out by the data.

If our claims can be justified, then this is quite important for the study of child grammar. The optional-infinitive analysis was created based on patterns and processes in languages other than English, patterns and processes which (as Wexler argued) are obscured by ambiguous English morphology. Following standard methodology in comparative syntax, we can nevertheless look for consequences of the optional-infinitive stage in English, and find that they do clearly exist. Thus we find a strong generalization that is all the more strong for the fact that it suggests a reanalysis of the original English data. If this method works in a number of cases, (as it did, for example, in Wexler's original papers), we can see the birth of a field of comparative language acquisition, to parallel the field of comparative syntax.

That the optional-infinitive stage exists in many languages is by now fairly uncontroversial. Many of its properties are quite clear. There has been, in fact, major activity in attempting to understand the underlying theory and cause of the optional-infinitive stage. A number of theories have been proposed (e.g., Wexler 1992, 1994, 1995, in press; Rizzi 1994; Hyams, this volume).

We will not review the theories here, but will concentrate on documenting that English falls into the optional-infinitive analysis. The theory which we will adopt is one of the variants of the theory presented in Wexler(1992, 1994), The intuition which underlies the Wexler (1992, 1994) theory to which we are referring is that in the optional-infinitive stage, TENSE is optional, and all other aspects of grammar are known to the child.[2] Wexler (1995, in press) suggests how a deficit in interpretive/pragmatic abilities might underlie the optionality of TENSE, but we will not discuss this here. We will simply take TENSE as optional.

The syntactic framework in which we will present this work is that of MINIMALIST THEORY, although it could have been presented in other versions of syntax, as it has been before. However, the minimalist analysis will allow us to show very clearly why the child's 'deficit' is not simply morphological, i.e., defined on word formation, but must be rooted in a difference in (one very small aspect of) the child's representation of the sentence, namely in the obligatoriness of $\langle +/- \rangle$ past features. Moreover, a new theory of the optional-infinitive stage developed in Wexler (1995), uses properties of minimalist syntax to help explain the optional-infinitive stage and its properties, so that the presentation here will be compatible with that theory.

Section 2 discusses briefly the general syntactic framework in which we are working. It also summarizes the characteristics of the optional-infinitive stage. Section 3 applies the optional-infinitive theory to child English, in particular the problem of the 'omitted' inflection -*s*. We make predictions concerning various phenomena and we also compare the predictions to those made by alternative theories. Section 4 discusses the natural production data evidence concerning these predictions and Section 5 is a report of a new experiment. The conclusion is contained in Section 6.

2. Background

According to the minimalist approach, lexical items are drawn from the lexicon and linked together under the operation of MERGE. Items are merged asymmetrically, meaning that the resultant structure has the identity of only one of the combined elements. This ensures that MERGE is a binary operation.

Lexical items are nouns, verbs, tense, agreement, determiners, etc. Lexical items need not be overt (e.g., tense and agreement). The phrases which they project (e.g., VP, NP, etc.) are maximal projections (XPs). The lexical items themselves are heads (X^0s). Heads which do not project may have simultaneous existences as maximal projections. In (1), β may be both a head and a maximal projection. The lower α is only a head and the superior is only an XP.

(1)

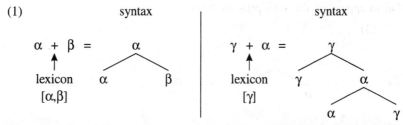

When two elements are merged, one must project a maximal projection. For example, if a verb (V) and an object (NP) are merged, they are both dominated by a verb phrase (VP), a projection of V. (While MERGE does not dictate which element must project, the structure generated must satisfy conditions of well-formedness not discussed here.)

MERGE continues its work until all items drawn from the lexicon have been integrated in some syntactic structure. During this time, certain sites in the structure may be targeted for the placement of moved items (e.g., the fronting of *wh*-words in questions). At any point during the derivation, the structure is subject to the operation SPELL-OUT, to being sent to the semantic (LF) and phonetic (PF) interfaces. If the structure meets the conditions of well-formedness demanded by each interface, the derivation is said to *converge*, if it fails any condition of either interface, it is said to *crash*.

(2)

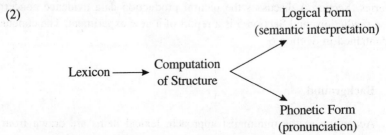

Lexicon ⟶ Computation of Structure

Logical Form
(semantic interpretation)

Phonetic Form
(pronunciation)

The minimalist view allows two possibilities for the realization of inflection on the verb.[3]

(i)   The verb (*walk*) and the morphological affixation (*-s*) are drawn as two separate elements and joined by MERGE, or

(ii)   The verb and the affixation are drawn as a whole, but with the appropriate inflectional and agreement features inherent in it.

We will not attempt to make a distinction between the two here. What will be important in this discussion is that the appropriate features either appear or fail to appear on the verb prior to SPELL-OUT.

(3)

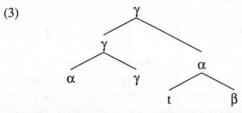

Any element bearing a strong feature (such as a tense or agreement feature) must have that feature checked by a functional category before the derivation is spelled out to the phonetic interface. This is driven by the principle of GREED. A feature is checked when the item bearing that feature moves into the checking domain of the appropriate functional category. This is satisfied when the item has adjoined to the head of the functional category. (3) shows us an example in which α has moved into the checking domain of γ. In English, the relevant features are weak, meaning that they needn't be checked before SPELL-OUT. The

movement of the verb is covert (at LF). This illustrates the principle of PRO-
CRASTINATION, which requires that any necessary movement be delayed as long
as possible, in this case, until LF.

(4)

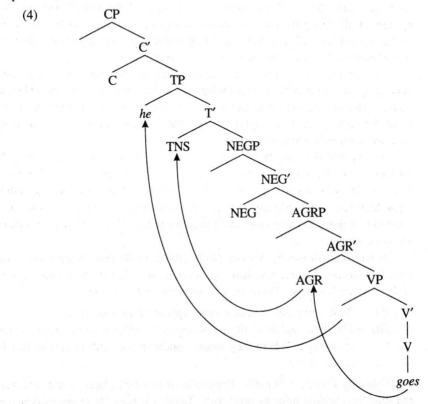

In (4), illustrating *he goes*, the verb must raise to AGR at LF to have its
agreement checked. In order to have its tense feature checked, it must continue
on to TNS. In this sentence, there is no negation, so NEG is not a necessary
intermediary landing spot. The verb raises directly from AGR to TNS. Notice
that this is irrelevant to the pronounced sentence, since movement occurs *after*
SPELL-OUT.

    In the other child form observed, *he go*, the only difference here is that the
main verb does not move at LF. Obviously, these examples cannot provide any
evidence which bears on whether movement has taken place.

If a lexical item is selected with a set of inflectional features, it must have those features checked by the appropriate inflectional category. Since we assume that the child's grammar is subject to UG constraints, this means that the child's grammar must check off the appropriate features, if the inflectional category appears at all. Since the optional-infinitive hypothesis holds that the inflection on the verb is indicative of the underlying feature, then we expect the distribution of inflected verbs to be different from the uninflected.

The prediction is that a functional category may/may not be present depending on whether the corresponding lexical item was selected. But when an item *is* selected, we expect to see it used grammatically. We predict no movement for agreement (least effort) when the category is absent, mandatory movement (greed) when it is present.

In English, the effects of this movement or lack of movement may be difficult to see because of impoverished inflectional morphology (which make it not so obvious whether a child is using a tensed form) and corresponding weak features, which require only covert movement. In languages with more overt morphology and also more overt movement, the effects of feature checking are more obvious.

It has been shown by Wexler (1990, 1992, 1994) that children acquiring French, German, Dutch, Swedish, Norwegian, and Danish all go through an optional-infinitive stage. There are two properties of this stage:

(i)   Both finite and nonfinite verbs appear in the root clause.
(ii)   The finite and nonfinite verbs appear in different word orders, corresponding to where they would appear in the adult grammar, that is, raised or not.

Consider French. It is unlike English in that [+INFL] bears a strong feature and must be checked prior to SPELL-OUT. Here, it is possible to see evidence of movement. In (5a), the matrix verb *sembler* is infinitival, and has not raised.[4] Indeed, as we see in (5b), raising an uninflected form results in ungrammaticality. The opposite is the case with the inflected form of *voir*. It *must* raise, as in (6). See the derivation in (7).

(5)   a.   *Ne pas sembler heureux est une condition pour écrire des romans.*
           'To seem not happy is a condition for writing novels.'
      b.   **Ne sembler pas heureux est une condition pour écrire des romans.*

(6)   a.   **Il ne pas voit Marie.*
           'He doesn't see her.'
      b.   *Il ne voit pas Marie.*

(7)

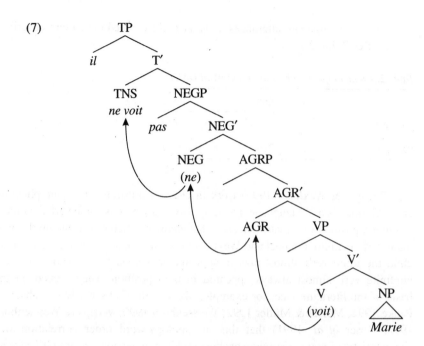

Whenever a verb appears before negation (*pas* here), we expect to see the verb in an inflected form (cf. (6b)). Where the negation-(*pas*) precedes the verb, as in (5a), we assume that the verb has not raised to TNS, and no inflection is observed in these instances. The child examples in Table 1 are from Pierce (1989):

Table 1. Examples of Inflection/Negation, Pierce (1989)

+finite...NEG	NEG...–finite
marche pas	*pas casser*
walks not	not break
ça tourne pas	*pas rouler en vélo*
this turns not	not roll on bike

The question is whether children respect this constraint on the distribution of verbs bearing inflection morphology. Pierce (1989) studied transcripts from four native-French speaking children aged 1;8–2;2.3. She found that the children overwhelmingly observed the constraint.

Out of 352 relevant utterances, only 11 (3%) violated the pattern described above. (See Table 2.)

Table 2. French Inflection/Negation and Word Order

	finite	-finite
pas verb	9	122
verb *pas*	216	2

Poeppel & Wexler's (1993) work in German illustrates the same phenomenon. German is a V2 language, meaning that it always has some verbal element in second position of a matrix clause. That element, whether it is an auxiliary or main verb, is finite. Poeppel and Wexler showed that in a 25–month old German child the finite verb almost always appeared in second (V2) position and the nonfinite verb almost always appeared in final position. They argued on the basis of the literature (see, for example, Mills 1985; Clahsen 1990; Clahsen & Penke 1992; Meisel & Müller 1992; Weissenborn 1990; Verrips & Weissenborn 1992; Boser *et al.* 1991) that this morphology/word order correlation was characteristic of young German-speaking children in the optional-infinitive stage. Wexler (1990, 1992, 1994) applied these kinds of arguments to a range of languages, showing that children in the optional-infinitive stage observed a characteristic word-order/morphology correlation: Although nonfinite root verbs frequently appeared, they appeared in the position corresponding to the (un-raised) nonfinite verb, whereas the finite verb appeared in the raised position determined by the adult language. He concluded that children in the optional-infinitive stage knew both the relevant UG principles and the parametric values (e.g., strong vs. weak features) of the adult language that was developing.

3. Theory of Optional Infinitives in English

The languages studied by Wexler (1990, 1992, 1994) provide us with examples of overt inflection/non-inflection. In these cases, we see that two-year-olds make some kind of distinction between them with respect to their distribution in sentences. Since this distribution is compatible with what is known about feature-checking, we assume that it is the result of grammatical knowledge held by the children. Wexler (1992, 1994) suggested that English children also go through the optional-infinitive stage, although there is no visible inflectional marking on the infinitive in English. Specifically, he suggests that, for example, when the English-speaking child says *he go* instead of *he goes*, this represents the workings of the optional-infinitive stage in English. Let us consider possible explanations for the incorrect, so-called *bare stem* form in child English.

What is the cause of the *he go/he goes* alternation in English-speaking two-year-olds? There are four possible hypotheses which explain the data:[5]

Hypotheses:
I.   Children randomly use the *-s* morpheme.
II.   Children randomly add the morpheme in third person singular contexts.
III. The [*-s* + verb] complex is a morphological variant of the stem.
IV.   Children pass through an optional-infinitive stage in which they optionally omit TENSE, and the form without *-s* is the untensed (nonfinite) form of the optional-infinitive stage in English (Wexler 1992, 1994).

If one wants to argue some variant of the view that children do not have functional categories (in modern approaches) or know inflectional morphemes (in more traditional approaches), then it is necessary to account for the fact that during most of the period of inflectional development, children are producing the tensed, agreeing form alongside the untensed, non-agreeing form, that is, they are producing *she goes* at the same ages (i.e., in the same files) as *she go*.[6] This fact, as Wexler (1992, 1994) points out, is what underlies Brown 's (1970) use of the *percent production in obligatory contexts* measure. Hypotheses I to III are variants of an attempt to capture both the use of *-s* and its optional use in some framework which assumes that children are missing functional categories. These hypotheses (I through III) are not necessarily distinct, depending on exact assumptions which could be made.

Hypotheses I through III reflect doubt over whether children around two years of age have complete knowledge of inflectional categories. This concern is expressed in two forms: one suggests that inflectional marking is optionally added or deleted, subject to interference from processing-load demands. The latter proposal would be in the spirit of Bloom (1990), although Bloom made no such claim.

The other proposal (Aldridge 1989) suggests that a verb plus its inflectional marking are taken as an unanalyzed whole,[7] and that such a unit is a variant of the "uninflected" form. On this view, *take* and *takes* are homonyms, i.e., there is no analysis of *takes* as [take+3SG]. As Radford (1994) writes, on Aldridge's view, "the absence of overt tense marking [e.g., in *Teddy cry*] is a low-level morphological error that has no syntactic correlate, so that *cry* has the same surface syntax as *cries* and carries covert tense.... What this implies ... is that *Teddy cry* has exactly the same superficial syntactic structure as *Teddy cries/cried*, with *cry* being a covert present/past tense form...."

It is quite clear that Hypothesis I can not be correct; children in this early stage do not use -*s* randomly, as Wexler (1992, 1994) points out.[8] Namely, -*s* is almost never used with other than third-singular subjects; for example, a child does not use -*s* with first singular subjects, e.g., *I goes*.[9] This fits with what Wexler (1992, 1994) and also Poeppel & Wexler (1993) claim about the optional-infinitive stage, that the child knows agreement, seldom using a finite verbal inflection with a subject which does not agree with it.

Hypothesis III is very close to Hypothesis I, and may not be distinguishable from it. Apparently, it also predicts that children use verbs with -*s* in the same environments as they use bare stem verbs, mistakenly predicting the occurrence of e.g., *I goes*.

Thus it is very difficult to find an 'inflected verbs are unanalyzed units' hypothesis that can begin to account for the agreement facts, namely that there are exceedingly few instances in the production data of finite verbal inflections with non-agreeing subjects. Our specification of Hypothesis II is an attempt to state such a hypothesis (just so we can argue against it, of course). Hypothesis II says that children know that verbs with -*s* have a third-singular feature, but they do not know any other grammatical aspects of the form. That is, the assumption of Hypothesis II is that children will use a verb with -*s* whenever the subject is third singular, but they do not know that the verb is tensed and is subject to distributional conditions on TENSE.

It is not clear to us, in fact, that Hypothesis II can be stated within a UG framework. At any rate, if Hypothesis II were actually to hold, we have to think of the child as having some kind of grammar, and in fact, not simply one without functional categories. This is because agreement is represented in terms of functional categories, and in fact, the usual 'no functional categories' theories (e.g., Radford 1990) state that children at an early age do not know agreement.[10] Thus even if Hypothesis II were to hold, it would not be compatible with a 'no functional categories' approach to the *she go/she goes* alternation. The implication of Hypothesis II is that children will not make agreement mistakes on -*s*; however, they will not demonstrate other knowledge of functional categories related to -*s*.

The question now becomes: can we find distributional evidence in English concerning the word order/morphology correlation which would distinguish Hypothesis II from Hypothesis IV (the optional-infinitive hypothesis)? The phenomenon of optional infinitives in English is not obvious for two reasons. First, only the third person singular bears overt morphology in present tense. The opportunity to make the relevant observations is limited in this sense. Secondly, and most importantly, the uninflected form is not unambiguously a proper infinitival. In the other languages in which Wexler found evidence for the optional-infinitive hypothesis, the infinitival inflection was visible, e.g., *-er, -ir, -re,* in French, *-en* in German, etc. But English infinitivals are a case of *zero morphology*; the infinitival form of the verb is phonetically identical to the bare stem. *Walk* may simply be the stem of *to walk*, for example.

The only present tense marker in English is third singular *-s*. Wexler (1992, 1994) argues that the omission of *-s* by children could follow from the optional-infinitive stage in the following way: the child either chooses ⟨+TNS⟩, yielding *she goes* or ⟨−TNS⟩, yielding *she go*. The assumption is that *go* in *she go* is the English infinitival form. This is suggested by examples such as (8):

(8)   a.   *I want Mary to go.*
       b.   *I saw Mary go.*

The embedded clause in (8b) is a 'small clause', typically taken to be a tenseless clause. Thus in both the 'infinitive' and small clause examples given in (8), we see that the form of the verb is *go*, the same form as in *she go*. This is what the optional-infinitive view predicts, given its assumption that English-speaking children may have root sentences with ⟨−TNS⟩. Here are some examples from CHILDES, with and without inflection (All CHILDES examples refer to MacWhinney & Snow 1985):

Table 3. Examples of 3rd Singular Verbs

child	file	age	example
Eve	14	2;0	*it only write on the pad.* *my finger hurts.*
Adam	01	2;3	*horse go # Mommy.*
Sarah	030	2;9	*he bite me.* *her cry.*
Adam	27	3;3	*dis go right here.*
Peter	08	3;3	*Patsy need a screw. This goes in there.*

Note that there is no distributional evidence for the optional-infinitive hypothesis here. English does not exhibit the surface word order movements that the other studied languages do. For example, it is not V2 (like German) and it does not raise the verb over negation on the surface (like French). Wexler (1992, 1994), however, suggests that English will have a manifestation of its own, involving negation.

(9)

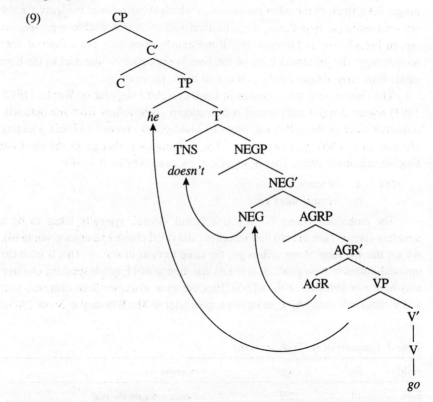

Consider again feature-checking in English. The main verb raises to have its tense feature checked.[11] If it raises directly to TNS over overt negation, it will be unable to properly govern its trace, violating the Head Movement Constraint. The only other option is to adjoin to the intervening negation marker before continuing. However, English does not allow negation to cliticize on to main verbs. The sentence *he not goes* is ungrammatical.[12]

The only way to save a negated sentence is through the insertion of a semantically null modal, such as *do*. *Do* is base-generated under AGR with the feature ⟨+TNS⟩. It raises to NEG, where it adjoins to the head there,[13] then continues on to TNS. It appears there with *n't* clitisized on to it. *Go*, here, is uninflected, and is not required to move.

Notice that the overt order is necessarily *he doesn't go* and not *he not does go*. Chomsky (1992) suggests that because *do* is semantically null, it is not visible at LF; it (like other auxiliaries in English) must move to have its features checked prior to SPELL-OUT.

Now consider what happens with sentences of the form:

(10)   *He doesn't walks.*

where both the modal and the main verb bear ⟨+TNS⟩. Only one of them can have its feature checked at TNS. The unchecked feature on the other will cause the derivation to crash.

Now, what do we expect from the optional-infinitive hypothesis (Hypothesis IV)? We have stated this hypothesis as the possibility of children optionally omitting TNS. When children choose TNS in their representation, they will have exactly the adult forms; for example, they will judge (10) as ungrammatical. Suppose now that they omit TNS in a representation of a negated sentence. As Wexler (1992, 1994) observes, it is in just such a case that we would expect the omission of *do*, since, as we have pointed out, *do* has been inserted so that a ⟨TNS⟩ feature may be checked. If there is no ⟨TNS⟩ feature to be checked, *do* will not be inserted, since ECONOMY considerations allow a transformational operation only when necessary to check a feature.[14] In such instances we would expect negative sentences like (11):

(11)   *she not go*

Since there is no TNS in (11), there is nothing to check; raising is not required at any level. In other words, since the verb is not marked for tense and TNS has not been selected as a lexical item, no feature-checking is required here. Economy principles restrict unnecessary movements, therefore the verb will not be raised vacuously. Thus (11) will be a grammatical form for the optional-infinitive child, that is, the optional-infinitive hypothesis predicts that negation may exist without *do*-support, in the form of sentences like (11).

In fact, as has been known since Klima & Bellugi (1966), children often omit *do* where it is required in negative sentences, yielding forms like (11). These authors took the existence of forms like (11) to indicate a 'medial NEG stage.' It was never clear why forms like (11) should exist; clearly it is a virtue of the optional-infinitive analysis that it in fact predicts that forms like (11) exist. However, other Hypotheses, for example, Hypothesis II, might take *do* to

(12)

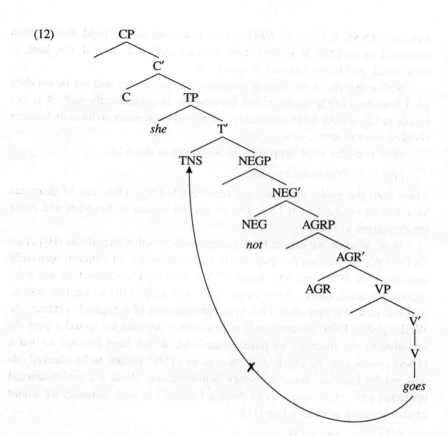

be made necessary by a functional category, and also predict that *do* may be omitted.[15] However, Wexler suggested distributional evidence that follows from the optional-infinitive hypothesis.

Consider forms similar to (11), but with the verb showing TNS, in particular -*s*, as in (13):

(13)   *she not goes*

The ⟨+TNS⟩ verb must raise to have features checked. The Head Movement Constraint in English restricts the verb from raising over negation. The optional-infinitive grammar will rule out such a sentence (12).

Note that in those instances when ⟨+TNS⟩ is either present on the verb or present in the phrase-marker, but not both, the sentence will automatically be ruled out, regardless of whatever else appears in the structure. This means, as Wexler (1992, 1994) argued, that the optional-infinitive hypothesis predicts that when *do* has been omitted, two-year-olds will never inflect negated sentences.

Other hypotheses, however, predict otherwise. Consider Hypothesis II, the most difficult of the alternative hypotheses to falsify, since it assumes the children know third singular features of -*s*. Let us assume that somehow Hypothesis II can allow the omission of *do*, perhaps by saying that *do* represents a functional category, even though this might be difficult to formalize. However, there does not seem to be any way that Hypothesis II differentiates between (11) and (13). The hypothesis allows both *she go* and *she goes*, by saying that verb + -*s* is allowed as a morphological (allomorphic) variant of the bare verb stem as long as the subject is third singular. Apparently, both (11) and (13) should be allowed by Hypothesis II.[16]

In summary, we have the following predictions:

Table 4. Predicted Forms

	she not go	*she not goes*
OI Hypothesis	✓	*
Hypothesis II	✓	✓

The purpose of this paper is to test these varying predictions. So far as we know, aside from Wexler (1992, 1994), this question has not been discussed (Klima & Bellugi 1966), in describing the MEDIAL NEG STAGE, didn't discuss verbal inflection).

4. Natural Production Data

4.1. *Use of Bare Negation*

Transcripts of 10 children from the CHILDES data base were examined.[17] The age range was from 1;6 to 4;1.[18] In brief, we searched for all sentences containing negation but no auxiliary and which should have had some inflectional marking.

Sentences counted were those containing some negation (either *no* or *not*) preceding a main verb. Sentences including a modal or auxiliary (such as *do* or *can*) were excluded. Questions were excluded. Since the purpose of the analysis was to investigate whether finite or nonfinite forms followed the medial negative (i.e., negatives where *do* should appear but does not), we only looked at verbs with singular third person subjects, since only third person singular morphology is visible on English main verbs. Only those sentences whose subjects (including null subjects) were unambiguously third person were included. Either -*s* or some form of the past tense were counted as inflected. Obviously progressive -*ing* was not included, since tense does not appear on -*ing* participles. Thus the sentences included in the analysis fell into two kinds, those with present or past tense on the main verb and those with an infinitival main verb, i.e., the bare stem. We will call these forms, both with and without tense, *bare negation* examples.[19]

(14) a. *not Fraser read it*   Eve 08
      b. *Saifi no knock on the door*   Apr 02
      c. *no Nathaniel has a microphone*   Nat 01

The table below counts all determinable-tense sentences lacking auxiliaries.

Table 5. Frequency of Tensed and Untensed Verbs

	aff	neg
−inflection	782	47
+inflection	594	5

+inflection: verb is marked for present or past tense.
−inflection: verb is the bare stem (i.e., the infinitive).
aff: sentence is affirmative
neg: sentence is negated with no or not, without do-support.

As we can see, about 43% of the affirmative sentences were inflected (e.g., *He goes*). Compare this to the inflection rate for sentences negated by *no(t)* (e.g., *He not goes*), 9.6% . This comparison suggests that the addition of the inflectional marker is disrupted by the presence of negation. Notice that five of the negated sentences were tensed; these are given in Table 6. A complete listing of all examples of bare negation with determinable tense is located in the appendix.

Note that the example from Peter 15 is a nonstandard case of inflection (where the particle is inflected), not repeated elsewhere in the transcripts studied. Indeed, in Peter 15, this same sentence is uttered without the -*s* appended to any word. Even though this seems clearly a performance error, it remains in all our counts. Thus the inflection rate for the negatives is probably too large. Eliminat-

Table 6. All Tensed Bare Negation Sentences

Abe	28	*it not works Mom*
Nath	01	*no Nathaniel has a microphone*
Peter	08	*no goes in there*
Peter	15	*but the horse not stand ups*
Peter	17	*no goes here!*

ing this example would give four inflected forms and 47 non-inflected forms for the medial-negation sentences. This is a 7.8% inflection rate vs. a 43% rate for the affirmatives.

It seems fair to conclude that verbs that appear after negation are not tensed; there is an extremely large difference between the inflection rate for affirmative and negative sentences. Moreover, the inflection rate for negative sentences is extremely small (in the range of 7 to 9 %); we can take this small rate of inflection to indicate performance errors.

Now consider the use of main verb (possessive) *have/has*. This is an especially clear example for the optional-infinitive hypothesis, since here it cannot be the case that the *-s* marker is simply dropped, leaving the stem form. For example, if the child says *she have a book*, this cannot be accounted for by saying that the child 'drops' the *-s*, since that would result in the utterance *she ha the book*.

Of the affirmative tense-determinable examples of *have/has*, 30.6% are inflected (e.g., *has*) vs. 12.5% of the negated examples.[20] This follows the pattern seen in the other verbs, namely that the verb is not tensed after negation. The following table shows the number of tense-determinable examples of main verb *have/has*, for affirmative and negative sentences.

Table 7. Have *with 3rd Person Subjects*

	aff	neg
−inflection	66	7
+inflection	29	1

Notice that the children often use infinitival *have* with third person singular subjects (69% of the time for affirmative sentences). This clearly means that the children cannot be using a strategy which says 'drop -s' to form what we are calling the 'nonfinite' verbs. Otherwise they would be saying *ha*, not *have*, in these cases. Clearly the children are giving the infinitival form of the verb.

One might argue, of course, that when the child uses *have* instead of *has*, the child is using incorrect agreement, that is, the child is using a finite form that is appropriate for any subject except a third singular one. However, there is evidence (see Poeppel & Wexler 1993; Wexler 1994) that children in the optional-infinitive stage know agreement; they very rarely make agreement errors, where 'agreement error' means the use of an incorrect finite form, i.e., a finite form used with a subject which does not agree with it in the adult language.

In the case of English, this means that we expect that the child will not use the -*s* inflection on the verb with anything but a third singular subject. In general this is the accepted wisdom in English language acquisition; -*s* may be omitted, but is rarely mis-applied. To confirm this, we examined instances of verbal inflection following *I* subjects (thus ignoring null subjects). The first person singular pronoun was selected because there were relatively few plural or *you* subjects in the corpus.[21] The corpus was the same as was used in the counts already presented. The sentences used were affirmative and did not include those with auxiliaries. The following table shows the numbers of such verbs that are 'bare' (i.e., correct, the 'stem') or have -*s* (i.e., are incorrect).

Table 8. Frequency of Verbs with 'I' *Subject*

stem	irregular past	-*ed*	-*s*
1349	325	47	3

As can be seen from the table, the use of -*s* in first person singular contexts is almost zero (3 forms with -*s*, and 1,349 bare forms). This 0% contrasts with the 43% use of -*s* that we have already discussed in third singular contexts. Moreover, it's clear that children *can* add inflection to the verb when the subject is first singular *I*. This can be seen from the numbers for the regular and irregular past tense.

Looking just at *have*, we see the following distribution of *have* versus *has* with an *I* subject.

Table 9. Frequency of Have/Has *with* 'I' *Subject*

have	has/haves
108	0

Again, the almost zero use of *has* with first singular subjects and the almost zero use of *s* with first singular subjects with other main verbs shows that the children know agreement; they simply almost never use finite forms with the wrong subjects. Thus we cannot think of *have* with third singular subjects as being a case of incorrect agreement, of the wrong finite form being used. Rather, as we have already argued, and as fits in with the general properties of the optional-infinitive stage, *have* with third singular subjects is an infinitival form.

4.2. Use of Inflection

It remains to be shown that the majority of the non-inflected utterances did not come from periods in the children's corpora when the majority of the utterances are not inflected. In other words, it could be the case that negation has no bearing on inflection, and all the relevant examples are drawn from transcripts in which verbs are simply more likely to be left uninflected. In particular, we should analyze separately the data of children from an age which is even more squarely within the optional-infinitive ages. In general, children before 2;6 in English very often omit third singular -*s*, so we will analyze the data separately for files from before and after age 2;6.

Table 10. Use of Inflection/Negation by Group

	younger children 1;6–2;6		older children 2;7–4:1	
	aff	neg	aff	neg
−inflection	596	31	186	16
+inflection	307	3	287	2
% +inf	34	9	61	11

It is clear from these tables that even children younger than 2;6 show a major difference in the amount of tense inflection on the verb in affirmative and medial negative sentences. (34% versus 9%). In fact, the example we earlier discussed from Peter 15 which has inflection on the preposition is one of the 3 cases of inflected verbs after medial negation for children younger than 2;6. Removing this case as a performance error yields 2 inflected forms out of 34 for the medial negation sentences. This means that children under 2;6 only inflect the verb in medial negation sentences 6% of the time. Thus, for the crucial instance of the *young* children, the proportion of inflected medial negation sentences is extremely close to zero. It seems quite reasonable to take this small number as performance errors. Furthermore, the older children show the same pattern.

The optional-infinitive hypothesis makes another prediction regarding the appearance of tense. As discussed in Section 2, the auxiliary *do* is assumed to be inserted in a sentence with *not* only so that a TNS feature can be checked off. As we showed earlier, *do* insertion is necessary in a sentence with *not* if and only if the sentence has TNS. Therefore, we would expect the occurrence of (the appropriate tensed form of) *do* in negated sentences to coincide with the occurrence of inflection in affirmatives. In other words, the child's propensity to add inflection in affirmatives ought to be more or less the same as his propensity to add inflection in negated sentences.

Note that this prediction is quite distinct from other ideas concerning *do*. For example, it might be thought (as it often has been thought) that medial-NEG sentences occurred because the child did not **know** *do* and that this lack of knowledge of *do* accounted for medial-NEG sentences.[22] Under such an analysis we would expect medial-NEG sentences to only occur at a time when *do* was not used at all. The optional-infinitive hypothesis, on the other hand, predicts that *do* insertion is linked to the use of TNS. To check the hypothesis, we compared the use of *do* in *not* contexts with the use of TNS in general.

The criteria for including items in Table 11 were as follows:

In the *don't-V* column, any form of *do* as an auxiliary was included, including *do not, does, doesn't, don't, didn't, does not* and *did not* as long as the context was third person singular. No form of *do* as a main verb was included. Examples of *don't-V* entries include:

(16) a. *that didn't went down*   Peter 17
      b. *he don't want some money*   Adam 19
      c. *Taki [?] doesn't want to*   Naomi 81

The *not-V* (medial-NEG) sentences were those containing *no* or *not*, either before or after a subject, or with no subject at all and without *do* or any other auxiliary verb, e.g., *Saifi no knock on the door*. Irregular past tense verbs as well as regular past tense verbs were counted as *-ed* verbs. Only bare stem verbs, and those ending with *-s* or *-ed* were included. Verbs with *-ing* were not included.

The percentages in Table 11 following were calculated only using the 'bare' sentences, meaning that no inflection whatsoever appeared in the sentences.

The prediction is that the two ratios will be roughly similar in a particular group. This is more or less borne out. The absolute ratios tend to follow each other from low in the early years to high in later years, with no more than a 13

Table 11. Frequency and Proportion of Bare Negatives, Do-Support and Tense

	grand		young		old	
	not-V	don't-V	not-V	don't-V	not-V	don't-V
bare	49	64	34	22	16	43
-s	5	2	3	0	2	2
-ed	0	5	0	0	0	5

	grand	young	old
proportion of do used in required negative contexts	.56	.37	.73
proportion of inflected verbs in affirmative sentences (from Tables 5 and 7)	.43	.34	.61

point gap. This is suggestive of the fact that do-support and inflectional mor-phology are related to TNS in the same way.

It is important to note that by counting only those instances of do-support from files with bare negation, a bias has been introduced which lowers the ratio of do-support to bare negation. Of all files containing negation, only the files containing bare negation were studied. Since there is not a great number of negated sentences in any transcript, bare negation sentences are over-represented in our comparison against the do-support sentences (which come from the same files). The more appropriate (and ambitious) tabulation would be to count do-support sentences in all transcripts, thereby driving their percentages up. We did not do that analysis because the main point of this paper was to study the interaction of medial negation and inflection; thus we only coded the data from files containing examples of medial negation.

Thus, we would like to stress what we have just pointed out; namely, it might turn out on fuller analysis that do is used much more often in required negative contexts than -s is used in required affirmative contexts.[23] If this turns out to be true, it actually could be understood in the following manner. In English, there are two negative morphemes, not and n't. The second is an affix; that is, it requires that it be attached to a host verb. Suppose children knew both not and n't and know their properties, namely that n't is an affix and not is not an affix. Thus, the children will know that n't requires a verb to host it. All this is just to assume that children know these elementary properties of English.

Now assume one thing further; namely, that children in production *prefer* to use *n't*. This is a natural assumption, as *n't* is the more colloquial form. *Not* is often more formal, used in more special contexts. On this assumption, children will select *n't* much more often than they will select *not*. Once the child has selected *n't* in production, she will have to use a verb to attach it to, since she knows that *n't* is an affix. Thus since there is no other auxiliary, the properties of English will force the use of *do*. Thus it follows that *do* will be used very often in negative contexts, rather than medial negation.

It is important that we have had to think of a reason that *do* is used *more* often than expected, compared to the use of obligatory TENSE. This means that we cannot explain the existence of medial-NEG sentences by saying that there is a problem with knowledge of *do* or of *do*-insertion. This result provides yet further evidence for the optional-infinitive stage in English; *do* is omitted optionally where required because TENSE is omitted optionally where required. There is no medial-NEG stage in the sense that *do* is *always* omitted; there is no hint of such a phenomenon in the data, rather the contrary. *Do*-omission is clearly optional, just like *-s* omission and other manifestations of the optional-infinitive stage.

Of course, as pointed out in the original discussion of the optional-infinitive stage in Wexler (1992, 1994), the younger the child in general, the smaller the proportion of tensed root verbs. The possibility was even noted that if a child was young enough, the proportion of tensed verbs might go to zero. In such a case, where TENSE was almost completely missing, we would expect *do* to be almost completely missing in negative sentences. Any indication that there was a particular problem with *do* might have been due to the fact that TENSE (and thus *do*) shows up only a small percentage of time in the youngest files.

4.3. *Appropriate Use of Tensed Forms*

Do children make correct use of tense? The optional-infinitives hypothesis maintains that while infinitive forms may be used optionally in places where tensed forms are used in adult speech, children do indeed have knowledge of tense, and will not use a tensed form incorrectly. Is this borne out in the data? Such a count can be done only by determining the implied time of action referred to by the sentences. Naturally, this is rather subjective in nature, especially when the coder was not present during the recording. Following standard practice, we have attempted as best we could to determine the time that the child was intending to refer to by her utterance. Given the mentioned limitations, these counts are meant to provide a rough idea of whether the assumption of knowledge of tense is supported even in this regard.

The following counts were conducted by examining the utterances surrounding the target sentence in order to determine whether the child was referring to past, present, or future events. Ambiguous contexts were excluded from the counts.

Statements concerning on-going activities were always interpreted as being in the present tense. Statements concerning what seemed to indicate future time or a desired state of affairs were interpreted as future. Statements concerning past events or events referred to by adults as past events were so interpreted. The counts resulted in the following table, in which an entry reflects the number of utterances with a particular morphological form (-*inf* means 'bare stem'):

Table 12. Time of Reference by Inflection

	present	past	future
-inf	771	128	39
-*s*	418	14	5
-*ed*	10	168	0

The first thing to note about this table is that *tensed* forms are used almost completely correctly; (a) present tense -*s* is used 418 (96%) times to indicate present and only 19 times to indicate past or future and (b) past tense -*ed* is used 168 (94%) times to mean past and only 10 times to mean present, and never to mean future. Thus the overwhelming number of uses of a tensed (finite) verb corresponds to the correct use of tense.

The use of the bare stem, on the other hand, shows a wider variation in meaning. Although 771 (82%) instances of the bare stem refer to present tense, 128 refer to the past and 39 refer to the future. Thus there is a considerably larger percentage of non-present contexts for –inf verbs (18%) than for -*s* verbs (4%). Note that although the difference between 4% and 18% may not appear to be very large, we essentially predict a 0% use of non-present contexts for -*s* verbs, and this is very close to what we found; essentially we consider the 4% to be performance errors, as was the less than 10% use of finite tense in medial neg contexts. The only 18% non-present contexts for –inf verbs may reflect a stronger tendency to use past morphology for past contexts; at any rate, there is no reason we would expect a larger percentage.

To be statistically precise, we should ask whether the –inf distribution is

really a different distribution than what we find for *-s*? We collapsed past and
future into nonpresent (Table 13) and examined –inf and *-s* with a test of χ^2.

Table 13. *Inflection by Temporal Context*

	present	nonpresent
-inf	771	167
-s	418	19

The result was highly significant ($\chi^2 = 46.15$, 1 *df*, p < .0001). This means
that the number of present context sentences containing verbs inflected with *-s*
is disproportionately large compared to the number of similar sentences with
uninflected verbs. Another way of looking at this would be to say that non-
present-context sentences were less likely to contain *-s*. Thus, we are lead to
conclude that the bare stem is less restricted than *-s* in its use in present/
nonpresent contexts.

This is exactly what the optional-infinitive hypothesis would expect. The
use of the nonfinite form, the optional-infinitive hypothesis assumes, indicates
that the child is filling in the tense specifications from context, just as the
nonfinite form in adult language has its tense specifications filled in by a higher
tense. Since context often specifies a present tense, we would expect many of
these. But, when needed, the nonfinite form may refer to past and future events.

Thus contextual, interpretive evidence supports the optional-infinitive
hypothesis. (See Behrens 1993 for similar results in optional infinitive German.)
Hypotheses which say that the 'bare stem' use of the verb with third singular
subjects reflects only the 'dropping' of *-s*, or an allophonic variant of the form
with *-s* (for example Hypothesis II above) would suggest that the bare stem (i.e.,
–inf) form would be used in the same contexts in which verb + *-s* is used. But
the table above shows this is quite clearly not the case; *-s* is used only 3% of
the time to refer to the past, whereas the bare stem is used 13% of the time to
refer to the past. Similarly, *-s* is used less than 1% of the time to refer to the
future, whereas the bare stem is used about 3% of the time to so refer. Even
more strikingly, from Table 12 we can calculate that whereas 41% of past
contexts contain a ⟨–inf⟩ verb, only 4.5% of past contexts contain an *-s* verb.

Clearly the bare stem can be used to refer to a wide variety of temporal
interpretations, whereas the finite forms are much more fixed. These contextual
results support the hypothesis of the optional-infinitive stage.

5. Elicitation Study

We also did an elicitation study, attempting to induce children to produce negated sentences, to see if they produced medial-NEG sentences, and what form of the verb was used in such sentences. One reason we did this was because there were a limited number of medial-NEG sentences in the CHILDES corpus. Presumably this is because children who would produce medial-NEG sentences would be younger children, who use tense less often, but younger children also use negation less often. Thus we attempted to induce young children to use negation.

There was a second reason we decided to do an elicitation experiment, namely to help to eliminate another hypothesis. Suppose somebody believed in one of the versions of the "no functional categories" view, perhaps in Hypothesis II. Although this hypothesis by itself cannot explain why medial-NEG sentences don't show TENSE, if an auxiliary hypothesis were added, the phenomenon could be explained. In particular, suppose one assumed that processing difficulties caused by the addition of an extra element (negation) caused a morpheme (TENSE) to be omitted.[24] Then, even if one assumed that bare stem verbs and verbs with s were simply allophonic variants of the other, (except that the forms with -s had third singular markings, i.e., Hypothesis II) the extra assumption about processing difficulty could explain why TNS was omitted when negation appeared.

Of course, this is a very complicated hypothesis, assuming both that children don't know the meaning of -s as present TNS and that the occurrence of morphemes causes other morphemes to be omitted. And even the auxiliary processing hypothesis could not explain the standard crosslinguistic optional-infinitive results, since the nonfinite morpheme still counts as a morpheme, and the surface-style 'processing-load' hypothesis would have to say why a finite morpheme should take up more room in 'memory' than a nonfinite morpheme. Nevertheless, we attempted to obtain more direct evidence that the auxiliary 'processing' hypothesis together with the 'no functional categories' hypothesis could not explain the data.

To do this, we could take advantage of the existence in English of adverbs, including negative adverbs like *never*, which do not require *do*-support, and do not interfere with the placement of inflection on the verb. If any extra element in the sentence interfered with the production of TENSE on the verb, then *never* should interfere as much as *not*. If this were the case, we would see no distinction between adverbs and negation. If children treat *go* and *goes* as allophonic variants, then *he never goes* and *he not goes* would have the same status; the proportion of tensed verbs after *never* should be equal to the proportion of tensed verbs after *not*; tense would be dispreferred in each case by the auxiliary processing hypothesis. That is, the addition of the negative element would make tense less likely.

Notice that in the optional-infinitive view, the infrequency of inflection after a verb in a negated sentence follows from the status of NEG as a functional head. But adjoined elements like adverbs are not potential barriers to raised elements. In children's speech, the optional-infinitive hypothesis expects an inflected verb after an adverb as often as when the verb is not preceded by an adverb; at any rate, the optional-infinitive hypothesis expects more inflected verbs after an adverb than after a NEG head (as indicated by the existence of *not* in the utterance). The optional-infinitive hypothesis predicts that only one of the following six forms, *he not goes,* is ungrammatical for optional-infinitive children:

Table 14. Predictions

[main verb]	*He go*
[main verb] + *s*	*He goes*
[main verb]	*He never go*
[main verb] + *s*	*He never goes*
[main verb]	*He not go*
*[main verb] + *s*	*He not goes*

In order to observe the use of adverbs by very young children, an elicitation study was devised. Testing was done at local day-care centers with the aid of a farm playset and a Sesame Street playset. Each child took turns playing with one, and was asked questions about ongoing activities. A fixed battery of questions was impossible to employ due to the rather limited attention span of children of this age. All questions are given in the context of free play. The questions were of the forms:

(16) a. *Does the cow always go in the barn, or does she never go?*

b. *Does the cow go in the barn or does she not go in the barn?*

That is, type (16a) uses an adverb which does not interfere with tense on the verb, whereas type (16b) uses *not*, which requires *do*-support. The two types alternated in precedence.

They were also asked questions of the form:

(17) a.   *Do you think he always goe<u>s</u> or do you think he never goe<u>s</u>?*
      b.   *Do you think that he goe<u>s</u>, or don't you think that he goe<u>s</u>?*

so they could hear questions with inflection on the main verb.

At the outset of testing, none of the children could answer the adverb questions. Typical responses are, "He does go," or just "Yeah," and "No." Of twenty-seven children evaluated,[25] only four were both successful with the full range of question types and also produced medial-NEG sentences. Other children either were too undeveloped to answer the questions fully enough or were so developed that they always used *do*-support. The four children are aged 2;1, 2;1 to 2;2, 2;3 and 2;8 to 2;9. The 2;8 child was a little delayed and his data fit with the others.

Sample Questions/Answers

EXP: *Do you think that he always sleeps in the yard, or do you think that he never sleeps in the yard?*
SUB: *Never sleeps in yard.*

EXP: *Does this cow go up there, or does this cow not go up there?*
SUB: *Not go up there.*

EXP: *Does that farmer go in, or don't you think the farmer goes in?*
SUB: *He not go in.*

EXP: *Do you think that chicken always plays in there, or do you think that chicken never plays in there?*
SUB: *Always play there.*

The following tables show, for these four children, the number and percentage of inflected and non-inflected tense-determinable verbs, for 3 different types of produced sentences; affirmative sentences, medial-NEG sentences with an adverb (e.g., *never* or *always*) which does not require *do*-support, and with *not*. By 'affirmative' sentences we mean sentences without an adverb or *not*; of course, some of the adverb sentences are affirmative, if the adverb is other than *never*; however, almost all the adverbs that children used were *never*.

Tables 15 show the three different kinds of sentences studied, and the frequency with which the main verb was inflected. The number on the left is the percentage of total utterances in that condition, and the number on the right reflects the raw count.

The tables differ in the following way: The first, 'grand total', shows all the utterances that the child made. The second table, 'responses to questions', shows only the utterances that the child made when asked a direct question, of the kind

Table 15. Sentence Type by Type of Inflection

	grand total					
	affirmative		adverb		*not*	
INFL	38%	60	28%	20	9%	4
not INFL	62%	98	72%	51	91%	42

	responses to questions					
	affirmative		adverb		*not*	
INFL	59%	23	26%	17	12%	4
not INFL	41%	16	74%	49	88%	29

	irrelevant or spontaneous					
	affirmative		adverb		*not*	
INFL	31%	37	60%	3	0%	0
not INFL	69%	82	40%	2	100%	13

we mentioned above. The third table, 'irrelevant or spontaneous', includes only the utterances that the child made that were *not* elicited directly by a question from the experimenter. Thus the entries in the first table are the sum of the corresponding entries in the second and third tables.

Looking at the grand totals, notice the difference in inflection between the negated sentences and the affirmative and adverb sentences. That is, the verb is inflected only 9% of the time when *not* is used, whereas it is inflected 28% of the time when an adverb is used and 38% of the time when neither *not* nor an adverb is used. The fact that the use of *not* pushes the use of inflection (TENSE) toward zero, while this is not true for adverbial (e.g., *never*) use, supports the optional-infinitive hypothesis and is not consistent with Hypothesis II supplemented by the auxiliary 'processing load' hypothesis. Moreover, the results in general are quite consistent with the results from the CHILDES natural production study; *not* in medial-NEG sentences pushes the use of tense toward zero (9%) whereas this is not true for sentences without *not*. Thus the optional-infinitive hypothesis is supported.

In fact, if we look at the third table, the 'irrelevant or spontaneous' utterances, we find an even more striking result. Here the use of inflection with sentences with no adverbs or *not* is 31%, with adverbs it is 60% (though there are only five such sentences overall) and with *not* it is 0% (out of 13 tokens overall). The reason there are fewer negatives in this table, of course, is that these represented the ones which were not elicited. Nevertheless, the difference between 0% for *not* and 31% inflection without *not* is quite striking and supportive of the optional-infinitive hypothesis. This is a particularly interesting condition because there was no question given to the child which could have influenced the response, a point which we will address shortly.

The second table, including only 'responses to questions,' also shows a major difference between *not* (12%) and affirmatives (59%) with respect to the incidence of inflection; the use of inflection for adverbs, however, falls in between the other 2 numbers (26%). The use of inflection is in the predicted direction; more inflection is used with adverbs such as *never* than with *not*. If processing difficulty of a surface form were accounting for these facts, then, if anything adverbs like *never* should cause *more* difficulty and show a lower rate of inflection; after all, *never* has two syllables rather than one; moreover, it is less common than *not*. All in all, the optional-infinitive hypothesis seems to be supported, although it would be good to have further studies, with more subjects, to see whether the difference between non-adverbial (affirmative) and adverbial sentences is reliable and whether there is any effect at all on inflection of having an adverb in the sentence.[26]

We have put into Table 16 the same data, broken down for each of the four children. These tables correspond to the *grand totals* section of Table 15; that is, they include all the children's utterances. Since there is not a large amount of data for each child, for simplicity, we have only given the grand totals for each child. The data in Table 16 show that the basic pattern that we have described above holds for each child; namely, there is a good deal more tense marking in an affirmative sentence than when there is a *not* in the sentence.[27]

While the results in Tables 15 and 16 show that the trend is in the predicted direction, there is a possible source of confounding with the question/answer paradigm. Since we are dealing with very young children, in an experimental setting, we should consider whether any kind of imitative response to the experimenter's question could make the responses come out in favor of the optional-infinitive hypothesis. Table 17 lists children's responses using inflected verbs depending on whether the child used the same inflection that the experimenter used in his question (copied infl), or whether the child used the opposite inflection. A child's utterance could also be classified as 'irrelevant,' a response

Table 16. Grand Totals for Each Child

	child 1 (2:1)		
	affirmative	adverb	*not*
INFL	17	3	2
not INFL	21	8	12

	child 2 (2;8–2;9)		
	affirmative	adverb	*not*
INFL	10	7	2
not INFL	10	14	11

	child 3 (2;1–2;2)		
	affirmative	adverb	*not*
INFL	17	4	0
not INFL	34	15	3

	child 4 (2;3)		
	affirmative	adverb	*not*
INFL	9	4	0
not INFL	3	8	1

which disregarded the content of the experimenter's preceding utterance. These responses are listed for each type of sentence (affirmative, adverb, or *not*) that the child produced.

In all cases, the children are more likely to answer using inflection if inflection had been used in the question. For example, if the question is, "Does he always go, or does he never go?" the child is more likely to answer "Never go" or "Always go," rather than "Never goe_s._"

Note that this result is not surprising for the affirmatives and the adverbs. The optional-infinitive hypothesis is that sometimes verbs appear in finite form and sometimes infinitival. Nothing is said about when one form will be chosen over the other, except in certain syntactic contexts (e.g., after *not,* as we have

Table 17. Frequency of Children's Inflection as a Function of Stimulus Inflection

	affirmative	adverb	*not*
copied INFL	46	46	24
counter INFL	29	18	14
irrelevant	83	7	8

been discussing). So we shouldn't be surprised to observe that children use inflection in a preceding question as a cue; both forms are possible and they are using the preceding question to influence their response. What we do not expect is for this cue to be used in the negated (*not*) sentences.

But consider the cases of *counter*–inflection (Table 18). Remember that the children do produce a sizable percentage of counter–inflection. The environments in which such utterances occur provide insight. The tables indicate whether inflection (-*s*) appears or does not (∅) appear in the 'stimulus' (i.e., experimenter's question) and whether inflection appears or does not appear in the children's response, for each type of child sentence, affirmative, adverb or *not*. For example, in the first, 'grand total' table, we see that when the child's sentence contains an adverb, there are 17 utterances in which the experimenter used an -*s* and the child did not use an -*s* and 16 utterances when the experimenter used an -*s* and the child used an -*s*. On the other hand, for sentences which contained an adverb, when the experimenter's question did not use an -*s*, the child's sentence failed to use an -*s* 30 times, and *did* use an -*s* only once.

Look at the second table, 'responses to questions'. For the affirmatives, a strong copying bias is evident when the experimenter used inflection. There are 15, or about 68%. For the adverb condition, there are 14, or about 48%. Now look at the *not* condition. Here there are only 4, or 25%. This reduction suggests that some grammatical knowledge is being tapped.

Unfortunately, there seems to be a bias against adding inflection where none was given (bottom row, each right hand cell). No comparison between sentence types can be made here.

Let us return to our predictions: Inflection ought to be optional for affirmatives and affirmatives with adverbs; 38–28% were so inflected. For the negated sentences, we predict no examples of inflection, and we have four (9%). Given that there is a copying bias, it is remarkable that only 9% of the *not* sentences showed inflection. Note that the random -*s*- hypothesis has no way of accounting for this split.

Table 18. Questions and Answers, Compared by Inflection

stimulus	grand total					
	affirmative		adverb		*not*	
	Ø	-s	Ø	-s	Ø	-s
-s	20	20	17	16	14	4
Ø	26	9	30	1	20	0

	responses to questions					
	affirmative		adverb		*not*	
	Ø	-s	Ø	-s	Ø	-s
-s	7	15	16	14	12	4
Ø	6	3	30	1	16	0

	irrelevant					
	affirmative		adverb		*not*	
	Ø	-s	Ø	-s	Ø	-s
-s	13	5	1	2	2	0
Ø	20	6	0	0	4	0

6. Conclusion

In this paper we have tested the hypothesis that young English children are in the optional-infinitive stage, and that this accounts for the optional lack of finite inflection on verbs, in particular for the lack of -s in third singular present tense. The evidence that we have adduced includes:

(a) Tense inflection is optionally missing from main verbs.

(b) Tense inflection is optionally missing from possessive *have*.

(c) Agreement is correct with main verbs; that is, -s is never used with first person singular subjects.

(d) Agreement is correct with possessive *have*; that is, *has* is never used with first person singular subjects.

(e) In medial-NEG sentences (i.e., with missing *do*), the verb does not show TENSE.

(f) TENSE is used far more often in affirmative sentences than in medial-NEG sentences.

(g) Present (*-s*) and past (*-ed*) morphemes refer almost exclusively to present or past events, respectively, but bare stems (the nonfinite forms of the optional-infinitive stage) refer to past, present or future events.

(h) Adverbs like *never* behave differently from *not* (in the elicitation experiment, where they were studied). Namely, they do not interfere with the use of TENSE on the verbs, as *not* does in medial-NEG sentences.

(i) At the age when children use medial-NEG sentences they also use sentences with *do*-support, in fact more than they use TENSE in general. Thus, medial-NEG sentences cannot be explained by lack of knowledge of *do*, or of *do*-support. Rather, medial-NEG sentences are the result of the optional-infinitive stage.

Any hypothesis concerning early inflectional development in English (or more generally) must deal with these phenomena. The evidence concerning the optional-infinitive stage in English that we have presented amply confirms Wexler's (1992, 1994) hypothesis that English shows the optional-infinitive stage. Moreover, we can now see the optional-infinitive stage as explaining and integrating a broad range of phenomena in early English morphological development.[28] At the beginning of this paper we talked about the possibility that inflectional development in general and English inflectional development in particular, were now subject to a more integrated and explanatory treatment. We believe that the data have provided support for such a position. We also believe that the success of research based on crosslinguistic analysis in explaining in a more integrated fashion data from a very well studied language shows that the promise of comparative language acquisition studies can be realized; there is much to learn about a particular language from analyses based on other languages. Of course, a major task that lies ahead is a better understanding of what is the underlying basis and cause of the optional-infinitive stage, why it exists in some languages and not others, and why it has the particular properties that it has. But that is a task for another day.

Appendix A. Cases of Tense-Determinable Medial Negation

Abe028
it not works Mom [#] it not works

Adam01
xxx TV not go

Adam03
oh no xxx do suitcase
no no xxx have one
oh no xxx happen

Adam04
no # fit
no it [?] fit

Adam13
dis not fit

Adam19
dat one not bump dat one # no
yeah # he not have hair
no dat blast off
dat no blast+off

Adam27
Mommy # de water not spill

Adam29
an(d) de man can see his # not # have
a bump

Adam43
not come to play # but she plays

Apr02
Saifi no knock on the door

Eve01
man no [?] taste it
man no taste it?

Eve08
not Fraser read it
no # Fraser read it

Eve13
not go go in the bushes

Eve14
Fraser not see him

Naom71
no [#] this go [#] this is broken

Naom81
this one [#] no blow bubbles

Nath01
no ba [#] no have de microphone
no nathaniel has a microphone a mi-
crophone

Nina01
no fit

Nina07
no. no. no lamb have it
no. no lamb have a chair either
no. no Nina stand up there

Nina09
no hop Mommy kangaroo. you Linda
kangaroo
no talk Mommy. no talk Mommy

Nina10
here. no dog stay in the room

Nina11
no Leila have a turn

Nina18
no fit [a box]

Peter08
no goes in there [#] no

Peter10
no [#] no fit in that

Peter11
Jenny [#] no [#] no [#] no have that

Peter13
no Jenny bug

Peter15
the horse not stand up
but the horse not stand upsən

Peter16
it not spill. put it in here. it not spill

Peter17
no the chair not go in here
no goes here

Sar030
no # op(en) a door

Sar040
he no bite ya

Sar046
tha(t) no(t) hurt

Sar091
has no hair

Shem01
now, no go here

Shem07
no go 'way the(re)

Shem13
not go in the water

Shem15
an' not work
wadio not work

Appendix B. Transcripts and Ages

file	age	file	age
Abe028	2;8	Apr02	2;1
Adam01	2;3	Eve01	1;6
Adam03	2;4	Eve05	1;8
Adam04	2;4	Eve08	1;9
Adam13	2;9	Eve13	2;0
Adam15	2;10	Eve14	2;0
Adam19	2;11	Naom71	2;9
Adam27	3;3	Naom81	3;2
Adam29	3;4	Nath01	2;5
Adam40	3;11	Nina01	1;11
Adam43	4;1	Nina07	2;0
Peter10	2;3	Nina09	2;1
Peter11	2;3	Nina10	2;1
Peter13	2;5	Nina11	2;1
Peter15	2;6	Nina18	2;3

Peter08	2;1	Sarah046	3;1
Peter09	2;2	Sarah091	4;1
Peter16	2;7	Shem01	2;2
Peter17	2;8	Shem07	2;4
Peter18	2;9	Shem13	2;5
Sarah030	2;9	Shem15	2;6
Sarah040	3;0		

Acknowledgements

We would like to thank Harald Clahsen for a close reading of the paper, and many valuable comments.

Notes

1. In fact, it appears as if the nonfinite forms occur in English even later than 2;7, perhaps even later than 3;0. See Rice, Wexler & Cleave (1995) for some quantitative data from both naturalistic production and elicitation tasks.

2. There is a possible variant to this way of stating the theory/generalization; namely, one could assume that TENSE exists in every root representation in the optinal-infinitive stage, but the values of +/− past are optionally missing, thus allowing infinitival verbs. If the TENSE projection is actually missing, it explains why the infinitival morphemes (English *to,*; French *à, de;* German *zu,* etc.), are not produced in the optional-infinitive stage along with the nonfinite verbs. Since these morphemes are usually taken to reside in the head of (nonfinite) TENSE, a missing TENSE head will be incompatible with the existence of these morphemes. See Wexler (1995, in press) for discussion. See also Bromberg & Wexler (1995) and Rhee & Wexler (1995).

3. Most analyses, as in Chomsky (1992) assume the 'lexicalist' approach exemplified by (b), that is, that the whole word is drawn from the lexicon, but this is not necessary; it depends on assumptions about how morphology works. We will not refer to the issue any further, since the particular analyses will not depend on which assumption is correct.

4. The examples in (5) are from Pollock (1984).

5. We do not wish to suggest that Hypotheses I and II have necessarily been proposed, although Hypothesis III has (Aldridge 1989). We are simply trying to lay out the logic of what might account for the *he go/he goes* alternation.

6. Of course, it is possible that there is a stage with no functional categories *before* the optional-infinitive stage. Radford (1994) appears to accept the existence of Wexler's (1991, 1992, 1994) optional-infinitive stage, as a transitional stage, though without

referring to those papers. It is difficult, however, to tell whether such a no functional category stage actually exists. The data supporting the no-functional-category stage (e.g., Radford 1990) are given as examples of children's utterances, but no quantitative evidence is given, so we do not know, for example, whether the children studied produce only verbs without tense inflection, or whether they sometimes produce inflected verbs. In studies which *do* provide quantitative evidence, it has proven difficult to show that there really is an early stage with *no* tense-marking. Wexler (1991, 1992, 1994) suggested that this might be the case, but left the question open empirically.

7.   We base our discussion of Aldridge (1989) on the presentation of it in Radford (1994).

8.   Since we do not have Aldridge (1989) available to us, we do not know if she takes into account the fact that *cry/cries* occur with different subject agreement features. Radford (1994) proposes (and rejects) an analysis in which *cry* does not have agreement or TENSE, but only *finite* features, so that it can be used with any kind of subject, but it is not clear that this is Aldridge's position.

9.   Evidence for this is provided in Section 4. For further evidence, see Rice, Wexler & Cleave (1995).

10.   Of course, one could try a theory in which agreement was not represented in a functional category, as Iatridou (1990) and Chomsky (1995) suggest. But the 'no functional categories' theories seem to want agreement not known to the child. At any rate, we will offer evidence that children in English in the optional-infinitive stage know more than agreement; that is the point of this paper.

11.   We are illustrating derivations with TNS higher then AGR, following an older tradition (e.g., Pollock 1989). The same points could be made with AGR higher than TNS; the exact syntactic analysis is not what is important here, but the general point, which will follow in all analyses.

12.   The question of why *do* must be inserted in English negatives is actively under discussion in minimalist theory, and there are a number of proposals, which vary in a number of ways, including whether or not the verb raises at LF if it does not raise on the surface, the role of distributed morphology, and of adjacency, etc. We have given just one simple formulation, for concreteness. We do not wish to be committed to this view of negation in English nor to claim that any of the current versions hold this view. The point we will make about distributional correlations holds no matter which account of *do*-insertion is correct. Wexler (1995, see also Bromberg & Wexler 1995) argues that TNS is completely missing from Optional Infinitives. Sentences such as (11) thus do not require or allow a verb to have TNS features.

13.   See Pollock (1989) for discussion on why main verbs fail to do this.

14.   And that is why *do* is not inserted in infinitival clauses in adult English:
      (i)   *I want her to not like me.*
      (ii)   **I want her to do not like me.*

15. Actually, the 'no functional categories' hypothesis, if made precise, would probably predict that *do* must be omitted, contradicting the empirical results that follow, which show that *do* is only optionally omitted, as predicted by the optional-infinitive hypothesis. For the 'no functional categories' hypothesis to predict that *do* may be optionally omitted, it would presumably have to say that *does* and *e*, the empty verb, are 'morphological variants' of each other, an assumption that might be difficult to coherently make.

16. Or any of the other variants, which are even more problematic empirically, e.g., Hypothesis I or III. So far as we can determine, earlier nonlinguistic descriptions, (e.g., Brown 1973) do not make any predictions at all, since they have no way of talking about the correlation between distribution and morphology. For example, they can talk about third singular German -*t* increasing in third singular contexts, but they do not have a way of describing its complementary distribution with the infinitival form, and that, moreover, the verb winds up in a diffent position. The insufficient descriptive categories of Brown (1973) and the traditions based on it are hardly surprising since much of the relevant grammatical theory was not yet developed (e.g., verb movement, etc.).

17. Brown corpora: Adam, Eve, Sarah   Sachs corpus: Naomi
    L. Bloom corpus: Peter   Clark corpus: Shem
    Suppes corpus: Nina   Higginson corpus: April
    Kuczaj corpus: Abe   Snow corpus: Nathaniel

18. We decided to try to find as many bare negation examples as possible; that is why we included children up until 4;1. Obviously most of the cases came from younger children (see Appendix A for the entire list). Since our main point was to compare the optional-infinitive account of bare verbs to other accounts, examples from all these ages might be taken as relevant. At any rate, since our results were so strong and categorical (i.e., there were almost no inflected bare negative verbs), the same results will hold if we cut off the data at some younger age, say 3;0 or 3;6.

19. There were only a very few examples in which negation preceded the subject, and we will not discuss this issue further. Pierce (1989) suggested that examples with negation preceding the subject showed a very early stage in which the subject did not raise out of the VP. We will not discuss the issue any further; the important point for us is that the optional-infinitive hypothesis predicts that if *do* is omitted, the verb will not be tensed, whether the subject has raised out of VP or not.

20. Two examples were 'haves,' an overregularization, similar to those noted in the past tense.

21. Also, *you* subjects could often be used in commands, and we did not want our results to be favored by the child's knowledge of imperatives.

22. For example, Sano & Hyams (1994) suggest that lack of knowldge of *do*-support is responsible for medial-NEG sentences.

23. This result, that *do*-insertion is used more often in required (*not*) contexts than TENSE is used in required contexts, appears also to be emerging from ongoing unpublished research in normal and SLI children by one of the authors (Wexler) together with Mabel Rice.

24. This is exactly in the spirit of P. Bloom (1990), following L. Bloom (1970). In particular, P. Bloom argues that there is a 'processing bottleneck', in particular a length limitation on children's utterances, which forces elements of the grammar to be omitted in production. See Hyams & Wexler (1993) for arguments against this position.

25. Ages range from 2;0 to 2;10.

26. We predicted that the proportion of TNS following *never* and other adverbs would not be zero, but would rather be equal to the proportion of TNS following affirmative sentences. The numbers come out someplace in the middle, as we have pointed out. Thus, in the grand totals, the proportion of TNS following adverbs is 28%, which is distinctly more than the 9% following *not*, but less than the 38% in affirmative sentences. The important thing is that, in the grand totals, the adverbs behave more like affirmative sentences than like *not*. More studies will be needed to determine whether there *is* an effect of adverbs, as opposed to the pure affirmative sentences. For example, there might be some kind of *semantic* reason that a negative adverb like *never* seems to require TNS more often than when no adverb appears in the sentence. (Harald Clahsen, p.c.).

27. Children 3 and 4 only have three and one utterances with *not*, respectively. Thus, for them, the inference is a bit weaker, though of course they conform to the pattern.

28. We have not discussed in this paper other manifestations of the optional-infinitive stage in English, for example, Wexler's analysis of sentences with auxiliary (progressive) and copula *be* omitted as resulting from the optional-infinitive stage. He proposes that *be* is required essentially only to bind TENSE. Thus, when TENSE is omitted from the representation of a sentence, *be* is also omitted. Such further evidence only strenghens and broadens the case for the optional-infinitive stage in English.

References

Aldridge, M. 1989. *The Acquisition of INFL.* Bloomington, Ind.: Indiana State University Linguistics Club.

Behrens, H. 1993. "Temporal Reference in German Child Language." Diss., University of Amsterdam.

Bloom, L. 1970. *Language Development: Form and Function in emerging grammars.* Cambridge, Mass.: MIT Press.

Bloom, P. 1990. "Subjectless Sentences in Child Language." *Linguistic Inquiry* 21.491–504.

Boser, K., B. Lust, L. Santelmann & J. Whitman. 1991. "The Theoretical Significance of Auxiliaries in Early Child German." Paper presented at the 16th Boston University Conference on Langauge Development, Boston, Mass.

Bromberg, H. & K. Wexler. 1995. "Null Subjects in Wh-Questions." *Papers on Language Processing and Acquisition*, ed. by C. Schütze, J. Ganger & K. Broinier. *MIT Working Papers in Linguistics*, 26.221–248. Massachusetts Institute of Technology, Cambridge.

Brown, R. 1973. *A First Language: The early stages*. Cambridge, Mass.: Harvard University Press.

Chomsky, N. 1989. "Some Notes on Economy of Derivation and Representation." *MIT Working Papers in Linguistics*, Vol. 10. Cambridge: Massachusetts Institute of Technology.

―――. 1992. *A Minimalist Program for Linguistic Theory*. *MIT Working Papers in Linguistics*. Cambridge, Massachusetts Institute of Technology.

―――. 1995. Chapter 4. Ms., Massachusetts Institute of Technology, Cambridge.

Clahsen, H. 1990. "Constraints on Parameter setting: A grammatical analysis of some acquisition stages in German child language." *Language Acquisition* 1.361–391.

Clahsen, H. & M. Penke. 1992. "The Acquisition of Agreement Morphology and Its Syntactic Consequences: New evidence on German child language from the Simone-Corpus." *The Acquisition of Verb Placement: Functional categories and V2 phenomena in language acquisition*, ed. by J. Meisel, 181–224. Dordrecht: Kluwer.

Clark, E. 1978. "Awareness of Language: Some evidence from what children say and do." *The Child's Conception of Language*, ed. by R. J. A. Sinclair & W. Levelt. Berlin: Springer.

Guasti, T. 1994. "Verb Syntax in Italian Child Grammar: Finite and nonfinite verbs." *Language Acquisition* 3.1–40.

Guilfoyle, Eithne & M. Noonan. 1988. "Functional Categories and Language Acquisition." *Canadian Journal of Linguistics* 37.241–272.

Higginson, R. P. 1985. "Fixing: Assimilation in Language Aquisition." Diss., Washington State University.

Hyams, N. This volume. "The Underspecification of Functional Categories in Early Grammar."

Hyams, N. & K. Wexler. 1993. "On the Grammatical Basis of Null Subjects in Child Language." *Linguistic Inquiry* 24.421–459.

Iatridou, S. 1990. "About AgrP." *Linguistic Inquiry* 21.551–577.

Klima, E. & U. Bellugi. 1966. "Syntactic Regularities in the Speech of Children." *Psycholinguistic Papers*, ed. by J. Lyons and R. Wales, 183–207. Edinburgh: Edinburgh University Press.

Kuczaj, S. 1976. " -ing, -s and -ed: A study of the acquisition of certain verb inflections." Ms., University of Minnesota.

Lebeaux, David. 1988. "Language Acquisition and the Form of the Grammar." Ph.D. Diss., University of Massachusetts, Amherst.

MacWhinney, B. & C. Snow. 1985. "The Child Language Data Exchange System." *Journal of Child Language* 12. 271–296.

Meisel, J. & N. Müller. 1992. "Finiteness and Verb Placement in Early Child Grammars. *The Acquisition of Verb Placement: Functional categories and V2 phenomena in language acquisition*, ed. by J. Meisel, 109–138. Dordrecht: Kluwer.

Mills, A. 1985. "The Acquisition of German." *The Crosslinguistic Study of Language Acquisition*. Vol. 1, *The Data*, ed. by D. Slobin, 141–254. Hillsdale, N.J.: Lawrence Erlbaum.

Pierce, A. 1992. *Language Acquisition and Syntactic Theory: A comparative analysis of French and English child grammars*. Dordrecht: Kluwer.

Platzack, C. 1990. "A Grammar without Functional Categories: A syntactic study of early Swedish child language." *Nordic Journal of Linguistics*, 13.107–126.

Poeppel, D. & K. Wexler. 1993. "The Full Competence Hypothesis of Clause Structure in Early German." *Language* 69.1–33.

Pollock, Jean-Yves. "Verb Movement, Universal Grammar, and the Structure of IP." *Linguistic Inquiry* 20.365–424.

Radford, A. 1990. *Syntactic Theory and the Acquisition of English Syntax*. Oxford: Basil Blackwell.

————. 1994. "Tense and Agreement Variability in Child Grammars of English." *Syntactic Theory and First Language Acquisition: Crosslinguistic Perspectives*, ed. by B. Lust, M. Suñer & J. Whitman. Hillsdale, N.J.: Lawrence Erlbaum.

Rhee, J. & K. Wexler 1995. "Optional Infinitives in Hebrew." *Papers on Language Processing and Acquisition*, ed. by C. Schütze, J. Ganger & K. Broinier. *MIT Working Papers in Linguistics*, 26.383–402. Massachusetts Institute of Technology, Cambridge.

Rice, M., K. Wexler & P. Cleave. 1995. "Specific Language Impairment as a period of Extended Optional Infinitive." *Journal of Speech and Hearing Research* 38.850–863.

Sachs, J. 1983. "Talking about the There and Then: The emergence of displaced reference in parent-child discourse." *Children's Language*. Vol. 4, ed. by K.E. Nelson. Hillsdale, N.J.: Lawrence Erlbaum.

Sano, T. & N. Hyams. 1994. "Agreement, Finiteness, and the Development of Null Arguments." Paper presented at NELS 24, University of Massachusetts, Amherst.

Snow, C. 1981. "The Uses of Imitation." *Journal of Child Language* 8.205–212.

Suppes, P. 1973. "The Semantics of Children's Language." *American Psychologist* 88.103–114.

Verrips, M. & J. Weissenborn. 1992. "The Acquisition of Functional Categories Reconsidered." Paper presented at the Workshop on Crossing Boundaries, University of Tübingen, Germany.

Weissenborn J. 1990. "Functional Categories and Verb Movement in Early German: The acquisition of German syntax reconsidered." *Spracherwerb und Grammatik: Linguistische Untersuchungen zum Erwerb von Syntax und Morphologie* (= *Linguistische Berichte,* Special Issue 3), ed. by M. Rothweiler, 190–224. Opladen: Westdeutscher Verlag.

Wexler, K. 1990. "Optional Infinitives, Head Movement, and the Economy of Derivations in Child Grammar." Paper presented at the annual meeting of the Society of Cognitive Science, MIT.

————. 1992. *Optional Infinitives, Head Movement, and the Economy of Derivations in Child Grammar.* Occasional Paper #45, MIT Dept. Brain & Cognitive Science.

————. 1994. "Finiteness and Head Movement in Early Child Grammar." *Verb Movement,* ed. by D. Lighfoot and N. Hornstein, 305–350. Cambridge: Cambridge University Press.

————. 1995. "Feature Interpretability and Optionality in Early Child Grammar." Paper presented at the Workshop on Optimality, Utrecht.

————. In press. "The Development of Inflection in a Biologically-based Theory of Language Acquisition. *Towards a Genetics of Language,* ed. by M. Rice. Hillsdale, N.J.: Lawrence Erlbaum.

Towards a Structure-Building Model of Acquisition

Andrew Radford
University of Essex

1. Introduction

There are two broad approaches to the study of the acquisition of syntactic structure which are found in the acquisition literature. One approach (the STRUCTURAL CONTINUITY approach) assumes that UG (the theory of Universal Grammar which is an integral part of the child's Language Faculty) provides the child with a 'template' which specifies the (universal) structure of phrases and clauses. On this view, adult sentences and their child counterparts of necessity have the same syntactic structure; they differ only in respect of their phonetic form, in that certain morphemes/lexemes which are overtly realised in adult sentences have a null realization in child grammars. The second approach (the STRUCTURE-BUILDING approach) assumes that although principles of UG determine how they are built up, syntactic structures are projections of the lexical items they contain, and lexical items vary from one language to another. For example, Spanish has clitic pronouns which might be argued to move to some position within a superordinate functional projection FP (cf. Uriagereka 1995), whereas English lacks clitic pronouns and so might be argued to lack the functional projection FP which houses them. If we make the traditional assumption that children acquire some types of lexical item before others (e.g., verbs before auxiliaries, nouns before determiners), and further assume that UG excludes the possibility of vacuous projections (i.e., projections containing an unfilled head and specifier: cf. Speas 1994), it follows from the LEXICAL PROJECTION view that children will gradually build up syntactic structures 'one projection at a time' (so that acquiring a new type of item will lead to the projection of a new type of phrase): in other words, the lexical projection view presupposes a structure-building account of acquisition.

In this paper, I shall adopt a specific version of the structure-building
approach, and posit that syntactic structures are MINIMAL LEXICAL PROJECTIONS
— i.e., they are the minimal syntactic projections of the lexical items they
contain. This assumption subsumes the principle of economy of representation
proposed in Chomsky (1989), and variants of it developed by Law (1991),
Boskovic (1993), Grimshaw (1993a, b), Safir (1993), Speas (1994), etc. It should
be emphasized that the MLP (= Minimal Lexical Projection) Hypothesis is an
approach to grammar rather than to acquisition, and hence determines the nature
of adult and child phrase structure alike. For example, adopting a specific
version of the MLP hypothesis, Grimshaw (1993a) argues that while interrogative clauses such as *Will it rain?* are CP constituents, declarative clauses such as
It will rain project no further than IP (since they contain no complementizer or
inverted auxiliary). She maintains (1993a:5) that "[a] clause is only as big as it
needs to be. It is an IP unless it has to be a CP (a VP unless it has to be an
IP)." Having outlined the key theoretical assumption which I am making in this
paper, let me now turn to delimit the precise topic of the paper — namely the
account offered by the structure-building model of the nature of the earliest
clause (i.e., subject + predicate) structures produced by one-year-old children
acquiring English as their L1 (for ease of reference, I will refer to these as
CHILDREN'S INITIAL CLAUSES, abbreviated to CICs).[1] At the stage in question
(which they typically go through somewhere between one-and-a-half and two
years of age), English-acquiring children produce verbal clauses headed by a
nonfinite verb, as illustrated by the examples in (1)–(3) below:

(1)	*baby talking*	Hayley(1;8)
	doggy barking	Bethan(1;9)
	Daddy coming	Helen(1;9)
	Wayne sitting on gate	Daniel(1;9)
	Mummy doing dinner	Daniel(1;10)
(2)	*Daddy gone*	Paula(1;6)
	Wayne taken bubble	Daniel(1;9)
	Jem drawn with Daddy pen	Jem(1;11)
	Mummy thrown it	Jem(1;11)
	bunny broken foot	Claire(2;0), from Hill (1983)
(3)	*Paula play with ball*	Paula(1;6)
	Bethan want one	Bethan(1;8)
	machine make noise	Kathryn(1;9), from Bloom (1970)
	Hayley draw boat	Hayley(1;8)
	baby eat cookies	Allison(1;10), from Bloom (1973)

If we assume that clauses (like all other constituents) are minimal lexical projections, then one way in which we might analyze CICs like (1–3) is to posit that they are *Small Clause* (= SC) constituents which are simple projections of a head nonfinite lexical V constituent, so that children's clauses at this stage have a structure along the lines indicated in (4) below:

(4)

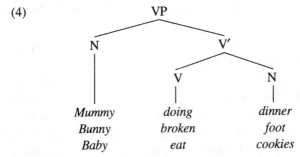

Mummy	*doing*	*dinner*
Bunny	*broken*	*foot*
Baby	*eat*	*cookies*

We might further assume that all theta-marking takes place under sisterhood, so that the complement is θ–marked by the head V, and the subject is θ–marked by its sister V-bar constituent. Just such a VP/SC/MLP analysis is suggested in Radford (1986, 1990), Lebeaux (1987, 1988), Guilfoyle & Noonan (1988), Kazman (1988) and Vainikka (1994).

Under the MLP analysis, all children's clauses at stage I are VPs which are direct projections of argument structure. It follows from this assumption that early child clauses have no functional architecture, and thus lack IP and CP projections. Evidence for the nonprojection of IP comes from the fact that children make no use of infinitival *to* or auxiliaries at this stage; for example, in contexts where adults require an IP headed by infinitival *to* (with an overt or null subject) children use a simple VP, as illustrated by the following examples taken from a longitudinal study of a boy called Daniel:

(5)	*want [have money]*	(1;7)
	want [Teddy drink]	(1;7)
	want [open door]	(1;8)
	want [Dolly talk]	(1;9)
	want [go out]	(1;10)
	want [lady get chocolate]	(1;11)

Likewise, corresponding to adult negative clauses containing the finite auxiliary *do,* children typically produce auxiliariless negative structures such as those in (6) below (from the Nina files on the CHILDES data base):

(6)	*no my play my puppet*	(2;0)
	no lamb have it	(2;0)
	no dog stay in the room	(2;1)
	no Leila have a turn	(2;1)

Evidence for the nonprojection of a CP constituent in CICs comes from the fact that children's earliest complement clauses such as those in (7) below lack complementizers:

(7)	*want [baby talking]*	Hayley(1;8)
	want [mummy come]	Jem(1;9)
	want [this go up]	Angharad(1;10)
	want [lady open it]	Daniel(1;10)

and from the fact that they omit complementizers on sentence-repetition tasks (cf. Phinney 1981). The fact that children produce complement clauses which do not require projection of a CP but not those which require CP is consistent with the SC analysis put forward here. Further evidence for the absence of CP comes from the fact that children do not produce structures containing inverted auxiliaries; for example, the earliest interrogative clauses produced by Claire (a child studied longitudinally by Hill 1983) at age 2;0–2;1 included structures such as the following:

(8)   *chair go? Kitty go? car go? that go? Jane go home? mummy gone?*

The adult counterpart of *Jane go home?* would be *Did Jane go home?*, with the preposed auxiliary *did* occupying the head C position of CP. Of course, it might be claimed that the absence of inverted auxiliaries in COMP is simply a consequence of the absence of auxiliaries in INFL: but if (as claimed by Gruber 1967; Cazden 1972; Miller & Ervin-Tripp 1973; and Wells 1979) inverted auxiliaries are typically acquired before noninverted auxiliaries, this will not be so. At any rate, the fact that children's clauses do not contain complementizers or inverted auxiliaries at this stage is consistent with the hypothesis that they are producing small-clause (VP) structures which lack a CP projection.

If we assume that a clause is a projection of a lexical verb (as argued by Jackendoff 1974, 1977; Williams 1975; Bresnan 1976; and Abney 1987) then VP structures are 'clauses' in the same way as IP and CP structures are: in the terminology of Radford 1993, V is the ULTIMATE HEAD of the clause; in the terminology of Grimshaw 1991, IP and CP are EXTENDED PROJECTIONS of V. There are some parallels between children's nonfinite VP structures and a class of adult English sentences which Akmajian (1984) terms MAD MAGAZINE SENTENCES — i.e., sentences such as that underscored below:

(9)   — *You've been cheating on me, admit it.*
           — *What? Me cheat on you? Never!*

The parallel with Mad Magazine Clauses (MMCs) extends to the fact that the latter appear to be simple VP projections headed by a nonfinite verb with an oblique subject, and do not allow INFL constituents like *to* (cf. *What? *Me to cheat on you? Never!*). Moreover, like child SCs, adult MMCs allow null subjects with variable reference (cf. *What? Deprive myself/yourself/himself of creature comforts? Never!*).[2]

Since it first appeared, the SMALL CLAUSE HYPOTHESIS (= SCH) has been attacked by a number of linguists on three main grounds — viz. (i) lack of *descriptive adequacy* (in that the SCH fails to provide an adequate account of the morphosyntax of particular phenomena in early child grammars — e.g., interrogatives, negatives, null arguments, Case, etc.); (ii) lack of universality (in that SCH is incompatible with known facts about the acquisition of languages with a more complex morphosyntax than English), and (iii) lack of explanatory adequacy (in that the SCH presupposes an essential discontinuity between adult and child grammars, and fails to explain why early child clauses should be 'smaller' than adult clauses, or how children's 'small clause' VPs develop into adult 'full clause' CPs). In each of the sections below, I answer specific criticisms which have been levelled at the SCH. For the most part, the data I consider in this paper will relate to the L1 acquisition of English; however, section 6 discusses the applicability of the SCH to other child languages.

2.   Null Subjects

A well-known characteristic of early grammars is that between a third and a half of CICs have null subjects (as noted, e.g., by Hyams 1986 and much subsequent work). Typical null subject CICs are illustrated in (10) below:

(10)   *want that. want Lisa. want baby talking*   Hayley(1;8)
          want one. gone out. got it. lost it. coming to rubbish

                                                                 Bethan(1;8)
          want crayons. want biscuit. want mummy come. pee in potty

                                                                       Jem(1;9)
          find mommy. taste cereal. close...door. go house. sit lap
                                          Kendall(1;10), from Bowerman (1973)

make arms. make pineapple. making one
Kathryn(1;10), from Bloom (1970)
want tiger. get tiger. shoot Tina Domenico(2;0)

What is the nature of the null subjects used in CICs?

Rizzi (1992) draws an important distinction between three different types of null subject, namely *pro*, PRO and *nc* (= NULL CONSTANT). *Pro* is the kind of null subject found in finite clauses in languages such as Spanish, Italian, Rumanian, etc., and is morphosyntactically licensed and identified (e.g., licensed through Case and identified via a rich set of agreement inflections carried by finite verbs — cf. Rizzi 1986). PRO is the type of null subject found in non-finite complements of control predicates; it is licensed through Case (receiving null Case from an appropriate Case assigner, e.g., a null complementizer), and is generally syntactically identified by a c-commanding antecedent (though it can be discourse identified where there is no c-commanding antecedent — e.g., in 'Mad Magazine' sentences such as *PRO kill himself? He hasn't got the guts!'*). Null constants represent a type of null definite description which must be A̅-bound by a non-quantificational specifier; however, Rizzi argues that binding requirements hold only if they are satisfiable in principle. It then follows that an *nc* will be exempt from the binding requirement only where it occupies a position where it cannot be so bound (i.e., where it cannot in principle have a c-commanding identifier) — i.e., only in a root specifier position. He suggests that the null subject found in diary style in adult English (cf. Haegeman 1990, and 1994:28–30) is a null constant, and hence restricted to occurring in a root specifier position — as in the following fictitious diary entry:

(11)   *(I) Don't know what I can do. (I) Can't tell my parents I've failed my exams. How could I have been so stupid! Will I ever learn?*

Although the bold-printed subjects in parentheses in (11) can be null, the underscored subjects cannot be null. If we posit that declarative clauses with null subjects in diary style are IPs which do not project up to CP, then the subject in Spec-IP will be in a root specifier position and so can be a discourse-identified null constant. Given the assumption that interrogative clauses are CPs, it follows that a null constant cannot be used as the subject of an interrogative clause — hence the fact that the underscored subjects cannot be null in the last two examples in (11).

It would seem implausible to suggest that the null subject in child sentences such as (10) is *pro*, since verbs in children's initial clauses are not inflected for agreement, and in any case adult English verb morphology is too impoverished to allow for morphological identification of null subjects.

A more plausible candidate would be PRO, if it is the case (as claimed by Roeper & Rohrbacher 1994 and Hyams 1994) that children use null subjects only in nonfinite clauses. However, the empirical adequacy of this latter claim is called into question by the fact that young children do indeed seem to produce null subjects in finite clauses. For example, Sano & Hyams (1994) report that 56.5% of the -ed-inflected verbs produced by Adam from 2;3 to 3;0 had null subjects; they cite examples such as the following, produced by Adam, Eve and Nina:

(12)   *goed on that way. dropped a rubber band. slapped Becca and Rachel*

Moreover, it is relatively common to find young children using null subjects with finite auxiliaries, as examples such as the following (produced by a different boy called Adam at age 2;2 in the course of a single 45–minute recording) show:

(13)   *don't know* (× 14: replies to 'What's this?', 'Is it a train?' etc.)
          don't paint that (= 'I didn't paint that.')
          don't work (× 3 = 'It doesn't work.')
          don't wanna draw on this one
          does (response to 'Yeah, it does.')
          won't (response to 'Does it work?')
          can't knock them down
          can't get it out
          can't stroke me now
          can't (× 3: reply to 'Can't you get it off?', 'Do you like having a bath?', 'Can you see anything, Adam?')

In the relevant recording, 41% of Adam's null subject sentences were headed by finite auxiliaries, 6% by past tense verbs, 18% by perfective participles, 11% by gerund forms, and 24% by (ambiguously finite/nonfinite) stem forms (e.g., *want see bonfire*). Given that PRO is restricted to occurring in nonfinite clauses, it seems more plausible to suppose that the null subjects found in finite clauses such as (12) and (13) are null constants (i.e., the kind of subjects found in adult diary style sentences like (11) above) rather than PRO. Of course, we could continue to maintain that the null subjects found in apparently nonfinite child clauses such as (10) are instances of PRO, but this would require a disjunctive characterization of children's null subjects (saying that they are PRO in nonfinite clauses, but null constants in finite clauses); and this would amount to abandoning any attempt at arriving at a unitary account of the syntax of children's null subjects.

If we accept that null subjects found in clauses such as (12) and (13) are null constants, then the only way of achieving a unitary characterization of null subjects in child English is to suppose that the null subjects found in CICs such as (10) are also null constants. Reasoning along these lines, we might suppose that a child null subject sentence such as *want tiger* is a VP which has a structure along the lines of (14) below:

(14)

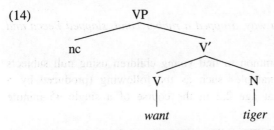

If (as here) the overall clause is analysed as a VP, the null subject (= *nc*) will be in Spec-VP and thus occupy a root specifier position. It therefore follows that it can be discourse-identified (by virtue of the fact that it has no c-commanding identifier). Thus, the VP analysis provides a relatively straightforward unitary account of the syntax of null subjects in CICs like (10)[3]. Of course, the account can be generalized to rather older children who produce sentences such as (12) and (13).

3.   Case

Subjects in CICs typically surface with oblique (i.e., objective/genitive) Case, as noted by Radford (1986:20–22), Kazman (1988:11–12), Aldridge (1989:82–85) (and as is clear from examples of objective subjects cited in many earlier works such as Gruber (1967), Menyuk (1969), L. Bloom (1970), Huxley (1970), Brown (1973), etc.). Typical examples (from Radford 1986 and Vainikka 1994) are given below:

(15)   *me talk*   Stephen(1;7)
        me do it   Bethan(1;8)
        me have biscuit   Angharad(1;10)
        my close it. my get my car   Nina(1;11)
        my need her. my make red table   Nina(2;0)

In a careful statistical study of the acquisition of Case marking, Vainikka (1994) argues that only 11% of the 1SG subjects used by Nina from age 1;11 to 2;1 were nominative *I*, the remainder being oblique subjects (predominantly genitive *my*, but also two instances of *me*). In Radford (1986), I reported that early pronominal subjects used by the children in my corpus typically carried objective Case; see Aldridge (1989) for exemplification.[4]

How are we to account for the Case-marking of subjects under SCH? There are three possibilities which we might envisage — viz. that the subject is assigned *structural Case, inherent Case*, or *default Case*. Vainikka (1994) proposes a structural account of genitive subjects, arguing that children extend the process by which N licenses a genitive specifier to other lexical heads, so that V too licenses a genitive specifier: cf. also Lebeaux (1987:36), who adopts a similar analysis. A variant of this analysis suggested by an anonymous reviewer is to posit that "CICs are in some sense categorially ambiguous between VPs and nominalizations, and that genitive Case is therefore available to the subjects of CICs. On such an approach, one might attribute the absence of genitive subjects in the adult language to the (categorial) selectional requirements of INFL in adult English." In much the same way, Radford (1992:240) outlines a structural account of the Case-marking of objective subjects, suggesting that SC subjects are assigned objective Case by virtue of standing in a Spec–head relation with an untensed (nonfinite) verb. If (following Roeper & de Villiers 1992a) we assume that young children at this stage have not yet acquired (cross-clausal) exceptional case marking (ECM), then it may be that children infer from ECM structures such as *Let [me have one]* that nonfinite verbs license objective subjects.[5] A residue of this 'nonfinite objective subjects' stage would then persist into the adult grammar in gerund constructions such as *Him turning up late was really irritating*, and in 'Mad Magazine' sentences such as *'What? Me cheat on you? Never!'* An alternative possibility is to suppose that the subjects of CICs carry inherent Case — i.e., Case assigned to constituents as a function of the thematic role which they fulfill. This position is reflected in interesting work by Nancy Budwig (1984, 1985, 1989). She notes that the youngest children she studied alternate between the use of nominative, objective and genitive subjects like *I/me/my*, and observes (1984:5) that "uses of *my* link up with utterances in which the child acts as a prototypical agent bringing about a change (for instance: *my blow the candles out* and *my do it*), while those containing *I* (for example, *I like peas* and *I no want those*) deviate from the agentive perspective." She observes that "the use of *I* is found most often in utterances expressing the child's experiential states and intentions." She also notes (p. 6) that in utterances with *me* subjects, "[t]he child refers to *self* as a subject affected by action." A natural interpretation of her observations is that that the relevant children assign inherent Case to subjects, with prototypical AGENTS being assigned genitive Case, prototypical EXPERIENCERS nominative Case, and prototypical PATIENTS objective Case.

A variant of the inherent-Case analysis would be to assume that Case reflects argumenthood, so that (e.g.) internal arguments (in VP complement position) receive objective Case, and external arguments (in VP specifier position) receive genitive Case (or perhaps nominative Case for some children). For the children reported in Radford (1986) who assign objective Case to subjects and complements alike, we might suppose that any thematic argument of a verb is assigned objective Case.

Under either variant of the inherent-Case analysis, Case is directly correlated with thematic/argument structure. Such a correlation would provide an account of why the subjects of unaccusative predicates sometimes surface in postverbal position in CICs such as the following (from Pierce 1989:78–79):

(16)   *(here) come Eve*   Eve(1;7)
        come Fraser   Eve(1;8)
        allgone grape juice   Eve(1;7)
        going (re)corder   Naomi(1;10)
        go Foster in town   April(2;9)
        come Cromer?   Adam(2;5)

The postverbal position of unaccusative 'subjects' can be accounted for straight-forwardly (as noted by Pierce 1989:81) if we assume that children directly project lexical entries onto morphosyntactic structures (and if we further assume that unaccusative 'subjects' are internal arguments). A second phenomenon which we can thereby account for is the observation made by Hyams (1986:63) that CICs are characterized by "a notable lack of ... expletive pronouns." Such pronouns would be absent precisely because they have no thematic role to play, and hence cannot be assigned Case and so are unlicensed. We might conjecture that expletives trigger subsequent acquisition of structural Case-marking of subjects, and at this point inherent Case-marking of subjects is catapulted out of the grammar (to use the metaphor developed in Randall 1992).

Pierce (1989:62) briefly discusses the idea that arguments are assigned inherent Case in early grammars, but dismisses it on the grounds that "Case assignment which overlaps with theta-role assignment is vacuous as a licensing condition." But against this, we might object that any grammar in which Case marking directly reflects theta-marking is surely optimal. For example, a direct mapping from theta-structure into Case structure would satisfy the *Isomorphism Principle* posited by Hyams (1986:162) which requires that grammars maximize the structural isomorphism between different levels of representation. What the inherent-Case analysis predicts is that children should have few problems learning the Case assigned to complements (because this is thematically determined), but would have potential problems learning the Case assigned to subjects (since this is structurally determined). And indeed, this prediction seems to be borne out: thus, not only do children have problems with assigning Case to finite subjects, but in addition, Roeper & de Villiers (1992) present experimental evidence that Case marking for the subjects of exceptional clauses is late-acquired. Independent support for this claim comes from the observation made by Chiat (1981:86) and Kazman (1988:11) that children frequently produce exceptional infinitive clauses with nominative subjects such as those bracketed below:

(17)   let [*he* go in your bed]   Sally(2;4)
         let [*she* go on your swing]   Sally(2;4)
         see [*he* walk]   Peter(no age specified)

and from the observation by Nishigauchi & Roeper (1987:119, fn. 19) that some young children produce complement clause structures such as:

(18)   help [*my* eat it]
         see [*my* ride it]
         see [*my* do it backwards]

One interpretation of data such as (17) and (18) is that for the children concerned, there is a direct mapping from thematic/argument structure onto morphosyntactic structure: the complement clause subject is assigned case as a function either of its thematic role (e.g., genitive because it is an AGENT), or of its argument status (e.g., nominative because it is an external argument).[6]

A final possibility would be to assume that SC-subjects receive *default* Case: more particularly, we might suppose that by virtue of being arguments they must be made visible through Case, and that when they occupy a position which is not inherently Case-marked, they receive default (objective) Case (cf. the proposal to this effect made by Roeper & de Villiers 1991a:8–10 and 1992a:220). It might be argued that a default-Case account involves no developmental discontinuity in that objective Case also serves a default function in adult grammars: e.g., in contexts where a nominal receives neither nominative Case, nor genitive Case, nor null Case, objective Case is assigned by default (so accounting for the objective Case carried by pronominal sentence fragments (cf. *Who did it? — Me*) and by the subjects of 'Mad Magazine' sentences (cf. *What? Me cheat at cards? Never!*). It goes without saying that the default analysis is applicable only to objective subjects (not to nominative or genitive subjects, for which an alternative account has to be developed).[7]

4. Negation

The earliest type of (non-anaphoric) negative structures produced by young children are typically presubject negatives, as illustrated by the examples in (17) below (from Pierce 1989:93–94; Déprez & Pierce 1993:34; and Déprez & Pierce 1994:61):

(19)	*not Fraser read it*	Eve(1;9)
	no the sun shining	Adam(2;4)
	no my play my puppet, play my toys	Nina(2;0)
	no Mommy doing. David turn	Nina(2;0)
	no lamb have it	Nina(2;0)
	no dog stay in the room	Nina(2;1)
	no Leila have a turn	Nina(2;1)

Déprez & Pierce (1994:61) report that of the earliest negative sentences produced by Eve at ages 18–21 months, Peter at 23–25 months and Nina at age 23–25 months, 96% (71/74) contained sentence-initial negatives.

Hyams (1992:378) remarks that "there does not seem to be any easy way of accommodating external negation into the small-clause analysis." I shall argue here that on the contrary, the SC-analysis permits us to arrive at a straightforward analysis under which the syntax of early negatives is determined by UG principles. Let us suppose (following Kazman 1988:17; Guilfoyle & Noonan 1988:37; Lebeaux 1988:39; and Radford 1990:154) that negatives are generated as VP-adjuncts, so that a sentence such as *no Fraser sharpen it* will have the syntactic structure (20) below:

(20) $[_{VP} no [_{VP} Fraser [_{V'} [_V sharpen] it]]]$

One of the UG principles which 'guides' the child to analyze negatives as clausal adjuncts is the ISOMORPHISM PRINCIPLE, posited by Hyams (1986:162), which specifies that grammars maximize the structural isomorphism between different levels of representation. Hyams herself (ibid.) notes that this principle will account for the position of negation: if we assume that the child identifies negatives as constituents which must have scope over (and so c-command) the entire clause at LF,[8] then it follows that the Isomorphism Principle will determine that negatives occupy preclausal position at PF as well, in order to maximize the isomorphism between LF and PF.

However, a second UG principle which plays a central role in determining the locus of negation is the MINIMAL PROJECTION PRINCIPLE, which might be characterized informally as follows:

(21)   *Minimal Projection Principle*
         Syntactic representations are the minimal projections of the lexical items they contain which are consistent with grammatical and lexical requirements.

Principle (21) is related to a number of conditions proposed in the literature. These include Chomsky's (1989) ECONOMY PRINCIPLE, Grimshaw's (1993a, 1993b) MINIMAL PROJECTION PRINCIPLE, Boskovic's (1993) MINIMAL STRUCTURE PRINCIPLE, Safir's (1993) STRUCTURAL ECONOMY PRINCIPLE and the principle of ECONOMY OF PROJECTION proposed in Speas (1994). One effect of this principle is to minimize extended projections (Recall that IP and CP are extended projections of V: cf. Grimshaw 1991). This would mean (e.g.) that in negating a simple (VP) projection such as *Fraser sharpen it*, the child will not develop an extended projection in which *no(t)* is generated as the specifier of an abstract functional projection FP, as in (22) below:

(22) $[_{FP}$ *no* $[_{F}$ $]$ $[_{VP}$ *Fraser* $[_{V}$ *sharpen*$]$ *it*$]]$

The reason is that the FP structure (22) will violate the economy principle (21), since the VP structure (20) is simpler by virtue of being a simple projection (i.e., (20) is a single-headed projection of V), whereas the alternative functional structure (22) is a more complex extended projection (i.e., it is a double-headed projection of F and V). In terms of the economy principle (which leads children to prefer single-headed structures to multiple-headed structures), we can explain the observation made by Solan & Roeper (1978), Roeper (1992) and Hoekstra & Jordens (1994) that children's initial strategy for incorporating new material into a clause is to adjoin it to the overall clause.

An interesting consequence of the adjunction analysis is that it enables us to provide a principled account of children's negative-null-subject sentences such as (23) below (produced by Kathryn at 1:10, from Bloom 1970):

(23)   *no fit. no fit here. no stand up. no go in. no go first. no go in there. no lock ə door. no find ə tank. no have ə this. no like celery, Mommy*

If we posit that *no* is a VP-adjunct in such cases, then a sentence such as *no go in* will have a structure along the lines of (24) below:

(24)

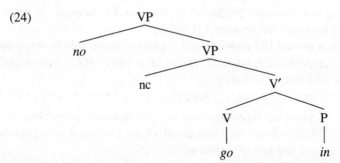

Since the null subject *nc* is in a root specifier position, it can be discourse-identified. Thus, the adjunction analysis of early-child negative clauses correctly predicts that we should find null-subject negative sentences. By contrast, if negatives are analyzed as root specifiers (as in (22) above), we wrongly predict that children will not be able to produce negative null-subject sentences (since the null subject will not be in a root specifier position, and so cannot be discourse-identified).[9]

A final point to note in connection with the VP-adjunct analysis of early-child negative sentences is that we maximize continuity with adult grammars, if we follow Zanuttini (1989) in positing that *not* is a VP-adjunct in adult English.

5.   *Wh*-Questions

Children's CICs typically contain a very limited range of *wh*-questions. Leaving aside potentially formulaic copula questions such as *what(s) dat?*, the earliest verbal *wh*-questions produced by young children are typically *wh*-complement questions (i.e., questions in which the *wh*-word is the complement of a verb) of the form *what N do(ing)?* or *where N go(ing)?* For example, Klima & Bellugi (1966) report sentences such as *what cowboy doing?* and *where horse go?* as the earliest *wh*-question types produced by Adam, Eve and Sarah. Bowerman's (1973) transcript of Kendall's speech at 1;11 includes the questions *where doggie go?* and *where pillow go?* The corpus included in Hill (1983:119–141) contains the following examples of verbal questions with overt *wh*-complements and overt subjects produced by Claire at age 2;0:

(25)   *where girl go? where pencil go? where cow go? (× 2) where Daddy go? where bathtub go? what kitty doing? what the dog doing? what squirrel doing? what lizard doing?*

Once *wh*-structures become more productive, we find a wider range of *wh*-complement questions, as illustrated by the following set of examples produced by Adam at age 2;4 (from Vainikka 1994):

(26)   *who me tickle? what say? what dat tell her? where dat come from? where find plier? where go drop it?*   Adam(2;4)

As noted earlier in relation to the examples in (8) above, a well-known characteristic of early *wh*-questions is that children at this stage do not make use of the presubject auxiliary found in adult questions — and the obvious question to ask is 'Why?' The traditional answer is that auxiliaries in *wh*-questions in colloquial speech tend to be 'weak' monosegmental clitic forms, or even null forms: cf.

(27)   *where'd he go?* [= *did*]
         where's she live? [= *does*]
         what you doing? [= *are*]
         where you been? [= *have*]

Given the hypothesis (put forward by McNeill 1966 and Gleitman & Wanner 1982) that items which lack acoustic salience fail to be parsed by young children, it follows that the child's 'intake' (in the sense of White 1982) for questions like (27) will be as in (28) below:

(28)   *where he go?*
         where she live?
         what you doing?
         where you been?

Thus, the absence of auxiliaries in early *wh*-questions is not difficult to account for. Moreover, if we assume that the child 'knows' that the *wh*-word is the complement of the verb, and that the canonical position of complements is postverbal, it follows that the child concludes that structures like (28) are CSV [= complement + subject + verb] structures which involve movement of a *wh*-complement. But how does the child determine the landing-site of the preposed *wh*-expression?

    The answer is that this is determined by the interaction of principles of UG. One is a SCOPE PRINCIPLE to the effect that interrogative *wh*-expressions (by virtue of being wide-scope quantifiers) must have scope over (i.e., must c-command) all the other constituents of the clause containing them, at PF and/or at LF (cf. Penner 1992:252). Given the positive evidence the child has that *wh*-expressions in English undergo overt movement, the child will 'know' that *wh*-expressions move in the syntax rather than at LF in English. But how does the child know where the *wh*-expression moves to?

This, too, is determined by principles of UG. One such principle is (a variant of) Rizzi's 1991 *wh*-criterion, which (in the version assumed here) requires that interrogative *wh*-expressions move to a (specifier or adjunct) position in which they are contained within a projection of an interrogative head. A second principle involved in determining the landing site for preposed *wh*-expressions is the minimal projection principle (21). This will interact with the scope principle and the *wh*-criterion to determine that interrogative expressions move into the minimal interrogative Ā-position in which they have scope over the other constituents in their containing clause. In the case of a typical child *wh*-question such as *what kitty doing?*, the minimal Ā-position into which the *wh*-operator *what* can move is VP-adjunct position. Thus, if we assume that *what* is adjoined to VP, the resulting structure will be (29) below:

(29)

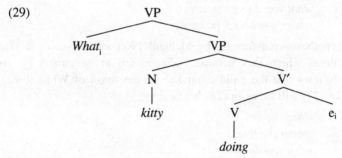

(where e_i is an empty category bound by the *wh*-pronoun *what*).[10] We might assume that the head verb *doing* carries an interrogative feature, so identifying the clause as interrogative.[11] The resulting structure (29) is a simple projection of V, and hence in keeping with the assumption that children do not form extended (functional) projections until forced to do so. As in the case of negative operators, the S-structure location of *wh*-expressions is determined for the child by the interaction of UG principles — including the SCOPE PRINCIPLE, the WH-CRITERION, and the MINIMAL PROJECTION PRINCIPLE.[12]

The minimal projection principle will lead the child to prefer the adjunction analysis (29) to an alternative CP/VP analysis such as that outlined in Radford (1994:232) and Roeper & Rohrbacher (1994), under which a sentence such as *What kitty doing?* might have the structure (30) below:

(30)

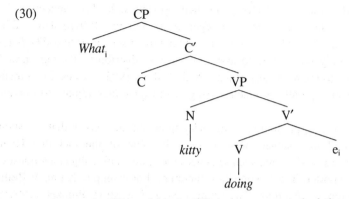

The reason is that the VP analysis in (29) is more economical than the CP/VP analysis in (30). Moreover, (30) violates the UG requirement that every head be filled at PF or at LF, since COMP remains empty throughout the derivation (unless we posit that *doing* moves to COMP — in which case, discontinuity problems arise, since no such movement of thematic verbs from V to C occurs in adult English). Since this in turn means that COMP must be weak, the CP/VP analysis involves an obvious discontinuity with adult English, in that a root interrogative COMP is always strong (and hence must be filled at PF) in adult English. Moreover, it is by no means clear that (30) satisfies the *wh*-criterion, since the head C of CP contains no interrogative item (Rizzi 1991 argues that COMP is only interrogative in root clauses if filled by an interrogative item — e.g., a preposed interrogative auxiliary).

An interesting possibility suggested by the adjunction analysis is that children initially analyse *wh*-words as quantifiers rather than operators. We might suppose that it follows from the semantics of *wh*-words that they are quantifiers, but that the range of quantifiers which function as operators varies parametrically, and hence has to be learned by the child. If we suppose that principles of UG determine that quantified expressions move to a clausal adjunct position (cf. May 1985) and that affective operators move to a clausal specifier position (cf. Rizzi 1990), it then follows that the quantifier analysis will 'force' children to assume an adjunction analysis. If Rizzi (1990) and Grimshaw (1993a) are right in claiming that polarity items can only occur within the scope of an affective operator, an additional prediction made by this analysis is that early *wh*-questions will not contain polarity items like existential *any* (and its compounds): this is a prediction to be tested in future research. An additional question to ask is whether the change of status of *wh*-words from quantifier to operator reflects a parallel change in their semantics. In this connection, it is interesting to note the claim by Roeper & de Villiers (1991b) that children initially assign *wh*-words a non-distributed reading in sentences like *Who bought what?*, and only later come to assign a pairwise distributed (bound variable) interpretation to them (cf. also Roeper & de Villiers 1992b). Does this semantic change trigger a parallel syntactic change from quantifier-adjunct to operator-specifier?

An interesting prediction of the *wh*-adjunction analysis is that we should expect to find null subject *wh*-questions. In spite of the fact that Hyams (1994:48, fn. 13) claims that such sentences are "rare", null-subject *wh*-questions are widely reported in the acquisition literature. For example, Klima & Bellugi (1966:200) report *what doing?* as a typical Stage I question: Plunkett (1992:58) reports that one of the earliest *wh*-questions produced by her son was *where go?*; and Vainikka (1994) provides the following examples of null-subject *wh*-questions produced by Adam, and Eve:

(31)   *where put?*   Eve(1;9)
        where go?   Adam(2;3)
        what say?   Adam(2;4)
        where find plier   Adam(2;4)
        where go drop it?   Adam(2;4)

Moreover, if we look at the corpus of utterances produced by Claire at age 2;0 (in Hill 1983), we find her producing null-subject utterances such as *what doing?* and *Where go?* In actual fact, 39% [11/28] of Claire's questions containing overt *wh*-words have null subjects. Roeper & Rohrbacher (1994) provide extensive exemplification of subjectless *wh*-questions found in the CHILDES database. Thus, Hyams' claim that such sentences are "rare" seems a doubtful one.

But how does the VP-analysis account for null subject *wh*-questions? If we suppose that null subjects are discourse-identified null constants and that *wh*-operators in early child grammars are adjoined to VP, it follows that a null subject *wh*-question such as *what say?* will have the structure (32) below (where *e* is an empty category bound by *what*). Since the null subject *nc* is in a root specifier position in (32), our grammar correctly predicts that the null constant (*nc*) can be discourse-identified, and hence that children will produce null subject *wh*-questions. Of course, if we assumed (e.g.) that the landing site for *wh*-operators was a superordinate specifier position (e.g., Spec-CP), we would wrongly predict that children would never produce null subject *wh*-questions

(32)

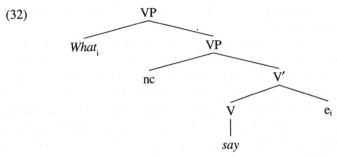

such as (31), since the null subject would no longer be in a root specifier position. Thus, sentences such as (31) provide empirical support for the VP-adjunction analysis. By the same token, the root null subject analysis predicts that once children come to move *wh*-expressions into CP-specifier position, they will cease to produce subjectless *wh*-questions — hence at this later stage they will not produce questions such as *what can do?*; and as Roeper & Rohrbacher (1994) have shown, this prediction is empirically substantiated.

6.   Universality

Hyams (1994:22) dismisses the SCH as a "historical accident", arising out of the fact that proponents of SCH looked at the acquisition of English; she suggests that it is only the fact that English has minimal and non-uniform finite verb morphology and relatively rigid SVC [= subject + verb + complement] word order which enables the SCH to account for CICs in English. However, she argues, if we look at the acquisition of (e.g., Romance or Germanic) languages with a richer verb morphology and verb syntax, "[w]e see that children acquire certain inflectional elements at a very early age, from the beginning of their multiword utterances. Moreover, they control syntactic operations such as verb raising and verb second (V2), which are dependent on the presence of functional heads" (Hyams, ibid.). Hyams' claims would appear to be borne out by numerous empirical studies arguing that in the initial stages of the acquisition of other languages such as French (cf., e.g., Pierce 1989), German (cf., e.g., Poeppel & Wexler 1993) and Italian (cf., e.g., Guasti 1992), children already differentiate finite from nonfinite verbs both in respect of their morphology and in respect of their syntax (in that, e.g., finite verbs are positioned before negatives and nonfinite verbs after negatives, and clitics attach to the left of finite verbs but to the right of nonfinite verbs).

However, a word of caution needs to be sounded. The claim that there is a potential 'small clause' stage cannot be disconfirmed simply by taking an arbitrarily chosen corpus (of the speech of one or more children around two years of age), and demonstrating that the child/children in question has/have already acquired the morphosyntax of finite verbs. After all, the fact that at time T_j (or during some period $T_j...T_k$, $k > j$) a given child has acquired the morphosyntax of finite clauses does not preclude the possibility that at an earlier time T_i ($i < j$) the child might not have done. The VP-period is a grammatical stage characterized by a cluster of co-occurring grammatical properties (described, e.g., in Radford 1986), not a *chronological age*: while — as suggested in Radford (1990) — most children seem to pass through this stage into the functional stage at around age 2;0 ($\pm$ 20%), some do so earlier and others later (e.g., Vainikka 1994 estimates that Eve passes out of the VP-stage at 1;8, Nina at 2;1, Adam at 2;3, and Sarah at 2;4). Moreover, while some children go through an extended period (of 3 or more months) in which they produce only nonfinite clauses, for others this period may be much shorter — indeed vanishingly short if we espouse the possibility suggested by Roeper (1992:340) that children may go through 'silent stages'. The fallacy of generalizing from the observation that child X at age Y was not at stage Z to the conclusion that 'There is no stage Z' is self-evident.

Instructive in this regard is Adone(-Resch)'s (1990, 1993, 1994) study of the acquisition of Mauritian Creole (a language in which finiteness is marked by tense/aspect/modality auxiliaries). All the two-year-old children in her corpus show productive use of one or more auxiliaries (the earliest to be acquired being progressive *pe*, perfective *fin*, past *ti* and future *pu*). Supporters of the FCH would no doubt invite us to conclude that here is additional evidence that children's earliest clauses contain functional categories. However, Adone-Resch's data also show that the youngest child studied (Laura, age 21 months) produced no auxiliaries at all (She omitted them 33 times in obligatory contexts — cf. Adone-Resch 1990:98), leading to the conclusion that "[s]he has not yet distinguished between finite and nonfinite verbs" (op. cit., p. 100), and that "[c]hildren like Laura have not yet developed an IP" (op. cit., p. 110). Typical utterances produced by Laura at age 1;9 (from Adone-Resch, op. cit., passim) are given below:

(33)   *mami sufe*   'Mummy blow'
        dada ale   'Daddy go'
        vid delo   '[I] pour water'

mete	'[I] put [it]'
peny atet	'[I] comb head'
aste to	'[I will] buy sweet[s]'
pas ade sa	'[I] Not look-at that'
pas one	'[I] not know'

Thus, Laura turns out to be the crucial 'missing link' in the overall picture of development. A natural conclusion to draw is that children like Laura have "a syntax without functional projections" (Adone 1993:8).

Much the same can be said of Pierce's (1989) study of the acquisition of French. She argues that the three children she studied show clear evidence of the acquisition of an IP-constituent, in that they differentiate finite from nonfinite verbs both morphologically and syntactically (e.g., the negative *pas* 'not' is positioned before nonfinite verbs but after finite verbs). However, if we read her work carefully, we uncover the observation that in the very first recording of Nathalie at age 1;9.3 (designated by Pierce as N1/T1), Nathalie uses only nonfinite verb forms, not finite verbs. Thus, Pierce (1989:41) observes that "Nathalie at N1 lacks tensed verbs", and concludes that there is an "absence of inflected forms in the very early stages" (op. cit., p. 42), noting that "[i]n Nathalie at T1, then, we catch a glimpse of a stage in French acquisition before verb raising to tense sets in." Thus, far from being 'freaks', children like Laura and Nathalie provide us with a crucial "glimpse" (to use Pierce's own word) of an earlier small-clause stage.

Hernández Pina's (1984) longitudinal study of her son Rafael acquiring L1 Spanish provides us with a further glimpse of the SC-stage. She notes that the root clauses produced by Rafael from 18 to 24 months of age were often headed by nonfinite verb forms (infinitives, gerunds, and participles): cf.

(34)	*nenes sentar*	'Children sit+infinitive'	
	Papa tuyando	'Daddy studying'	(1;10)
	roto caja	'Broken box'	(1;10)

She also notes that during the same period Rafael produced a number of imperatives and 3SG present indicative forms such as:

(35)	*¡Satata ab[r]e!*	'[Let] Fuensanta open [it]'	(1;7)
	mete dedo	'[I] puts [my] finger [there]'	(1;10)

Although it might be supposed that clauses like (35) are finite (and hence justify positing an IP-projection), Pierce (1989) and Tsimpli (1992) argue that this is not so, pointing out that Rafael's verbs show no tense, agreement or mood contrasts at this stage (e.g., imperative and indicative verbs have the same form): both Pierce and Tsimpli argue that verbs occupy the head V position of VP, and that subjects are in Spec-VP. If their claims are substantiated, it is plausible to suppose that Rafael's earliest sentences are small-clause (VP) constituents. Much the same seems to hold of the earliest stages in the acquisition of Welsh. A longitudinal study of a boy called Kevin between 18 and 30 months by Aldridge *et al.* (1995) argues that from ages 1;7–1;11, Kevin produces only VP-structures with SVC order, as illustrated by the examples below:

(36) a. *tŵr disgyn*   'Tower fall'   Kevin(1;8)
     b. *Ginger dwad*   'Ginger come'   Kevin(1;9)
     c. *cath licio hwnna* 'Cat like that'   Kevin(1;10)
     d. *dyn isda yfana*   'Man sit there'   Kevin(1;10)
     e. *mam cosi Lisa*   'Mum tickle Lisa'   Kevin(1;11)

During this period, Kevin produces no examples of VSC order (i.e., of structures where we might suppose that V has raised to INFL or COMP), and no examples of auxiliaries (despite the high frequency of auxiliaries in his input): VSC and auxiliary structures only start to appear at 2;0–2;1. Given the Minimal Lexical Projection Hypothesis, there seems to be no good reason to assume that Kevin can form extended (functional) projections of VP at this point in his development. Thus, one reply which might be given to Hyams' claim that SCH does not extend to languages other than English is that there are a number of published studies of the acquisition of languages other than English which point to a very different conclusion. (Evidence for a stage at which verbs and their arguments are VP-internal has been reported for Swedish in Platzack 1990, for Greek in Tsimpli 1992, for French and German in Meisel 1994, and for Basque in Meisel & Ezeizabarrena, this volume). However, let us suppose that at least some speakers of some languages do not pass through a visible small-clause stage. Let us further suppose (for the sake of argument) that Echeverría (1978:65) and Clark (1985:713) are right in claiming that children's early clauses in Spanish show examples of CVS order alongside the dominant SVC order.[13] Let us also suppose (in the spirit of Koopman & Sportiche 1991) that CVS structures involve movement of the verb to INFL (perhaps with the complement moving to Spec-IP), so resulting in S-structures of the form (37) below:

(37) $[_{IP}$ complement$_i$ $[_I$ verb$_j]$ $[_{VP}$ subject $[_V$ t$_j]$ t$_i]]$

If all these suppositions are well founded, we would appear to have evidence for the early existence of at least some functional architecture above VP.

Leaving aside the (crucial) question of whether these suppositions are indeed well founded, the following comment might be made about this type of argumentation. It follows from the minimal projection principle (21) that children will project only the minimal structure needed to accommodate the lexical items in a given (child) sentence. As we have seen, for a language with a relatively impoverished verbal morphosyntax (e.g., English), a simple VP-structure enables the child to project a wide range of clause structures (declaratives, negatives, interrogatives, etc.) at an early stage. However, for a language like Spanish with a much richer verbal morphosyntax, we might suppose that the child recognizes at a very early stage that verbs carry a rich tense/mood/agreement morphology and can occupy noncanonical presubject position. We might therefore suppose that UG principles force the child learning such a language to project an IP constituent at the outset: this will be the case, e.g., if UG principles require that verbs with a rich agreement morphology raise to INFL (as claimed by Rohrbacher 1994). On such a scenario, only children acquiring languages with an impoverished verbal morphosyntax will be expected to show evidence of a visible small-clause stage; for children acquiring languages with a relatively rich verbal morphosyntax (e.g., Spanish or German), we expect the small-clause stage to be invisible. Thus, the conclusion we reach is exactly the opposite of that reached by Hyams — namely that the languages which teach us most about the earliest stages of acquisition are those in which verbs have a relatively impoverished morphosyntax — e.g., English.

7. Explanatory Adequacy

Given that the ultimate goal of any theory is explanatory adequacy, two crucial questions which the SCH has to answer are (i) why the earliest clausal structures developed by young children are lexical VPs, and (ii) how these early clauses subsequently develop into functional IP and CP structures.

A number of different answers have been given to the 'Why VPs?' question. One is a LEXICAL LEARNING account, which holds that (in consequence of the economy principle) children project only those lexical items which they have acquired at any given stage of development, and that they acquire contentives before functors. It follows from these assumptions that their earliest clauses are projections of the four major categories of contentive — noun, verb, adjective and preposition. Of course, this account raises the question of why contentives are acquired before functors: traditional answers given to this question are that functors are late-acquired because of their lack of acoustic salience (Gleitman & Wanner 1982:17), or their greater cognitive/semantic complexity (Hyams 1986:82), or their greater grammatical complexity (Radford 1990:264–266), or the fact that they are subject to substantial parametric variation across languages (cf. the functional parametrization hypothesis of Chomsky 1989).

A second type of explanation (cf. Radford 1990:266–268) is a STRUCTURAL (more specifically, TELEOLOGICAL) one. We might argue that it is in the nature of the grammatical structure being acquired that some parts of the structure must be 'in place' before others can develop. For example, if we adopt the view of Grimshaw (1991) that all clauses share a common VP 'core', and that IP and CP are extended projections of VP, then it follows that children cannot in principle develop IP or CP projections until they have developed VP.[14]

A third type of explanation which might be offered is a MATURATIONAL one (cf., e.g., Cinque 1988). That is, we might suppose that the principles which enable the child to project argument structures onto lexical syntactic structures (i.e., structures which are projections of lexical categories) come 'on line' at an early age (e.g., 1;6), whereas the principles which enable the child to form extended (functional) projections of lexical structures come on line somewhat later (e.g., 2;0). The onset of the functional period would coincide with dendritic development in Broca's area, and with an increase in 'neural connectivity' (for relevant studies, see Simonds & Scheibel 1989; Greenfield 1991; and Wakefield & Wilcox 1995).

Consider now the 'How?' question — i.e., the problem of "explaining how the functional categories are acquired if they are initially absent" (Hyams 1994:21). The problems posed for the SC-analysis in this regard are very much parallel to those posed by any functional analysis which (like that of Pierce 1989; Déprez & Pierce 1993, 1994; and Platzack, this volume) posits that subject, verbs and complements all remain within VP in CICs. In Radford (1990), I suggested that the capacity to form functional projections matures, so that different functional projections (CP, IP, DP, etc.) are acquired more or less simultaneously, at around the age of 24 months. Here, I outline the alternative possibility that functional projections are acquired sequentially in a bottom-up fashion, with young children building up functional architecture 'one layer at a time'. Given lack of space (and the absence of micro-studies sufficiently detailed to allow us to chart children's development on a daily basis at crucial points in their development), the account of development which I offer below is of necessity partial and tentative, and is limited to a discussion of the development of phrase structure (more specifically of the functional architecture in clauses).

Following Guilfoyle & Noonan 1988 and Vainikka 1994, let us suppose that the first stage after the VP stage is an IP stage (starting at around 2;0 and lasting for several weeks or months) during which VP has an extended projection into IP.[15] The earliest type of INFL constituent developed by English-acquiring children is typically an auxiliary of some kind: for example, Radford & Aldridge (1987) report on a group of children whose first INFL constituents were a subset of modal auxiliaries (and infinitival *to*). Pierce (1989:85–89) suggests that copula/auxiliary *be* is the first INFL constituent to be acquired by Naomi. Vainikka (1994) argues that the first INFL constituents produced by Nina are modals at age 2;1.15 with past tense +*d* appearing (and being overgeneralized) at the same time (file 10), and the dummy auxiliary *do* appearing shortly afterwards (2;1.29). Nominative Case is acquired at the same time as modals/tense (Nina produces only one *I* subject at 2;1.6, but 56 at 2;1.15), suggesting a direct correlation between the acquisition of tense and nominative Case (cf. the claim by Watanabe 1993 that tensed verbs license nominative subjects). Vainikka notes (in relation to 1SG subjects) that modals are used only with *I* subjects, whereas nonauxiliary verbs are used with either nominative or oblique subjects: cf.

(38)   *I̲ seed you*   Nina(2;1.15)

        m̲y̲ ate outside   Nina(2;1.15)

She suggests that clauses with nominative subjects are IPs, and that clauses with oblique subjects are VPs. This implies that when they first acquire a given type of functional extended projection, children only optionally project the relevant functional architecture (cf. the suggestion in Rizzi 1994 that children between 2;0 and 2;6 optionally project functional categories in root clauses). What this means is that (e.g.) when children first enter the IP-stage, they alternate between projecting V into VP or IP, so that their clauses at this (second) stage are sometimes VPs, sometimes IPs. We might suppose that complement clauses at this stage can similarly be IP or VP constituents, so accounting for the fact that as the complement of verbs like *want* children use both infinitival IP complements headed by *to*, and *to*-less VP complements (and hence alternate between (e.g.) I want [*Daddy to do it*] and want [*Daddy do it*]).

The IP/VP-analysis makes interesting predictions about the syntax of *wh*-expressions. We might expect *wh*-phrases in VP-structures to be adjoined to VP (as in Stage I), with the subject in Spec-VP carrying oblique Case — and structures such as (39) below seem to represent this type of clause:

(39)   *who me tickle?*   Adam(2;4)
          what me write   Adam(2;10)
          where me sleep?   Adam(2;11)
          why me go? why me going?   Adam(2;11)
          what my doing?   Eve(1;10)
          what my need?   Eve(2;0)
          Mommy, where my sit?   Sarah(3;0)
          how my bang my head?   Sarah(3;0)

But what of IP-structures? Pierce (1989) and Déprez & Pierce (1993:60 and 1994:74) argue that the earliest auxiliaries used by young children do not trigger raising of the subject from Spec-VP to Spec-IP, so that the subject remains in Spec-VP 'below' the auxiliary, even in declarative sentences such as the following (produced by Naomi at 1;11):

(40)   *is shoes off*   *is kitty sleep*
          is it hard   *is it broken*

If the subject does not raise to Spec-IP, it follows that Spec-IP will be available as a landing-site for preposed *wh*-phrases, so resulting in [*wh*–AUX–S] (*wh*-phrase + auxiliary + subject) structures such as (41) below in which the *wh*-phrase might be analyzed as being in Spec-IP and the (italicized) oblique subject in Spec-VP:[16]

(41)   *where is him?*   Nina(2;5)
          how old are me?   Sarah(3;1)
          what's them?   Jonathan(2;4)
          where's me?   Michelle(2;5),
                        trying to find her picture in a photo album)

Indeed, the presumed Spec-VP position of the subject may be the reason why the copula seems to agree with the preceding *wh*-expression rather than the following subject in sentences such as (42) below, given that agreement is canonically a relation between INFL and Spec-IP:[17]

(42)   *what colour is these? what's the wheels doing?*   Holly(2;0)
          where's my pictures?   Nina(2;1)
          what's these?   Adam(2;2)
          what's these? what's those?   Jonathan(2;4)
          where's my hankies   Katy(2;4)
          what's those?   Alistair(2;6)
          what's you doing?   Ellen(2;9)

what's animals' names?	Kelly(3;0)
where is his feet?	Jonathan(3;3)
where is you?	Elspeth(3;3)
(= 'Where are you?')	

We might further conjecture that early inverted *yes-no* questions such as (43) below:

(43)	*is this doggie?*	Naomi(1;10.19)
	is it raining?	Naomi(1;11.6)
	is it gone?	Naomi(1;11.6)
	is it going to work?	Naomi(1;11.6)
	can me have biscuit?	Angharad(1;10)

are IP structures in which Spec-IP is occupied by a null *yes/no* question operator (as suggested by Guilfoyle & Noonan, 1988:40: cf. Katz & Postal 1964 and Grimshaw 1993a, 1993b for arguments that adult English root *yes/no* questions involve a null counterpart of *whether*).

However, if we posit that at a later stage, the subject raises to Spec-IP (and consequently carries nominative Case), then we should expect (at this second phase of the IP/VP-stage) to find that *wh*-phrases can no longer move to Spec-IP (since this is now filled by the nominative subject), and instead adjoin to IP (as suggested by Guilfoyle & Noonan 1988:40). Potential examples of this kind of structure include the following (from Bellugi & Klima 1966:205):

(44)	*where the other Joe will drive?*
	where I should put it when I make up?
	what he can ride in?
	why he don't know how to pretend?
	why kitty can't stand up?
	how he can be a doctor?
	how they can't talk?
	which way they should go?

Just as *wh*-expressions adjoin to VP when they immediately precede oblique subjects but to IP when they immediately precede nominative subjects, so too it seems that topic phrases can be adjoined either to the left of a VP with an oblique subject, or to the left of an IP with a nominative subject: cf.

(45)	*a train me got. a car me got*	Nina(2;5)
	my tights I want	Nina(2;5)

Thus, there seems to be parallelism between the syntax of topics and the syntax of *wh*-phrases at this point. In this connection, we should point out that Grimshaw (1993a) argues that *wh*-phrases are adjoined to IP in French interrogative structures such as (46a) below, and that topic phrases are likewise adjoined to IP in adult English structures such as (46b):

(46) a. *Qui il a rencontré?*
        who he has met
        'Who did he meet?'
     b. *You must understand that this kind of behaviour we cannot tolerate.*

In the light of potential parallels between topic structures and *wh*-structures in adult grammars, it is not implausible to suggest that there are similar parallels in child grammars. If the relevant *wh*-expressions function as quantifiers, and both quantifiers and topics undergo adjunction to IP, the parallelism is not unexpected.

At around two and a half years of age, children begin to acquire a COMP projection — as is suggested by the fact that they begin to use overt complementizers: cf.

(47)   *see if swimming water's there*   Jem(2;3)
       you know that the flute is in there   Hannah(2;7)
       leave a little space for them to get out   Helen(2;7)

At this point, we start to find other items seemingly miscategorized as complementizers, so that children create novel complementizers of their own; for example, the following child seems to replace the adult prepositional complementizer *for* by the preposition *in*:

(48)   *don't wait in me go on it*   Ruth(2;6)

An intriguing example of a novel complementizer created by a young child is noted by Akmajian & Heny (1975:17) who report a three-year-old girl producing interrogative structures such as:

(49)   *is I can do that?*   *is you should eat the apple?*
       is Ben did go?   *is the apple juice won't spill?*

A similar pattern is noted by Davis (1987), who reports the following examples of child *yes/no* questions:

(50)   *are you want one?*   *are you got some orange juice?*
       are this is broke?   *are you sneezed?*
       are you don't know what Sharon's name is?

(For further examples, see Roeper 1992:341). It seems that the children concerned miscategorized *is* and *are* as root *yes/no* question complementizers. The assumption that adult inverted auxiliaries may be miscategorized by children as complementizers makes it all the more plausible to posit that inverted auxiliaries are positioned in C in Child English at this stage.

At the point where we have evidence of the acquisition of complementizers, it seems reasonable to suppose that children enter a third (CP) stage in their acquisition of clause structure — a stage at which an additional potential landing-site for *wh*-expressions becomes available — namely Spec-CP. If *wh*-expressions move to Spec-CP, we expect to find that auxiliaries move from INFL to COMP (in order to satisfy Rizzi's 1991 *wh*-criterion), and that the subject will raise from Spec-VP to Spec-IP and carry nominative Case, so resulting in adult-like structures such as:

(51) *what's he doing? what's he do?*   Eve(2;0, file 13)

   how did he get out?   Nina(2;9, file 32)

   why can't we open this piano?   Nina(2;9, file 33)

   can I have it? can I do that? shall I close it? are we going
   on an aeroplane now? what's she doing? what's she say-
   ing? what's he got? why was he gone?   (Heather 2;2)

Jill de Villiers (1991) argues that there is a significant correlation between the point at which children acquire embedded questions containing a given *wh*-item and the point at which they acquire root inversion questions with the same *wh*-item (e.g., a correlation between the emergence of embedded *what?* questions and root [*what* + auxiliary + subject] questions). Why should this be?

One likely answer is that embedded *wh*-questions 'force' the child to posit an additional functional projection. The reason is that UG-principles (cf. Chomsky 1986) ban adjunction to arguments (e.g., to selected complements of lexical heads), so that the child 'knows' that embedded *wh*-questions cannot involve *wh*-adjunction to IP. Once the child has acquired CP (and comes to 'realize' that all finite complement clauses are CPs), the child concludes that *wh*-phrases in embedded clauses move to Spec-CP; if we assume that Spec-CP is the canonical landing site for affective operators, this may lead the child to analyse *wh*-words as operators rather than simple quantifiers. Given that UG-principles prohibit movement into the head position of a lexically selected complement (cf. Rizzi & Roberts 1989), the child will 'know' that auxiliaries cannot move from INFL to COMP in embedded questions, so that there will be no auxiliary inversion in embedded questions.[18] It seems reasonable to suppose that the child further assumes that if Spec-CP is the landing site for preposed *wh*-expressions in embedded clauses, Spec-CP will also be available as a landing site for preposed *wh*-expressions in root clauses as well. In a root *wh*-question, Spec-CP will then be filled by a preposed *wh*-expression and the head COMP position will be filled by moving an auxiliary from INFL to COMP (in order to satisfy the *wh*-criterion), so resulting in '*wh*-inversion' structures like (51).

As noted by Roeper (1991), independent evidence of AUX-movement from INFL to COMP in root interrogative clauses at this later (CP-)stage comes from the phenomenon of auxiliary copying, illustrated by the following examples (from Stromswold 1990):

(52)   *why did you did scare me?*   Nina(3;2)
         does it doesn't move?   Nina(2;10)
         did I didn't mean to?   Adam(3;4)
         is this is a dog?   Nina(2;10)
         is my old baby blanket is clean?   Ross(3;0)
         is the clock is working?   Shem(2;5)

If we assume that copying is a process by which both links in the relevant movement chain are lexicalized, it is reasonable to conclude that structures such as (52) provide us with evidence of AUX-movement to COMP — and hence of a CP-projection (a claim which echoes earlier work by Hurford 1975; Fay 1978; and Mayer *et al.* 1978).

It might seem natural to expect that once children acquire *wh*-movement to Spec-CP and auxiliary inversion, they have come to master the syntax of adult *wh*-questions. However, many children seem to go through a stage at which they make optional use of inverted auxiliaries in questions (e.g., they alternate between *what can I have?* and *what I can have?*) — a pattern reported in a wide range of naturalistic studies dating back to Bellugi & Klima (1966). Stromswold (1990) reports supporting elicitation data, noting (p. 256) that her child subjects "judged ungrammatical questions like **What Kermit eats?* to be just as good as grammatical questions like *What does Kermit eat?*" One way of analyzing the relevant data is to suppose that questions which contain inverted auxiliaries are CP-structures in which the *wh*-phrase is in Spec-CP, but that questions which lack inverted auxiliaries are IP-structures (a relic of the earlier IP-stage) in which the *wh*-phrase is adjoined to IP. If this is so, children at this stage would alternate between CP- and IP-interrogative structures. If (as reported by Stromswold 1990) children generally invert with *wh*-arguments but sometimes do not invert with *wh*-adjuncts (Stromswold 1990:198–199 reports that the three-year-olds in her study had 100% inversion in argument-*where*-questions versus 50% for adjunct-*where*-questions), it would seem that Spec-CP is the landing site for *wh*-arguments, but that *wh*-adjuncts are either adjoined to IP or moved to Spec-CP. Interesting in this connection are the complex set of lexical effects which Labov & Labov (1978) report in their daughter Jessie's acquisition of auxiliary inversion in *wh*-questions. From the graph which they present on p. 23 of their article, it would appear that when Jessie was 3;8, she showed obligatory use of auxiliary inversion in *how*-questions, no use of inversion in *why*-questions, and sporadic use of inversion in *where*- (around 45%) and *what*- (around 25%) questions. Stromswold (1990:253) reports similar lexical effects on an elicitation task: she notes that children preferred *what*-questions with inverted auxiliaries (e.g., *what does Kermit eat?*), but *why*-questions without auxiliaries (e.g., *why Kermit eats cookies?*). How can we explain this inversion asymmetry between the different types of *wh*-question?

Obligatory inversion after *how* would indicate that Jessie at the relevant stage had identified Spec-CP as the (unique) landing-site for *how*. The total absence of inversion after *why* would indicate that she had not yet identified Spec-CP as a licit landing site for *why*, and simply adjoined *why* to IP (with the minimal projection principle ensuring that the clause would not further project into a vacuous CP). Optional inversion after *where/what* would suggest that Spec-CP had been identified as a possible landing site for *where/what*, but the optionality of inversion suggests that IP-adjunct position remained an alternative landing site (again, with the clause projecting no further than IP in such cases). What all of this tells us is that there is a strong component of lexical learning involved in the acquisition of *wh*-questions. Only when the child has learned that Spec-CP is the only licit PF structure position for moved interrogative *wh*-phrases in English can we say that the full adult clause structure has been acquired.

One possible interpretation of the relevant facts is to posit that when (e.g.) *what* triggers auxiliary inversion it functions as an operator (and so moves into Spec-CP), but when it is used without inversion, it functions as a simple quantifier (and so is adjoined to IP): the assumption that *wh*-items may have dual status as operators or quantifiers provides one way of accounting for the observation made by Grimshaw (1993a) that interrogative *wh*-expressions in adult French may either move to Spec-CP (and trigger movement of an auxilary or non-auxiliary verb to COMP), or be adjoined to IP (and hence occupy presubject position); when they move to Spec-CP, *wh*-items in French function as operators (and so license polarity items), but when they are adjoined to IP, they function as quantifiers (and so do not license polarity items). If (as we speculated earlier) children 'know' (from their semantic properties) that *wh*-items are quantifiers, but have to learn (on an item-by-item basis) whether they function as simple quantifiers, operators or both, the pattern of acquisition observed by Labov and Labov (1978) and Stromswold (1990) can readily be accounted for. Any given *wh*-item which is analysed as an operator will move into Spec-CP, and the *wh*-criterion will ensure that movement to Spec-CP triggers auxiliary inversion.

Thus far, we have suggested that when children reach the early CP-stage, they may alternate between CP- and IP-structures. However, Radford (1995) presents evidence (from a longitudinal study of a girl called Iris) that even three-year old children at the early CP stage may continue to produce nonfinite small-clause VP structures as root clauses alongside finite IP- and CP-structures. As we would expect, there is abundant evidence that by age 2;9, Iris has developed I- and C-projections. Typical IP-structures she produces (with finite verbs, auxiliaries, preverbal negatives, infinitival *to,* nominatives, etc.) include the following:

(53)   *Mum, I'll help Fraser too. we are going now. I might*
         see Pauline in there. you may like one soup, Mummy.
         we want him. I play piano   (2;9)
         I saw a rabbit. I want hankies. you're tired   (3;0)
         I'm going to sit on these. we had a nice one. he lay on
         that one   (3;3)

Typical CP-structures which she produces (with inverted auxiliaries and preposed *wh*-expressions) include:

(54)   *may I hang some up? what is that? what's this*   (2;9)
         can I have some tea, Mummy? will you put my gloves
         on? why doesn't he have slippers like that?   (3;0)
         can I have a drink of juice? can you? what am I going
         to do?   (3;3)

Yet, in spite of the fact that there is clear evidence that by age 2;9 Iris can project operator clauses into CP and other clauses into IP, she also produces clauses which seem to be simple VPs. For example, we find her producing root nonfinite clauses with objective or null subjects: cf.

(55)   *me going haircut Fraser. me being play piano. me*
         pull up my trousers. me put this on table? us do
         again. me want see outside. Mummy, done it! go see
         Mummy? got bit cheese, Fraser?   (2;9)

> *me going to use this one. me sit down here. me take*
> *microphone off. me put them on? me get in bath?*
> *want sit here. going to have a go on the swing*   (3;3)

Likewise, she often produces to-less infinitive complements: cf.

(56)   *me going haircut Fraser. me want see outside. want*
         sit in my chair   (2;9)
         want go in the car   (3;0)
         want sit here   (3;3)

Significantly, she also produces nonanaphoric presubject negatives such as (57) below:

(57)   *no Fraser play with me doll house*   (2;9)
         no me got one. no me got him   (3;3)

The relevant clauses in (55)–(57) seem to be VPs, even though their adult counterparts are IPs.

We find a similar picture in relation to the syntax of questions. Alongside adultlike *yes/no* CP-structures (with an inverted auxiliary in C) we find simple VP questions (with null or objective subjects): cf.

(58)   *me put this on table? got bit cheese, Fraser? go see*
         Mummy?   (2;9)
         me put them on? me get in bath? want to go to bed?   (3;3)

Similarly, alongside adultlike CP *wh*-structures with a *wh*-pronoun in Spec-CP, we find Iris producing *wh*-VPs like (59) below, with objective or null subjects:

(59)   *where candle go? why me turning? why turning?*
         what get in shops? what put on top?   (2;9)
         how Fraser have his dinner? where Fraser put his
         plate? where Fraser gone? how me going to get on?
         how me going to have a bath? how me get in that?
         how going put it on? why no gonna use that one?   (3;3)

The fact that Iris produces (what appear to be) VP-structures such as (55)–(59) at the very same stage that she is producing CP/IP-structures such as (53)–(54) suggests that in the earliest phase of the CP-stage (and hence throughout the earlier IP-stage), children like Iris only optionally project functional heads like I and C: in the terminology of Rizzi (1994), we might say that children like Iris optionally *truncate* structures.[19]

8. Summary and Conclusion

In Section 1, I provided a brief outline of the SCH, and of the criticisms which have been leveled at it. In subsequent sections, I attempted to show that SCH provides a principled account of numerous characteristics of CICs. In § 2, I argued that the SCH can provide a principled account of null subjects in CICs if we assume (with Rizzi and Hyams) that null subjects can be discourse-identified in root specifier positions. In § 3, I suggested that subjects might be assigned inherent Case, structural Case or default Case. In § 4 and § 5, I argued that early negative and interrogative sentences typically involve adjunction of the negative/interrogative constituent to VP, and that the superficial location of the negative or interrogative constituent is determined by UG-principles relating to scope, the *wh*-criterion and *minimal projection*. In § 6, I argued that there is empirical evidence for a small-clause stage in other child languages, but that we cannot exclude the possibility that the SC-stage might be 'silent' for (at least some) children acquiring languages with a rich verbal morphosyntax. In § 7, I looked at the interrelated questions of why early-child clauses are VPs (high-lighting the possible role of lexical, structural and maturational factors), and how children subsequently develop IP- and CP-projections. I suggested a three-stage VP > IP > CP model in which functional architecture is acquired in a bottom-up fashion, but is initially optionally projected (so that at Stage I clauses are VPs, at Stage II they are VPs or IPs, and at Stage III they are VPs, IPs or CPs). In the case of *wh*-questions, such an analysis predicts (*inter alia*) that as clauses 'grow bigger', moved *wh*-expressions will come to occupy ever higher positions within the clause, moving from VP-adjunct position to IP-specifier position to IP-adjunct position, and finally CP-specifier position. Thus, the 'bottom-up' model of acquisition presented here provides an intuitively plausible model in which children pass from an initial stage when they form only simple projections to subsequent stages in which they come to form ever more complex extended projections.

Acknowledgements

Earlier (oral) versions of this paper were presented at the Child Language Seminar at Bangor in March 1994, at the University of Wales Linguistics Colloquium at Gregynog on 30th April 1994, and at the University of Durham on 26th September 1994. I am grateful to the audiences at these talks, to Harald Clahsen, Claudia Felser and an anonmymous reviewer for helpful comments on earlier versions of the paper.

Notes

1. As noted, the broad aim of my paper is to show that the STRUCTURE-BUILDING MODEL can provide an insightful account of children's early syntactic development. In general, I shall not attempt to argue that the CONTINUITY MODEL cannot account for the relevant data. In fact, I have serious doubts about whether the continuity model is in principle empirically falsifiable, given that proponents of the model have gone down the road of positing that functional heads may be underspecified or improperly specified in certain respects: this allows one to assume that children's functional heads differ in specification from their adult counterparts, and thus amounts to positing an inherently unconstrained theory of child grammars. Note also that I am assuming that the small-clause stage described here precedes Wexler's (1994) optional infinitive stage and Rizzi's (1994) truncation stage, since at the stage Wexler and Rizzi are talking about, children alternate between finite and nonfinite root clauses.

2. The parallels between child SCs and adult MMCs are far from exact, however. Children allow *wh*-elements or topics at the left periphery of SCs as is clear from the examples in the text, but adults do not allow such structures — cf. the ungrammaticality of topic structures such as *What! *Rhubarb me eat?! Never!*

3. The analysis in the text accounts only for null subjects. As has been noted by, e.g., P. Bloom (1990), English children also make sporadic use of null objects. One way of accounting for null objects would be to suppose that they involve topicalization — e.g., a null topic adjoined to VP which binds an empty category in object position. Since the null topic would be in a root (VP-adjunct) position, it could be discourse-identified. If we assume (following Hyams & Wexler 1993:431) that topicalization is infrequent in early child English (as indeed it is in adult English), we then have a natural account of the relative scarcity of null objects in CICs.

4. Vainikka (1994) reports that the earliest recorded clausal structures produced by Eve and Sarah typically have nominative subjects. However (as Vainikka herself notes), we should not exclude the possibility that nominative subjects herald the development of IP-structures. This might mean that a child who alternates between *me/I want cookie* has entered the stage where IP is optionally projected, and that *me want cookie* is a VP-structure, and *I want cookie* is an IP-structure. Nor indeed should we exclude the possibility of structural nominative Case-assignment in some early child grammars whereby verbal subjects are assigned nominative Case, with the result that adult ECM clauses have nominative subjects — cf. the examples in (17) in the text. See Rispoli (1994a, b, c, 1995), and Powers (1995) for interesting discussion of the Case properties of subjects in child grammars.

5. ECM-structures seem to be productive in early child grammars: for example, Vainikka (1994) notes that Adam produces this construction 75 times in seven files between ages 2;6 and 2;9, using the main verbs *let, see* and *want*. Stromswold & Snyder (1995) report that the mean age of first recorded use of causative and perceptual structures like *make him go* for 12 English-speaking children on CHILDES was 2;4.

6. Susan Powers (1995:445) argues that Budwig's inherent-Case analysis is potentially falsified by minimal pairs such as:

    (i) a. *I need her*   Nina(2;0)
         b. *my need her*   Nina(2;0)
    (ii) a. *I love*   Naomi(2;3)
         b. *me love boat*   Naomi(2;3)

    Of course, given the possibility that two-year olds may alternate between 'small' and 'big' clauses, we cannot rule out the possibility that the a-examples are 'big clause' IP structures, and the b-examples are 'small clause' VP structures.

7. Harald Clahsen (p.c.) has pointed out to me that nominative is the default Case in German, and that German-acquiring children overgeneralize nominative Case to complements, but not objective Case to subjects. This might be argued to be consistent with the assumption that (pro)nominal arguments receive default Case in early child grammars.

8. A technical problem (pointed out to me by Claudia Felser) which arises from this analysis is that if we assume that c-command requires dominance by all the segments of a given category, then *no* in (34) has no c-command domain (since *no* is dominated by only one segment of VP). We can overcome this problem, e.g., by positing c-command holds vacuously in such cases, or requires dominance by the root segment, or by positing that for X to c-command Y entails that every segment which dominates X also dominates Y.

9. An anomymous reviewer has pointed out the possibility that null-subject negatives might be analyzed as having a complex functional architecture in which the null subject is raised out of Spec-VP into specifier position within a functional projection dominating NEGP (e.g., into Spec-IP): we could then maintain that the null subject is a null constant occupying a root specifier position. However, any such possibility would be precluded (within the framework used here) by the minimal projection principle, since the analysis would involve positing two functional extended projections of VP (one housing the negative, the other housing the null subject), and thus be less economical than the VP-adjunct analysis (24) in the text. Such an analysis would also wrongly predict that overt subjects precede negatives at the relevant stage. Moreover, it is far from clear why (if such child negatives contain an INFL node) *do*-support (which is obligatory in adult IP negatives) is not used.

10. A VP-adjunction analysis of early *wh*-movement is proposed (e.g.) in Guilfoyle & Noonan (1988:37), Radford (1990:134), and Vainikka (1994:passim). The precise nature of the empty category bound by the *wh*-expression in early *wh*-questions produced by children is unclear. It may be a null resumptive pronoun (as suggested by Roeper *et al.* 1986; Nishigauchi & Roeper 1987), or a null constant (cf. Roeper & de Villiers 1992a, b; Vainikka & Roeper 1993), or a variable. It might be argued that the VP-adjunction analysis violates principles of UG. If we suppose (following Déprez & Pierce 1994:77 and Stromswold 1994) that Spec-CP is universally the landing site for

preposed *wh*-operators, then it follows that VP-adjunction position is not a licit landing-site for preposed *wh*-phrases. However, it cannot be that principles of UG determine that Spec-CP is the (universal) landing site for moved *wh*-phrases, since there is strong evidence of parametric variation across languages with respect to *wh*-landing sites. For example, Grimshaw (1993a) argues that in French root interrogatives, *wh*-expressions surface either in preverbal Spec-CP position or in presubject ADJ-IP (IP adjunct) position. Similarly, Rudin (1988) and Kraskow (1994) argue that both landing sites are licensed in Slavic languages, so that in a multiple *wh*-question, we can find one *wh*-phrase moving to Spec-CP, and another to ADJ-IP. In a similar vein, Boskovic (1993) argues that null operators in English relative clauses are moved to Spec-CP in *that*-relatives, but are adjoined to IP in *that*-less relatives. Moreover, Chomsky (1986) argues that *wh*-complements adjoin to VP before moving into Spec-CP. Hence, it seems unlikely that principles of UG exclude the possibility of adjoining a *wh*-expression to VP.

11. One reason for assuming that verbs carry interrogativeness features is the fact that in languages like (West Greenlandic) Eskimo, verbs carry interrogative inflections (cf. Sadock 1984). However, we can arrive at a similar conclusion in relation to the *wh*-criterion of Rizzi (1991), from which it follows that in English and Italian sentences such as:

(i)   *What is it?*
(ii)   *Cosa fa   Gianni?*
          what does Gianni
          'What is Gianni doing?'

the underlined verb (which moves from V to INFL to COMP) must carry an interrogativeness feature if the requirement imposed by the *wh*-criterion for an interrogative specifier like *what/cosa* to be associated with an interrogative head is to be met.

12. As Peter Coopmans has pointed out to me, if *wh*-constituents and negatives move to occupy a scope position, we might ask what determines the relative position of the two in negative *wh*-questions. One would expect the relative syntactic position of the two to reflect the semantic scope relation between them, and hence that (since *wh*-phrases require wide scope) the *wh*-constituent will be higher than (and to the left of) the negative. It may be that examples such as the following (produced by Adam at age 2;11, file 17) provide support for this claim:

(i)   *why not me break plate?*   *why not me drink it?*
          why not me sleeping?   *why not me careful?*

However, it might alternatively be that *whynot* is a compound *wh*-word for Adam at this stage.

13. It should be noted, however, that the children studied by Echeverría were more than two years old, and arguably well past the SC-stage. Hernández Pina (1984) does not report early CVS-structures — though does report early CV-structures which might be taken to be CVS-structures with null subjects (but could equally be interpreted in many

other ways — e.g., Tsimpli 1992 argues that such structures are VPs in which the complement can either precede or follow the verb within V-bar).

14. Note, however, that the structural account does not in principle exclude the possibility that (say) VP and IP might be acquired simultaneously. In other words, the account excludes the possibility of IP being acquired before VP, but allows for the twin possibilities that either VP is acquired before IP, or IP is acquired at the same time as VP. We might therefore expect that there is a clearcut VP stage in the acquisition of some languages, but no such stage in the acquisition of other languages.

15. An alternative possibility is that the first functional head to be acquired is a neutralized/underspecified COMP/INFL-category which, following den Besten (1982), we might term CONFL (See Aldridge 1989:128–132 for discussion of one such CONFL analysis). The FP-analysis of early-child German clause structures by Clahsen & Penke (1992) and Clahsen *et al.* (1993) is a variant of the CONFL analysis.

16. The suggestion that early *wh*-questions involve *wh*-movement to Spec-IP is found, e.g., in Plunkett (1992:73), Déprez & Pierce (1993:59) and Vainikka (1994). Stromswold (1990) maintains that none of the children in her study passed through a stage in which they failed to raise the subjects of auxiliaries; this might mean that the earliest IP-stage which the children in her study went through in the acquisition of *wh*-questions was an IP-adjunction stage. If Vainikka (1994) is correct in claiming that children continue to use genitive subjects in Spec-VP at this stage, we should (as an anonymous reviewer has pointed out) expect to find sentences such as *where is my?* 'Where am I?' alongside *where is me?* I have no examples of such data in my corpus. Indeed, in my corpus, objective subjects are roughly six times as frequent as genitive subjects, and the only clear and productive examples of genitive subjects involve *my*. This raises the question of whether *my*-subjects are indeed genitive (If they are, why do we never find, e.g., *our* used as a subject?), or whether *my* is an analogical nominative, formed by adding the nominative morpheme /aɪ/ to the first person singular stem /m/, giving a form /maɪ/ which is transcribed as *my* and then (wrongly?) analyzed as genitive.

We should also expect to find (as the same reviewer points out) examples of questions containing an inverted auxiliary followed by an oblique subject: see Rispoli (1995:36–37) for extensive exemplification of structures such as *can me write my name?* (This particular example produced by an unnamed child aged 2;7).

17. Vainikka reports Nina at 2;1.15 saying *There was monkeys.* Presumably we have a related case of Spec-head agreement within IP here, with expletive *there* carrying the default person/number specification 3SG, and hence co-occurring with the 3SG verb form *was.* Henry (1995) reports structures such as these in adult Belfast English; and such structures are also found in Shakespearean English. Lest the claim that *wh*-phrases move to Spec-IP seems to violate principles of UG, it should be pointed out that Solá (1992) and Jimenez (1994) argue that certain types of *wh*-phrase in adult Catalan and Spanish move to Spec-IP.

18. Sporadic examples of inversion in embedded *wh*-questions are reported in the literature
    — cf., e.g., Plunkett (1991:131) and the following examples from Stromswold
    1990:296–297):
    (i)   *I don't know who is dat*
              I don't know what is his name
              I don't know what do you think it was
              I don't know what is that bunny called
              I don't know what ingredient do you use to make gumdrops
              I don't know what's that
              I know what time is it
              I better see what was this
              Look at what are dey building

Stromswold also reports that three-year-old children judge embedded *wh*-questions with
auxiliary inversion to be grammatical. Déprez & Pierce argue that embedded questions
like (i) are IPs in which the *wh*-expression moves to Spec-IP and the auxiliary is base-
generated in INFL. However, Henry (1995) argues that similar complement clause
questions found in adult Belfast English are CPs in which the auxiliary has moved to
COMP.

19. It scarcely needs to be said that much of the evidence presented in § 7 is atomist in
    nature. To establish a reliable chronology of the various stages which children go
    through in the acquisition of syntax requires a detailed quantitative analysis of far
    larger and finer-grained corpora than any currently available. On the other hand, to
    conclude (in the words of an anonymous reviewer) that the kind of unquantified
    evidence presented here is 'anecdotal' in nature and 'very nearly useless' seems to me
    to be very nearly perverse. For example, utterances like (55)–(59) produced by Iris
    clearly need to be given a proper syntactic description irrespective of whether they
    represent 17.497% or 32.691% (or whatever) of the clausal structures she produced at
    the time: calculating the precise frequency of the relevant utterances is not going to
    provide any insights into the nature of the grammar that gave rise to them. Sadly, all
    too often quantitative data are used as a way of 'discarding' crucial counterexamples
    to proposed analyses, on the grounds that the relevant examples are 'rare', hence
    'occasional performance errors.' Many advances in our understanding of adult syntax
    have come from probing the syntax of structures (e.g., parasitic-gap structures) which
    any computer corpus would show to be extremely 'rare'. If, as Tom Roeper has
    conjectured, children pass through numerous fleeting or 'silent' stages, we should
    expect that crucial evidence relating to such stages would be 'rare'. The watch-word of
    the developmental linguist should not be 'Count every example' but rather 'Every
    example counts!'

References

Abney, S. P. 1987. "The English Noun Phrase in its Sentential Aspect." Diss., Massachusetts Institute of Technology, Cambridge.

Adone-Resch, M. C. D. 1990. "The Acquisition of Mauritian Creole as a First Language." Diss., University of Düsseldorf.

Adone, M. C. D. 1993. "IP and its Development in Mauritian Creole." Ms., University of Hamburg.

Adone, D. 1994. *The Acquisition of Mauritian Creole*. Amsterdam: John Benjamins.

Akmajian, A. 1984. "Sentence Types and the Form–Function Fit." *Natural Language and Linguistic Theory* 2.1–23.

Akmajian, A. & F. W. Heny. 1975. *An Introduction to the Principles of Transformational Syntax*. Cambridge, Mass.: MIT Press.

Aldridge, M. 1989. *The Acquisition of INFL*. Bloomington: Indiana University Linguistics Club.

Aldridge, M., R. D. Borsley & S. Clack. 1995. "The Acquisition of Welsh Clause Structure." *Proceedings of the 19th Annual Boston University Conference on Language Development*. 2 Vols, ed. by D. MacLaughlin & S. McEwen, 37–47. Somerville, Mass.: Cascadilla Press.

Besten, H. den. 1982. "On the Interaction of Root Transformations and Lexical Deletive Rules." *On the Formal Syntax of the Westgermania: Papers from the "3rd Groningen Grammar Talks", Groningen, January 1981.* (= *Linguistik Actuell*, 3), ed. by W. Abraham, 47–131. Amsterdam: John Benjamins.

Bloom, L. 1970. *Language Development*. Cambridge, Mass.: MIT Press.

Bloom, P. 1990. "Subjectless Sentences in Child Language." *Linguistic Inquiry* 21.491–504.

Boskovic, Z. 1993. "Selection and Categorial Status of Infinitival Complements." Ms., University of Connecticut and Haskins Laboratories.

Bowerman, M. 1973. *Early Syntactic Development*. London: Cambridge University Press.

Bresnan, J. W. 1976. "On the Form and Functioning of Transformations." *Linguistic Inquiry* 7.3–40.

Brown, R. 1973. *A First Language: The Early Stages*. London: George Allen and Unwin.

Budwig, N. 1984. "Me, My and 'Name': Children's early systematizations of forms, meanings and functions in talk about the self." *Papers and Reports on Child Development*, 24.

———. 1985. "The Expression of Transitivity by a 2–Year-Old Child." *Sprachtheorie, Pragmatik, Interdisciplinäres*, ed. by W. Kürschner, R. Vogt & S. Siebert-Nemann, 291–302. Tübingen: Niemeyer.

————. 1989. "The Linguistic Marking of Agentivity and Control in Child Language." *Journal of Child Language* 16.263–284.

Cazden, C. 1972. *Child Language and Education*. New York: Holt, Rinehart and Winston.

Chiat, S. 1981. "Context-specificity and generalizations in the acquisition of pronominal distinctions." *Journal of Child Language* 8.75–91.

Chomsky, N. 1986. *Barriers*. Cambridge, Mass.: MIT Press.

————. 1989. "Some Notes on Economy of Derivation and Representation." *MIT Working Papers in Linguistics* 10.43–74.

Cinque, G. 1988. "Parameter-Setting in 'Instantaneous' and 'Real-Time' Acquisition." *The Behavioural and Brain Sciences* 12.336–337.

Clahsen, H. & M. Penke. 1992. "The Acquisition of Agreement Morphology and Its Syntactic Consequences: New evidence on German child language from the Simone-corpus". *The Acquisition of Verb Placement: Functional Categories and V2 Phonemena in Language Acquisition*, ed. by J. Meisel, 181–223. Dordrecht: Kluwer.

Clahsen, H., M. Penke & T. Parodi. 1993. "Functional Categories in Early Child German." *Language Acquisition* 3.395–429.

Clark, E. V. 1985. "The Acquisition of Romance with Special Reference to French." *The Crosslinguistic Study of Language Acquisition*. Vol. 1, *The Data*, ed. by D. I. Slobin, 687–780. Hillsdale, N.J.: Lawrence Erlbaum.

Davis, H. 1987. *The Acquisition of the English Auxiliary System and Its Relation to Linguistic Theory*. Diss., University of British Columbia.

Déprez, V. & A. Pierce. 1993. "Negation and Functional Projections in Early Grammar." *Linguistic Inquiry* 24.47–85.

————. 1994. "Crosslinguistic Evidence for Functional Projections in Early Child Grammar." *Language Acquisition Studies in Generative Grammar*, ed. by T. Hoekstra & B. D. Schwartz, 57–84. Amsterdam: John Benjamins.

Echeverría, M. D. 1978. *Desarrollo de la comprensión de la sintaxis española*. Serie Lingüistica 3. University of Concepción.

Fay, D. 1978. "Transformations as Mental Operations: A reply to Kuczaj." *Journal of Child Language* 5.143–149.

Gleitman, L. & E. Wanner. 1982. "Language Acquisition: The state of the state of the art." *Language Acquisition: The state of the art*, ed. by E. Wanner & L. Gleitman, 3–48. Cambridge: Cambridge University Press.

Greenfield, P. 1991. "Language, Tools and the Brain." *Behavioural and Brain Sciences* 14.531–595.

Grimshaw, J. 1991. "Extended Projections." Ms., Brandeis University.

————. 1993a. "Minimal Projection, Heads, and Optimality." Ms., Rutgers University.

————. 1993b. "Minimal Projection, Heads, and Optimality." Conference handout, Rutgers University [revised version of Grimshaw 1993a].

Gruber, J. 1967. "Topicalization in Child Language." *Foundations of Language* 3.37–65.

Guasti, M.-T. 1992. "Verb Syntax in Italian Child Grammar." *Geneva Generative Papers* 2.145–162.

Guilfoyle, E. & M. Noonan. 1988. "Functional Categories and Language Acquisition." Text of paper presented at the 13th Annual Boston University Conference on Language Development.

Haegeman, L. 1990. "Non-overt Subjects in Diary Contexts." *Grammar in Progress*, ed. by J. Mascaro and M. Nespor, 167–179. Dordrecht: Foris.

————. 1994. *Introduction to Government and Binding Theory*. 2nd ed. Oxford: Basil Blackwell.

Henry, A. 1995. *Belfast English and Standard English: Dialect variation and parameter setting*. Oxford: Oxford University Press.

Hernández Pina, R. 1984. *Teorías psico-sociolingüísticas y su aplicación a la adquisición del español como lengua materna*. Madrid: Siglo XXI.

Hill, J. A. C. 1983. *A Computational Model of Language Acquisition in the Two-Year-Old*. Bloomington: Indiana University Linguistics Club.

Hoekstra, T. & P. Jordens. 1994. "From Adjunct to Head." *Language Acquisition Studies in Generative Grammar*, ed. by T. Hoekstra & B. D. Schwartz, 119–149. Amsterdam: John Benjamins.

Hurford, J. 1975. "A Child and the English Question Formation Rule." *Journal of Child Language* 2.299–301.

Huxley, R. 1970. "The Development of the Correct Use of Subject Pronouns in Two Children." *Advances in Psycholinguistics*, ed. by G. Flores d'Arcais and W. Levelt, 141–165. Amsterdam: North Holland.

Hyams, N. 1986. *Language Acquisition and the Theory of Parameters*. Dordrecht: Reidel.

————. 1992. "The Genesis of Clausal Structure." *The Acquisition of Verb Placement: Functional Categories and V2 Phonemena in Language Acquisition*, ed. by J. Meisel, 371–400. Dordrecht: Kluwer.

————. 1994. "V2, Null Arguments and COMP Projections." *Language Acquisition Studies in Generative Grammar*, ed. by T. Hoekstra & B. D. Schwartz, 21–55. Amsterdam: John Benjamins.

————. This volume. "The Underspecification of Functional Categories in Early Grammar."

Hyams, N. & K. Wexler. 1993. "On the Grammatical Basis of Null Subjects in Child Language." *Linguistic Inquiry* 24.421–459.

Jackendoff, R. S. 1974. *Introduction to the X'-Convention*. Bloomington: Indiana University Linguistic Club.

————. 1977. *X'-Syntax: A study of phrase structure*. Cambridge, Mass.: MIT Press.

Jimenez, M.-L. 1994. "Subject–Verb Inversion in Spanish." Abstract of paper presented to meeting of Linguistic Society of America, January 1994.

Katz, J. J. & P. M. Postal. 1964. *An Integrated Theory of Linguistic Descriptions*. Cambridge, Mass.: MIT Press.

Kazman, R. 1988. "Null Arguments and the Acquisition of Case and INFL." Ms., Carnegie Mellon University.

Klima, E. S. and U. Bellugi. 1966. "Syntactic Regularities in the Speech of Children." *Psycholinguistic Papers*, ed. by J. Lyons & R. Wales, 183–207. Edinburgh: Edinburgh University Press.

Koopman, H. & D. Sportiche. 1991. "The Position of Subjects." *Lingua* 18.211–258.

Kraskow, T. 1994. "Slavic Multiple Questions: Evidence for *wh*-movement." Abstract of paper presented to meeting of Linguistic Society of America, January 1994.

Labov, W. & T. Labov. 1978. "Learning the Syntax of Questions." *Recent Advances in the Psychology of Language*, ed. by R. N. Campbell & P. T. Smith, 1–54. New York: Plenum Press.

Law, P. 1991. "Effects of Head Movement on Theories of Subjacency and Proper Government." Diss., Massachusetts Institute of Technology, Cambridge.

Lebeaux, D. 1987. "Comments on Hyams." *Parameter Setting*, ed. by T. Roeper & E. Williams, 23–39. Dordrecht: Reidel.

————. 1988. "Language Acquisition and the Form of the Grammar." Diss., University of Massachusetts, Amherst.

May, R. 1985. *Logical Form*. Cambridge, Mass.: MIT Press.

Mayer, J. W., A. Erreich & V. Valian. 1978. "Transformations, Basic Operations and Language Acquisition." *Cognition* 6.1–13.

McNeill, D. 1966. "Developmental Psycholinguistics". *The Genesis of Language: A psycholinguistic approach*, ed. by F. Smith & G. A. Miller, 15–84. Cambridge, Mass.: MIT Press.

Meisel, J. 1994. "Getting FAT: Finiteness, Agreement and Tense in Early Grammars." *Bilingual First Language Acquisition: French and German grammatical development*, ed. by J. Meisel, 89–129. Amsterdam: John Benjamins.

Meisel, J. & M.-J. Ezeizabarrena. This volume. "Subject–Verb and Object–Verb Agreement in Early Basque."

Menyuk, P. 1969. *Sentences Children Use*. Cambridge, Mass.: MIT Press.

Miller, W. & S. Ervin-Tripp. 1973. "The Development of Grammar in Child Language." *Studies of Child Language Development*, ed. by C. Ferguson and D. Slobin, 355–380. New York: Holt, Rinehart & Winston.

Nishigauchi, T. & T. Roeper. 1987. "Deductive Parameters and the Growth of Empty Categories." *Parameter Setting,* ed. by T. Roeper & E. Williams, 91–121. Dordrecht: Reidel.

Penner, Z. 1992. "The Ban on Parameter Resetting, Default Mechanisms, and the Acquisition of V2 in Bernese Swiss German." *The Acquisition of Verb Placement: Functional Categories and V2 Phonemena in Language Acquisition,* ed. by J. Meisel, 245–281. Dordrecht: Kluwer.

Phinney, M. 1981. "Syntactic Constraints and the Acquisition of Embedded Sentential Complements." Diss., University of Massachusetts, Amherst.

Pierce, A. 1989. "On the Emergence of Syntax: A Crosslinguistic Study." Diss., Massachusetts Institute of Technology, Cambridge.

Platzack, C. 1990. "A Grammar without Functional Categories: A syntactic study of Early Swedish child language." *Nordic Journal of Linguistics* 13.107–126.

————. This volume. "The Initial Hypothesis of Syntax: A minimalist perspective on language acquisition and attrition."

Plunkett, B. 1991. "Inversion and Early Wh-Questions." *Papers in the Acquisition of WH,* ed. by T. L Maxfield & B. Plunkett, 125–153. Amherst, Mass.: Graduate Linguistic Student Association.

————. 1992. "Continuity and the Landing Site for Wh-Movement." *Bangor Research Papers in Linguistics* 4.53–77.

Poeppel, D. & K. Wexler. 1993. "The Full Competence Hypothesis of Clause Structure in Early German." *Language* 69.1–33.

Powers, S. 1995. "The Acquisition of Pronouns in Dutch and English: The far continuity." *Proceedings of the 19th Annual Boston University Conference on Language Development.* Vol. 2, ed. by D. MacLaughlin & S. McEwen, 439–450. Somerville, Mass.: Cascadilla Press.

Radford, A. 1986. "Small Children's Small Clauses." *Bangor Research Papers in Linguistics* 1.1–38.

————. 1990. *Syntactic Theory and the Acquisition of English Syntax.* Oxford: Basil Blackwell.

————. 1992. "Comments on Roeper and de Villiers." *Theoretical Issues in Language Acquisition,* ed. by J. Weissenborn, H. Goodluck & T. Roeper, 237–248. Hillsdale, N.J.: Lawrence Erlbaum.

————. 1993. "Head-Hunting: On the trail of the nominal Janus". *Heads in Grammatical Theory,* ed. by G. Corbett *et al.,* 73–113. Cambridge: Cambridge University Press.

————. 1994. "The Syntax of Questions in Child English." *Journal of Child Language* 21.211–236.

————. 1995. "Children — Architects or Brickies?" *Proceedings of the 19th Annual Boston University Conference on Language Development.* 2 Vols, ed. by D. MacLaughlin & S. McEwen, 1–19. Somerville, Mass.: Cascadilla Press.

Radford, A. & M. Aldridge. 1987. "The Acquisition of the Inflection System." *Perspectives on Language in Performance.* Vol. 2, ed. by W. Lörscher & R. Schulze, 1289–1309. Tübingen: Günther Narr.

Randall, J. H. 1992. "The Catapult Hypothesis: An approach to unlearning." *Theoretical Issues in Language Acquisition,* ed. by J. Weissenborn, H. Goodluck & T. Roeper, 93–138. Hillsdale N.J.: Lawrence Erlbaum.

Rispoli, M. 1994a. "Pronoun Case Overextensions and Paradigm Building." *Journal of Child Language* 21.157–172.

———. 1994b. "Paradigms and Pronoun Case Errors." Paper presented at the Boston University Conference on Language Development, January 7th 1994.

———. 1994c. "Paradigms and Pronoun Case Errors." Paper presented at the Stanford Child Language Research Forum, April 17th 1994.

———. 1995. "Mechanisms of Pronoun Case Errors: Biased retrieval, not syntactic incompetence." Ms., Northern Arizona University.

Rizzi, L. 1986. "Null Subjects in Italian and the Theory of *pro.*" *Linguistic Inquiry* 17. 501–557.

———. 1991. "Residual Verb Second and the *Wh*-Criterion." Technical Reports in Formal and Computational Linguistics 3, University of Geneva.

———. 1992. "Early Null Subjects and Root Null Subjects." *Geneva Generative Papers* 0.102–114. [Revised version in *Language Acquisition Studies in Generative Grammar,* ed. by T. Hoekstra & B. D. Schwartz, 151–176. Amsterdam: John Benjamins.]

———. 1994. "Some Notes on Linguistic Theory and Language Development." Ms., University of Geneva.

Rizzi, L. & I. Roberts. 1989. "Complex Inversion in French." *Probus* 1.1–30.

Roeper, T. 1992. "Acquisition Principles in Action." *The Acquisition of Verb Placement: Functional Categories and V2 Phonemena in Language Acquisition,* ed. by J. Meisel, 333–370. Dordrecht: Kluwer.

Roeper, T., S. Akiyama, L. Mallis & M. Rooth. 1985. "The Problem of Empty Categories and Bound Variables in Language Acquisition." Ms., University of Massachusetts, Amherst.

Roeper, T. & J. de Villiers. 1991a. "Introduction: Acquisition of *Wh*-Movement." *Papers in the Acquisition of WH,* ed. by T. L Maxfield & B. Plunkett, 1–18. Amherst, Mass.: Graduate Linguistic Student Association.

———. 1991b. "The Emergence of Bound Variable Structures." *Papers in the Acquisition of WH,* ed. by T. L Maxfield & B. Plunkett, 225–265. Amherst, Mass.: Graduate Linguistic Student Association.

———. 1992a. "Ordered Decisions in the Acquisition of *Wh*-Questions." *Theoretical Issues in Language Acquisition,* ed. by J. Weissenborn, H. Goodluck & T. Roeper, 191–236. Hillsdale N.J.: Lawrence Erlbaum.

————. 1992b. "The One-Feature Hypothesis for Acquisition". Ms., University of Massachusetts, Amherst.

Roeper, T. & B. Rohrbacher. 1994. "Null Subjects in Early Child English and the Theory of Economy of Projection." Ms., University of Massachusetts, Amherst and University of Pennsylvania.

Rohrbacher, B. 1994. *The Germanic VO Languages and the Full Paradigm: A theory of V-to-I Raising*. Amherst, Mass.: Graduate Linguistic Student Association.

Rudin, C. 1988. "On Multiple Questions and Multiple *Wh*-fronting." *Natural Language and Linguistic Theory* 6.445–501.

Sadock, J. M. 1984. "West Greenlandic." *Interrogativity*, ed. by W. S. Chisholm. Amsterdam: John Benjamins.

Safir, K. 1993. "Perception, Selection and Structural Economy." Ms., Rutgers University [to appear in *Natural Language Semantics*].

Sano, T. & N. Hyams. 1994. "Agreement, Finiteness and the Development of Null Arguments." *Proceedings of NELS 24*. Amherst, Mass.: Graduate Linguistic Student Association.

Simonds, R. & A. D. Scheibel. 1989. "The Postnatal Development of the Motor Speech Area: A preliminary study." *Brain and Language* 37.42–58.

Solá, J. 1992. "Agreement and Subjects." Diss., University of Barcelona.

Solan, L. & T. Roeper. 1978. "Children's Use of Syntactic Structure in Interpreting Relative Clauses." *Papers in the Structure and Development of Child Language* (= *UMASS Occasional Papers in Linguistics*, vol 4).

Speas, M. 1994. "Null Arguments in a Theory of Economy of Projection." Paper presented at the Boston meeting of the LSA, January.

Stromswold, K. 1990. "Learnability and the Acquisition of Auxiliaries." Diss., Massachusetts Institute of Technology, Cambridge.

————. 1994. "The Nature of Children's Early Grammar: Evidence from inversion errors." Paper presented at the Boston meeting of the LSA, January.

Stromswold, K. & W. Snyder. 1995. "The Acquisition of Datives, Particles and Related Constructions: Evidence for a parametric account." *Proceedings of the 19th Annual Boston University Conference on Language Development*. 2 Vols., ed. by D. MacLaughlin & S. McEwen, 621–628. Somerville, Mass.: Cascadilla Press.

Tsimpli, I.-M. 1992. "Functional Categories and Maturation: The prefunctional stage of language acquisition." Diss., University College London.

Uriagereka, J. 1995. "Aspects of the Syntax of Clitic Placement in Western Romance." *Linguistic Inquiry* 26.79–123.

Vainikka, A. 1994. "Case in the Development of English Syntax." *Language Acquisition* 3.257–325.

Vaikikka, A. & T. Roeper. 1993. "Abstract Operators in Early Acquisition." Ms., University of Massachusetts, Amherst.

Villiers, J. de. 1991. "Why Questions?" *Papers in the Acquisition of WH*, ed. by T. L Maxfield & B. Plunkett, 155–173. Amherst, Mass.: Graduate Linguistic Student Association.

Wakefield, J. & M. J. Wilcox. 1995. "Brain Maturation and Language Acquisition: A theoretical model and preliminary investigation." *Proceedings of the 19th Annual Boston University Conference on Language Development.* 2 Vols., ed. by D. MacLaughlin & S. McEwen, 643–654. Somerville, Mass.: Cascadilla Press.

Watanabe, A. 1993. "The Notion of Finite Clauses in AGR-based Case Theory." *MIT Working Papers in Linguistics* 18.281–296.

Wells, C. G. 1979. "Learning and using the auxiliary verb in English." *Language Development*, ed. by V. Lee, 250–270. London: Croom Helm.

Wexler, K. 1991. "Optional Infinitives, Head Movement and the Economy of Derivations in Child Grammar." *Verb Movement,* ed. by D. Lightfoot & N. Hornstein, 305–350. Cambridge: Cambridge University Press.

White, L. 1982. *Grammatical Theory and Language Acquisition.* Hingham, Mass: Kluwer.

Williams, E. 1975. "Small Clauses in English." *Syntax and Semantics* 4.249–273.

Zanuttini, R. 1989. "Two Types of Negative Markers." *Proceedings of NELS 20.* Amherst, Mass.: GLSA publications.

The Underspecification of Functional Categories in Early Grammar

Nina Hyams
University of California, Los Angeles

1. Introduction

Let me begin by pointing out certain parallelisms between the behavior of the I and D systems in early syntax. First, verbs often surface in root contexts without finite morphology, as illustrated in (1) (Pierce 1989; Weverink 1989; Jordens 1990; Wexler 1994). The examples given are from French (1a, b), German (1c, d), Dutch (1e–g). Wexler refers to this phenomenon as the OPTIONAL INFINITIVE STAGE because such examples occur alongside finite sentences.

(1) a. *pas manger la   poupée*
    not eat-INF the doll
    'The doll doesn't eat.'

  b. *Michel dormir*   (Pierce 1989)
    Michel sleep-INF

  c. *zahne putzen*
    teeth brush-INF
    '(Someone) brushes (his) teeth.'

  d. *Thorstn das haben*   (Wexler 1994)
    Thorstn that have-INF
    'Thorsten has that.'

  e. *pappa schoen wassen*
    daddy shoes wash-INF
    'Daddy washes (the) shoes.'

  f. *ik ook lezen*
    I also read-INF
    'I also read.'   (Weverink 1989; Schaeffer 1994)

The sentences in (1) suggest that the finiteness of root clauses, an obligatory property of adult languages, is optional in the child's language.

Just as the clause in early language need not be marked for temporal specificity, that is, finiteness, so nominals may remain unmarked with respect to nominal specificity. Thus, parallel to the nonfinite sentences in (1) we have the sentences in (2), which lack determiners and are also characteristic of early language.

(2) a. *open door*
     b. *Wayne in garden*
     c. *Hayley draw boat*   (Radford 1990)
     d. *Niekje ook boot maken*
         Niekje also boat make-INF
         'Niekje also makes [ ] boat.'
     e. *Papa heft ook trein*
         Daddy had also train
         'Daddy also had [ ] train.'
     f. *mag ik weer wan blokjes toren bouwen*
         may I again of blocks tower make
         'May I make [ ] tower of blocks again.'
                                                    (Dutch, Schaeffer 1994)

There is a further parallel between the verbal and nominal domains. Both finiteness and specificity trigger head movement. Finite verbs raise to I, as in French, or to C as in V2 languages such as Dutch and German. In the grammar of this stage nonfinite verbs remain *in situ*, as in (1a), where the verb appears to the right of negation, and in (1d–f), where the nonfinite verb is in sentence final position. Similarly, in languages such as Dutch, in which specific object NPs undergo obligatory movement, a process known as SCRAMBLING, children fail to scramble determinerless nominals (Hoekstra & Jordens 1994; Schaeffer 1994). This is illustrated in the examples in (3), in which the object appears to the right of the adverb or negation, when it should appear to the left.

(3) a. *niet neus snuiten*
         not nose blow-INF
         'Don't blow [ ] nose/I don't want to blow my nose.'
     b. *vind ook huis mooi*
         find also house beautiful
         'I like [ ] house too.'

c.   *ikke ook kietje aai*
I   also knee stroke
'I want to stroke [ ] knee, too.'

d.   *heb jij   nog niet thee opedaan*
have you yet not tea   up-done
'Haven't you written down 'tea' yet.'

On an intuitive level, we might say that what finite morphology and determiners have in common is that they are 'anchor' points, that is, points at which the sentence fixes itself with respect to discourse. Tense places the event or state denoted by the verb at a time relative to the time of discourse, while definite determiners pick out FAMILIAR entities (Heim 1982), that is, discourse referents. The parallel pragmatic function of these elements suggests the intriguing possibility that the optionality of these functional elements in early speech is an effect of the pragmatic principles in early language. This is the approach we will pursue in developing an account of the facts in (1) through (3). More generally, we will outline a possible solution to the problem of why children are inconsistent in their use of certain functional elements during what we will call the OPTIONAL SPECIFICITY STAGE. We will propose, in essence, that the early grammar contains the full set of functional categories, but that the functional heads may be UNDERSPECIFIED in a sense to be made precise. Moreover, we will suggest that the difference between the early grammar and the adult grammar with respect to the option for having underspecified functional heads is a result of differences between the pragmatic system of children and that of adults. This is in contrast to the position of Lebeaux (1988), Guilfoyle & Noonan (1988), Aldridge (1988), Radford (1990) and others, who have proposed that the early grammar lacks the functional projections, D(ET), I(NFL) and C(OMP), and that the difference between the early and adult grammar is structural, hence strictly syntactic.

The structure of the paper is as follows: First, we will discuss the null subject phenomenon. We will propose that null subjects in early English are directly related to the root infinitive phenomenon, illustrated in the examples in (1), and not an independently mis-set parameter, as originally proposed in Hyams (1983, 1986). On the analysis that we will outline, both English null subjects and root infinitives are derived from the underspecification of I. We will also discuss the behavior of D in the early grammar and suggest that the optionality of determiners and object scrambling in early Dutch follows from the underspecification of D. Finally, we will relate the underspecification of I and

D to the discourse role played by these functional heads. The analysis of the null subjects is based on Sano & Hyams (1994), and my discussion of Dutch determiners and scrambling is based on Schaeffer (1994, in prep.).

To set things in context, we will begin by briefly discussing the null-subject analysis proposed in Hyams (1983, 1986), which is an instance of a more general hypothesis which we may refer to as the PARAMETER MIS-SETTING HYPOTHESIS.

2. Parameter Mis-setting or Fast Setting

As is well known, children optionally produce null subjects even in languages such as English, in which null subjects are not typically licensed, as in (4) (CHILDES, MacWhinney & Snow 1989; Brown 1973).

(4)   a.   *drop bean*
       b.   *fix Mommy shoe*
       c.   *go on track*

There is a fairly wide consensus at this point that the null subject phenomenon relates to properties of the developing INFL system, but it has proved difficult to specify the precise nature of the relationship. In earlier work (Hyams 1983, 1986), I argued that AGR in child grammars is initially specified as pronominal (following ideas of Luigi Rizzi (cf. Rizzi 1982) for adult *pro*-drop languages), and thereby licenses a little-*pro* subject. On this view young children speak a language with the essential properties of an adult *pro*-drop language like Italian and the early grammar of English, for example, represents a MIS-SETTING along a specific parameter of UG. Unfortunately, this view has proved untenable for both empirical and conceptual reasons. It also runs into a particular logical problem. We consider these in turn.

On the empirical end, we now know that there are significant differences in the distribution of null subjects in early English and adult *pro*-drop languages. For example, Valian (1991) has noted that in early English null subjects do not occur in embedded contexts, and sentences like that in (5a) are unattested, while sentences such as (5b) do occur in early and adult Italian, as Rizzi (1992) has shown. (@ indicates that a sentence type is unattested in early language.)

(5)   a.   @*I said that ___ went home.*
       b.   *Ho detto che ___ andava a casa.*
             'I said that ___ went home.'

There are further distributional differences between early English and adult *pro*-drop languages that we will discuss shortly and these will be essential to the account of the early null subject phenomenon which we will present below. For now, however, we simply make the point that the available empirical evidence does not support the view that English speaking children speak an adult-like *pro*-drop language.

On the conceptual end, the notion that children have a MIS-SET parameter — which remains mis-set long enough to show overt effects — is also problematic. The most striking result that has emerged from the last few years of cross-linguistic investigation into early grammars is that language particular properties show up very early in development. Consider, for example, head direction; at no point do English-speaking children assume a head-last grammar, nor do Japanese-speaking children assume a head-initial grammar. Consider also the movement parameters. There is considerable evidence that French-speaking children have verb raising to I from the earliest stages (Déprez & Pierce 1992; Pierce 1992; Meisel & Müller 1992; and Verrips & Weissenborn 1992), as shown by the examples in (6), and the contingencies in Table 1 (Table 1 is adapted from Pierce 1992).

(6)   [+finite]   [−finite]

    a. *elle a pas la bouche*   d. *pas la poupée dormir*
        she has not the mouth   not the doll   sleep-INF
        'She doesn't have a mouth.'   'The doll doesn't sleep.'

    b. *veux pas lolo*   e. *pas atrapper une fleur*
        want not water   not pick   a   flower
        '(I) don't want water.'   '[ ] doesn't pick a
                                    flower.'

    c. *ça tourne pas*   f. *pas tomber bebé*
        that turns not   not fall   baby
        'That doesn't turn.'   'The baby doesn't fall.'
        (Pierce 1992)

Table 1. Finiteness vs. Position of negation in Early French*

		[+finite]	[−finite]
neg	V	11	77
V	neg	185	2

* p = 0001. From Pierce (1992).

The contingency table shows the position of the finite and nonfinite verbs with respect to negation. As we can see, in early French the finite verb raises across negation to I, as in the adult language and thus appears to the left of *pas*.

English-speaking children, in contrast, never assume verb raising to I for lexical verbs, and hence errors of the sort in (7a) are unattested. On the other hand, English-speaking children do raise auxiliaries to I at the point at which they begin to use auxiliaries, as is correct in English. So we also do not find errors of the sort in (7b–d). (cf. Stromswold 1990;, Harris & Wexler, this volume).

(7)   a. *@I dance not*
        b. *@I not be/am bad*
        c. *@the sun not is shining*
        d. *@I not have gone*

Thus, if we wish to think in terms of parameters, French- and English-speaking children fix the V-to-I parameter very quickly. Consider next German and Dutch children. Although there is some disagreement as to the position of the fronted verb in the V2 languages spoken by young children,[1] it is clear that children acquiring verb-second languages such as German, Dutch, and Swedish show V2 effects very early on, while English-speaking children and children acquiring the Romance languages do not. It is widely reported (cf. Meisel 1990; Clahsen & Penke 1992; Verrips & Weissenborn 1992; Meisel & Müller 1992; Poeppel & Wexler 1993) that German children place the finite verbs in second position, while leaving the nonfinite verb in sentence-final position. De Haan & Tuijnman (1988) and Jordens (1990) report similar findings for Dutch, and Platzack (1992) for Swedish.[2] Table 2 shows the finiteness/verb-position contingency for the one child studied by Poeppel & Wexler (1993). (Cf. also Clahsen & Penke 1992, who report quantitative data on another child, Simone.)

Table 2. Finiteness vs. Verb Position in Early German*

	[+finite]	[−finite]
V2 position	70	1
final position	6	1

* p = 0001. From Poeppel & Wexler (1993).

These cases illustrate that the effects of the environment are felt quite early in development and that in the general case, parameters are set very quickly. It thus seems that a FAST SETTING MODEL is more appropriate, one in which parameters are set early and without error (Hyams 1993, 1994b). In this specific sense the instantaneous model (Chomsky 1965), as a model of the acquisition of core grammar, may be close to correct. This renders less plausible the view that English children go through a protracted period in which they have a mis-setting of the *pro*-drop parameter.[3]

There is also a logical problem with the parameter mis-setting hypothesis. Considerations of learnability require that parameters be set on the basis of unambiguous triggers (Sano 1992; Roeper & Weissenborn 1991). This means that the data which the child uses to fix a parameter at one of its values, say value *x*, must be consistent only with value *x*, and not compatible with value *y*. For example, in Hyams (1986) I proposed that English-speaking children fix the *pro*-drop parameter on the basis of lexical expletives, since these are incompatible with a *pro*-drop setting. Overt referential subjects would not be a good trigger because they are possible in both *pro*-drop and non-*pro*-drop languages alike. Similarly, SVO word order could not be a trigger for the V2-parameter, since SVO order is possible in SOV languages with V to C, but also in languages which have a base-generated SVO order. If parameters were set by ambiguous data, we could not explain how the child converges on the adult grammar, rather than swinging to and fro between two grammars in a kind of pendulum effect. It thus follows that there can be no *intermediate* stage of development characterized as a parameter mis-setting since this would have been set on the basis of data which are compatible with both the correct value and the incorrect value for the target language.[4]

2.1. *An Alternative Analysis of the Null Subject Phenomenon*

Sano & Hyams (1994) have developed an alternative analysis of the early English *pro*-drop phenomenon. We believe that the null-subject property of early English is directly related to the root-infinitive phenomenon discussed above and that both phenomena are effects of the underspecification of I. Similar analyses have been proposed independently by Roeper & Rohrbacher (1994), Kramer (1993), and, much earlier, and under somewhat different assumptions, by Guilfoyle (1984). Rizzi's (1992, 1994) truncation hypothesis also connects the null-subject and root-infinitive phenomena.[5]

Jordens (1990) and Weverink (1989) were the first to observe that Dutch children pass through a stage in which they freely allow infinitives in root clauses. Wexler (1994) notes that this generalization holds across a wide range of child languages. Examples from French, German, Dutch were given in (1). Wexler extends this analysis to child English, arguing that uninflected verbs such as those in (8), that occur during the so-called TELEGRAPHIC STAGE, are actually infinitives, which in English happen to be indistinguishable from stems. This important hypothesis brings English nicely in line with the other languages discussed above, in which the infinitive is overtly marked.[6]

(8)   a.   *Eve sit floor*
      b.   *where penny go?*
      c.   *that truck fall down*
      d.   *open door*
      e.   *Hayley draw boat*
      f.   *Daddy want golf ball*
      (CHILDES; MacWhinney & Snow 1989; Radford 1990)

Although Wexler does not deal in any detail with the null subject issue, (cf. Wexler 1994, note 44) his optional-infinitive analysis of English bare forms suggests the hypothesis that null subjects are related to the root-infinitive option in early grammar, in contrast to the adult grammar. So let us explore this idea in more detail.

An important descriptive generalization of linguistic theory is that nonfinite clauses have a specific kind of subject — dubbed PRO — and that PRO may only occur as the subject of a nonfinite clause (or phrase). Within a government-based theory (Chomsky 1982), the distribution of PRO is derived from the PRO-theorem, i.e., the requirement that PRO be ungoverned. Within more recent minimalist terms (Chomsky 1992), the distribution of PRO follows from Case theory and from the assumption that PRO is a MINIMAL NP ARGUMENT. Chomsky & Lasnik (1992) propose that as a minimal NP, PRO is the only argument which bears NULL CASE.[7] Null Case, like nominative Case, is assigned or checked in Spec-IP. While nominative Case is a realization of Spec–Head agreement between a lexical subject (or *pro*) and a finite I, null Case is the realization of the same relation where I lacks tense and agreement features, that is, a nonfinite I. Thus, infinitival I (and the head *-ing* of gerunds) check null Case, and the distribution of PRO, schematized in (9), follows.[8]

(9)   a.   [$_{IP}$ *John*/*PRO [$_I$ ⟨+finite⟩] [$_{VP}$ *walks*]]
                     [+nom Case]
           b.   [$_{IP}$ **John*/PRO [$_I$ ⟨–finite⟩] [$_{VP}$ *walk*]]
                     [+null Case]

Returning now to the child's grammar, we can see exactly how the root infinitive phenomenon might relate to the null subject phenomenon. Sano & Hyams propose that in the early grammar, *I may be left underspecified*. For the present, let us say that an underspecified I contains no tense or agreement features. Thus, when I is underspecified, we have a licit context for PRO, that is, null Case is checked in Chomsky & Lasnik's terms, as in (9b). When I is specified, the finite verb checks nominative Case and PRO is excluded, as in (9a).

On this view, then, the English child's null subjects are not the result of a mis-setting of a null-subject parameter, as I originally argued, but rather they are the effect of an independent aspect of child grammars, the optional under-specification of I, the same property that gives rise to root infinitives. Moreover, we assume (in contrast to my earlier view), and following proposals by Guil-foyle (1984), Guilfoyle & Noonan (1989) and Radford (1990), that the null subject of early English is PRO, in contrast to the null subject of Italian, which is *pro*.[9]

Below we will provide a more precise characterization of underspecification, and we will also address the explanatory problem of why underspecification is possible in the early grammar, but not in the adult's. For now let us simply assume that underspecification means that tense and agreement features are absent. Let us now turn to some empirical evidence for the underspecification hypothesis.

3.   Empirical Considerations

3.1. *Null Subjects and Inflected* be

There are a number of clear predictions which follow from the under-specification analysis. The most obvious is that null subjects in early English will not occur with finite verbs inflected for agreement since this would entail a specification of I-features and hence the null Case of PRO would not be checked. In English, the verb *be* provides the only unambiguous case of agreement morphology and so this is the place to test the prediction. We expect that null subjects will not occur with inflected forms of the verb *be*. In Table 3, we show the number of null subjects occurring in sentences with uncontracted *am, are, is* in the corpora of Eve, Adam and Nina (CHILDES; MacWhinney & Snow 1989; Brown 1973; Suppes 1973).[10]

Table 3. The Proportion of Null Subjects in Sentences Containing Uncontracted am, are, is (Sano & Hyams 1994)

file	age	am	are	is
Eve 01–20	1;6–2;3	0/4	0/36	0/109
Adam 01–20	2;3.4–3;0.11	0/1	0/71	13/114 (=11.4%)
Nina* 01–21	1;11.16–2;4.12	0/0	0/19	2/50 (=4%)

* Nina 08 is not available, hence Nina 01–21 consists of 20 files.

As can be seen in Table 3, children use null subjects very infrequently with *am/are/is*. A comparison with these children's overall null subject use highlights this result. Table 4 lists the proportion of null-subject sentences out of sentences containing lexical verbs (i.e., non-copulas, non-auxiliaries) for Eve and Adam (from Hyams & Wexler 1993) and the proportion of null-subject sentences out of all utterances for Nina files 01 and 13 (from Pierce 1992).

Table 4. The Overall Proportion of Sentences with Null Subjects

child	age	proportion
Eve	1;6–2;1	26%
Adam	2;5–3;0	41%
Nina	1;11.16	44%
	2;2.6	11%

Although the data in Table 4 do not cover the whole period covered in Table 3, it is obvious that the children produce null subjects with uncontracted *am/are/is* far less frequently than with lexical verbs.

A second point to note regarding *be* concerns its optionality. As is well known, *be* is often omitted in obligatory contexts (Brown 1973), as in the participle cases in (10), and in predicative constructions, as in (11) (CHILDES; MacWhinney & Snow 1989; Radford 1990).

(10) a. *Adam laughing*
     b. *I brushing*
     c. *Becca making a table*
(11) a. *Geraint naughty*
     b. *Mommy busy*
     c. *hand cold*
     d. *potty dirty*

Hyams & Jaeggli (1987) propose that omission of *be* is directly related to the specification of I-features. We suggested that *be* is an expletive verb inserted into the derivation to carry tense and agreement features (see also Scholten 1987; Moro 1993) or in current terms to 'check' those features, but which does not contribute to the semantic structure of the sentence. It follows that if I is underspecified, *be* will be omitted.[11]

3.2. *Null Subjects and Modals*

Another prediction of our analysis is that the null subject of child English should not co-occur with modals, which are inherently finite in English and hence exclude PRO. The data in Valian (1991) show that this is the case for the corpora of 21 children that she examined. While modals do occur during the stage at which children produce null subjects, they occur almost exclusively with overt subjects, as shown in Table 5.

Table 5. The Proportion of Overt Subjects in Sentences Containing Modals (Valian 1991)

	group I	group II	group III	group IV
mean age/MLU	2;0/1.77	2;5/2.49	2;5/3.39	2;7/4.22
%	94	95	98	99

3.3. *Null Subjects and* -ed, -s

Let's turn now to tense and agreement on lexical verbs, marked by *-ed* and *-s*. Our analysis predicts that null subjects will occur only with nonfinite forms and not with verbs inflected with past-tense and number/person morphology. However, if we look at Table 6, we see that the predicted incompatibility between null subjects and finiteness does not appear to hold for the past-tense morpheme *-ed*. Table 6 shows the proportions of null subjects with verbs inflected with *-ed*.[12]

A comparison with the corresponding data in Tables 3 and 4 for each child indicates that null subjects occur substantially more with the morpheme *-ed* than with *am/are/is* (cf. Table 3), and that the proportion is close to the overall proportion of null subjects in Table 4.[13] Clearly, null subjects co-occur with *-ed*. The examples in (12) are from Adam, Eve and Nina (CHILDES; MacWhinney & Snow 1989).

Table 6. The Proportion of Null Subjects with Verbs Inflected with -ed

file		age	proportion	%
Eve	01–20	1;6–2;3	9/40	22.5
Adam	01–20	2;3–3;0	13/23	56.5
Nina	13–21	2;2–2;4	3/16	18.8

(12) a. *goed on that way*   (subject = cow)
      b. *dropped a rubber band*   (subject = I)
      c. *slapped Becca and Rachel*   (subject = I)

Turning to *-s*, we find that it appears with null subjects at the frequencies given in Table 7. As we can see, null subjects occur less frequently with *-s* than with *-ed* (cf. Table 4), but not as infrequently as with *am/are/is* (cf. Table 3).

Table 7. The Proportion of Null Subjects in Sentences Containing -s

file		age	proportion	%
Eve	01–20	1;6–2;3	5/50	10
Adam	01–20	2;3–3;0	16/62	25.8

On the face of it, these data appear to show that children do use null subjects in finite clauses, contrary to our hypothesis. Sano & Hyams propose that at this stage verbs in *-ed* and *-s* are ambiguous between a finite and participial form. When finite, V-*ed* and V-*s* check nominative Case in the standard way and hence require lexical subjects. As participles, they are like the gerundive *-ing* head discussed above, in that they check null Case. By hypothesis, it is this latter option that is realized in the null-subject sentences under discussion. The structure that we assume for the aspectual use of *-s* and *-ed* is roughly as in (13) (irrelevant details omitted). The verb is inside a low Aspect Phrase of the sort proposed by Belletti (1990) for (Italian) past participles.

(13) $[_{IP}$ PRO $[_I$ 0 $]$ ... $[_{ASPP}$ V-*ed*/V-s_i ... $[_{VP}...t_i...]]]$

We may assume that *-ed* marks perfective aspect, while *-s* marks participial number agreement. This latter suggestion follows in the spirit of Kayne's (1989) proposal that English *-s* marks singular number and not person, as is standardly assumed. It is also consistent with the observation that participles typically mark number and gender, but not person. The structure in (13) is independently motivated by the early progressive sentences given in (10), and also past-participle sentences, such as the Italian ones given in (14) (from Antelmi 1992).

(14)   a.   *visto mao*
            seen kitty

       b.   *rotta   a   pallina*
            broken the ball

       c.   *porta chiusa*
            door closed

       d.   *cotta   a   pappa*
            cooked the food

       e.   *vista etta*
            seen this

Thus, the sentences in (12) would be analyzed as *I [have] goed on that way, I [have] dropped a rubber band,* etc. with an empty I. This proposal is reminiscent of a traditional view which holds that children acquire aspect before tense (Bronckart & Sinclair 1973; Antinucci & Miller 1976; Bloom *et al.* 1980; under a different set of assumptions, Tsimpli 1992).[14] The claim we make is a weaker one, but which is nevertheless strong enough to capture the relevant facts, which is that finite morphology is ambiguously aspectual in the early stage, and when it is aspectual it provides a licit context for PRO and when it marks tense, it does not. Thus, in contrast to the STRICT ASPECT-BEFORE-TENSE hypothesis noted above, we maintain that the early grammar expresses tense as well as aspect. In Section 4 we address the issue of how temporal interpretations are assigned in the early grammar, and also the question of how children recover from the aspectual analysis of *-ed* and *-s*.

3.4. *Null Subject and Finite Subordinate Clauses*

A further empirical point concerns Valian's (1991) observation that English speaking children do not use null subjects in embedded finite contexts, in contrast to Italian children (cf. Rizzi 1992). Valian reports that in 21 children ranging in age from 1;10 to 2;8, there were *no occurrences* of null subjects in 123 finite subordinate clauses. Roeper & Weissenborn (1990) confirm this for French and German, though they do not provide quantitative data (but see note 3). This follows on the analysis we are proposing since the embedded finite I excludes PRO.

3.5. *Underspecified Categories or No Categories?*

To sum up thus far, we have proposed that null subjects in child English are not an independent property, but rather are related to the early optionality of root infinitives. Both phenomena are derived from the underspecification of I. This proposal is empirically supported by the fact that null subjects do not appear in unambiguously finite contexts, for example, in constructions involving *am/are/is* and embedded finite clauses. We have proposed that apparent cases of past tense and agreement morphology in null-subject sentences are aspect markers, hence *minimal* in the sense required to check the null Case of PRO.

An important respect in which the underspecification analysis proposed here differs from Radford's and other 'small clause' (Lebeaux 1988; Guilfoyle & Noonan 1988) and truncation (Rizzi 1994) approaches to root infinitives, is that we assume that children have an obligatory I projection from the earliest stage. On our analysis children's early infinitives do not differ structurally (or morphologically) from adult infinitives. A nonfinite I is necessary for the assignment of null Case in both the early and adult grammar. Thus, it is precisely the presence of I in the early grammar which provides a licensing context for PRO and hence explains the distribution of null subjects in early English. Within a system that posits no I projection in root infinitives, we are forced to assume a new kind of empty category with distinct properties from those that exist in similar structures in the adult language (cf. for example, Rizzi 1994), since neither *pro* nor PRO is licensed as subject of a small clause or truncated tree. The small-clause/truncation analyses also fail to explain the morphological characteristics of root infinitives, which is that they have infinitival morphology in those languages where this is a distinctive form (cf. the examples in (1)). By hypothesis, this inflection is picked up/checked somewhere; the obvious candidate is I. The child's system does differ from the adult's in that infinitives are used in contexts which are infelicitous in the adult language, namely in root declarative contexts. This suggests that the locus of difference between the early and adult grammar is in the pragmatic system. We develop this proposal further below.

4.   A Theory of Underspecification

Let us now examine more carefully the idea of underspecification. There are two issues:

(i)   Can we make the notion more precise; that is, exactly what do we mean when we say that a functional node is underspecified?

(ii) Why is it the case that categories can be underspecified in the child's grammar but not in the adult's?

There is much evidence to suggest that the internal structure of nominal phrases is strongly parallel to that of clauses (Szabolsci 1983, 1994; Abney 1987). For example, the head of DP, a determiner such as *the*, is parallel to a complementizer which heads CP, like *that*, and there are functional projections which intervene between the head and its complement (Valois 1991; Ritter 1989). Various syntactic operations at the clausal level have DP-analogues; for example, it is suggested that N raising to D parallels V-to-C (Hoekstra, p.c.). Clauses and DPs are also parallel with respect to their interpretive properties. Thus, as noted earlier, I marks finiteness, which is TEMPORAL SPECIFICITY, just as D marks NOMINAL SPECIFICITY. A finite I situates the event described by the verb at a specific interval of time, either past or present (relative to Speech or Reference Time).[15] And specific NPs refer to NPs in the discourse domain.

Traditionally, the temporal specification of the clause has been thought of as anaphoric, which is to say dependent for its interpretation on an antecedent. For example, Partee (1973) notes a number of parallels between temporal and nominal anaphora. In particular, she observes that a past tense can be used to refer to a particular time not introduced by previous linguistic context, just as a pronoun may be without a linguistically specified antecedent when its referent is understood to be salient to the hearer. Thus, (15a) (Partee's example) may be uttered while driving down the freeway, just as (15b) may be uttered as the first sentence of a conversation. Partee's point is that in (15a) the temporal reference is not specified while in (15b) the nominal reference is not specified; the reference is implicit in both cases.

(15)   a.   *I didn't turn off the stove.*

      b.   *She left me.*

Extending the nominal/temporal parallelism, Partee likens the past tense to a third person pronoun in that the antecedent may be either implicit as in (15a, b) or explicit as in (16a, b).

(16)   a.   *Yesterday, John washed the car.*

      b.   *John said he would wash the car.*

      c.   *John knows the answer.*

The antecedent to a past tense is explicitly represented in (16a) by the temporal adverb *yesterday.* Similarly, the pronoun *he* in (16b) may take *John* as its linguistically specified antecedent. On the other hand, a genuinely temporal present tense in a simple sentence, such as (16c), is like a first person pronoun in that it is indexical; both are evaluated relative to discourse context. A genuinely temporal present tense refers to Speech Time, just as first person refers to the speaker.

Following in the spirit of Partee's notion of temporal anaphora (and also Enç's 1987 binding-theoretic account of tense), Guéron & Hoekstra (1989, 1994) propose a binding analysis according to which I may be either anaphoric or pronominal.[16] When I is anaphoric, it is bound (co-indexed) with a temporal operator (TO) (in Spec-CP), whose default value is the *here and now,* or *speech time,* and I has the value of *present* tense, as in (17a). When I is pronominal, it is free from the TO (contra-indexed), and has the value *past,* as in (17b).[17]

(17)   a. (TO_i) *John* $[I_i]$ *knows the answer.*   present
        b. (TO_i) *John* $[I_j]$ *drove his car.*   past

Following Guéron & Hoekstra, we refer to the relation between the TO and I as an I-CHAIN (their TENSE CHAIN). The function of the I-chain is to make the predicate referential by hooking the V + I-complex up to temporal operator and hence the discourse world.

This is a very sketchy presentation of the Guéron & Hoekstra analysis, but it suffices for our purposes. Given this framework, suppose we now understand the specification of I as its TEMPORAL INDEX (either co-indexed or contra-indexed to the temporal operator). The index on I provides the verb with its temporal interpretation, either simultaneous with or prior to Speech Time. This temporal index, and the I-chain it creates, may have a morphological reflex, for example, English *-ed, -s.*

We have said about young children that I can be underspecified, giving rise to the root infinitive phenomenon. We are now in a position to understand what this means. In terms of our present discussion, underspecification means UN-INDEXED or not part of an I-chain. Thus, our claim is that in the early grammar, I may be co-indexed or contra-indexed with the operator, as in the adult grammar, or it may fail to bear an index altogether, as in (18):

(18) (TO_i) *Baby doll* $[I_0]$ *cry.*

When I is unindexed, there will be no morphological features realized on the verb and the infinitive surfaces, as in (18). If we were to say nothing else at this point, this would mean that the verb in the child's utterance in (18) had no temporal interpretation. In fact, it has been suggested (Meisel 1990; Boser *et al.* 1991; Kramer 1993; Hoekstra & Jordens 1994) that root infinitives have a modal interpretation (but cf. Clahsen & Penke 1992; Clahsen *et al.*, this volume, for arguments that German root infinitives may also have a declarative interpretation). Thus, Meisel reports that the German child's sentence in (19) means something like *The bear must/should/ought to sleep.*

(19)   *bar schlapen*
         bear sleep
         'The bear should/must/ought to sleep.'

Though there is a modal interpretation for some root infinitives, it is not the only one in English child language (cf. also Kramer 1993 for Dutch root infinitives.) Root infinitives generally denote ongoing events or states. We thus assume that when I is without an index, it somehow receives a declarative — usually present tense interpretation. This does not involve syntactic binding as in the case where I is co-indexed with the operator, as in (17a). Rather, we propose that in this case there is a pragmatic assignment of a temporal value, from discourse or non-linguistic context. We can think of this assignment as TEMPORAL COREFERENCE, as distinct from binding. Following in the spirit of Partee's proposal that the use of tense parallels that of pronouns, we are suggesting that a present tense I can be either anaphoric, as described by Guéron & Hoekstra, and illustrated in (17a), or it can enter into coreference, in which case the event described by the verb just happens to take place in the present, though there is no binding relation between the operator and I. We thus have temporal anaphora and temporal coreference, analogous to nominal anaphora and nominal coreference, as described in Reinhart (1983). Root infinitives involve temporal coreference.[18]

So now the obvious question is why is the coreference, i.e., root infinitive, option blocked in the adult grammar? Again, we suggest a parallel with the nominal system. In the adult language coreference between two NPs is ruled out just in case the resulting interpretation would be indistinguishable from that of bound anaphora. This is the essence of the pragmatic principle first formulated by Reinhart (1983), and later modified by Grodzinsky & Reinhart (1992), and under a different set of assumptions by Chien & Wexler (1990). The Grodzinsky & Reinhart formulation is given as Rule I in (20).

(20)   Rule I
         NP A cannot corefer with NP B if replacing A with C, C a
         variable bound by B, yields an indistinguishable interpretation.

In other words, if you can use bound anaphora, use it, and if you do not use it, the hearer will infer that you mean something different.

To illustrate, Rule I rules out the sentence in (21a) with a coreference interpretation (indicated by underlining the coreferent NPs), since there is a well-formed instance of bound anaphora which means the same thing, that is, the sentence in (21b). Recall that Rule I governs coreference possibilities and not syntactic binding. The local binding relation in (21c) (indicated by co-indexing) is ruled out by Condition B of the binding theory (Chomsky 1981).

(21) a. *_John_ likes _him_.
  b. $John_i$ likes $himself_i$.
  c. *$John_i$ like him_i.

Over a wide range of cases, Rule I and the Binding Theory converge, ruling out both local binding and local coreference. There are, however, sentences which are thrown out by the Binding Theory, but which satisfy Rule I. Consider the sentences in (22).

(22) a. _I dreamed I was Mel Gibson and then I kissed me._
  b. _I dreamed I was Mel Gibson and then I kissed myself._
  (a ≠ b)

(22a) is good under a coreference interpretation precisely because it means something different from (22b). The binding theory rules out binding between _I_ and _me_ in the second conjunct of (22a), yet Rule I allows coreference, precisely because (22a) does not describe a self-kissing event as does (22b).

Suppose we extend Reinhart's principle or something close to it, to temporal coreference, as in (23), which we henceforth refer to as Rule T.

(23) Rule T
   I(nfl) A cannot corefer with I(nfl) B if replacing A with C, C a variable bound by B, yields an indistinguishable interpretation.

The principle in (23) would then rule out temporal coreference whenever the resulting interpretation is indistinguishable from temporal anaphora. This would get us exactly the desired result; in the adult grammar a root infinitive, i.e., coreference, is ruled out by Rule T when its interpretation is indistinguishable from the anaphoric present tense, such as that represented in (17a).

Continuing the parallel with the nominal system, we now expect that root infinitives should be possible in the adult language under other interpretations. In this regard, consider the sentences in (24).

(24) a. *John dance. Never in a million years!*
      b. *My brother marry Mary. Over my dead body!*
      c. *Herman eat bean sprouts. Why?*

The adult sentences in (24) contain root infinitives, but they are perfectly well-formed in the context provided. Notice, however, that these root infinitives are possible because they have a modal-like interpretation; that is, they are distinguishable from a declarative tense interpretation. So, the root infinitives in (24) are felicitous according to Rule T.

One final question remains, why can children produce root infinitives with an indistinguishable temporal interpretation, while this is ruled out in the adult grammar? Or in other words, in what way does the child's system differ from the adult's? We propose that the difference is due to the same factor or a similar one to that which is responsible for children's apparent Condition B violations. As is well known, young children accept sentences such as that in (21a). According to Chien & Wexler (1990) and Grodzinsky & Reinhart, this is because children either have not yet developed (Chien & Wexler) or cannot implement (Grodzinsky & Reinhart) Rule I (in (20)), the principle which blocks coreference where bound anaphora is possible. Our proposal is that Rule T is similarly unavailable in the early grammar and as a result temporal coreference is possible with a declarative tense (non-modal) interpretation, even where temporal anaphora is available. Thus, root infinitives are possible in both the adult and child language, but they are felicitous in a broader set of pragmatic circumstances in the child's grammar than in the adult's due to the absence or inaccessibility of Rule T.[19]

To sum up the discussion thus far, we are claiming that the optional specificity stage (and the derivative null-subject phenomenon) has its roots in the child's developing semantics and pragmatics. The child's tense semantics, that is, her assignment of temporal specificity, is like the adult's when I is specified. Thus, we are rejecting the notion that children have aspect but not tense in the early stages (see also Weist 1984; Fantuzzi 1994; Hoekstra & Hyams 1995a, b; Sano & Hyams 1994; Sano 1995). However, because of the inaccessibility of the pragmatic principle Rule T, children have a further interpretive option, unavailable to the adult, which is for I to be underspecified, hence nonfinite or nonspecific. When this happens, it receives a deictic interpretation, generally referring to Speech Time since this is the default value of the temporal operator. (But see note 18.)

Although there are obviously many technical details to be worked out, the analysis just outlined accords well with our intuition that children are somehow

more bound to the here and now than adults, an intuition which people have
tried to capture in various ways, for example, the aspect-before-tense hypothesis
referred to earlier or the idea proposed in Smith (1980) (and adopted by Tsimpli
1992) that for children Event Time and Reference Time are frozen at Speech
Time. We capture this intuition by allowing children's underspecified I to
receive the deictic here-and-now value which corresponds to the default value of
the temporal operator. This is one of three values assigned to I, which may also
be anaphoric, hence present, or pronominal, hence past, as in the adult grammar.

The option of having both coreference and anaphoric binding of T further
assimilates the semantics of temporal anaphora to that of nominal anaphora in
the spirit of Partee's original insights. It also allows us to maintain a very strong
form of SYNTACTIC CONTINUITY. There is nothing in the child's *grammar* which
must change in order for root infinitives to be pushed out. It places the problem
in the domain of pragmatics where we have independent evidence of developmental delays (e.g., Chien & Wexler 1990; and see also Wales 1986; Weist
1986 for an overview of children's use of deixis and tense). Once Rule I appears
(either through maturation of the rule itself (Chien & Wexler 1990), or of the
mechanisms involved in the implementation of the rule (Grodzinsky & Reinhart
1993)), the deictic assignment of temporal reference is blocked and I must be
finitely specified, that is, indexed to the temporal operator. Root infinitives are
now impossible, except in cases such as those in (24). At this point children will
give up the aspectual analysis of *-ed* and *-s* in favor of the tense analysis of
these morphemes since a representation such as that in (13) also contains an
underspecified I.

5. Extensions to the D-system

Let's turn now to another aspect of the early grammar, the underspecification of D, which we will propose follows from principles similar to
those just outlined for temporal interpretation of I. The analysis of determiners
is more sketchy than the analysis of I, but we hope to at least point in the
direction of a possible explanation for the behavior of the D system in early
language.

As noted earlier, D and I have an important property in common, which is
that they are both points at which the sentence is anchored into a discourse
representation. As discussed above, a finite I situates the event described by the
verb at a specific interval of time, either past or present (relative to Speech or

Reference Time). In a similar way, D specifies the relation of its NP-complement to the DPs in the discourse representation. Thus, a definite/specific DP such as *the boy* or *he*, refer to a FAMILIAR NP, one which has already been implicitly or explicitly introduced into discourse, while an indefinite/non-specific DP, for example *a boy*, can introduce a NOVEL NP (Heim 1982).[20]

There are well-known syntactic effects of definiteness and specificity. For example, there is a definiteness restriction on the postverbal subject of an existential construction, as illustrated in (25a, b); specific animate objects in Spanish require *a*-insertion, while nonspecific objects do not, as in (25c, d) (from Zubizarreta 1992); and postverbal subjects in Italian show weak definiteness effects, as in (25e, f).

(25)   a.   *There is a boy in the garden.*

          b.   **There is the boy in the garden.*

          c.   *Juan vio a Maria.*

               'Juan saw (a) Maria.'

          d.   *Juan busca una muchacha que sepa hablar ingles.*

               'Juan is looking for a girl that knows English.'

          e.   ?*Ha scritto la   lettera Gianni.*

               has written the letter   Gianni

               'John has written the letter.'

          f.   *Ha scritto la   lettera una studentessa.*

               has written the letter   a   student

               'A student has written a letter.'

Specificity effects also show up in scrambling constructions in German, Dutch and other languages. We focus on Dutch. In Dutch specific DPs (including proper names and pronouns) move to the left of negation and adverbs in a process known as SCRAMBLING, as illustrated in (26a, b). Non-specific DPs do not scramble in the general case, as in (26c).

(26)   a.   ... *dat Jan het boek$_i$ niet/stilletjes* t$_i$ *leest*   [definite DP]

               '... that Jan the book not (quietly) reads.'

          b.   ... *dat Jan het$_i$ niet/stilletjes* t$_i$ *leest.*   [pronoun]

               '... that Jan it not/quietly reads.'

          c.   ... *dat Jan niet/stilletjes ein boek leest.*   [indefinite DP]

               '... that Jan not/quietly a book reads.'

Within recent theory (Wyngaerd 1989; Mahajan 1990; Koopman & Sportiche 1991), scrambling is analyzed as a movement of the object NP out of the VP to the Spec of a higher functional position, symbolized as (FP), roughly as illustrated in the embedded clause in (27). (Irrelevant details and projections omitted).[21]

(27)   ... [$_{IP}$ Jan [$_{FP}$ het boek$_i$ stilletjes/niet [$_{VP}$ t$_i$ t$_j$] [$_I$ leest$_j$]

Let us return to the child's grammar. As is well known, determiners are often unexpressed in the early grammar. Some examples were given in (2), and these are repeated below.[22]

(2)   a.   open door
       b.   Wayne in garden
       c.   Hayley draw boat   (Radford 1990)
       d.   Niekje ook boot maken
             Niekje also boat make-INF
             'Niekje also makes (the) boat.'
       e.   Papa   heft ook trein
             Daddy had also train
             'Daddy also had [ ] train.'
       f.   mag ik weer wan blokjes toren bouwen
             may I again of   blocks tower make
             'May I make [ ] tower of blocks again.'

(Dutch, Schaeffer 1994)

Hoekstra & Jordens (1993) and Schaeffer (1994) note that there are many determinerless nominals in Dutch child language. (See also Clahsen et al. 1994 and Eisenbeiss 1994 for German). Schaeffer reports the percentages of determiners for the two children she studied, as in Table 8.[23]

Table 8. Percentage of NPs with and without Determiners during Niek and Laura, Stage 1. (Adapted from Schaeffer 1994)

		with determiner	without determiner
Niek	(2;7-3;5)	4 (7%)	61 (93%)
Laura	(1;9-3;4)	8 (31%)	23 (69%)

Schaeffer proposes that in the early grammar D can be underspecified with respect to (nominal) specificity, just as I can be underspecified with respect to temporal specificity, i.e., finiteness. This has two consequences: First, it accounts for the optionality of determiners since determiners on her account are simply a morphological realization or spell-out of the specificity feature. This is reminiscent of our earlier discussion of *be,* where we said that since *be* is a spelling out of I features, it would not be realized in the case of an underspecified I-node. Second, the underspecification of D in Dutch has a syntactic consequence, which is that nominals which are underspecified with respect to specificity should not scramble. As we see in Table 9, this prediction is by and large confirmed. 82% of Niek's and 100% of Laura's determinerless nominals occur in unscrambled position (see also Hoekstra & Jordens 1994).

Table 9. Proportion of Non-Scrambled Determinerless Nominals for Niek and Laura, Stage 1. (From Schaeffer 1994)

		scrambled	non-scrambled
Niek	(2;7-3;5)	11 (18%)	50 (82%)
Laura	(1;9-3;4)	0	18 (100%)

Some examples of non-scrambled determinerless nominals were given in (3) and are repeated below.

(3)   a.   *niet neus snuiten*
           not nose blow-INF
           'Don't blow [ ] nose/I don't want to blow my nose.'
      b.   *vind ook huis   mooi*
           find also house beautiful
           'I like [ ] house too.'
      c.   *ikke ook kietje aai*
           I   also knee stroke
           'I want to stroke [ ] knee, too.'
      d.   *heb jij   nog niet thee opedaan*
           have you yet not tea up-done
           'Haven't you written down [ ] 'tea' yet.'

Interestingly, Schaeffer shows that the results in Table 9 are completely reversed for pronouns. As shown in Table 10, pronouns — which we take to be inherently specific — are most often correctly scrambled.[24]

The results in Table 10 show that Dutch children do not have a problem with the movement involved in scrambling per se, but rather with the specificity element that triggers scrambling. Since pronouns are inherently marked, they scramble, while in NPs the specificity feature must be marked by a D.[25]

Table 10. Proportion of Scrambled and Non-Scrambled Pronouns for Niek and Laura,
Stage 1. (From Schaeffer 1994)

	scrambled	non-scrambled
Niek (2;7-3;5)	15 (71%)	6 (29%)
Laura (1;9-3;4)	7 (70%)	3 (30%)

Schaeffer notes that one of the questions left unanswered by this account is
how underspecified DPs are semantically interpreted in the early grammar. To
begin to answer this question, we might try to assimilate Schaeffer's analysis
into framework outlined earlier for I. Suppose we assume, essentially following
Heim (1982), that DPs introduce into the sentence variables that must be bound.
Nonspecific/indefinite DPs introduce novel variables. (We will have little to say
here about these.) The interesting case for our purposes are the specific/definite
DPs, which in Heim's framework, introduce familiar variables. Familiar
variables must find an antecedent in the discourse, or else have a contextually
salient referent. So, following Guéron & Hoekstra (1994), let us further assume
that parallel to the T-operator, there is a D-operator which has as its default
range the contextually salient and presupposed DPs, i.e., the discourse domain.
We might think of the D-operator as analogous to the signing space in signed
languages such as ASL. It contains the speaker, the hearer and a set of discourse
referents, each of whom is indexed, just as the referents in ASL are assigned
points in space (T. Hoekstra, p.c.).

In the adult system the head of DP, D, may be specific, by which we now
mean that it bears the index of the D-operator, hence picks out a familiar NP, or
it is nonspecific, that is, contra-indexed, and thus introduces a novel NP.
Turning to the child's system, let us assume, as we did for I, that the child has
the co-indexing and contra-indexing possibilities plus a third option, which is for
D to be unindexed. Although D may be underspecified, the NPs must nevertheless be semantically interpreted. As in the case of root infinitives, which receive
a default here and now interpretation, we propose that unindexed DPs are
assigned a default, FAMILIAR interpretation. This assignment is done pragmatically or deictically. There are thus two ways to arrive at a familiar interpretation in
the child's grammar — grammatically, by co-indexing, or via a pragmatic or
deictic assignment.[26] The latter would not represent a case of binding, however,
but rather of coreference. The coreference interpretation assigned to a determinerless DP is not an option available in the adult grammar for the reasons

outlined earlier; it would yield an interpretation which is indistinguishable from the bound variable interpretation and is thus ruled out by some appropriate version of rule I/T, given in (28)/(31), a rule which is unavailable to the child. In this way, the analysis of I in the early grammar is extended in full to D allowing us to capture the parallel properties of these two heads, outlined in (28).

(28)　a.　Underspecification of I →
　　　　　　i.　root infinitives
　　　　　　ii.　null Case (→ null subjects)
　　　　　　iii.　deictic *here and now* interpretation
　　　　b.　underspecification of D →
　　　　　　i.　determinerless DPs
　　　　　　ii.　no scrambling
　　　　　　iii.　deictic *familiar* interpretation

6. Conclusion

We have proposed that the various properties which characterize the early grammar, specifically root infinitives, null subjects, determinerless DPs, and the optionality of scrambling, can be handled in a unified way as the effects of underspecified functional heads. We understand an underspecified head as one which is not indexed with a linguistic antecedent and hence whose interpretation must be deictically assigned. Underspecification has morphosyntactic reflexes in the form of absence of finite morphology, determiners, the presence of null subjects in non-*pro*-drop languages such as English. The possibility of under-specification (which is only marginally available in the adult language, cf. (24)) reduces ultimately to the availability of an interpretive rule which links under-specified Ds and Is directly to the discourse domain. The deictic interpretation is unavailable in the adult grammar because of the bleeding relationship between grammar and pragmatics, which requires that variables — whether temporal or nominal — be grammatically interpreted where possible (Reinhart 1993). On this view, then, the shift to the adult grammar, and hence away from root infinitives, null subjects, and determinerless nominals, involves a restructuring (or several restructurings) not of the syntax proper, but rather of the mapping between grammar and pragmatics. We see in the child's development of nominal and temporal specificity, as with other developmental phenomena, an interaction of distinct modules — pragmatics, semantics, syntax, morphology and this interaction is characterized by a staggered or uneven development in different domains, with the syntax and semantics outpacing the pragmatic component.

By way of conclusion we might consider whether grammatical underspecification, as it is described here, relates in an interesting way to phonological underspecification (cf. Steriade 1994). One difference between the two is that underspecified phonological segments get filled in, while underspecified functional heads do not. Given economy considerations and current minimalist assumptions (Chomsky 1992), conditions on grammatical representation are motivated purely by properties of the two interface levels LF and PF. The auditory/perceptual requirements of PF will force the specification of phonological features since underspecified segments are unpronounceable. Grammatical categories must be specified only as required by the interpretive/conceptual system. We have proposed that in the early grammar there is a deictic option for the assignment of temporal and nominal reference, thereby satisfying interpretive requirements. Hence, grammatical specification is preempted. The differences between the two kinds of underspecification thus follow from independent properties of the interface levels.[27]

Acknowledgements

I would like to thank Tetsuya Sano and Jeannette Schaeffer, whose ideas I have liberally borrowed, Harald Clahsen, and Peter Coopmans, Anne Roussou, Jürgen Meisel, Filippo Beghelli and 3 anonymous reviewers for their many helpful comments and suggestions. Finally, my appreciation to Teun Hoekstra for his invaluable help and encouragement. An earlier version of this paper was presented at the Great Britain Child Language Seminar in Bangor, Wales, in March 1994. This research is partially supported by a UCLA Academic Senate, Faculty Research Grant, 1993–1994.

Notes

1.   Weissenborn (1990), Poeppel & Wexler (1993), Hyams (1992, 1994a) argue that V
      raises to C as in the adult grammar. Meisel & Müller (1992) argue that I raises to C
      from a VP-internal position, and Clahsen et al. (this volume) to an unspecified FP; in
      the latter two proposals the early grammar, though different from the adult grammar,
      mimicks the V2-effect.

2. Platzack (1992) and de Haan & Tuijnman (1988) actually argue that young children do not have V2. Their data clearly show, however, that children place finite verbs in second position and nonfinite verbs in final position. See Hyams (1992) and Wexler (1994) for discussion.

3. Potentially problematic for the Fast Setting Model are the so-called LATE NULL SUBJECTS discussed in Hamann (1992, 1994) and Duffield (1993) (his rogue nulls). Hamann and Duffield independently isolate a late stage in German during which children have postverbal null subjects (hence not null topics, which are permissible in German and frequently observed in early language, cf. Weissenborn 1991; de Haan & Tuijnman 1988; Jaeggli & Hyams 1987), as in (i).

(i)   *das will   hier haben.*
             that want here have
             '(I) want that here.'

Duffield and Hamann both suggest that the German children have Italian-like null subjects during this stage. If so, this would provide a counterexample to the hypothesis that parameters are set quickly and without error. There is, however, reason to doubt the Italian analysis of late null subjects. First, the frequency of these null subjects is quite low as compared to null subjects in Italian (children and adults); 12–18% in early German vs. 70% in Italian. (cf. Valian 1991 who argues against my original *pro*-drop analysis of English on the basis of frequency difference between Italian and English null subjects.) Second, and more revealing, is the fact that if these are Italian null subjects, their appearance should correlate with the acquisition of 'rich' agreement. In fact, Hamann notes that agreement is fully productive in Elena prior to the late null subject stage, and Duffield observes that Simone acquires the second person *-st,* the point of acquisition of AGR according to Clahsen & Penke (1994), significantly earlier than his rogue nulls appear. Third, late nulls, if Italian-like, should appear in embedded contexts (cf. (5)). Examples such as those in (ii) do occur, but they are extremely rare (under 1% of all embedded clauses for the children studied by Duffield).

(ii)   *... nein, weil ___ zu gross ist.*
             no   because too big   is
             '... no, because [ ] is too big.'

According to Hamann, the late null subject stage ends with the acquisition of the expletive *es.* It thus seems likely, as she proposes, that the occurrence of late null subjects (particularly those in embedded contexts) in German, but not in English, for example, is related to the fact that German allows null expletives in postverbal position, and in embedded contexts, as in (iii, iv).

(iii)   *Mir   wurde pro geholfen.*
             me(DAT) was   helped
             'I was helped.'
(iv)   *... daß pro getanzt wurde.*
             that   danced was
             '... that there was dancing.'

According to Hamann, who follows Tomaselli (1990), German null expletives are licensed under government by the verb in C, hence directly related to the V2-property. If this is so, then German speaking children are not speaking Italian, which is not a V2-language and which licenses null subjects through Spec–Head agreement with AGR(S) (Rizzi 1986).

4. This logical argument does not preclude a situation such as the one described in Hyams (1993, 1996), in which a parameter (e.g., the *pro*-drop parameter) comes fixed at an *initial* parameter setting which may be altered on the basis of positive evidence. But it does preclude an intermediate parameter mis-setting, fixed on the basis of some datum. However, the view that parameters come fixed at an initial setting raises the well-known TRIGGERING PROBLEM, that is, the question of why the parameter remains mis-set for as long as it does despite the availability of triggering data. This problem, which was apparent as soon as the *pro*-drop story was proposed (cf. Hyams 1986; Borer & Wexler 1987), provides one of the main motivations for the maturational theory proposed in Borer & Wexler.

5. The term 'root infinitive' is from Rizzi (1994). Rizzi proposes that root infinitives are truncated structures, i.e., VPs, and that child grammars, in contrast to adult grammars, need not project to a CP-root. We discuss some problematic aspects of the truncation hypothesis below, but see Hoekstra & Hyams (1995a, b) for further discussion of this approach.

    Roeper & Rohrbacher (1994) also adopt a truncation-type analysis, though under somewhat different assumptions from Rizzi.

6. It is important to note that the root infinitive phenomenon is not a universal property of child language. In particular, we do not find root infinitives in Romance *pro*-drop languages such as Italian, Spanish and Catalan (cf. Grinstead 1994; Guasti 1992). Nor does it occur in Japanese (Sano 1995). We do not address the issue of cross-linguistic variation here, but see Hoekstra & Hyams (1995a, b) for an account of these facts.

7. Chomsky & Lasnik observe that PRO behaves like other arguments in that it moves from non-Case positions and is barred from moving from Case positions. If PRO, like other NPs, contains Case features, then this behavior is explained. Space limitations prevent a more thorough presentation of their arguments, but see Chomsky & Lasnik (1992, Section 4.3) for discussion.

8. For ease of exposition, here and throughout we do not split INFL into its different heads, TENSE, AGR and so on (Pollock 1989). However, the analysis proposed here can readily be translated into a split-INFL system. See Hoekstra & Hyams (1995a, b) for a specific proposal.

9. Kramer (1993) independently arrives at a similar analysis based on acquisition data from one German-speaking child and two Dutch children. She observes a high correlation between lexical subjects and finite verbs on the one hand, and between null subjects and root infinitives on the other. On the basis of these data, Kramer argues

two points; first, that the Case Filter is operative in early child grammar and hence lexical subjects must occur with finite verbs (or with a null modal + infinitive), and second, that the (predominant) null subject in these early (non-*pro*-drop) languages is PRO.

It should be noted that early English poses an apparent problem with respect to Case since we find a very high proportion of lexical subjects with root infinitives which cannot plausibly be argued to involve a null modal or modal interpretation. See Section 3 for discussion. Hoekstra & Hyams (1995b) present a number of arguments that the lexical subject of root infinitives is a dislocated constituent.

10. We do not consider contracted forms of *be*, e.g., *I'm, he's*, etc. since the copula is a clitic in these cases, and the subject is required for independent phonological reasons.

11. Wexler (p.c.) further observes that this may account for the interesting and previously unexplained fact that children do not use the nonfinite form of *be* during the optional infinitive stage, in contrast to their behavior with lexical verbs. Thus, '*I be good*' occurs rarely, if at all. As Wexler notes, this also follows on the assumption that *be* is expletive and hence needed only for feature checking.

Anecdotal evidence also suggests that when *be* is used as a root infinitive, it has a lexical meaning, roughly equivalent to *I am behaving/acting good (like a good boy)* (M. Jaeggli, p.c.). This would follow as well.

12. We excluded from the count subject *wh*-questions such as *What happened?* because such sentences do not allow null subjects for obvious reasons.

13. Note that because Nina began to produce the morpheme *-ed* only after the age of 2;2, her 18.8% in Table 6 should be compared to the 11% in Table 4 which is at the comparable age.

14. Tsimpli (1992) follows Radford in assuming that children do not project functional categories during this early stage. On her analysis aspect is a lexical property, which unlike tense and agreement, requires no association with a functional head position, and is thus available in a 'prefunctional' grammar of the sort she assumes, and prior to tense.

15. It is difficult to give a crosslinguistically valid morphological characterization of finiteness since languages differ with respect to which particular heads spell out the finiteness, e.g., person, tense, number, gender, etc., and there is even variation within a particular language, e.g., in the past tense English marks finiteness with a tense morpheme *-ed*; in the present with an agreement morpheme, *-s*. For the matters which we wish to emphasize in this paper we will simply represent finiteness as a property of I. For a discussion of crosslinguistic morphological variation and how this relates to development, see Hoekstra & Hyams (1995a, b).

16. Guéron & Hoekstra identify T as anaphoric/pronominal. However, we will recast their ideas in terms of I for the reasons noted in note 15.

17. More precisely, on Guéron & Hoekstra's account, the T-operator determines the value of C, which contains the Reference Time (in Reichenbach 's 1948 sense) of the sentence. Their tense chain is a complex object containing tense features and an e-(ventuality) role provided by a lexical verb or other predicate, and is headed by the tense operator.

Parallel to the tense chain is the D(et)-chain which we refer to in our discussion of the determiner system below.

18. The analysis proposed in the text is for root infinitives with a present-tense declarative interpretation. For root infinitives with a modal reading, such as that in (19), we assume that there is a null modal in I bound by a modal operator. Much less frequently a root infinitive will have a past-tense interpretation. In these cases we assume the T^0 takes a marked past value and underspecified T refers directly to this interval.

19. The fact that there is a considerable lag between the time the child sorts out the pragmatics of the temporal system and that of the anaphor system suggest that Reinhart's Rule I and Rule T are not one and the same, but are rather specific instances of a more general bleeding relationship between grammar and pragmatics such that if an interpretation can be assigned grammatically, then this precludes a (non-distinct) pragmatic assignment. Thus, children give up declarative root infinitives by roughly age 3, while the principle blocking local coreference between a pronoun and NP-antecedent is not apparent for several years; at age 6 children still accept sentences such as that in (21c) (Chien & Wexler 1990).

20. The relation between definiteness and specificity is a complicated one. Since the details are not really crucial to what follows, we will make some simplifying assumptions: definite DPs are specific (except where generic as in *The dolphin is a beautiful animal,* in which case the determiner is expletive (Vergnaud & Zubizarreta 1992); indefinite DPs may be specific or non-specific. Thus, *John wants to marry a girl with blue eyes* may mean that a prerequisite for John marrying is that the girl, whoever she is, have blue eyes, or John wants to marry a specific girl, say Mary, who has blue eyes. In what follows we are primarily concerned with specific DPs. (For detailed discussion of these issues see Heim 1982; Diesing 1992, and papers in Reuland & ter Meulen 1987.)

21. For ease of exposition we assume that adverbs and the negative marker *niet* occur in the same position. There is a great deal of debate over the exact position of negation and the various adverbials, which has rather important implications for acquisition. For discussion, see Schaeffer (in prep.).

22. Examples such as that in (i) show that determiners (at least in object position) can appear in nonfinite clauses, and they can also be omitted in finite clauses, as in (ii, iii).

    (i)   *pas atrapper une fleur*
                [ ] not pick   a   flower
    (ii)   *veux pas lolo*
                (I) want not water
    (iii)   *Papa   heft ook trein*
                Daddy has also train

It is unclear at this point whether there is a correlation in early English (or French or Dutch) between root infinitives and determinerless nominals in either subject or object position. Clahsen *et al.* (this volume) report a correlation in German between root infinitives and underspecified subjects, where the latter include both determinerless DPs and null subjects (mainly null subjects). Their RI/null subject correlation seems to parallel the English results reported in Sano & Hyams, Roeper & Rohrbacher, and Kramer's Dutch results, discussed in the text. In order to determine whether there is, in addition, a correlation between root infinitives and determinerless DPs in these languages, quantitative analyses must be done. This issue is taken up in Hoekstra & Hyams (1995b).

23. We would like to thank Jacqueline van Kampen for making Laura's data available to us.

24. We should note that most of the nonscrambled pronouns are demonstratives, which can be left unscrambled when they are focused.

25. We have not included proportions for scrambled vs. non-scrambled full DPs because scrambling in these cases (unlike the pronoun case) is dependent on a variety of factors including focus. For example, in a neutral context a definite DP-object must scramble, as in (i), but if the object has contrastive focus then it may not scramble even if definite/ specific, as in (ii) (T. Hoekstra, J. Schaeffer, p.c.).

(i)   *Roll de bal maar.*
         roll the ball go-ahead
         'Go ahead roll the ball.'

(ii)   *Roll maar   de ball.*
         roll go-ahead the ball (not the marble)
         'Go ahead roll the ball, (not the marble).'

From transcripts it is difficult to establish obligatory contexts for scrambling of definite DPs in a way that would make a proportion meaningful.

26. Hamann (1992) presents some interesting evidence supporting the idea that the default or unmarked interpretation of D is deictic. She observes that in early German there is a preference for tonic subject pronouns (85% of all cases) over atonic pronouns at the same time that children 'overextend' topic drop, that is, they drop topics in contexts in which it would be infelicitous to do so in the adult language, where the referent is not clearly given. Hamann suggests that these two phenomena follow from the child's early preference for deictic or direct discourse anchoring of anaphoric expressions. She points out that the tonic pronouns, like first and second person pronouns, are deictic, that is, they can be directly interpreted in discourse, while the atonic pronouns are anaphoric and must be bound by a linguistically specified antecedent, and hence they are a later development. Similarly, children's null topics are directly anchored in discourse and are not anaphorically related to a linguistic antecedent, as would be required in the adult language.

27. My thanks to Alec Marantz and David Pesetsky for bringing the issue of phonological vs. grammatical underspecification to my attention.

References

Abney, S. 1987. "The English NP in its Sentential Aspect." Diss., Massachusetts Institute of Technology, Cambridge.

Aldridge, D. 1988. "The Acquisition of Infl." *Research Monographs in Linguistics,* UCNW, Bangor.

Antelmi, D. 1992. "L'ipotesi maturazionale nell'acquisizione del linguaggio. Diss., Padova University.

Antinucci, F. & R. Miller. 1976. "How Children Talk about What Happened." *Journal of Child Language* 3.167–189.

Belletti, A. 1990. *Generalized Verb Movement.* Torino: Rosenberg & Sellier.

Bloom, L., K. Lifter & J. Hafitz. 1980. "Semantics of Rules and the Development of Verb Inflection in Children." *Language* 56.386–412.

Borer, H. & K. Wexler. 1987. "The Maturation of Syntax." *Parameter Setting* (= *Studies in Theoretical Psycholinguistics*), ed. by T. Roeper and E. Williams, 123–172. Dordrecht: Reidel.

Bronckart, J.P. & H. Sinclair. 1973. "Time, Tense and Aspect." *Cognition* 2.107–130.

Brown, R. 1973. *A First Language.* Boston: Harvard University Press.

Boser, K., B. Lust, L. Santelmann & J. Whitman. 1991. "The Theoretical Significance of Auxiliaries in Early Child German." Paper presented at Boston University Child Language Conference, October, 1991.

Cardinaletti, A. 1990. *Pronomi nulli e pleonastici nelle lingue germaniche e romanze.* Diss., University of Venice.

Chien, Y.-C. & K. Wexler. 1990. "Children's Knowledge of Locality Conditions on Landing as Evidence for the Modularity of Syntax and Pragmatics." *Language Acquisition* 1.225–295.

Chomsky, N. 1965. *Aspects of the Theory of Syntax.* Cambridge, Mass.: MIT Press.

———. 1981. *Lectures on Government and Binding.* Dordrecht: Foris.

———. 1992. A Minimalist Program for Linguistic Theory. *MIT Occasional Papers in Linguistics,* 1.

Chomsky, N. & Howard Lasnik. 1993. "Principles and Parameter Theory." *Syntax: An International Handbook of Contemporary Research,* ed. by J. Jacobs, A. von Stechow, W. Sternefeld and T. Vennemann. Berlin: Walter de Gruyter.

Clahsen, H., S. Eisenbeiss & A. Vainikka. 1994. "The Seeds of Structure: A syntactic analysis of the acquisition of Case marking." *Language Acquisition Studies in Generative Grammar* (= *Language Acquisition and Language Disorders,* 8), ed. by T. Hoekstra & B. Schwartz, 92–118. Amsterdam: John Benjamins.

Clahsen, H. & M. Penke. 1992. "The Acquisition of Agreement Morphology and its Syntactic Consequences: New evidence on German child language from the Simone-corpus." *The Acquisition of Verb Placement: Functional categories and V2 phenomena in language acquisition,* ed. by J. Meisel, 181–224. Dordrecht: Kluwer.

Diesing, M. 1992. *Indefinites.* Cambridge, Mass.: MIT Press.

Duffield, N. 1993. "Roots and Rogues: Null Subjects in German child language." Ms., Heinrich-Heine University, Düsseldorf.

Eisenbeiss, S. 1994. "Raising to Spec and Adjunction Scrambling in German Child Language." Paper presented at the Workshop on the Acquisition of Clause-internal Rules: Scrambling and cliticization. University of Berne, Switzerland.

Enç, M. 1987. "Binding Conditions for Tense." *Linguistic Inquiry* 18.633–657.

Fantuzzi, C. 1994. "Bootstrapping Mechanisms in the Acquisition of Verbal Aspect." Paper Presented at the Second Language Research Forum, Baltimore.

Grinstead, J. 1994. Consequences of the Maturation of Number Morphology in Spanish and Catalan. MA Thesis, University of California at Los Angeles.

Grodzinsky, Y. and T. Reinhart. 1993. "The Innateness of Binding and Reference." *Linguistic Inquiry* 24.69–102.

Guasti, M.-T. 1993/1994. "Verb Syntax in Italian Child Grammar: Finite and nonfinite verbs." *Language Acquisition* 3.1–40.

Guéron, J. & T. Hoekstra. 1989. "T-Chains and the Constituent Structure of Auxiliaries." *Constituent Structure: Papers from the 1987 GLOW Conference*, ed. by A. Cardinaletti, G. Cinque, G. Giusti, 35–99. University of Venice.

———. To appear. "The Temporal Interpretation of Predication." *Small Clauses (Syntax and Semantics*, 28), ed. by A. Cardinaletti and M.-T. Guasti. New York: Academic Press.

Guilfoyle, E. 1984. "The Acquisition of Tense and the Emergence of Lexical Subjects." *McGill Working Papers in Linguistics.*

Guilfoyle, E. & M. Noonan. 1988. "Functional Categories and Language Acquisition." Paper presented at the 16th Annual Boston University Conference on Language Development, Boston.

Haan, G. J. de & K. Tuijnman. 1988. "Missing Subjects and Objects in Child Grammar." *Language Development*, ed. by P. Jordens & J. Lalleman, 110–122. Dordrecht: Foris.

Hamann, C. 1992. "Ambiguous Input and Late Empty Subjects in German Child Language." Ms., University of Geneva.

———. 1994. "Null Arguments in German Child Language." Ms., University of Geneva.

Heim, I. 1982. "The Semantics of Definite and Indefinite NP's." Diss., University of Massachusetts, Amherst.

Hoekstra, T. & P. Jordens. 1994. "From Adjunct to Head." *Language Acquisition Studies in Generative Grammar,* (= *Language Acquisition & Language Disorders,* 8), ed. by T. Hoekstra and B. D. Schwartz, 119–149. Amsterdam: John Benjamins.

Hoekstra, T. & N. Hyams. 1995a. "The Syntax and Interpretation of "Dropped" Categories in Early Grammar: A unified account." *Proceedings of WCCFL 14.*

———. 1995b. "The Role of Number in Nominal and Verbal Finiteness." Ms., University of California at Los Angeles, Leiden University. [in progress]

Hyams, N. 1983. "The Acquisition of Parametrized Grammars." Diss., City University of New York.

————. 1986. *Language Acquisition and the Theory of Parameters.* Dordrecht: Reidel.

————. 1992. "The Genesis of Clausal Structure." *The Acquisition of Verb Placement: Functional categories and V2 phenomena in language development,* ed. by J. Meisel, 371–400. Dordrecht: Kluwer.

————. 1993. "An Overview of Null Subjects." Talk presented at the Trieste Encounters in Cognitive Science, Workshop on Cross-Linguistic Acquisition Studies, Scuola Internazionale Superiore di Studi Avanzati (SISSA). Trieste, Italy.

————. 1994a. "V2, Null Arguments and COMP Projections." *Language Acquisition Studies in Generative Grammar (= Language Acquisition & Language Disorders,* 8), ed. by T. Hoekstra & B.D. Schwartz. Amsterdam: John Benjamins.

————. 1994b. "Commentary: Null Subjects in Child Language and the Implications of Cross-linguistic Variation." *Syntactic Theory and First Language Acqusition,* ed. by B. Lust, G. Hermon & J. Kornfilt. Vol. 2. Hillsdale, N.J.: Lawrence Erlbaum.

Hyams, N. & Kenneth Wexler. 1993. "On the Grammatical Basis of Null Subjects in Child Language." *Linguistic Inquiry* 24.421–459.

Jaeggli, O. & N. Hyams. 1987. "Morphological Uniformity and the Setting of the Null Subject Parameter." *Proceedings of NELS 18, 1987,* ed. by J. Blevins & J. Carter, 238–253. Amherst, Mass.: Graduate Linguistic Student Organization.

Johnson, K. 1990. "The Syntax of Inflectional Paradigms." Ms., University of Wisconsin, Madison.

Jordens, P. 1990. "The Acquisition of Verb Placement in Dutch and German." *Linguistics* 28.1407–1448.

Koopman, H. & D. Sportiche. 1991. "The Position of Subjects." *Lingua* 85.211–258.

Kramer, I. 1993. "The Licensing of Subjects in Early Child Language." *MIT Working Papers in Linguistics.*

Kayne, R. 1989. "Notes on English Agreement." Ms., City University of New York.

Lebeaux, D. 1988. *Language Acquisition and the Form of Grammar.* Diss., University of Massachusetts, Amherst.

MacWhinney, B. & C. Snow. 1985. "The Child Language Data Exchange System." *Journal of Child Language* 12.271–296.

Mahajan, A. 1990. "The A/Ā-Distinction and Movement Theory." Diss., Massachusetts Institute of Technology, Cambridge.

Meisel, J. 1990. "INFL-ection, Subjects and Subject–Verb Agreement." *Two First Languages: Early grammatical development in bilingual children (= Studies in Theoretical Psycholinguistics,* 16) ed. by J. Meisel, 237–298. Dordrecht: Foris.

Meisel, J. & N. Müller. 1992. "Finiteness and Verb Placement in Early Child Grammars: Evidence from simultaneous acquisition of French and German in bilinguals." *The Acquisition of Verb Placement: Functional categories and V2 phenomena in language development* (= *Studies in Theoretical Psycholinguistics*, 16), ed. by J. Meisel, 109–138. Dordrecht: Kluwer.

Moro, A. 1993. "I predicati nominali e la struttura della frase." Diss., University of Venice.

Partee, B. 1973. "Some Structural Analogies Between Tenses and Pronouns in English." *Journal of Philosophy* 70.

Pierce, Amy. 1989. "On the Emergence of Syntax: A cross-Linguistic study. Diss., Massachusetts Institute of Technology, Cambridge.

——. 1992. *Language Acquisition and Syntactic Theory: A comparative analysis of French and English child grammars.* Dordrecht: Kluwer.

Platzack, C. 1992. "Functional Categories and Early Swedish." *The Acquisition of Verb Placement: Functional categories and V2 phenomena in language development* (= *Studies in Theoretical Psycholinguistics*, 16), ed. by J. Meisel, 63–82. Dordrecht: Kluwer.

Poeppel, D. & K. Wexler. 1993. "The Full Competence Hypothesis of Clause Structure." *Language* 69.1–33.

Pollock, J.-Y. 1989. "Verb Movement, UG, and the Structure of IP." *Linguistic Inquiry* 20.365–424.

Radford, A. 1990. *Syntactic Theory and the Acquisition of English Syntax.* Oxford: Basil Blackwell.

Reichenbach, H. 1947. *Elements of Symbolic Logic.* New York: Free Press.

Reinhart, T. 1983. *Anaphora and Semantic Interpretation.* London: Croom Helm.

Reuland, E. & A. ter Meulen, eds. 1987. *The Interpretation of (In)definiteness.* Cambridge, Mass.: MIT Press.

Ritter, E. 1989. "Two Functional Categories in Noun Phrases: Evidence from Modern Hebrew." *Perspectives on Phrase Structure: Heads and Licensing* (= *Syntax and Semantics*, 26), ed. by S. Rothstein. New York: Academic Press.

Rizzi, Luigi. 1992. "Early Null Subjects and Root Null Subjects." *Geneva Generative Papers* 0.(1/2). Geneva University.

——. 1994. "Some Notes on Linguistic Theory and Language Development." *Language Acquisition* 3.371–394.

Roeper, T. & B. Rohrbacher. 1994. "True *pro*-Drop in Child English and the Principle of Economy of Projection." Ms., University of Massachussets, Amherst.

Roeper, T. & J. Weissenborn. 1990. "How to Make Parameters Work: Comments on Valian." *Language Processing and Language Acquisition* (= *Studies in Theoretical Psycholinguistics*, 10), ed. by L. Frazier and J. de Villiers, 147–162. Dordrecht: Kluwer.

Sano, T. 1992. "The Acquisition of Referentially Dependent Items and Their Development." *Proceedings of WCCFL 11.*

———. 1995. A Study of Universal Grammar with Special Reference to Child Grammar. Diss., University of California at Los Angeles.

Sano, T. & N. Hyams. 1994. "Agreement, Finiteness and the Development of Null Arguments." *Proceedings of NELS 24,* 543–558.

Schaeffer, J. 1990. The Syntax of the Subject in Child Language: Italian compared to Dutch. MA Thesis, Utrecht University.

———. 1994. "On the Acquisition of Scrambling in Dutch." *Proceedings of the Boston University Conference on Language Development I,* ed. by D. MacLaughlin & S. McEwen, 521–532.

Scholten, T. 1988. "Principles of Universal Grammar and the Auxiliary Verb Phenomenon". Diss., University of Maryland.

Smith, C. 1980. "The Acquisition of Time Talk." *Journal of Child Language* 7.263–278.

Steriade, D. 1995. "Underspecification and Markedness." *A Handbook of Phonological Theory,* ed. by J. Goldsmith. Oxford: Basil Blackwell.

Stromswold, Karin. 1990. "Learnability and the Acquisition of Auxiliaries." Diss., Massachusetts Institute of Technology, Cambridge.

Suppes, P. 1973. "The Semantics of Children's Language." *American Psychologist* 88.103–114.

Szabolsci, A. 1983. "The Possessor that Ran away from Home." *The Linguistic Review* 3.89–102.

———. 1994. "The Noun Phrase." *Hungarian Syntax (= Syntax and Semantics,* 27), ed. by F. Kiefer and K. Kiss, 179–214. New York: Academic Press.

Tomaselli, A. 1990. *La sintassi del verbo finito nelle lingue germaniche.* Padova: Unipress.

Tsimpli, I. 1992. "Functional Categories and Maturation: The prefunctional stage of language acquisition. Diss., University College, London.

Valian, V. 1991. "Syntactic Subjects in the Early Speech of American and Italian Children." *Cognition* 40.21–81.

Valois, Daniel. 1991. "The Internal Syntax of DP." Diss., University of California at Los Angeles.

Vergnaud, J.-R. & M.-L. Zubizarreta. 1992. "The Definite Determiner and the Inalienable Constructions in French and English." *Linguistic Inquiry* 23.595–652.

Verrips, M. & J. Weissenborn. 1992. "Routes to Verb Placement in Early German and French: The independence of finiteness and agreement." *The Acquisition of Verb Placement: Functional categories and V2 phenomena in language development (= Studies in Theoretical Psycholinguistics,* 16), ed. by J. Meisel, 288–311. Dordrecht: Kluwer.

Wales, Roger. 1986. "Deixis." *Language Acquisition,* ed. by P. Fletcher and M. Garmen, 401–428. 2nd ed. Cambridge: Cambridge University Press.

Weissenborn, J. 1991. "Null Subjects in Early Grammars: Implications for parameter-setting theories." *Theoretical Issues in Language Acquisition,* ed. by J. Weissenborn, H. Goodluck and T. Roeper. Hillsdale, N.J.: Lawrence Erlbaum.

Weist, R. 1986. "Tense." *Language Acquisition,* ed. by P. Fletcher and M. Garman, 356–374. 2nd ed. Cambridge: Cambridge University Press.

Weverink, M. 1989. "The Subject in Relation to Inflection in Child Language." MA thesis, Utrecht University.

Wexler, K. 1994. "Optional Infinitives, Head Movement and the Economy of Derivations." *Verb Movement,* ed. by David Lightfoot and Norbert Hornstein, 305–350. Cambridge: Cambridge University Press.

Wyngaerd, G. vanden. 1989. "Object Shift as an A-movement Rule." *MIT Working Papers in Linguistics,* Vol. 11. Massachusetts Institute of Technology, Cambridge.

Zubizarreta, M.-L. 1992. "Word Order in Spanish and the Nature of Nominative Case." Ms., University of Southern California.

Lexical Learning in Early Syntactic Development

Harald Clahsen
University of Essex

Sonja Eisenbeiss & Martina Penke
University of Düsseldorf

1. Introduction

The present state of research into syntactic development in children presents us with a dilemma which results from two conflicting sets of observations. On the one hand, several studies provide evidence for *very early language-particular achievements* in syntactic development; when children begin to produce two- and multi-word utterances, differences between early English, early Chinese and early Italian, for example, with respect to null arguments seem to mimic differences between the corresponding adult grammars: English children drop many subjects in topic position ('diary drop'), but only very few objects (= less than 10% according to Andrew Radford, personal communication); Chinese children drop subjects and objects in topic position ('topic drop'), and Italian children drop subjects and objects in pre- and postverbal position (= '*pro*-drop'), cf. Valian (1991). Other examples of very early language-particular achievements include verb raising in V2–languages (Poeppel & Wexler 1993, among others) and subject–verb agreement in languages such as Italian (Guasti 1992). On the other hand, there is evidence for *later syntactic developments*, for example the late acquisition of scrambling in German (cf. Eisenbeiss 1994a, 1994b), the late disappearance of root clause infinitives (cf. e.g., Clahsen & Penke 1992) in the acquisition of languages such as German and Dutch, the lack of a subject–verb agreement paradigm and generalized V2 in early German (cf. Clahsen *et al.* 1994), etc.

Whereas the early achievements seem to indicate that children know verb raising, properties of null arguments and agreement even before they start producing sentences, the evidence for later syntactic developments suggests that this cannot be the full story, and that the child acquires certain language-particular properties of verb placement, null arguments, agreement and object placement at a later age. This dilemma has given rise to a theoretical debate between the Full Competence Hypothesis (FCH) and the Lexical Learning Hypothesis (LLH). According to the FCH, children have the full adult-like clause structure around the age of 2 years (cf. Weissenborn 1990; Poeppel & Wexler 1993; Boser *et al.* 1992, among others), whereas under the LLH it is only when the child learns new properties of heads that functional projections are added to existing phrase-structure representations (cf. Clahsen 1990; Clahsen & Penke 1992; Clahsen *et al.* 1994). The purpose of the present article is to further elaborate the Lexical Learning Hypothesis, both theoretically and empirically. In the first part of the article, we will outline some theoretical essentials of the LLH, and in the second part we will present some new empirical findings on German child language and analyze them from a Lexical Learning perspective.

2.   Some Elements of a Lexical Learning Approach to Syntactic Development

The LLH claims that all UG-principles are available to the child from the outset of language development and that syntactic development is driven by the learning of new lexical and morphological items and their features (cf. Clahsen 1990). Under the LLH, differences between early achievements and later developments are taken to reflect the child's gradual acquisition of lexical and functional heads and their features. Under this approach no additional constraints or stipulations are required to solve the developmental problem of language acquisition (cf. Clahsen 1992); it should therefore only be deviated from if specific data leave no other choice.

In the following, we will outline three essential elements of the Lexical Learning approach, (i) weak continuity, (ii) head-driven projections and structural economy, and (iii) morphological bootstrapping.

2.1. *Weak Continuity*

Under the weak-continuity assumption, all components of Universal Grammar (UG) are available to the child from the outset of acquisition, but language-particular grammatical knowledge increases over time (cf. Clahsen *et al.* 1993). With respect to phrase-structure development, weak continuity states that UG-components such as X'-theory constrain children's phrase-structure trees from the beginning of acquisition, but that the full adult-like phrase-structure tree of the particular language the child is acquiring emerges gradually, based on UG principles and the input data.

2.2. Head-driven Projections and Structural Economy

The kinds of structural descriptions and syntactic derivations that are posited for children's grammars crucially depend on theoretical assumptions about what constitutes a legitimate versus an illegitimate description or derivation in adults' grammars. In the Lexical Learning approach, two major assumptions about phrase-structure positions are adopted from recent syntactic theory; these should hold for children's as well as for adults' grammars:

(1) a. Head-driven projections
         There is no fixed set of labels for functional projections CP, IP,
         ... provided by UG; rather, functional projections are feature
         bundles, and their properties are determined by their head
         features (cf. Chomsky 1995).
     b. Structural economy
         At any point in a derivation, a structural description for a
         natural language string employs as few nodes as grammatical
         principles and lexical selection require (Safir 1993:12).

According to standard X'-theory, UG is assumed to provide a fixed set of functional categories CP, IP, TP, AGR-, etc. Acquisition researchers used this fixed set of functional categories to analyze child language data. In Chomsky's (1995) theory of MERGER, however, the assumption that UG provides for a fixed set of syntactic projections has been given up in favour of the idea (adopted from categorial grammar) that projections are feature bundles and their properties are determined by their head features. We think that this move has desirable consequences for our understanding of the acquisition of syntactic structure. Suppose, for example, that in some adult grammar the head category X of the functional projection XP has the features F_1, F_2, ...F_n, but that at some early stage, the child has not yet fully determined the feature content of X, and has only acquired F_1. Instead of being forced to select a potentially inappropriate phrase-structure label from a fixed list of options, under the assumption of head-driven projections, we would posit a functional projection XP that has no properties other than those imposed by F_1. In this case, the child's X and XP positions are underspecified compared to the corresponding adult grammar, and the child still has to learn that in addition to F_1, XP also hosts the features F_2, ...F_n. We think that in this way we will achieve a more realistic view of grammatical development in which phrase-structure representations are gradually expanded throughout early childhood as a function of the child's acquisition of new features.

The structural economy principle we have adopted from Safir (1993) is part of a set of economy requirements on syntactic representations. Following Chomsky (1993), syntactic derivations have to be optimal in the sense that they must satisfy as many constraints as possible. Movement operations, for example, are subject to economy requirements, such as the 'shortest movement' condition (Chomsky 1993:15 ff.). In addition to the economy of derivation requirements, UG is also assumed to impose specific economy conditions on representations. Speas (1993) argued, for example, that each maximal projection must receive independent content from either its specifier or its head. Hence, the specifier of IP can be left empty if its head position is filled, whereas if I^0 is not filled Spec-IP cannot be left empty; (this contrast would account for the difference between null-subject languages such as Italian and non-null-subject languages such as English). Grimshaw (1993) argued along the same lines that a MINIMAL PROJECTION PRINCIPLE requires a projection not be empty, i.e., its Spec or head must be filled.

In analyzing children's and adults' sentences, these economy principles lead us to posit only as much structure as is required. Rather than automatically analyzing all constructions headed by a verb as full CPs whenever possible, these economy considerations allow us to describe the various stages of language acquisition (including the later developments mentioned above) in linguistic terms, namely in terms of phrase-structure building.

2.3. Morphological Bootstrapping

Children have to learn the language-specific content of syntactic heads as this is not specified in UG. This applies to the lexical content of heads such as N^0 and V^0, as well as to the morphological content of inflectional heads such as I^0, D^0, Agr^0, etc. That *rock* can be a verb in English, but that it can only be a noun in German is not part of UG. The same holds for inflectional heads: that the adult language has a unique second person singular affix is something the German-speaking child has to learn whereas the English-speaking child does not have to bother. Theoretical and typological research demonstrate close correlations between overt inflectional affixes and syntactic phenomena such as head movement (Holmberg & Platzack 1991; Roberts 1993; Rohrbacher 1994). Rohrbacher (1994:80) shows, for example, that V-to-I raising occurs in exactly those languages which distinctively mark the person features ⟨1st⟩ and ⟨2nd⟩. The intuition behind the idea of morphological bootstrapping is that the child exploits such correlations in acquisition such that the child's learning of overt morphological affixes has consequences for his/her phrase-structure representations.

We will not attempt to develop a comprehensive theory of morphological bootstrapping here; rather we will focus on one specific idea that has emerged from earlier work of our research group (cf. Clahsen & Penke 1992; Clahsen *et al.* 1994; Eisenbeiss 1994b) with respect to the role of morphology in syntactic development. The idea is that functional categories such as IP, AGRP, etc. or syntactic features may come into the child's phrase-structure representations as a consequence of the child's learning a regular inflectional paradigm of distinct inflectional affixes. There are different possibilities of spelling out this claim in technical terms.

Following Rohrbacher (1994), only those elements of a regular paradigm that distinctively mark relevant categories such as PERSON and NUMBER are inserted into the phrase-structure representations along with lexical elements such as nouns and verbs. This means, for example, that a German-speaking child who has learnt the subject–verb agreement paradigm will insert affixes such as the second person singular form -*st* into I^0 (or AGR(S)^0) and will consequently have to raise the verb. Hence such inflectional affixes are syntactically active in the same way as other heads.

Our idea of the role of overt inflectional affixes in syntactic development can also be spelled out in terms of feature-checking theories, such as Chomsky (1993, 1995). We would, however, have to make the assumption that elements of a regular paradigm that distinctively mark relevant categories induce syntactic features that are 'strong' in Chomsky's sense.[1] Hence, if Rohrbacher's descriptive generalization mentioned above is correct, we would expect to find that, as a consequence of the child's acquisition of a regular agreement paradigm that distinctively marks ⟨1st⟩ and ⟨2nd⟩, a 'strong' V-feature comes into the child's grammar. According to Chomsky, strong features need to be checked in the syntax, e.g., by overt head movement. Hence, irrespective of whether we adopt a weak lexicalist approach such as Rohrbacher's or a feature-checking system such as Chomsky's the consequences are the same: once affixes from regular paradigms distinctively mark relevant inflectional features or categories, these affixes become syntactically active. If this view is correct, we would expect to find close morphology–syntax connections in child language development. In the following sections we will show that such developmental correlations do exist and that they can be interpreted in terms of syntactic consequences of the child's learning of inflectional morphology (cf. Clahsen & Penke 1992).

3. Results

In the second part of this article, we will investigate the acquisition of phrase structure and its developmental links to the acquisition of inflectional morphology in German child language. We will first show that early child grammars may initially lack certain functional projections that do exist in the corresponding adult grammar. Next, we will examine syntactic effects of the acquisition of regular inflectional paradigms. Finally, we will investigate how the acquisition of syntactic features and categories in the nominal domain is linked to the creation of clause structure in child language development. Our findings are based on 88 recordings from longitudinal corpora of five monolingual German children covering the age period of 1;10–3;6 (cf. Table 1).

Table 1. Data

child	source	age	number of recordings
Annelie	LEXLERN	2;4–2;9	6
Hannah	LEXLERN	2;0–2;7	7
Mathias	Clahsen	2;3–3;6	18
Simone	Miller	1;10–2;7	42
Svenja	LEXLERN	2;9–3;3	15
totals		1;10–3;6	88

3.1. *Early Child Grammars*

Consider first how the grammar of a German child looks like before s/he has acquired regular agreement and Case paradigms. In previous studies (Clahsen 1990; Clahsen *et al.* 1993), we described an early developmental stage (around the age of 2 years) with the following properties:

(2)   —   Regular subject–verb agreement and regular accusative and
           dative Case marking have not been acquired.
      —   Finite verbs (i.e., modals, auxiliaries, forms of *sein* 'to be' and
           verbs inflected with the affix -*t*) appear in first or second position,
           whereas nonfinite verbs remain in clause-final position.
      —   In contrast to adult German, subjects do not intervene between
           the finite verb and the negation marker.
      —   Children do not produce *wh*-elements or complementizers.

Clahsen (1990) argued that at this stage the child has a phrase-structure tree with
one functional projection in the verbal domain, F(inite)-P. The head of this
projection is the host of the syntactic feature ⟨+F(inite)⟩, and in this way
functions as a landing site for finite verbs. This projection cannot be identified
with IP or AGRP in the traditional sense since its specifier position is not
restricted to subjects. On the other hand, the projection cannot be CP either,
because the head position of this projection can only be filled with finite verbs
at this early stage, and because the Spec position of this projection cannot be
filled with *wh*-elements (cf. Clahsen *et al.* 1995).[2]

(3)

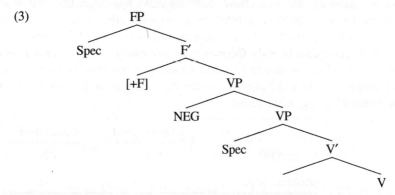

The functional projection FP is an example of an underspecified phrase-structure
position which may arise during language development. In this case, the
functional head appears in the target position (generating V2–patterns for finite
verbs), but the complete feature grid of that position as it is in adult German is
not yet fully specified.

   Recent studies adopting the full competence approach have questioned the
postulation of the tree in (3) with two distinct verb positions, one for finite and
the other for nonfinite verbs. Basically, three major variants of the FCH can be
distinguished. First, Poeppel & Wexler (1993) among others proposed an

account of early German child language in which IP and CP necessarily project together. Thus, children's grammars generate two functional categories above VP, rather than just one as in (3). The second variant is Déprez & Pierce's (1993) idea of the optionality of movement. Déprez & Pierce assume that the full set of functional projections is operative when the child starts to produce sentences, but they additionally claim that movement operations such as verb raising to Comp are initially optional. To support this account, they quote some examples from three German-speaking children between the ages of 1;10 and 2;2 in which finite verbs occur in clause-final position of matrix sentences (cf. Schaner-Wolles 1994 for similar data). Déprez & Pierce take these examples as evidence for the optionality of verb raising and the availability of a head-final IP in early child German. The third variant is Rizzi's (1993) MATURATIONAL THEORY. Rizzi assumes that in adult grammars a constraint is operative which requires all root clauses to be headed by CP. He claims that the hierarchical structuring of functional projections is determined by UG, and to capture child–adult differences he suggests that the constraint 'CP = root' matures around the age of 2;5. Before this age, bare sub-CPs are available as clause types, thereby allowing for root-clause null subjects, non-target-like VP-internal subjects (Guilfoyle & Noonan 1988), bare nonfinite verbs in matrix declaratives (Radford 1990), and other characteristic properties of early child language.

Verb placement in early German is an interesting test case for the debate between Full Competence and Lexical Learning approaches as the predictions they make are partly different. Consider the four logical possibilities for the placement of simple main verbs:

(4)

	verb-second	clause-final
finite verb	(i)	(ii)
nonfinite verb	(iii)	(iv)

Under the first variant of the FCH as well as under the FP-analysis in (3), one would expect to find (4i) and (4iv) in the data, but not (4ii) and (4iii). Pattern (4iii) is ruled out, because under both analyses the V2–position is restricted to finite verbs and cannot host nonfinite verbs. In the FP-analysis, (4ii) should not occur, because the clause-final verb position is restricted to nonfinite verbs. In Poeppel & Wexler's FCH analysis, (4ii) should not occur, because all finite verbs are raised to COMP in main clauses. If, however, Rizzi's or Déprez & Pierce's accounts are correct, three of the four possibilities should be represented in the data, namely (4i), (4ii) and (4iv), but not (4iii). The patterns (4i) and (4iv) are analyzed in terms of full CP-trees, and (4ii) is derived from CP-truncation in Rizzi's theory and from the optionality of verb raising in Déprez & Pierce's account.

The second set of predictions concerns the placement of verbal elements in verb clusters, i.e., in auxiliary + participle and modal + infinitive patterns. Under the three variants of the FCH, the child's grammar generates two clause-final verb positions, one for nonfinite verbs within VP and another one for finite verbs within IP. In contrast to that, the FP-tree in (3) has only one clause-final verb position for nonfinite verbs. According to Rizzi (1993) and Déprez & Pierce (1993), finite verbs sometimes fail to appear in COMP, either because the CP-layer has been truncated or because the finite verb has not been moved. Therefore, verb clusters such as $[..[_{IP}...[_{VP}...V_{-fin}]\ V_{+fin}]]$ with nonfinite verbs (infinitives and participles) preceding finite verbal elements (auxiliaries, modals) are predicted to occur in the data. Under the FP-analysis and the first variant of the FCH-account, however, such verb clusters should not occur. In the FP-tree in (3), there is only one clause-final verb position, for nonfinite verbs. Thus, in verb clusters the finite verbal element should always precede the nonfinite verbal elements. In Poeppel & Wexler's theory, the CP-layer is generated in all sentences, and finite verbs are raised to COMP. Therefore, verb clusters in which the nonfinite verb precedes the finite one should not occur (except in embedded clauses in which COMP is filled with a lexical complementizer).

These two predictions were examined in our data. Note that from one of the children under study, Svenja, we do not have any data representing this early stage of grammatical development. Recordings started when Svenja was 2;9, and at this age the child had already acquired the subject–verb agreement paradigm and other syntactic properties of adult German (see below for further details). The following analysis of early child grammars is therefore restricted to the remaining four children. The quantitative results are shown in Table 2.

3.1.1. Placement of Finite and Nonfinite Verbs

In order to test the placement patterns in (4) and the first set of predictions against the data, we must distinguish ambiguous verb-second and verb-final patterns from unambiguous ones. Consider the surface patterns (X)VY and YV which are ambiguous in several ways. In (X)VY patterns, for example, the verb could be in the ⟨+F⟩-position or it could be in the V^0-position with Y being extraposed. YV-patterns are also ambiguous in that the verb could either be in

Table 2. Verb Placement of Finite and Non-Finite Verbs and in Verb Clusters

	Simone	Mathias	Annelie	Hannah
finite/non-finite verbs				
V_{+fin} in V2-position	93% (511)	87% (69)	88% (117)	80% (4)
V_{+fin} in V-final position	7% (41)	13% (10)	12% (16)	20% (1)
V_{-fin} in V2-position	2% (4)	2% (1)	1% (1)	X
V_{-fin} in V-final position	98% (189)	98% (52)	99% (80)	X
verb clusters				
$V_{+fin} < V_{-fin}$	72	35	40	0
$V_{-fin} < V_{+fin}$	8	0	0	0

the V^0- or in the $\langle +F \rangle$-position with Y being topicalized in the latter case. We did not include these two ambiguous patterns into our analysis; rather we only compared unambiguous V2–patterns with unambiguous V-final structures. V2–patterns are unambiguous if the verb appears before NEG, so giving rise to the order V NEG, or if the verb appears before two other constituents (V X Y). V-final patterns are unambiguous if the verb appears after NEG, so giving rise to the order NEG V or if the verb follows two other constituents (X Y V).

Table 2 presents percentages of use of the four logical possibilities for the placement of finite and nonfinite verbs in main clauses; the figures in parentheses provide the total number of finite and nonfinite verbs in the two verb positions. Only unambiguous patterns were included.

Table 2 shows a clear distinction between the placement of finite and nonfinite verbs. 91% of the finite verbs appear in the V2–position (4i), whereas 98% of the nonfinite verbs are placed clause-finally (4iv). Some examples of these predominant verb-placement patterns are given in (5) and (6). These data indicate that the V2–position is the landing site for finite verbs whereas non-finite verbs remain within VP.

(5)   Finite V in V2–position (4i)
       ich hab hier reintecken tasche   A(2;6)
       I   have here put-in   bag
       'I have put (this) into the bag.'

(6)   Nonfinite V in clause-final position (4iv)
         mone   auch lump ausziehen   S(1;11)
         Simone also rag take-off

Furthermore, Table 2 demonstrates that pattern (4iii), i.e., nonfinite verbs appearing in the V2–position, is practically non-existent (1%–2%); two examples are given in (7). By contrast, pattern (4ii) is represented in the data: about 10% of the finite verbs do occur in clause-final position: cf. the examples in (8).

(7)   Nonfinite V in V2–position (4iii)
    a.   *das da   rutschen nich runt*   M(3;0)
         this one slip   not down
    b.   *habe Maxe   auch*   S(2;1)
         have Max (subject) too

(8)   Finite V in V-final position (4ii)
    a.   *da   ni   fährt*   A(2;4)
         there not drives
    b.   *mäuschen   da   reinklettert*   H(2;4)
         little-mouse there in-climbs

Taken together, these data allow us to exclude one of the four logical possibilities for verb placement, namely (4iii): nonfinite verbs do not occur in the V2–position. Pattern (4ii) cannot, however, be excluded, despite the fact that clause-final finite verbs are relatively rare compared to the dominant patterns (4i) and (4iv).

3.1.2. *Verb Placement in Verb Clusters*

Recall that in verb clusters (auxiliary + participle/modal + infinitive) the FP-analysis requires the finite verbal element to precede the nonfinite verbal elements, whereas under Rizzi's (1993) and Déprez & Pierce's (1993) variants of the FCH, clause-final verb clusters in which auxiliaries or modals follow nonfinite verbal elements should also be possible.

Table 2 presents the total number of main clauses consisting of a verb cluster and an additional constituent. Two placement patterns within verb clusters are distinguished in Table 2:

— $V_{+fin} < V_{-fin}$: The finite verb precedes the nonfinite element.
— $V_{-fin} < V_{+fin}$: The nonfinite verb precedes the finite verb.

Table 2 shows that the finite element of a verb cluster almost always precedes the nonfinite element. In such cases the finite verb is placed in the V2–position; cf. the examples in (9). Verb clusters with the finite verb following the nonfinite verb are extremely rare. Only in the data from Simone did we find eight cases of this kind (10). Note however, that six of these utterances (10a–f) result from VP-topicalizations; independent evidence (11) indicates that Simone topicalizes VPs from the age of 1;10 onwards. This leaves us with two exceptions, (10g) and (10h). In all other cases, the finite verb precedes the nonfinite verb in verb clusters. This supports the FP-analysis and specifically the assumption that there is only one clause-final verb position in early child grammar, namely the V^0–position.

(9)   Finite V before nonfinite V

    a.   *ich habe das mach*   M(3;0)
       I   have that done

    b.   *kann nich de knete   essen*   S(2;1)
       can   not   the plasticine(OBJ) eat

    c.   *der   muß auch kochen*   A(2;6)
       this-one must also cook

(10)   Nonfinite V before finite V

    a.   *bonbon habe möcht*   S(2;0)
       candy   have want
       '(I) want to have (a) candy.'

    b.   *lala   habe möcht*   S(2;0)
       pacifier have want

    c.   *gummibärche habe möcht*   S(2;0)
       jellybaby   have want

    d.   *wasser gieße   hab*   S(2;0)
       water   poured have

    e.   *mäuse   abisse* [=*abgerissen*] *habe*   S(2;0)
       mice(OBJ) teared-off   have

    f.   *aua   macht hat*   S(2;2)
       ouch made has

    g.   *junge aua   macht hat*   S(2;2)
       boy   ouch made has

    h.   *mone   abgerisse hat*   S(2;0)
       Simone teared-off has

(11)   *baun will   ich*   S(1;10)
         build want I
         'I want to build (something).'

3.1.3. Discussion

Full Competence accounts (Rizzi 1993; Déprez & Pierce 1993; Poeppel & Wexler 1993) postulate phrase-structure representations with two clause-final verb positions for German child language, one for finite and another for nonfinite verbs. In the present data, however, we found a clear asymmetry in the placement patterns of finite verbs, which makes it hard to believe that the child's grammar does in fact generate two different verb positions in the right periphery of the clause. Specifically, we found that simple finite verbs are sometimes left in clause-final position, but that in verb clusters that consist of finite and nonfinite elements the finite verbal element is almost always raised. These findings are incompatible with the first variant of the full competence hypothesis, cf. Poeppel & Wexler (1993), in which IP and CP necessarily project together. In such a theory, the fact that children sometimes leave finite verbs in clause-final position rather than raising them to C^0 would be left unexplained. By contrast, Rizzi (1993) and Déprez & Pierce (1993) provide an account for the patterns used by the children: main clauses with finite verbs in second position are regarded as adult-like CPs in both accounts, and main clauses with simple finite verbs in clause-final position are derived either from CP-truncation (Rizzi) or from the optionality of verb raising (Déprez & Pierce). Notice, however, that none of these approaches can explain the asymmetry between simple finite verbs and verb clusters, i.e., the fact that simple finite verbs are sometimes left in clause-final position, whereas auxiliaries and modals in verb clusters are almost always raised.

Like the three variants of the FCH, the original FP-analysis in (3) cannot account for the complete set of findings. A slight modification is required to derive the observed distribution. Whereas in (3) the V-position was restricted to nonfinite verbs, i.e., verbs specified for the feature ⟨–fin⟩, we would now suggest a second underspecified position in the child's grammar at this early stage. This position is specified for the categorial feature ⟨+V⟩, and the corresponding projection is head-final; cf. the revised tree in (12). Compared to the corresponding position of adult German, i.e., the V^0-position, which is restricted to nonfinite verbs, the position hosting ⟨+V⟩ in (12) is neutral with respect to finiteness. Therefore, both finite and nonfinite verbal elements may appear in this position.

(12)

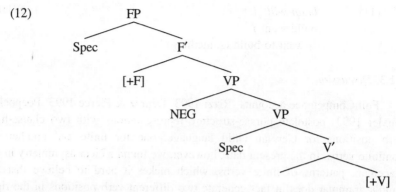

The revised FP-analysis in (12) accounts for the complete set of findings. The position hosting the feature ⟨+Finite⟩ in (12) is restricted to finite verbs. Therefore, nonfinite verbs cannot occur in this position. The clause-final position of (12) is restricted to verbs, but it is not yet specified for finiteness. Therefore, this position can host finite or nonfinite verbs. There is, however, only one clause-final verb position in (12) and, therefore, the finite verbal elements of verb clusters must be raised to the position hosting ⟨+F⟩. We conclude that in the early stage of language development, the child's grammar generates underspecified phrase-structure positions and that at this stage, there is only one functional projection in the sentential domain, namely FP in (12).

Clahsen & Eisenbeiss (1992) made a similar point for the development of the nominal domain. They argued that the grammar of early child German generates only one functional projection in the nominal domain, and that the head of this projection hosts the feature ⟨DEF(inite)⟩, but is underspecified with respect to the Φ-features ⟨Gender⟩ and ⟨Number⟩. The characteristic properties of DP/NPs in early child German can be derived from this analysis; for example, the fact that children distinguish between definite and indefinite determiners early on, but that at the same time, they do not inflect determiners and adjectives for gender and number (cf. Clahsen *et al.* 1994). Similarly, the underspecified position hosting ⟨DEF⟩ may be filled with determiners or adjectives, so giving rise to the complementary distribution between determiners and adjectives that has been found in children's early noun phrases (cf. Clahsen *et al.* 1994).

These parallels suggest that the notion of underspecification is not just a peripheral phenomenon of the development of verb placement, but that it might have some general significance and may contribute to a better characterization of children's early functional projections, both in the verbal and in the nominal domain.

3.2. Syntactic Effects of the Acquisition of Inflectional Paradigms

According to the Lexical-Learning approach, syntactic development is driven by the learning of new lexical and morphological items. The specific Lexical Learning effect we will investigate is concerned with regular inflectional paradigms. Our hypothesis is that once the child has acquired a new regular inflectional paradigm, the corresponding grammatical features will be incorporated into the child's phrase-structure tree. This may lead to new phrase-structure layers or to the specification of previously existing underspecified functional positions. We will test this hypothesis by investigating the syntactic effects of the acquisition of the regular subject–verb agreement paradigm of German.

We assume that the paradigm of subject–verb agreement is acquired if more than 90% of the forms are used correctly in obligatory contexts. Our claim is that the acquisition of the regular subject–verb agreement paradigm leads to the creation of the functional projection AGR(S)P. If this is correct, syntactic effects of AGR(S)P should be visible once the subject–verb agreement paradigm has been acquired. In the following, we will test two specific predictions of the presence of AGR(S)P, the first one concerning movement of finite verbs and the second one concerning movement of the subject over the negation.

The quantitative results with respect to these two predictions are shown in Table 3.

3.2.1. Verb Raising

Recall, with respect to verb movement, that before the acquisition of subject–verb agreement the child had only a small number of finite verb forms to lexicalize the V2–position (modals, auxiliaries, forms of *sein* and verbs ending in -*t*), cf. Clahsen (1990), Clahsen *et al.* (1993). Once the subject–verb agreement paradigm has been acquired, the child can generate finite forms for all verbs, and verbal inflections are categorized as agreement affixes. This should have indirect consequences for the placement of verbs as it is now possible for the child to lexicalize the V2–position not only with a restricted class of verbs, but rather with the unrestricted class of verbs generated by the paradigm. This developmental change can be seen most clearly on verbs inflected with -$\emptyset$ or -*e*. These verb forms did not belong to the restricted class of finite verbs which

Table 3. Verb and Subject Raising in Relation to the Acquisition of Subject–Verb-Agreement

		Simone	Mathias	Annelie	Hannah	Svenja
acquisition of subject–verb-agreement paradigm at age		2;4	3;1	2;8	2;6	≤ 2;9
		position of verbs with *-Ø/-e*				
Stage I	totals	(136)	(89)	(69)	(7)	—*
	V2-position	59%†	54%	71%	43%	
	V-final position	41%	46%	29%	57%	
Stage II	totals	(202)	(66)	(44)	(10)	(570)
	V2-position	93%	94%	95%	100%	98%
	V-final position	7%	6%	5%	0%	2%
		subject–negation patterns				
Stage I	V Subj Neg	2	0	0	0	—*
	V Neg Subj	6	2	2	0	
Stage II	V Subj Neg	9	2	1	0	15
	V Neg Subj	0	1	0	0	1

* Stage I is not represented in the data we have from Svenja.
† In the Southern German dialect spoken by Simone *-e* is in free variation with *-n*. *-e* can therefore mark first person singular, any of the plural forms or the infinitive. Because of these ambiguities, *-e* was excluded from this analysis for Simone.

could lexicalize the V2–position in the FP-stage. Once the affixes *-Ø* and *-e* are integrated into the agreement paradigm, verbs inflected with *-Ø* or *-e* are finite verb forms and should always be moved into the V2–position.

   Table 3 presents percentages of V2 — and V-final placement patterns for regular verbs inflected with *-Ø* or *-e* in main clauses in Stages I (before agreement) and II (after the acquisition of the agreement paradigm). The figures in parentheses present the total number of verbs on which these percentages are calculated. The ages at which the children acquire the subject–verb-agreement paradigm are given in the first line of Table 3.

   The data demonstrate a clear developmental change in the placement of verbs inflected with *-Ø* and *-e*: In Stage I, verbs inflected with *-Ø/-e* are only optionally raised (with frequencies ranging between 40% and 70%), whereas in Stage II, i.e., after the acquisition of the subject–verb agreement paradigm, these verbs are almost always placed in the V2–position, with frequencies of over 93% for all children. We suggest that this developmental change is an effect of the children's acquisition of the morphological paradigm. Clahsen & Penke (1992) have shown, on the basis of morphological criteria (e.g., correctness of use in obligatory contexts), that in Stage I the affixes -$\emptyset$/-e are not yet used as 1sg. markings. Moreover, the affixes -$\emptyset$/-e can be finite verb forms as well as stems in German. The morphological ambiguity of these verb forms is reflected in their placement patterns in that V2–placement for these verbs is far from obligatory in Stage I. However, once the affixes -$\emptyset$ and -e are used as agreement affixes, namely in Stage II, verbs inflected with -$\emptyset$ or -e are finite verb forms and are obligatorily raised into the V2–position. The developmental link between verb raising and paradigm learning shows that syntactic development is dependent upon the acquisition of morphological features.

3.2.2. Subject Raising

The second effect of the acquisition of the subject–verb agreement paradigm concerns movement of subjects over negation. If the acquistion of regular subject–verb agreement leads to the creation of AGR(S)P, Spec-AGR(S)P should be available as a landing site for movement, as soon as the general paradigm has been established. Before the acquisition of the general paradigm, i.e., at the FP-stage, there is no landing site for the subject between the finite verb in the position hosting $\langle +F \rangle$ and the NEG-position. Therefore, the occurrence of adult-like V–Subj–NEG patterns should correlate with the acquisition of the subject–verb agreement paradigm. Consider for illustration the adult German sentence (13a):

(13) a. *Mir schmeckt die Wurst   nicht.*
          me taste   the sausage not
          'The sausage doesn't taste good to me.'

      b. [$_{CP}$ *mir* [*schmeckt*$_i$] [$_{AGR(S)P}$[$_{Spec}$ *die Wurst*$_j$] e$_i$] [$_{VP}$ *nicht* [$_{VP}$ [$_{Spec}$ e$_j$] e$_i$]]]

Before the acquisition of subject–verb agreement, the child's grammar does not generate a landing site for the subject between the finite verb in the $\langle +F \rangle$-position and the NEG-position; cf. the tree in (12). Hence sentences such as (13) with the subject appearing between the finite verb and NEG should not occur. After the acquisition of subject–verb agreement, the child's grammar generates the Spec-AGR(S)P position in (13b). Hence sentences such as (13a) are expected to occur: the finite verb is raised, the subject is moved from Spec-VP to Spec-AGRP, and the negation marker remains in its underlying position.

Table 3 shows the total number of verb–subject–NEG and verb–NEG–subject patterns in main clauses before and after the acquisition of the subject–verb–agreement paradigm. We have not included pronominal subjects in this analysis, as they seem to behave differently from non-pronominal subjects in early child German. Specifically, there is evidence that children cliticize subject pronouns to finite verbs. This can be seen from cases of subject doubling in which a pronominal copy of the lexical subject is attached to the finite verb, e.g., *mann is-er nicht oben* [man is-he not upstairs]. Such cases have been documented for German children under the age of 3;0 (cf. Clahsen 1986). The cases of subject doubling always involve a pronominal subject immediately after the finite verb, and never two non-pronominal subjects. This shows that nonpronominal subjects do not occur in the clitic position. These observations have consequences for the present analysis. Consider a verb–subject–NEG pattern with a pronominal subject. Given the evidence for cliticization of pronominal subjects, a $V-subj_{[+pron]}-NEG$ pattern is ambiguous, because the pronominal subject could either be directly attached to the finite verb or it could be in Spec-AGR(S)P. By contrast, subject–negation patterns with non-pronominal subjects are unambiguous, as the option of cliticization to the finite verb is not available in this case. For these reasons, we restricted the analysis in Table 3 to nonpronominal subjects.

Table 3 shows that in Stage I subjects almost always appear after the negation — resulting in incorrrect placement patterns (cf. (14)), whereas after the acquisition of the subject–verb agreement paradigm the children produce adult-like patterns with the subject appearing before NEG (cf. (15)).

(14)   V—NEG—subject patterns

   a.   *da   is nich pappa pauf*   A(I:2;6)
         there is not   daddy on (it)

   b.   *darf nich Julia haben*   M(I:2;9)
         may not   Julia have
         'Julia must not have (it).'

(15)   V–subject–NEG patterns
        hoffentlich eß   das piepmatz   das nich auf   M(II:3;1)
        hopefully   eats the cheeping-bird that not up
        'Hopefully the cheeping bird does not eat that.'

3.2.3. *Preliminary Summary*

The two movement effects we found and the developmental link to the acquisition of the subject–verb agreement paradigm are rather unexpected under the Full Competence Hypothesis, because the acquisition of overt inflectional paradigms is said to be irrelevant for the acquisition of phrase-structure representations (cf. e.g., Verrips & Weissenborn 1992). Under the Lexical Learning Hypothesis, however, specific syntactic effects are to be expected when the child learns new inflectional paradigms. Our results provide support for the LLH and specifically for the claim that the acquisition of regular subject–verb agreement leads to the integration of AGR(S)P into the child's grammar. This change in the child's grammatical system is reflected in the appearance of new phrase-structure positions that can function as landing sites for movement.

Similar findings have been obtained by Eisenbeiss (1994a, 1994b) for the development of AGR(O)P. Under the Lexical Learning Hypothesis, we would expect that the acquisition of regular accusative case marking leads to the integration of AGR(O)P into the child's grammar and that syntactic effects of AGR(O)P should only be visible after the acquisition of regular accusative Case marking. In the syntactic literature, object scrambling is assumed to involve movement to Spec-AGR(O)P in adult German. Thus, object scrambling over NEG should only occur in child German after AGR(O) has been established, i.e., after the acquisition of accusative Case. Before that point, there is no landing site for the object between the finite verb in the position hosting ⟨+F⟩ and the NEG-position (cf. (12)). Eisenbeiss shows that these predictions hold: object scrambling occurs once the child has acquired regular accusative Case marking.

3.3. *Connections between the Acquisition of DP and AGR*

In recent studies, language acquisition researchers have started to explore developmental links between functional categories in the nominal and the sentential domain. Radford (1990) argued that there is an early stage of syntactic development in which children's grammars do not generate functional categories at all and in later stages functional categories in both domains mature in parallel. Hyams (this volume) takes the view that functional categories are present at the earliest stage of syntactic development, and she argues that early child grammars lack a certain pragmatic principle that requires the functional categories T and D to be specified for finiteness and definiteness. Once this pragmatic principle is available to children, children are said to use functional categories in adult-like ways. Hence, similar to Radford, Hyams postulates parallel developments in the nominal and the sentential domain.

What does the Lexical Learning approach have to say about developmental connections between the nominal and the sentential domain? According to the LLH, the course of syntactic development is determined by the interaction of UG-principles and the gradual acquisition of lexical and morphological items and their grammatical features. This implies that functional categories may develop independently and at different times. Thus, dissociations in the development of functional categories may arise — such that one functional category X has been acquired but not Y.

In the following, we will demonstrate that functional categories in the sentential and the nominal domains do not always develop in parallel, but that there are in fact developmental dissociations. This raises the question of whether children's grammars violate principles of Universal Grammar in such cases. The UG component that is responsible for interactions between the nominal and the sentential domain is CHECKING THEORY (Chomsky 1993) according to which DP-internal N-features ⟨Gender⟩ and ⟨Number⟩ have to be checked by an appropriate AGR-category, i.e., fully specified DP-subjects have to be checked by AGR(S), fully specified direct DP objects by AGR(O), and fully specified indirect DP-objects by AGR(IO). If children use fully specified DPs before the corresponding AGR-projections have been established, then given Checking Theory, they are faced with a licensing conflict. How do they solve such conflicts and do they violate the principles of Checking Theory in such circumstances?

We will investigate these questions for subjects, direct objects and indirect objects. The analyses are based on the data summarized in Table 1.

3.3.1. *The Acquisition of DP*

In the development of the DP two clearly distinct stages can be distinguished (cf. Clahsen *et al.* 1994; Eisenbeiss 1994a). Initially, determiners, genitives and adjectives occur in complementary distribution, and determiners and attributive adjectives show a high percentage of agreement errors. Later, the genitive -*s* is used productively, determiners become obligatory, combinations of determiners and prenominal adjectives occur, and the percentage of agreement errors drops significantly. Other studies on DP-development in early German have largely confirmed these findings from our project (cf. Müller 1992; Penner & Weissenborn, this volume).

We have argued that all of the later developments which occur at about the same time result from the children's creation of fully specified DPs. This would imply that at the later stage the child's grammar generates the two N-features ⟨Gender⟩ and ⟨Number⟩. Thus, given Checking Theory and our assumptions on phrase structure we expect to find overt evidence for AGR-projections from this stage onwards. Line (1) of Table 4 provides the age of the children under study when they have reached this later stage (cf. Clahsen *et al.* 1994; Clahsen & Eisenbeiss 1992; Eisenbeiss 1994).

Table 4. The Acquisition of DP in Relation to the Development of AGR-Projections

		Annelie	Hannah	Mathias	Simone	Svenja
(1)	acquisition of DP at age	2;8	2;6	3;1	2;4	≤2;9
	subjects					
(2)	acquisition of AGR(S) at age	2;8	2;6	3;1	2;4	≤2;9
(3)	root-clause infinitives without DP-subjects after acquisition of DP	100% (12)	100% (10)	100% (7)	100% (93)	100% (23)
(4)	subject–verb agreement in sentences with DP-subjects	93% (123)	93% (72)	92% (91)	90% (459)	93% (576)
	direct objects					
(5)	acquisition of Agr(O) at age	2;8	2;6	3;1	≤2;4	2;9
(6)	accusative Case on DP-object after acquisition of DP	100% (9)	75% (4)	100% (8)	93% (27)	99% (73)
	indirect objects					
(7)	acquisition of Agr(IO) at age	>2;9	2;6	>3;6	2;4	>3;3
(8)	three-place predicates without DP-IOs after acquisition of DP	100% (8)	—	73% (11)	—	96% (81)

3.3.2. Subjects

The first question to be addressed is whether in children's sentences fully specified DPs used as subjects are properly licensed in terms of Checking

Theory. According to Checking Theory, AGR(S)P is the relevant structural domain for checking DP-subjects. We counted all subject noun phrases showing overt morphological realizations of the N-features ⟨Gender⟩ and ⟨Number⟩ as fully specified DP-subjects.[3] We assume that the acquisition of the regular subject–verb agreement paradigm leads to the creation of the functional projection AGR(S)P. In previous studies (cf. Clahsen & Penke 1992), we have argued that the paradigm of subject–verb agreement is acquired if more than 90% of the forms are used correctly. Line (2) in Table 4 shows this point of development for each child.

Table 4 shows that the children under study acquire DP and AGR(S) simultaneously, and hence licensing conflicts do not arise for subjects. As is clear from several acquisition studies, however, children continue to use root clause infinitives, i.e., utterances without finite verbs, even after the acquisition of subject–verb agreement (cf. e.g., Poeppel & Wexler 1993; Clahsen & Penke 1992). This allows us to make two predictions concerning the co-occurrence of fully specified DP-subjects and AGR(S):

(16) a.   Root-clause infinitives, i.e., utterances without AGR(S), should not have fully specified DP-subjects.

      b.   Utterances with a fully specified DP-subject must have AGR(S).

Root-clause infinitives (since they do not generate AGR(S)P) cannot license fully specified DP-subjects. Thus, if children obey Checking Theory, root-clause infinitives should not contain DP-subjects, and this should be the case even after children have acquired DPs.

Line (3) in Table 4 presents percentages of root-clause infinitives that do not contain fully specified DP-subjects after the children have acquired DP, i.e., from the age given in the first line. The figures in parentheses provide the total number of root-clause infinitives in the relevant age period. These data show that fully specified DP-subjects are absent from root-clause infinitives: out of 147 root-clause infinitives there were none that contained a DP-subject. Instead, the children either drop the subject (116 cases) or they use subjects that are not specified for the relevant N-features, i.e., proper names, first and second person pronouns (29 cases).

With respect to prediction (16b), line (4) in Table 4 shows that 92% (1,210 cases) of the sentences with fully specified subject DPs contain a verb that is correctly marked for subject–verb agreement. In the remaining cases, the verb has either been dropped (4%) or the verb is finite but incorrectly inflected (4%).[4]

These data show that in sentences with fully specified DP-subjects children generate an AGR(S)-projection as well. Hence, for subjects there are no licensing conflicts and no violations of Checking Theory.

3.3.3. Direct Objects

Co-occurrence requirements similar to those for subjects should hold for direct objects as well. According to Checking Theory, the N-features of direct object DPs have to be checked in AGR(O)P. We assume that overt accusative marking is evidence for the presence of AGR(O) and that the acquisition of the regular accusative paradigm leads to the creation of AGR(O)P. Thus, a DP-object with N-features may only appear if the features in AGR(O) are overtly realized, i.e., if the DP-object bears accusative Case.

Following Eisenbeiss (1994a, b) we assume that the regular accusative paradigm is acquired if more than 90% of adjectives and strong determiners in accusative contexts are used correctly. Line (5) in Table 4 shows this point of development for each child.

As is clear from Table 4, the children under study acquire DP and AGR(O) simultaneously; compare lines (1) and (5) of Table 4. Therefore, there are no licensing conflicts. Nevertheless, even after the accusative Case paradigm is acquired, the children sometimes produce Case-marking errors on direct objects, e.g., nominative forms instead of accusative forms. According to Checking Theory, such errors should not occur with fully specified DP-objects, because otherwise the relevant licensing domain for checking the N-features of the DP-object, namely AGR(O)P, would be missing. Thus, if children obey Checking Theory, we predict that sentences with a DP-object must have overt accusative Case marking.

With respect to this prediction, line (6) of Table 4 shows the percentages of DP-objects that have correct overt accusative Case markings.[5] The figures demonstrate that sentences with a DP-object have overt accusative Case marking. This holds for 97% of the DP-objects produced by the children. These results on direct objects are parallel to those on subjects: in both cases, there are no licensing conflicts and no violations of Checking Theory.

3.3.4. Indirect Objects

Consider finally the co-occurrence relationships between fully specified DPs used as indirect objects and the relevant AGR-projection. According to Checking Theory, the N-features of indirect objects are licensed by AGR(IO). Thus, before the acquisition of AGR(IO) children are unable to check the N-features of indirect object DPs. Eisenbeiss (1994a, b) has shown that the acquisition of the regular dative paradigm leads to the creation of AGR(IO)P; we assume that the regular dative paradigm is acquired if more than 90% of adjectives and strong determiners in dative contexts are correct.[6]

Line (7) of Table 4 shows the age of the acquisition of AGR(IO) for each child. By comparing these with the ages given in line (1) of Table 4, we can distinguish two groups of children:

I.   Hannah and Simone acquire DP and AGR(IO) simultaneously.
II. Annelie, Mathias and Svenja acquire DP before AGR(IO).

For the group-I children licensing conflicts do not arise. In fact, all the indirect object DPs used by these children had correct dative Case marking.

The data from the children in group II are more interesting because these children are faced with a licensing conflict. The acquisition of AGR(IO) is delayed with respect to DP-development in these children, and therefore, their grammars do not provide the relevant AGR-projection needed to check the N-features of indirect objects. Do children violate Universal Grammar, specifically Checking Theory in such circumstances?

We found that, even in this situation of conflict, children obey UG principles. Line (8) of Table 4 shows that 94% of the three-place predicates used by the children of group II do not contain a fully specified indirect-object DP, even though these children know how to generate a fully specified DP. The children either omit the indirect object (cf. (17)), or they use a PP (cf. (18)):

> (17) a.   *dann hau ich ein*   Svenja(3;2)
>   then beat I   one
>   b.   *ich hab die   senkt [= geschenkt]*   Annelie(2;9)
>   I   have these given
>
> (18) a.   *dann hau ich bei die Joana eine*
>   then beat I   at the Joana one   Svenja(3;2)
>   b.   *und das das schenk ich bei die jujana [= Indianer]* Svenja(3;0)
>   and that   give   I   at the Red Indians
>   c.   *die andern Sachen schenk ich für uns*   Svenja(3;2)
>   the other things give   I   for us

In these cases, there are no violations of Checking Theory. The cases in (17) do not contain an indirect object, and in (18) the relevant ⟨Number⟩ and ⟨Gender⟩

features of the GOAL-arguments are checked by the PP. Thus, even those children who acquire AGR(IO) later than DP do not violate Checking Theory.

3.3.5. *Preliminary Summary*

In contrast to what one would expect from Radford's (1990) Maturation Hypothesis and from Hyams' (this volume) Full Competence account, functional categories in the sentential and the nominal domain do not necessarily develop in parallel. We found that DPs and the corresponding AGR-projections may develop independently and at different times. Specifically, the acquisition of AGR(IO) may be delayed with respect to the development of DP.

We interpreted developmental connections between the nominal and the sentential domain in terms of Chomsky's (1993) Checking Theory. This theory states that fully specified DPs have to be licensed by appropriate AGR-projections, DP-subjects by AGR(S), DP-objects by AGR(O) and indirect objects by AGR(IO). We found that the licensing requirements are obeyed in children's sentences:

— Root-clause infinitives do not contain DP-subjects, whereas utterances with DP-subjects show overt S–V agreement.
— DP-objects show overt accusative Case marking.
— Indirect DP-objects show overt dative Case marking.

Given Checking Theory, the developmental dissociation of AGR(IO) and DP yields a licensing conflict for those children who acquire AGR(IO) later than DPs. We found that even under these circumstances, however, children do not violate Checking Theory. To solve the licensing conflict, they either omit the indirect object, or they realize the GOAL-Argument as a PP.

4.   Summary and Conclusion

We presented an account of the development of phrase structure that is based on the Lexical Learning approach. Three essential elements of this approach were described. First, it assumes *weak continuity*: all components of Universal Grammar (UG) are available to the child from the outset of acquisition, but language-particular grammatical knowledge increases over time. Second, it adopts two constraints from syntactic theory on what constitutes a legitimate phrase-structure representation, (i) head-driven projections and (ii) structural economy. These constraints ensure that in analyzing children's and adults' sentences we posit only as much structure as is required. The third element of our account is the idea of MORPHOLOGICAL BOOTSTRAPPING according to which functional categories such as IP, DP, AGRP, etc. or syntactic features may come into the child's phrase-structure representations as a consequence of the child's learning the morphological content of inflectional heads such I^0, D^0, Agr^0, etc.

In the second part of this article we presented some new empirical findings and an analysis of early child German in terms of the Lexical Learning approach.

The first set of findings concerns the nature of functional categories in early child grammars. We analyzed verb-placement patterns in an early developmental stage at which the child does not yet have the regular subject–verb agreement paradigm and found the following distribution:

(i)   Finite verbs frequently occur in the V(erb)-Second position and rarely (10%—20%) in clause-final position.

(ii) Nonfinite verbs only occur clause-finally, and not in the V2–position.

(iii) In verb clusters (auxiliary + participle/modal + infinitive), the finite verbal element almost always precedes the nonfinite element.

Three major variants of Full Competence were discussed none of which could explain the findings in (i) to (iii) above. Instead, we have analyzed this set of observations in terms of the clause structure (12) with two underspecified phrase-structure positions hosting the features $\langle +F \rangle$ and $\langle +V \rangle$ respectively. FP is the highest projection in (12), and it is left-headed. This gives rise to V2–patterns, but since the head position of FP is restricted to verbs marked for the feature $\langle +Finite \rangle$, nonfinite verbs cannot occur in this position. By contrast, the clause-final verb position of (12) is only specified for the categorial feature $\langle +V \rangle$, and it can therefore be filled by finite or nonfinite verbs. This accounts for the placement patterns of simple verbs and it correctly rules out clause-final verb clusters.

The second group of empirical findings concerns developmental connections between the acquisition of subject–verb-agreement and phrase-structure syntax. We found that once the general paradigm of subject–verb agreement has been acquired, verbs inflected with $-\emptyset/-e$ almost always appear in the V2–position and adult-like V–subj–NEG patterns occur. From the perspective of the FCH, the acquisition of overt inflectional paradigms is irrelevant for the acquisition of phrase-structure representations, and thus the FCH does not even attempt to explain these findings. The LLH, however, provides for a straightforward account. Under the LLH phrase-structure representations are gradually expanded throughout early childhood and this process of gradual expansion is a function of the child's acquisition of new lexical and morphological elements. This means, for example, that when new inflectional paradigms are learned the corresponding features are integrated into the child's grammar. The acquisition of the subject–verb agreement paradigm leads to the creation of the phrase-structure position AGR(S), and regular accusative case marking to the creation of AGR(O). These functional projections make new landing sites for movement available to the child, e.g., Spec-AGR(S)P and Spec-AGR(O)P, and thus we find a developmental correlation between for example subject raising over NEG and subject–verb agreement. Before the acquisition of the Case/agreement paradigms, AGR(S)P and AGR(O)P are not generated by the child's grammar and thus the Spec-positions are not available as landing sites for movement. This is corroborated by the observed word-order errors in the early stage (cf., e.g., (14)).

The third group of findings concerns developmental links and co-occurrence restrictions between DPs and AGR-Ps in child language. We found that the use of fully specified DPs (i.e., specified for ⟨Gender⟩ and ⟨Number⟩) as subjects and direct objects developmentally co-varies with the creation of AGR(S) and AGR(O). Such a close developmental connection does not, however, exist for indirect objects as some children create the relevant AGR-projection for indirect objects considerably later than they acquire DPs. Hence, DPs and the corresponding AGR-projections may show up at different times in development and this supports our view that functional categories gradually emerge based on X-bar theory and lexical/morphological evidence from the input.

We used Chomsky's (1993) Checking Theory to account for developmental connections between DPs and AGRPs. Checking principles require that N-features of DPs have to be checked in the domain of AGRPs and hence the developmental and structural links between DPs and AGRPs in child language. We found that children do not violate Checking Theory, and we have argued that checking principles are available to the child from the beginning.

In conclusion, we have found that the sentences children produce are in several ways similar to the sentences of the corresponding adult grammar, and the Full Competence Hypothesis accounts for these similarities. However, we have also found that in early stages of syntactic development the sentences children produce differ from the adult grammar, and the FCH is faced with serious problems accounting for these differences. We tried to account for both the similarities and the differences between child and adult grammars in terms of the Lexical Learning approach. The similarities are captured by assuming functional categories in early syntactic development, and the differences are attributed to underspecification, i.e., the lack of certain grammatical features in early stages. The observed developments towards the adults' grammar were explainable in terms of morphological bootstrapping.

Notes

1. As Chomsky (1993, 1995) is not particularly concerned with the role of overt morphology for the syntax, this assumption is not made in his theory. We need to make this assumption, however, in order to spell out the idea of morphological bootstrapping in a feature-checking framework.

2. Some researchers (cf. Verrips & Weissenborn 1992, among others) interpret the lack of embedded clauses with lexical complementizers in early child German as peripheral phenomena, i.e., as accidental lexical gaps resulting from the fact that the child has not yet learnt the required lexical items. If this was indeed the case, then we would expect to find omissions of certain complementizers, substitution errors and some correctly used complementizers, since this is the typical pattern that occurs in cases of lexical gaps, e.g., when children learn the past tense forms of irregular verbs in English. In the sentences German-speaking children produce before the age of approximately 2 years, there is nothing like this pattern; rather complementizers are simply absent. Thus, there is no evidence of accidental gaps in the children's lexicon at this stage; cf. Clahsen *et al.* (1995) for more discussion.

3. These features are overtly realized, either on determiners, third person pronouns or on prenominal adjectives. First person singular and second person pronouns and proper nouns were not treated as fully specified DPs as they are not overtly marked for ⟨Gender⟩ and ⟨Number⟩.

4. In these cases, the children produce inflectional errors, but the verb forms are always finite:
    (i)   *und der teller isse* [correct = *ist*] *auch dreckig*   H(II: 2;7)
            and the plate is   also dirty
    (ii)   *wo's* [correct: *sind*] *die nüsse?*   S(II: 2;5)
            where's   the nuts?

5. Notice that only masculine singular DP-objects were considered here, because these have distinct accusative Case markings, e.g., *der Hut* 'the hat' vs. *den Hut* 'the-ACC hat'. This does not hold for feminine and neuter nouns, nor for plurals. DP-objects with weak determiners (indefinite articles, possessive pronouns, *kein (no)*) were not taken into account as well.

6.   Eisenbeiss (1994b) has shown that the replacement of the dative suffix -*m* by the accusative suffix -*n* may be due to morphophonological reasons. Therefore, noun phrases with this type of error were not included in the analysis.

References

Boser, K., B. Lust, L. Santelmann, & J. Whitman. 1992. "The Syntax of V-2 in Early Child German Grammar: The strong continuity hypothesis." *Proceedings of NELS 22*, 57–66. Amherst, Mass.: Graduate Linguistic Student Association.

Chomsky, N. 1993. "A Minimalist Program for Linguistic Theory." *The view from building 20*, ed. by K. Hale & S. J. Keyser, 1–52. Cambridge, Mass.: MIT Press.

———. 1995. "Bare phrase structure." *Government and Binding Theory and the Minimalist Program*, ed. by G. Webelhuth, 383–439. Cambridge: Basil Blackwell.

Clahsen, H. 1986. "Verb Inflections in German Child Language: Acquisition of agreement markings and the functions they encode." *Linguistics* 24.79–121.

———. 1990. "Constraints on Parameter Setting: A grammatical analysis of some acquisition stages in German child language." *Language Acquisition* 1.361–391.

———. 1992. "Learnability Theory and the Problem of Development in Language Acquisition." *Theoretical Issues in Language Acquisition: Continuity and change in development*, ed. by J. Weissenborn, H. Goodluck. & T. Roeper, 53–76. Hillsdale, N.J.: Lawrence Erlbaum.

Clahsen, H. & M. Penke. 1992. "The Acquisition of Agreement Morphology and its Syntactic Consequences: New evidence on German child language from the Simone-corpus." *The Acquisition of Verb Placement: Functional categories and V2 phenomena in language acquisition*, ed. by J. Meisel, 181–224. Dordrecht: Kluwer.

Clahsen, H. & S. Eisenbeiss. 1992. "The Development of DP in German Child Language." Paper presented at the Cognitive Science Group, Rutgers University.

Clahsen, H., M. Penke & T. Parodi. 1993. "Functional Categories in Early Child German." *Language Acquisition* 3.395–429.

Clahsen, H., S. Eisenbeiss & A. Vainikka. 1994. "The Seeds of Structure: A syntactic analysis of the acquisition of Case marking." *Language Acquisition Studies in Generative Grammar* (= *Language Acquisition & Language Disorders*, 9), ed. by T. Hoekstra & B. D. Schwartz, 85–118. Amsterdam: John Benjamins.

Clahsen, H., C. Kursawe & M. Penke. 1995. "Introducing CP: The development of *wh*-questions and embedded clauses in German child language." *Essex Research Reports in Linguistics* 7.1–28

Déprez, V. & A. Pierce. 1993. "Negation and Functional Projections in Early Grammar." *Linguistic Inquiry* 24.25–67.

Duffield, N. 1993. "Roots and Rogues: Null subjects in German child language." Ms., Heinrich-Heine University, Düsseldorf.

Eisenbeiss, S. 1994a. "Raising to Spec and Adjunction Scrambling in German Child Language." Paper presented at the 'Workshop on the Acquisition of Clause-Internal Rules: Scrambling and Cliticization', University of Berne, January 1994.

————. 1994b. "Kasus und Wortstellungsvariation im deutschen Mittelfeld: Theoretische Überlegungen und Untersuchungen zum Erstspracherwerb." *Was determiniert Wortstellungsvariation?* ed. by B. Haftka, 277–298. Opladen: Westdeutscher Verlag.

Grimshaw, J. 1993. "Minimal Projection, Heads, and Optimality." Ms., Rutgers University.

Guasti, M.-T. 1992. "Verb Syntax in Italian Child Grammar." *Geneva Generative Papers* 1.145–162.

Guilfoyle, E. & M. Noonan. 1989. "Functional Categories and Language Acquisition." Ms.: McGill University.

Holmberg, A. & C. Platzack 1991. "On the Role of Inflection in Scandinavian Syntax." *Issues in Germanic Syntax*, ed. by W. Abraham & E. Reuland, 93–118. Berlin: Mouton de Gruyter.

Hyams, N. This volume. "The Underspecification of Functional Categories in Early Grammar."

Kayne, R. 1993. "The Antisymmetry of Syntax." Ms., City University of New York.

Müller, N. 1992. "The Role of Agr-features GENDER and NUMBER in the Grammar of Bilingual Children (German/French)." Paper presented at the 17th Boston University Conference on Language Development, October 1992.

Penner, Z. & J. Weissenborn. This volume. "Strong Continuity, Parameter Setting and the Trigger Hierarchy: On the acquisition of the DP in Bernese Swiss German and High German."

Poeppel, D. & K. Wexler. 1993. "The Full Competence Hypothesis of Clause Structure in Early German." *Language* 69.1–33.

Pollock, J.-Y. 1989. "Verb Movement, Universal Grammar, and the Structure of IP." *Linguistic Inquiry* 20.365–424.

Radford, A. 1990. *Syntactic Theory and the Acquisition of English Syntax: The nature of early child grammars of English*. Oxford: Basil Blackwell.

Rizzi, L. 1993. "Some Notes on Linguistic Theory and Language Development: The case of root infinitives." *Language Acquisition* 3(4).371–394.

Roberts, I. 1993. *Verbs in Diachronic Syntax: A comparative history of English and French*. Dordrecht: Kluwer.

Rohrbacher, B. 1994. "The Germanic VO Languages and the Full Paradigm: A theory of V-to-I raising." Diss., University of Massachusetts, Amherst.

Safir, K. 1993. "Perception, Selection, and Structural Economy." *Natural Language Semantics* 2.47–70.

Schaner-Wolles, C. 1994. "Intermodular Synchronization: On the role of morphology in the normal and impaired acquisition of a verb-second language." *How tolerant is Universal Grammar?* ed. by R. Tracy & E. Lattey. Tübingen: Niemeyer.

Speas, M. 1993. "Null Arguments in a Theory of Economy of Projection." Ms., University of Massachusetts at Amherst.

Valian, V. 1991. "Syntactic Subjects in the Early Speech of American and Italian Children." *Cognition* 40.21–81.

Verrips, M. & J. Weissenborn. 1992. "Routes to Verb Placement in Early German and French: The independence of finiteness and agreement." *The Acquisition of Verb Placement: Functional categories and V2 phenomena in language acquisition,* ed. by J. Meisel, 283–332. Dordrecht: Kluwer.

Weissenborn, J. 1990. "Functional Categories and Verb Movement in Early German: The acquisition of German syntax reconsidered." *Spracherwerb und Grammatik: Linguistische Untersuchungen zum Erwerb von Syntax und Morphologie* (= *Linguistische Berichte,* Special Issue 3), ed. by M. Rothweiler, 190–224. Opladen: Westdeutscher Verlag.

———. 1992. "Null Subjects in Early Grammars: Implications for parameter-setting theories." *Theoretical Issues in Language Acquisition: Continuity and change in development,* ed. by J. Weissenborn, H. Goodluck. & T. Roeper, 269–299. Hillsdale, N.J.: Lawrence Erlbaum.

Strong Continuity, Parameter Setting and the Trigger Hierarchy
On the Acquisition of the DP in Bernese Swiss German and High German

Zvi Penner
Universität Bern

Jürgen Weissenborn
Universität Potsdam

1. Introduction

The aim of this paper is to present an articulated version of the STRONG CONTINUITY HYPOTHESIS of language development within the framework of a parametrized UG approach to language acquisition. We claim that in order to predictively account on the one hand for language particular developmental sequences and on the other hand for crosslinguistic similarities and differences between developmental sequences, the theory of parameter setting needs to be complemented by a theory of the accessibility of triggers in the input (Weissenborn 1990). We will apply our approach in a comparative investigation of the acquisition of the DP in two varieties of German, namely Bernese Swiss German and High German, which differ only marginally in this domain.

More specifically, we will argue that, analogous to the development of Complementizer Phrases (CP) (Penner & Müller 1992), fullfledged DPs are part of the child's grammar from early on. Evidence comes from the early occurrence of DP-internal movement (e.g., N-to-D and Possessor Raising in periphrastic possessive constructions) as well as from the existence of strongly inflected adjectives and dummy place holders in functional positions.

This is not incompatible with the observation that the *instantiation* of the structural positions inside the DP can be partially inconsistent with the target grammar (e.g., default agreement spelled out in D^0 or the absence of possessive -*s* in High German). We propose that these inconsistencies are the manifestation of an intermediate grammar which is the result of the strict order of parameter setting, rather than of the successive development of structural positions or the acquisition of agreement paradigms as proposed by Clahsen *et al.* (this volume).

We will suggest, following Penner (1994a, 1994b, and 1994c) that potential triggering data are treated hierarchically. At the initial stage, the child SYNTACTICALLY BOOTSTRAPS only those target parameters which are CANONICAL in nature,[1] i.e., parameters the values of which are disambiguated by highly reliable devices such as root/non-root asymmetries (e.g., main vs. subordinate clauses) or expletive markers. Triggers which are not encoded in this manner become accessible at a later stage. The fact that not all triggers are accessible at the same point in time leads to the observed inconsistencies of the initial stage with respect to the target.

Our hypothesis is partially at variance with recent analyses of the acquisition of the DP in German which claim that the development of the DP is triggered by the acquisition of Case features (see Clahsen *et al.*, this volume). This claim predicts that High German and Bernese Swiss German should show different developmental schedules for the DP because Bernese Swiss German, as in Dutch and related German dialects, displays reduced Case patterns which are not comparable to the High German four-way Case marking system (nominative, accusative, genitive, and dative). We will show that this prediction is not borne out. This result suggests that in German Case marking (as well as DP-internal agreement) is probably acquired independently from the DP.

Finally we will point out that syntactic bootstrapping alone does not suffice to explain the course of development, but that we may have to assume that the initial choice of parametric options is determined by a SYNTACTIC PRECEDENCE PRINCIPLE (Weissenborn 1993), which predicts that the child should prefer movement options which fulfill scope requirements over *in-situ* options which would have to be considered as marked.

2. Strong Continuity, Parameter Setting and the Trigger Hierarchy

As defined here, the notion of STRONG CONTINUITY of language development is opposed to the notion of DISCONTINUITY on the one hand, and to WEAK CONTINUITY on the other hand.

— By DISCONTINUITY we understand that the child's representation may violate the principles of UG, e.g., Felix's (1984) assumption that the child's initial word order may not obey the X′-scheme.

— By WEAK CONTINUITY we understand UG-constrained representations which are inconsistent with the target parametric system (e.g., Borer &

Wexler 1987; Hyams 1986; Lebeaux 1988; Roeper & de Villiers 1991; among others).

The notion of STRONG CONTINUITY refers to the assumption that the representations of early grammar violate neither the UG-principles nor the parameters of the target language.[2]

STRONG CONTINUITY should be thought of as a modular term (i.e., relativized continuity). The main claim of this hypothesis is that the early grammar obeys the parametrically-determined wellformedness conditions of the target language defined either as (a) or (b). Option (c) is excluded:

a. In some cases parameter setting can be fully target-consistent from the beginning. That is, certain parameter values can be fixed very early, e.g., at the pre-linguistic or the one-to-two-word stage.

b. In some cases a given parameter can be set stepwise (or gradually). This will result in an early grammar which is only partially consistent with the target.

Whether a given parameter is of the type (a) or (b) depends on the accessibility hierarchy as defined below.

c. The case of parameter mis-setting (i.e., violation of the target value) is excluded.

It follows from (b) that the child's representations initially may not fully match the target ones. But it puts strong constraints on how the child's grammar may possibly differ from the grammar of the adult. One such contraint is for example, the LOCAL WELLFORMEDNESS CONSTRAINT proposed by Weissenborn (1993, 1994).[3] That is, the Strong Continuity Hypothesis as proposed here makes precise predictions with respect to the possible licensing conditions on the representations which may emerge in early grammar: they are the same as in the target system (Penner 1993, 1994a). To give just one example, the Strong Continuity Hypothesis predicts that illicit infinitival *wh*-questions like the one in (1):

(1)   *wer hocker haben?*
         who chair   have+INF

corresponding to the declarative infinitival sentence in (2):

(2)   *mone   hocker haben*   S(2;00.05)
         (Si)mone chair   have+INF

should not occur, given that the licensing conditions for the occurrence of a *wh*-pronoun are not fulfilled in the absence of the finite verb. As shown in Weissenborn (1993, 1994) this is indeed the case.[4] On the other hand, as we will see in our discussion of the development of the DP, there are licit deviations from the target like underspecification with respect to the feature content of a given functional position from which the child can retreat on the basis of positive evidence.[5]

As mentioned in (a) above, the Strong Continuity Hypothesis allows for the possibility that certain parameters (e.g., directionality, *pro*-drop, *wh-in-situ*, verb-final, etc.) can be set extremely early. The main question here concerns the order of parameter setting. Whether or not a given parameter can be set at an early stage depends on how the triggering information is encoded in the input. That is, how ACCESSIBLE the relevant trigger is.

Informally, the following considerations underlie our notion of ACCESSIBILITY.[6] We assume that the order of parameter setting is determined by an ACCESSIBILITY HIERARCHY. The basic hypothesis is that for each parameter there is at least one unambiguous trigger (Roeper & Weissenborn 1990). This trigger is CANONICAL if it is optimally accessible to syntactic bootstrapping. Canonicity results under the following conditions:

— The trigger is embedded in a triggering frame which involves a ROOT/NON-ROOT CONTRAST like main versus subordinate clause or vocative (non-argument nominals) versus non-vocative (argument nominals). A typical example of canonical triggering information of this type concerns the familiar V2-PARAMETER: V-to-C movement takes place only in main (root) clauses. That is, the V2-rule can be deduced from minimal pairs of root/non-root sentences of the type in (3):

(3)   *Ich liebe ihn, obgleich du   ihn   nicht liebst.*
          I   love him although you him not   love
          'I love him although you don't love him.'

As can easily be seen from (3), the so-called DIRECTIONALITY PARAMETER, that is, VO versus OV ordering, can be deduced from the same root/non-root contrast as well. Other examples of parameters related to this contrast are:

a.   Topic-drop (including subject null constants in the sense of Rizzi 1992),

b.   *Pro*-drop (or clitic deletion of the second person in German dialects), and

c.   *tun*-insertion (*do*-support as a V2-marker in German dialects), all of which are pure root phenomena (for a detailed analysis, see Penner 1994a). On the contrary, as can be seen from the vocative/non-vocative contrast in (4):

(4) a. (*der) Hans komm   nach Hause!   vs.
        the Hans come(IMPER) home
    b. der Hans kommt nach Hause   vs.
        the Hans comes home

Article insertion in German is a pure *non-root* phenomenon. We will discuss this topic in detail below.

— The canonicity of triggers increases if they are encoded as EXPLETIVE rather than SUBSTANTIVE heads. Expletives are semantically empty heads like for instance:
    a. the semantically empty definite articles which co-occur with intrinsi-cally-referential nominals like proper names (e.g., *der Max* 'the Max'),
    b. dummy verbs like the verb *tun* 'do' in German (e.g., *er tut niemals lachen* 'he does never laugh'),
    c. the 'superfluous' complementizer *daß* 'that' in the so-called doubly-filled-COMP constructions (e.g., *ich weiß, warum daß er lacht* 'I know why (that) he laughs'),
    d. copying effects (e.g., verb-doubling constructions in Swiss German of the type *er geit ga schaffe* 'he goes go work'), etc.

Substantive heads, on the other hand, involve 'contentful' features like, for instance, the ⟨+Referentiality⟩-marked definite article in the discourse sequence *I saw Mr. Brown_i yesterday. The man_i is very sick.*

Our basic assumption is that triggers encoded as expletive heads are more accessible than those encoded as substantive heads. The high canonicity of expletive triggers follows from ECONOMY CONSIDERATIONS: given that semanti-cally uninterpretable symbols at LF are illicit (in the sense of Chomsky 1993), the expletive heads must be identified by the child as unequivocally marking a given syntactic position as *not empty*. So, for instance, the occurrence of expletive definite articles in German unambiguously indicates that D^0 must be overtly spelled out, independently of whether or not a given nominal is marked for semantic features like ⟨+Referentiality⟩. That is, overt D^0 is required by a parametrically-driven formal wellformedness condition.

Not all expletive heads are equally accessible to syntactic bootstrapping. We propose the following distinction:

a. Triggers encoded as STRUCTURALLY COMPLEX expletives are more accessible than STRUCTURALLY SIMPLE ones. So, for instance, an expletive head which spells out a twofold agreement relationship with both the specifier and the complement position is more accessible in terms of triggering than an expletive head which merely spells out complement–head agreement.[7] $\succ$ (٩)

b. Expletive triggers may also vary with regard to the articulation of the agreement morphology. The main distinction is between particle-like expletives which lack overt agreement morphology (i.e., possessive -s in High German) and expletive heads with full-fledged agreement morphology (i.e., possessive pronouns in Bernese Swiss German). The basic assumption is that the latter outranks the former on the accessibility hierarchy.[8]) (2d ↦ (22)

Canonicity decreases if the bootstrapping can not operate on information encoded as root/non-root asymmetries or expletive heads. This concerns triggering information which is PARADIGMATICALLY encoded either as inflectional paradigms (for example, the dialect-specific pattern of strong versus weak adjectives in German, see below) or as idiosyncratic, word- or class-specific information. This is, for instance, the case of the distribution of V2-complements in German which, in contrast to V2 in main clauses, is determined by idiosyncratic and class-specific properties of the matrix verb. As can be seen from the examples in (5), the V2-order of the complement clause may alternate with a *daß* 'that' clause if embedded under assertive verbs of the *say* type, but not under factive verbs of the *forget* type:

(5) a. *Er sagt, er hat den Mann gesehen.*
   he says he has the man seen
   'He says he has seen the man.'

b. *Er sagt, daß er den Mann gesehen hat.*
   he says that he the man seen has
   'He says that he has seen the man.'

c. **Er hat vergessen, er hat den Mann gesehen.*
   he forgot   he has the man seen
   'He forgot he has seen the man.'

d. *Er hat vergessen, daß er den Mann gesehen hat.*
   he forgot   that he the man seen   has
   'He forgot that he has seen the man.'

If the triggering system of a given parameter involves both canonical and non-canonical triggers, a tension will emerge between the early 'finger print knowledge' which can be deduced from the canonical trigger information and the still unspecified (or underspecified) non-canonical information.[9] This tension will give rise to a series of INTERIM SOLUTIONS by virtue of which the child will articulate her knowledge of the parameter. The most wide spread interim solution is PLACE HOLDER INSERTION, i.e., insertion of a proto-morphological item to mark a syntactic position like D^0 or C^0 (see, among others, Bottari *et al.* 1992; Penner & Müller 1992; Peters & Menn 1993; and the literature cited therein).

So, for instance, if the child is capable of syntactically bootstrapping the structure of the subordinate CP-structure, but initially fails to assess the language-specific instantiation of the feature content of the subordinate complementizer (i.e., whether the embedded COMP-position is specified for INFL or not), the 'finger print knowledge' can be articulated by a dummy marker (e.g., schwa 'ə' or other proto-morphological items) of the C-position in conjunction with the clause-final verb placement which is typical of the subordinate clause in German as in (6) (from Stern & Stern 1928):[10]

(6)   *vatel sagen ə kaffee trinken kann*   E(2;0)
        father tell   coffee drink   can

Given the hierarchical architecture of the triggering system, the notion of STRONG CONTINUITY can be specified as follows:

— Parameters which are uniformly canonical can be set at the onset of or even before the multiple-word stage.[11] As mentioned above, we assume continuous parametric consistency with regard to e.g., object placement, clause-final verb placement, scrambling, topic drop, subject null constants, etc.[12]

— By contrast, the parameters the triggering information of which is not canonically encoded, do not lend themselves to this kind of syntactic bootstrapping. They are predicted to be acquired at a later stage.

— Parameters the triggering information of which involves both canonical and non-canonical encoding are predicted to display a mixed status. On the one hand, parametric constraints are predicted to be respected in the sense of Weissenborn's Local Wellformedness Constraint due to what we have referred to above as FINGER PRINT KNOWLEDGE of the target parameters. On the other hand, we expect the grammar to provide interim solutions (e.g., dummy place holders) whenever a given syntactic position remains underspecified. As discussed in detail in Weissenborn (1994) and Penner

(1994a, 1994b) this tension is probably what we find in the realm of the COMP-related rules in German (V2 in main clauses, subordination, question formation, etc.).

With this system in mind, let us now closely look at the development of the DP.

3. The Development of the DP

Thus far, we have argued that syntactic bootstrapping plays a central role in assessing the values of core parameters such as directionality of object placement, V2, *pro*-drop, and scrambling. Does this hypothesis carry over to the development of the DP in High German and Swiss German?

3.1. *The Parametric Specification of the DP in German*

The following analysis rests on Penner (1993, 1994a, 1994c) and Penner & Schönenberger (1995). Extending the basic hypothesis of Longobardi (1994), we will assume the universal wellformedness condition on nominals in (7):

> (7)   Universal DET Requirement
>
>   Non-vocative nominals (i.e., nominals in argument positions) must involve a D position.

How is the UNIVERSAL DET REQUIREMENT met in adult High German and Bernese? The parametric choice of German can be stated as follows:

> (8)   The DP-Parameter in German
>
>   The Φ-features of both the Spec-DP and the Complement-DP position are copied onto D^0.

This double-agreement configuration can be schematically represented as in (9):

(9)

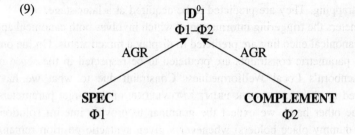

At the level of instantiation we distinguish between a PARTIAL AGREEMENT CONFIGURATION and a COMPLETE AGREEMENT CONFIGURATION. The partial agreement configuration emerges whenever the Spec-DP position remains empty. This is the case of the definite article in German. Recall that we distinguish between substantive (as for instance the ⟨+Referentiality⟩-marked definite article in the discourse sequence *I saw Mr. Brown~i~ yesterday. The man~i~ is very sick*) and expletive definite articles. The expletive definite articles occur in generic nominals (e.g., *die Milch* 'the milk'), situative and discourse unica (e.g., *die Sonne*, 'the sun', *der Papst* 'the pope', *der Briefträger*, 'the mailman', etc.), and proper names (e.g., *die Maria*, '(the) Mary'). The underlying structure of the expletive definite article in German is as in (10):

(10)   The partial agreement configuration of the expletive definite article in German

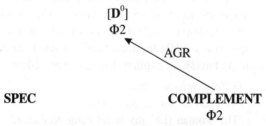

$$[\mathbf{D}^0]$$
$$\Phi 2$$

AGR

SPEC   **COMPLEMENT**
$$\Phi 2$$

The relevant features of expletive definite articles in High German are as in (11):

(11) a. No overt difference between substantive and expletive definite article in the non-oblique Case (nominative and accusative).[13]

b. Optional with generics in the subject position. Obligatory deletion of the expletive article with generics in the object position.

c. Optional with proper names in both subject and non-subject position.

The relevant examples are:

(12) a. *(Die) Milch, die   ich gestern   getrunken habe, war*
          the milk   which I   yesterday drank   have was
          sauer.   (referential)
          sour

b. *(Die) Milch ist weiß.*   (generic)
          the milk is white

    c.   *Ich trinke gerne (*die) Milch.*   (generic)
        I   drink like   the milk
    d.   *(Der) Hans hat (die) Maria gesehen.*   (proper name)
        the Hans has the Maria seen

The corresponding properties in Bernese are as in (13):

(13) a. Expletive definite articles are always cliticized to the noun regardless of whether the DP is in an oblique (i.e., prepositional phrases corresponding to the dative/genitive in High German) or a non-oblique (i.e., corresponding to the nominative/ accusative in High German) position. Substantive definite articles are exempted from cliticization.

       b. Expletive definite articles are *obligatory* with proper names.

This means that in contrast to High German, expletive definite articles in Swiss German are consistently morphologically marked. This is illustrated in (14). Note that the CLITIC expletive article *d'* in (14a) marks the nominal 'woman' as a unicum (i.e., 'my wife'), while the TONIC definite article *di* in (14b) marks the nominal 'woman' as having an explicit discourse antecedent:

(14) a. *D'Frou isch cho tanze.*   Swiss German
          Die Frau ist tanzen gekommen.   High German
          'The woman (i.e., my wife) came to dance.'

      b. *I ha di/*d' Frou ganz gärn.*   Swiss German
          Ich mag die Frau sehr gern.   High German
          'I like the woman very much.'

      c. *I ha d'Anna geschter gseh.*   Swiss German
          Ich habe die Anna gestern gesehen.   High German
          'I have (the) Anna yesterday seen.'

Following Longobardi (1994) and Penner & Schönenberger (1995), we will further assume that the deletion and the cliticization of the expletive definite article in High and Swiss German are instances of SYNTACTIC N-to-D movement, the structure of which is given in (15):

(15) a. $[_{DP} [_{D'} (d')Milch_i [_{NP} [_{N'} t_i]]]]]$
          the milk
    b. $[_{DP} [_{D'} (d')Anna_i [_{NP} [_{N'} t_i]]]]]$
          the Anna

    An aside on Case in Bernese Swiss German is in order here. It should be kept in mind that Bernese Swiss German lacks morphological Case marking comparable to the four-way Case system (nominative, accusative, dative, and genitive) of High German. Basically, the nominal system of Bernese distinguishes between oblique and non-oblique Case. The non-oblique Case comprises the nominative/accusative. The oblique Case groups together the dative and the genitive and is realized as a prepositional phrase marked by the endings -*m* (masculine and neuter singular) and -*r* (feminine singular) suffixing the preposition.

We now turn to the possessive constructions and the implementation of the Universal DET Requirement. Following Schönenberger & Penner (in prep.), we assume that possessors in German are generally treated as operators and that the requirement on Q(UANTIFIER) RAISING of the possessor to its scope position may be met either in the syntax or at LF. The latter option is realized as post nominal possessors which are placed in the complement position of N (note that Bernese Swiss German only has the (a)-option):

(16) a. [$_{DP}$ [$_{D'}$ *die* [$_{NP}$ [$_{N'}$ *Mutter von Hans*]]]]]
    the   mother of Hans

  b. [$_{DP}$ [$_{D'}$ *die* [$_{NP}$ [$_{N'}$ *Mutter des Schülers*]]]]]
    the   mother the student:GEN

Syntactically Q-raised possessors are DP-internally (i.e., to Spec-DP) topicalized elements. For the purpose of our discussion, we have to distinguish between the more liberal *von* 'of' type in (17):

(17) [$_{DP}$ *von der Anna* [$_{D'}$ *die* [$_{NP}$ [$_{N'}$ *Schuhe*]]]]]
  of the Anna the   shoes
  'Anna's shoes'

and the Bernese Swiss German and colloquial High German pattern[14] as in (18) which we will refer to as the DATIVE POSSESSIVE:

(18) a. *em*   *Vater si*   *Huet*
   to.the:DAT:MASC:SG father his:MASC:SG|MASC:SG hat:MASC:SG
   'father's hat'

  b. *dem*   *Vater sein*   *Hut*
   to.the:DAT:MASC:SG father his:MASC:SG|MASC:SG hat:MASC:SG
   'father's hat'

The dative possessive, which is typical of the dialectal and spoken varieties of German consists of three terms, namely:

— a dative- (or prepositionally-)marked possessor noun
— the possessed object (possessum)
— an *expletive* possessive pronoun which agrees both with the possessor and the possessum with respect to number and gender.

The assumption is that the raised possessor in the dative possessive structure participates in an AFFECT CONFIGURATION in the sense of Haegeman's (1992) AFFECT-CRITERION and Rizzi's (1991) WH-CRITERION. Haegeman (1992) argues that the affective elements are subject to the Affect Criterion:

(19)   The Affect Criterion

a.   An [AFFECTIVE] operator must be in a Spec–head configuration with an [AFFECTIVE] X^0.

b.   An [AFFECTIVE] X^0 must be in a Spec–head configuration with an [AFFECTIVE] operator.

The Affect Criterion thus requires that the raised possessor occur in an Affect Configuration, the main property of which is SPEC–HEAD AGREEMENT. This requirement is met by creating an Affect Configuration in the Spec-DP-D^0 segment which participates in a complete agreement configuration in the above sense. This is schematized in (20):

(20)   The dative possessive as a complete agreement configuration[15]

em   Vater   si   Huet
to.the father his hat
'father's hat'

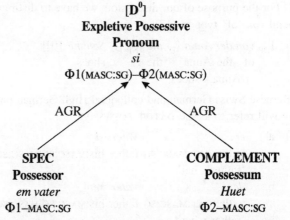

We will further hypothesize that the so-called -*s* possessive marker in High German of the type:

(21)   *Vaters Hut*
'father's hat'

is a special variant of (20). We contend, following Ramat (1986), that both *Vaters Hut* and the more dialectal possessive constructions with a dative possessor *dem Vater sein Hut* are equally derived from the raising structure (20) with the difference that in the former the expletive possessive head by means of which the complete agreement configuration (and the Affect Criterion) is spelled out is a *particle-like* head, rather than a fully articulated possessive pronoun with two distinct agreement morphemes. The underlying agreement configuration of the High German possessive construction *Vaters Hut* is given in (22):[16]

(22)   *Vater-s Hut*
         'father's hat'

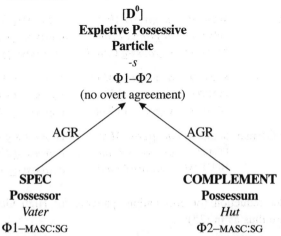

[D⁰]
Expletive Possessive
Particle

-*s*

Φ1–Φ2
(no overt agreement)

AGR   AGR

SPEC   **COMPLEMENT**
Possessor   Possessum
Vater   *Hut*
Φ1–MASC:SG   Φ2–MASC:SG

A brief remark on the so-called weak/strong asymmetry of adjective agreement is in order here. It is a well-known fact that agreement features in the DP can be instantiated in an asymmetrical manner. This is what happens with the adjective inflection. Roughly, the adjective is weakly inflected (i.e., having undergone gender marking reduction) when following the definite article and strongly inflected (characterized by its three-way gender distinction) if preceded by the indefinite article. This is illustrated for High German (23):

(23)   'the/a big man/woman/child'

MASC:SG	*d-er*	*gross-e Mann*	*ein*	*gross-er Mann*
FEM:SG	*d-ie*	*gross-e Frau*	*ein-e*	*gross-e Frau*
NEUT:SG	*d-as*	*gross-e Kind*	*ein*	*gross-es Kind*

Penner & Schönenberger (1995) and Penner (1994a) show in detail that, while the weak/strong asymmetry *per se* is a common feature of High and Swiss German, there is a great deal of crossdialectal variation with regard to the instantiation of this rule. More precisely, the patterns of gender marking reduction may significantly vary from one variety to the other. This is illustrated for Swiss German dialects in (24):

(24)   'the/a big man/woman/child'

		gender reduction	three-way gender distinction
Bernese	MASC:SG	dr grooss Maa	e grooss-e Maa
	FEM:SG	di grooss-i Frou	e grooss-i Frou
	NEUT:SG	ds grooss-e Ching	es grooss-es Ching
Lucernese	MASC:SG	de grooss Maa	e grooss-e Maa
	FEM:SG	di grooss Frau	e grooss-i Frau
	NEUT:SG	s grooss-e Chind	es grooss-es Chind
Basel German	MASC:SG	dr grooss-i Maa	e grooss-e Maa
	FEM:SG	di grooss-i Frau	e grooss-i Frau
	NEUT:SG	s grooss-i Chind	e grooss-es Chind
St. Galler German	MASC:SG	de grooss Maa	en grooss-e Maa
	FEM:SG	di grooss Frou	e grooss-i Frau
	NEUT:SG	s grooss Chind	e grooss-es Chind

The gender reduction (or elimination) patterns for High German and Swiss German are thus as in (25):

(25)

High German	zero distinction		-e
Bernese	three-way distinction	MASC	zero
		FEM	-i
		NEUT	-e
Lucernese	two-way distinction	MASC/FEM	zero
		NEUT	-e
Basel German	zero distinction		-i
St. Galler German	zero distinction		zero

It follows from these data that, while the weak/strong asymmetry is found in all varieties of German, the implementation of this rule involves a significant idiosyncratic, hence unpredictable component.

An additional aspect of the dialect-specific character of the weak/strong asymmetry concerns its distribution. It is worth mentioning here that in High German the possessive -*s* (and dative possessives) patterns with the INDEFINITE article, displaying strong adjective agreement (*Vaters lieb-es Mariechen*, 'father's dear Mary', *dem Vater sein liebes Mariechen*, [to.the father his dear Mary], while in Bernese the dative possessives pattern with the DEFINITE article, displaying *weak* adjective agreement (*em Vater sis lieb-e Mareli* [to.the father his dear Mary].

3.2. *Encoding the Relevant Triggers*

To what extent does the DP in German lend itself to syntactic bootstrapping at the initial stages? When scanning the input, searching for the relevant triggers, the child encounters the following cues:

1. As already alluded to at the outset, expletive definite articles as well as possessive constructions are pure non-root phenomena. More precisely, the input contains root/non-root asymmetries as in (26)–(27) which render the rules of Possessor Raising and expletive insertion salient in the sense of the trigger accessibility hierarchy discussed above:

    (26)   The insertion of expletive definite articles in, e.g., proper names and kinship terms (obligatory in Bernese Swiss German, while optional in High German) is a pure non-root (i.e., non-vocative) phenomenon:

    a.   Bernese Swiss German
          (*dr) Hans chum hei!   vocative
          the Hans come home
          *(dr) Hans chunnt hei.   non-vocative
          the Hans comes home
    b.   High German
          (*der) Hans komm nach Hause!   vocative
          the Hans come home
          (der) Hans kommt nach Hause.   non-vocative
          the Hans comes home

(27)   Dative possessives in Bernese Swiss German and -s possessives
          in High German (i.e., Possessor Raising and the insertion of the
          expletive possessive pronoun/particle) are pure non-root phe-
          nomena:

    a.   Bernese Swiss German

        Mareli!   vocative
        Mary

        em   Vater sis   *Mareli*   non-vocative
        to.the father his:MASC:SG|NEUT:SG Mary
        'father's Mary'

    b.   High German

        Mariechen!   vocative
        Mary

        Vaters   Mariechen   non-vocative
        father's Mary

2.   In both cases D^0 is spelled out as an expletive head, a fact which as
explained above should considerably facilitate the triggering procedure in
the sense of syntactic bootstrapping.

3.   The expletive heads are not equally accessible:

    a.   The expletive *possessive* head is generally more accessible than the
expletive definite article, given that the former is located within a
complete agreement configuration (see (20)), while the latter is a
structurally incomplete DP (a DP involving an empty Spec as
schematized in (10) above).

    b.   The expletive possessive pronoun in the dative constructions is more
accessible than the possessive -s in High German, given that the
former is a morphologically articulated element (full-fledged morphological spell out), while the latter is merely a particle-like element.

4.   Evidence in favor of the expletive possessive pronoun as an occupant of D^0
comes from possessive constructions containing an adjective. Recall that in
Bernese, but not in High German, the expletive possessive pronouns pattern
with the definite article with regard to adjective agreement. The relevant
root/non-root asymmetries are given in (28):

(28) a.   Bernese Swiss German
            liebs Mareli!   vocative
            dear Mary [strongly inflected]
            em   Vater sis   *liebe Mareli*   non-vocative
            to.the father his:MASC|NEUT:SG dear Mary [weakly inflected]
      b.   High German
            liebes Mariechen!   vocative
            dear Mary [strongly inflected]
            dem   Vater sein liebes Mariechen   non-vocative
            to.the father his dear Mary [strongly inflected]

That is, in Bernese Swiss German the evidence associated with the expletive head of the possessive constructions is rendered more salient due to vocative/non-vocative asymmetries. This kind of input support is not available in High German. Note that while the weak/strong asymmetry is mirrored by root/non-root contrasts, the dialect- and item-specific organization of the inflectional paradigm itself is not rendered visible in this way (cf. (24) above).

Given these considerations, we assume that the triggers of the rules of Possessor Raising and expletive insertion (in both possessive constructions and DPs with definite articles) in Bernese and High German are part of the *canonical* system. Within the system developed here, the trigger of the weak/strong asymmetry of adjectives is more accessible in Bernese than in High German. On the contrary, the *implementation* of expletive insertion in D^0 as well as of the weak/strong asymmetry of adjectives involves idiosyncratic information and is thus *non-canonical*. We expect the canonical triggers to be available to the child at a very early stage. However, given that the implementation of the expletive insertion involves non-canonical information as well, the realization of the D^0 position is unlikely to be target-like from the onset. More precisely, on the one hand, we expect the full-fledged DP structure (including Possessor Raising, expletive insertion, and N-to-D movement) to be available at an early stage. On the other hand, we predict the D^0 position to be initially spelled out by an interim device (most likely a place holder).

The more fine-grained order of acquisition, however, is predicted to be different in the two varieties of German. In Bernese Swiss German the triggers embodied in the dative possessives are unequivocally more accessible than the ones of the definite article. High German lacks this clear hierarchy, given that the expletive head of the possessives is a particle-like element and given the unavailability of support in the form of weak/strong asymmetries.

3.3. *The Data: The Acquisition of the DP in Bernese and in High German*

The following analysis focuses on the development of the definite article and possessor raising structures.[17]

3.3.1. *The Acquisition of the DP in Early Bernese Swiss German*

The order of acquisition of the DP in early Bernese Swiss German can be presented as follows:[18]

The Initial Phase (1;02–1;06.14)
In this period there is no evidence for D^0 filling by means of functional heads. Until the age of 1;06.13 only bare nouns of the type:[19]

(29) a.   *ditsi [= güetzi] mei [= nei]*   J(1;02.18)
           cookies   no
           'There are no more cookies.'

      b.   *Tatti [= Grossvati] ga*   J(1;05.02)
           Grandfather   go
           'Go to grandfather!'

are attested. At first glance these structures seem to be structurally ambiguous between the (target-consistent) N-to-D and the (target-inconsistent) empty D^0 option, i.e., between (30a) and (30b):

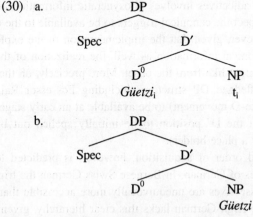

(30) a.   DP
                           ╱   ╲
                      Spec   D′
                                   ╱   ╲
                                 D^0 NP
                              Güetzi$_i$ t$_i$

      b.   DP
                           ╱   ╲
                      Spec   D′
                                   ╱   ╲
                                 D^0 NP
                                           Güetzi

A closer look at the data reveals, however, that the vast majority of the nominals attested at this stage (97%) can be analyzed as *vocatives* in the above sense. On this view, these nominals would be exempted from the Universal Det Requirement.

The Acquisition of Dative Possessives
The acquisition of the dative possessive is comprised of three sub-phases:

Phase 1 (1;06.14–1;07.28)
In this period only bare possessor raising structures (e.g., N–N possessives) are attested. At this phase, two occurrences of possessive structures occur, namely:

(31) a. *Nomi Bett*   J(1;06.14)
      Naomi bed
      'Naomi's bed'

    b. *Mami Bébé*   J(1;07.28)
      mother baby
      'the baby's mother'

Phase 2 (1;07.29–1;10.18)
The first occurrences of D^0-filling by means of an expletive possessive pronoun emerge in this phase. There are in total 18 possessive structures in this period, 11 of which (61%) are instances of truncated possessive structures in which the possessum is IMPLICIT (non-overt) as in (32):

(32)   *Mami sis*   J(1;07.29)
          Mother its:NEUT:SG|NEUT:SG
          'Mother's'

Six cascs (33%) are still bare possessor raising structures (N–N possessives) of the type in (33) (and (31)):

(33)   *Nomi puli*   J(1;08.05)
          Naomi shirt
          'Naomi's shirt'

One case (5.5%) can be analyzed as a POSSESSOR-IN-SITU construction, namely:

(34)   *(j)agge (Ju)wal*   J(1;07.01)
          jacket Juwal
          'the jacket of Juwal'

Note that the possessive pronouns occupying the D^0-position in this phase are unspecified with respect to agreement features. They are thus unequivocally place holders. In the D^0-position we find not only the unmarked (or 'universal') possessive pronoun of the neuter singular (as in (32) above), but also illicit forms such as, for instance, the possessive pronoun inflected for the first person singular as in (35):

(35)   *Nomi   mis*   J(1;07.02)
         Naomi mine:1:SG|NEUT:SG
         'Naomi's' (points to Naomi's alarm-clock)

Phase 3 (from 1;10.19–)
The first complete dative possessives are attested. In these possessive structures,
both the possessor and the possessum nominals are explicitly spelled out. The
first occurrence is:

(36)   *Nadaw sis   Ue [= Uhr]*   J(1;10.19)
         Nadaw:NEUT:SG watch:FEM:SG
         'Nadaw's watch'

It is worth noting that the emergence of the attributive adjectives displaying
default inflection, but with weak/strong distinction (see (37) below) correlates
with the acquisition of the complete dative possessives.

(37)   *Bibi [= Bébé] (chl)iises*   J(1;10.15)
         baby   small:NEUT:SG (strongly inflected)
         'small baby'

In the period between 1;10.19 and 2;05.01 71 dative possessives are attested. Of
these, 32 (45%) are complete structures of the type in (37). Bare possessor
raising structures (e.g., N–N possessives without D^0-filling of the type (32))
comprise 10% of the data. The latest of these bare possessor raising structures
occurs at 2;01.16. As for agreement spell-out in D^0, a close inspection of the
data reveals that at the time period under discussion, no gender (and number)
distinctions are expressed by the expletive possessive pronoun. The latter is
realized either as *sis* (MASC/NEUT:SG|NEUT:SG) or *sine* (MASC/NEUT:SG|MASC:SG),
regardless of the feature content of both the possessor and the possessum. Thus,
there is no evidence for an underlying paradigm at this stage and the requirement on D^0-filling seems to be fulfilled by means of place holder insertion.

   It is further worth noting that the obligatory dative marking (by means of
an oblique preposition) is absent altogether until the age of 2;3.14. In the period
between 2;03.14 and 2;05.01, out of the 16 dative possessives that occur, 4
(25%) are Case-marked as in (38) below:

(38)   *am   Juwal sine*   J(2;03.14)
         to-the:DAT Juwal his:MASC:SG
         'Juwal's'

Given this observation, it seems unlikely that the acquisition of the full-fledged
structure of the DP in Bernese Swiss German must be preceded by the general-

ization of morphological Case marking. In fact, the data seem to support the opposite assumption namely, that Case marking in the possessor position applies only after the syntactic rule of possessor raising and D^0-filling by means of an expletive possessive pronoun, has applied. Given that the possessive pronoun in dative possessives displays the status of a morphologically unmarked (or default-marked) head there is also no evidence for any dependency of the syntactic structure on the acquisition of overt agreement spell-out.

The Acquisition of the Expletive Definite Article

Phase 1 (19–24 months)
The first occurrence of a definite article is attested at 1;07.13 one month after the emergence of the possessor raising structures (cf. (31)):

(39)   *d'Outo ab*   J(1;07.13)
          'the car down'

In this phase, the definite article occurs rather marginally and unsystematically (mean value: 6%). This is shown in the table in (40):[20]

(40)   1;07.01–1;07.30   3% (3 out of 95)
          1;08.01–1;08.31   0% (0 out of 133)
          1;09.01–1;09.30   6% (6 out of 99)
          1;10.01–1;10.31   16% (17 out of 104)
          1;11.01–1;11.30   6% (5 out of 82)

Formally, the definite article at this stage displays the status of a place holder, being uniformly spelled out as *d-*.

Phase 2 (1;9.10–2;02.06)
At 1;9.10 the first distinction at the level of case marking is observed: *d-* is used to mark the non-oblique Case (nominative/accusative), while *m-* spells out the oblique Case as in (41):

(41)   *m'Outo*   J(1;09.10)
          'in/to the car'

Let us emphasize that while the oblique/non-oblique distinction is occasionally expressed by the child, it is by no means systematically marked in the period under discussion.

Phase 3

In the 27th month a significant increase (45%) in the use of expletive definite articles in the domain of proper names and kinship terms is observed. In the period between 2;4 and 2;6 the expletive definite article occurs with proper names and kinship terms 70% of the time and, 87% of the time (6 cases of missing articles out of 45) by age 2;7. Importantly, there are no cases of using the definite article in vocative contexts at this time.

At the level of overt spell-out, the variation in the determiner becomes apparent:

(42) a. *ds*   *Nomi*   *Chätschgummi gää* J(2;02.06)
         the:NOM:NEUT:SG Naomi:NEUT:SG chewing.gum give
         'Naomi gives a chewing gum.'

     b. *dr*   *Ima*   *chunnt*   J(2;02.23)
         the:MASC:SG mother:FEM:SG comes

Note, however, that gender marking is far from being systematic until the age of 2;7. On the one hand, we still find free alternation between the forms of the determiner:

(43) a. *d'* (FEM:SG = target form) *Imma*
         də (= place holder, nonexistent in target language) *Imma*
         dr (*MASC:SG) *Imma*
         'the Mommy'

     b. *ds* (NEUT:SG = target form) *Nomi*
         də (= place holder, nonexistent in target language) *Nomi*
         ar (OBL:FEM:SG) *Nomi*
         'the Naomi'

On the other hand, we still observe productive use (35%) of the morphologically unmarked place holder *də*. Agreement marking at this stage is thus either inconsistent or omitted altogether.

The development of the expletive definite article with unica is slightly slower than with proper names and kinship terms. With this type of nominal, the expletive definite article is used 18% at 2;3, 65% at 2;4, 70% at 2;5 and 80% (15 instances of missing articles out of 74 occurrences of unica) at the end of the 31st month.

Given these data, the developmental sequences can be summarized as follows:

1;2–1;7   bare nouns (no evidence for a functional projection, probably nominals in vocative contexts)

1;11–2;1   evidence for DP; the acquisition of (complete dative) possessives

2;07   the acquisition of the expletive article in proper names and kinship terms; with slightly slower acquisition of expletive articles in unica

In more technical terms:

— The emergence of the DP-structure is initially (1;06.14–1;07.28) spelled out by means of possessor raising. The corresponding tree is (44) (cf. (29) above):

(44)

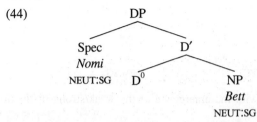

Initially (a short-lived stage (1;07.13–1;07.28)) D^0-filling via expletive insertion is restricted to (clitic) place holders functioning as markers of the definite article. The underlying structure is as in (45) (cf. (30) above):

(45)

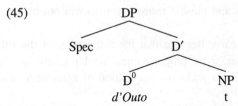

The distribution of these place holders at this intermediate stage is marginal and unsystematic.

— At the following stage D^0-filling by means of expletive insertion is acquired stepwise. First in truncated possessives of the type (32) (in the period between 1;07.29–1;10.18) and then in complete possessive structures of the type (37) (100% after 2;01.19) into a position made available by possessor raising. Thus we observe the transition from:

(46)

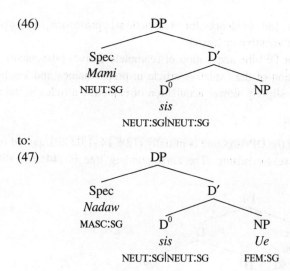

to:
(47)

This transition correlates with the emergence of the weak/strong distinction in adjective inflection.

— Once the tree in (47) has been established, a systematic process of generalizing the Expletive Insertion Rule via definite articles begins. In this process, which lasts from 2;3 to 2;7 (and later), the acquisition of expletive insertion in proper names and kinship terms seems to win out over expletive insertion in unica.

— There is no evidence in early Bernese that the acquisition of the rule of expletive insertion in possessives, proper names, kinship terms, and unica is dependent on (or correlates with) the acquisition of agreement of Case marking.

3.3.2. *The Acquisition of the DP in Early High German*[21]

We will first present the data concerning the development of the definite article and then turn to the development of possessor raising structures.

3.3.2.1. The Development of the Definite Article. The overall developmental sequence for DPs, excluding one-word utterances, structures with proper names, and possessor raising structures is shown in Figure 1:

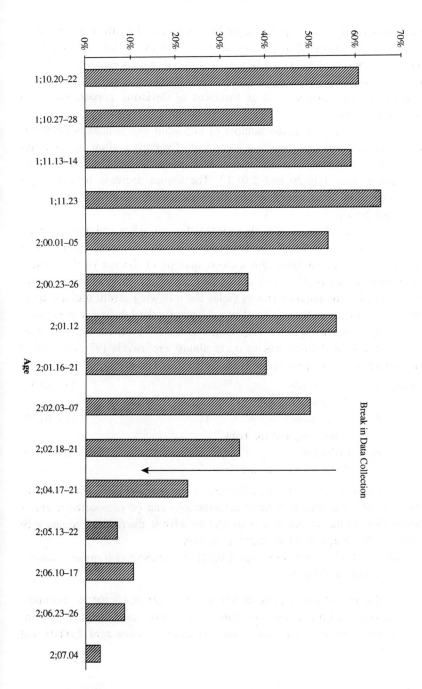

Figure 1. Non-Adult-Like Nominal Structures, i.e. Illicit Omissions of a Determiner, in % of the total nominal structures

The complementary set to the non-adult-like structures, i.e. illicit omissions of a determiner, is constituted by close-to-adult or adult-like structures comprising definite, indefinite, and quantified NPs as well as NPs with possessive pronouns. They also include the use of reduced forms of the definite article, (i.e., *de, e, er* instead of *der, die, das*) as well as instances of deviating gender, Case and agreement marking.[22,23]

As shown in Figure 1, the number of non-adult-like structures decreases steadily with age although there is a great deal of variation, allowing for peaks of non-adult like structures at later dates which come close to the initial values, e.g., compare ages 1;10.20 and 2;01.12. The abrupt decrease between ages 2;02.21 and 2;04.17 is explained by the absence of recordings during the intermediate period.[24]

Figure 1 alone does not give us a clear indication when and how the child discovers the option to fulfill the Universal DET Requirement by means of insertion of a functional head. But a close analysis of the use of the definite article which occurs in 575 cases out of the 1253 (i.e., 46%) of the close-to-adult or adult-like nominal structures yields the following result: initially, as in Bernese Swiss German, there is no clear evidence for the fulfillment of the Det-Requirement by means of a functional head in the D^0 position. Between ages 1;10.20 and 2;00.01 definite articles occur almost exclusively (97 cases out of 98) in formulaic expressions of the type shown in (48):

(48) a. *wos de baby*   S(1;10.20)
         'Where is the baby?'
      b. *das de baby*   S(1;10.20)
         'That/there (is) the baby.'
      c. *wo'se lala*   S(1;10.20)
         'Where's the pacifier?'

Of these definite articles, 84 (i.e., 87%) are of the reduced type. It is not clear whether the reduced article in these constructions can be considered a place-holder or whether the *wh*-operator or the deictic adverb, the reduced copula verb and the reduced article form an unanalyzed unit.

After age 2;00.01 and up to age 2;02.21 we observe two major changes, which are shown in Table 1.

— First, the use of the definite article is no longer restricted to formulaic expressions. Within a few days this use becomes more frequent in non-formulaic contexts (164 cases versus 91 cases between ages 2;00.03 and 2;02.21).

Table 1. Distribution of Reduced and Full Definite Articles in Formulaic and Non-formulaic Expressions

ages	formulaic expressions			non-formulaic expressions		
	reduced DET	full DET	total	reduced DET	full DET	total
1;10.20–2;00.01	84 (87%)	13 (%13)	97	1	0	1
2;00.03–2;00.05	6 (60%)	4 (%40)	10	1 (9%)	10 (%91)	11
2;00.23–2;00.26	3 (%60)	2 (%40)	5	2 (7%)	27 (%93)	29
2;01.12–2;01.21	5 (%14)	31 (%86)	36	16 (25%)	49 (%75)	65
2;02.03–2;02.21	8 (%20)	32 (%80)	40	15 (25%)	44 (%75)	59
2;04.17–2;04.19	13 (%17)	63 (%83)	76	5 (18%)	23 (%82)	28

— Second, simultaneously the relation between the number of full forms and
reduced forms of the definite article is reversed: we find now 78% (199) of full
forms versus 22% (56) of reduced forms between ages 2;00.3 and 2;02.2.

These changes clearly indicate that the option of fulfilling the Universal DET
Requirement by means of a place-holder or a full-fledged functional head has
become available to the child. How can we account for this sudden change? The
explanation is offered by a third observation, namely,

— the fact that *slightly* before the moment we observe the two changes
mentioned above at age 2;00.01, the definite article, first also in its reduced
form, starts to be used with proper names.

This is exactly what we would predict from the point of view of our triggering
model. That is: we expect the expletive article with proper names in the input to
act as the trigger for the insertion of functional elements in D^0.[25] The identification of this trigger information by the child is reflected by the slightly earlier use
of the definite article with proper names than with common nouns. The occurrence of definite articles with proper names clearly indicates that the child has
realized that the Universal DET Requirement can be fulfilled by the insertion of
an expletive functional element. Just as for Bernese we assume that this change
is the result of the encoding of the trigger information both as canonical and
expletive. Remember that the use of the expletive article with proper names in
the target is optional. It is this optionality which makes the High German
expletive article with proper nouns a weaker trigger than the obligatory expletive
article in Bernese. This is one of the reasons why the generalization of article
insertion in the relevant context takes longer in High German than in Bernese.

3.3.2.2. *The Development of Possessor Raising Structures.* First, of the three types
of possessor raising structures in High German the possessive *-s* construction is
the earliest one. We find an isolated example already at age 1;11.13 (*mones*
'Simone's'). All the other examples, 22 of them, are bare noun structures of the
type N + N (*maxe bauch* 'Maxe belly'). As already pointed out by Clahsen *et al.*
(this volume), from age 2;00.23 onwards the structures spelling out the possessive
-s become predominant: up to age 2;02.21 34 cases out of 54 N + N-possessives
show the possessive *-s*. After age 2;04.17 up to age 2;07.04 there are almost no
bare N + N-structures to be found (i.e., only 3 out of 39). The remarkable point
here is that we do not find any possessor *in situ* structures at this time.

Second, dative-possessor-raising structures, contrary to Bernese, are very

rare. There are only two of them, with the expletive possessive omitted in both
cases, as shown in (49):

(49) a. *de   mone   is det net   perl*   S(2;00.23)
          der:DAT Simone ist das nicht (ihre) Perle
          The Simone is this not (her) pearl.

      b. *der   mone   balla is weg*   S(2;01.12)
          the:DAT Simone (her) ball   is gone

      c. *der Jan is Nina ihr bruder*   S(2;11.18)
          the Jan is Nina's   brother

But interestingly, these structures are also very early. The first dative possessive
with spell out of the expletive possessive pronoun is found much later; see (49c)
above.

Third, the *von*-possessives like (50):

(50)   *von der uni   das   puttgegang*   S(2;07.04)
          of   the university that-one broken
          (referring to tape recorder)

are observed only at the end of our observation period together with the
unmoved structure (51):

(51)   *die schwester von 'bias*   S(2;07.04)
          'the sister of Tobias'

We propose that in High German like in Bernese the early emergence of
constructions in which the possessor precedes the possessed object reflects the
fact that the child has acquired Possessor Raising to Spec-DP due to the
aforementioned vocative/non-vocative asymmetries. That is, the full DP-representation with the relevant Affect Configuration is available from early on by
virtue of syntactic bootstrapping. This assumption is supported by the absolute
absence at this early stage of constructions in which the possessed object
precedes the possessor.

That the earliness of Possessor Raising is common both to Bernese and
High German, although:

— the Bernese Case system is crucially different from the High German one,
   and

— there is no evidence that Possessor Raising correlates with Case assignment.

This indicates that the Case feature itself cannot be crucial for the acquisition of
the structural features of the German DP. This is at variance with recent

proposals which link the development of DP to the development of Case marking which itself is related to the semantic notion of possession as proposed by Clahsen *et al.* (this volume).

In High German as in Bernese, the D^0-position is initially underspecified as shown by the absence of functional spell-outs or the insertion of place-holders. This is due to the fact that its acquisition involves non-canonical information components, that is the language-particular inflectional paradigms and the weak/strong patterns of adjectives.

In Bernese, where, as discussed above, the expletive possessive pronoun is a more salient trigger than the expletive definite article, the child first generalizes overt determiners in dative possessives. There is a short intermediate stage at which the overt D(eterminer) spell-out is optional. As soon as the child uncovers the weak/strong asymmetry of adjectives and the additional fact that the expletive possessive pronoun is followed by a weakly inflected adjective, D spell-out becomes obligatory. The generalization of the definite article follows: it is first established in the nominal class which is the most prominent one with regard to expletivity within the domain of definite articles, namely proper names. Note that at the stage in question expletive possessive pronouns and the expletive definite articles are realized as dummy place holders. It takes longer for the expletive definite article in unica (which are not inherently definite) to be acquired. It is worth noting here that the fact that early definite articles are uniformly realized as clitics indicates that the child applies N-to-D movement as schematized in (15) repeated here.

(15) a. $[_{DP} [_{D'} (d')Milch_i [_{NP} [_{N'} t_i]]]]$
            the milk
     b. $[_{DP} [_{D'} (d')Anna_i [_{NP} [_{N'} t_i]]]]$
            the Anna

In High German, no such apparent hierarchy is observable. On the one hand, the productive use of expletive definite articles (with unica) clearly precedes -*s* insertion in possessive structures. We ascribe the prominence of the expletive definite article to the fact that the article is morphologically more salient than the particle-like possessive -*s/si*. On the other hand, -*s* insertion in possessive structures is clearly generalized before article insertion. In our system, this follows from the fact that -*s* possessives, in contrast to article insertion, are instances of complete agreement configurations, hence more accessible in terms of triggering.

4. Summary and Conclusions

To summarize, in our paper we have shown that the early stages of the acquisition of DP in Bernese Swiss German as well as in High German can be accounted for by a refined version of the Strong Continuity Hypothesis formulated in terms of a theory of syntactic bootstrapping which is based on a set of universal formal constraints, i.e., the Universal DET Requirement and the Affect Criterion, and an articulated theory of parameter setting. That is, if the possessor-raising analysis is basically correct and if we further assume that bare nouns are initially instances of N-to-D movement, we may assume that the child starts out with a full DP-representation, thus obeying both UG and language-particular, i.e., parametrized, requirements. In this sense, early DPs behave on a par with the so-called pre-conjunctional subordinate clauses (Penner & Müller 1992).[26]

We have further proposed that the triggering order, i.e., the order in which parameters are set is determined by an accessibility hierarchy based on the distinction between canonical and non-canonical trigger information, whereby the former is defined as trigger information encoded in root/non-root contrasts and expletives, and the latter in paradigmatic–idiosyncratic contexts. We predicted that canonical trigger information should be easier to access than non-canonical trigger information. That is, the main claim is that at an early point in development, most likely even before the multiple-word stage, the child bootstraps the canonically encoded parameters. This is what we call the 'finger print knowledge of the child', by means of which the child is capable of assessing the global parametric value of the DP in German (i.e., the Possessor Raising option, the status of D^0 as a 'copy' of the agreement features of the Spec and complement position, and the weak/strong asymmetry). Since the non-canonical paradigmatic component of this task cannot be acquired by means of syntactic bootstrapping, the D^0 position is marked by dummy place holders as a target-consistent interim solution. We claim that the difference between the developmental sequences of the acquisition of DP in Bernese Swiss and High German boils down to fact that in High German the possessive expletive head is less accessible in terms of morphological articulation.

In conclusion, we want to address the question whether the explanation of the developmental sequences in Bernese and High German given so far is sufficient to account for the totality of the observed developmental phenomena. The answer seems to be no. Thus our framework makes no predictions with regard to the fact that apparently the DP-internal topicalization structures in (50) occur before the unmoved structure in (51):

(50)   *von der uni*   *das puttgegang*   S(2;07.04)
           of   the university that broken
           'The one of the university is broken.'

(51)   *die schwester von (To)bias*   S(2;07.04)
           'the sister of (To)bias'

even though both options seem to be equally accessible to the child. Based on similar observations and a proposal made in Weissenborn (1993) on the development of *wh*-questions in French, where *wh*-movement (52) occurs developmentally before *wh-in-situ* (53):

(52)   *où*   *il*   *est?*   F(1;10.26)
           where he is

(53)   *il*   *est où?*   F(2;08.25)
           he is   where

We want to suggest that this specific order of occurrence can be accounted for if we assume a meta-principle which requires that whenever the target language allows for the fulfillment of scope requirements both in the syntax and at LF, the syntactic option is preferred in the initial grammar. LF-movement, that is the *in-situ* option, must then be considered as the marked option.

As can easily be seen, the same explanation would allow us to account for the relative order of occurrence of the DP-structures in (50) and (51). We will call the meta-principle just described the SYNTACTIC PRECEDENCE PRINCIPLE (54):

(54)   The Syntactic Precedence Principle
           Given a language L which allows for a parameter P the choice of more than one value V1 and V2 such that
     (i)   V1 and V2 are equally accessible in terms of the Accessibility Hierarchy, and
     (ii)   V1 allows for the fulfillment of scope requirements in the syntax while V2 meets the scope requirement at LF then, early grammar prefers V1 over V2.

This meta-principle poses an interesting problem because it seems to conflict with the prediction resulting from another meta-principle namely Chomsky's (1993) PRINCIPLE OF ECONOMY OF DERIVATION which would predict that the unmoved option should be preferred. This does not mean that we want to exclude the possibility that the Economy Principle plays a role in acquisition as recently proposed by Roeper (1991), Wexler (1994), and de Villiers & Roeper (1994), among others. But, in cases of conflict between both meta-principles the latter apparently is overridden by the former which seems to define, parallel to our ACCESSIBILITY HIERARCHY for parameter triggers, a HIERARCHY OF PARAMETRIC CHOICES. This latter hierarchy points to specific properties of the acquisition mechanism which remain to be determined.

Acknowledgements

We would like to thank T. Roeper, M. Schönenberger, and two anonymous reviewers for their comments. Thanks also to Ulrike Frank for her help with the German data and to Susan Powers for preparing and checking the English of the final manuscript. Other than that, the usual disclaimers apply.

Notes

1. In the spirit of Landau & Gleitman (1985).

2. Notice that our definition of Strong Continuity is not identical to the same notion as used by other authors under which the child's representations need not obey the parametric values of the target grammar (cf. Boser *et al.* 1991; Whitman 1994; Whitman *et al.* 1991).

3. The LOCAL WELL-FORMEDNESS CONSTRAINT: The representation of any utterance of the child is locally wellformed with respect to a representation of the adult grammar.

4. The same observation has been made independently for French by Crisma (1992).

5. Similarly, within the theory developed in Hyams (1994) the target-inconsistency of the *pro*-drop phenomena in early English as well as the so-called root infinitives (Wexler 1994) do not constitute violations of the parametric system of the target language, but are rather taken to be derived from the underspecification of the COMP slot.

6. For details see Penner (1994a, 1994b, and 1994c) on normal and disordered language acquisition. The notion of accessibility incorporates some ideas developed in Roeper & Weissenborn (1990).

7. For details see (9) below.

8. For details see (20) and (22) below.

9. This metaphor characterizes knowledge as incomplete, but compatible with the information to be detected.

10. The schwa ə in these examples is interpreted as a dummy place holder for the adult complementizer *daß*.

11. Similar assumptions have already been made by Roeper (1973).

12. Consider the following examples in the realms of object placement and scrambling. As shown in Penner *et al.* (1994) for Swiss German and High German there are hardly any violations to be found. Consider first the Swiss German data. In J.'s corpus (1;2–2;4), 374 transitive infinitives or past participles with overt objects of the type in (i) are attested:

(i)   a.   *Bauue hole*   J(1;08.22)
           ball   get
       b.   *Dip fundet*   J(1;08.25)
           jeep found
       c.   *hole Buech*   J(2;01.25)
           fetch book

In this period only 1.3% directionality violations are attested. That is, given these data, it is unlikely that Kayne's (1993) hypothesis of the universal SVO base order is confirmed (but see Platzack 1994). The same holds for High German. In the Simone corpus we find between age 1;10.20–2;02.21 618 nonfinite transitive utterances of the type in (ii-a, b), only 10 of which (i.e., 1.6%) contain objects to the right of the verb (ii-c):

(ii)   a.   *zähne putzen*   S(1;10.22)
           'teeth brush'
       b.   *schuh ausziehn*   S(1;11.13)
           'shoe take off'
       c.   *nich buttmache lumlum*   S(2;00.01)
           'not break balloon'

Our second example concerns the development of scrambling. As discussed in Penner *et al.* (1993), and contrary for example to Clahsen *et al.* (this volume), scrambling can be observed from the outset as shown in the examples in (iii):

(iii)   c.   *ja tee mone habe(n)*   S(2;00.06)
           'yes tea (Si)mone have'
       d.   *des auch mone hol(en)*   S(2;01.21)
           'this also (Si)mone get'

Examples like (iv):

(iv)   *häschen braucht nich windel*   S(2;01.19)
           'bunny needs not diaper'

cannot be considered counterexamples, given that a sentence like the following in which negation is stressed:

(v)   *Hans hat nícht den Kuchen gegessen*
           'Hans has not the cake eaten.'

is perfectly acceptable with the sentential reading of negation. Early scrambling as instances of subject movement is shown in (vi-a, b):

(vi) a. *maxe auch (mu)sik mache(n)*   S(1;11.14)
             'Max also music make'
      b. *mone nich das eis haben*   S(2;00.06)
             'Simone ice cream have'

13. As discussed in detail in Penner & Schönenberger (1995), cliticization of the definite article in High German is restricted to prepositional phrases.

14. The dative possessive is more complex because the expletive possessive pronoun *si* agrees with both the possessor and the possessum and thus participates in a complete agreement configuration. This is not the case in (17).

15. In this sense the possessive pronoun is an expletive element on a par with *daß* in doubly filled complementizer constructions which constitutes a special case of Affect Configuration as well.

16. Note that the term PRE-NOMINAL GENITIVE for possessive constructions of the type (21) (see Clahsen *et al.*, this volume, and others) is inadequate, given that the *-s* prefix is attached to any possessor in the Spec-CP position regardless of its gender specification, while the *-s* endings of the post-nominal genitive (*das Haus des Vaters* 'the house of the father') is restricted to the masculine and neuter singular. The feminine genitive takes no *-s* (*das Haus der Mutter* 'the house of the mother') . In fact, on the assumption that topicalized elements, being in Ā-positions, are exempted from the Case Filter, Case assignment to the possessor in the Spec-DP position seems to be superfluous (or optional). There is thus no theoretical reason to postulate that the possessive *-s* spells out the obligatory Case marking of the possessor.

17. Quantified and indefinite DPs will have to be dealt with in other research.

18. The Bernese data are mainly taken from Juwal's diary which consists of two corpora. The first corpus (age range: 1;2–2;8, total number of utterances: 5,000) contains a daily collection of all the developmentally relevant data from the onset (first one-word utterances) until after the acquisition of V2. The second corpus focuses on the late development of subordination.

19. The bracketed text gives the adult or target form [= target].

20. We will assume, following Penner (1994a) and Penner *et al.* (1994), that bare object nouns are initially treated generically as 'prefixes' rather than full arguments. So, for instance, the noun *ball* in *ball spielen* 'play ball' is initially treated by the child on a par with the 'prefix-like' object *klavier* in *klavier spielen* 'play piano' in which case the object is not a true argument DP, hence exempted from the Universal DET Requirement. In this sense, the number of genuine 'violations' is much smaller.

21. The data are from the Simone Corpus collected by Max Miller. We analyzed 40 transcripts ranging from age 1;09.11 to 2;07.04 comprising 16,678 utterances.

22. Note that the reduced forms are not found in the input. They represent thus genuine examples of place holders.

23. In 488 uses of the full forms of the definite article we find 20 cases of gender error
     (i.e., 4%) which are distributed over the whole period of observation. There are seven
     occurrences of Case errors (i.e., 1%), two of which are related to the inappropriate
     choice of accusative Case instead of dative Case with prepositions which take both
     Cases, i.e., *in* 'in' and *hinter* 'behind'.

24. A presentation of our data grouping them together as in Clahsen *et al.*'s (1994) analysis
     yields the following results:

		total N	non-adultlike	% non-adultlike
a.	1;10.20–2;00.23:	1,191	667	56
b.	2;00.26–2;02.21:	1,100	457	42
c.	2;04.17–2;07.04:	974	125	13

     Although our analysis yields numbers which are slightly different from the ones in
     Clahsen *et al.* (1994) the comparison of the above grouped presentation with Figure 1
     shows that the differences, especially the one between (a) and (b) mask the considerable
     within-group variation (see Figure 1). This becomes even more apparent if we split each
     group into two down the middle yielding the groups (a') and (a''), (b') and (b''), (c') and
     (c''). We then find significant differences (chi-square test, Pearson coefficient) between
     (a') and (a'') (p = 0.05), and (c') and (c'') (p = 0.001), a result which is not expected under
     Clahsen *et al.* (1994) analysis which takes only into account the difference between (a),
     (b), and (c), and which predicts relative homogeneity within groups with respect to the
     frequency of occurrence of deviating utterances. Also, the comparison between (b) and
     (c) seems questionable to us, given the absence of recordings for two months which
     accentuates the difference between (b) and (c).

25. Up to age 2;00.03 we observe 3,472 uses of proper names in the input out of which 679
     (20%) are used with an unreduced definite article.

26. Pre-conjunctional subordinate clauses are conjunctionless subordinate clauses which
     typically occur prior to the acquisition of the complementizer. Penner & Müller (1992)
     assume that the gap as in (i), co-occurring in the unmarked case with the verb-final
     structure (Bernese Swiss German, J(1;11) (Penner 1994a):
     (i)   *Hund chunnt, Angscht*
           dog   comes fear
           'I am afraid (when) the dog comes.'
     or the monosyllabic place holder, as in (ii) (Stern & Stern Corpus):
     (ii) *ich will 'n Eimer mitnehmen in Garten ə ich schippen kann*   G(2;10)
           I   want a bucket with-take in garden I   shovel   can
           'I want to take a bucket with me to the garden in order to shovel.'
     are fillers of the yet underspecified COMP-position.

References

Borer, H. & K. Wexler. 1987. "The Maturation of Syntax." *Parameter Setting* (= *Studies in Theoretical Psycholinguistics*), ed. by T. Roeper and E. Williams, 123–172. Dordrecht: Reidel.

Boser, K., B. Lust, L. Santelmann & J. Whitman. 1992. "The Syntax of V2 in Early German Grammar: The strong continuity hypothesis. *Proceedings of NELS 22*, 51–66. Amherst, Mass.: Graduate Linguistic Student Association.

Bottari, P., P. Cipriani & A. M. Chilosi. 1992. "Proto-syntactic Devices in the Acquisition of Italian Free Morphology." *Geneva Generative Papers* 1.83–101.

Chomsky, N. 1993. "A Minimalist Program for Linguistic Theory." *The View from Building 20*, ed. by K. Hale & S. J. Keyser, 1–52. Cambridge, Mass.: MIT Press.

Clahsen, H., S. Eisenbeiss & M. Penke. This volume. "Lexical Learning in Early Syntactic Development." [Paper presented at the Workshop on Generative Studies in the Acquisition of Case and Agreement, University of Essex.]

Clahsen, H., S. Eisenbeiss & A. Vainikka. 1994. "The Seeds of Structure: A syntactic analysis of the acquisition of Case marking." *Language Acquisition Studies in Generative Grammar* (= *Language Acquisition and Language Disorders,* 8), ed. by T. Hoekstra & B. D. Schwartz, 92–118. Amsterdam: John Benjamins.

Crisma, P. 1992. "On the Acquisition of *Wh*-questions in French. *Geneva Generative Papers* 0.115–122.

Eisenbeiss, S. 1994a. "Raising to Spec and Adjunction Scrambling in German Child Language." Paper presented at the 'Workshop on the Acquisition of Clause-Internal Rules: Scrambling and Cliticization', University of Berne, January 1994.

Felix, S. 1984. "Maturational Aspects of Universal Grammar. *Interlanguage,* ed. by A. Davis, C. Criper & A. Howatt, 133–161. Edinburgh. Edinburgh University Press.

Haegeman, L. 1992. "Sentential Negation in Italian and the Neg Criterion." Ms., University of Geneva.

Hyams, N. 1986. *Language Acquisition and the Theory of Parameters.* Dordrecht: Reidel.

——. 1994. "The Underspecification of Functional Categories in Early Grammar. Paper presented at the Great Britain Child Language Seminar, Bangor, Wales.

Kayne, R. 1994. *The Antisymmetry of Syntax.* Cambridge, Mass.: MIT Press.

Landau, B. & L. Gleitman. 1985. "Language and Experience: Evidence from the blind child." Cambridge (Mass): MIT Press.

Lebeaux, D. 1988. "Language Acquisition and the Form of the Grammar." Diss., University of Massachusetts, Amherst.

Longobardi, G. 1994. "Reference and Proper Names: A theory of N-movement in syntax and Logical Form. *Linguistic Inquiry* 25.609–665.

Mazuka, R. 1994. "How Can a Grammatical Parameter Be Set Before the First Word?" Ms., Duke University.

Penner, Z. 1993. "The Earliest Stage in the Acquisition of the Nominal Phrase in Bernese Swiss German: Syntactic bootstrapping and the architecture of language learning." Arbeitspapier Nr. 30, Institut für Sprachwissenschaft der Universität Bern.

————. 1994a. "Ordered Parameter Setting in First Language Acquisition, The role of syntactic bootstrapping and the triggering hierarchy in determining the developmental sequence in early grammar: A Case Study in the Acquisition of Bernese Swiss German." Habilitation Thesis, University of Bern.

————. 1994b. "Learning-Theoretical Perspectives on Language Disorders in Childhood: Developmental dysphasia in Swiss German." Ms., University of Bern.

————. 1994c. Störungen im Erwerb der Nominalphrase: Ein spontan-sprachliches Diagnoseverfahren zur Feststellung von Entwicklungsstörungen im Schweizerdeutschen. Luzern: Edition SZH.

Penner, Z. & N. Müller. 1992. "On the Early Stages in the Acquisition of Finite Subordinate Clauses: The syntax of the so-called pre-conjunctional subordinate clauses in German, Swiss German, and French. Geneva Generative Papers 1.163–181.

Penner, Z. & M. Schönenberger. 1995. "The Distribution of DP Agreement Features in German Dialects: Expletive DETs and the so-called weak/strong asymmetry." Topics in Swiss German Syntax, ed. by Z. Penner, 331–346. Bern: Peter Lang.

Penner, Z., M. Schönenberger & J. Weissenborn. 1994. "Object Placement in Early German." Linguistics in Potsdam 1.93–108.

Penner, Z., R. Tracy & J. Weissenborn. 1993. "The Relevance of Focus Particles for Language Acquisition." Paper presented at the 6th International Congress for the Study of Child Language, Trieste.

————. 1994. "The Acquisition of Focus Particles and Negation." Paper presented at the Workshop on the L1– and L2– Acquisition of Clause-Internal Rules: Scrambling and Cliticization, Bern.

Penner, Z. & J. Weissenborn. 1993. "The Acquisition of the DP in German: The role of grammatical features and the acquisition path." Paper presented at the Conference on Generative Approaches to Language Acquisition, Durham.

Peters, A. & L. Menn. 1993. "False Starts and Filler Syllables: Ways to learn grammatical morphemes." Language 69.742–777.

Platzack, C. 1994. "Parameter Setting and Brain Structure." Paper presented at the Workshop of Generative Studies in the Acquisition of Case and Agreement. University of Essex.

Ramat, P. 1986. "The Germanic Possessive Type '*dem Vater sein Haus*'." *Linguistics across Historical and Geographical Boundaries*, ed. by D. Katovsky & A. Szwedek, 579–590. Berlin: Mouton de Gruyter.

Rizzi, L. 1991. "Residual Verb Second and the *Wh*-Criterion." Technical Reports in Formal and Computational Linguistics 3, University of Geneva.

———. 1992. "Early Null Subjects and Root Null Subjects." *Geneva Generative Papers* 0.102–114. [Revised version in *Language Acquisition Studies in Generative Grammar*, ed. by T. Hoekstra & B. D. Schwartz, 151–176. Amsterdam: John Benjamins.]

Roeper, T. 1973. "Approaches to a Theory of Language Acquisition with Examples from German Children." Diss., Harvard University, Cambridge, Mass.

———. 1991. "How a Marked Parameter is Chosen: Adverbs and *do*-insertion in the IP of child grammar. *Papers in the Acquisition of WH* (= University of Massachusetts Occasional Papers, special edition), ed. by T. Maxfield & B. Plunkett, 175–202. Amherst, Mass.: Graduate Linguistic Student Association.

Roeper, T. & J. de Villiers. 1991. "The Emergence of Bound Variable Structures." *Papers in the Acquisition of WH* (= University of Massachusetts Occasional Papers, special edition), ed. by T. L Maxfield & B. Plunkett, 225–256. Amherst, Mass.: Graduate Linguistic Student Association.

Roeper, T. & J. Weissenborn. 1990. "How to Make Parameters Work: Comments on Valian." *Language Processing and Language Acquisition* (= *Studies in Theoretical Psycholinguistics*, 10), ed. by L. Frazier and J. de Villiers, 147–162. Dordrecht: Kluwer.

Schönenberger, M. & Z. Penner. In preparation. "Possessor Raising in Swiss German."

Stern, C. & W. Stern. 1928. *Die Kindersprache*. Leipzig: Barth (Reprint Darmstadt 1975: Wissenschaftliche Buchgesellschaft).

Villiers, J. de & T. Roeper. 1995. "Barriers, Binding the Acquisition of the NP/DP Distinction." *Language Acquisition* 4.73–104.

Weissenborn J. 1990. "Functional Categories and Verb Movement in Early German: The acquisition of German syntax reconsidered." *Spracherwerb und Grammatik: Linguistische Untersuchungen zum Erwerb von Syntax und Morphologie* (= *Linguistische Berichte*, Special Issue 3), ed. by M. Rothweiler, 190–224. Opladen: Westdeutscher Verlag.

———. 1992. "Null Subjects in Early Grammars: Implications for parameter-setting theories." *Theoretical Issues in Language Acquisition: Continuity and change in development*, ed. by J. Weissenborn, H. Goodluck. & T. Roeper, 269–299. Hillsdale, N.J.: Lawrence Erlbaum.

————. 1993. "Matrix Infinitives and Economy in Language Development: Comments on Wexler." Paper presented at the OTS 5th Anniversary Conference 'The Robustness of the Language Faculty: Coping with Incomplete Information", Utrecht, October.

————. 1994. "Constraining the Child's Grammar: Local well-formedness in the development of verb movement in German and French. *Syntactic Theory and First Language Acquisition: Crosslinguistic perspectives.* Vol. 1: *Heads, Projections, and Learnability,* ed. by B. Lust, M. Suñer & J. Whitman, 215–247. Hillsdale, N.J.: Lawrence Erlbaum.

Wexler, K. 1994. "Optional Infinitives, Head Movement and the Economy of Derivations." *Verb Movement,* ed. by D. Lightfoot and N. Hornstein, 305–350. Cambridge: Cambridge University Press.

Whitman, J. 1994. "In Defense of a Strong Continuity Account of the Acquisition of Verb-second." *Syntactic Theory and First Language Acquisition: Crosslinguistic perspectives.* Vol. 1: *Heads, Projections, and Learnability,* ed. by B. Lust, M. Suñer & J. Whitman, 273–287. Hillsdale, N.J.: Lawrence Erlbaum.

Whitman, J., K.-O. Lee & B. Lust. 1991. "Continuity of the Principles of Universal Grammar in First Language Acquisition: The issue of functional categories. *Proceedings of NELS 21,* ed. by Tim Sherer, 383–397. Amherst, Mass.: Graduate Linguistic Student Association.

Subject–Verb and Object–Verb Agreement in Early Basque

Jürgen M. Meisel   Maria-Jose Ezeizabarrena
Universität Hamburg

1. Introduction

Much of the research on grammatical agreement between the verb and its arguments and certainly most of the work on these phenomena in first language development has been concerned with subject–verb agreement, almost exclusively based on Indoeuropean languages, especially from the Germanic and Romance families. This focus unduly limits our perspective on an important aspect of grammar and leaves a number of crucial questions unanswered. There exist, for example, no *a priori* reasons for treating agreement with different types of verbal arguments as one uniform phenomenon, rather than distinguishing between two (subject–object) or more (differentiating between complements) sorts of agreement. Although a uniform treatment appears to be preferable for reasons of parsimony, it remains to be seen whether this is indeed a viable solution. Language acquisition studies can, in our opinion, shed some light on these problems.

In the present paper, we report on a study dealing with the acquisition of Basque, a non-Indoeuropean language. Basque has a rich verbal and nominal morphology, marking Case and agreement overtly. We are concerned mainly with agreement, but since, according to Universal Grammar, Case assignment is closely related to it, this will also be dealt with where appropriate.

The second section of this paper introduces the relevant properties of the adult target system in which the verb agrees with its subject as well as with direct and indirect objects. It is also a morphologically ergative system. Section 3 alludes to some notions of grammatical theory which play a crucial role in the ensuing discussion. It is tentatively suggested that verb–argument agreement can be defined uniformly as reflecting a specifier–head relationship allowing for feature sharing to happen, a decisive role being attributed to ⟨person⟩ in this process. Case, in Basque, is claimed to be assigned under agreement. The fourth section introduces the children studied and briefly refers to the data collection procedures. Section 5 offers a fairly detailed description of the findings obtained with two bilingual children and summarizes the results from a study of a third bilingual and one monolingual child. The picture which emerges shows that subject–verb agreement is acquired before object–verb agreement. Initially, only forms marking third person singular subjects are used, then other grammatical persons are differentiated. Direct-object agreement seems to come in earlier than agreement with indirect objects, but the data are not unambiguous on this point. The discussion of these results, in Section 6, raises the question of what kinds of developments in the grammatical knowledge of the children might be underlying the observed changes in language use. We want to argue that they result from the fact that parameterized options of Universal Grammar become accessible successively as the parameters are set at the target value. Section 7 then gives a summary of the results and refers to possible implications for grammatical theory.

2.   Agreement and Case in Basque

Basque is an SOV language which, although allowing considerable variation in word order, exhibits rather strict head-final order. Basque verbs appear in two types of inflectional paradigms. All verbs can be used as PERI- PHRASTIC (or ANALYTIC) constructions, consisting of a main verb and an auxiliary. In this case, the main verb carries ASPECTUAL information, i.e., perfective (-0),[1] imperfective (-t(z)en), or future (-ko). TENSE, MOOD and PERSON agreement, however, are marked solely on the auxiliary. Except for some modal particles and the interrogative particle al, no element can intervene between the main verb and its auxiliary in affirmative sentences. With ergative agreement markings (see below) the auxiliary edun must be selected, otherwise izan is used.[2]

(1)   a.   *Joan   naiz.*
             GO:PERF INTR:SUBJ.1SG:PRES
             'I have gone.'
       b.   *Ikusi   dut.*
             SEE:PERF TRANS:DO.3SG:SUBJ.1SG:PRES
             'I have seen (it).'

    c.   *Joango naiz.*
         go:FUT INTR:SUBJ.1SG:PRES
         'I will go.'
    d.   *Ikusiko dut.*
         see:FUT TRANS:DO.3SG:SUBJ.1SG:PRES
         'I will see (it).'
    e.   *Joaten   naiz.*
         go:IMPERF INTR:SUBJ.1SG:PRES
         'I (usually) go.'
    f.   *Ikusten   dut.*
         see:IMPERF TRANS:DO.3SG:SUBJ.1SG:PRES
         'I see (it).'

In addition to being used in periphrastic constructions, a small number of frequently occurring verbs, e.g., *egon* 'to stay, to be', *eduki* 'to hold, to have', *jakin* 'to know', *ekarri* 'to bring', *eraman* 'to take (to), to carry', *joan* 'to go (directional)', *ibili* 'to go, to wander', *etorri* 'to come', *ikusi* 'to see', exhibit SYNTHETIC forms. In these cases, it is the main verb which is inflected for tense, mood and person agreement.

    (2) a.   *noa*
              SUBJ.1SG:go:PRES
              'I go'
         b.   *nindoan*
              SUBJ.1SG:go:PAST
              'I went'
         c.   *dakit*
              know:DO.3SG:SUBJ.1SG:PRES
              'I know (it)'
         d.   *nekien*
              SUBJ.1SG:know:DO.3SG:PAST
              'I knew (it)'

Verbs agree with their subjects, direct objects and indirect (dative) objects; all three arguments can be lexically empty (*pro*). Depending on the type of argument the verb agrees with, Basque exhibits four types of agreement:

I.   Single agreement marking for the subjects of unaccusative verbs (ABS), as in (1a) and (2a).

II.   Bivalent verbs marking subjects (ABS) and dative objects (DAT) of unaccusative verbs:

(3)   *Gustatzen   zait.*
        please:IMPERF SUBJ.3SG:IO.1SG
        'It pleases me.'/'I like it.'

III. Double marking with bivalent verbs, agreeing with subjects (ERG) and
     direct objects (ABS) of transitive verbs, as in (1b) and (2c).
IV. Triple marking for subjects (ERG), direct objects (ABS), and dative objects
     (DAT) of trivalent verbs:

(4)   *Ekarri   dizkiot.*
        bring:PERF TRANS:DO.3PL:IO.3SG:SUBJ.1SG:PRES
        'I have brought them to him/her.'

It should be added that transitive verbs can be detransitivized, resulting in
what has been called an IMPERSONAL or REFLEXIVE meaning; in these constructions the transitive auxiliary is replaced by an intransitive one which agrees with
the internal argument:

(5)   a. *Sagarrak ikusi   ditut.*
            apples   see:PERF TRANS:SUBJ.1SG:DO.3PL
            'I have seen the apples.'
        b. *Sagarrak ikusi   dira.*
            apples   see:PERF INTR:SUBJ.3PL
            'The apples have been seen.'

Position and form of person agreement morphemes vary, for the same
grammatical person, depending on number and type of argument, tense, etc.

Table 1. Position of Agreement Affixes for Synthetic Verbs

present	past
ABS+root	ABS+root
ABS+root+DAT	ABS+root+DAT
ABS+root+ERG[3]	ABS+root+ERG/ERG+root+ABS[4]
ABS+root+DAT+ERG[5]	ERG+root+ABS+DAT[6]

The following tables show the agreement affixes for present tense. Note
that the affix *d-* is usually not classified as a true person marker. Rather, it is
said to mark present tense, and it stands in opposition to other tense and mood
markers, e.g., *z-* for the past. These prefixes must be used in the absence of first
or second person prefixes. In this sense, *d-* encodes 'not first/not second person';
see Euskaltzaindia (1987:139). Note further that Basque does not have genuine

third person pronouns; the items listed under 3SG and 3PL in Tables 2–5 are demonstratives.

As these tables show, subjects in transitive and in agentive sentences ('active' refers to both types) carry ergative case markings. Basque distinguishes, in fact, 15 Cases, but we will only be concerned with what are called 'grammatical Cases', i.e., absolutive, ergative, and dative, leaving aside those which are not related to agreement and which may better be classified as postpositions, e.g., locative, adlative, ablative, etc.; see Larrañaga (1994) concerning the acquisition of these Cases.

Table 2. Present Tense Subject Agreement with Unaccusative Verbs

	subject pronoun	verbal affix	
1SG	*ni*	*n-*	
2SG	*zu*	*z-*	
3SG	*hura*	*d-*	
1PL	*gu*	*g-*	*-Ø/-z*
2PL	*zuek*	*z-*	*-te*
3PL	*haiek*	*d-*	*-de/-z*[7]

Table 3. Present Tense Subject Agreement with Active Verbs

	subject pronoun	verbal affix
1SG	*nik*	*-t*[8]
2SG	*zuk*	*-zu*
3SG	*hark*	*-Ø*
1PL	*guk*	*-gu*
2PL	*zuek*	*-zue*
3PL	*haiek*	*-te/-e*

Although Basque is a morphologically ergative language, it relies on a subject-object (S-structure) distinction for a number of syntactic processes, including assignment of (abstract) Case. Thus, it does not qualify as a syntactically ergative language. Oyharçabal (1992) refers to Basque as an 'ergaccusative' language. He argues that ergative as well as dative Case are inherent Cases assigned by the verb at D-structure together with theta-roles.

Table 4. Present Tense Direct Object Agreement

	object pronoun	verbal affix
1SG	ni	n-
2SG	zu	z-
3SG	hura	Ø-
1PL	gu	g-
2PL	zuek	z- -te
3PL	haiek	-it-/-z[7]

Table 5. Present Tense Indirect Object Agreement

	object pronoun	verbal affix
1SG	niri	-t(a) (-)[8]
2SG	zuri	-zu(-)
3SG	hari	-o(-)/-a(-)[9]
1PL	guri	-gu(-)
2PL	zuei	-zue(-)
3PL	haiei	-e(-)

Absolutive Case, on the other hand, is said to be a structural Case which can be assigned to subjects as well as to objects, thus corresponding to nominative as well as to accusative Case. He further proposes that Basque verbs assign only inherent Case. Structural Case, on the other hand, is assigned by functional heads, once per clause.

Following Oyharçabal (1992:311), we assume that Basque exhibits a sentence structure like (6) (abstracting away from other inflectional categories and ignoring the COMP system).

AGR(O), according to this theory, assigns accusative Case in transitive sentences to DPs which have not received inherent Case, and AGR(S) assigns nominative Case in unaccusative sentences to DPs also not inherently Case-marked. Consequently, DPs must move in order to receive structural Case. Even though Case-marked in its D-structure position, DP_{erg}, too, can and normally must move, namely to the specifier position of the functional projection to which the case-assigning head moves; see Oyharçabal (1992:319). This approach to Case seems to capture adequately the fact that, in Basque, ergative and dative Case assignment is a property of the verb. Previous analyses had suggested that

(6)

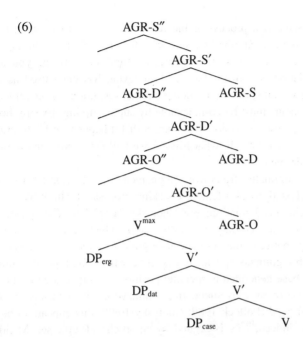

ERG and ABS be assigned by AGR (or INFL) to subject position, and DAT and ABS by the verb to indirect and direct object position, respectively; see Ortiz de Urbina (1989a).

3. Aspects of a Theory of Agreement

As becomes apparent from these last remarks, there exists some disagreement as to exactly how verb–argument agreement and Case assignment work. This is obviously not a specific problem of Basque grammars. Theories of agreement and of Case are, in fact, currently under revision, and studies on language development, we believe, can make a significant contribution to this debate. Before turning to the child data, we want to outline very briefly some theoretical assumptions on which our discussion is based. This will allow us to render explicit what kind of grammatical knowledge the child must have access to in order to make use of agreement in its grammar. At the same time, it should reveal to what extent the explanations offered are theory-dependent and, consequently, subject to revisions as the theory changes.

Agreement is seen as a process or the result of a process by which two elements come to share a number of syntactic features. Feature sharing is possible if the two elements stand in a specific structural relationship; typically a specifier–head relation (Chomsky 1986). Co-indexing has been used as an indication of shared features, thus introducing another condition for agreement, i.e., that the two elements must be co-indexable by superscripting. Exactly how superscripting works, however, is not clear, except that it happens at D-structure level; see Chomsky (1981:259). In what follows we will focus our attention on configurational requirements.

In fact, in the minimalist framework, agreement and structural Case are morphological manifestations of a feature checking process which, universally, happens in a specifier–head relation; see Chomsky (1992:10). The question, then, is whether there is indeed only one configuration which allows for feature sharing (or checking) between the verb and its arguments. Adopting this stance requires that all verb arguments appear in a position where this type of config- uration holds, either base-generated in specifier positions, as suggested by Cheng & Demirdache (1993) or by movement. In a framework which makes use of AGR as a functional head (Pollock 1989; Chomsky 1989), this appears to be a natural consequence indeed,[10] as is argued by Sportiche (1990); see Mendi- koetxea (1992) for a discussion of these issues in Romance languages and in Basque. In other words, at least for languages which exhibit agreement with direct and indirect objects, one is led to assume the existence of the functional categories AGR(O) and AGR(D), resulting, for Basque, in a sentence structure like the one proposed by Oyharçabal (1992); see (6), above. Although in this paper we assume the existence of AGR(O) and AGR(D) in addition to AGR(S), and although we believe that our analysis is consistent with the minimalist framework, we prefer, at this point, not to commit ourselves to this theoretical position. Instead, we will ask, where appropriate, which of the competing solu- tions is supported by the analysis of the child data.

So far, we have been talking about feature sharing, without, however, addressing the issue of which features we are referring to. As is well known, verb–argument agreement universally can involve person, number, and gender. With respect to Basque, we may ignore gender in the current discussion, even though the inflected verb can agree with the addressee in gender in so-called 'allocutive forms'; see Oyharçabal (1993). This is not a case of verb–argument agreement, though, since the addressee is not instantiated as an argument selected by the verb. Also, these forms have disappeared in many varieties of the language and are not attested in our data. Note that Basque does not have gender marking in other contexts, e.g., on nouns. As for the remaining features, we assume that agreement crucially depends on ⟨person⟩. Platzack & Holmberg (1989), among others, have argued in favor of the special status of ⟨person⟩, demonstrating that verb raising in Scandinavian languages correlates with person but not with number agreement. This issue is discussed at some length by Mendikoetxea (1992) who, furthermore, shows that the status of the ⟨person⟩ feature is the same in subject as well as in object agreement; see also Meisel (1994a) for arguments indicating that, in French and German child language, AGR is initially instantiated only as person agreement.

As a consequence of the claim that AGR is a phrasal head, we will further assume, following Roberts (1993:43f), that V-to-AGR movement results in the incorporation of the verb into AGR by substitution of a head into another head position. Ignoring, for the present purpose, Tense and Aspect, this amounts to saying that an X^{-1} feature within AGR morphologically selects the verb, i.e., "a structural slot is created for the incorporee at D-structure as a function of the lexical properties of the incorporation host ... leading to the creation of a complex head" (Roberts 1993:43). In tune with what has been said above about the special status of person agreement, we want to claim that ⟨person⟩ is the X^{-1} feature of AGR acting as the triggering element for V-to-AGR movement. Furthermore, it is a plausible assumption, we contend, that it is this complex head, [V + AGR], which triggers feature sharing, in spite of the fact that it is the subject and the object, respectively, which passes its features on to the verb, and not *vice versa*.[11]

As for the relationship between Case assignment and agreement, it is commonly agreed that nominative Case assignment is subject to the agreement requirement. More generally, Koopman & Sportiche (1991) propose two ways for assigning structural Case: Case assigment under government and Case assigment under agreement. As for nominative assignment, Roberts (1993:19) suggests that the choice between Case-assignment configurations (government or agreement) is parameterized, allowing for the possibility that a language chooses both options. In Basque, both nominative and accusative Case are assigned under agreement and, according to Mendikoetxea (1992:233), are linked to the ⟨person⟩ feature.

Inherent-Case assignment, on the other hand, is lexically dependent. As suggested by Sportiche (1990:16), it "depends on both the lexical choice of the Case assigner and on the thematic relation between the Case assigner and the category receiving Case." He further proposes (Sportiche 1990:74) that although inherent Case is always governed Case and agreement Case is always structural

Case, the reverse does not necessarily hold, i.e., governed Case need not be inherent Case, since direct objects may be assigned accusative Case in complement position and nominative Case can be governed Case, e.g., in some VSO languages; see Koopman & Sportiche (1991). This is in accordance with Oyharçabal's (1992) view of ergative and dative Case assignment in Basque.

4. The Gasteiz-Hamburg Corpus

In this section, we will briefly describe the procedures of data collection and analysis, and give short biographical sketches of the three children we are concerned with in our study. For more information on these issues, see Mahlau (1994).

This analysis is part of a longitudinal study of one monolingual Basque and three bilingual, Basque–Spanish, children. They are growing up in middle class families in the Spanish part of Euskal Herria (The Basque Country). The bilinguals are Jurgi, Mikel, and Peru. Both languages were present in their environment, from birth on. They were recorded during the following age periods:[12]

(7)   Jurgi   1;10.21–5;03.06
        Mikel   1;06.27–5;00.12
        Peru   1;11.00–5;03.24

This study grew out of the collaborative work of two research teams, one at the University of Hamburg (Germany), the other at the University of the Basque Country (Vitoria-Gasteiz). The recordings were initiated in 1987 and ended in 1991.[13]

The data consist of video-recordings which were transcribed and stored and coded on computer. Up to age 4;0, the recordings of about 60 minutes, each, took place every two weeks, approximately, afterwards only once per month. Two adults were present during the recording, one handling the technical equipment, the other interacting with the child; they switched roles in the middle of the session, and each adult consistently addressed the child in one language, Basque or Spanish, respectively. The recording sessions took place in the child's home. The researchers also took notes on what happened during each session.

Jurgi is the second-born child of parents who have both spoken Basque since early childhood. They consistently use Standard Basque when addressing the children, although they speak Spanish as well as Basque to one another.

They are both university professors. During the time period investigated, the child spent much of the week with a nanny who only used the Biscayan variety of Basque with him. According to his parents, Basque is his stronger language. Jurgi and Peru are friends.

Mikel is the second-born child of a Basque-speaking mother (Biscayan variety) and a Spanish-monolingual father. The parents speak Spanish to one another, and they address the children in Basque and Spanish, respectively, carefully avoiding changes in language choice. Mikel uses Basque with his sister and with his peers. He appears to be a balanced bilingual.

Peru is a first-born child; his sister was born when he was four and a half years of age. His father, a university professor, acquired Basque in early childhood; his mother, a highschool teacher, learned Basque as an adult. The family language is Standard Basque, exclusively. During the period investigated, Peru spent several hours every day with a nanny who speaks only Spanish. The majority of his peers are bilinguals, like himself. He, too, appears to be a balanced bilingual.

The present study is based on an analysis of the recordings up to age four, for each of these children. In what follows, we give some MLU values. We are well aware of the limitations of MLU values, but we believe that they can give at least an approximate idea of the children's grammatical development at a given age. As will become apparent, during the ensuing discussions, the three children studied exhibit considerable variation with respect to rate of development.

Table 6. MLU Values Jurgi

recording	age	MLU
20	2;04.07	1.13
22	2;05.03	1.40
30	2;07.19	1.86
32	2;08.10	2.34
40	2;11.09	2.27
46	3;01.17	2.53
50	3;03.14	3.44
56	3;05.09	2.77
64	3;07.21	3.10
68	3;09.13	3.51
73	3;10.23	3.92
81	4;00.25	5.03

Table 7. MLU values Mikel

recording	age	MLU
8	1;09.22	1.44
14	1;11.06	1.96
16	2;00.00	2.43
25	2;02.11	2.41
32	2;04.11	3.95
36	2;05.10	3.17
47	2;08.19	3.41
50	2;10.04	4.24
61	3;01.04	4.45
70	3;03.01	5.37
77	3;05.10	4.56
82	3;06.26	5.03

Table 8. MLU values Peru

recording	age	MLU
12	2;02.14	1.56
20	2;04.15	2.10
28	2;07.30	3.27
31	2;09.05	3.25
39	2;11.25	3.27
43	3;01.24	3.45
46	3;03.07	3.75
53	3;05.09	4.25
62	3;07.27	4.64
64	3;09.02	4.66

5.   The Development of Agreement in Basque

5.1. *Early Verb Forms*

In what follows, we will describe the development of grammatical agreement observed in the speech of two of the children recorded, Mikel and Jurgi, and we will compare the results with those obtained for another child, Peru, studied by Larrañaga (1992).

Phase 1a. When the children begin to use the first verbs, these appear in holophrastic utterances. At this point, verb inflection is not yet used. The forms attested are non-inflected main verbs, infinitives or so-called 'participles' without auxiliaries and lacking aspectual suffixation. In adult language, this form can also be used in imperatives. Context and intonation, however, show that only one example in each of the children's speech samples serves as an imperative, e.g., (8b).

(8) a.   *apurtu*   M(1;06)
          'break'

     b.   *eman!*   J(2;02)
          'give'

Phase 1b: Mikel(1;07–1;08). As of age 1;07 (Mikel), finite verb forms begin to appear. Yet this use is restricted to the formulaic expressions *eztakit* 'I don't know'[14] and to third singular forms of the verbal element 'to be', i.e., the copula *da* and locative and copula *dau*, both corresponding to English 'is' (3SG). We suggest that the limited number of early instances should be regarded as formulaic uses rather than as instances of productive verb inflection.

Table 9. Number of Early Finite and Non-Finite Verb Forms

child	age	finite verb forms	V_{fin}	$V_{non\text{-}fin}$
Mikel	1;06–1;08	*da* 'is', *dau* 'is'	4	4
Jurgi	1;10–2;03	—	—	10

5.2. Subject–Verb Agreement

Phase 2: 3SG agreement; M(1;09–1;11), J(2;04–2;07). Productive use of subject agreement markings can be said to start at ages M(1;09) and J(2;04). One indication of productivity is that the number of occurrences of finite forms increases significantly, e.g., for Mikel from 3 in recording 1;07.27 to 19 in 1;09.04. Furthermore, Mikel now also combines inflected auxiliaries (transitive and intransitive) with main verbs, thus using adult-like periphrastic forms. As for Jurgi, he only now begins to use finite forms, four at age 2;04, four in recording 2;05.03, one in 2;05.17, two at 2;06, and 18 at 2;07; this amounts to saying that he begins late, yet he appears to skip what we called Phase 1b. His early uses, however, are initially still restricted to forms corresponding to English 'is', including the locative 'be', i.e., up to J(2;08) there are no periphrastic verb constructions as yet. The sudden emergence of finite forms in his speech, however, seems to justify the conclusion that Jurgi too uses these forms productively.

It is important to note that these early agreement markers in the speech of both children only refer to subjects, and, moreover, they are all forms of the third person singular. As a result, they do not always conform to adult usage, i.e., when the third person singular form refers to the speaker (1SG) or to a third person plural subject. This is the case in three out of six occurrences of this form during the period ranging from Mikel (1;09.04–1;11.06).

(9)   *kendu (eg)in da*   (= *dot?*)   M(1;09.04)
        take away INTR.3SG TRANS:SUBJ.1SG:DO.3SG)
        'It has been taken away.' (I have taken it away)

Interestingly enough, the first aspectual markers emerge, as well, during this period of time.

Table 10. Emergence of Aspect Markers

	-t(z)en [−FUT/−PERF]	-Ø [−FUT/+PERF]	-ko/-go [+FUT/−PERF]
Mikel	1;09	1;09	2;00
Jurgi	3;02	2;08	2;07

Phase 3: *Subject–verb agreement; M(2;00–2;03, J(2;08–3;00)*. Four months after the emergence of third person singular forms, at ages M(2;00) and J(2;08), the children begin to distinguish between grammatical persons in subject–verb agreement, in unaccusative as well as in active constructions. Note that this implies that when using the third person singular two different morphemes (*d-*, -*Ø*) are required — a further indication for productive use of subject–verb agreement. During this phase, both children make no more errors in person agreement.

(10) a.   *banoie*   [INTR:1SG] M(2;04.11)
           AFF:go:SUBJ.1SG
           '(Yes) I go.'

      b.   *hemendik bai dauz beste kotxiek*   [INTR:3PL] M(2;04.11)
           here   AFF are other cars
           'About here, yes (there) are more cars.'

c. *hau ken(d)u gu(ra d)o(t)*   [TRANS:1SG] M(2;00.00)
   that take-off want:TRANS:SUBJ.1SG:DO.3SG
   'I want to take this off.'

d. *ipini (d)ozu?*   [TRANS:2SG] M(2;03.11)
   put:PERF TRANS:SUBJ.2SG:DO.3SG
   'Did you put it (there)?'

e. *hola (i)piniko (d)o(g)u e?*   [TRANS:1PL] M(2;00.00)
   like this put:FUT TRANS:SUBJ.1PL:DO.3SG
   'Shall we put it like this, eh?'

f. *txerritxo bat zera zu*   [INTR:2SG]   J(3;01.17)
   piggy one are you
   'You are a piggy.'

g. *txitxita (=jantzita) nago*   [INTR:1SG]   J(3;01.17)
   dressed:PERF am
   'I am dressed.'

h. *ezin dut*   [TRANS:1SG]   J(2;08.10)
   cannot TRANS:SUBJ.1SG:DO.3SG
   'I cannot (do it).'

5.3. Object–Verb Agreement

Phase 4: Direct-object–verb agreement; M(2;04–2;06, J(3;01–3;02). Empirical evidence for direct object agreement marking is rather scarce in our data.[15] One reason is that not many objects are lexically realized since Basque allows null objects. A further complication is that initially only contexts for third person singular object agreement appear in the data, but third person singular in the adult language is marked by a zero morpheme, making it difficult to decide when third person singular agreement has been acquired. The ages given in Tables 11 and 12,[16] below, are based on the observation that the required verb form appears in the appropriate contexts. Unambiguous direct evidence is available only months later, when third person plural and first person singular affixes are used.

(11) a. *ekarri (do)zuz bi kotxiek?*   M(2;04.11)
   bring:PERF TRANS:SUBJ.2SG:DO.3PL two cars-the
   'Did you bring the two cars?'

   b. *hanka(?k) daukoz eta ho(r)tza(k) dauko(z)*   J(3;01.17)
   paw(s) has:DO.3PL and tooth(teeth) has DO.3SG(PL)
   'It has paw(s) and it has tooth (=teeth).'

c.   *ez nauzu*   *ikusten*   J(3;11.23)
no TRANS:SUBJ.2SG:DO.1SG see:IMPERF
'You don't see me.'

We thus consider direct object marking as acquired only after some other form than third person singular is used. The same criterion, i.e., use of more than one form, was applied in deciding when subject–verb agreement is acquired, except that in this case two different forms for third person singular agreement were available. With subject agreement, the zero form -$\emptyset$ stands in opposition to *d*-; no such contrast exists for the zero form $\emptyset$– which marks direct-object agreement. As becomes evident from Tables 11–13, direct-object agreement is acquired four to five months later than subject agreement. Yet even then instances of markings other than third person singular are scarce, and errors still occur after this point; in (11b), for example, plural affixes on the noun and on the second verb are omitted. Also, Mikel occasionally uses a trivalent verb form (S–IO–DO) where a bivalent form (S–DO) is required; we find 12 uses of this type, in addition to 80 examples of adult-like S–IO–DO constructions. An error of this kind is found as late as age 3;11.

(12)   *kotxe batek zapaldu (eg)in   (d)otza (=dau)*   M(3;11.17)
car   one E run.over do:PERF TRANS:SUBJ.3SG:DO.3SG:IO.3SG
'A car has run him over.'

Thus, agreement with objects not only emerges later than with subjects, it continues to be a source of errors for some time. In Mikel's data, for example, we find at least one example at ages 2;04, 2;05, 2;08, 2;09, 2;10, respectively, where the DO.3PL markings (-*z*, -*it*-, -*z*-) are missing. Similarly, Jurgi fails to provide these markings in one example at age 3;01, in all of seven contexts at 3;03, and in one out of two contexts at 3;04. What may even be more telling, Jurgi uses at least one example at age 3;00 where a DO.3PL marking should have been supplied but was not.

Phase 5: Indirect-object–verb agreement; M(2;07, J(3;03). Affixes marking indirect object agreement are the last agreement markers to be realized in their appropriate contexts. Determining the exact point at which they emerge is, again, difficult. In Mikel's data one finds a couple of uncertain occurrences as early as 2;04.[17] Yet both children, once they begin to use these forms, employ them with transitive as well as with unaccusative verbs; this certainly happens no later than at ages M(2;07) and J(3;03), respectively.

Table 11. Acquisitional Sequence of Agreement Affixes: Mikel

	subject		direct object	indirect object	
age	unaccusative	active	transitive	unaccusative	transitive
1;09	3SG *d-*				
1;10		3SG *-Ø*	3SG *-Ø*		
2;00		1SG *-t*			
2;00		1PL *-gu*			
2;03		2SG *-zu*			
2;04	1SG *n-*		3PL *-z*		
2;04	3PL *d--z*				
2;07	1PL *g-*			1SG *-t*	1SG *-t*
2;07					2SG *-zu*
2;08		3PL *-te*			
2;09				3SG *-o*	
2;10			3PL *-it-*		
2;11	2SG *z-*				
3;01					3SG *-o*
4;0		2PL *-zue*		2SG *-zu*	3PL *-e*

(13) a. *galdu   jata*   M(2;07.01)
         lost:PERF INTR:SUBJ.3SG:IO.1SG
         'I lost it.'

     b. *jo (eg)ingo (d)otzut*   M(2;07.01)
         hit do:FUT TRANS:SUBJ.1SG:DO.3SG:IO.2SG
         'I will hit you.'

Mikel deviates from the adult standard in never using bi-valent S-DO forms with overt markings for the direct object, i.e., for first or second person. Where such a form is required, he substitutes for it a trivalent (S–DO–IO) form.

(14)   *zapalduko (d)otzut*
         stomp:FUT TRANS:SUBJ.1SG:DO.3SG:IO.SG
         (= *zaitut*)   M(3;06.26)
         (TRANS:SUBJ.1SG:DO.2SG)
         'I will stomp on you.'

Table 12. Acquisitional Sequence of Agreement Affixes: Jurgi

	subject		direct object	indirect object	
age	unaccusative	active	transitive	unaccusative	transitive
2;04	3SG *d-*				
2;08		1SG -*t*	3SG Ø-		
2;09	1PL *g-* (-*z*)				
2;10		3SG -Ø			
3;01	1SG *n-*		3PL -*z*		
3;01	2SG *z-*				
3;02	3PL *d-* -*z*				
3;03		2SG -*zu*		2SG -*zu*	1SG -*t*
3;04		1PL -*gu*	3PL -*it-*		
3;05				3SG -*o*	
3;07	2PL *z-* -*te*			1SG -*t*	
3;08		3PL -*te*			
3;09		2PL -*zue*			
3;11			1SG *n-*		

Jurgi, on the other hand, sometimes fails to provide dative agreement, and, except for the sentence given as (15), he never uses triple markings during the recordings analyzed here.

(15)   *niri   jo egin   dit*   J(3;03.14)
         me:DAT hit do:PERF SUBJ.3SG:DO.3SG:IO.1SG
         'He has hit me.'

Where triple markings are required, he provides verb forms with single or double markings instead, see (16), eliminating the direct object and marking the indirect object as ABS instead of DAT. Personal agreement affixes, however, are present in virtually all contexts requiring them.

(16)   *emango zaitut*   (= *dizut*)   J(3;09,13)
         five:FUT trans:SUBJ.1SG:DO.2SG TRANS:SUBJ.1SG:DO.3SG:IO.2SG
         'I will give you.' (= 'I will give it to you.')

Let us add that the number of dative object markings, too, is quite limited. In Mikel's data we find a total of 138 contexts of which 28 exhibit the use of dative NPs; for Jurgi, the corresponding figures are 23/10. To the extent that one may make generalizations based on such a narrow empirical foundation, agreement between the dative object and the verb appears to be acquired without major difficulties.

It could be argued,[18] especially for indirect object agreement, that the late appearance of object agreement markings merely reflects the fact that the necessary contexts are initially not present in the children's language use. In our view, the reverse chain of causality is correct, i.e., the children do not use such constructions because they do not have available the formal means of expression. One kind of evidence which points in this direction is that none of the four children in our corpus, neither the two studied here nor Peru or the monolingual Oitz, use such constructions before the time when object agreement is claimed to have been acquired. Pye (1992) reporting on the acquisition of another language with object agreement, K'iche' Mayan, does not mention such contexts either. Example (17) might, in fact, be an exception to this generalization.

(17) a. *garajie kendu   (eg)in   dau*   M(2;04,00)
          garage take.away do:PERF TRANS:SUBJ.3SG:DO.3SG
          '(Someone) has taken away the garage.'

      b. *nork kendu   dotzu   garajie?*   Mother
          who take.away TRANS:SUBJ.3PL DO.3SG garage
          'Who took it away (from you-DAT)?'

The reaction by the mother could be interpreted as an implicit correction, adding the indirect-object agreement marking. But since the form provided by the child results in a grammatical construction as well, it is not possible, we believe, to classify such cases as contexts requiring indirect-object agreement. Only when the indirect object is lexically realized do we have unambiguous evidence. Note that such evidence is available, once the first indirect-object agreement markers have appeared. Jurgi at age 3;03, for example, uses eight sentences where indirect-object agreement should have been marked on the verb, but he provides the corresponding verb forms only twice. From then on, the indirect object is marked in all required contexts. We thus believe that the conclusion that object agreement is acquired after subject agreement is empirically justified.

5.4. *Summary*

To summarize, then, we find that subject as well as object agreement markings are used almost without errors from the very beginning (Phases 3 and 4, respectively), as far as the choice of the correct person features is concerned.

Problem areas are plural markings and the choice between bivalent and trivalent verb forms. Interestingly enough, this does not necessarily cause the children to omit affixes or to replace them by one of lower valency; Mikel, indeed, tends to go in the opposite direction, providing trivalent instead of bivalent forms.

In conclusion, we have shown that the acquisition of grammatical agreement in Basque proceeds in five steps, characterized by four developmental achievements. During an initial period (Phase 1) nothing indicates that the children's grammar might allow them to make use of agreement; specifically, verbal morphology is not used productively for this purpose.

A first major change (Phase 2) can be observed at ages M(1;9) and J(2;4), with the emergence of affixes for third person singular subject agreement. This is clearly the case with unaccusative verbs, but, it is not impossible that the children already distinguish between unaccusative and active verbs at this point. Although it is difficult to decide on this question based on the use of verbal affixes, given that third person singular of active verbs is marked by zero forms, it is important to note that they never combine the third person singular transitive auxiliary with unaccusative verbs, as is pointed out by Ezeizabarrena (1994). Also during this period, the children begin to mark aspect on main verbs. The next important change, initiating what we call Phase 3, happens at ages M(2;0) and J(2;8). From now on, grammatical persons other than third person singular are marked by verbal affixes. This is true for subject–verb agreement with unaccusative as well as with active verbs. A few months later, during phase 4, direct-object–verb agreement is marked for third person singular and third person plural. The last development, possibly happening simultaneously with the previous one, concerns indirect-object–verb agreement, emerging no later than at ages M(2;07) and J(3;03). In this case, all three grammatical persons appear more or less simultaneously.

During Phases 4 and 5, the children continue to add further forms to their repertoire, enabling them to differentiate more person and number markings for the previously acquired subject and direct object agreement. Note that, with the exception of third person singular during Phase 2, we do not attribute any theoretical importance to the chronology of emergence of the various grammatical persons. It varies considerably across individuals, and it does not seem to follow a language-specific pattern either; see Meisel (1990) for some discussion of this point concerning German and French, for example. We contend that the specific order to be observed in individual cases depends on pragmatic factors as well as on pecularities of the data collection procedures. Similarly, the fact that plural forms tend to appear later than singular forms does not primarily reflect a grammatical phenomenon; see Koehn (1994).

We would like to add that our findings are in accordance with those from another bilingual child of the same corpus, Peru, who has been studied by Larrañaga (1992). We present her results in the same way as the previously discussed ones in Table 13. It is also important to take into account the analysis of the linguistic development of the monolingual boy Oitz; see Barreña (1993, 1994). Given that in Spanish, the other language of the bilingual children studied here, verbs are inflected for subject but not for object agreement, the order of acquisition which we found could result from the influence of Spanish.[19] Barreña (1994:246) confirms that Oitz first acquires subject verb agreement. So, although the chronology of acquisition concerning direct-object and indirect-object agreement requires further empirical testing, see our discussion of Phase 5 in section 4.2, temporal precedence of subject over object agreement is confirmed by monolingual Basque data.

Table 13. Acquisitional Sequence of Agreement Affixes: Peru

age	subject		direct object	indirect object	
	unaccusative	active	transitive	unaccusative	transitive
2;03	3SG *d-*				
2;04		1SG *-t*	3SG *Ø-*		
2;04		3SG *-Ø*			
2;07		2SG *-zu*			
2;09	1SG *n-*	1PL *-gu*	2SG *-z*		
2;10	1PL *g-*				3SG *-o*
3;00				2SG *-zu*	
3;01	3PL *d- -z*				
3;02		3PL *-te*		1PL *-gu*	2SG *-zu*
3;04					1SG *-t*
3;05	2SG *z-*		3PL *-it-*		
3;06				1SG *-t*	
3;07	2PL *z- -te*				
3;09			1SG *n-*		

The question now is how to explain these changes in the course of development of Early Basque. Note that surface properties, e.g., saliency of the affixes concerned, hardly qualify as an explanation. Tables 11–13 indicate quite clearly that neither their prefixal as opposed to suffixal nature, nor their phonological properties pattern with their order of acquisition. We therefore want to ask what kind of grammatical knowledge might underly them.

6. Discussion: The Acquisition of Verb–Argument Agreement

6.1. *The Initial State of Child Grammars*

In investigating the problem of what kind of knowledge the children have access to at each point of development, we are assuming that parameterized options of UG may, initially, not be instantiated in children's early grammars. Following Chomsky (1989) and others, parameters relate to functional heads. This includes the possibility that not all functional categories made available by UG are implemented in the grammar of every language. If this is correct, it follows for language acquisition that children have to discover the set of categories required by the grammar of their language. In other words, UG makes the entire set of functional categories accessible to the children, but they have to decide for each of them whether to make use of it or not. One possible prediction following from these assumptions is that, initially, no functional category is implemented; positive evidence is needed in order to make this parametric choice. Early grammars, thus, are hypothesized to contain only projections of referential categories, most importantly verbs and nouns. Ignoring, for the purpose of this discussion, categories not directly related to verb inflection, one can say that early sentence structures resemble VPs with subjects remaining in their base position in Spec-VP; see Kuroda (1988) and Koopman & Sportiche (1991). This view corresponds in essence to what Guilfoyle & Noonan (1992) called the STRUCTURE BUILDING HYPOTHESIS; see also Radford (1986, 1990). Yet although we assume that this approach to grammatical development is basically correct, the main purpose of the ensuing discussion is not to defend the claim that early grammars lack functional categories. A theory which proposes that functional projections are present but cannot be used, during early phases of language acquisition, appears to be equally compatible with our hypotheses.

6.2. Marking Agreement by Default

The first observation we could report, with respect to possible evidence for grammatical agreement, has been that third person singular subject agreement forms are the first to appear in all children, during what we labeled as Phase 2. This happens first in unaccusative constructions.

This raises the question whether the affix used here, *d-*, is indeed marking person agreement, rather than present tense; see Section 1, above. The arguments put forth against its classification as an agreement prefix are the following: First, the fact that forms of first and second person agreement are by and large the same across the verbal paradigm for different tenses, whereas *d-* does not normally mark third person; second, that the form of the agreement affix normally resembles the form of the corresponding personal pronoun. Both these arguments, however, are clearly not compelling. It is a well known fact that, in many languages, third person markings can differ from first and second person, either by being less marked or, on the contrary, by carrying more overt markings than the other grammatical persons, as seems to be the case in English. As for the second argument, it does not apply, at all, since *hura, hark*, etc. (see Tables 2–5) are demonstratives. This phenomenon, too, is familiar from many other languages, e.g., Romance pronouns have evolved out of Latin demonstratives, and in colloquial German, articles like *der, die, das* [the:MASC,FEM,NEUTER], themselves ancient demonstratives, function as third person pronouns. The third and perhaps most serious argument says that, across the verbal paradigm, the position of the third person singular subject agreement morpheme, in constructions corresponding to those exhibiting the *d-*, is lexically not filled; one should therefore expect a zero marking (as in *zaio* in (19)) rather than *d-*; see (18) for the transitive and (18) and (19) for the intransitive auxiliary.

(18)
n-	*aiz*	
SUBJ.1SG ROOT:PRES		
'(I) am'		

d- *a*
SUBJ.3SG ROOT:PRES
'(s/he) is'

n- *intze-n*
SUBJ.1SG ROOT:PAST
'(I) was'

z- *e* *-n*
SUBJ.3SG ROOT PAST
'(s/he) was'

d- u - t
ROOT SUBJ.1SG PRES
'(I) have (it)'

d- u -Ø
ROOT SUBJ.3SG PRES
'(s/he) has (it)'

n- *u* *-en*
SUBJ.1SG ROOT PAST
'(I) had (it)'

z- *u* *-en*
SUBJ.3SG ROOT PAST
'(s/he) had (it)'

(19)   *n-   atzai -o*   *n-   intzai -o   -n*

SUBJ.1SG ROOT IO.3SG:PRES   SUBJ.1SG ROOT IO.3SG PAST

'(I) am/have (for him)'   '(I) was/had (for him)'

Ø-   zai -o   *z-   itzai -o   -n*

SUBJ.3SG ROOT IO.3SG:PRES   SUBJ.3SG root IO.3SG PAST

'(s/he) is/has (for him)'   '(s/he) was/had (for him)'

Although this seems, indeed, to be plausible from a paradigmatic point of view, the question remains whether *d-* merely functions as a tense marker. Note, first of all, that the temporal distinction, *d-* present (*da, du*, etc.) *versus z-* past (*zen, zuen*, etc.) only holds for third person forms. In addition, during the developmental period with which we are concerned here, i.e., before Phase 3, one does not find any other tense marking. As has been shown by Almgren & Barreña (1991), Larrañaga (1992), and Ezeizabarrena (1994), the first past tense markings appear at ages M(2;10), J(3;03), and P(2;10), respectively. Consequently, it is justified, we contend, to analyze *d-* as a person agreement prefix, at least for child language. In fact, its definition by Euskaltzaindia (1987:139) as coding "not first/not second person" appears to be quite adequate.

Interestingly enough, the observation that third singular verb forms are the first to emerge in child language has been reported from other languages, as well. In Meisel (1994a), this issue is studied in some detail, and it is argued that third person singular forms represent the default value of agreement, as is obviously the case in mature grammars which usually resort to this solution if no thematic nominal element is available in the specifier position, e.g., with expletive or with empty (*pro*) subjects, with impersonals, or if the element in this position is not a nominative thematic NP, e.g., German *ihrer wurde gedacht* [of them+GEN was+3SG thought] 'they were remembered', rather than **ihrer wurden gedacht* [of them + GEN were+3PL thought].

Remember, now, that agreement has been defined as feature sharing of two elements which stand in a specific structural relation, typically a specifier–head relation. In fact, what figures in agreement is this configuration (Georgopoulos 1991:148); agreement affixes are what Koopman & Sportiche (1991:221) call the "morphological reflex of a relation between INFL and its specifier, or more generally, between a head and its specifier." The fact, then, that we find an early phase of grammatical development during which, crosslinguistically, children use default markings for agreement, more specifically for subject–verb agreement, strongly suggests (a) that the structural configuration of specifier–head relationship is already present in the case of subject–verb agreement, and (b) that feature sharing is not yet possible. Note that if this interpretation of the facts is correct, one should expect to find person agreement errors in early speech. No such errors were found by Meisel (1994a) in French and German child language, and it was suggested that this might be due to low frequency of occurrence of forms other than third person in the input and in the children's language use. As has been reported in section 5.1., above, some instances of person agreement errors have been found in the Basque data, none of them occurring after Phase 2.

We are now left with the problem of explaining why only default markings are possible at this point, or, put differently, what it is that developing grammars still lack. The hypothesis developed by Meisel (1994a) is that, during this phase, both the verb and the subject remain in VP. It does not matter, for the sake of this argument, whether this is because AGR″ has not yet been implemented into the grammar or whether movement does not happen in spite of the presence of a functional category. The crucial point is that even without movement, the two elements stand in a specifier–head relation. This explains why verb–object agreement is not marked by default, for the object cannot yet be moved into a specifier position and, consequently, cannot be in the required configurational relation with the verb. Let us distinguish, in analogy to Case marking, between 'Agreement', the grammatical relation, and 'agreement', its morphological reflex. One can then argue that the former but not the latter is available. This amounts to saying that the default form of the verb is inserted as a whole into syntactic structure from the morphological component, much like suppletive verb forms in the adult grammar.

6.3. Subject–Verb Agreement

Let us now look at the achievements of Phase 3 in order to better understand what kind of grammatical knowledge had not been accessible previously. As was shown in Section 4, the new developments during Phase 3 are characterized by the appearance of agreement affixes for grammatical persons other than third person singular. In fact, first person singular emerges first in the speech of all three children, and second person affixes follow three to five months later.

Remember now that, in Section 2, we argued that agreement is crucially defined in terms of person agreement, that it is this feature of AGR which triggers V-to-AGR movement, and that the complex head [V + AGR] triggers feature sharing. We can now hypothesize that the default option of third person singular, defined as [−1st, −2nd] does not qualify as AGR in the sense just mentioned. In other words, it is not 'strong' enough (Chomsky 1989) to force movement. Strong AGR requires at least one further distinction, e.g., [+1st, −2nd]. If this is correct, we should find that increasing strength not only surfaces as adult-like agreement marking, but that it also triggers movement.

Evidence from other languages indeed supports these claims, as has been shown by Meisel (1994a) for German and French, reviewing a number of facts concerning verb placement. One such case is the placement of finite verbs in second position of German main clauses, preceded by either the subject or by some other topicalized constituent. As was first demonstrated by Clahsen (1986) for German child language, this V2–effect depends crucially on the presence of agreement markings on the verb. Verbs lacking these suffixes consistently appear in final position. Another crucial bit of evidence is the position of verbs in relation to the negative elements. Following Pollock (1989) and Weissenborn & Verrips (1989), one can use the position of verbs with respect to the negative element as an indicator of verb movement, since finite verbs, in French and in German main clauses, precede the negator, and infinitival verbal elements normally follow it. This distribution is also found in early child language, as soon as verb forms carrying agreement markings are used in negative constructions. The conclusion drawn from observations of this kind, in Meisel (1994a), is that agreement triggers verb movement once it involves more than one grammatical person.

A similar argument can be made for Basque. The perhaps clearest case is provided by negative constructions. In Section 2 above, it was pointed out that in affirmative sentences, the verb typically appears in clause-final position, and the auxiliary of periphrastic constructions immediately follows the main verb. Yet in the case of propositional negation, the verbal element carrying agreement features attaches to the negator *ez* 'not' and is fronted. In periphrastic constructions, this results in a separation of the ordinarily tightly connected unit V + AUX. The unmarked word order is illustrated by example (20). Other word order patterns are possible if one wants to focus an element; it, then, is placed after the auxiliary.

(20)   *Ikasleak   ez   zituen   liburuak   hartu.*
         student:DEF:E NEG A3PL:E3SG:PAST book:DEF:A:PL take
         'The student did not take the book.'

Although there is some controversy as to whether the negator is base-generated in this position and attracts the verb (Laka 1989), or whether there exists a head-final NEG″ with the negator moving to AGR and further to COMP, together with the verb (Ortiz de Urbina 1989b), both analyses agree in stating that the verbal element carrying agreement has to move. An examination of negative constructions in child language reveals that this movement shows up at the beginning of what we labeled as Phase 3, i.e., at ages Mikel(1;11) (suggesting, perhaps, that he enters this phase slightly earlier than indicated by Table 11), Peru(2;04), and Jurgi(2;08); see Meisel (1994b). What is perhaps even more revealing is that, before this point of development, Peru(2;03) and Jurgi(2;07) negate sentences by placing the negator *after* the uninflected main verb, as in (21).[20] Note that *ez* never appears postponed after the verbal element carrying agreement affixes; see Ezeizabarrena (1991).

(21) a.   *apu(r)tu ho(ri) ez*   J(2;07)
            break   this NEG

      b.   *Itzi   jan ez*   P(2;05)
            Itziar eat NEG

These observations confirm our hypothesis according to which movement of the verb out of VP is indeed possible as of Phase 3, i.e., AGR triggers V-to-AGR movement once it is specified for more than one grammatical person.

There exists, however, one bit of evidence, mentioned in Section 4.1., which might represent a problem for this analysis, namely some early occurrences of aspect markings on main verbs, during Phase 2; see Table 10. Laka (1990) suggests that aspect projects to a maximal phrase, ASP″, subcategorizing VP. She further proposes that auxiliaries as well as synthetic verbs raise to AGR (or INFL, in her analysis), whereas main verbs in periphrastic constructions remain in ASP. Under this analysis, early aspect markings on main verbs seem to suggest that these are raised to ASP already during Phase 2, and, consequently, the auxiliary should move to AGR(S). In view of the fact that all the other evidence available at this point speaks against a verb raising analysis during Phase 2, this conclusion does not appear to be plausible. Applying the by now well known criterion for productivity of a form, i.e., that two different markings are supplied, we want to argue that the earliest uses of aspect marking must be regarded as rote-learned forms. Only when the criterion is met, at ages M(1;11) and J(2;08), do we have evidence in favor of productive use. This fixes the point of acquisition of aspect exactly at the transition between Stage 2 and 3, immediately before or simultaneously with the acquisition of subject agreement.

The last issue we want to raise in this section concerns the distinction between what has been called 'active' (i.e., ergative intransitive and transitive) and unaccusative verbs. As becomes evident from Tables 11–13, this distinction is acquired early, certainly during Phase 3, but quite possibly earlier. Note that, although third person singular subject agreement is coded by means of a zero affix, a different auxiliary needs to be selected with unaccusative as opposed to active verbs, i.e., *da* 'is' versus *du* 'has'. Remember also that, as pointed out in § 5.3., the transitive form is never used in intransitive constructions, not even during Phase 2. One can thus conclude that the transitive–intransitive distinction does not represent a problem for the children. The development of subject agreement, characterizing Phase 3, however, primarily happens with active verbs. Only one child, Jurgi, begins to use an agreement affix for a person other than third person singular with unaccusative verbs during this period, i.e., the first person plural *g- -z*. The question of whether the cause for the developmental precedence of agreement with active verbs can be traced back to grammatical factors must remain unanswered for the time being.

6.4. *Object Verb Agreement*

Turning now to Phases 4 and 5, our discussion in Section 5 has shown that object–verb agreement emerges after subject–verb agreement. At least for direct object agreement, this is not a trivial result, since, from a functional point of view, one might have predicted the reverse order, assuming that subjects tend to be topics, whereas objects are focused upon. In fact, Slobin (1973:180) reports that in "languages which provide an inflection for marking the object of action (accusative), this is typically an extremely early inflection to emerge;" and Slobin & Bever (1982), in a comprehension study with children in the age range from 2;0 to 4;4, found that object-inflected forms in Turkish are comprehended most easily and that, in Serbo-Croatian, "sensitivity to object-marked forms develops sooner than to subject-marked forms in situations in which the correct performance is to interpret the first noun as the object and the second noun as subject" (p. 250), and they report on similar findings for German and Hebrew. The same kind of result could have been expected for object agreement markings on verbs.

We might add that a more grammatically oriented approach, based on the hierarchical order of functional categories in sentence structure, does not succeed much better. We are referring here to the assumption which, implicitly or explicitly (Meisel 1994a), holds that the functional category subcategorizing VP will become accessible first to the child, and the highest functional category will be last. Although there is considerable disagreement as to how these categories are layered in sentence structure (see Ouhalla 1991), it seems to be uncontroversial that AGR(S) dominates AGR(O). To make things worse, AGR(D) appears between AGR(S) and AGR(O) in the structure given as (6) in Section 2, but agreement with dative objects seems to be the last to be acquired.

To phrase the issue at stake here somewhat differently, one can say that if we want to explain the developmental chronology of argument agreement in terms of independent principles or mechanisms provided by grammatical theory, we need to identify grammatical constraints from which it follows that object agreement is dependent on subject agreement. Note that this is desirable not only in order to account for the acquisitional facts described here. Georgopoulos (1991:152 ff.) claims that, universally, object agreement is only possible if there is also subject agreement, a generalization reminiscent of Burzio's generalization, according to which a verb assigns a theta-role to the subject if it assigns Case to the object (Burzio 1986). Even if the claim that object agreement is dependent on subject agreement should turn out not to be universally valid (see Dryer 1992) — a problematic issue here is whether the affixes in question are indeed agreement markers — the fact that languages with object agreement but lacking subject agreement are uncommon or non-existent requires an explanation which, in all likelyhood, will also account for the observed developmental order.

A solution can perhaps be developed along the lines sketched by Georgopoulos (1991). She postulates that object Agreement is a reflection of a VP-internal specifier–head relation, in fact that all agreement is based on specifier–head coindexing. In order for this to be possible, however, she has to assume that in constructions with trivalent verbs, one argument, i.e., the subject, is not base-generated in VP, for if it was assigned its theta-role there, the position would not be accessible to the object. "Thus, the generalization emerges that specifier–head coindexing in VP (i.e., object agreement) can occur only with those transitive heads that θ-mark their external subject" (Georgopoulos 1991:151). This yields, indeed, the desired result that subject agreement is sanctioning object agreement. With respect to language acquisition, this means that object agreement is not possible in developing grammars unless they provide the learner with the mechanisms necessary to place the subject in a position external to VP, e.g., IP (or TP). A similar analysis is possible in a framework like the one developed by Koopman & Sportiche (1991) and Sportiche's (1990) who assume a second specifier position adjoined to VP.

Another possible solution is to say that object agreement is not an instance of a specifier–head but of a head–complement relation, following the traditional account of Case assignment. In this case, one would have to further stipulate that specifier–head agreement is in some sense more basic than head–complement agreement. Chomsky (1992:9), in fact, suggests that among the two local relations, specifier–head and head–complement, the latter is the 'more local' one — leading to exactly the opposite predictions for the developmental sequence in question. Perhaps more importantly, such an approach implies abandoning the idea of a unified theory of agreement which treats all cases as instances of the relation between a functional head and its specifier.

If we want to maintain the unified theory, both solutions mentioned should be abandoned. Following Chomsky (1992), both agreement and structural Case universally involve NP and AGR, and head-government is dispensed with. Yet if a unified theory obliges us to assume that there are several AGR phrases, it will also have to incorporate the idea that AGR(S) agreement is a prerequisite for AGR(O) agreement. This takes us back to where we started from. The most obvious candidate in our search for a general and independently motivated principle of grammar to explain this fact is the Extended Projection Principle, according to which sentences must have subjects,[21] regardless of the verb's argument structure. From this, we may deduce that AGR(S) has to be the first functional projection to be instantiated in early sentence structures.

We would like to point out in this context that this finding obliges us to abandon the hypothesis according to which the layering of functional projections in sentence structure reflects or determines, for that matter, the order of grammatical development. Note that if one is to assume that the order of affixes mirrors the hierarchical order of AGR phrases, Basque also poses a number of problems. As is evident from the facts displayed in Table 1, subjects and direct objects do not appear in a fixed order, for, with bi- and trivalent verbs in the past tense, the direct-object agreement marker is prefixed when the subject marker is suffixed, and *vice versa*. It should also be noted that with trivalent verbs, markers for indirect-object agreement are closer to the stem than ergative subject markers in present tense, but not with past-tense forms. These facts cast doubt on the claim that the order of morphemes mirrors sentence structure even though Laka (1988) maintains that the mirror principle can be saved if one assumes what she calls "ergative displacement".

6.5. *Agreement and Case assignment*

A glance at Case assignment will close our discussion. Remember that in Basque, ABS, which may really be NOM and ACC, is the structural Case, assigned under Agreement. DAT is clearly an inherent Case determined by the verb. Classifying ERG is somewhat more problematic. It is traditionally regarded as a structural Case because it is assigned to subjects, but the arguments given by

Oyharçabal (1992) leave little doubt, we believe, that it is an inherent Case, assigned by the verb, depending on the thematic relation with its external argument. Note that in all instances, following Oyharçabal (1992), Case assignment (or checking) involves movement to the specifier position of a functional category.

What are the predictions, then, for language acquisition? Structural Case assignment should not be possible unless Agreement is accessible in developing grammars, but lexically dependent Case relies on such requirements, too, since dative and ergative DPs must also move to functional projections. The fact that it requires, in addition, inductive learning of lexical properties makes it difficult to predict when and how this will happen. For the same reason, one should expect to find more variation, depending on the particular lexical item, i.e., the verb, with respect to inherent Case.

The acquisition of Case assignment and case marking has been studied in some detail by Larrañaga (1994), for one child, Mikel. ABS forms are, indeed, found right from the first recording onwards, in subject as well as in object position, i.e., also in contexts where ERG is required. Yet, due to the fact that ABS is zero marked, one cannot be certain from when on exactly it can be regarded as an instance of Case assignment. As of 2;00, there is evidence that the zero marked nouns are indeed Case-marked. One indication is that (as of 2;00) Mikel uses nominal subjects; up to then the subject position had been either lexically empty or filled by demonstratives. We may thus say that NOM is attested as of 2;0, i.e., precisely at the same time when we want to claim that AGR(S) agreement is possible. Note that at this point, zero marked forms are not necessarily bare nouns, for they can carry the specificity marker -a or lexical Case.

This leads us to the next observation. So-called semantic Cases are used earlier than grammatical Cases. The first to appear is ABL(-ative) at age 1;07.27; LOC and ADL follow at ages 1;09.04 and 1;09.22, respectively. From 2;00.22 onwards, LOC is always supplied correctly, with only two exceptions. Provided these are indeed Cases, not postpositions, lexical Case is used as of 1;09. In fact, the crucial idea remains the same, even if these devices are classified as postpositions, since they are lexically selected by the verb and assigned to the noun under government.

ERG appears for the first time at age 1;09.04, but only with one isolated example; the next instances are attested as of 2;01.06, but there are only three examples in spite of many contexts where it is required. As of 2;04.00, ERG seems to be well-established. With first person singular and second person singular pronouns, it is now consistently supplied. With third person singular, it is still occasionally replaced by ABS. The picture which emerges in Larrañaga's (1994) analysis supports the idea that ERG requires lexical learning; there is certainly no sudden increase as one might have expected. Still, it is somewhat surprising that ERG causes problems up to age 2;04, in spite of the fact that auxiliary selection is handled without apparent problems even before age 2;00, and although Mikel acquires the verbal agreement suffixes corresponding to ERG subjects for all three grammatical persons between ages 2;00 and 2;03. In fact, ERG Case ceases to be a problem, as soon as direct-object agreement is established. It remains to be seen whether these two facts are indeed causally related.

DAT Case markings are first attested at age 2;04, as well. This is interesting since, at this point, indirect-object agreement has not yet been acquired. From 2;01.26 up to 2;05.11 one finds one example per recording where ABS is used in DAT contexts. The real surprise, however, shows up at age 2;07 when DAT is attested again. This is exactly the point at which indirect object agreement is acquired; in addition, from this recording onwards, DAT markings are used 100% correctly, i.e., in all required contexts, and only there. A developmental pattern of this sort is normally an indication of parameter setting, rather than inductive learning.

In sum, then, the acquisition of structural Case confirms our predictions given that nominative is acquired precisely at the point of development when AGR(S) comes in. As for accusative, its emergence cannot be determined due to the nature of our data. Problems arise concerning ergative and dative Case. Yet this too was to be expected; it confirms, in fact, Oyharçabal's (1992) classification of ERG as a lexically dependent Case. Since ergative DPs must move to the specifier of AGR(S)″, these markings should not appear before Phase 3. This is indeed what we find. What remains to be explained, however, is why ERG is not used consistently before 2;04 and why ergative markers are occasionally lacking even afterwards. Part of the explanation for this may indeed be that lexical learning plays a role here, although auxiliary selection and the use of ergative verbal affixes do not seem to represent learning problems. Note, however, that according to Oyharçabal's (1992) analysis, AGR(S) and AGR(O) assign nominative and accusative respectively to DPs which have not been Case-marked inherently. Assignment of ABS or ERG to subject and of ABS to direct object position is thus mutually dependent. One might therefore hypothesize that this interdependence of mechanisms involving lexical as well as functional elements are the source of the observed difficulties which cannot be resolved satisfactorily unless both AGR(S) and AGR(O) are accessible to the child. As for DAT, the 100% correct uses at precisely the point of development when AGR(D) has been shown to be available appears to confirm very nicely the grammatical relation between indirect-object agreement and dative Case. What spoils this picture is the fact that some DAT markings are attested earlier. We can think of two explanations for this: either these occurrences indicate that DAT is initially treated as a 'semantic case' like LOC or ADL, or Barreña (1994) was right when he argued that indirect-object agreement emerges earlier, and this would mean that our analysis of uncertain examples has been too cautious (see 5.1, above). In order to decide this issue, more empirical evidence is required.

7. Conclusion

We have argued that the observed changes in language use should be explained in terms of developments of grammatical knowledge. Principles-and-Parameters Theory predicts that such developments depend crucially on parameterized options of Universal Grammar which relate primarily or exclusively to functional categories. Assuming that not all functional categories made available by UG are implemented in the grammar of every language and that their featural composition may vary across languages (Meisel 1994c), one should allow for the posssibility of functional categories temporarily not being accessible to the child.

Following the spirit of these ideas, we explained the exclusive use of third person singular subject-agreement markings during an initial period as a default marking for agreement. The necessary structural configuration is available, but movement to AGR(S) is not possible. Remember that person agreement features had been identified as the triggering elements for V-to-AGR; see section 2. At this point of development, however, AGR is characterized as [−1st, −2nd] and is, thus, not able to force movement — not unless it contains at least one positive value, i.e., [+1st, −2nd] or [−1st, +2nd].

An important result of our study, we believe, is that subject agreement is acquired before object agreement. Since virtually all research on the acquisition of agreement was concerned with subject agreement,[22] little information on this issue had been available so far. In fact, functional considerations might have predicted that object agreement would be acquired first. In our understanding, an adequate explanation of the observed developmental chronology requires a grammatical account from which it follows that object agreement is dependent on subject agreement. This is not only suggested by our analysis of child language, it is also reflected by the typological generalization according to which object agreement is possible if there is also subject agreement. We suggest that the order of development is forced by the Extended Projection Principle.

Another issue raised in this paper concerns the different kinds of object agreement. Unfortunately, however, the developmental facts which we were able to uncover are ambiguous in this case. We tentatively concluded that direct object agreement precedes indirect object agreement. Yet due to the fact that almost all instances of direct-object agreement are cases of third person agreement and third person singular is marked by a zero form in Basque and third person plural is attested only very rarely, it is impossible to take a firm stand on this issue. A definitive answer to this question has to be postponed until unambiguous data are available, possibly from a language where singular forms of direct-object agreement are not marked by zero forms.

On a further issue, however, we believe we have presented convincing evidence. It is frequently assumed, implicitly or explicitly, that the order of acquisition of functional categories reflects their hierarchical position in sentence structure. This turns out to be wrong, for subject agreement developmentally precedes object agreement, yet there is general consensus that AGR(S)″ dominates AGR(O)″ as well as AGR(D)″. If, in addition, our tentative conclusion that direct-object agreement is acquired before indirect-object agreement turns out to be correct, this constitutes further evidence against this hypothesis, since AGR(D) can be argued to subcategorize AGR(O).

Finally, we want to call attention to one more finding, one for which we have no explanation to offer at this point, but which is potentially of significant interest. Our analysis of the child language data indicated quite clearly that no transitive affix is used with intransitive verbs, not even during our Phase 2 when only third person singular subject-agreement forms are attested. The children, thus, have no problems with auxiliary selection with unaccusative *versus* active verbs, at a point of development when this distinction is not yet marked morphologically, neither on the verb nor on verbal arguments. Whether this reflects underlying grammatical knowledge or whether it needs to be explained in semantic or pragmatic terms is a question which must, for the time being, remain unanswered.

Acknowledgements

We want to thank those who read and commented on a first version of this paper, Andoni Barreña, Susanne E. Carroll, Andolin Eguzkitza, Georg Kaiser, Itziar Laka, Pilar Larrañaga, Natascha Müller, and two anonymous reviewers.

Notes

1. Traditionally, the participial forms *-tu*, *-i*, and *-n* are classified as aspect markers for 'perfect' (Goenaga 1980:157-163).

2. Abbreviations: A, ABS = absolutive; AFF = affirmative; Ø, DAT = dative; DO = direct object; E, ERG = ergative; FUT = future; IO = indirect object; IMPERF = imperfective; INTR = intransitive; PERF = perfective; PL = plural; PRES = present; SUBJ = subject; SG = singular; TRANS = transitive.

3. If the object is third person plural, the order is ROOT:ERG:.+ABS, in the Bizkaiera dialect.

4. If the direct object is third person.

5. If the direct object is third person plural, the order is ROOT:DAT:ERG:ABS, in the Bizkaiera dialect.

6. If the object is third person plural, the order is ERG:ROOT:DAT:ABS, in the Bizkaiera dialect.

7. The choice of the suffix varies depending on the particular lexical item as well as on the dialect. There exist, in fact, more variants of the plural morpheme for all three persons, frequently appearing discontinuously. They can be ignored here, because they are not frequent and are not attested in our corpus.

8. If another morpheme follows this suffix, it is frequently replaced by the infix **-da-**.

9. In the Bizkaiera dialect.

10. There exist reasons to doubt that AGR is indeed the head of an independent projection, rather than being an X^{-1} feature of the verb; see Meisel (1994a). We will not, however, discuss this issue here. Instead, we simply adopt this framework for the present purpose; but see, for example, Georgopoulos (1991) for a suggestion as to how a unified theory of agreement in a Spec–head configuration might work without having to assume additional functional projections.

11. As has been pointed out, correctly, by one of the two reviewers, this question is irrelevant if agreement is seen as a case of feature checking, since this is a 'symmetrical' process.

12. Years;months.days. In giving the days of the children's age, we are not attempting to be excessively precise. Rather, this identifies the recording we are referring to.

13. The team in the Basque Country, directed by Itziar Idiazabal, consisted of Andoni Barreña, Amaia Basauri, Mari Jose Ezeizabarrena, Kristina Elosegi, Margareta Almgren, Izaskun Soloeta, Idoia Imaz, Elena Urzelay and Susana Irizar. The researchers of the team at the University of Hamburg, directed by Jürgen M. Meisel, were Mari Jose Ezeizabarrena, Pilar Larrañaga, and Axel Mahlau. Nuria Acacio, José Cárdenes, Aurora Hernández-Cembellín, Juan Mercado and Luis Moreno collaborated as research assistants. We want to thank all of them for their contributions without which this study

would not have been possible. We also gratefully acknowledge the financial support with which we have been endowed during six years. The team in the Basque Country was supported (1988–1992) by the Municipality of Vitoria-Gasteiz through several research fellowships and by the University of the Basque Country through a research grant in 1989. The team in Hamburg has been supported by several research grants to J. M. Meisel (1990–1994) by the Deutsche Forschungsgemeinschaft (DFG). The fact that the two groups could meet twice a year, during the period from 1989 to 1993, is due to several travel grants by the Ministry of Education and Science, in Spain, and the DAAD (Deutscher Akademischer Austauschdienst) in Germany.

14. These formulaic uses of *eztakit* have not been included in Table 9. Jurgi also uses *attoz* 'come!'.

15. For detailed information about frequencies of use, here as well as in the following discussion, see Ezeizabarrena (1995).

16. Tables 11–13 display the present tense agreement affixes, listed in the chronological order of their acquisition.

17. Barreña (1993) argues that Oitz, a monolingual Basque child, acquires indirect-object agreement before direct-object agreement, and he suggests that Mikel acquires indirect-object agreement at age 2;04, interpreting the examples which we qualified as 'uncertain' as sufficient evidence. An example is the following, literally meaning approximately 'it does not please me' in the sense of 'I don't like it':

    (i)   *ez   to   gustetan*
             not AUX please

    The question is how to interpret the child form 'to'. In our interpretation it stands for adult *dot*; Barreña argues that it replaces adult *jata*. There exist four examples of this sort. We believe that, whatever interpretation one favors, they do not represent sufficient evidence for claiming that indirect-object agreement has been acquired.

18. This has been pointed out by both reviewers.

19. This point was brought up by one of the reviewers.

20. In adult language, this is possible in some imperative-like constructions.

21. This was pointed out by Luigi Rizzi at the Essex meeting, and also by one of the reviewers.

22. See, however, Kaiser (1994), who analyzes French clitics as instances of object agreement.

References

Almgren, M. & A. Barreña. 1991. "Aditzaren eta aditz-multzoaren jabekuntz-garapena bi haur euskaldunengan, elebakarra bata eta euskara-gaztelera elebiduna bestea." *Adquisición del lenguaje en niños bilingües y monolingües*, ed. by I. Idiazabal, 137–168. Donostia: Euskal Herriko Unibertsitatea.

Barreña, A. 1993. *Haur euskaldunen hizkuntzaren jabekuntza-garapena: INFL et KONP funtzio-kategorien erabileraz*. Diss., University of the Basque Country.

———. 1994. "Sobre la adquisición de la categoría funcional COMP por niños vascos." *La adquisición del vasco y del español en niños bilingües*, ed. by J. Meisel, 231–284. Frankfurt am Main: Vervuert.

Burzio, L. 1986. *Italian Syntax*. Dordrecht: Kluwer.

Cheng, L. L. S. & H. Demirdache. 1993. "External arguments in Basque." *Generative Studies in Basque Linguistics*, ed. by J. I. Hualde & J. Ortiz de Urbina, 71–87. Amsterdam: John Benjamins.

Chomsky, N. 1981. *Lectures on Government and Binding: The Pisa Lectures*. Dordrecht: Foris.

———. 1986. *Barriers*. Cambridge, Mass.: MIT Press.

———. 1989. "Some Notes on Economy of Derivation and Representation." *MIT Working Papers in Linguistics* 10.43–74.

———. 1992. "A Minimalist Program for Linguistic Theory." *MIT Occasional Papers in Linguistics*, 1.

Clahsen, H. 1986. "Verb Inflections in German Child Language: Acquisition of agreement markings and the functions they encode." *Linguistics* 24.79–121.

Dryer, M. S. 1992. "The Greenbergian Word Order correlations." *Language* 68.81–138.

Euskaltzaindia. 1987. *Euskal Gramatika: Lehen Urratsak II*. Bilbao.

Ezeizabarrena, M. J. 1991. "Ezeztapenerako formen bilakaera bi haur elebidunen eta elebakar baten hizkuntz jabekuntzan." *Adquisición del lenguaje en niños bilingües y monolingües*, ed. by I. Idiazabal, 183–196. Donostia: Euskal Herriko Unibertsitatea.

———. 1994. "Primeras formas verbales de concordancia en euskera." *La adquisición del vasco y del español en niños bilingües*, ed. by J. Meisel, 181–229. Frankfurt am Main: Vervuert.

———. 1995. *Adquisición de la morfología verbal en euskera y castellano por niños bilingües*. Diss., University of Hamburg.

Georgopoulos, C. 1991. "On A- and Ā-agreement." *Lingua* 85.135–169.

Goenaga, P. 1980. *Gramatika bideetan*. Donostia: Erein.

Guilfoyle, E. & M. Noonan. 1992. "Functional Categories and Language Acquisition." *The Canadian Journal of Linguistics* 37.241–272.

Kaiser, G. 1994. "More about INFL-ection and Agreement: The acquisition of clitic pronouns in French." *Bilingual First Language Acquisition: French and German grammatical development*, ed. by J. Meisel, 131–160. Amsterdam: John Benjamins.

.

Koehn, C. 1994. "The Acquisition of Gender and Number Morphology within NP." *Bilingual First Language Acquisition: French and German grammatical development*, ed. by J. Meisel, 29–51. Amsterdam: John Benjamins.

Koopman, H. & D. Sportiche. 1991. "The Position of Subjects." *Lingua* 85.211–258.

Kuroda, S. Y. 1988. "Whether we Agree or Not: A comparative syntax of English and Japanese." *Lingvisticae Investigationes* 12.1–47.

Laka, I. 1988. "Configurational Heads in Inflectional Morphology: The structure of the inflected forms in Basque." *Anuario del Seminario de Filología Vasca "Julio de Urquijo"* 22.343–365.

————. 1989. "Constraints on Sentence Negation: The case of Basque." *MIT Working Papers in Linguistics* 10.199–216.

————. 1990. "Negation in Syntax: On the nature of functional categories and projections." Diss., Massachusetts Institute of Technology, Cambridge.

Larrañaga, M. P. 1992. "Der Erwerb des baskischen Indikativs: Eine Fallstudie am Beispiel eines bilingualen Kindes." M.A. Thesis, University of Kiel.

————. 1994. "La evolución del caso en euskera y castellano." *La adquisición del vasco y del español en niños bilingües*, ed. by J. Meisel, 113–150. Frankfurt am Main: Vervuert.

Mahlau, A. 1994. "El proyecto BUSDE: Corpus y metodología." *La adquisición del vasco y del español en niños bilingües*, ed. by J. Meisel, 21–34. Frankfurt am Main: Vervuert.

Meisel, J. M. 1990. "INFL-ection, Subjects and Subject–Verb Agreement." *Two First Languages: Early grammatical development in bilingual children* (= *Studies in Theoretical Psycholinguistics*, 16) ed. by J. Meisel, 237–298. Dordrecht: Foris.

————. 1994a. "Getting FAT: Finiteness, Agreement and Tense in Early Grammars." *Bilingual First Language Acquisition: French and German grammatical development*, ed. by J. Meisel, 89–129. Amsterdam: John Benjamins.

————. 1994b. "La adquisición de la negación en euskera y en castellano. Sobre la separación temprana de sistemas gramaticales por niños bilingües." *La adquisición del vasco y del español en niños bilingües*, ed. by J. Meisel, 151–180. Frankfurt am Main: Vervuert.

————. 1994c. "Simultaneous First Language Acquisition: A window on early grammatical development." *D.E.L.T.A.* 9.353–385.

Mendikoetxea, A. 1992. "Some Speculations on the Nature of Agreement." *Syntactic Theory and Basque Syntax* (= Anejos del Anuario del Seminario de Filología Vasca "Julio de Urquijo", 27), ed. by J. Lakarra & J. Ortiz de Urbina, 233–264. San Sebastián: Diputación Provincial del Guipúzcoa.

Ortiz de Urbina, J. 1989a. *Some Parameters in the Grammar of Basque*. Dordrecht: Foris.

————. 1989b. "Dislocaciones verbales en estructuras de polaridad." *Anuario del Seminario de Filología Vasca "Julio de Urquijo"* 23.393–410.

Ouhalla, J. 1991. *Functional Categories and Parametric Variation.* London: Routledge.

Oyharçabal, B. 1992. "Structural Case and Inherent Case Marking: Ergaccusativity in Basque." *Syntactic Theory and Basque Syntax* (= Anejos del Anuario del Seminario de Filología Vasca "Julio de Urquijo", 27), ed. by J. Lakarra & J. Ortiz de Urbina, 309–342. San Sebastián: Diputación Provincial del Guipúzcoa.

————. 1993. "Verb Agreement with Nonarguments: On allocutive agreement." *Generative Studies in Basque Linguistics,* ed. by J.I. Hualde & J. Ortiz de Urbina, 89–114. Amsterdam: Benjamins.

Platzack, C. & A. Holmberg. 1989. "The Role of AGR and Finiteness in Germanic VO Languages." *Scandinavian Working Papers in Linguistics* 43.51–76.

Pollock, J.-Y. 1989. "Verb Movement, Universal Grammar, and the Structure of IP." *Linguistic Inquiry* 20.365–424.

Pye, C. 1992. "The Acquisition of K'iche' Maya." *The Crosslinguistic Study of Language Acquisition.* Vol. 3, ed. by D.I. Slobin, 221–308. Hillsdale, N.J.: Lawrence Erlbaum.

Radford, A. 1986. "Small children's Small Clauses." *Bangor Research Papers in Linguistics* 1.1–38.

————. 1990. *Syntactic Theory and the Acquisition of Syntax.* Oxford: Basil Blackwell.

Roberts, I. 1993. *Verbs and Diachronic Syntax: A comparative history of English and French.* Dordrecht: Kluwer.

Slobin, D.I. 1973. "Cognitive Prerequisites for the Development of Grammar." *Studies of Language Development,* ed. by Ch.A. Ferguson & D.I. Slobin, 175–208. New York: Holt, Rinehart & Winston.

Slobin, D.I. & T.G. Bever. 1982. "Children Use Canonical Sentence Schemas: A crosslinguistic study of word order and inflections." *Cognition* 12.229–265.

Sportiche, D. 1990. "Movement, Agreement and Case." Ms., University of California at Los Angeles.

Weissenborn, J. & M. Verrips. 1989. "Negation as a Window to the Structure of Early Child Language." Ms., Max Planck Institut für Psycholinguistik, Nijmegen.

Acquisition of Italian Interrogatives

Maria Teresa Guasti
Fondazione scientifica San Raffaele

1. Introduction

This article presents a study of the acquisition of Italian negative questions and offers a comparison with the acquisition of similar structures in English.

In a recent study Thornton (1993), Guasti *et al.* (1995) have found an asymmetry between positive and negative questions: whereas positive questions were adult in form, negative ones were not. Three main structures were found with auxiliaries, modals and *do*. Here, for simplicity we report each type with *do*.

(1) a. *What John doesn't like?*
  b. *What do you don't like?*
  c. *What do you not like?*

Children failed to apply SUBJECT-AUXILIARY INVERSION (SAI) in negative questions, as observed by Bellugi (1971) (see (1a)). Most frequently, they produced negative questions with a double auxiliary, as in (1b). Finally, they also formed questions with negation *not,* as in (1c). The problem appears to be the raising of the clitic negation *n't* to C, along with the auxiliary. Although the movement of the clitic negation to C is parasitic on movement of the auxiliary to C, conceptually the two are distinct.

From a theoretical point of view, SAI has been analyzed as involving movement of I to C. Rizzi (1990) has proposed that I-to-C applies not only in English questions, but also in Italian ones. Since negative *non* is also a syntactic clitic that moves to C along with I (see Belletti 1990), the question arises whether there is an asymmetry between negative and positive interrogatives in early Italian as there is in early English. The present study is an investigation of this issue.

The article is organized as follows. As a first step, I present the theoretical background, that is the analysis of questions I assume. Second, I review Guasti *et al.*'s study and point out what we may expect to find in early Italian. Third, I report the results of the experiment on early Italian. Fourth, I compare early Italian and early English and evaluate the possible explanations of the two sets of data.

2.   English and Italian Interrogative Sentences

In English, main interrogatives feature SAI. Thus, the order in (2a) with the subject intervening between the *wh*-operator and the auxiliary is ungrammatical. In (2b), SAI has applied as proved by the fact that the auxiliary precedes the subject.

(2)   a.   *What John has done?*
       b.   *What has John* t *done?*

SAI is not possible in embedded interrogatives, as seen in (3).

(3)   a.   *I wonder what has John done.*
       b.   *I wonder what John has done.*

Given the main/embedded dichotomy, SAI is viewed as a form of residual V2. It results from movement of the auxiliary *has* from I to C. Rizzi (1990) analyzes the contrast between (2) and (3) in terms of the *wh*-criterion (see May 1985) reported in (4). This is a universal wellformedness condition on the way *wh*-expressions are assigned scope.

(4)   a.   Each *wh*-operator must be in a Spec–head relation with a ⟨+wh⟩ X.
       b.   Each ⟨+wh⟩ X must be in a Spec–head relation with a *wh*-operator.

In main questions, the *wh*-feature is generated on I and moved along with I to C. The *wh*-operator raises to Spec-CP: because of these two movements the X ⟨+wh⟩ is in a Spec–head relation with the *wh*-operator and *vice versa,* thus satisfying the two clauses of the *wh*-criterion.

(5) $[_{CP}$ *what*$_j$ $[_C$ *has*$_i$ $[_{IP}$ *John* t$_i$ *done* t$_j$]]]?
                                   ⟨+wh⟩

As for embedded questions, the matrix verb selects the *wh*-feature on the embedded C. Then, clause (b) of the *wh*-criterion requires that the *wh*-operator moves to Spec-CP, as in (6).

(6)   *I wonder* [*what* [C [*John has done*]]].
                  ⟨+wh⟩

The embedded verb cannot raise to C, since C is not radically empty as in main questions: its movement would be a violation of the structure preservation condition (Rizzi & Roberts 1989).

As in the English example in (2a), in Italian interrogatives (and more generally in Romance ones), the subject cannot intervene between the *wh*-operator and the verb, as (7b) illustrates. However, unlike in English, the subject cannot follow the auxiliary, as in (7a). The acceptable orders are (7c) and (7d), where the subject is sentence final or in a left-dislocated position.

(7)   a.   *Cosa ha Gianni fatto?*
             what has Gianni done
       b.   *Cosa Gianni ha fatto?*
             what Gianni has done
       c.   *Cosa ha fatto Gianni?*
             what has done Gianni
             'What has Gianni done?'
       d.   *Gianni, cosa ha fatto?*
             Gianni what has done
             'What has Gianni done?'

Rizzi interprets the requirement of adjacency between the *wh*-operator and the verb by claiming that I-to-C movement and movement of the *wh*-operator to Spec-CP also apply in Italian, in agreement with the *wh*-criterion. Therefore, we expect that (7b) is ungrammatical: the *wh*- and the verb are not in the expected Spec–head configuration. Second, he conjectures that the Italian verb in C does not have the option of assigning case under government to the subject in Spec-IP, whereas it can do so in English. Consequently, (7a) is also ungrammatical. However, Italian, unlike English, has the option of leaving the subject in a postverbal position or the option of moving it to a left-dislocated position. Thus, I-to-C movement combined with the availability of a postverbal subject position or a left-dislocated position yields the structures in (7c) and (7d), respectively.

As opposed to English, in Italian the subject of an indirect question appears in a sentence-final position, as in (8a). However, a preverbal subject is acceptable if the mood of the embedded question is subjunctive as in (8c) and marginal if the mood is indicative, as in (8b). Notice that whereas the order *wh*–S–V may be acceptable under certain conditions in embedded questions, the same order is absolutely prohibited in main questions (see 7b)). Thus, there is a main/embedded asymmetry in Italian as well, though not so strong as in English.

(8)   a.   *Mi*   *domando cosa ha fatto Gianni.*
              (I) to-myself wonder   what has done Gianni
     b.   ??*Mi*   *domando cosa Gianni ha fatto.*
              (I) to-myself wonder   what Gianni has done
     c.   *Mi*   *domando cosa Gianni abbia   fatto.*
              (I) to-myself wonder   what Gianni has:SUBJ done

We can explain the pattern in (8) as follows. As in English, the feature ⟨+wh⟩ is generated in C and no I-to-C movement applies. The contrast between (8a) and (8b) suggests that the *wh*-feature may also be selected on I as in main questions. Then, I-to-C applies and we have the same order found in main questions. I take Rizzi's framework as a starting point for my analysis of the Italian acquisition data. As we will go on, we will evaluate it with respect to an alternative analysis of Romance questions and we will consider some possible revisions.

3.   Negative and Positive Interrogatives in English

In this section, I report the results and the discussion of the experiment carried out by Guasti *et al.* (1995). These authors designed an elicited production experiment to study English-speaking children's formation of negative questions.

The structures targeted included *wh*-questions with different extraction sites (subject, object, adjunct) and *yes/no* questions. Questions with modals, with the auxiliary (*be*) and *do* were also part of the test battery. To control for children's knowledge of SAI, Guasti *et al.* (1995) elicited positive questions. In addition, they analyzed negative declaratives to verify children's use of negation. Ten children between 3;8 and 4;7 participated in the experiment. Each child participated in four sessions.

Guasti *et al.* (1995) evoked the range of targeted question structures from the child subjects using the methodology of elicited production. On each trial, an experimenter acted-out a story in front of the child and a snail puppet, who was played by another experimenter. The experimenter told the child subject that the snail was too shy to talk to grown-ups and would only talk to children. This provided the child with a reason to communicate with the snail. At the end of the story, the experimenter asked the child to find out from the snail what had happened in the story. In order to evoke the target questions, the experimenter provided a lead-in given in (9) for the different extraction sites.

(9)   a.   Protocol for object extraction

           Experimenter: *I heard the snail doesn't like some things. Ask him what.*

           Target: *What don't you like to eat?*

      b.   Protocol for adjunct extraction

           Experimenter: *There was one place Gummy Bear couldn't eat the raisin. Ask the snail where.*

           Target: *Where couldn't Gummy Bear eat the raisin?*

      c.   Protocol for subject extraction

           Experimenter: *One of these guys doesn't like cheese. Ask the snail who.*

           Target: *Who doesn't like cheese?*

All of the negative declarative sentences produced by the children in the Guasti *et al.* (1995) experiment were adult in form and most of them contained the clitic form of negation *n't*. Children's positive questions were almost all adult-like, thus showing that children have mastery of I-to-C movement (or SAI). Eight of the 10 subjects produced adult-like questions 90% of time, i.e., featuring SAI and the youngest child (age 3;8) only 40% of the time. A dramatic contrast was observed with negative questions. Whereas subject extraction questions were adult-like, as (10) shows, object and adjunct extraction questions were non-adult in form.

(10)   *Who doesn't like cheese?*

Three main varieties of question structures appeared in the children's transcripts. These are reported in (11) through (13).

Non-inversion structure

(11)   *What the mummy can't do?*   Rosy(3;11)

Doubling structure

(12)   a.   *What kind of bread do you don't like?*   Rosy(3;11)

        b.   *What will Cookie Monster won't share?*   Anna(4;3)

        c.   *How can the Indian boy can't paddle?*   Chris(3;10)

Not-*structure*

(13)   *Why can you not eat chocolate?*   Darell(4;1)

In (11), I-to-C does not occur. The sentence in (12) features SAI, but it is not grammatical in the adult language. In this structure, the clitic negation *n't* is used but it fails to raise to C (along with the auxiliary). In (13), the full form of negation *not* is used. This form of negation has to remain in the IP. Although the structure in (13) is grammatical in the adult language, it is not the structure an adult would have used in the situation set up in the experiment. Finally, a few children produced another structure, in (14), where the negation appears in C, but it is also retained in the IP.

NEG/Doubling structure

(14)   *Who doesn't Captain Hook doesn't like?*   Emily(4;2)

All the structures were found both for *yes/no* and *wh*-questions, except for the Non-inversion one, which was absent with *yes/no* questions. Moreover, all the structures were present irrespective of the type of *wh*-operator (object or adjunct) and of the type of auxiliary/modal/*do*.

Guasti *et al.* (1995)'s results show first that children master SAI. Second, they suggest that children have problems in raising the clitic negation to C, along with the auxiliary/modal/*do*. Movement of the negation *n't* to C is parasitic on movement of I-to-C, since *n't* cannot move to C without I, but in principle the two operations are distinct.

In English, the negation *n't* may remain in the IP, as in negative declaratives or, it may raise to C as in negative questions. Guasti *et al.* (1995) propose that children choose the option of leaving the negation in the IP. They will change their default hypothesis, based on positive evidence from the language they are exposed to. The choice to place the negation in the IP is the source of the different structures produced by children (see Thornton 1994 for a discussion of comprehension data about the placement of the negation).[1]

Given the assumptions outlined above, subject extraction questions are expected to be well formed: the inflection and consequently *n't* does not raise to C. The absence of I-to-C is displayed by the lack of *do*-support in positive questions, as seen in (15).

(15)   *$*Who_i$ does t_i eat apples?*

I-to-C cannot apply in subject extraction questions because of the ECP, as proposed by Rizzi (1990). If I raised to C, the subject trace in Spec-IP would not be properly governed, i.e., head-governed by I within I'.[2] Similarly, in negative questions on the subject I cannot raise to C and *a fortiori* the negation *n't* remains in the IP. In this way, the constraint holding in children's grammar is satisfied. Subject questions have the structure in (16).[3]

(16) $[_{CP} \; Who_i \; C_i \; [_{IP} \; t_i \; doesn't_{i/j} \; [_{NEGP} \; t_j \; like \; cheese?]]]$

As for the other structures, the following observations hold. The full form of negation, *not*, must stay in the IP (in the adult language). By choosing it, children sidestep the problem of having to raise the negation to C. Thus, they resort to a structure that is grammatical in the adult language, though not the most appropriate in the context set up in the experiment (see (13)).

To retain the negation *n't* in the IP, I-to-C is relaxed in the non-inversion structure in (11), thus violating the *wh*-criterion.

Finally, in the AUX-doubling questions in (12), the *wh*-criterion is satisfied by raising the Inflection to C. The auxiliary is doubled to leave the negation *n't* in the IP. In the NEG/AUX-doubling (see (14)), the least frequent structure, the negation is raised to C, but it is also found in the IP. This structure is a bridge between the child and the adult grammar.

This study demonstrates the existence of a stage during which English-speaking children leave the negation in the IP.[4] Because of this choice, they produce non-adult negative questions extracting from object and adjunct positions. However, they produce adult subject negative questions, since here, the verb and the negation do not raise to C, in line with Rizzi's analysis. Notice that if one claimed that I-to-C applies to subject questions, this striking contrast between subject and non-subject negative questions could not be captured.[5] From a cross-linguistic perspective, it is worth asking whether children learning other languages, involving raising of the negation to C, go through a similar stage. If they do, one expects to find non-adult negative interrogatives in other early languages as well. If they do not, then the factor responsible for the difference needs to be identified.

4.   Possible Expectations for Early Italian

Both in Italian and in English the subject cannot intervene between the *wh*- and the verb, as in (2a) and (7b). As said in Section 2, Rizzi interprets this adjacency requirement by saying that the verb raises to C in Italian interrogative sentences, as it does in English ones. Since the negation is cliticized on the verb, it is carried over to C, as seen in (17).[6]

(17)   *(Gianni)*, [$_{CP}$ *a chi* [$_C$ *non diede* [$_{IP}$ *il   libro (Gianni)*)]]]?
        Gianni   to whom NEG gave   the book Gianni
        'Who didn't Gianni give the book to?'

Therefore, the structure of an Italian and of an English question is the same, *modulo* the position of the subject. This can either stay in a left peripheral position or at the end of the sentence. If Italian children have difficulties in raising the negation to C, and choose to retain it in the IP, as their English peers do, they should resort to some non-adult structure. We may expect Italian-speaking children to produce the non-inversion structure, which would take the form in (18). The subject intervenes between the *wh*-operator and the verb. This proves that the verb and the negation *non* have not raised to C.

(18)   **Cosa Gianni non prende?*
        what Gianni NEG takes
        'What doesn't Gianni take?'

Notice that in Italian declarative sentences, the subject can stay either in a preverbal position or in a postverbal one, as seen in (19):

(19)   a.   *Gianni telefona.*
                Gianni called
        b.   *Telefona Gianni.*
                called   Gianni
                'It is Gianni that called.'

Thus, one may object that (18) may fail to appear in early Italian production because Italian-speaking children have the option of leaving the subject in the postverbal position. Notice that awareness of this option does not guarantee the absence of structures such as (18). For one thing, in declaratives, the subject may occur in a postverbal position. If the child does not produce (18), it is because she knows that the subject cannot intervene between the *wh*-operator and the verb. In Rizzi's framework, absence of (18) would mean that children raise the verb to C.

    Let us continue and examine other expectations. Italian and English differ with respect to the possibilities of V-movement (see Pollock 1989; Belletti 1990). In English only auxiliaries and modals raise to C, whereas in Italian any verb can move to C. Given these observations, the Italian counterpart of the AUX-doubling structure should take either of the forms in (20). A main non-negated verb is raised to C and a copy of it along with the negation is present in the IP (notice that modals are lexical verbs in Italian).

(20) a. *Cosa prende (Gianni) non prende (Gianni)?
what takes Gianni NEG takes Gianni

b. *Cosa può (Gianni) non può prendere (Gianni)?
what can Gianni NEG can take Gianni

In Italian, *non* may be used as constituent negation with any kind of elements. Possibly, in this case, it is not a clitic (see Cardinaletti & Guasti 1993). Although some caution is necessary, we may regard the constituent negation *non* as the counterpart of English *not*. Under this view, another structure that Italian-speaking children may produce is in (21).

(21) *Cosa prende non Gianni?
what takes NEG Gianni

The verb has raised to C, but negation remains in the IP.

Finally, Italian *yes/no* questions differ from their English counterparts in that I-to-C movement is not required. A *yes/no* question may have the same order, though not the intonation, found in declaratives, as seen in (22).

(22) Gianni non ha scritto?
Gianni NEG has written
'Hasn't Gianni written?'

Given this, in adult *yes/no* questions the negation stays inside the IP. Therefore, whether or not Italian-speaking children start off with the hypothesis that the negation must remain in the IP, *yes/no* questions should be adult in form. Therefore, the relevant area of investigation is *wh*-questions.

5. The Study of Italian Interrogative Sentences

5.1. *Experiment*

In this experiment children's production of positive and negative questions was assessed by using the elicited production task (see Crain 1991; Thornton 1990). The experiment on early Italian is a repetition of the experiment carried out by Guasti *et al.* (1995) for English. Except for a few adjustments, the same procedure and the same stimuli were used. With respect to the Guasti *et al.* study, the present research required elicitation of fewer sentences. Guasti *et al.*

(1995) evoked questions containing different auxiliaries and modals the only verbs that raise to C in English. This was necessary to check whether the failure to raise the negation to C holds for all of these verbs. Fewer controls were necessary for Italian, since auxiliaries and lexical verbs behave in the same way with respect to raising. They all raise to C. Therefore, the target questions contained a variety of verbs.

5.2. Subjects

Eleven children between 3;1 and 4;8 participated in the study. The children were all monolingual speakers of Italian from mixed socioeconomic backgrounds. They were all enrolled at the public preschool in Casalmaggiore, Cremona, Italy.

5.3. Procedure

The children were tested individually and the sessions were audiotaped for transcription. The target questions were elicited in two sessions for five children and in one session for the remaining six. Each session lasted about thirty minutes; with enthusiastic children, they lasted longer. Data were collected over a period of one month. Negative and positive yes/no and wh-questions were elicited. Questions produced spontaneously were also included in the sample.

5.4. Elicitation Task

A single experimenter took part in the elicitation experiment. She played two roles: that of a snail puppet that was too shy to talk to 'grown-ups' and only talked to children and that of a 'grown-up' who wanted to talk to the snail, but who could not. Therefore, she invited the child to ask questions to the snail. These queries were either about the snail itself or about stories that were staged with toys by the experimenter.

5.5. Experimental Stimuli

As in the experiment on English, I elicited wh- and yes/no questions. I included yes/no questions for the sake of comparison, although I did not expect to find non-adult structures, for the reasons discussed above. The extraction site in wh-questions varied from subject, to object, to adjunct. I employed lexical verbs and auxiliaries. Recall that in Italian, auxiliaries and lexical verbs all move in the same way.

The experimenter staged an event using props and toys in front of the child and the snail. For example the object extraction in (23) was accompanied by a story in which a boy (Paolo) was preparing things to go on vacation. He took several things (clothes, a dish, a spoon), but there was one thing he could not fit into his bag. At the end of the story, the experimenter asked the child to ask the snail puppet a question about the story. Lead-ins were useful to evoke the targeted structure. They were formed by two sentences. In the first part of the lead-in, the subject of the targeted (non-subject) question was overt either as a full NP or a pronoun. In the second one, only the *wh*-word was mentioned. The protocols used are in (23) through (26).

(23)   Protocol for object extraction

Experimenter: *C'è qualcosa che Paolo non prende. Domanda alla lumaca cosa.*
'There is something that Paolo doesn't take. Ask the snail what.'

Target: *(Paolo) (che) cosa non prende (Paolo)?*
Paolo   che what NEG takes   Paolo
'What doesn't Paolo take?'

(24)   Protocol for adjunct extraction

Experimenter: *C'è un posto dove il bambino non può andare. Domanda alla lumaca dove.*
'There is a place where the child can't go. Ask the snail where.'

Target: *(Il bambino), dove non può andare (il bambino)?*
the child   where NEG can go   the child
'Where can't the child go?'

(25)   Protocol for subject extraction

Experimenter: *Qualcuno non vuole aiutare la mamma. Domanda alla lumaca chi.*
'Someone doesn't want to help the mother. Ask the snail who.'

Target: *Chi non vuole aiutare la mamma?*
who NEG wants help   the mummy
'Who doesn't want to help the mummy?'

(26)   Protocol for *yes/no* question
Experimenter: *Tu pensi che a lei non piaccia il gelato? Magari sta scherzando.*
              Prova a chiederle se non le piace.
              'Do you think that she doesn't like the ice-cream. Maybe she is
              joking. Try to ask her if she doesn't like it.'
Target: *Non ti   piace (il   gelato)?*
              NEG to.you likes   the ice-cream
              'Don't you like the ice-cream?'

Since Italian is a null-subject language, it is generally possible to omit the
subject, which is placed in parentheses in the target questions above.

The stories used to evoke negative questions were useful to elicit positive
questions, as well. After the child had asked the targeted negative question, the
experimenter invited the child to ask the snail a positive question. For example
in the case of (23), the experimenter let the child remark that there were things
that Paolo took. Then, she invited the child to ask the snail what. In this way,
positive questions were also collected as controls.

5.6. Data

I first present the data across the group of children and then I turn briefly
to individual data. The main finding of the experiment on Italian is that children
produced adult negative questions, in addition to adult positive ones. For
questions extracting from object or adjunct position, four structures were found,
all legitimate in the adult language.

(27) a.   *che cosa compa?*   Dante(3;11)
           what   buys
           'What does he buy?'

      b.   *quando taja l'albero?*   Lia(3;11)
           when   cuts the tree
           'When does he cut the tree?'

      c.   *dove non può mangiare l'arancia?*   Clara(4;7)
           where NEG can eat   the orange?
           'Where can't he eat the orange?

      d.   *quando non dormi?*   Lia(3;11)
           when   NEG sleep
           'When don't you sleep?'

(28) a. *cosa può fare il   cowboy?*   Adriano(3;1)
        what can do   the cowboy
        'What can the cowboy do?'

     b. *cosa sei tu?*   Aurelio(4;2)
        what are you

     c. *cosa non ta [sa] fare il   bambino?*   Dante(3;11)
        what NEG can   do   the child?
        'What can't the child do?'

     d. *perchè non vuole andare a scuola la bambina?* Davide(4;7)
        why   NEG want go   to school the girl
        'Why doesn't the girl want to go to school?'

(29) a. *e   la pera, dov'è?*   Aurelio(4;2)
        and the pear where is
        'Where is the pear?'

     b. *e   lui, cosa fa   là   da solo?*   Adriano(3;1)
        and he   what makes there alone
        'And he, what does (he) make there alone?'

     c. *Luigino, dove non può andare?*   Davide(4;7)
        Luigino where NEG can go
        'Where can't Luigino go?'

(30) a. *Che cos'è che   prende?*   Miriam(4;4)
        what   is that (he) takes

     b. *Dov' è che non può andare?*   Miriam(4;4)
        where is that NEG can go

     c. *Che cos'è, lumaca, che non ha preso?* Davide(4;7)
        what   is snail   that NEG has taken

     d. *Cos' è che non prende il   bambino?*   Aurelio(4;2)
        what is that NEG takes   the child

Since Italian is a null-subject language, a common form of question was with a null subject, as in (27). When the subject was expressed, it was placed either in sentence-final position as in (28) or in a left dislocated position, preceding the *wh*-operator (29). Finally, children produced questions, which have the structure of a cleft, in (30). Poletto (1993) observes that in standard Italian the cleft structure is limited to certain pragmatic contexts (e.g., when the interrogation is on a well-known set of objects or in echo contexts). As she acknowledges, in the Northern variety of Italian, which was the variant investigated, the cleft structure does not require any particular presupposition and is commonly used in spoken language. All the four structures were found with positive and also with negative questions.

In Table 1, I summarize the numbers and percentages of positive and negative *wh*-non-subject questions produced by the group of the eleven children. The first column includes questions with a preverbal subject, the second questions with left-dislocated subjects, the third with subjects at the end of the sentence; the fourth column includes null-subject questions, the fifth cleft structures and the last one includes structures that were not classified.[7]

Table 1. Numbers and Percentages of Negative Questions by Question Types

	structures*										
	wh S V		S *wh* V		*wh* V S		null S		cleft		other	
positive Q	0		3	3%	13	15%	67	77%	3	3%	0	
negative Q	3	2%	3	2%	19	16%	73	64%	13	11%	2	1%

* Subject questions are not included; subjects = 11.

As is apparent from Table 1, children did not produce any non-adult structures. The verb/doubling is never attested. As for the non-inversion structure some remarks are in order. To establish whether children produce non-inversion structures or not, we have to look only at questions where the subject is lexical. Null-subject questions are irrelevant, since one cannot see where the verb is with respect to a null subject. For the question at issue, only the first three columns are relevant. If we confine our attention to these three columns, we can conclude that children do not produce non-inversion structures. A comparison between the first and the other two columns shows that children do not place the subject between the *wh*-operator and the verb. If children did not raise the verb to C, we should have found questions with the subject appearing between the *wh*-operator and the verb. But this did not happen. In the framework of Rizzi's analysis, we may interpret these data by saying that Italian-speaking children do indeed raise the verb and the negation to C. The two examples in the first column with the order *wh*-S-V are not problematic. They are *perchè*-questions '*why*-questions'. Interestingly, with *perchè,* inversion is optional even in adult Italian. Thus, these examples are not errors.[8,9]

(31) a. *lumaca, perchè la bambina non è andata a scuola?*
          snail   why   the girl   NEG is gone   to school
          'Snail, why didn't the girl go to school?'   Davide(4;7)

b. *perchè la signora non può bere il caffè senza zucchero?*
     why   the madame NEG can drink the coffee without sugar
     Why can't the madame drink the coffee without sugar?'
                                                                    Arianna(4;5)

Tables 2 and 3 report individual data for positive and negative questions, respectively.

Table 2. Individual Children Positive Answers

		structures*				
child	age	wh S V	S wh V	wh V S	null S	cleft
Dante	3;11				6	
Lia	3;11				8	
Ascanio	4;8			2	5	
Omero	4;6			1	5	
Aurelio	4;2		1	8	11	
Adriano	3;1		1	2	14	
Valeria	3;9				2	1
Arianna	4;5				4	
Clara	4;7				2	
Miriam	4;4				4	2
Davide	4;7		1		6	

* Subject questions are not included.

Of the eleven children, two Lia and Miriam produced only null-subject questions. The other children formed questions with an overt subject and this was correctly placed. Two children expressed the subject in both positive and negative questions, three others only in positive and four others only in negative questions. Thus, for our point, only the production from six of the children is revealing. This clearly proves the absence of any non-adult form of negative questions. Strictly speaking, for the other five children we cannot say for sure that they do not produce non-inverted negative structures, because the sentences they produce were without a subject. However, in spite of these limitations, it seems reasonable to conclude that in early Italian there is no stage during which children retain negation in the IP and fail to raise it to C, along with the verb. If this were the case, we should find non-inversion structures, contrary to the

Table 3. Individual Children Negative Answers

		structures*				
child	age	*wh* S V	S *wh* V	*wh* V S	null S	cleft
Dante	3;11			1	12	
Lia	3;11				5	
Ascanio	4;8				8	1
Omero	4;6			7	5	1
Aurelio	4;2				11	2
Adriano	3;1				5	
Valeria	3;9			1	11	1
Arianna	4;5	1		8	1	
Clara	4;7	1			9	
Miriam	4;4				2	5
Davide	4;7	1	3	2	4	3

* Subject questions are not included.

facts. The same conclusion is supported by the absence of doubling structures of the type in (20) and of structures such as (21).

For the sake of completeness, I should point out that subject extraction questions and *yes/no* questions were all grammatical, as expected. Subject questions took two forms. Either the one with the *wh*-operator next to the verb, as in (32a, b) or a cleft structure, as in (32c, d):

(32) a. *chi te   l' ha regalato?*   Aurelio(4;2)
        who to.you it has given
        'Who gave it to you?'

     b. *chi non può andare in   barca?*   Valeria(3;9)
        who NEG can go   into (the) ship
        'Who can't go into the ship?'

     c. *chi è che aiuta la mamma?*   Adriano(3;1)
        who is that helps the mummy

     d. *chi è che non va   sull'altalena?*   Miriam(4;4)
        who is that NEG goes on the see-saw

Yes/no questions occurred in three forms: with a null subject, with a preverbal subject or with a postverbal subject, as shown in (33). All three structures are grammatical in adult Italian.

(33) a. *viene in su quello là?*   Aurelio(4;2)
comes up the one   there
'Does the one there come up?'

b. *quette non gli piacciono?*   Dante(3;11)
these NEG to.him like?
'Doesn't he like these?'

These results show that Italian-speaking children's negative questions are adult-like and consequently that Italian-speaking children do not choose to retain negation in the IP.

6. Discussion

In contrast to their English-speaking peers, Italian-speaking children form adult negative interrogatives. According to Rizzi's theoretical framework, these data reveal that Italian-speaking children can raise the negation outside the IP. In other words, they can raise negation along with the verb to C. In this respect, they seem to behave differently from their English peers. Given this, acquisition data suggest that some difference must exist between the two languages in as far as the raising of the negation to C is concerned. I call this THE HEAD-RAISING ACCOUNT. Alternatively, one may reject the analysis of Italian questions I have assumed so far. Then, one can interpret the English and Italian data by arguing that Italian questions are not CPs, as English ones, but just IPs. Thus, neither I-to-C movement nor movement of the negation to C ever take place in Italian questions. According to this account, Italian-speaking children retain negation in the IP, as adults do, because this is the only choice allowed by the grammar of Italian questions. I call this THE STRUCTURAL ACCOUNT. In the following sections, I discuss these two accounts.

6.1. *The Structural Account*

I start by evaluating the second hypothesis from the perspective of theoretical linguistics. I first spell out the proposal according to which Italian questions are IPs. Second, I discuss how this analysis could accommodate the acquisition data. Finally, I argue that in spite of its simplicity the IP-analysis cannot be endorsed.

As pointed out in Section 1, English SAI occurs in main questions, but not in embedded questions. Given this main/embedded asymmetry, SAI has been regarded as a form of residual verb-second, involving I-to-C. Since Italian (and Romance) does not have a clear-cut asymmetry, the hypothesis that I-to-C occurs in this language may be questionable. Such an observation has been the basis for claiming that Romance questions do not feature I-to-C movement and that they do not have the same structure as their English counterparts. Solá (1992) and Bonet (1989) have proposed for Catalan (and for other Romance languages) that questions are IPs. The *wh*-operator lands in Spec-IP and the verb carrying the *wh*-feature remains in I, as in (34).

(34)   [$_{IP}$ *Cosa* [$_I$ *ha fatto Gianni*]]?
          what   has done Gianni
          'What has Gianni done?'

Since the *wh*-operator is in Spec-IP, the subject cannot appear there, thus explaining the adjacency between the *wh*-operator and the verb. The configuration in (34) satisfies the *wh*-criterion. The *wh*-operator is in a Spec–head relation with the main inflection carrying the *wh*-feature and *vice versa*.

This analysis offers a framework to accommodate the results from early Italian and to reconcile them with the outcome from early English. Since questions are IPs, the clitic negation *non* can only remain inside the IP, as in (35). In this respect, Italian and English-speaking children make the same choice: they retain the negation in the IP. Only in Italian is this choice legitimate in the adult grammar, however.

(35)   [$_{IP}$ *Cosa non ha fatto Gianni?*]
          what NEG has done Gianni
          'What hasn't Gianni done?'

The differing performance of Italian-speaking children with respect to their American peers is a consequence of the different structure of questions in the two languages. In other words, the option of retaining the negation inside the IP is the adult option. By choosing it, Italian-speaking children do what is required in their target language. On the contrary, the same choice made by English-speaking children is responsible for the formation of non-adult structures. To recall, in English, questions are CPs and require raising of I plus the negation to C.

Although this account is very simple and attractive, it faces several theoretical problems that lead me to reject it. In particular, the IP-analysis of Italian questions entails a view of the null subject *pro* not supported by the empirical evidence.

The idea that questions are IPs and that Spec-IP is filled with a *wh*-operator entails that a null subject must be located in the postverbal position as a lexical subject (see (36)).

(36)   *Cosa ha fatto* pro/ *Gianni?*
         what has done they Gianni

Empirical evidence discussed by Rizzi (1987) shows that *pro* has the same distribution as preverbal subjects and not as postverbal subjects (see Solà for potential counterevidence and Guasti's, in press, criticism of it). In other words, *pro* is in a preverbal subject position. For example, a null subject patterns with a preverbal and not with a postverbal subject if we consider the distribution of floating quantifiers. The relevant paradigm is given in (37).

(37) a.   *Tutti i soldati sono   andati via.*
      b.   *I soldati   sono tutti andati via.*
      c.   *Sono   andati via tutti i soldati.*
      d. *   *Sono tutti andati via   i soldati.*
      e.   *Sono tutti andati via.*
      '(All) the soldiers are (all) gone away (all) the soldiers.'

In (37b), the preverbal subject has stranded the floating quantifier *tutti* 'all' in a lower position. The ungrammaticality of (37d) indicates that a postverbal subject cannot strand a floating quantifier. If *pro* could occupy the postverbal position, (37e) should be unacceptable as (37d) is, contrary to facts. Thus, a null subject must occur in a preverbal position, that is (37e) is the null subject version of (37b).

Additional evidence is discussed by Cardinaletti (1994) and Guasti (in press). Cardinaletti notes that in copular constructions (see Moro, in press) a null subject cannot stay in the postverbal position, whereas an overt subject can. Consider the following examples.

(38) a.   *Io sono il   dottore.*
            I am   the physician
      b.   *Il dottore sono io.*
            the physician am   I

In (38a), the subject occurs in the preverbal position, whereas in (38b), it occupies the postverbal position and the predicate *il dottore* (the physician) is in a preverbal position. If we omit the subject in (38a), we obtain the grammatical sentence in (39a). On the contrary, we cannot omit the postverbal subject in (38b), as the ungrammatical sentence in (39b) shows. A lexical subject can stay in the postverbal position, but a null one cannot: it must raise to a preverbal position.

(39) a.   pro *sono il   dottore*
            am   the physician
      b. **il dottore sono* pro

In summary, the facts discussed show that a null subject cannot stay in the postverbal position, but only in SpecIP. In turn, this implies that Italian questions cannot be IPs.[10] This conclusion entails that the accurate performance of Italian-speaking children cannot be attributed to the fact that the structure of Italian questions does not need movement of the negation to C. The alternative analysis of questions that I have assumed, the one of Rizzi, maintains that in Italian as in English, the clitic negation has to raise along with the verb to C. In this framework, we may attribute the different performance of Italian and of English-speaking children to some intrinsic difference between the two languages as far as movement of the negation and of the verb to C are concerned.

6.2. The Head-Movement Account

I attribute the crosslinguistic differences in children's production to the existence in English of a special class of auxiliaries and consequently to the different scope of verb movement in Italian and English. In the latter language, only auxiliaries and modals raise, whereas in the former all verbs raise as shown by Belletti (1990) and there is no distinctive class of auxiliaries or modals. Auxiliaries and modals are of category I. Thus, in English interrogatives, an element of the category I moves to C, whereas in Italian it is an element of category V that raises to C. This entails that C in Italian must be compatible with the category V, whereas it need not in English. Let us then suppose that C must have some V(erbal)-features in order to be able to host the verb. To pursue this analysis, I elaborate on Rizzi (1992) and propose that the functional categories C and I are the result of a combination of features, as is assumed for lexical categories. These specifications do not replace those proposed by Rizzi (1992), but they add to them. I suggest that I is specified for the features $\langle +I, +V \rangle$, in English and in Italian. It will be $\langle +V \rangle$ since it contains features related to the verb. The node C will be $\langle +V \rangle$ and $\langle +I \rangle$, if it can host an inflected verb, $\langle +I \rangle$ and not specified for $\langle V \rangle$, if it can host only elements of categories I. In English, C is $\langle +I, V \rangle$ since it cannot host a verb; in Italian, C is $\langle +I, +V \rangle$ since it hosts an inflected verb.

Let us now see how these hypotheses can account for the acquisition of interrogatives in English and Italian. What children have to decide is whether or not negation must stay in the projection containing V-related features. Their initial decision is that negation must stay in the projection containing V-related features. In English, this projection is the IP since only I is specified $\langle +V \rangle$. Therefore, English-speaking children will not have problems with negative declarative sentences, since negation stays in the IP. However, they will have trouble with negative questions. The *wh*-criterion requires movement of I to C. Thus, the clitic negation attached to I will have to move to C. This requirement conflicts with children's initial choice to· place negation inside the projection containing V-related features. English-speaking children solve this conflict by retaining the negation inside the IP, as claimed by Guasti *et al.* (1995). This decision about the placement of the negation will lead them to produce the non-adult structures illustrated in Guasti *et al.*' (1995) study.

Suppose now that Italian-speaking children, as their English peers, also decide that negation must stay in the projection containing V-related features. As in English, IP contains V-related features. But CP also contains V-related features, since, contrary to English, C has the feature ⟨+V⟩. Under appropriate conditions, C attracts an element of category V, in Italian. Thus, Italian-speaking children do not have to face any conflict. They raise the verb to C, because they have to satisfy the *wh*-criterion. Since CP contains V-related features, the negation cliticized on the verb also raises to C. In this way, they comply with the constraint that the negation be retained inside the projection containing V-related features. In addition, they conform with the requirements of their target grammar. In other words, the *wh*-criterion, on the one hand, and the fact that CP contains V-related features, on the other, allow Italian-speaking children to produce grammatical interrogatives. By contrast, English-speaking children only raise the auxiliary or modal to C, in agreement with the *wh*-criterion. Negation must stay in the IP, because only this projection contains V-related features.

Under the view proposed here, the different performance of Italian and English-speaking children is a consequence of the different specification of the CP-node in the two languages and ultimately of the movement properties of verbal elements: whereas all verbs move in Italian only auxiliaries and modals do in English.

7. Conclusions

Italian-speaking children produce negative interrogatives that are adult in form. This result contrasts with Guasti *et al.*'s (1995) findings about the acquisition of English negative interrogatives. Guasti *et al.* (1995) showed that there is a stage during which English-speaking children's positive questions are adult-like, but their negative questions are not. Elaborating on Guasti *et al.* (1995)'s proposal, I have argued that the asymmetry between the two sets of data depends on the different scope of V-movement in the two languages. Whereas in Italian all verbs raise to C, in English only auxiliaries and modals, i.e., elements of category I, move to C. My proposal is that Italian-speaking children do indeed choose to place the negation inside the V-related projection, but this projection is the CP in Italian and the IP in English.

Appendix A

For Romance questions, we may envisage a third alternative analysis of questions that represents a compromise between the IP-analysis and the CP-analysis. Suppose, as a reviewer has suggested, that questions in Romance are CPs as in English, but that I-to-C does not occur in the former set of languages, at least overtly, while it does in the latter one (see Suñer 1994; Guasti, in press, for a discussion of this view). Thus, the structure of an Italian question is:

(A1) $[_{CP}$ *Cosa* C $[_{IP}$ *mangia Gianni*]]?
         'What does Gianni eat?'

This proposal needs to be qualified further. We need to explain how the *wh*-criterion is satisfied and why the subject cannot intervene between the *wh*-operator and the verb, as in (A2):

(A2)   **Cosa Gianni mangia?*
         what Gianni eats

In other words, we have to find an analysis of all the facts discussed in Section 2 which follow from Rizzi's account in terms of movement of I-to-C. For the purposes of this article, suppose that this analysis is correct and let us see how it copes with the acquisition data presented. Notice that the merits of my observations can only be evaluated with respect to a developed version of this CP without I-to-C analysis.

If Italian-speaking children do not have to raise the verb and consequently the negation to C, probably they will not have the problems faced by their English peers. They would not produce the doubling structure in (20) *cosa prende non prende Gianni?* [what takes NEG takes Gianni]) which arises as a consequence of the movement of a non-negated verb to C. The same observation may be extended to the counterpart of the structure in (21) *cosa mangia non Gianni?* [what eats NEG Gianni]. However, to explain the fact that Italian-speaking children do not produce the non-inversion structure, in (18) *cosa*

Gianni non prende? [what Gianni NEG takes] we need to make some additional assumptions concerning the placement of the subject. As I said in the main text (Section 4), we cannot simply appeal to the fact that in Italian the subject can be in the postverbal position, because this is just an option. To solve this dilemma one may elaborate on Bobaljik's (1994) idea that the *wh*-element and the verb need to be adjacent in order to satisfy the *wh*-criterion, as a reviewer has suggested. Adjacency may be obtained by placing the subject in the postverbal position. However, one may want to reduce this adjacency requirement to some more primitive property, as Rizzi has done. Another possibility is to pursue the idea that there is some incompatibility between the activation of *wh*-features on the main inflection and the preverbal subject (see Guasti, in press). For the moment, I leave these issues open, but notice that this point is crucial for the whole approach to be attractive.

If this new analysis of Romance interrogatives is viable, then one difference between early English and early Italian may lie in the occurrence versus non-occurrence of the I-to-C movement. Although this third line of investigation may be promising, it is evident that it requires a careful examination, which is outside the topic of this article.

Appendix B

Natural production data from children younger than those tested in the present study reveal that Italian-speaking children never place the subject between the *wh*-element and the verb, producing ungrammatical structures such as those in (B1):

(B1)   *cosa Gianni mangia?*
          what Gianni eats

I examined the Italian data available through the CHILDES database (MacWhinney & Snow 1985) and contributed by Cipriani *et al.* (1992) #4698 from the Istituto Stella Maris of Calambrone, Pisa. I used the Combo utility (MacWhinney & Snow 1985) to search the transcripts from three monolingual Italian-speaking children (Martina 1;8 to 2;7), Diana (1;10 to 2;6) and Guglielmo (2;2 to 2;11) and cull all the lines containing an interrogation mark. As a group, the three children produced 171 spontaneous questions. Of this number, 67 had an overt subject that was either placed at the end of the question or in a left-dislocated position. Just 3 examples had the order *wh*–S–V and all these were examples headed by the *wh*-operator *perchè* 'why'. As I said earlier, just in the case of *perchè*, the order *wh*–S–V is legitimate in the adult grammar. These results are interesting because they contrast with what we know about the acquisition of English interrogatives. Bellugi (1971) claimed that the acquisition of English questions proceeds in a piecemeal fashion, with an initial failure to invert. Thus, in early English production we find sentences such as (B2).

(B2)   *what you eat?*

The data on early Italian interrogatives present a very different scenario. Given the framework adopted here, early Italian data suggest that I-to-C is in place from the beginning of children's relevant productions. Although it is beyond the scope of this paper to deal with this asymmetry between early Italian and early English, nevertheless I would like to offer some speculative remarks on the topic. This discrepancy may be a consequence of the different scope of verb movement in the two languages. In a language where all verbs raise (to I and furthermore to C) there is no question of what element to move. Once verb movement is in place, children apply it whenever it is needed (to satisfy some specific constraints, e.g., to check V-features or *wh*-features). This proposal predicts that Italian-speaking children not only produce adult questions from the very beginning, but that they have mastery of verb movement in declarative sentences. This prediction is indeed borne out. Guasti (1993/1994) argues that Italian-speaking children have knowledge of verb movement from the onset. Thus, it is not surprising that they use the same knowledge in questions.

English differs from Italian in that the property of verb movement cuts across two classes of items: auxiliaries move, whereas main verbs do not. Children have to figure out which items belong to the former set and which to the latter one and this may cause them problems. They may have to learn auxiliaries on an item by item basis. When English-speaking children do not know auxiliaries, they may produce sentences such as (B3). It may be that the source for children's non-inversion questions is the syntax of *do*-support (as suggested in Stromswold 1990). *Do* does not have any semantic content and its role consists in supporting inflectional features, under certain circumstances. Children may initially conjecture that their language does not have *do*. If so, they are expected to form questions of type (B3) where the inflection (-*s*) is attached to the verb, rather than to *do* (which is absent from children's grammar).

(B3)   *What John eats?*

At the moment, I am unable to test these predictions and leave the issue for future research.

Acknowledgements

Many thanks to the director of the public preschool in Casalmaggiore (Cremona, Italy) where the data were gathered. I am also indebted to the teachers and to the children who took part in the experiments. This study was planned at the Scuola Internazionale di Studi Avanzati in Trieste in July 1993 during the Trieste Encounters in Cognitive Science (TECSA) organized by Luigi Rizzi and Ken Wexler. I am grateful to the organizers and the audience of this summer school. This research has been partially founded by the Pôle-Rhone Alpes for Cognitive Sciences. A different version of this article was presented at the post-Glow Workshop on Language Acquisition in Vienna (April, 1994). I am grateful to the organizers and the audience of this event and especially to Anna Cardinaletti. Thanks go to Liliane Haegeman for comments on an earlier version of this paper, to Luigi Rizzi, Rosalind Thornton, Giorgio Graffi for discussing these issues with me and to two anonymous reviewers.

Notes

1. The asymmetry found in early English between positive and negative questions exists in the grammar of an adult language, Paduan, a 'dialect' spoken in Northern Italy, discussed by Poletto (1993). In positive questions, we have inversion between the clitic subject and the verb and this is an indication that the verb has moved to C (all the examples are from Poletto 1993:245):

   (i)   *Quando zelo vegnuo?*
           when   is.he come
           'When has he come?'

   Inversion is not possible in negative questions, that is we cannot move the verb to C in this context, as seen in (ii). Lack of inversion does not solve the problem, however, as (iii) illustrates.

   (ii)   **Cosa no galo fato?*
           what NEG has.he done

   (iii)   **Cosa nol   ga fato?*
           what NEG.he has done

   Negative questions in Paduan are expressed by a cleft structure. We may notice that this structure is similar to the early English AUX-doubling structure.

   (iv)   *Cosa ze che nol   ga fato?*
           what is that NEG.he has done

2. Rizzi (1990) proposes that AGR is autonomously selected in C. Thus, C becomes a proper governor for the subject trace.

3. Since I does not raise to C, the question arises as to how the *wh*-criterion is satisfied. Rizzi proposes that the *wh*-criterion is satisfied by the representational chain that includes the *wh*-operator, its trace in subject position and the two heads, C and I. Each head is coindexed with its specifier, that is the *wh*-operator and the subject trace, respectively. The *wh*-operator and its trace are also co-indexed. As a result all the four elements of the chain have the same index and this guarantees the fulfillment of the *wh*-criterion.

4. This choice to retain negation in the IP may be related to Progovac 's (1993) claim that negation within the IP differs substantially from negation within the CP.

5. A reviewer suggests that the *wh*-feature might be always generated in C. Under this view, one may say that I-to-C movement is triggered to support the *wh*-feature. Although interesting, this hint has some drawbacks. First, it cannot make a distinction between subject and non-subject questions: I-to-C is always required. But this does not seem to be correct. Second, as far as I can see, it cannot express the main/subordinate distinction with respect to I-to-C movement.

6. The clitic status of the negation *non* is discussed in Belletti (1990) and in Cardinaletti & Guasti (1993). This status may be observed in the Italian stylistically marked AUX-to-COMP construction (Rizzi 1982). These structures involve movement of a nonfinite or subjunctive auxiliary to C. When negation is present negation moves with the verb to C, as clitic pronouns do.

   (i)   [$_{CP}$ *Non l'avesse* [$_{IP}$ *Gianni mangiata*]], *sarebbe   stato meglio*
          NEG it had   Gianni eaten   (it) would.have been better
          'If he hadn't eaten it, it would have been better.'

7. The two questions under the column 'other' are an *in-situ* question and a question where the subject is placed between the modal and the infinitive. Both questions are unacceptable in Italian. Notice that (i) was produced after some hesitation. Since there are just two examples, the phenomenon does not appear relevant.

   (i)   *quell'uomo lí,   cos'è,   non sa   fare che cosa?*   Davide(4;7)
          that man   there what is   NEG can do   what
          'That man there, what is, (he) can't do what?'

   (ii)   *dove   non puó questo pupazzo sedersi?*   Arianna(4;5)
          where NEG can this   puppet sit.down
          'Where can't this puppet sit down?'

8. By looking at Table 1, one may observe that the non-inversion structure is not found with positive questions. The reason is that in the sample of questions collected, there is just one positive question with *perchè*. Thus, this lack is simply due to the absence of occasions for producing *perchè*-positive questions.

9. The result of this production experiment are at odds with Schaeffer's (1993) comprehension findings about Italian questions. Example (i) is a question on the subject as shown by the English translation in (iii). Schaeffer found that Italian children interpret (i) as a question on the object and not on the subject, contrary to adults. In other

words, for children (i) corresponds to the English translation in (ii) and not to that in
(iii).

(i) *Che bambini hanno suonato?*
     what children have played
(ii) *What have children played?*
(iii) *Which children have played?*

This view entails that they analyze *che* in (i) as the object and *bambini* 'children' as
the subject of the sentence. According to this result, children's grammar allows a
subject to intervene between the *wh*-operator and the verb. Production data strongly
support the opposite view, since children never put the subject between the *wh*-operator
and the verb. It would be very interesting to test whether the same set of children
perform as Schaeffer describes in her comprehension task and as I describe in the
production task. If so, the issue should be raised as to the source of this mismatch. I
leave this issue open for future research.

10. In the CP structure *pro* is located in the preverbal subject position, Spec-IP. In Section
     1, I said that a lexical NP subject cannot stay in Spec-IP, because the verb in C cannot
     assign Case under government to an element in this position. Since *pro* requires Case,
     one may wonder how it can receive such case in Spec-IP. I assume that *pro*, unlike a
     NP, is made visible by incorporating with the verb in C, something which happens also
     in French complex inversion, according to Rizzi & Roberts (1989) (see Friedemann
     1990).

References

Belletti, A. 1990. *Generalized Verb Movement*. Turin: Rosenberg & Sellier.

Bellugi, U. 1971. "Simplification in Children's Language." *Language Acquisition: Models and methods*, ed. by R. Huxley and E. Ingram. New York: Academic Press.

Bobaljik, J. 1994. "What does adjacency do?" Ms., Massachusetts Institute of Technology, Cambridge.

Bonet, E. 1989. "Subjects in Catalan." Ms., Massachusetts Institute of Technology, Cambridge.

Cardinaletti, A. 1994. Subject position. *GenGenP* 2(1).

Cardinaletti A. & M. T. Guasti. 1993. "Negation in Small Clauses." *Probus* 5.39-61.

Cipriani, P., A.-M. Chilosi, P. Bottari & L. Pfanner. 1992. *L'acquisizione della morfosintassi: Fasi e processi*. Padova: Unipress.

Crain, S. 1991. "Language Acquisition in the absence of experience." *Brain and Behavioral Science* 14.597-650.

Friedemann, M.-A. 1990. "Le pronom interrogatif que et le monté du verbe. *Rivista di Grammatica Generative* 15.123–139.

Guasti, M. T. 1993/1994. "Verb Syntax in Italian Child Grammar: Finite and nonfinite verbs." *Language Acquisition* 3.1-40.

———. In press. "The Controversial Status of Romance Questions." *Probus.*

Guasti, M. T., R. Thornton & K. Wexler. 1995 "Negation in Children's Questions: The case of English." Proceedings of the 19th Boston Conference on Language Acquisition and Language Development, ed. by D. MacLaughlin & S. McEwen, 229–239. Somerville: Cascadilla Press.

Haegeman, L. 1993. "The Syntax of Negation." *GenGenP* 2.

Kayne, R. 1990. "Notes on English Agreement." *CIEFL Bulletin*, Hyderabad, India.

May, R. 1985. *Logical Form: Its structure and derivation.* Cambridge, Mass.: MIT Press.

MacWhinney, B. & C. Snow. 1985. "The Child Language Data Exchange System." *Journal of Child Language* 12.271-296.

Ouhalla, J. 1990. "Sentential Negation, Relativised Minimality and the Aspectual Status of Auxiliaries." *The Linguistic Review* 7.183-231.

Moro, A. In press. "The Raising of Predicates." Predicative noun phrases and the theory of clause structure. Cambridge: Cambridge University Press.

Pesetsky, D. 1983. "Paths and Categories." Diss., Massachusetts Institute of Technology, Cambridge.

Poletto, C. 1992. "La sintassi del soggetto nei dialetti italiani settentrionali. Diss., University of Padova/Venice.

———. 1993. "Subject Clitic/Verb Inversion in North Eastern Italian Dialects." *The Dialects of Italian*, ed. by A. Belletti, 204–251. Turin: Rosenberg & Sellier.

Pollock, J.-Y. 1989. "Verb Movement, UG and the Structure of IP." *Linguistic Inquiry* 20.265-424.

Progovac, L. 1993. "Negation and COMP." *Rivista di linguistica* 5.329-347.

Rizzi, L. 1982. *Issues in Italian Syntax.* Dordrecht: Foris.

———. 1986. "Null Objects in Italian and the Theory of pro." *Linguistic Inquiry* 17.501-557.

———. 1987. "Three Issues in Romance Dialectology." Paper presented at the GLOW Workshop on Dialectology, Venice.

———. 1990. "Residual Verb Second and the *Wh*-Criterion." *Technical Reports in Formal and Computational Linguistics.* University of Geneva.

———. 1992. "Speculations on Verb Second." *Grammar in Progress*, ed. by J. Mascaró, & M. Nespor, 375–386. Dordrecht: Foris.

Rizzi, L. & Roberts, I. 1989. "Complex Inversion in French." *Probus* 1.1-30.

Schaeffer, J. 1993. "Non-inverted Main Wh-Questions in Italian and English Child Language." Ms., University of California at Los Angeles.

Solà, J. 1992. "Agreement and Subjects." Diss., University of Barcelona.

Suñer, M. 1994. "V-movement and the Licensing of Agreement Wh-Phrases in Spanish." *Natural Language and Linguistic Theory* 12.335–372.

Stromswold, K. 1990. "Learnability and the Acquisition of Auxiliaries. Diss., Massachusetts Institute of Technology, Cambridge.

Thornton, R. 1990. "Adventures in Long-Distance Moving: The acquisition of complex wh-questions. Diss., University of Connecticut, Storrs.

———. 1993. "Children Who Don't Raise the Negative." Paper presented at the LSA, Los Angeles.

———. 1994. "Children's Negative Questions: A production/comprehension asymmetry. To appear in Proceedings of ESCOL.

Zanuttini, R. 1991. "Syntactic Properties of Sentential Negation: A comparative study of Romance languages." Diss., University of Pennsylvania.

Root Infinitives, Clitics and Truncated Structures

Liliane Haegeman
University of Geneva

1. Introduction

1.1. *Root Infinitives in Acquisition*

In the acquisition literature the independent use of infinitival clauses, from now on referred to as root infinitives and illustrated in (1), has received a lot of attention (cf. Radford 1994 for a survey of some of the literature).

(1) a. *voir l'auto papa*   French
         see the car daddy
     b. *Thorstn das hab'm*   German
         Thorsten that have   (Wexler 1992; Rizzi 1994b)

Root infinitives are not excluded in the adult language *per se* but their use and interpretation differs from that in the child grammar (cf. Haegeman, forthcoming a; Wijnen 1994) and their structural properties are different (Haegeman, forthcoming b; Rizzi 1994b, and sections 1.2.1 and 2.4.2).

The root infinitive is used with a relatively high frequency in the child grammar of English (Radford 1990, 1994),[1] Dutch (Haegeman, forthcoming a; Jordens 1990; Krämer 1994; Weverink 1989; Wijnen 1994), German (Boser *et al* 1992) French (Crisma 1992; Friedemann 1992; Pierce 1989) and Swedish (Platzack 1990). In the analyses proposed for the child root infinitive, Tense is usually argued to be deficient in some way, either because it is absent (Rizzi 1994b; Wexler 1991), or because of its specific properties (Sano & Hyams 1994). While analyses converge on singling out the deficiency of Tense as the property that makes root infinitives possible, there is a split in the literature with respect to the structure assigned to root infinitives. Specifically, and simplifying very much, some authors assume that root infinitives are full CPs (Boser *et al.* 1992; Sano & Hyams 1994; Wexler 1992; Wijnen 1994); others propose that the structure of root infinitives is impoverished in that some or all of the functional clausal projections are missing. In seminal work Radford (1990, 1994) proposes that root infinitives are bare VPs, without any functional projections; Platzack (1990), Rizzi (1994b) and Grimshaw (1993) propose analyses in terms of clausal truncation, allowing for some, though not all, clausal functional projections.

1.2. *Truncation*

Rizzi (1994a, b) accounts for the properties of child root infinitives in terms of a full competence hypothesis (cf. Poeppel and Wexler 1993) with maturation of constraints. He assumes that the full set of clausal functional projections are available initially and that their hierarchy (2a) is determined — at least to a large extent — by UG (1994b:378).[2]

(2)   a.   CP > AGR(S)P > NEGP > TP > AGR(O)P > VP

Rizzi proposes that the adult root clause is dominated by CP, as stated in (2b):[3]

(2)   b.   Root ⇒ CP

In order to account for the observed differences between the child grammar and the adult grammar, Rizzi proposes that (2b) is subject to maturation: it is not yet operative in the child grammar, where functional projections can be truncated. This means that children can produce root clauses which are dominated by CP, but that they are free also to produce reduced structures where CP, and possibly other projections, are truncated. Truncation is dependent on the structural hierarchy: if a projection is truncated at a point in the clausal hierarchy, all the dominating projections of the clause are also missing. Child root infinitives are truncated under TP. Rizzi thus maintains the full competence hypothesis while at the same time explaining differences between the adult grammar and the child grammar. For alternatives to the full competence hypothesis I refer the reader to the important discussion in Clahsen *et al.* (this volume) and in Wijnen (1994).

1.2.1. *Maturation of CP as the Root*

1.2.1.1. *Tense Variables.* Rizzi postulates that the Tense variable in nonfinite clauses is a non-overt category and hence subject to the EMPTY CATEGORY PRINCIPLE (ECP) (2c) (cf. Rizzi 1990b).

(2) c. Empty Category Principle

ec ⟨–pronominal⟩ must be chain-connected to an antecedent.

The non-overt Tense variable in embedded infinitives will be chain-connected to a higher Tense as illustrated in Italian (3a). Declarative root infinitives such as Italian (3b) are ungrammatical: they contain a non-overt Tense which cannot be chain-connected to an antecedent.

(3) a. *Penso di giocare al pallone.*

I think to play   football

b. **Giocare al pallone.*

play   football

[(3c)–(3e)] differ form declaratives in that they involve some kind of operator, as is overtly the case for questions and not implausible for the other cases. One possible line of thought could then be that the operators involved may unselectively bind the Tense variable... Rizzi (1994b:375).

[3] c. *Che cosa dire in questi casi?*   [question]

what   to.say in these cases

d. *Io fare questo? Mai!*   [counterfactual]

'Me do that? Never!'

e. *Partire immediatamente!*   [jussive]

'Leave immediately!'

1.2.1.2. *Tense and CP.* One important question is whether Rizzi's axiom (2b) is a primitive of the grammar. One way of deriving the axiom is to relate it to Tense interpretation. Enç (1987) treats "tense as a referential expression denoting intervals (...) treating tenses on a par with nominals allows us to account for certain relations between temporal expressions appealing to general notions of linguistic theory" (1987:638–639). She proposes that Tense must be related to a specifier in order to be interpreted, this specifier being COMP. In matrix sentences COMP denotes speech time. If T^0 can only be interpreted via C^0 then (2b) derives from THE PRINCIPLE OF FULL INTERPRETATION. Guéron & Hoekstra (1992) refine the role of C^0 in T^0-interpretation:

Nous proposons que le Temps [± fini] dépend de la présence d'un opérateur temporel dans le nœud COMP; le Temps de l'événement que la phrase dénote se calcule à partir d'un Temps de référence dans COMP. (1992:70)[4]

Nous proposons que le morphème Temps lié par un opérateur temporel dans COMP fonctionne comme une variable pronominale. (1992:74)[5]

Guéron (1993) relates T^0, situated in the IP-system, to the E-Tense in Reichenbach's (1947) Tense representation; the Tense as associated with C^0 is the R-Tense, the referential time (cf. Hamann 1987).

Suggestive evidence that the verbal T^0 is anchored by C^0 is the observation that the choice of complementizer is determined by the T^0 of the complement. In English, for instance, *that* selects a finite clause, *for* selects an infinitive. Let us assume that T^0 in the IP-system is related to C^0 by virtue of a co-indexation relation. Further evidence for the link between T^0 and C^0 is found in Irish, where the form of the complementizer depends on the past/non-past distinction of the Tense of the clause it introduces (Cottell 1994).

(4) a. *Silim*   *go*   *dtuigeann*   *Brid Gaeilge.*
         think:PRES:1SG COMP:NON-PAST understand:PRES Bridget Irish
         'I think that Bridget understands Irish.'

     b. *Silim*   *gur*   *thuig*   *Brid Gaeilge.*
         think:PRES:1SG COMP:PAST understand:PAST Bridget Irish
         'I think that Bridget understood Irish.'

Rizzi's axiom (2b), which identifies root clauses as CP, follows from the anchoring requirement on T^0: T^0 must be anchored and the relevant anchor is C^0. In the grammatical adult root infinitives Spec-CP hosts the modal or imperative operator. Let us assume that the operator in Spec-CP will co-index with C^0, licensing C^0 and allowing C^0 in turn to identify the infinitival T^0. We have to exclude ungrammatical declarative root infinitives such as (3b) in Italian. Let us assume that a non-overt root infinitival C^0 has to be licensed by a specifier–head relation with an operator (imperative or modal). There being no such operator in a root declarative (3b), C^0 remains unlicensed, hence T^0 cannot be interpreted, and (3b) violates Full Interpretation.

1.2.1.3. CP as a Context Anchor. Let us further explore the intuition that T^0 is anchored to C^0, as postulated by Enç (1987) and Guéron & Hoekstra (1988, 1992). The question arises whether the anchoring C^0–T^0 can be made more precise. One line to pursue is to follow Guéron & Hoekstra (1988, 1992) and also Guéron (1993), who propose that the temporal specification of C^0 corresponds to the Referential Tense, i.e., Reichenbach's point *R*. Reichenbach (1947:288) explicitly connects *R* with the context.

> From a sentence like 'Peter had gone' we see that the time order expressed in the tense does not concern one event, but two events, whose positions are determined with respect to the point of speech. We shall call these time points the point of the event and the point of reference. In the example the point of the event is the time when Peter went;

the point of reference is a time between this point and the point of speech. In an individual sentence like the one given it is not clear which time point is used as the point of reference. *This determination is rather given by the context of speech. In a story, for instance, the series of events recounted determines the point of reference which in this case is in the past, seen from the point of speech, some individual events lying outside this point are then referred, not directly to the point of speech, but to this point of reference determined by the story.* (Reichenbach 1947:288, italics mine)

Following Guéron (1993), I propose that the Tense encoded on C^0 is the R-Tense, C^0 is the point at which a clause is connected to the context (cf. Hamann 1987).

Support for the hypothesis that C^0 is the point of contact between clause and discourse is that the CP layer typically tends to be associated with discourse related elements. For instance, the illocutionary force of an utterance is encoded at the CP level: *wh*-movement is assumed to move a *wh*-phrase to Spec-CP in English, and the inflected verb, carrying the feature [+*wh*] moves to C^0. Following Rizzi (class lectures, 1994) the CP-level also comprises projections whose specifiers host topics and foci, two entities which also have a clear discourse connection, topic being what is 'given' in the context, 'focus' what is contrasted with the context. We propose that C^0 is the anchoring point of the clause in the context. Under this hypothesis, the maturation of (2b), i.e., of the CP-layer as an obligatory part of the root sentence, would be a function of the maturation of the Tense anchoring to C^0 or the more general discourse anchoring of the utterance which replaces the deictic anchoring. A further extension of this idea would be to explore the relation between Reference in the time interpretation with Reference in the DP and relate the maturation of CP to the maturation of Reference in the grammar along the lines suggested in Roeper (1992).

1.2.2. *Truncation in Child Language*

Rizzi (1994b) proposes that child root infinitives are truncated structures, i.e., structures which do not project the full array of categories (2a). To be more precise, root infinitives are (extended) projections of V (Grimshaw 1991) lacking TP and any of the dominating functional projections in (2a). In root infinitives there is no non-overt T^0, hence (2c) is irrelevant for T^0.

If root infinitives are truncated structures, the absence of *wh*-root infinitives follows. Crisma (1992) examines the French Philippe corpus from the CHILDES data base (MacWhinney & Snow 1985). Her findings are summarized in Table (1) below: the file names correspond to the ages of the child in years, months, days. The column labeled 'declaratives' represents the total of declaratives; that labeled *wh*-questions gives the total of *wh*-questions. For each clause type, I also give the breakdown in terms of finite clauses and root infinitives. It is clear that while root infinitives are used as declaratives, they are not used as *wh*-interrogatives in this corpus. See also Weissenborn (1992).

Table 1. Sentence Types: Finite Sentences and Root Infinitives in French. Crisma (1992).

files	declaratives	finite declarative	root infinitive declarative	*wh*-questions	finite *wh*	root infinitive *wh*
2;1.19–2;2.17	491	374	117	35	35	0
2;2.6–2;3.21	511	433	78	79	79	0
2;6.13–2;7.18	611	596	15	199	199	0

If the root infinitives lack AGR(S)P and if subject clitics (or weak pronouns (WP), cf. Starke and Cardinaletti 1993) are licensed by AgrS, the absence of subject clitics in French child root infinitives, signalled by Pierce (1989) and Friedemann (1992), is expected. These findings are confirmed in recent work by Hamann *et al.* (this volume) in a quantitative analysis of natural production data. The study concerns a monolingual subject, acquiring French. Their findings are summarized in Table 2. For a breakdown of their figures see their Table 3.

Table 2. Subject Realization According to Sentence Types (Hamann et al., Table 6)

age	verbal utterances		with clitic subject	with 0 subject	with lexical subject	protosyntactic device	*y a*
total	finite	568	273	153	81	47	14
	root infinitive	73	5	59	3	2	14

Observe that out of 278 subject clitics as many as 273 (98.2%) occur in a finite clause and only five (1.8%) occur in a root infinitive. In Section 4.2 we will see that while subject clitics are absent from French root infinitives object clitics are available.

Rizzi's truncation approach also leads us to expect the absence of negative root infinitives in French: if TP is absent, NEGP, which dominates it according to (2a), will also be absent. Friedemann (1992) finds only six negated root infinitives out of 137 negated sentences in the Philippe and Grégoire corpus, i.e., 4.3%. The rate of negated root infinitives vs negated finite clauses is much lower than that between the non-negated patterns. Finally, the absence of aspectual auxiliaries in root infinitives can be made to follow from the absence of T^0: following Guasti (1993) Rizzi assumes that auxiliaries have to associate with T^0.[6]

1.3. Outline of the Paper

This paper studies the Dutch child root infinitive in terms of Rizzi's truncation approach. I will compare the truncation account with accounts such as that developed by Boser et al. (1992) and a similar analysis by Wijnen (1994), where root infinitives are interpreted as finite clauses with a null auxiliary in C^0. Section 2 introduces aspects of the Dutch clause structure; this section relies extensively on my own work on West-Flemish (Haegeman 1994a). In Section 3 I examine the root infinitive in the Hein data from the CHILDES corpus (MacWhinney & Snow 1985, coders: Wijnen and Boers), a corpus of spontaneous production collected over 10 months. The first recording is at two years and four months, the last at three years and one month.[7] Section 4 turns to the distribution of clitics in child root infinitives in French and in Dutch, and its relevance for the syntax of clitics in general.

2.   The Structure of the West-Germanic SOV languages

2.1. Two Zones for Scrambling (Haegeman 1994a)

In earlier work on West-Flemish I have argued that the domain between C^0 and the finite V contains at least three zones:[8]

(5)   The clausal domain in the West-Germanic SOV languages
        C [Zone 1]   adverb   [Zone 2] *niet* [Zone 3] V_{fin}
           'long scrambling'   object shift   PredP

Zone 1 is the domain of 'long scrambling', a domain between the complementizer and the highest sentential adverb. This domain contains the definite subject, clitic objects and weak pronoun objects, and some scrambled objects. Zone 2 is lower than Zone 1 and corresponds to the domain of OBJECT SHIFT. Zone 2 is the domain in which sentence adverbials and definite DPs are found. Strong pronouns are found in Zone 2, but not clitics or weak pronouns (cf. below for discussion). Zone 3 is the domain between negation and the finite V (Haegeman 1994a).

Given the presence of clitics (and multiple clitics in West-Flemish) in Zone 1, I assume it consists of head-initial functional projections whose heads check specific or presuppositional features in the sense of Bennis (1986). The functional heads are not V-related, V-movement to C^0 can bypass these heads (Haegeman 1994a). It is not clear whether AGR(S)P is one of the projections constituting Zone 1, or whether it is an independent projection dominating these projections or dominated by them. For the discussion of Dutch child root infinitives the three analyses lead to the same conclusions. Zone 2 is composed of the (recursive) V-related AGR(O)P. Zone 3 is upwardly delimited by the negative element *niet* which, based on Haegeman (1995), I take to be in Spec-NEGP. Adopting a traditional SOV point of view for Dutch and West-Flemish syntax (see note 8), Zone 3 corresponds to the VP; in an SVO approach Zone 3 is interpreted as Predicate Phrase (Koster 1994; Zwart 1993a, b).

Definite DP-objects undergo object shift and move at least to Zone 2. Following Vanden Wyngaerd (1989), Zwart (1993a, b) and many others I assume that this kind of scrambling is A-movement to a specifier of AGR(O)P. Definite DPs with a presuppositional feature undergo long scrambling and move to Zone 1. If we assume that object shift moves a DP to Spec-AGR(O)P and if *niet* occupies Spec-NEGP (Haegeman 1995), we are led to conclude that in Dutch AGR(O)P dominates NEGP. I return to this point in Section 2.2.

In work on West-Flemish and Dutch (Haegeman 1993b, 1993c) I distinguish three types of object pronominalization: strong pronouns, i.e., *mij* 'me', *jou* 'you', *hem* 'him', *haar* 'her', *ons* 'us', *jullie* 'you', *hun* 'them' and *hen* 'them, weak pronouns, i.e., the reduced forms of the strong pronouns: *me* 'me', *je* 'you', *'m* 'him', *'r* 'her', *ons* 'us', *jullie* 'you' and the clitics *ze* 'them', *'t* 'it' (cf. also Cardinaletti & Starke 1993). What is crucial for the present study is that both clitics and weak pronouns first scramble to Zone 2, then they both move to Zone 1. Weak pronouns occupy the specifier of a functional projection. Object clitics also move to the specifier of a functional projection in Zone 1, where their head is extracted and cliticizes to a functional head. The contrast between clitic objects (i.e., heads) and weak pronouns (maximal projections) will often not be relevant.

In (6a) *Maria* and *t* are in Zone 1; in (6b) *Maria* and *dat boek* are in Zone 1, in (6c) *Maria* and *dat boek* remain in Zone 2; in (6d) *aan Maria* is in Zone 3.

(6)　a.　*dat Jan 't Maria gisteren　niet gegeven heeft.*
　　　　 that Jan it Maria yesterday not given　 has

　　 b.　*dat Jan Maria dat boek gisteren　niet gegeven heeft.*
　　　　 that Jan Maria that book yesterday not given　 has

c.   *dat Jan gisteren Maria dat boek niet gegeven heeft.*
d.   *dat Jan gisteren   dat boek niet aan Maria gegeven heeft.*
    that Jan yesterday that book not to   Maria given   has

For reasons of space I cannot substantiate my analysis here and I refer the reader to my work (Haegeman 1991a, b, 1994a).

2.2. *The Hierarchy of Functional Projections*

If the leftward movement of the object to a position preceding the marker of sentential negation, *niet* 'not', is A-movement to the specifier of AGR(O)P and if *niet* is the specifier of NEGP, this implies that AGR(O)P dominates NEGP. Such an analysis of the West-Germanic languages leads to the hypothesis that NEGP does not have a universally fixed position in the clausal hierarchy: in languages such as Dutch, AGR(O)P dominates NEGP, while in Romance languages and in English NEGP dominates AGR(O)P (cf. (7)). Admittedly, the proposal involves a weakening of the role of UG in determining the hierarchy of clause structure, an option allowed for in Rizzi's proposal (cf. Rizzi 1994b:381). However, observe that I do not assume that the hierarchy of functional projections is entirely language specific. While the position of NEGP may vary, the relative positions of AGR(S), AGR(O) and TP are constant. The subject-AGR features are checked in a position above TP and the object-AGR features are checked above VP and below TP. The relative ordering of AGR(S), TP, AGR(O) and VP can be derived independently: AGR(S) is involved in nominative Case checking, which is associated with T, and AGR(O) is associated with the checking of accusative Case, which is a function of V. Anticipating the discussion below, note that if Dutch child root infinitives are truncated at the TP-level, negative root infinitives are not structurally excluded.

(7)   The hierarchy of functional projections
    a.   West-Germanic: ...   > TP > AGR(O)P > NEGP > VP
    b.   Romance   NEGP > TP > AGR(O)P   > VP

2.3. *Clitic Projections*

In Dutch, object weak pronouns are maximal projections which move to the specifier positions of functional projections in Zone 1. Object clitics are hosted by functional heads in Zone 1. Ignoring the position of AGR(S)P, the clause structure looks as follows:

(8)   CP > FP* >TP > AGR(O)P > NEGP > PREDP > VP

The recursive functional projection FP* whose head hosts clitics and whose specifier hosts, among other things, weak pronouns, is reminiscent of Sportiche's (1992) 'clitic projection'. Sportiche (1992) proposes that Romance clitics are base-generated as the heads of functional projections dominating AGR(S)P; the argument DP corresponding to the clitic is realized as *pro* and moves to the specifier position of the clitic head. Sportiche's analysis unifies scrambling in Dutch and German and cliticization: scrambling is the overt movement of an argument DP to the specifier of the clitic projection. The unification of the syntax of clitics in Germanic and Romance is of course highly attractive, but raises problems. In infinitival clauses in French, for instance, clitics do not appear as high in the structure as would be the case in finite clauses, as shown in the contrast between (9a–d) and (9e):

(9) a. *Ne pas toujours les   inviter serait   une erreur.*
         ne not always   them invite would-be an error

     b. *Ne pas les inviter toujours serait une erreur.*

     c. *Ne les pas inviter toujours serait une erreur.*

     d. *Ne les inviter pas toujours serait une erreur.*

     e. *Je ne les   invite pas toujours.*
         I *ne* them invite not always

In (9a) the clitic and the infinitive onto which it cliticizes remain lower than the adverb *toujours*. In (9b) they precede the adverb, but they remain lower than Spec-NEGP *pas*. These data suggest minimally that Romance clitics do not have to be base-generated as heads of the high clitic projections (FP* in (8)). If clitics move to a functional head, the clitic in (9a) must be adjoined to some functional head, possibly AGR(O), to which V^0 also has moved; from that position V^0 and the clitic may move higher. In (9b) the negative head (*ne*) precedes *pas* and we propose it has moved to AGR(S), leaving a trace in NEG^0. If heads cannot adjoin to traces, then the clitic-V^0 complex *les inviter* in (9b) has moved to some functional head lower than NEG^0, possibly T^0. In the West-Germanic languages considered, clitics move to the relevant functional projections (FP*) both in finite clauses and in infinitives, as we will see presently. Also, unlike Romance clitic movement, Germanic clitic movement is independent of V-movement. In Section 4.2 we see that acquisition data support the contrast between French clitics and their Dutch counterparts, suggesting again that the former can remain lower in the structure than the latter.

2.4. *Infinitives and Root Infinitives in Adult Dutch*

2.4.1. *Infinitives*

The structure outlined for the Germanic languages characterizes both finite and infinitival clauses in adult Dutch. Zone 1 is instantiated in dependent infinitival clauses:

(10) a. *I zal   proberen om t Jan vandaag nog te bezorgen.*
          I will try   for it Jan today   yet to deliver
      b. *Ik zal proberen om t niet meer te doen.*
          I will try   of it not more to do

2.4.2. *Root Infinitives*

In the present Section I show that Zone 1 is available in adult Dutch root infinitives.

Adult Dutch root infinitives can be used as elliptical answers. An elliptical root infinitive cannot have an overt subject; it can contain a clitic object, which means that FP* must be available:

(11)   *Wat ga je   doen?*
         what go you do
         — *(*Ik/*me) t   onmiddellijk aan de politie vertellen.*
         I   me it:CL immediately to   the police tell

Root infinitives are also used with imperative force. Such 'jussive' infinitives can be negated. Objects again may be realised as clitics. Overt subjects are ungrammatical.

(12)   *(*Jij) ze   morgen   niet vergeten!*
         you them tomorrow not forget
         'Don't forget them tomorrow.'

Given the presence of both clitics and adverbs I infer that Dutch adult root infinitives have the full clausal structure, including the functional projections of Zone 1 which host clitics. For the sake of completeness, note that there are also exclamative root infinitives with overt subjects. The overt subjects of such root infinitives are DPs and nominative strong pronouns; accusative subjects are excluded. Again, exclamative root infinitives may contain clitics, this means that the functional projection FP is available.

(13)   *Ik/*mij t aan de politie vertellen? Nooit!*
         I   me it to   the police tell   never

I also assume that the root infinitives in adult Dutch involve the CP-level. One piece of support for this claim is that indeed in certain instances the root infinitive contains a *wh*-operator:

(14)   *Waarom niet eerst naar huis   gaan?*
         why   not first to   home go
         'Why not first go home?'

Root infinitives often have jussive force (cf. (12)). If the illocutionary force is encoded in C (cf. Section 1.2.1.3) then we postulate that the jussive root infinitive is dominated by the relevant layer. For elliptical root infinitives Spec-CP contains a null operator interpreted by co-indexation in the discourse.

3.   Root Infinitives in the Acquisition of Dutch

3.1. *Overall Totals*

For this study I have used the spontaneous speech corpus of one Dutch child, Hein, which is part of the CHILDES material. Hein is studied longitudinally over a period of 10 months, from two years, four months to three years, one month. The overall distribution of the root infinitives in the Dutch Hein corpus is given in Table 3. File numbers correspond to ages: Hein 2;04 is recorded at the age of two years, four months, for instance. The criteria used for the classification of clauses were both syntactic (i.e., the position of the verb) and morphological. In the following examples the verb is finite, and it has the regular inflection: in (15a) *is* is the third person singular of *zijn* 'be', in (15b) *kijk* is the second person singular of *kijken* 'look', and in (15c) *komt* is the third person singular of *komen* 'come'.

(15) a.   *Doenja is weg*   Hein(2;04)
          Doenja is away
     b.   *daar kijk je   door   naar buiten*   Hein(2;04)
          there look you through outside
     c.   *Gijs komt*   Hein(2;04)
          Gijs comes

In (16a) and (16b) the verb forms (*kom* and *blijf*) are the stem forms, but they occupy the position associated with inflected forms, i.e., the second position.

(16) a. *Bee kom   dadelijk*   Hein(2;04)
          Bee comes immediately
      b. *waarom blijf daar-?*   Hein(2;06)
          why   stay there

What is essential for my classification is that forms such as those in (16a) and (16b) have the syntactic position of finite forms, and contrast with the infinitival forms in (16c) and (16d) which occupy a final position.[9]

(16) c. *zo ikke in doen.*   Hein(2;04)
          so I   in put
      d. *jij   doen*   Hein(2;04)
          you do

Table 3. Distribution of Finite Clauses and Root Infinitives in Hein

age	total utterances	finite clauses + root infinitives	finite clauses	%	root infinitives	%
2;4	1,405	385	296	77	89	23
2;5	1,153	304	203	67	101	33
2;6	1,946	741	608	82	133	18
2;7	1,399	364	283	78	81	22
2;8	1,939	532	452	85	80	15
2;9	1,545	468	403	86	65	14
2;0	1,762	525	461	88	64	12
2;1	1,675	418	349	83	69	17
3;0	1,002	355	340	96	15	4
3;1	754	397	373	94	24	6
total	14,580	4,489	3,768	84	721	16

We see that root infinitives range from 33% at the age of two years, five months to as low as 4% at the age of three years. In Table 4 I give corresponding percentages for root infinitives in the Thomas files, in Table 5 those for the Niek Files, both also taken from the CHILDES files.

The proportion of root infinitives systematically decreases with age (see also Krämer 1994 and Wijnen 1994).

Table 4. Root Infinitives in Thomas

age	total utterances	clauses with verbs	root infinitives	% root infinitives
2;3	547	138	77	56
2;4	1,999	566	252	45
2;5	2,240	617	173	28
2;6	239	103	21	20
2;7	3,152	1,169	168	14
2;8	2,033	697	97	14
2;9	1,588	512	60	12
2;10	2,315	1,051	68	6
2;11	855	359	23	6
total	14,986	5,212	939	18

Table 5. Root Infinitives in Niek

age	total utterances	clauses with verbs	root infinitives	% root infinitives
2;8	319	45	36	80
2;9	512	77	57	74
2;10	433	68	39	57
2;11	499	123	80	65
3;0	1,180	253	86	34
3;1	2,040	736	190	26
3;2	165	63	14	22
3;4	2,752	977	90	9
3;5	429	173	14	8
3;6	3,519	1,721	89	5
3;7	338	112	01	1
3;8	1,638	544	14	3
3;9	1,115	723	32	4
3;10	1,299	626	21	3
total	16,238	6,241	736	12

3.2. *The Structure of Root Infinitives: Functional Projections*

Rizzi (1994b) argues that root infinitives are truncated structures lacking TP and the projections dominating it. The evidence cited by Rizzi (see Section 1.2.2.) obtains for Dutch.

3.2.1. *CP*

The Hein corpus contains 90 *wh*-questions, 88 of which are finite and two of which are root infinitives, both found in one file (2;06). The proportion of *wh*-root infinitives is clearly much lower than would be expected from the average ratio finite/infinitival clauses; overall there are 84% finite clauses and 16% root infinitives; if this proportion was constant for interrogative root infinitives we might have expected to find some 15 *wh*-root infinitives. The only two *wh*-root infinitives in the corpus are given in (17):[10]

> (17) a. *hoe heten?*   Hein(2;06)
>   how call
>
>   b. *waarom <niet> [//] nu &ni [/] niet wassen*   Hein(2;06)
>   why   not   now   not wash

The examples in (18) illustrate some of the finite interrogatives of file Hein 2;06:

> (18) a. *en wat doen ze   daar?*
>   and what do   they there
>
>   b. *waarom blijf daar-?*
>   why   stay there
>
>   c. *waar's taart nou?*
>   where is cake now
>
>   d. *wie staat daar?*
>   who stands there

The near absence of *wh*-questions in root infinitives is predicted if child root infinitives lack CP.

For root infinitives Boser *et al.* (1992) postulate structure (19), where a null auxiliary moves to C^0 and the subject moves to Spec-CP, in order to identify and license the null auxiliary.

> (19) $[_{CP}$ *der*$_i$ $[_{C^0}$ AUX$_{j/i}$] [t$_i$ *eine Hose anziehen* $[_{I^0}$ t$_j$]]]
>   this   a   pants on.put

Boser *et al.*'s analysis (1992) correctly excludes root infinitives with initial non-subjects, a point to which I return in Section 3.2.2.2. The absence of subject interrogatives such as (20) is unexpected under their analysis: in (20) the interrogative subject *wer* 'who' would move to Spec-CP where it can license the non-overt auxiliary:

> (20)   *$[_{CP}$ *wer*$_i$ $[_{C^0}$ AUX$_{j/i}$] [t$_i$ *eine Hose anziehen* $[_{I^0}$ t$_j$]]]
>   who   a   pants on.put

In the Hein corpus there are 14 subject *wh*-questions, eight with *wie* 'who' and six with *wat* 'what'. As there are 16% root infinitives in the corpus, Boser *et al.*'s account would lead us to expect to find that 16% of subject interrogatives are realized as root infinitives, i.e., we might have expected to find two or three *wh*-subjects in the root infinitives, contrary to fact.

3.2.2. Subjects and Subject Clitics

3.2.2.1. *The Realization of the Subject.* Table 6 is a survey of the finite sentences and root infinitives with overt subjects in the Hein corpus. The overt realization of the subject is consistently much lower in root infinitives than in finite clauses. 68% of finite clauses have an overt subject, against only 15% of root infinitives (see also Krämer 1994).

Table 6. Overt Subjects in the Hein Corpus

age	finite S	overt subject	%	root infinitives	overt subject	%
2;4	296	170	57	89	20	22
2;5	203	132	65	101	17	17
2;6	608	411	68	133	25	19
2;7	283	201	71	81	12	15
2;8	452	292	65	80	10	12
2;9	403	269	67	65	8	12
2;10	461	321	70	64	5	8
2;11	349	259	74	69	1	1
3;0	340	246	72	15	3	20
3;1	373	268	72	24	5	21
total	3,768	2,569	68	721	106	15

In finite clauses overt pronominal subjects are realized both as strong pronouns and as weak pronouns (Cardinaletti & Starke 1993); in root infinitives there are no weak pronoun subjects. If weak pronouns are licensed in the specifier position of the highest functional projection in Zone 1, the absence of subject weak pronouns in root infinitives follows from an analysis of root infinitives in which it is assumed that the relevant functional projection of Zone 1 is truncated. That overt subjects in general are rarer in root infinitives than in the finite clauses is also at least partially accounted for: if a nominative subject is licensed in the specifier of one of the functional projections that constitute Zone 1; the root infinitive, lacking the relevant functional projection, does not have a position to license the nominative subject.[11,12]

Table 7. The Distribution of Subject Personal Pronouns

age	utterance	finite S	subj. strong pronoun	subj. weak pronoun	root infin- itive	subj. strong pronoun	subj. weak pronoun
2;4	1,405	296	98	9	89	15	0
2;5	1,153	203	50	25	101	13	0
2;6	1,946	608	110	60	133	16	0
2;7	1,399	283	69	33	81	7	0
2;8	1,939	452	117	68	80	10	0
2;9	1,545	403	99	65	65	7	0
2;10	1,762	461	100	77	64	4	0
2;11	1,675	349	91	45	69	0	0
3;0	1,002	340	63	51	15	3	0
3;1	754	373	174	39	24	3	0
total	14,580	3,768	971	472	721	78	0

In analyses which posit a full CP-structure (with the clausal functional heads) for child root infinitives, the absence of subject weak pronouns is hard to account for. Even in the more restricted approach developed by Boser *et al.* (1992) it is not clear why weak pronoun subjects do not appear in root infinitives. One might try to exclude weak pronoun subjects in root infinitives by arguing that weak pronouns are phonetic clitics and that cliticization to a non-overt host is disallowed, but this is not a natural assumption for Dutch where object clitics such as *t* are hosted by non-overt functional heads, as illustrated in (21) (cf. Zwart 1991; 1992a; 1992b; 1993a, b; Haegeman 1993a, b, c; 1994a):

(21)   *Ik denk dat Maria t   Jan wel zal zeggen.*
         I think that Maria it:CL Jan well will say

Cliticization to a non-overt functional head is attested in the child data:

(22)   *zo kan jij   't   ook doen he?*
         so can you it:CL also do   he   Hein(3:01)[13]

3.2.2.2. *The Position of the Subject.* In finite clauses in the Hein material overt subjects occur both in a position to the left of the finite V and in a position to the right of the finite V.

(23) a. *hij doet 't niet*   Hein(2;04)
          he does it not
      b. *zo kan jij 't ook doen, he?*   Hein(3;01)
          so can you it also do   he

According to the traditional analysis where all V2 is movement of V to C, the position to the left of the finite verb in root clauses is Spec-CP. In other accounts (Haegeman, forthc. b; Travis 1984; Zwart 1992b, 1993a, b) a sentence-initial subject in root clauses may occupy either Spec-AGR(S)P or, when topicalized, Spec-CP. Similarly, while in traditional approaches to V2 all sentence-initial material is taken to be in Spec-CP, recent proposals distinguish Spec-TOPP from Spec-CP (cf. Zwart 1993a, b). As theoretical Germanic syntax is in a state of flux, the descriptive term 'preverbal position' in (22a) refers to the initial position in a V2-sentence.[14]

Table 8. Position of Overt Subjects in Finite Clauses in Hein

	preverbal	postverbal
2;4	76	94
2;5	44	88
2;6	239	172
2;7	85	116
2;8	149	143
2;9	126	143
2;10	146	175
2;11	124	135
3;0	126	120
3;1	108	160
total	1,223	1,346
%	48	52

When the subject does not occupy the sentence-initial position, this position often remains empty, i.e., presumably it is filled by a zero operator or a zero topic.[15] Table 9 gives a survey of the numbers of sentences with overt non subject material to the left of a finite V.

In root infinitives with an overt subject, the subject is predominantly in first position: among the 106 examples with overt subjects (cf. Table 6), only 5 have the subject in non-initial position: (24) is the exhaustive list of examples with a non-initial subject:

Table 9. Non-subject Sentence-Initial Material in Finite Clauses

	overt material left of finite V	postverbal subject
2;4	22	94
2;5	22	88
2;6	25	172
2;7	23	116
2;8	49	143
2;9	55	143
2;10	82	175
2;11	99	135
3;0	64	120
3;1	59	160

(24) a. *zo ikke in doen*   Hein(2;04)
          so I   in do
      b. *nu   jij   doen*   Hein(2;04)
          now you do
      c. *en   dan ik slapen*   Hein(2;04)
          and then I sleep
      d. *eerst [$B] Hein aanzetten*   Hein(3;01)
          first   Hein on-put
      e. *wel de wolf van #&x [//] klein(e) geitjes nog opeten*
          well the wolf of ...   little   goats still eat
                                                                   Hein(3;01)

Examples (24a–c) occur in file 2;04; (24d–e) occur in file 3;01 in which root infinitives have become rare in general. If we compare the rate of non subject-initial root infinitives with the rate of non subject-initial finite clauses the figures are sharply different. 1,223 finite sentences have the subject to the left of V, and 500 sentences have a non-subject to the left of V. This means that 500 out of 1,723 sentences with overt material preceding the finite verb have a non-subject preceding the overt subject, i.e., some 30%. In only five root infinitives out of the 106 root infinitives with an overt subject does a non subject precede the subject, i.e., about 5%, and the examples cluster in two files. These data confirm Poeppel & Wexler's (1993) conclusion for German that non-subject-initial root infinitives are performance errors. Boser *et al.* (1992) correctly exclude non subject-initial root infinitives.

3.2.2.3. *Overt Subjects in Root Infinitives.* If root infinitives lack AGR(S)P then the subject cannot be assigned Case in the same way as the overt subject of finite clauses, i.e., by AGR(S). Following suggestions in Rizzi (1994b) for French, I propose that overt subjects in root infinitives occupy an $\overline{A}$-position, possibly an adjoined position, and receive default Case, and that in Dutch the default Case is nominative. This hypothesis is supported by the observation that the default form of the first pronoun in Dutch is *ikke* 'I' (25a) and that this form tends to be used as the subject of child nonfinite utterances, including root infinitives (25b). The form *ik* 'I' is more typically used for finite clauses (see Haegeman, forthcoming a, for details) (25c).

> (25) a. *wie weet dat?*   *ikke*
>   who knows that   me
>
>   b. *zo ikke in doen*
>   so I   in put
>
>   c. *ik heef* &t6 [/] *toch* # &O\[/] *ook* &6 *witte buik   ikke?*
>   I have   yet   also   white tummy I
>   Hein(2;08)

Observe that in (25c) *ik* is the subject of the finite verb and *ikke* occurs in a right-dislocated position. I assume that in that position it receives default nominative.

3.2.3. *The Distribution of Objects and the Absence of Zone 1*

Recall that I propose that objects in Dutch move either to the specifier of AGR(O)P, i.e., below TP and AGR(S)P, or they may also move to the specifiers of the higher clitic projections of Zone 1 (FP* in (8)). In root infinitives there is evidence for the Zone 2, i.e., AGR(O)P, but the data suggest that Zone 1 is truncated.

3.2.3.1. *Object Clitics and Root Infinitives.* Object pronominals may be realized as strong pronouns, weak pronouns and clitics. I will group weak pronouns and clitics as object clitics/weak pronouns: they move to Zone 1, unlike strong pronouns, which may remain in Zone 2.

Table 10 gives the distribution of object clitics/weak pronouns in the Hein corpus. In general there are very few instances: a total of 53 in the entire corpus. The scarcity of object cliticization was also noted for French in Friedemann (1992) and in Hamann *et al.* (this volume). I return to French in Section 4. In Dutch child root infinitives there are no object clitics/weak pronouns at all. If object clitics/weak pronouns were equally distributed in finite and nonfinite sentences, we might have expected to find eight instances in the root infinitives.

Table 10. Object Clitics/Weak Pronouns in the Hein Corpus

age	finite S	object clitics/ weak pronouns	non-finite	object clitic/ weak pronouns
2;4	296	2/3	89	0
2;5	203	2	101	0
2;6	608	1	133	0
2;7	283	4	81	0
2;8	452	10	80	0
2;9	403	12	65	0
2;10	461	3	64	0
2;11	349	2	69	0
3;0	340	7/8	15	0
3;1	373	10	24	0
total	3,768	53/5	721	0

A quick perusal of the Niek corpus (CHILDES 1985) and of the Thomas corpus (CHILDES 1985) confirms the absence of object clitics/weak pronouns (Tables 11 and 12).

Table 11. Object Clitics/Weak Pronouns in the Thomas Corpus

age	finite clauses	object clitics	root infinitives	object clitics
2;3	61	0	77	0
2;4	314	2	252	0
2;5	444	1	173	0
2;6	82	0	21	0
2;7	1,001	5	168	0
2;8	600	5	97	1
2;9	452	1	60	0
2;10	983	10	68	0
2;11	336	1	23	0
total	4,273	25	939	1

Table 12. Object Clitics/Weak Pronouns in the Niek Corpus

age	finite clauses	object clitics	root infinitives	object clitics
2;8	11	0	36	0
2;9	20	0	57	0
2;10	29	0	39	0
2;11	43	0	80	0
3;0	167	0	86	0
3;1	546	1	190	0
3;2	49	0	14	0
3;4	887	7	90	0
3;5	159	0	14	0
3;6	1,632	7	89	0
3;7	111	2	1	0
3;8	530	26	14	0
3;9	691	13	32	0
3;10	605	37	21	0
total	5,480	93	763	0

The absence of object clitics in root infinitives follows from the absence of Zone 1, the functional projections whose heads host clitics and whose specifiers host weak pronouns or other DPs that have undergone scrambling. Pursuing the truncation strategy we assume that neither CP, nor the functional projections which host object clitics in Zone 1, are present in root infinitives. An analysis of root infinitives as CPs (even in the restrictive version of Boser *et al.* 1992) does not offer any explanation for the absence of object clitics. Recall that in adult Dutch root infinitives object cliticization is possible, as discussed in Section 2.4. For object clitics in French root infinitives see Section 4.

3.2.3.2. *Object Pronouns.* In the Hein corpus there are only 53 object clitics/weak pronouns in all, six weak pronouns and 47 clitics. Strong pronoun objects are even rarer in the corpus: there are only nine strong pronouns which can be unambiguously interpreted as complements of verbs. I illustrate strong pronouns in (26): (26a) is a root infinitive, (26b) is finite.

(26) a. *&n &n jij   even mij helpen?*   Hein(2;04)
          you once me help

      b. *Hein [?] gaat jou plagen*   Hein(2;09)
          Hein   goes you tease

Four out of nine strong pronouns occur in root infinitives, which is about 50% of all examples. This might be interpreted in the following way. Clitics/weak pronouns are licensed in Zone 1, strong pronouns can also occur in Zone 2. If Zone 1 is truncated in root infinitives and if Zone 2 is available, a point to which I return presently, then strong pronouns are the only option for object pronominalization in root infinitives. The data in the Niek corpus confirm this pattern. In this corpus there are 15 full pronouns in finite clauses and six in root infinitives.

The global low occurrence of object pronouns in the acquisition data requires further study, though. It is important to point out that the figures given so far concern the distribution of personal pronouns used as complements of verbs. Complements of prepositions are often realized as pronouns. In the Hein corpus 68 pronouns occur as complements of P and a further 38 strong pronouns are used as possessives.

A first hypothesis is that pronouns which undergo leftward movement are rare, in contrast with pronouns which remain *in situ*. However, Dutch demonstrative pronouns have a strong tendency for leftward movement, and yet demonstrative pronoun objects are well attested in the child grammar, both in finite clauses and in root infinitives. In the Hein corpus there are 243 instances of objects realized as demonstrative pronouns; these are distributed over finite clauses and root infinitives: 44, i.e., 14%, occur in root infinitives, which is comparative to the general ratio of root infinitives to finite clauses (16%). The presence of demonstrative objects shows that object pronominal elements as such are not unavailable in the child grammar.[16]

3.2.3.3. *The Realization of Objects: Summary.* The proportion of pronouns is much higher for subjects than for objects. Out of 990 overt objects 53 are realized as clitics/weak pronouns, nine are strong pronouns, 243 as demonstratives and the remaining 685 are lexical DPs. Out of 2,675 overt subjects, 1,094 are strong pronouns and 472 are weak pronouns.

3.3. *Scrambling*

While Zone 1 is absent in root infinitives, there is evidence that Zone 2 is available. Recall that, following much recent work, I assume that scrambling to Zone 2 is leftward Case-driven A-movement to the specifier of a functional projection, AGR(O)P. The presence of scrambled elements in root infinitives is evidence for Zone 2.[17]

It has been argued (Barbier 1994; Schaeffer *et al.* 1994) that leftward movement is attested in the acquisition data, though this is a relatively late development (cf. Clahsen *et al.* 1994). Leftward movement is particularly frequent with demonstratives (cf. Jordens & Hoekstra 1991). In the finite clauses in the Hein corpus there are 43 instances in which the presence or absence of leftward movement can be diagnosed on the basis of the position of adverbials, and in 36 of these the movement option is chosen.[18] Though limited, these data provide some evidence for postulating AGR(O)P.

(27) a. *ditte # nu   opeten*   Hein(2;05)
          this   now eat

      b. *&mnm jij[?] die even pakken?*   Hein(2;06)
          mm   you   that once take

      c. *die niet lezen*   Hein(2;10)
          that not read

3.4. *NEGP*

I have provided arguments that child root infinitives in Dutch are truncated structures lacking CP, and the functional projections constituting Zone 1. From the leftward object movement, I conclude that AGR(O)P (Zone 2) is available. Following Rizzi's truncation theory, if AGR(O)P is available, NEGP is also projected. I now turn to NEGP.

3.4.1. *Direct Evidence for NEGP*

When a functional projection is truncated the dominating projections are also truncated. On the basis of the hierarchy of functional projections of Romance (2a) the truncation of TP in French entails that NEGP is also missing. This is confirmed by the French data discussed in Friedemann (1992): of all negative sentences only 4.3% are root infinitives. Table 13 provides a summary of the distribution of sentential negation in the Hein corpus:

Out of 635 negative sentences in the Hein corpus, only 38 i.e., 6%, are root infinitives. On the other hand, out of 3,859 non-negative sentences, 683, i.e., 17% are root infinitives. In the first part of the material, where root infinitives are more frequent, we get slightly higher percentages of negative root infinitives. Out of 318 negative sentences in files 2;04–2;08, 29 (i.e., 9%) are root infinitives; but again the figures for negative root infinitives are lower than for non-negative ones: of 2,008 non-negative sentences, 455, i.e., 23%, are root infinitives.[19] If

Table 13. Sentential Negation in the Hein Corpus

age	finite clauses	negated	infinitive clauses	negated
2;4	296	83	89	7
2;5	203	44	101	8
2;6	608	62	133	6
2;7	283	38	81	2
2;8	452	62	80	6
2;9	403	66	65	2
2;10	461	93	64	5
2;11	349	81	69	2
3;0	340	38	15	0
3;1	373	30	24	0
total	3,768	597	721	38

NEGP is structurally available, as argued above, the question arises why there is some reluctance to use negative root infinitives I return to this point in section 3.5.

3.4.2. *Pre-negative Adverbs*

In Dutch adverbs such as *ook* 'also', *even* 'once', *nou, nu* 'now', *eerst* 'first', *straks* 'in a moment', *weer* 'again' precede the sentential negation *niet*.

(28) a. *Ik heb ook/eerst/even niet gewerkt.*
          I have also/first/once not worked
      b. **Ik heb niet ook/eerst/even gewerkt.*

The presence of pre-negative adverbials is additional evidence that root infinitives contain NEGP. (29) illustrates root infinitives from Hein 2;04 containing such adverbials (see also Schaeffer 1994).

(29) a. *Bea ook werken*
          Bea also work
      b. *jij mij even helpen?*
          you me once help

3.5. *TP*

On the basis of the distribution of scrambled objects, and of adverbs, and on the basis of the absence of subject weak pronouns, of object clitics/weak pronouns and of *wh*-phrases I conclude that CP and the functional projections constituting Zone 1 are absent in root infinitives, while the functional projections constituting Zone 2, and NEGP are present. So far, I have not discussed the availability of TP. I propose that in Dutch TP dominates NEGP. The relevant partial structure of the clause is as in (30):

(30)   TP > AGR(O)P > NEGP > (PredP) > VP

If TP is truncated in child root infinitives, their structure would be as in (31):[20]

(31)   AGR(O)P > NEGP > (PredP) > VP

Two observations offer support that TP is not available; these are discussed in Sections 3.5.1 and 3.5.2.

3.5.1. *Absence of Auxiliaries*

All the verbs in child root infinitives are lexical verbs: modal auxiliaries (*moeten* 'must', *kunnen* 'can', *willen* 'want,' etc.) and aspectual auxiliaries (*hebben* 'have' and *zijn* 'be') are entirely absent. Following Guasti (1993) and Rizzi (1994b) I assume that this follows from the absence of TP, auxiliaries have to be licensed by T^0 (cf. § 1.2.2). It might be argued that the absence of auxiliaries is due to the fact that there are no nonfinite forms of auxiliaries at the early stage of the grammar. This argument, though, is problematic: while perfective *hebben* 'have' is absent from root infinitives, possessive *hebben* 'have' is used as shown in (32):

(32) a.   *dit hebben*   Hein(2;05)
            this have

       b.   *jij xxx nie die hebben?*   Hein(2;07)
            you   not that have?

3.5.2. *Reluctance to Use Negation*

A problem left open is the reluctance to use negation in Dutch child root infinitives (see Hamann 1994 for German). Since direct objects precede the sentential negation *niet* I assume that AGR(O)P dominates NEGP. If root infinitives are truncated above AGR(O)P, as argued above, then the low occurrence of negated root infinitives is unexpected. One hypothesis in line with the previous discussion is that sentential negation depends on Tense in that NEG^0 has to be licensed by T^0 (cf. Zanuttini 1991, forthc.; Laka 1990, 1994). The projection NEGP as such is available in the Dutch child root infinitive, but because TP is truncated, NEG^0 cannot be licensed by T^0. The reluctance to use negative root infinitives follows from the absence of TP.[21]

Adult root infinitives are full CPs. As shown in (12) and (14), adult root infinitives can be negated.

3.6. Conclusion

Dutch root infinitives are truncated structures from which TP and all the projections dominating it, AGR(S)P, the clitic projections and CP, are absent. Alternative approaches in which root infinitives are interpreted as CPs will fail to account for the absence of *wh*-root infinitives and for the lack of weak pronoun subjects, clitic/weak pronoun objects, and the low occurrence of negative root infinitives.

4.   Clitics and Clitic Projections in Romance and in Germanic

4.1. Subjects and Subject Clitics

The absence of subject clitics in French root infinitives is observed in Crisma (1992), Friedemann (1992) and is confirmed in Hamann *et al.* (this volume), discussed already in Section 1.2.2. The lack of clitic subjects in root infinitives in French is parallel to that found for the Dutch material, where subject weak pronouns also exclusively appear in the finite clauses.

4.2. Objects and Object Clitics

We have seen (§ 3.2.3.) that object clitics/weak pronouns are rare in the Dutch child data, and that they are absent from root infinitives. In the Hein corpus there are 685 lexical objects and 53 clitic/weak pronoun objects; object clitics/weak pronouns are absent from root infinitives. The absence of object clitics in root infinitives is confirmed for the Thomas corpus (Table 11) and for the Niek corpus (Table 12). When we compare the proportion of object forms realized as clitics we see that it is much lower than that of subject clitics (cf. Section 3.2.2.1., Table 7).

4.2.1. *Object Clitics and Root Infinitives in French and in Dutch*

Friedemann (1992) shows that in the first files of the French Philippe corpus the number of object clitics is very low: only 42 instances are found in the files 2.1–2.3, while there are 625 lexical object DPs.[22] In contrast with Dutch, clitic objects do appear in French root infinitives: six out of 42 instances (14%) occur in root infinitives. Some examples are given in (33):

(33) a. *les   mettre dans le garage*   Philippe(2;1)
        them put   in   the garage

    b. *l'ouvrir fermé*   Philippe(2;2)
        it.open closed

    c. *les vis   les   mettre là*   Philippe(2;2)
        the screws them to.put there

The same observation is made in Hamann *et al.*'s (this volume) study of a child acquiring French. This child is the same age as the Dutch children studied. It is clear from their data (cf. their Table 6) that object clitics are relatively rare and emerge late.

While Dutch root infinitives lack *both* subject weak pronouns and object clitics/weak pronouns, in French root infinitives, object clitics, in contrast with subject clitics, are attested. The availability of clitics in the French root infinitives and their absence in the Dutch parallels follows from an account in which object clitics have a different landing site in the two languages. The distributional differences between Dutch object clitics and their French counterparts is not directly compatible with a unified approach to cliticization in Dutch and French, as proposed by Sportiche (1992), who argues that there are identical clitic projections dominating AGR(S)P which host the clitics *both* in Romance and in Germanic and whose specifiers host the scrambled DPs in Germanic. If my analysis is on the right track then the projections whose heads host the clitics in Germanic are the non-L-related functional projections in Zone 1, and they are higher in the structure than the V-related AGR(O)P-projections whose heads host the clitics in Romance and which correspond to Zone 2 (cf. (9)). While Zone 1, which dominates TP, is missing in root infinitives, Zone 2 is available in root infinitives in French (as shown by the presence of clitics) and in Dutch.

4.2.2. *Late Emergence of Object Clitics*

Apart from the contrastive behavior of object clitics in root infinitives, there remains the striking parallelism between the early Dutch discussed here (cf.

Haegeman 1994b) and the early French data discussed in Hamann *et al.* (this volume). Both in early Dutch and in early French, complement clitics are significantly delayed with respect to the emergence of subject clitics.

Hamann *et al.* (this volume) point out that the delayed occurrence of object clitics contrasts sharply with the emergence of subject clitics which are earlier and more frequent: in the first seven files of their corpus only one genuine example of an object clitic is found as opposed to 74 occurrences of 5 different kinds of subject clitics. They point out that this cannot be related to a failure of pronominalization for complements since in the same period the child produces both subject and object forms of the demonstrative *ça*, with six subject forms and 12 object forms. They propose that the later development of object clitics as opposed to the subject forms can be interpreted in terms of Cardinaletti & Starke's (1993) theory of markedness. In this approach, French subject clitics are analysed as weak pronouns, i.e., maximal projections, while object clitics are genuine clitics, i.e., heads. Under this analysis object clitics are more deficient than subject weak pronouns, hence they emerge later.

Given the parallelism between the early French data discussed by Hamann *et al.*, and the Dutch data discussed in the present paper — a parallelism signalled by Hamann *et al.* themselves — an account for the rare and delayed occurrence of object clitics in French should ideally also account for the analogous early Dutch data. However, Hamann *et al.*'s analysis in terms of Cardinaletti & Starke's markedness hierarchy — clitics are more marked than weak pronouns, and weak pronouns are more marked than strong pronouns — does not seem to me to be able to capture the distribution of object pronominals in the Dutch material. In early Dutch, object clitics and weak pronouns are rarer than subject weak pronouns, but Cardinaletti & Starke's hierarchy seems to be irrelevant for object pronominalization. In the Hein corpus, there are 47 object clitics and there are six object weak pronouns.[23] Moreover, there are only nine strong pronouns. This distribution is unexpected in terms of the theory of markedness referred to by Hamann *et al.*: weak pronouns should be more frequent than clitics, and strong pronouns, not being structurally deficient at all, should be the least marked option.

As observed in the French data, object pronominalization as such is not problematic. Demonstrative objects are found (Section 3.2.3.2) and are more frequent than personal pronouns: in the Hein corpus there are 243 demonstrative verb complements. What seems to be problematic is the realization of the verb complement as a personal pronoun with person, number and gender features, regardless of its specific realization as a clitic, a weak pronoun or a strong pronoun. The late emergence of object clitics and object pronominals in Dutch and French requires further study.

5. Conclusion

This paper examines the structural properties of Dutch child root infinitives in the light of Rizzi's truncation theory. I argue that root infinitives are truncated structures projected up to AGR(O)P. Evidence for the truncation analysis is the absence of wh-phrases, the absence of subject clitics, and the absence of object clitics/weak pronouns in root infinitives. The reduced use of negative root infinitives suggests that NEGP, though in place, cannot be fully exploited. The reluctance to use negative root infinitives derives from the absence of TP.

The presence of object clitics in French root infinitives and their absence in the Dutch counterparts suggests that both types of root infinitives are projections of the AGR(O)P-type and that Dutch clitics move higher in the structure than their French counterparts. This conclusion is incompatible with a rigid version of Sportiche's clausal structures.

Further research is required to account for the general rare appearance of object clitics in both languages. A related issue which remains to be analyzed is the delayed occurrence of overt object personal pronouns in Dutch.[24]

Acknowledgements

This paper was presented at the conference on the Generative Studies of the Acquisition of Case and Agreement at the University of Essex in 1994 and at the Séminaire de Recherche of the Faculty of Letters of the University of Geneva. I thank both audiences for their comments. Thanks to Adriana Belletti, Hans Broekhuis, Siobhan Cottell, Teresa Guasti, Cornelia Hamann, Christopher Laenzlinger, Luigi Rizzi, Manuela Schoenenberger, Ur Shlonsky, Ken Wexler, Frank Wijnen, Jan Wouter Zwart and two anonymous reviewers for discussion of parts of the paper. Special thanks are due to Harald Clahsen whose invitation has been the incentive for my work on acquisition and whose comments have been an important help in the shaping of this paper. Obviously none of these mentioned can be held responsible for the way I have used their suggestions.

My research on negation is part of project 11–33542.92 subsidized by the Fond National Suisse de la Recherche Scientifique.

Notes

1. Radford (1990) refers to the analogous data in English as stem forms missing inflection.

2. Rizzi allows for variation with respect to the position of NEGP (1994b:381).

3. Rizzi (1994) proposes (i), but as the equation is not bi-directional, since not all CPs are root clauses, I use the notation in (2b) in the text.

    (i)   Root = CP

4. "We propose that Tense ⟨±finite⟩ depends on the presence of a temporal operator in the COMP-node; the time of the event which the clause denotes is calculated on the basis of the reference time in COMP."

5. "We propose that the Tense morpheme bound by a temporal operator in C functions as a pronominal variable."

6. I deliberately use the vague notion 'associate with'. In finite clauses in French and in English the auxiliary will move to T^0, but in infinitival clauses auxiliaries need not move to T^0, neither in French nor in English:

    (i)   a.   *Ne pas souvent être invité est triste.*

              ne pas often   be   invited is   sad

         b.   *To not often be invited is sad.*

    One option is to say that the auxiliary moves to T^0 at LF (contra Chomsky 1993). Another is to assume that T^0-antecedent governs the auxiliary in (i), and that they form a representational CHAIN.

7. Hein's (approximate) MLU (2;04: 2.7; 2;5: 2.8; 2;6: 3.7; 2;7: 4.1.; 2;8: 3.8.; 2;9: 3.3; 2;10: 3.8; 2;11: 3.8, 3;00: 3.6., 3;01: 4.2.) is comparable to that of Philippe (Pierce 1989).

8. I assume the traditional analysis of Dutch in which VP and V-related functional projections (T, AGR(O)P, AGR(S)P) are head-final. Under more recent proposals (Kayne 1994; Zwart 1993), the functional projections are head-initial, which would have important ramifications. This is not the place to go into this issue and I refer the reader to the ongoing debate in the literature.

9. A further analysis of the inflected forms with respect to the question whether the inflected form is correctly used certainly would be important. This point is beyond the scope of the present paper though (cf. Clahsen *et al.*, this volume, for such an analysis of the German data).

10. The examples in (17) might be interpreted as *wh-in-situ*.

11. The reader will recall that I did not commit myself to the position of AGR(S)P with respect to Zone 1. In Section 3.2.3 I provide evidence that all the projections of Zone 1 are lacking.

302　　　　　　　　LILIANE HAEGEMAN

12. In Table 7, a subject strong pronoun is exemplified by a pronoun such as *ik*; a subject weak pronoun is a pronoun such as *'k*. For discussion see Cardinaletti & Starke (1993).

13. As pointed out by an anonymous referee for this volume, Sano & Hyams' (1994) analysis would account for the absence of overt subjects in root infinitives. In their analysis root infinitives lack V-movement and one might say that this is what blocks overt realization of the subject. However, this account does not carry over to the observed absence of object clitics and weak pronouns in root infinitives (§ 3.2.3.1 below).

14. Clahsen *et al.* (this volume:145 ff.) show that in early stages of the acquisition of German, *nicht*, the marker of negation, may precede the definite subject. If these data are systematic we must conclude that the subject perhaps does not move out of VP in this stage. See also Friedemann (1992) for parallel discussion in French. For reasons of space I cannot pursue the distribution of non initial subjects in the material.

15. Especially in the early files there are a lot of non-overt preverbal positions.

16. Possibly, absence of object pronouns is related to the development of the determiner system and of reference (see Clahsen *et al.* 1994; Haegeman 1994b; Roeper 1992).

17. If Zone 1 is unavailable in root infinitives, then scrambling to the specifiers of FP is not available, though. Sometimes movement to Zone 2 is referred to as OBJECT SHIFT, and that to Zone 1 as LONG SCRAMBLING.

18. Against Clahsen *et al.* (this volume), where it is assumed that adverbs can adjoin to projections, I assume that adverbs occupy the specifiers of functional heads as the insertion of an adverb contributes to the licensing of clitics in West-Flemish. In Haegeman (in prep.) I argue that the adverbial licenses a functional head which can host a clitic. If adverbs are specifiers of functional projections the pre-adverbial position of the demonstratives shows minimally that they are moved to AGR(O)P outside of VP.

19. Thanks to Cornelia Hamann for help on these counts.

20. In earlier versions of the paper I proposed (30) as the structure for root infinitives. In (30), T^0, being the head of the root, satisfies the ECP vacuously (Rizzi 1994a). However, the absence of auxiliaries in root infinitives is unexplained in (30), while it follows from (31), as will be discussed. Also, the reluctance to use negation follows from (31) on the assumption that sentential negation is licensed by T (Zanuttini forthc.), while it does not follow quite as naturally from (30). I abandon (30) in favor of (31).

21. Hoekstra & Jordens (1991) show that early root infinitives often have *neen* rather than *niet* to express negation. The form *neen* is also used for independent sentential negation in Dutch. *Neen* might be seen as a default negation in the absence of TP. The use of *ikke* as the nominative subject in the child root infinitive as discussed in Section 3.2.1.3 is then analogous to the use of *neen* for sentential negation, in that just as *neen* is the independent default negation, *ikke* is the independent default pronoun. Note in passing

that nothing in Boser *et al.*'s (1992) account leads us to expect the reluctance to negate root infinitives.

22. Philippe's MLU is similar to Hein's (cf. note 7).

23. Based on evidence from Flemish I assume (Haegeman 1994a) that *ze* 'them' and *t* 'it' are clitics, and that *je* 'you', *'m* 'him' and *'r* 'her' are weak pronouns. The classification may be disputed: perhaps there are no genuine object clitics in Dutch. However, regardless of the status of clitics/weak pronouns my point still stands that strong pronouns, which should be the less marked in the hierarchy postulated by Hamann *et al.* (this volume) are significantly less frequent than the deficient forms.

24. A further issue which I address in independent work (Haegeman forthc. b) is the relation between the root-infinitive phenomenon and the occurrence of root null subjects in child data.

References

Barbier, I. 1994. "An Experimental Study of Scrambling and Object Shift in the Acquisition of Dutch." Paper presented at the Gala Conference, Durham. Ms., Cornell University.

Bennis, H. 1986. *Gaps and Dummies.* Dordrecht: Foris.

Boser, K, B. Lust, L. Santelmann and J. Whitman. 1992. "The Syntax of CP and V2 in Early Child German (ECG). The Strong Continuity Hypothesis'. *NELS proceedings*, ed. by K. Broderick, 51–65. Amherst, Mass: Graduate Linguistic Student Association.

Cardinaletti, A. & M. Starke. 1993. "On Dependent Pronouns and Pronoun Movement." Paper presented at the GLOW Conference, Lund.

Chomsky, N. 1993. "A Minimalist Program for Linguistic Theory." *A View from Building 20,* ed. by K. Hale & J. Keyser, 1–52. Cambridge, Mass.: MIT Press.

Clahsen, H., S. Eisenbeiss & M. Penke. This volume. "Lexical Learning in Early Syntactic Development."

Cottell, S. 1994. "Negation in Irish." Ms., University of Geneva.

Crisma, P. 1992. "On the Acquisition of *Wh*-Questions in French." *GenGenP* 0.115–122.

Enç, M. 1987. "Anchoring Conditions for Tense." *Linguistic Inquiry* 18.633–657.

Friedemann, M.-A. 1992. "The Underlying Position of External Arguments in French: A study in Adult and Child Grammar." *GenGenP* 0.123–144.

Grimshaw, J. 1991. "Extended Projection." Ms., Brandeis University.

———. 1993. "Minimal Projection and Clause Structure." Ms., Rutgers University.

Guasti, M.-T. 1993. "Causatives and Perception Verbs." Turin: Rosenberg & Sellier.

————. 1993/4. "Verb Syntax in Italian Child Grammar: Finite and nonfinite verbs." *Language Acquisition* 3.1–40.

Guéron, J. 1993. "Sur la syntaxe du temps." *Langue Française* 100.102–124.

Guéron, J. & T. Hoekstra. 1988. "T-chains and the Constituent Structure of Auxiliaries." *Constituent Structure*, ed. by A. Cardinaletti, G. Cinque & G. Giusti, 35–99. Dordrecht: Foris.

————. 1992. "Chaînes temporelles et phrases réduites." *Structure de la phrase et théorie du liage*, ed. by H.G. Obenauer & A. Zribi-Herz, 69–91. Presses Universitaires de Vincennes.

Guilfoyle, E. 1984. "The Acquisition of Tense and the Emergence of Lexical Subjects in Child Grammar of English." *McGill Working Papers in Linguistics* 1.120–131.

Haegeman, L. 1991a. "On the Relevance of Clitic Placement for the Analysis of Subject-initial Verb Second in West-Flemish." *Groninger Arbeiten zur Germanistischen Linguistic* 34.29–66.

————. 1993a. "Some Speculations on Argument Shift, Clitics and Crossing in West-Flemish." *Dialektsyntax* (=*Linguistische Berichte*, Special Issue), ed. by J. Bayer, 131–160. Opladen: Westdeutscher Verlag.

————. 1993b. "The Morphology and Distribution of Object Clitics in West-Flemish." *Studia Linguistica.* NS.47.57–94.

————. 1993c. "Object Clitics in West-Flemish and the Identification of A/Ā-Positions." *GenGenP* 1.2.1–31.

————. 1994a. "The Typology of Syntactic Positions: L-relatedness and the A/Ā-distinction." *Minimalism and Kayne's Asymmetry Hypothesis* (= *Groninger Arbeiten zur Germanistischen Linguistik*, Special Issue), ed. by Jan-Wouter Zwart, 37.115–157.

————. 1994b. "Root Infinitives, Tense and Truncated Structures." *GenGenP* 2.1.12–41.

————. 1995. *The Syntax of Negation.* Cambridge: Cambridge University Press.

————. Forthcoming a. "Root Infinitives, Tense and Truncated Structures in Dutch." *Language Acquisition.*

————. Forthcoming b. "Root Infinitives and Root Null Subjects in Early Dutch." To appear in the Proceedings of GALA, ed. by C. Koster & F. Wijnen.

————. In preparation a. "Adverbials and AgrP."

Haegeman, L. & R. Zanuttini. 1991. "Negative Heads and the Neg Criterion." *The Linguistic Review* 8.233–251.

Hamann, C. 1987. "The awesome seeds of reference time." *Essays on Tensing in English*, ed. by A. Schopf, 27–69. Tübingen: Max Niemeyer.

————. 1992. "Late Empty Subjects in German Child Language." *Technical Reports in Formal and Computational Linguistics* 4. University of Geneva.

————. 1994. "Negation, Infinitives and Heads." Ms., University of Geneva.

Hamann, C., L. Rizzi & U. Frauenfelder. This volume. *On the Acquisiton of the Pronominal System in French.*

Jordens, P. 1990. "The Acquisition of Verb Placement in Dutch and German." *Linguistics* 28.1407–1448.

Hoekstra, T. & P. Jordens. 1991. "From Adjunct to Head." Ms., University of Leiden.

Koster, J. 1993. "Predicate Incorporation and the Word Order of Dutch." *Paths towards Universal Grammar: Studies in honor of Richard S. Kayne,* ed. by G. Cinque, J. Koster, J.-Y. Pollock, L. Rizzi & R Zanuttini, 255–276. Washington: Georgetown University Press.

Krämer, I. 1994. "The Licensing of Subjects in Early Child Language." *MIT Working Papers in Linguistics* 19.197–212.

Laka, I. 1990. "Negation in Syntax: On the nature of functional categories and projections." Diss., Massachusetts Institute of Technology, Cambridge.

———. 1994. "Negation in syntax: The view from Basque." *Rivista di Linguistica* 5.2. Thematic issue on *The Syntax of Sentential Negation,* ed. by L. Haegeman, 245–273.

Lebeaux, D. 1989. "Language Acquisition and the Form of the Grammar." Diss., University of Massachusetts, Amherst.

MacWhinney B. & C. Snow. 1985. "The Child language Data Exchange system." *Journal of Child Language* 12.271–296.

Pierce, A. 1989. "On the Emergence of Syntax: A crosslinguistic study." Diss., Massachusetts Institute of Technology, Cambridge.

Platzack, C. 1990. "A Grammar without Functional Categories: A syntactic study of early Swedish Child Language." *Nordic Journal of Linguistics* 13.107–126.

Poeppel, D. & K. Wexler. 1991. "The Status of Functional Categories in Early German Grammar. Ms., Massachusetts Institute of Technology, Cambridge.

———. 1993. "The Full Competence Hypothesis of Clause Structure in Early German." *Language* 69.1–33.

Radford, A. 1990. *Syntactic Theory and the Acquisition of English Syntax.* Oxford: Basil Blackwell.

———. 1994. "Clausal Projections in Early Child Grammar." *Essex Reports in Linguistics* 3.32–72.

Reichenbach, H. 1947. *Elements of Symbolic Logic.* New York: Free Press.

Rizzi, L. 1990a. "Speculations on Verb Second." *Grammar in Progress,* ed. by J. Mascaró & M. Nespor, 375–386. Dordrecht: Foris.

———. 1990b. *Relativized Minimality.* Cambridge, Mass.: MIT Press.

———. 1994a. "Early Null Subjects and Root Null subjects." *Language Acquisition Studies in Generative Grammar,* ed. by T. Hoekstra & B.D. Schwartz, 151–177. Amsterdam: John Benjamins.

———. 1994b. "Some Notes on Linguistic Theory and Language Development: The case of root infinitives." *Language Acquisition* 3.371–393.

Roeper, T. 1992. "Reflections on Reference in Language Acquisition." Ms., University of Massachusetts, Amherst.

Sano, T. & N. Hyams. 1994. "Agreement, Finiteness, and the Development of Null Arguments. *Proceedings of NELS 24,* ed. by M. Gonzáles, 543–558. Amherst, Mass.: Graduate Linguistic Student Association.

Schaeffer, J. 1994. "On the Acquisition of Scrambling in Dutch." Ms., Utrecht University.

Sportiche, D. 1992. "Clitics, Voice and Spec–Head Licensing." Paper presented at the GLOW Conference, Lisbon, May 13th.

Travis, L. 1984. "Parameters and Effects of Word Order Variation." Diss., Massachusetts Institute of Technology, Cambridge.

Weissenborn, J. 1992. "Null Subjects in Early Grammars: Implications for parameter-setting theories." *Theoretical Issues in Language Acquisition: Continuity and change in development,* ed. by J. Weissenborn, H. Goodluck. & T. Roeper, 269–299. Hillsdale, N.J.: Lawrence Erlbaum.

Weissenborn, J. & Z. Penner. 1994. "The Acquisition of Case and Agreement in the German DP." Paper presented at the conference on Generative Studies of the Acquisition of Case and Agreement, University of Essex.

Weverink, M. 1989. "The Subject in Relation to Inflection in Child Language." MA Thesis, Utrecht University.

Wexler, K. 1992. "Optional Infinitives, Head Movement and the Economy of Derivations in Child Grammar." *Verb Movement,* ed. by D. Lightfoot & N. Hornstein, 305–350. Cambridge: Cambridge University Press.

Wijnen, F. 1994. "Incremental Acquisition of Phrase Structure: A longitudinal analysis of verb placement in Dutch child language." Ms., University of Groningen.

Wyngaerd, G. vanden. 1989. "Raising to Object in English and Dutch." *Dutch Working Papers in English Language and Linguistics* 14.1–19. Leiden University.

Zanuttini, R. 1991. "Syntactic Properties of Sentential Negation: A comparative study of Romance languages, Diss., University of Pennsylvania.

———. 1993. "Re-examining negative Clauses." Ms., University of Pennsylvania.

———. Forthcoming. "On the Relevance of Tense for Sentential Negation." *Parameters and Functional Heads. Essays in Comparative Syntax,* ed. by L. Rizzi & A. Belletti. Oxford: Oxford University Press.

———. 1995. "Speculations on Negative Imperatives." *Rivista di Linguistica* 6.1. Thematic issue on *The Syntax of sentential Negation,* ed. by L. Haegeman, 119–141.

Zwart, C. J. W. 1991. "Clitics in Dutch: Evidence for the position of INFL. *Groninger Arbeiten zur Germanistischen Linguistik* 33.71–92. Amsterdam: John Benjamins.

———. 1992a. "Subject Initial Verb Second in West-Flemish: A reply to Haegeman." *Groninger Arbeiten zur Germanistischen Linguistik* 35.72–1.

———. 1992b. "Notes on Clitics in Dutch." Paper presented at the ESF workshop on clitics, Lund, May 22.

———. 1993a. "SOV Languages are Head-initial. Ms., University of Groningen.

———. 1993b. "Dutch Syntax." Diss., University of Groningen.

On the Acquisition of Subject and Object Clitics in French

Cornelia Hamann
University of Geneva

Luigi Rizzi
University of Geneva

Uli H. Frauenfelder
University of Geneva

1. Introduction

It has long been recognized that the study of pronouns can play a key role in the understanding of the system of mental representations for language. The richness and diversity of pronominal systems and the fact that these systems obey sharp formal and interpretative constraints has proved instrumental for the investigation of topics of great theoretical significance such as the fine-grained functional structure of clauses, different types of licensing mechanisms, and locality constraints. So it is not surprising that much attention has been devoted to the acquisition of pronouns within the recent trend of linguistically motivated developmental psycholinguistic studies.

This paper reports some preliminary results on the acquisition of French pronouns. The study is based on a quantitative analysis of a natural production corpus, collected in the framework of an interdepartmental project involving the units of General Linguistics and Psycholinguistics of the University of Geneva. A clear result emerging from this study is that around the age of two the child already masters the morpho-lexical distinction between clitic and free forms, as well as its syntactic consequences: clitics are never placed in non-clitic positions in the early productions. Second, a sharp dissociation exists between the acquisition of subject and complement clitics, the latter being significantly delayed. This observation confirms findings by Pierce (1989, 1992), Friedemann (1992), Haegeman (this volume). It supports the view that subject and complement clitics are distinct theoretical entities and, in spite of their common properties, should not be fully assimilated. A third finding is that subject clitics appear to be sensitive to the tensed/untensed distinction while object clitics are not.

The paper is organized as follows: After a short summary of the assumed theoretical background and a presentation of the questions we intend to ask (Section 1), the natural production corpus is presented (Section 2). Section 3 focuses on the results of a quantitative analysis of the occurrence and distribution of pronominal forms in early productions. Section 4 concludes the paper by relating the results to the adopted theoretical framework.

1.1. *Background*

Romance pronominal clitics differ from full nominal and pronominal expressions with respect to a number of properties: they cannot be used in isolation (1a, b), cannot be conjoined (2a, b), cannot be modified (3a, b), cannot receive focal stress as in (4a, b), cannot be separated from the verb (unless by another clitic, or under very special circumstances in some Romance varieties). All in all, their distribution is severely restricted with respect to full nominal and pronominal expressions; see Kayne (1975) for the original discussion of these properties. Using such properties as a kind of crude test for clitichood, we would be lead to assimilate subject and object unstressed pronouns in French:

(1) a. *Qui est venu? *Il.*
         who is come   he
     b. *Qui as-tu   vu? *Le.*
         who have-you seen him

(2) a. *Il et elle viendront.*
         he and she will.come
     b. *Je le et la connais.*
         I him and her know

(3) a. *Ils   deux viendront.*
         they two will.come
     b. *Je les deux connais.*
         I them two know

(4) a. *IL viendra (pas Marie)*
         he will.come not Marie
     b. *Je LE connais (pas Marie)*
         I him know   not Marie

(5) a. *Il probablement viendra.*
         he probably   will.come
     b. *Pierre le   probablement connaît.*
         Pierre him probably   knows

However, a simple inspection of the structural representation of clauses strongly suggests that the assimilation between the two cases cannot be complete:

(6)

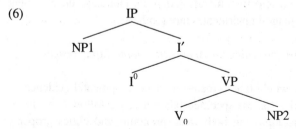

If we assume that the clitic position is associated to I^0 (the surface position of the inflected verb in French), a clitic can legitimately bind a trace in object position (possibly through a number of intermediate steps, if the object pronoun first moves to the Spec of some intervening functional projection on its way to the cliticization site), but not in subject position, due to the fact that I^0 does not c-command NP1. Adopting some version of the VP-INTERNAL SUBJECT HYPO-THESIS (hence postulating a subject trace lower than I^0 in (6)) would not solve the problem since, under a sufficiently strong version of the Extended Projection Principle (Chomsky 1981), position NP1 is obligatory and must be filled by a legitimate element.

A traditional way of tackling this problem is to assume that subject clitics are full NPs in the syntax, i.e., occupy position NP1 at S-structure, so that on this level (and at LF), there is no trace binding to worry about. They undergo a cliticization process only in the phonology, where the proper binding require-ment is irrelevant (Kayne 1983; Rizzi 1986). If phonological cliticization is limited to linearly adjacent positions, this option is not open to object clitics, which must undergo syntactic movement and give rise to representations which satisfy proper binding. The common properties of subject and object clitics follow, in this approach, from the fact that they are all clitics in the phonology, even though their syntactic status is very different. More recently, it has been proposed (Cardinaletti & Starke 1994) that French subject and object clitics instantiate two different kinds of structurally impoverished elements: the former are WEAK PRONOUNS, constrained to occur in a strict specifier–head configura-tion with the licensing head; the latter are genuine clitics, undergoing head movement to be associated to their licensing head. The common properties of subject and object clitics follow, under this approach, by their being IMPOVER-ISHED ELEMENTS, even though to a different extent.

What these approaches have in common is the fact that subject and object clitics are very different entities on the abstract levels of mental representation

S-structure and LF. This leads us to expect dissociations between the two classes arising along a number of empirical dimensions: syntactic behavior, cross-linguistic distribution, selective manifestation in language development and selective loss in language impairment, among others.

1.2. Some Questions Concerning the Acquisition of the Clitic System

In this paper we would like to focus on the developmental evidence bearing on the theory of clitics (unless specified otherwise, we follow here the normal use of this term, encompassing both weak pronouns and clitics proper in the Cardinaletti & Starke 1994 terminology). The first question to ask concerns the acquisition of the peculiar distributional properties of clitics:

How early does the child show mastery of the morpholexical distinction between clitic and non-clitic forms, as well as of the syntactic consequences of this distinction?

According to current approaches in which lexical, morphological and syntactic properties are strictly integrated, the two parts of this question are two sides of the same coin. So we want to know how early the child correctly places clitic forms in the restricted class of clitic positions and free forms in the full range of normal NP positions.

The second question concerns the possible existence of differences in the time-course of the acquisition of subject and object clitics. The answers to these questions may provide empirical reasons for differentiating subject and object clitics in adult French:

Do subject and object clitics arise simultaneously in the course of acquisition? If not, how can we interpret the observed order?

In earlier studies on the acquisition of French, it has been concluded that object clitics are found relatively late in development, cf. Clark (1985). This claim was challenged in Weissenborn (1988) where the occurrence of the object clitics *en, le, te, la, les* is documented in the speech of three French children between the ages of 2;00 and 2;04 (Weissenborn 1988:6, 7). Subsequently, Pierce (1989, 1992) found evidence for the early mastery of the system of subject clitics in French. Friedemann (1992) observed a delay in the mastery of French object clitics, a result that was also found by White (this volume) for L2 French. Haegeman (this volume) observes that object clitics are much rarer than subject clitics in early Dutch. On the basis of the new empirical material offered by our French corpus, we would like to contribute to this unresolved issue concerning the timing of the acquisition of object clitics.

The third question combines aspects of the first two:

How do subject and object clitics distribute in tensed and untensed clauses in acquisition?

In adult French, subject and object clitics mirror the distribution of free subject and object NPs with respect to the tensed/untensed distinction: objects (clitic or not) can occur in both tensed and untensed clauses, while subjects (clitic or not) are restricted to tensed clauses:

(7)   a.   *Que Jean aime Marie, c'est normal.*
          that Jean loves Marie it.is normal

      b.   **(Jean) aimer Marie, c'est normal.*
          Jean love Marie it.is normal

(8)   a.   *Qu' il l' aime, c'est normal.*
          that he her loves it.is normal

      b.   **(Il) l' aimer, c'est normal.*
          he her love it.is normal

What kind of pattern do we find in acquisition? The question is made interesting by the existence of root infinitives in early grammars. Around the age of two, children typically produce root infinitives, main clauses with the verb in the infinitival form (Wexler 1994; Rizzi 1994 and references cited there). Root infinitives, contrary to adult embedded infinitives, appear to be able to co-occur with lexical subjects (examples from Pierce 1989):

(9)   a.   *monsieur conduire*
          man   drive

      b.   *tracteur casser maison*
          tractor destroy house

What about subject clitics in root infinitives? Pierce (1989, 1992), based on the French corpus available on CHILDES (MacWhinney & Snow 1985) and the Lightbown (1977) corpus, showed that subject clitics tend not to occur in this construction, an important property which sheds light on the structural constitution of root infinitives. Do object clitics show the same asymmetric distribution? We would like to address these questions on the basis of the new French corpus.

2. Method

One monolingual child acquiring French, Augustin, was studied longitudinally over a period of approximately 10 months. He was recorded ten times at his home in Neuchâtel in 45 minute sessions. The first 30 minutes of each session were transcribed. The recording sessions occurred roughly every three to four weeks. However, there was a two months break between the seventh and eighth recording sessions and a two and a half months break between the eighth and ninth recording sessions. Augustin was born on January 20, 1991. The subject's age, at the first recording, was two years, zero months and two days and two years, nine months and 30 days at the final recording. Generally, the mother and the experimenter were both present at recordings.

Recordings and transcriptions were made by two students at the Faculté de Psychologie et des Sciences de l'Education at the University of Geneva. Moreover, these transcriptions were hand corrected by three further students of the Faculté des Lettres.

The following conventions were used. If the child utterance was made up of fully comprehensible adult words, an orthographic transcription was given and no interpretation was added as in (10a). If a child utterance did not quite correspond phonetically to the adult utterance but was easily comprehensible, it was rendered in orthographic phonetic transcription, cf. *ça toune* and an interpretation was added between brackets (*ça tourne*) 'that turns' as in (12a). When the phonetic deviance from adult utterances was more marked (and often systematic as in [t] for [s]) a phonetic transcription was given in square brackets. The phonetic symbols correspond to the computer-coded phonemic notation of SAMPA as discussed in Wells (1989) for European languages, which is similar to UNIBET used in the CHILDES database, cf. MacWhinney (1991). If possible, an interpretation was added (10b). Sometimes, when the rest of the utterance was clearly comprehensible as in (10d), a phonetic chunk was left uninterpreted. In some cases a phonetic transcription was completely uninterpretable. Such a case was included in the transcription for further verification, but not included in the counts of utterances or otherwise.

3.   Results

3.1. *Proportion of Verbal Utterances*

Romance clitics are verbal clitics, in that they require a verbal element as their host. A preliminary count which is relevant for studying the acquisition of the clitic system is then the number of verbal utterances, as well as the ratio verbal utterances / total of utterances. Before addressing the main theoretical questions, we must make sure that there is a sufficient number of potential clitic environments in the transcriptions to warrant further analysis.

Of the total of 2,191 utterances in the Augustin corpus there were 771 verbal utterances, i.e., 35.2%. During the period of observation, there was a considerable increase in the use of verbal utterances. In the first seven record-ings (age ranging from 2;0.2 to 2;4.22) verbal utterances range from 15.7% to 26.6% of the total, while in the last three recordings (ages 2;6.16 to 2;9.30, including two longer breaks of two and two and a half months) the proportion of verbal utterances ranges from 53.2% to 56.6%. The remarkably sharp increase in the number of verbal utterances produced by Augustin is reminiscent of the findings that Valian (1991) obtained in her cross-sectional study for English.

Table 1 shows the numbers and ratio of utterances and utterances contain-ing a verb form. This count and calculation includes all occurrences of finite verbs as in (10a), all infinitives (10b, c, d), even those introduced by prepositions (10d), and all occurrences of past participles (10e). It also includes the occur-rences of verb forms ending in [e] together with an auxiliary or modal proform as in (10f) where no decision is possible as to the status of this form as infini-tive or participle, but the form nevertheless is clearly verbal. An auxiliary–verb complex was counted as one verbal form (10g). The count also includes imperatives (10h).

Table 1. Number of Utterances and Verbal Utterances of All Kinds in the Augustin Corpus

sample	age	total number of utterances (u)	number of verbal utterances (v)	percentage of verbal utterances (v/u)
A.01	2;0.2	270	57	21.1
A.02	2;0.23	150	30	20.0
A.03	2;1.15	140	22	15.7
A.04	2;2.13	224	55	24.5
A.05	2;3.10	164	45	27.4
A.06	2;4.1	224	62	27.6
A.07	2;4.22	204	54	26.5
A.08	2;6.16	218	116	53.2
A.09	2;9.2	309	175	56.6
A.10	2;9.30	288	155	53.8
	total	2,191	771	35.2

(10)   a.   *on joue*   A(2;0.2)
                we play

        b.   Experimenter: *Tu veux quoi?*
                                  you want what
            A: [*ote tu ta*]   (*ôter   tout ça)*   A(2;0.2)
                                                empty all   this

        c.   *manger, maman, manger*   A(2;0.2)
                eat   mummy eat
                (A wants to open a box of chocolates)

        d.   [*katschuk*] *pour faire pan pan*   A(2;9.2)
                              to   do   pom pom

        e.   [*kake*] (*cassé*)   A(2;0.2)
                broken

        f.   [*e pa deA~Ze sa*] ([*e*] *pas derang*[*e*] *ça*   A(2;0.2)
                                     (*veux/vais pas déranger ça)*
                                     want/will not disturb   this
                                     (*ai/est   pas dérangé ça)*
                                     have/is not disturbed this

        g.   *est pa(r)ti papa*   A(2;0.2)
                is   left   Daddy

        h.   *attends, attends* [*KitE*]]   A(2;0.2)
                wait   wait

3.2. Distributional Constraints

In order to address the first question concerning the acquisition of the distributional properties of clitics, we must start from an inventory of clitic and non-clitic positions. In adult French, the major clitic position is the immediate preverbal position (adjacent to the verb, or separated from the verb by another clitic, as in *Je la lui donne* [I it him give]); two kinds of immediate postverbal positions are occupied by clitics in special constructions: main questions for subject clitics (*est-il parti?* [is-he left]) and non-negative imperatives for object clitics (*prends-le* [take-it]).

Elsewhere, clitics are excluded: they cannot occur in non-verbal utterances, i.e., they cannot be used in isolation (11a), in postcopular predicate position (11b), in postverbal object position (11c), as objects of prepositions (11d), as right or left dislocated elements (11e–f):

(11) a. *Qu' as- tu vu? *le* (cf. ok: *ça*)
what have-you seen him that

b. *Jean est le* (cf. *Jean est intelligent, Jean l'est*)
Jean is it Jean is ˙ intelligent Jean it.is

c. *Jean dit toujours le* (cf. *Jean dit toujours ça*)
John says always it John says always that

d. *Jean parle de le* (cf. *Jean parle de ça*)
John speaks of it John speaks of this

e. *Je le connais, le* (cf. *Je le connais, lui*)
I him know him I him know him

f. *Le, je le connais* (cf. *Lui, je le connais*)
him I him know him I him know

Are these distributional constraints respected in the child's utterances? The answer is yes, apparently without exception. In the corpus we found 282 occurrences of unambiguous subject or object clitic forms *je, tu, il, on, ils, ce, me, te, se, le, les, y, en* (we exclude here the 32 occurrences of *elle*, a subject clitic which is ambiguous with the oblique form: *elle vient* 'she comes', *pour elle* 'for her'; see Tables 4 and 5 for individual occurrences). None of these occurrences were found in a non-verbal utterance, or in any other non-clitic position found in list (11).

It is particularly instructive to compare the restricted distribution of clitic forms with the very wide distribution of the non-clitic demonstrative pronoun *ça*. In the adult grammar, in addition to preverbal subject position, *ça* freely occurs as a postcopular pro-predicate in the expression *c'est ça* 'that's it', as a post-verbal object, as a prepositional object (the expression *comme ça* 'like this' is presumably to be assimilated to this case), in right- and left-dislocated position (particularly in the expressions *c'est beau, ça* 'it is nice, that' and *ça, c'est beau* 'that, it is nice'), modified by the universal quantifier *tout*, and in nonverbal utterances, for instance as a short answer to a question. This wide distribution is mirrored exactly by the early productions of Augustin. Consider the following examples:

(12) a. *ça toune* (*ça tourne*) A(2;3.10)
that turns

b. *[teta]* (*c'est ça*) A(2;0.2)
it.is that
'That's it.'

c. *manger ça?* A(2;0.2)
eat that

Table 2. Occurrences of ça in Different Verbal Environments in the Augustin Corpus

age	subject	predicate c'est ça	object	prepositional object	comme ça	right dislocation	left dislocation	tout ça	utterances	total
2;0.2	2	1	4	0	1	1	0	0	0	9
2;0.23	0	0	3	0	1	3	0	0	1	8
2;1.15	1	0	0	0	1	0	0	1	0	3
2;2.13	1	0	0	0	2	0	0	0	0	3
2;3.10	1	0	1	1	5	3	0	0	2	12
2;4.1	0	0	0	0	3	2	1	0	1	6
2;4.22	0	1	4	0	6	6	6	0	2	20
2;6.16	0	0	2	0	2	3	2	0	2	18
2;9.2	2	1	4	1	7	4	3	1	0	21
2;9.30	0	1	2	3	18	2	0	0	0	29
total	8	3	20	6	46	24	12	2	8	129

d. *ôter   ça*   A(2;4.22)
    empty that
e. *e fais avec ça*   (*je fais avec ça*)   A(2;6.16)
    I do with that
f. *c'est pour ça*   A(2;9.2)
    it is for   that
g. [*e kate   ta*]   (*est cassé ça*)   A(2;4.1)
    is broken that
h. *c'est quoi, ta*   (*c'est quoi, ça*)   A(2;6.16)
    it is what that
i. *ça, c' est quoi?*   A(2;6.16)
    that it is what
l. *qu' est-ce que tu   veux enlever?* — A: *ça*   A(2;4.22)
    what is it that you want take.away   that
m. *qu' est-ce qu' il y   a   encore dans la boite?*
    what is- it that it there has still in   the box
    — A: *encore ça*   A(2;4.1)
        still   that
n. *qu' est-ce que tu   veux réparer?* - A: *ça*   A(2;6.16)
    what is it that you want repair   that

Of the 129 occurrences of *ça*, no less than 121 are found in a position from which a clitic would be excluded in the adult grammar (see Table 2), while all the 282 unambiguous clitic forms are correctly placed in clitic position. Already in the first two recordings (ages 2;0.2 and 2;0.23), 15 of the 17 occurrences of *ça* are in positions from which a clitic would be banned in the adult grammar, whereas all the 21 occurrences of clitics (see following tables) are placed in clitic position. We thus seem to have rather robust evidence that, from the earliest syntactically relevant productions, the child masters the lexical distinction between clitic and non-clitic forms, as well as the major syntactic consequences of this distinction.

3.3. *Subject vs. Object Clitics*

Table 3 presents the occurrence of subject and object clitics in the Augustin corpus.

There is a clear difference in the appearance of subject and object clitics in the corpus. Different kinds of subject clitics already occur at the age of 2;0 (see also Table 4), while the first genuine object clitic occurs at the age of 2;2.13 in

Table 3. Occurrences of Subject and Object Clitics in Verbal Utterances in the Augustin Corpus

age	verbal utterances	subject clitics	% of verbal utterances	object clitics	% of verbal utterances
2;0.2	57	17	29.8	0	0
2;0.23	30	4	13.3	0	0
2;1.15	22	4	18.2	0	0
2;2.13	55	16	29.1	1	1.8
2;3.10	45	12	26.6	0	0
2;4.1	62	10	16.1	0	0
2;4.22	54	11	20.4	1	1.9
2;6.16	116	25	21.6	2	1.7
2;9.2	175	80	45.7	10	5.7
2;9.30	155	99	63.4	22	14.2
total	771	278	36.1	36	4.7

the form of an enclitic: *ateinds-le* (*éteinds-le*) [turn.off it]. In fact, this is the only occurrence of an object clitic in the first six recordings (2;0.2–2;4.1), and we find only one more object clitic in the next recording. Observe that in the first seven recordings: 2;02.–2;4.22, 74 occurrences of subject clitics have been identified. It is only after the age 2;6 that we find a substantial number of object clitics. In the same period, the number of subject clitics increases dramatically.

The counts for subject clitics in Table 3 are based on the occurrences of *je, tu, il, elle, on, nous, ils, elles* and *c'*. Clearly identifiable pro-forms which did not match the adult forms perfectly, but could be considered phonetic approximations, were also counted as clitics. Thus Augustin used either *'l* or *i* for *il*, depending on whether the following verbal element started with a consonant or a vowel, as in:

(13) a. [*i   ku   apE*]   (*il court après*)   A(2;0.2)
          he runs after

     b.   *'l   est gros*   (*il est gros*)   A(2;0.2)
          he is fat

That the form *'l est* is not just a misanalysis of the auxiliary form is suggested by the occurrence of alternations such as the following, sometimes in the same recording:

(14) a.   *est tout tout tout* [*kake*] (*caché*)   A(2;0.2)
          is all all all   hidden
      b.   *'l est gros*   A(2;0.2)
          he is fat

Utterance (14a) is a case of a null-subject sentence, a familiar phenomenon in child language, while (14b) is the variant with an overt pronominal subject. In some difficult cases, the decision whether the sentences contained an overt subject clitic or not was taken on the basis of an analysis of the acoustic waveform. For the example (14a), Figure 1a shows an abrupt onset of the vowel [E] in *est*, whereas Figure 1b shows a much more gradual transition which corresponds to a liquid consonant in utterance (14b).

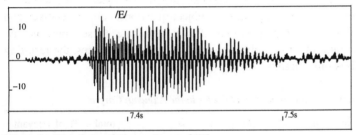

Figure 1a. Waveform of Abrupt Onset of [E]

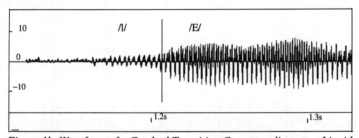

Figure 1b. Waveform of a Gradual Transition Correspondiong to a Liquid

An alternation similar to '*l/i* could be observed for *je*. Here, Augustin used [j] as in [j] *ai fini* 'I have finished' before vowels and often a schwa or [e] before consonants. In order to remain on the safe side and avoid possible confusion with homophonous proto-syntactic devices (Bottari *et al.* 1992), only the [j] form was counted as a clitic. Another problem was the occurrence of examples involving the adult *il y a* [it there has] 'there is/are') construction which is phonetically reduced to *y a* even in informal adult speech. These examples were not counted as occurrences of *il*. They were included in the count for the object clitic *y*, however.

As to a separation of *il* and *ils*, which are phonetically indistinguishable (except in LIAISON contexts), we counted the plural form only in two utterances in which the verbal agreement unambiguously required a plural subject:

(15) a. *ils   sont où   les ciseaux*   A(2;9.2)
          they are where the scissors
      b. *ils   sont là.*   A(2;9.30)
          they are there

Following these guidelines we obtain Table 4 which shows the occurrence of individual subject clitics. It should also be noticed that the total set of verbal utterances given in Table 3 includes contexts in which subject clitics would be banned in adult grammars: imperatives, subject questions, subject relatives and infinitives introduced by prepositions. If we eliminate these contexts and recalculate the ratio of subject clitics to *relevant* verbal utterances, the resulting proportion raises only slightly.

Table 4. Occurrences of Different Subject Clitics in the Augustin Corpus

age	je	tu	il	elle	on	ils	c'	total	% of relevant verbal utterances
2;0.2			4		11		2	17	33.3
2;0.23			3				1	4	16.6
2;1.15					4			4	25.0
2;2.13			4	1	9		2	16	36.3
2;3.10			5		7			12	35.3
2;4.1		1	4		1		4	10	18.2
2;4.22			10				1	11	22.9
2;6.16			10	1	2		12	25	24.7
2;9.2	18	12	13	12	3	1	21	80	55.2
2;9.30	22	11	13	18	7	1	27	99	73.9
total	40	24	66	32	44	2	70	278	42.6

It is important to note that the third person clitics (*il, on, c'*) are attested from the earliest recorded productions, while first and second person singular clitics are massively attested only in the latest recordings. The late occurrence of *je* in our count could be due to the restrictive way of distinguishing the occurence of a clitic and a proform as discussed above. Non-third person plural clitics are not attested at all in the Augustin corpus.

Table 5 gives the occurrence of object and other complement clitics in this corpus. To make sure that the absence of object clitics is not due to Augustin's fortuitous failure to use verbs taking complements, we computed the percentage for object clitics as a function of the total number of the occurrences of complement-taking verbs. This count includes all occurrences of verbs with an overt direct or indirect object or a complement (locative or other). It also includes verbal utterances without an overt complement if the verb obligatorily takes a complement. To facilitate the matching with object clitics, double complement taking verbs were counted twice. Unclear cases, where it could not be decided whether an object clitic, some unidentifiable proform or a null object was present, were excluded. This recalculation does not change the picture very much, since object clitics are virtually absent until relatively late. The observed differences between subject and object clitics remain very sharp.

Table 5. Occurrences of Different Object Clitics in the Augustin Corpus

age	me	te	se	le	la	les	en	y	total	% of relevant verbal utterances
2;0.2										0
2;0.23										0
2;1.15										0
2;2.13			1						1	3.8
2;3.10										0
2;4.1										0
2;4.22	1								1	5.0
2;6.16	1							1	2	3.9
2;9.2	1	2	1	2		2	2		10	14.3
2;9.30	1		4			4	13		22	23.9
total	4	2	5	3		2	6	14	36	10.5

The following is an exhaustive list of the object and other complement clitics produced by Augustin. The first and third example are part of a song sung by the child, hence have not been counted. The fixed expression *s'il te plait* was also not included in the actual count. *Vas-t-en,* on the other hand was included because Augustin uses *s'en aller* productively as exemplified by his use of *elle s'en va.*

Two of the following examples show enclitic forms in positive imperatives
(the first at 2;2.13 is the first genuine occurrence of an object clitic form; the
second one is *vas-t-en* at 2;9.2). We did not find any cases of erroneous pro-
clitic forms in positive imperatives, which occur in other corpora according to
Haverkort & Weissenborn (1991). Nor did we find a third person dative clitic.

(16)   *topez-la*   (*trempez-le*)   A(2;1.15)
        soak it   song
        ateinds-le   (*éteinds-le*)   A(2;2.13)
        switch.off it
        topez-la   A(2;2.13)
        soak it   song
        papa, i(l) me dit   comme i(l) faut   papa   A(2;4.22)
        dad   he me tells how   it   must (be)
        me met un autre short   A(2;6.16)
        me put   other shorts
        y   a un petit chat   A(2;6.16)
        there is a   little cat
        on les r... joue avec   A(2;9.2)
        we them   play with
        e me gratter   A(2;9.2)
          me scratch   infinitive
        (xxx) que les   gratter (xxx)   A(2;9.2)
            only them scratch   infinitive
        T'   as   vu, en   a   par-terre aussi
        you have seen from.it has on-floor too   A(2;9.2)
        e   t'amuse avec elle   A(2;9.2)
        you entertain with her
        ne s'amuse   avec elle, moi   A(2;9.2)
        not himself.entertains with her I
        parce qu' il le coupe puis le plie   A(2;9.2)
        because he it cuts   then it folds
        s' il te   plaît   A(2;9.2)
        if it you pleases   fixed
        va-t- en, maman   A(2;9.2)
        go-you away mummy
        nan, d'abord se   ranger comme ça   A(2;9.30)
        no   first   oneself put   like   that   infinitive

se ranger comme...comme ça	A(2;9.30)
oneself put like like that	infinitive
pis y a des arbres et pis des [mejO~]	A(2;9.30)
then there is trees and then [ ]	
(xxx) y a une boule de [manjia]	A(2;9.30)
there is a ball of [ ]	
elle dit (xxx) y a une boule de [manjia]	A(2;9.30)
she says there is a ball of [ ]	
nan, je me repose	A(2;9.30)
no I myself rest	
qu' est-ce qui y a?	A(2;9.30)
what is it that it there is	
y a des motos de course	A(2;9.30)
there is motorbikes of race	
y a meme pas quelqu'un sur cette moto	A(2;9.30)
there is even not somebody on this motorbike	
Euh, y a deux roues	A(2;9.30)
uh there is two wheels	
Là, y a pas de place	A(2;9.30)
there there is not of place	
y a plus rien	A(2;9.30)
there is any more nothing	
ah, nan, y en a ... a pas là	A(2;9.30)
ah no there of.it is is not there	
y en a pas	A(2;9.30)
there of.it is not	
T' as vu, y a pas de gomme	A(2;9.30)
you have seen there is not of eraser	
y a pas de place comme ça	A(2;9.30)
there is not of place like that	
elle s' en va	A(2;9.30)
she herself from.it goes	
elle s' en va [pate]	A(2;9.30)
she herself from.it goes	

Our data thus confirm the existence of major differences in the time-course of the acquisition of subject and·object clitics. They are consistent with recent findings of White (this volume) concerning L2-acquisition and the results presented in Crysmann & Müller (1994) on bilingual French-speaking children (though their observation on the occurrence of reflexives before the occurrence of genuine object clitics could not be reproduced). Subject clitics are attested from the earliest recording in the Augustin corpus, they remain stable throughout the period from 2 to 2;6 and in the last recordings (2;9) their proportion of occurrence jumps to over half of the relevant verbal utterances. Object clitics are nearly absent in the period 2–2;6 and show an increase only in the last two recordings (2;9). This finding is clearly illustrated in Figure 2:

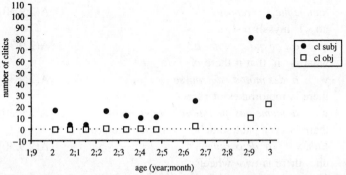

Figure 2. Number of Subject and Object Clitics as a Function of Age

To confirm the relevance of this finding, we want to know how frequent object clitics (and, more generally, complement clitics) are in the adult French productions in this corpus. If object clitics were comparatively rare in adult productions as well, the observed acquisition pattern would be less significant. In order to respond to this potential objection, we calculated the ratio of all subject and object (and other complement) clitics produced by the adults involved in the recordings (experimentor, mother, father, cousin, aunt, uncle). The following table compares adult and child production.

Table 6. Adult and Child Clitics in the Augustin Corpus

	adults		child (A)	
subject clitics	2,332	76.4%	278	88.5%
object clitics	719	23.6%	36	11.5%
total	3,051		314	

The results show that adults produce fewer complement clitics than subject clitics as is to be expected given the Extended Projection Principle and the fact that French is not a null-subject language. However, the adult ratio is almost 1:3, much higher than the 1:9 ratio of the child productions. Moreover, even this huge difference in the ratios does not do full justice to the developmental effect shown by Tables 4 and 5 because complement clitics are clearly mastered by the child in the latest recordings. Remember that in the first seven recordings only two complement clitics are produced by the child in comparison to 74 subject clitics, whereas in the last recording the child produces 22 complement clitics and 99 subject clitics, a ratio already close to the adult ratio. So our recordings seem to have captured the asynchronous development of clitics, with subject clitics already productive at 2;0 and complement clitics becoming productive after 2;6 in this child's production.

3.4. *Clitics in Finite and Nonfinite Clauses*

Another clear distinction between subject and object clitics emerges when their distribution with respect to tensed verbs and infinitives is considered. The investigation of this phenomenon is particularly interesting because Augustin is well within the ROOT INfiNITIVE period, i.e., he produces non-adult infinitives in declaratives next to inflected structures. Such infinitives correspond to 10.9% of his verbal utterances.

For the count of finite constructions imperatives and the complex constructions where the auxiliary or modal is a proform like [e] were excluded, cf. (10f). Thus the count includes finite forms like *mange* and clear AUX + participle and AUX/MOD + infinitive complexes. The count of root infinitives includes all the clear cases of non-adult infinitives, but also the cases where the pragmatic situation allows an infinitive in adult speech, cf. (10b). Infinitives introduced by prepositions were not counted, cf. (10d). For convenience these examples are repeated here:

(10) a. *on joue* A(2;0.2)
      we play

   b. Experimenter: *Tu veux quoi?*
      you want what

   A: [*ote tu ta*]   (*ôter   tout ça*   A(2;0.2)
      empty all that

c. *manger, maman, manger*   A(2;0.2)
    eat   mummy eat
    (A wants to open a box of chocolates)
d. *[katschuk] pour faire pan pan*   A(2;9.2)
           to   do   pom pom
e. *[kake] (cassé)*   A(2;0.2)
    broken
f. *[e pa deA~Ze sa]* (*[e] pas derang[e] ça*   A(2;0.2)
           (*veux/vais pas déranger ça*)
           want/will not disturb   that
           (*ai/est   pas dérangé ça*)
           have/is not disturbed that
g. *est pa(r)ti papa*   A(2;0.2)
    is left   Daddy
h. *attends, attends [KitE]]*   A(2;0.2)
    wait   wait

Bare participles, though nonfinite forms, were not included. Special subject proforms (proto-syntactic devices, in the terminology of Bottari *et al.* 1992) as in the following cases were included on the other hand.

(17) a. *[o] jouer [kitEl]*   (*[o] jouer, Christelle*)   A(2;2.13)
                            play   Christelle
     b. *[a tikot a bE jakEt]*   (*[a] tricote la belle jaquette*)
                           knit   the nice cardigan
                                        A(2;2.13)
     c. *[e te pa]*   (*[e] sais   pas*)   A(2;2.13)
                            know not
     d. *[@] dois [fE]*   (*[@] dois faire*)   A(2;9.30)
                            must do

The occurrences of postverbal subjects were not included separately in the table. Postverbal lexical subjects were simply counted as lexical subjects. If a right-dislocation occurred as in an adult construction (i.e., with a preverbal clitic subject) then this case was counted as involving a subject clitic, not a lexical subject.

(18) a. *est plus beau ça*   A(2;4.22)
       is more nice that   lexical subject
     b. *c' est que là,   que là   il va,   mon crayon*   A(2;9.2)
       it.is that there that there it goes my pencil   subject clitic

Table 7. Occurrences of Clitics and Other Subjects in Finite Structures and Root Infinitives in the Augustin Corpus

age	verbal utterances		with clitic subject		with clitic object		with Ø-subject		with lexical subject		with s-proform (proto-syntactic device)		(il) y-a case	
	fin	inf	fin	inf	fin	inf	fin	inf	fin	inf	fin	inf	fin	inf
2;0.2	42	7	17				16	7	9					
2;0.23	14	9	4				6	8	2	1	2			
2;1.15	8	7	4				2	5	2	2				
2;2.13	38	6	16		1		11	5	9		2	1		
2;3.10	29	4	9	3			9	1	7		4			
2;4.1	48	5	9	1			25	4	8		6			
2;4.22	38	8	11		1		14	8	9		4			
2;6.16	93	7	25		2		30	7	22		15		1	
2;9.2	133	8	80		8	2	28	7	12		13	1		
2;9.30	125	8	98	1	20	2	12	7	1		1		13	
total	568	69	273	5	32	4	153	59	81	3	47	2	14	

All in all, we observe that, out of 278 subject clitics, 273 occur in a tensed clause and only five with an infinitive, i.e., 98.2% of all subject clitics occur in tensed clauses and only 1.8% in infinitives. This corroborates the results of Pierce (1989) for L1- and of White (this volume) for L2-acquisition of subject clitics. On the other hand, four of 36 clitic objects occur with an infinitive and 32 with a tensed verb in the Augustin corpus. Thus 88.9% of all object clitics occur with tensed verbs and 11.1% with an infinitive.

Table 8. Percentage of Finite Structures and Root Infinitives in Clitic Constructions

	finite verbs	infinitives
subject clitics	98.2%	01.8%
object clitics	88.9%	11.1%

Even though the overall number of object clitics is small, the asymmetry with subject clitics emerges clearly. As root infinitives are about 10% of the verbal utterances in the whole corpus, object clitics appear to distribute homogeneously across the tensed/untensed distinction. On the other hand, subject clitics show a very strong tendency to occur in tensed environments. A look at the exhaustive list of the EXCEPTIONAL subject clitics occurring with infinitives makes this result even stronger:

(19) a.   *on   ôter*   A(2;3.10)
           we/one empty
     b.   *on   ôter*   A(2;3.10)
           we/one empty
     c.   *on   ôter*   A(2;3.10)
           we/one empty
     d.   *on   jouer aux (pe)tites autos*   A(2;4.1)
           we/one play with little   cars
     e.   *on   mettre sur ça*   A(2;9.30)
           we/one put   on this

All the five exceptional cases involve the subject clitic *on*; three of them occur in the same recording and with the same verb so that the idiosyncrasy is extremely limited. One might be tempted to conclude that Augustin treats *on* as a strong pronoun. This cannot be the case, however, because *on* only occurs in clitic positions and not in the positions possible for strong pronouns discussed earlier for *ça*. It is not inconceivable, however, that some or all of the above cases could be analyzed as involving the use of the proto-syntactic device [*o*] or

[n] found elsewhere in the corpus, rather than as genuine occurrences of the subject clitic.

4. Conclusion

The present study has traced the acquisition by Augustin of the French clitic system longitudinally during a ten-month period. On the basis of the resulting corpus, we have been able to document a number of important characteristics of his language development. The first clear finding is that around the age of two, the child already masters the major constraints that limit the distribution of clitics and weak pronominal forms. Already in the earliest recordings of our corpus, the child produces a variety of subject clitics, which are always placed in the correct position. The first occurrences of object and complement clitics (in later recordings) are also correctly placed in a position adjacent to the verb. Augustin's sensitivity to such distributional constraints is further demonstrated by comparing his constrained production of clitics with the very free distribution of the non-clitic pronominal form *ça*, which is produced in a large array of environments from very early on. As in many other similar cases (the acquisition of finite and nonfinite verb forms, for instance, cf. Déprez & Pierce 1993), the acquisition of the morpholexical properties of an item goes hand in hand with the mastery of its syntactic properties.

The second finding is that the occurrence of object and complement clitics appears to be significantly delayed with respect to subject clitics. Only two genuine examples of object clitics are found in the first seven recordings of Augustin's productions (2;0.2–2;4.22); in the same period he has already produced 74 occurrences of five different kinds of subject clitics. That this cannot be attributed to some general tendency to pronominalize subjects and avoid pronominalization of objects is clearly shown by the distribution of the non-clitic pronominal form *ça* in the same period, which occurs six times in subject position and 12 times in object position. Our result on the delayed occurrence of object clitics confirms findings by Friedemann (1992) on a different French corpus, by White (this volume) on the L2-acquisition of French clitics, and by Haegeman (this volume) on early Dutch. We will not attempt here to provide a theoretical explanation for this difference. We will simply observe that the order [subject clitics > object clitics] is consistent with the theory of markedness and acquisition that derives from Cardinaletti & Starke's (1994) typology of pronouns: subject clitics, as 'weak pronouns', (maximal projections constrained to occur in strict specifier–head configurations with special licensing heads) are less deficient (hence, less marked) elements than object clitics, simple heads incorporated into the verbal host. This order of acquisition is also consistent with the assumption that subject and object clitics occupy different positions and thus bring into play different functional categories, as suggested by Sportiche (1992) for French, by Haegeman (this volume) for Dutch and by Crysmann & Müller (1994) or White (this volume) for the bilingual or L2-acquisition of French.

The third finding is that there is an additional difference between subject and complement clitics with respect to the tensed/untensed distinction. The rare object clitics of the Augustin corpus distribute homogeneously in tensed clauses and root infinitives, whereas subject clitics are basically limited to tensed environments. If the Augustin corpus clearly confirms previous findings about the (near) absence of subject clitics in root infinitives, it does not show a dissociation between subject clitics and lexical subjects in root infinitives, as other corpora of early productions have shown (see Pierce 1989, 1992 on French, Haegeman (this volume) on Dutch). In fact, as Table 7 indicates, out of 69 cases of root infinitives only three have a lexical subject (and two have a proto-syntactic device arguably in subject position), the largely predominant subject type for root infinitives being the null subject. We do not know at the moment whether the more or less limited occurrence of lexical subjects in root infinitives is submitted to arbitrary individual variation (i.e., some children could make up a special Case-assignment rule for subjects of root infinitives, thus making lexical subjects possible, while other children would not) or whether it relates to some other variable property of the early systems. In contrast, the (near) non-occurrence, in the early stages, of subject clitics in root infinitives appears to be stable, to the best of our current knowledge, across individual learners and languages.

Finally, the possible occurrence of object clitics in root infinitives has a clear implication for the analysis of both root infinitives and Romance cliticization, as Haegeman (this volume) points out. If root infinitives are truncated structures (Rizzi 1994), then the point of truncation must be at least as high as the functional head which hosts object clitics. Conversely, if the point of truncation is necessarily lower than TP (Rizzi, *op. cit.*), then the landing site of French complement clitics must be lower than T^0 (possibly $AGR(O)^0$ as in Belletti 1993). So acquisition data may bear directly on the much-debated question of the landing site of Romance cliticization, and help to drastically narrow down the range of possible candidates.

Acknowledgements

Our thanks are due to Christelle Girot and Isabelle Schindelholz, who made the recordings and the original transcriptions, to Nathalie Martinez, Lucienne Rasetti, and Daniela Renggli, who double-checked and hand-corrected these transcriptions, to Paola Merlo, who helped with the computerized data analysis, to Christine Meunier, who analyzed the waveforms, and to Eric Haeberli, Liliane Haegeman, Andrew Radford and two anonymous reviewers for helpful comments on earlier versions of this paper.

The research presented here was supported in part by grant N° 1213-042212.94 of the Swiss National Science Foundation.

References

Belletti, A. 1993. "Case Checking and Clitic Placement: Three issues on Italian/Romance clitics." *GenGenP* 1.101–118.

Bottari, P., P. Cipriani & A.M. Chilosi. 1992. "Proto-syntactic Devices in the Acquisition of Italian Free Morphology." *GenGenP* 0.83–101.

Cardinaletti, A. & M. Starke. 1994. "The Typology of Structural Deficiency." Ms., University of Venice and University of Geneva.

Chomsky, N. 1981. *Lectures on Government and Binding*. Dordrecht: Foris.

Clark, E. 1985. "The Acquisition of Romance with Special Reference to French." *The Crosslinguistic Study of Language Acquistion*, ed. by D. Slobin, 687–782. Hilldsdale, N.J.: Lawrence Erlbaum.

Crysmann, B. & N. Müller. 1994. "On the Non-parallelism in the Acquisition of Reflexive and Non-reflexive Object Clitics. *On the Acquistion of Scrambling and Cliticization*, ed. by C. Hamann & S. Powers (to appear).

Déprez, V. & A. Pierce. 1993. "Negation and Functional Projections in Early Grammar." *Linguistic Inquiry* 24.25–67.

Friedemann, M.-A. 1992. "The Underlying Position of External Arguments in French." *GenGenP* 0.123–144.

Haegeman, L. This volume. "Root Infinitives, Clitics and Truncated Structures."

Haverkort, M. & J. Weissenborn. 1991. "Clitic and Affix Interaction in Early Romance." Paper presented at the 16th BU Conference on Language Development.

Kayne, R. 1975. *French Syntax*. Cambridge, MAss.: MIT Press.

———. 1983. *Connectedness and Binary Branching*. Dordrecht: Foris.

Lightbown, P. 1977. "Constituency and Variation in the Acquisition of French." Diss., Columbia University.

MacWhinney, B. 1991. *The Childes Project: Tools for analysing talk*. Hillsdale, N.J.: Lawrence Erlbaum.

MacWhinney, B. & C. Snow. 1985. "The Child Language Data Exchange System." *Journal of Child Language* 12.271–296.

Pierce, A. 1989. "On the Emergence of Syntax: A crosslinguistic study. Diss., Massachusetts Institute of Technology, Cambridge.

————. 1992. *Language Acquisition and Syntactic Theory.* Dordrecht: Kluwer.

Rizzi, L. 1986. "On the Status of Subject Clitics in Romance." *Studies in Romance Linguistics*, ed. by O. Jaeggli & C. Silva-Corvalan, 391–419. Dordrecht: Foris.

————. 1994. "Some Notes on Linguistic Theory and Language Development: The case of root infinitives." *Language Acquisition* 3.371–393.

Sportiche, D. 1992. "Clitic Constructions." Ms., University of California, Los Angeles.

Valian, V. 1991. "Syntactic Subjects in the Early Speech of American and Italian Children." *Cognition* 40.41–81.

Weissenborn, J. 1988. "The Acquisition of Clitic Object Pronouns and Word Order in French: Syntax or morphology?" Paper presented at the 3rd International Morphology Meeting, Krems, July.

Wells, J. C. 1989. "Computer-coded Phonemic Notation of Individual Languages ot the European Community." *Journal of the International Phonetic Association* 19.31–54.

Wexler, K. 1994. "Optional Infinitives, Head Movement and the Economy of Derivations." *Verb Movement*, ed. by D. Lightfoot & N. Hornstein, 305-350. Cambridge: Cambridge University Press.

White, L. This volume. "Clitics in Child L2-French."

Clitics in L2 French

Lydia White

McGill University

1. Introduction

There is currently a lively debate over the nature of initial and early representations in the second language (L2) interlanguage grammar, particularly over the question of whether functional categories are present or absent (e.g., Epstein *et al.*, in press; Grondin & White 1995; Lakshmanan 1993/1994; Schwartz, in press; Schwartz & Sprouse 1994; Vainikka & Young-Scholten 1994). To some extent, this parallels the debate in first language (L1) acquisition. However, in L2 acquisition there is an extra dimension to be considered. If functional categories prove to be present in the early interlanguage grammar, the question arises as to their source: are they present because L2 learners access them directly via UG (Epstein *et al.*, in press) or are they present because L2 learners initially use the L1 grammar as a theory to account for the L2 data (Schwartz, in press; Schwartz & Sprouse 1994)? A number of researchers have argued for the presence of functional categories in the early stages of L2 acquisition; however, in many cases one is unable to decide between the L1 versus immediate access to UG as the potential source of such categories, because the L1s and L2s in question make use of similar functional projections. For example, Grondin & White (1995) argue for the presence of DP, IP, and probably CP, in early child L2 French; Lakshmanan (1993/1994) and Lakshmanan & Selinker (1994) argue for the same categories in early child L2 English. In both cases, the L1 is a potential source of knowledge of the categories in question. Some research looks at L2 acquisition of Japanese by native speakers of English (Kaplan 1993) or L2 acquisition of English by native speakers of Japanese (Epstein *et al.*, in press). On the assumption that Japanese has no functional categories (Fukui & Speas 1986), the L1 and L2 differ and the potential influence of the L1 on the initial state could be investigated. However, current analyses of Japanese assume the existence of functional categories; thus, an examination of the acquisition of Japanese or English by native speakers of English or Japanese does not, in fact, allow one to distinguish between immediate UG access or L1-mediated access in the initial state.

A related issue is whether there are changes in functional categories over time in the acquisition of a second language. According to those researchers who propose full and immediate access, there will be no essential changes in the grammar of functional categories over time, although there may be changes in the extent to which they are used (Epstein *et al.*, in press). In other words, one might expect quantitative changes but not qualitative ones. For researchers who assume absolute L1 influence (Schwartz, in press; Schwartz & Sprouse 1994), changes in functional categories are predicted if the L1 and L2 differ; the L2 learner would start off with L1 categories and change to categories appropriate for the L2 as these are triggered by L2 input, suggesting the possibility of qualitatively different stages in the L2 development of functional categories, although all stages would be UG-constrained.

In this paper, I argue that looking at L2 acquisition of French clitics by native speakers of English is a good way to determine the extent of L1 influence on the initial state and early interlanguage, as well as the issue of whether interlanguage grammars go through qualitative changes with respect to functional categories. English lacks syntactic clitics, in contrast to French. Sportiche (1992, 1993) argues that clitics head their own projections. The native speaker of English, then, would have no clitic projections realized in the L1 grammar; there is nothing in the English input to motivate them. Thus, if an L2 learner of French shows early evidence of syntactic clitics and their projections, this suggests that potential functional categories made available by UG but not instantiated in the L1 can be triggered on the basis of L2 input. Furthermore, if clitic projections are available from the earliest stages, it would support the hypothesis that there are no qualitative changes in the interlanguage grammar with respect to properties of functional categories.

2.   Strong and Weak Pronouns in French

French pronouns vary in their form, depending on whether they are strong or weak, as can be seen in Table 1. Strong pronouns occur in most environments where full DPs are found (Kayne 1975). Weak pronouns, on the other hand, are clitics which attach to a verbal host. (Table 1 only presents subject and direct-object clitic forms. In addition, there are other clitics which will not be investigated in this study, namely indirect object clitics; the subject clitic *c'* 'it'; the locative clitic *y;* the genitive clitic *en;* the reflexive clitics.)

Table 1. Pronouns and Clitics in French

	strong pronouns	subject clitics	object clitics
1SG	*moi*	*je*	*me*
2SG	*toi*	*tu*	*te*
2SG MASC	*lui*	*il*	*le*
2SG FEM	*elle*	*elle*	*la*
1PL	*nous*	*on, nous*	*nous*
2PL	*vous*	*vous*	*vous*
3PL MASC	*eux*	*ils*	*les*
3PL FEM	*elles*	*elles/ils**	*les*

* Third person feminine plural is *elles* in Standard French, *ils* in colloquial Quebec French.

Kayne (1975) offers a number of diagnostic tests for French clitics. Although subject clitics seem to occur in the same surface position as subject DPs, as in (1a), other properties show that they behave differently from DPs and from strong pronouns.[1,2] These differences include the fact that nothing can intervene between the clitic and the verb, as in (1b);[3] clitics cannot be modified, as in (1c); they cannot be conjoined, as in (1d); they cannot be contrastively stressed, as in (1e).

(1)   a.   *Jean partira bientôt.*
         Il partira bientôt
         'Jean/He will leave soon.'
      b.   *Jean, souvent, mange du fromage.*
         **Il, souvent, mange du fromage.*
         'Jean/He, often, eats cheese.'
      c.   *Tous les garçons partiront bientôt.*
         'All the boys will leave soon.'
         **Ils tous partiront bientôt.*
         Eux tous partiront bientôt.
         'They all will leave soon.'

    d.   *Jean et Pierre partiront bientôt.*
          'Jean and Pierre will leave soon.'
          **Jean et il partiront bientôt.*
          Jean et lui partiront bientôt.
          'Jean and he/him will leave soon.'
    e.   **IL partira le premier.*
          LUI partira   le premier.
          he   leave:FUT the first
          'HE will leave first.'

Weak object pronouns are in complementary distribution with direct object DPs and with strong pronouns. Whereas direct objects in French follow the verb, clitic object pronouns precede it, as shown in (2):

    (2)   a.   *Marie connaît mon frère.*
              Marie knows my brother
         b.   *Marie le   connaît.*
              Marie him knows
         c.   **Marie connaît le.*
              Marie knows him

However, in positive imperatives, the verb precedes the object, as in (3a). Strong forms of the pronoun are required for first and second person rather than weak; compare (3b) and (3c).

    (3)   a.   *Regarde le!*
              look.at him
         b.   *Regarde moi!*
              look.at me
         c.   **Regarde me!*

A weak pronoun may not be the complement of a preposition, in contrast to a strong pronoun or DP:

    (4)   a.   *Marie parle avec Jean.*
         b.   *Marie parle avec lui.*
         c.   **Marie parle avec le.*
            'Marie is talking to Jean/him.'

Object clitics share many of the properties of subject clitics discussed above. In French, material can intervene between the verb and the DP direct object. However, nothing can intervene between the clitic and the verb, except for other clitics, as shown in (5):

(5) a. *Jean voit souvent Marie.*
         Jean sees often   Marie
     b. **Jean la   souvent voit.*
         Jean her often   sees

Object clitics, like subject clitics and unlike DPs, cannot be conjoined or contrastively stressed, as shown in (6a) and (6b):

(6) a. **Jean la   et   le   voit.*
         Jean her and him sees
     b. **Jean LA préfère.*
         Jean her prefers
         'Jean prefers HER.'

Clitics cannot occur alone. For example, where a pronoun is required as the answer to a question, the strong form must be used rather than the clitic:

(7)   *Qui as-tu   vu?*
         who did.you see
         *Lui/*Le.*
         him

It should be noted that there are some differences between Quebec French and Standard French with respect to clitics; these will be discussed where relevant.

3. Analysis of Clitics

There has been considerable and long-standing debate in the literature as to the status of Romance clitics, including the question of whether they are base-generated or arrive in their surface positions by movement, whether they are heads or XPs and whether they are syntactic clitics or morphological affixes. (See Auger 1994 for review.)

Those arguing for movement include Kayne (1975). As noted above, clitics and DPs are often in complementary distribution, and clitics usually satisfy the argument structure of the verb in question (e.g., (2) above). This can be explained if clitics are DPs which move from a D-structure DP position and adjoin to the verb. Arguments against movement, and in favor of base-generation of clitics in their S-structure positions, have centered on the issue of clitic doubling (Borer 1986; Rivas 1977; Strozer 1976). In some Romance dialects but not in

Standard French, clitics can appear together with a co-indexed DP or PP, rather than their being in complementary distribution. Subject-doubling, as in (8), is common in Quebec French (Auger 1994; Carroll 1982; Roberge & Vinet 1989; Roberge 1990):

> (8)   *Jean il part.*
> Jean he leaves

Furthermore, there are cases where the clitic appears to have no possible source from which it could have moved (Sportiche 1992), such as the ethical dative construction and the dative of possession, as illustrated in (9):

> (9) a. *Je t'acheterais   un cadeau à Pierre.*
>   I you.would.buy a   present to Pierre
>   'I tell ya, I would buy Peter a present.'   (Sportiche's gloss)
>   b. *Elles leur ont tiré dans le ventre.*
>   they them have shot in   the stomach
>   'They shot them in the stomach.'
>   c. **Elles ont tiré dans le ventre à ces   garçons.*
>   they have shot in   the stomach to these boys
>   'They shot these boys in the stomach.'

In (9a), the clitic *t'* is not linked to any argument in the sentence. In (9b) a dative clitic indicating possession is permitted, even though the presumed source in (9c) is ungrammatical.

Sportiche (1992) argues that both theories of clitic placement have something essentially correct about them and that the conflict between base-generation and movement theories can be resolved by assuming that each kind of clitic (nominative, accusative, dative) is base-generated as the head of its own projection, which he calls clitic 'voices'. There is a relationship of Spec–head agreement between the clitic and some XP, which can be *pro,* which has moved to the Spec of the clitic projection. Clitics are treated as a kind of agreement morpheme, but with properties somewhat different from regular subject or object agreement.

Under this analysis, the subject moves from VP-internal subject position to Spec of NomV, while the nominative subject clitic is base-generated in Nom. Clitic doubling is permitted in principle; independent factors rule it out in certain dialects. In the case of accusative object clitics, the clitic is base-generated in Acc. A *pro* object moves to Spec-Acc. This claim thus implies that French is a *pro*-drop language, allowing both subject and object *pro* (see also Auger 1994; Kaiser 1994; Roberge 1990). The tree for nominative and accusative voices is given in (10). (I leave aside here the question of where the clitic projections are with respect to AGR(S) and AGR(O). Sportiche concludes that the clitic projections are higher than the agreement projections, i.e., NomV is higher than AGR(S) and AccV is higher than AGR(O).)

(10) *(Jean) il la voit.*
      Jean he her sees

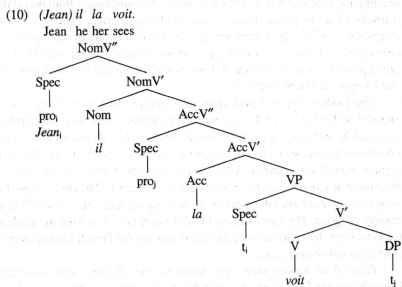

4. Hypothesis and Data

English pronouns are not clitics.[4] The question then arises as to whether and when L2 learners of French acquire the appropriate properties of pronominal clitics. The hypothesis to be investigated here is that child L2 learners of French will correctly analyse French weak pronouns as clitics even in the earliest stages, and will have the associated projections in their grammars. If it proves to be the case that early utterances show evidence of clitics, this supports the claim that functional categories are present in L2 grammars, i.e., that there is not a preliminary purely lexical stage as argued for by Vainikka & Young-Scholten (1994). Furthermore, since clitic projections are not present in the L1, presence of clitics in the L2 would be evidence against the claim that L2 learners in early stages project only structures consistent with the L1 grammar. The first claim is independent of the particular analysis of clitics adopted here, while the second depends on Sportiche's analysis of clitics. We return to this issue in the discussion.

The use of subject and object clitics is examined in a corpus of spontaneous longitudinal production data (approximately 3,450 utterances) from two children (identified here by pseudonyms, Kenny and Greg) learning French in Montreal (Lightbown 1977). This corpus was gathered over a period of three years; thus, developments in the use of clitics can be investigated. (Other aspects of functional projections in the speech of these children are examined in Grondin 1992 and Grondin & White 1995.)

The mother tongue of both children is English. Kenny and Greg were first exposed to French in a bilingual nursery program, where they participated in activities in both languages. Subsequently, they were both enrolled in a French immersion kindergarten class but within a few weeks they were transferred to a regular French kindergarten, with French speaking peers; from this point on, their input at school consisted almost entirely of French. The children produced very few spontaneous utterances in French during their time in the bilingual nursery program. The data examined in this paper are taken from the kindergarten year, once the children had transferred into regular French kindergarten, and from first and second grades.

From their kindergarten year onwards, the children were recorded at intervals ranging from one to five months, in play sessions with a research assistant, each session lasting approximately one hour. Kenny was also interviewed on three occasions during his nursery school programme; however, he did not say much on these occasions. In some of the sessions, both children were present and interacted with each other as well as with the assistant. Kenny's sessions took place at regular intervals, usually on a monthly or bimonthly basis. As far as Greg was concerned, the first interview yielding spontaneous production data took place after five months of exposure to French in Kindergarten; there was a four-month interval between this recording session and the next one. This means that the data from Kenny are more likely to reveal evidence relating to the status of clitics in the initial or early stages and more likely to allow one to track the development of clitics. Table 2 provides details. Note that months of exposure refers to months of exposure from the Kindergarten year onward; the nursery school exposure is not included.

Table 2. Age of Subjects and Months of Exposure to French from Kindergarten Year onwards

months of exposure	grade*	age		interview #	
		Kenny	Greg	Kenny	Greg
2	K	5;10	5;6	IV	—
3	K	5;11	5;7	V	—
4	K	6;0	5;8	VI	—
5	K	6;1	5;9	VII	II
7	K	6;2	5;11	VIII	—
8	K	6;3	6;0	IX	—
9	K	6;4	6;1	X	III
9.5	K	6;5		XI	—
10	K	6;6	6;2	XII	IV
11	K	6;7	6;3	XIII	V
14	G1	6;10	6;6	XIV	VI
15	G1	6;11	6;7	XV	VII
18	G1	7;2	6;10	XVI	VIII
20	G1	7;4	7;0	XVII	IX
25	G2	7;9	7;5	XVIII	X
27	G2	7;11	7;7	XIX	XI
29	G2	8;1	7;9	XX	XII

* K= Kindergarten, G1 = Grade 1, G2 = Grade 2

5. Subject Clitics

5.1. *Evidence for Segmentation of Clitics*

Before looking in detail at the L2 acquisition of subject clitics, it is necessary to establish that any weak forms that occur in the data are indeed independent morphemes. In other studies on use of first person weak forms in L2 French, it has been suggested that *j'ai* 'I've' is an unanalyzed form, i.e., that one cannot assume that this form consists of a clitic and a verb. Harley & Swain (1984) argue that *j'ai* in L2 French of children in French immersion programmes in Canada is in fact a pronoun rather than a clitic plus auxiliary. As evidence, they point out that children use *j'ai* with a past participle when the intended meaning is present, as in (11a), that they use *j'ai* with present forms of the verb instead of the past participle, as in (11b), and that they use *j'ai* together with another auxiliary, as in (11c):

(11) a. *J'ai marché à la maison toujours.*
I've walked home   always
'I always walk home.'

    b. *J'ai crois qu'il a juste fait comme ça.*
I've thinkthat.he has only done like   that
'I think that he only did this.'

    c. *J'ai a oublié.*
I've has forgotten
'I have forgotten.'

Another possibility is that *j'* might be misanalyzed as part of the verb. Harley & Swain report such cases, as in (12):

(12)   *il j'aime ça*
he I.like that
'He likes that.'

There is little evidence in the data examined here that the children treat *j'ai* as a pronoun or that they fail to analyse *je* or *j'* as separate morphemes. Although there are occasional errors of the type in (11b), these are few and far between and they mostly occur in the later interviews. In the early interviews, there is evidence that *je*, *j'* 'I' and *ai* 'have' are independently analyzed. As can be seen in (13) and (14), both weak and strong pronominal forms occur with the same verbs, suggesting that the verb and the clitic do not form an unanalyzed unit.

(13) a. *je sais pas*
I know not

    b. *moi sais*
me know

    c. *moi je sais*
me I know   Kenny(month 2)[5]

(14) a. *moi j'ai deux fermes*
me I've two farms

    b. *moi ai fait ...*
me have made

    c.   *moi fais   ici*
        me make here
    d.   *moi je fais   ici*
        me I make here   Greg(month 5)

Furthermore, both children use *je* and *il* with a variety of verbs, suggesting that these are not restricted to routines but are independent and productively used morphemes, as shown in (15):

(15) a.   *i' pas vient*
           he not comes
      b.   *i' crie*
           he shouts
      c.   *i' tombe*
           he falls
      d.   *je vais*
           I go
      e.   *je va   aller à la   toilette*[6]
           I will:3SG go   to the bathroom   Kenny(month 4)

    It is nevertheless conceivable that forms like *je* and *il* could be unanalyzed when they occur in potential routines. For this reason, certain expressions which were very frequent in the children's language even early on have been excluded from the analysis, since they may well have been learned as unanalyzed chunks, thus not providing evidence for the presence of clitics in the grammar. Excluded expressions are: *je sais* 'I know'; *je ne sais pas* 'I don't know'; *il y a* 'there is/are'; *il y en a* 'there is/are some of them'; *s'il vous plait* 'please'; *c'est* 'it's; *c'est ça* 'that's it; *ça c'est* 'that it's ....'.[7]

5.2. *Patterns of Subject Usage*

    Strong and weak pronouns are used by Kenny and Greg as subjects from the earliest interviews, as well as DP-subjects. First appearance of strong pronouns and of subject and object clitics is shown in Table 3.[8] Most common in the early interviews are first person forms (*moi* and *je*), probably because of the nature of the sessions rather than absence of other pronouns in the grammar; second (*toi*, *tu*) and third person (*il/ils*, usually pronounced *i*) are also found. *On*, *elle*, *vous* show up later; again, one should be cautious about interpreting this as late emergence. *Nous* is used considerably later than other weak pronouns; in colloquial French, first person plural is usually expressed by *on* and this is what these children use too. (Subject *ça* and *c'* 'it' were frequently used by both children throughout the time that they were observed; these have been excluded from analysis because of the fact that they occur mostly in potential routines.)

Table 3. First Appearance of Pronouns (in Months)

		strong pronouns		subject clitics			object clitics	
		Kenny	Greg		Kenny	Greg		Kenny	Greg
1SG	*moi*	2	5	*je*	2	5	*me*	20	—
2SG	*toi*	3	14	*tu*	7	9.5	*te*	11	20
3SG MASC	*lui*	4	15	*il*	3	9.5	*le*	11	9.5
3SG FEM	*elle*	18	18	*elle*	9	9.5	*la*	20	20
1PL				*on*	8	10			
1PL	*nous*	25	25	*nous*	18	29	*nous*	29	29
2PL	*vous*	18	18	*vous*	9	15	*vous*	9	14
3PL FEM	*eux*	27	29	*ils*	5	9	*les*	3	18
3PL FEM	*elles*	—	—	*elles*	—	—	*les*	—	14

The main patterns of subject usage to be discussed are given in (16). In some cases, the verb is finite, in other cases nonfinite. The incidence of these patterns over time is presented in Tables 4 and 5.

(16)   DP–V
         clitic pronoun–V (Cl V)
         strong pronoun–V (Pr V)
         strong pronoun–clitic pronoun–V (Pr Cl V)
         DP–clitic pronoun–V (DP Cl V)
         null subject–V

It can be seen from Table 4 that Kenny's subjects are typically DPs or clitic pronouns with finite verbs.[9] Utterances with strong pronoun subjects are also found, sometimes containing a finite verb, sometimes a nonfinite. Greg's behavior is similar (Table 5). In addition, both children use clitic doubling (Pr–Cl–V and DP–Cl–V), Greg much more extensively than Kenny.

To establish whether the weak pronominal forms are indeed clitics in the grammars of these children, one can examine whether they are used in ways which are consistent with Kayne's (1975) tests. Only three of Kayne's tests can be examined in these data, namely the position of the clitic in relation to the verb, the issue of conjunction and the question of contrastive stress.

Table 4. Subjects in Kenny's Speech

		IV	V	VI	VII	VIII	IX	X	XI	XII	XIII	XIV	XV	XVI	XVII	XVIII	XIX	XX
interviews		IV	V	VI	VII	VIII	IX	X	XI	XII	XIII	XIV	XV	XVI	XVII	XVIII	XIX	XX
months		2	3	4	5	7	8	9	9.5	10	11	14	15	18	20	25	27	29
DP V	finite	0	2	5	8	11	8	2	9	9	9	8	14	18	9	12	24	17
	nonfinite	1	0	0	0	0	2	0	0	0	0	0	0	0	0	0	0	0
Cl V	finite	0	2	9	0	4	6	6	3	8	7	10	29	85	92	130	133	156
	nonfinite	0	0	0	0	1	0	0	0	0	0	0	0	0	1	0	1	5
Pr V	finite	2	0	1	4	3	3	2	2	12	7	24	15	3	1	0	1	3
	nonfinite	0	1	0	0	4	5	6	5	4	6	7	9	2	2	0	2	0
Pr Cl V	finite	0	1	0	1	0	0	0	0	4	0	3	6	7	9	20	10	14
	nonfinite	0	0	0	0	0	0	0	0	1	0	0	0	0	0	0	1	0
DP Cl V	finite	0	0	0	2	0	0	0	0	0	2	0	0	0	0	7	1	11
	nonfinite	0	0	0	0	0	0	0	0	0	0	0	0	0	0	0	0	0
null S	finite	1	2	2	1	13	6	3	9	8	11	9	18	6	8	4	0	5
	nonfinite	0	3	0	4	2	0	0	0	0	2	2	2	1	1	4	0	2
total subjects		4	11	17	20	38	30	19	28	46	44	63	93	122	123	177	173	213

Table 5. Subjects in Greg's Speech

interviews		II	III	IV	V	VI	VII	VIII	IX	X	XI	XII
months		5	9	10	11	14	15	18	20	25	27	29
DP V	finite	2	9	6	4	18	32	19	21	40	21	43
	nonfinite	0	2	1	0	0	1	0	0	0	0	0
Cl V	finite	1	8	4	4	26	93	66	133	306	225	208
	nonfinite	0	0	0	1	1	4	1	0	0	0	0
Pr V	finite	9	0	4	1	7	3	4	2	0	0	2
	nonfinite	1	1	5	1	5	2	2	3	1	0	0
Pr Cl V	finite	9	6	6	4	52	53	15	15	55	31	46
	nonfinite	0	0	0	2	4	0	0	0	0	0	0
DP Cl V	finite	0	2	0	2	3	1	3	0	6	1	3
	nonfinite	0	0	0	0	0	0	0	0	0	0	0
null S	finite	1	3	4	0	10	18	11	4	2	2	8
	nonfinite	0	0	8	3	6	3	4	1	4	0	0
total subjects		23	32	38	22	132	210	125	179	414	280	310

In all the data over the whole time period, there are practically no cases of material intervening between the clitic and the finite verb (except other clitics, which is permitted). The cases that do occur are mostly found in later interviews:

(17) a. *on juste veut pas*   Greg(month 20)
   one just wants not
   'We just don't want to.'

 b. *on juste peut voir*   Greg(month 25)
   one just can see

However, this lack of material between weak pronoun and verb would be of little interest if there were a total lack of material intervening between other kinds of subjects and verbs. Material intervening between strong pronouns and the verb is occasionally found:

(18) a. *moi aussi ai fait le rouge*
   me also have made the red (one)

 b. *moi juste fais pas tout le soleil*   Kenny(month 15)
   me only make not all the sun

Furthermore, frequent throughout the data, especially from Greg, are cases of strong pronouns or DPs which are separated from the verb by a weak pronoun, as in (19a) and (19b). There are no cases of the weak form preceding the strong, as in (19c):

(19) a. *moi je veux pas*   Kenny(month 3)
      me I want not

     b. *moi j'ai   deux lapins*
        me I.have two rabbits   Greg(month 5)

     c. **je moi veux pas*
        I me want not

In addition, there are also some cases, mostly after the first year of exposure, of material intervening between a strong pronoun and a weak pronoun, as in (20a) and (20b). In contrast, there are no cases like (20c).

(20) a. *moi aussi j'ai   besoin*   Kenny(month 27)
        me too   I.have need
        'I need (it) too.'

     b. *moi avril je va   être huit ans*   Greg(month 27)
        me April I will:3SG be eight years
        'In April I'll be eight.'

     c. **moi je aussi ai   besoin*
        me I too   have need

Such findings suggest that the weak forms have to be next to the verb, consistent with their analysis as clitics.

No cases of conjoined weak pronoun subjects are found but there are other kinds of conjoined subjects as shown in (21):

(21) a. *le kangourou et le bébé-kangourou live there* Kenny(month 5)
     b. *moi et   toi est trop grand pour la porte*   Kenny(month 15)
        me and you is too big   for the door

This suggests that while the children allow conjunction they do not permit conjunction of weak forms, again consistent with their analysis as clitics.

As far as contrastive stress is concerned, no cases of stressed subject clitics are found anywhere in the data; in contrast, stressed strong pronouns are found throughout. Some examples are given in (22):

(22) a. *TOI faire ça*   Kenny(month 7)
        YOU do:INF that

b.   *LUI il a un chapeau, pas lui*   Kenny(month 29)
       HIM he has a hat   not him
c.   *MOI j'ai deux lapins*
       ME I.have two rabbits   Greg(month 5)

Failure of certain forms to show up in production data does not, of course, guarantee that they are absent or prohibited in the grammar; their absence in the data could, after all, be due to a sampling error. Nevertheless, the production data from these children are consistent with the hypothesis that weak pronouns are indeed clitics in child L2 French.

Furthermore, there are a number of verbless utterances in the data; in these utterances, a clitic is never found as the subject, whereas a strong pronoun is, again suggesting that the children know that weak pronouns require a verbal host. Examples are given in (23), where the context suggests that the missing verb is *avoir* 'to have':

(23) a.   *toi animaux*   Kenny(month 3)
          you animals
      b.   *moi deux*   Kenny(month 4)
          me two

Additional evidence for the clitic status of the weak pronouns is that they almost invariably occur with a finite verb (see Tables 4 and 5). Assuming that subject clitics are a form of agreement which must ultimately attach to a verb, we expect them to occur only with finite verbs, since these raise in French to pick up agreement and clitics whereas nonfinite verbs do not (Pollock 1989; see also Pierce 1992). If weak pronouns were analyzed as independent pronouns on the basis of the L1, we might expect them to be found also with nonfinite verbs, given that the children do produce utterances with pronominal subjects and nonfinite verbs (see below).

Strong pronouns are used as subjects by both children without the presence of a doubled clitic. From months 7 to 15, Kenny produces a high proportion of utterances with strong pronoun subjects, ranging from 18% to 49% of all subjects produced at a particular interview. These utterances sometimes contain a finite verb, sometimes a nonfinite. Greg's behavior is similar (Table 5); he uses a high proportion of strong pronouns as subjects from months 5 to 14, ranging from 3% to 43% of all subjects produced. Examples are given in (24). It is noticeable, however, that the majority of instances of strong pronouns with a finite verb consist of just two forms, namely *moi est* 'me is' and *moi fais* 'me do'.

(24) a. *toi parle   français*   Kenny(month 5)
          you speak:fin French
      b. *moi chercher*[10]   Greg(month 5)
          me search:INF

Such sentences are ungrammatical in adult French but are also found in L1 acquisition (Clark 1985; Pierce 1992).[11]

Nonfinite and finite main verbs occur during the same interviews, the nonfinite verbs being used almost exclusively with strong pronoun or null subjects. In Kenny's case, nonfinite verbs are found in almost all interviews, ranging from 11% to 36% of main verbs used until month 15, after which there is a dramatic decrease in their occurrence. Similarly, Greg uses nonfinite verbs as main verbs with strong pronoun and null subjects to a considerable extent up till month 14, incidence ranging from 12% to 37%, with a reduction thereafter.

The occurrence of finite and nonfinite verbs together is reminiscent of the optional root infinitive stage found in L1 acquisition (Rizzi 1994b; Wexler 1994) and suggests that child L2 learners may go through a similar stage. Rizzi (1994b, 1993/1994) argues that root infinitives are truncated structures; as such, one does not expect subject clitics to show up in them, since the relevant head which hosts the clitic will be absent in the truncated structure. The L2 data are consistent with this analysis.

Rizzi argues that optional infinitives and truncated structures in general are permitted in the grammar until the learner discovers that a root sentence must be a CP. He further proposes that attainment of this knowledge is maturational (Rizzi 1994a). The occurrence of optional infinitives in the L2 data suggests, however, that this is unlikely to be a maturational issue. Kenny and Greg are older than children who are past the truncated structure stage in L1 acquisition.

Further evidence which suggests that these learners do not know that a root clause must be a CP is that Kenny and Greg use null subjects (without a clitic) (see Tables 4 and 5). These null subjects are usually found in initial position in a root clause, suggesting that they may in fact constitute instances of root null subjects or null constants, permitted in cases where the root is an IP (Rizzi 1994a). There is a drop in the proportion of null subjects at the same time as there is a drop in the incidence of optional infinitives, around months 15 to 18, suggesting that this might be the point at which the L2 learners discover that a root clause in the L2 must be a CP. While the data are suggestive that L2 learners have an optional infinitive or truncated structure stage, and hence that the explanation of optional infinitives in acquisition cannot be maturational, further investigation of the nature of root clauses in L2 acquisition is required. To sum up, the data are consistent with the claim that Kenny and Greg have subject clitics in their grammars. Weak pronouns are found almost exclusively adjacent to finite verbs and they are used in ways which are consistent with Kayne's tests for clitics. This is true in the early interviews and subsequently; that is, there do not appear to be any radical shifts over time. Weak forms do not appear to be analyzed as independent pronouns, as might be expected if an L1-based analysis were being imposed on the L2 data.

6. Object Clitics

We turn now to a consideration of object clitics in the child L2 data. The first appearance of accusative object clitics is reported in Table 3. Examples of the patterns of usage and non-usage to be discussed are given in (25); developments over time in these sentence types are documented in Tables 6 and 7. There were few instances of dative clitics in the data and these will not be reported or discussed.

(25)   V–DP
       V–ça
       clitic pronoun – V (Cl V)
       imperative V–clitic pronoun (imperative Cl)
       omitted clitics
       V–clitic pronoun (V Cl)
       V–strong pronoun (V Pr)
       preposition–strong pronoun (P Pr)
       preposition–clitic pronoun (P Cl)
       extra clitics

With the exception of imperatives, object clitics (reported in the tables as Cl V) are found sporadically, if at all, until month 11 in both children. Late appearance of object clitics has also been reported in the L1 acquisition of French (Clark 1985; Hamann, Rizzi & Frauenfelder, this volume) and in bilingual acquisition of French (Kaiser 1994; Müller, Crysmann & Kaiser 1994). It should, however, be noted that there are relatively few non-imperative contexts for object clitics in the early months. Kenny, in particular, produces practically no utterances with direct objects (reported as V DP and V ça) until month seven, so the lack of object clitics may be accidental up to that point.

Table 6. Objects in Kenny's Speech

interviews	IV	V	VI	VII	VIII	IX	X	XI	XII	XIII	XIV	XV	XVI	XVII	XVIII	XIX	XX
months	2	3	4	5	7	8	9	9.5	10	11	14	15	18	20	25	27	29
V DP	0	1	1	0	4	5	1	8	15	2	13	23	34	49	39	94	63
V ça	0	0	0	0	3	1	0	2	6	9	6	21	16	12	1	3	2
Cl V	0	1	0	0	0	0	1	0	0	5	1	3	3	1	25	14	14
imperative Cl	0	8	2	2	0	0	1	1	1	1	10	2	1	5	0	0	1
omitted clitics	0	0	0	0	0	0	0	0	0	0	2	2	4	3	5	5	1
V Cl	0	0	0	0	0	2	0	0	0	0	0	0	0	0	0	0	0
V Pr	0	0	0	1	2	0	0	2	1	4	13	5	1	1	0	0	0
P Pr	0	8	10	0	0	0	0	2	0	0	0	0	7	9	2	2	2
P Cl	0	0	0	0	0	0	0	0	0	2	0	0	0	0	0	0	0
extra clitics	0	0	0	0	0	0	0	0	0	0	0	0	0	0	20	4	0

Table 7. Objects in Greg's Speech

interviews	II	III	IV	V	VI	VII	VIII	IX	X	XI	XII
months	5	9	10	11	14	15	18	20	25	27	29
V DP	10	5	12	5	47	54	33	45	100	88	90
V ça	1	9	21	5	22	10	4	7	25	13	13
Cl V	0	1	1	2	4	0	2	30	22	17	7
imperative Cl	5	0	1	0	11	3	1	1	1	2	1
omitted clitics	0	3	3	1	4	4	3	6	12	15	5
V Cl	0	0	0	0	1	0	0	2	1	3	0
V Pr	0	0	0	0	0	3	1	1	0	0	2
P Pr	0	0	0	0	2	5	1	6	16	15	9
P Cl	0	0	0	0	0	0	0	0	0	0	0
extra clitics	0	0	0	0	0	0	0	1	1	1	0

However, between months 7 and 11, he produces objects but not object clitics.

It is also possible that the children develop a strategy for avoiding object clitics. For example, there are a number of cases where the non-clitic pronoun *ça* 'that' is used as an object (see Tables 6 and 7), where a clitic pronoun might have been more felicitous, as can be seen in (26). In Kenny's case, there is a sharp decline in V *ça* structures in the last three interviews at the same time as there is a sharp increase in use of accusative clitics.

(26) a. *pas ouvrir ça*   Kenny(month 5)
          not open that
      b. *le papa-vache fait ça*   Kenny(month 7)
          the father.cow does that

Hamann *et al.* (this volume) also note that *ça* is frequently found in their L1 acquisition data. They point out that *ça* is found in positions from which clitics would be excluded, suggesting that the L1 acquirer has mastered the distinction between clitic and non-clitic pronouns. The same argument can be made for our L2 data. If Kenny and Greg were treating object clitics as independent pronouns, one would expect them to be found in the same contexts as *ça*, and at the same stages. This does not occur.

Examples of correct placement of weak object clitic pronouns in front of the verb in non-imperative contexts are given in (27):

(27) a. *je le sais*   Kenny(month 11)
          I it know
          'I know.'

      b. *on le laisse comme ça*   Greg(month 11)
          we it leave like   that
          'We'll leave it like that.'

Imperatives, usually involving first and second person objects, are found in the data from the earliest interviews (see Tables 6 and 7). Both children correctly use the strong forms of first and second person pronouns in this context, as can be seen in (28a) and (28b). Kenny also correctly uses the weak form of a third person pronoun in month four, as in (28c), but this could be a routine.

(28) a. *excuse   moi*   Kenny(month 5)
          excuse:2SG me

      b. *regardez   moi*   Greg(month 5)
          look.at:2PL me

      c. *mets   les   là*   Kenny(month 4)
          put:2SG them there

The presence of object pronouns in imperatives in the earlier interviews does not constitute clear evidence for early emergence of object clitics, since the most commonly occuring forms, *moi* and *toi*, are identical to the strong pronoun forms. Thus, it is possible that the children analyse these as strong pronouns rather than as clitics.

Once object clitics are produced by the children, they are quite often omitted. That is, there are contexts for clitics where no clitic is found, as documented in Tables 6 and 7. Kenny produces such structures from month 14 onwards, Greg from month 9. An example is given in (29):

(29) *j'ai encore fait   trop grand*   Greg(month 15)
      I've already made (it) too big

As with subject clitics above, we will now look at Kayne's tests to try to establish, descriptively, whether the children's use of weak object pronouns is consistent with their analysis as clitics. The position of the clitic in relation to the verb, the issue of conjunction and the question of stress will be examined, as well as the question of whether weak pronouns are ever used in isolation or after a preposition.

Weak pronoun objects must be placed adjacent and to the left of the verb (see (2b) above). Only other clitics may intervene. Weak pronouns may not follow the verb, as shown in (2c). The occurrence of errors like (2c) has been reported in the L2 acquisition literature (e.g., Tarone *et al.* 1976); such errors suggest the misanalysis of object clitics as independent pronouns, a potential L1-based analysis. A rare number of such errors is found in the data from Greg in the later interviews; these are reported in Table 7 as V Cl. An example is given in (30a). Kenny never produces such forms (see Table 6). Pronoun placement errors are also found with a strong pronoun following the verb, ungrammatical in French, as in (30b); again, these are rare in the data (reported in Tables 6 and 7 as V Pr).

> (30) a. *moi j'ai   trouvé le*   Greg(month 14)
>   me I.have found it
>   b. *moi j'ai fait   toi aussi*   Greg(month 15)
>   me I've made you too
>   'I drew you as well'

There are also a few utterances where a schwa-like sound fills a position that would be grammatical for a pronoun like *ça* but not for a clitic, as shown in (31):

> (31) *moi dit _ dans anglais*   Kenny(month 7)
>   me say in   English

In sum, regarding the placement of weak pronominal forms, on the whole they are correctly placed to the left of the verb, with no intervening material, suggesting that they are indeed analyzed as clitics. If they were being analyzed as independent pronouns on the basis of L1 English, one would expect a much higher incidence of errors like (30a), especially in early stages.

No cases of conjoined weak object pronouns are found but there are other kinds of conjoined objects, as can be seen in (32). (Conjoined NPs in general are quite common.)

> (32) a. *non moi je veux jouer avec train, le bébé-lion et   éléphant*
>   no me I want to.play with train the baby.lion and elephant
>   Greg(month 10)
>   b. *j'ai faite ça et ça et ça et ça*   Greg(month 11)
>   I've done that and that and that and that

As for stress, no cases of stressed object clitics are found anywhere in the data; as mentioned above, stressed strong pronouns are found throughout. Examples of stressed strong pronouns in non-subject position are given in (33):

(33) a. *c'est de MOI*   Kenny(month 3)
          it's of me
          'It's MINE.'

      b. *c'est à TOI celui-là*   Greg(month 20)
          it's to you that.one
          'That one's YOURS.'

Clitics cannot occur alone (for example, in answer to a question, as in (7) above), nor can they occur as the complement of a preposition. Pronouns that occur alone or in verbless utterances (and there are many of these) in these children's production are always strong pronouns, never weak. Both children produce PPs; as can be seen in Tables 6 and 7, where PPs contain a pronoun, the strong pronoun is always found (P Pr), never the weak (P Cl). Again, on an L1-based analysis of weak pronouns as independent forms, one might expect such errors to occur.

In general, then, the data are consistent with the claim that weak object pronouns are clitics in the grammars of these children, parallel to weak subject pronouns. The data suggest, however, that object clitics appear later than subject clitics. There appears to be no misanalysis of clitics as independent pronouns, as might be expected in early stages if the absolute-L1-influence hypothesis is correct.

7. Clitic Doubling, Spec–head Agreement and Other Matters

In this section, further properties of child L2 clitics are considered, including non target-like usage and the issue of what kind of Spec–head agreement is involved. Recall that Sportiche argues that clitics head their own projections. As can be seen in (10), in the case of subject clitics, the projection is Nom Voice; the clitic is base-generated in the head (Nom), the subject DP moves to Spec of NomV and there is Spec–head agreement between the clitic and the subject.[12] On this theory, French is a *pro*-drop language, with *pro* in Spec-NomV whenever this position is not filled by a lexical DP or strong pronoun; *pro* is licensed by Spec–head agreement.[13]

This analysis allows for the possibility of clitic doubling, with the clitic in

Nom and the subject in SpecNom. In Quebec French (the dialect our subjects are exposed to), subject doubling is common (Auger 1994; Roberge 1990; Roberge & Vinet 1989). As described in Section 5.2, weak pronouns are found in the subjects' speech in conjunction with a strong pronoun or with a DP, as in (34a) and (34b). Greg, in particular, frequently produces doubled subjects.

(34) a. *moi j'ai   le cirque*   Greg(month 5)
          me I.have the circus

     b. *le bébé i' va   là   ici   aussi*   Greg(month 11)
          the baby he goes there here also

Although some utterances involving a clitic together with another subject may in fact prove to be cases of left dislocation, the tapes show that there is only sometimes a pause between the strong pronoun or DP and the subject clitic, while the context suggests no special kind of topicalization, indicating genuine clitic doubling.

As has already been mentioned, Sportiche's analysis assumes that French is a null subject language, with a subject *pro* in Spec agreeing with the clitic in Nom. Adult French does not allow null subjects in the absence of clitics. Subject clitics provide the 'rich' agreement that licenses *pro*, French verbal agreement alone being insufficient for this (Auger 1994; Kaiser 1994; Roberge 1990). On the whole, the data from Kenny and Greg are consistent with the assumption that the clitic serves as the relevant agreement property for these child L2 learners, as it does for native speakers.

Regarding the position of the subject clitic, since in most cases the clitic correctly surfaces next to the finite verb, one cannot exclude the possibility that it is generated as an agreement marker directly on the verb rather than being base-generated in Nom. However, some rare deviant utterances suggest that the clitic must be generated higher than the verb. These utterances involve clitics and negative placement, as in (35):

(35) a. *i' pas vient*   Kenny(month 4)
          he not comes

     b. *te pas fais*   Greg(month 15)
          you not do

     c. *moi je pas jouer   avec l'auto*   Greg(month 11)
          me I not play:INF with the.car

In these examples, the clitic is to the left of negation, consistent with the assumption that clitics are base-generated in the head of a higher projection. What is wrong with these sentences relates to verb raising; in (35a) and (35b), the tensed verb has failed to raise, while in (35c) a nonfinite verb co-occurs with a clitic, which in fact requires a raised finite verb. (In other instances of negation in the speech of these children, the tensed verb is correctly found to the left of *pas*, while infinitives are found to the right, without clitics. See Grondin & White 1995, for details.)

What kind of Spec–head agreement is involved? Sportiche suggests that the subject must raise to the Spec of the clitic projection to check features of person, number, gender and Case. Clitics in Kenny's and Greg's speech always show correct person agreement; in sentences with doubling, there are no errors like (36). In sentences without doubling, agreement is to the person features of the subject *pro*.

(36) **moi il joue*
me he plays

Correctness of gender agreement is harder to check. For example, if *il* is used for feminine subjects, this could only count as a gender agreement error if one could show that the children know that the noun in question has feminine gender. In the example in (37), the masculine determiner *le* is used for a feminine noun (*tête*); the masculine clitic *il* is also used. Thus, agreement is consistently masculine, even though the noun in question carries feminine gender for native speakers of French:

(37)   *Où   est-ce qu'il   est le   tête d'éléphant?*
where is.it   that.it:MASC is the:MASC head of.elephant
'Where is the elephant's head?'

Greg(month, 20)

In other cases, there is apparent gender confusion, even late in the acquisition process, as shown in (38):

(38) a.   *la maison-là   i'   est gros; celui-là   elle*
the house.there:FEM he is big   that.one.there:MASC she
a   son   porte fermée   Kenny(month 29)
has its:MASC door shut

b.   *mon   maman elle parle anglais*   Greg(month 9)
my:MASC mother she speaks English

As for number, the clitics *je, tu* and *on* 'we'; (singular form, plural meaning) are always used correctly; singular and plural *il/ils* are homophonous, so it is harder to determine whether number is used correctly in these cases.[14]

Agreement for clitics contrasts with agreement on verbs, where there are occasional person errors and where number errors are found for a considerable period of time (see Grondin 1992; see also Meisel 1994, for evidence that number agreement emerges later than person agreement in bilingual children). In (39), the plural subject has singular verb agreement and a clitic form that could be singular or plural:

(39) *les petits animaux i'*   *va*   *là*   Greg(month 9)
     the little animals they go:3SG there

Regarding Case, subject clitics have the correct Case form: there are no cases of accusative *me* or *le* for nominative *je* or *il*. In one or two very rare instances in later months, *te* (accusative) is used instead of *tu* (nominative), as shown in (40) (and also in (35b)). However, as pointed out by a reviewer, this may well involve phonological reduction rather than a Case error:

(40) *pourquoi te*   *fais ça?*   Kenny(month 15)
     why   you:ACC do that

As far as Spec–head agreement with object clitics is concerned, Sportiche argues that accusative object clitics are base-generated in Acc and a *pro* moves to Spec-AccV, as shown in (10). Lexical DPs cannot move to this position, however. Sportiche claims that this is because of a doubly-filled clitic filter.[15] A *pro* object is licensed by Spec–head agreement; it must move so that features of person, number, gender and Case can be checked, as was the case for *pro* subjects. For the children studied here, Case on object clitics is always correct, in that nominative Case is never found on an accusative clitic. Person agreement is also correct; most non-subject clitics that occur are in fact third person. There are occasional number and gender agreement errors.

A structure produced by both children, but especially Kenny in later months, is to insert extra clitics (see Tables 6 and 7). These clitics almost always consist of the 2nd person singular clitic *te/t'* as shown in (41):

(41) *je t'ai*   *fais*   *une erreur*   Kenny(month 29)
     I you've made a   mistake
     'I made a mistake.'

The existence of such clitics is used by Sportiche as an argument against the movement analysis for the clitic itself, since they have no obvious source position. Sportiche (personal communication) handles these in the same way as other clitics in his analysis; the clitic is base-generated in a clitic voice, linked obligatorily to a theta-less XP-position containing a *pro*.

8. Discussion

In this paper, it has been argued that child L2 learners of French show evidence of clitics in their interlanguage grammars. The data fail to provide evidence for a stage where only L1 functional categories are projected, contra the absolute-L1-influence hypothesis, or where L2 subject or object clitics are misanalyzed as independent pronouns, another possibility that might stem from the L1 grammar.

However, one might question the extent to which assumptions about the L2 initial state can be made on the basis of the data presented here. It is, of course, difficult, if not impossible, to prove on the basis of production data what the initial state is like or how long it lasts. This is particularly true if some predicted phenomenon is absent; production data gathered from an earlier stage might have shown something different. It is certainly possible that the data examined here may not be relevant to the issue of the initial state. The data discussed so far are drawn from the Kindergarten year onwards, not from the prior year of exposure to French in the bilingual nursery school, during which time the children hardly spoke French at all (Lightbown 1977). Furthermore, Greg's interviews start only after five months exposure to French in Kindergarten.

Kenny's interviews start after two months in Kindergarten. His early interviews, then, are more likely to be revealing of the initial state. Subject clitics are found throughout, used in ways consistent with Kayne's tests: clitics occur next to the verb and are used exclusively with finite verbs; there are no errors involving the use of a clitic where a strong pronoun form is required, that is, no evidence that clitics are misanalyzed as independent pronouns. In addition, there are some data from the three interviews conducted with Kenny during the bilingual nursery school year. In these interviews, seven utterances containing verbs were found; two of these contain a clitic subject, namely *je*. (Otherwise, most utterances gathered in these three interviews consisted of isolated nouns or DPs, numbers and routines.)

The available data, then, suggest that Kenny has the subject clitics in his grammar at the earliest interviews, consistent with the hypothesis that the initial state projects subject clitics or that they are acquired very early in the course of L2 acquisition. Greg also has subject clitics at his first interview; however, given the timing of this interview, the data cannot be taken as conclusive evidence about early stages in the acquisition of clitics.

We turn now to the issue of developmental changes, focussing particularly on whether there is any evidence of qualitative changes in the children's grammars over the course of development, something which might be expected if the initial grammar is the L1 grammar with subsequent changes in response to L2 input. Three phases can be distinguished in the data:

I.   Up to and including month 11 (the end of the Kindergarten year), both children use subject clitics but their incidence is not particularly high. With the exception of imperatives, object clitics are hardly found at all.

II.   At months 14 to 15, there is a significant increase in the number of utterances containing verbs, leading to an increase in the incidence of subjects in general and subject clitics in particular, including clitic doubling in Greg's case. At about this time, there is also a decrease in the proportion of optional infinitives, as well as of strong pronouns occurring as subjects without a doubled clitic. Object clitics are found but not frequently.

III. There is a dramatic increase in object clitics at month 25 for Kenny and at month 20 for Greg.

The change from the first phase to the second in terms of usage of subject clitics seems to be quantitative rather than qualitative, as does the change in usage of object clitics from the second phase to the third phase. That is, there do not appear to be essential changes in how the clitics are used, only in the number of clitics that are found. However, it is possible that there is a qualitative difference between the first and second phases as far as object clitics are concerned, in which case it could be argued that the interlanguage grammar in the first year does not have an accusative clitic projection. This could support the absolute-L1-influence hypothesis, since it looks as if a projection not present in the L1 is added at a later stage of L2 development, in response to L2 input. However, given that later emergence of object clitics is also reported for L1 and bilingual acquisition (Clark 1985; Hamann et al., this volume; Kaiser 1994), it is not clear that their later appearance in L2 acquisition is related to the lack of clitics in the mother tongue. Indeed, the later emergence of object clitics might be taken as support of the lexical learning hypothesis (Clahsen et al. 1994; Vainikka & Young-Scholten 1994); the early presence of subject clitics, however, does not support this hypothesis.

My analysis of the L1 as not playing a role in the early stages of clitic acquisition depends crucially on there being a difference between English and French with respect to clitic projections. This follows from Sportiche's theory of clitics. However, there are other analyses of clitics which assume that subject clitics are a realization of agreement and are found in Infl (Rizzi 1986; Roberge 1990) or AGR(S) in current terms; object clitics are realization of AGR(O). If these accounts are correct, the absolute L1 influence hypothesis might hold, since the English-speaking L2 learner of French could initially project AGR(S) and AGR(O) on the basis of English. The L2 acquisition task, then, would not be to acquire new functional projections (clitic projections) but to work out that the realization of AGR(S) and AGR(O) differs in the two languages, with clitics being a form of agreement in the L2 but not the L1.

Although I have argued that the L1 grammar does not have significant effects on the L2 acquisition of clitic projections, I do not wish to deny that L1 grammars are used in general as an initial or interim theory of the L2. I have argued extensively for this position over the years, for example by claiming that L1 parameter settings are applied to the L2 until positive L2 data lead to resetting (e.g., White 1985; 1989; 1991).

However, I would like to suggest that there will be situations where the L1 grammar cannot constitute an initial theory of the L2. These will involve cases where some property of UG has not been activated in the L1 and has therefore remained unspecified. I propose, then, that the initial state of the L2 learner consists both of L1-based knowledge (such as L1 parameter settings) and unspecified aspects of UG. The unspecified properties can interact immediately with the L2 input, with the result that the L2 acquisition path will be close to that found in L1 acquisition for the properties in question. L2 acquisition of clitics by English learners of French constitutes such a case; in the case of functional projections that are not realized in the L1, it is not clear what aspect of the L1 grammar could constitute an initial theory of the L2, unless the forms in question are misanalyzed as not being functional categories at all. As we have seen, this does seem not to happen in the data reported here. Instead, the L2 learner appears to be sensitive early on to properties of the L2 input that suggest the need for functional categories not instantiated in the L1. It is noteworthy that the L2 data reported here are quite similar to the L1 data reported in Hamann *et al.* (this volume), both in terms of the distributional properties of clitics versus other pronouns and DPs, and in terms of the later appearance of object clitics.

In conclusion, in the spirit of recent proposals that L2 research should turn in more detail to investigations of the precise properties of interlanguage grammars, including the nature of functional categories and the role of the L1 grammar (Epstein *et al.*, in press; Eubank 1993/1994, 1994; Schwartz & Sprouse 1994; White, in press), weak pronouns and their status as clitics has been explored in this paper. It has been shown that subject clitics are present from the earliest interviews, while appearance of object clitics is later. It has been argued that the interlanguages of child L2 learners of French contain clitic projections.

Here, I have only been concerned with L2 acquisition by young children but in principle the same issues could be explored for older learners, thus addressing the question of whether adult learners also can acquire functional projections not instantiated in the L1 and whether this takes place immediately or after an initial phase of L1 influence.

Acknowledgements

I should like to thank Patsy Lightbown for generously making her data available, Julie Auger, Usha Lakshmann, Bonnie Schwartz, Rex Sprouse and three anonymous reviewers for comments and suggestions, as well as Philippe Prévost for his invaluable assistance in hunting for clitics in the data. This research was conducted with the assistance of research grants from FCAR and SSHRCC.

Notes

1. Examples are taken from Kayne (1975).

2. One difference that will not be pursued in this paper is that subject clitics can invert with the verb in questions, in contrast to DPs. Subject clitic inversion is practically non-existent in the child L2 data to be examined here (Grondin & White 1995).

3. Example (1b) is ungrammatical with a full DP if the adverb is not parenthetical (Pollock 1989).

4. Keyser & Roeper (1992) argue that English verbs are associated with an abstract clitic position. However, as they note, their notion of clitic is different from the traditional one. I assume that English lacks the standard kind of clitics which are the focus of this paper.

5. These examples involve *sais*, which in general has been excluded from the analysis in case *je sais* and *je ne sais pas* are learned as routines. However, it seems clear that routines are not involved here. *Moi sais* is not grammatical and would not occur in the input, for example.

6. *Je va* occurred quite frequently in the data. This has a first person clitic but the third person singular form of the verb. *Je va* is common in colloquial Quebec French (Auger 1994).

7. As a result of the decision to omit potential routines/unanalyzed chunks, as well as to exclude certain kinds of clitics from the analyses here, there are some numerical discrepancies between the data reported in this paper and those reported in Grondin (1992), Grondin & White (1995).

8. As can be seen from Table 1, the strong pronoun and clitic forms are sometimes identical (*elle, nous, vous, elles*). In such cases, I have assumed that a form is a clitic if it occurs in a clitic-like context, otherwise a strong pronoun.

9. See Grondin & White (1995) for evidence that both children have DPs (rather than bare NPs) in the earliest interviews.

10. One problem in deciding whether the children are using finite or nonfinite forms arises from the fact that French has many homophonous morphemes, particularly in the case of regular verbs of the first conjugation. For example, the morpheme pronounced [e] is ambiguous. It can mark the second person plural present tense (written as *-ez*), or the infinitive (written as *-er*) or the past participle (written as *-é*). In the latter two cases, [e] is nonfinite. I have taken the child's use of this form to be nonfinite unless there are other indications to the contrary. In the case of second and third person conjugation verbs, on the other hand, there are clear distinctions between infinitives and finite forms, although there are still ambiguities between participles and finite forms for some verbs.

11. A third person strong pronoun can occur as the subject of a finite verb in adult French, provided that it is stressed. See (1e) for an example.

12. I assume, however, that the clitic and its projection is not obligatory, since French can have sentences with DP subjects but no clitics. In such cases, the subject remains in Spec-AGR(S), unless one assumes the presence of a null clitic.

13. The claim that French is a *pro*-drop language is shared by other theories, including theories that do not assume that clitics head their own projections (e.g., Auger 1994; Roberge 1990; Roberge & Vinet 1989).

14. In standard French, *elle/elles* are also homophonous. In colloquial Quebec French, *ils* (pronounced *i*] is used for both masculine and feminine 3rd person plural. Kenny and Greg do not use *elles* at all (see Table 3).

15. Sportiche argues that a doubly filled clitic filter operates in those dialects which prohibit doubling. However, a problem with this proposal, for Quebec French at least, is that although an object DP may not occur in Spec-Acc together with a clitic in Acc, a subject may be clitic-doubled. This suggests that such a filter cannot be the right explanation.

References

Auger, J. 1994. "Pronominal Clitics in Québec Colloquial French: A morphological analysis." Diss., University of Pennsylvania.

Borer, H. (ed.). 1986. *The Syntax of Pronominal Clitics* (= *Syntax and Semantics*). Orlando: Academic Press.

Carroll, S. 1982. "Redoublement et dislocations en français." *La syntaxe comparée du français standard et populaire: Approche formelle et fonctionnelle*, ed. by C. Lefebvre, 291–357. Montreal: Office de la langue français.

Clahsen, H., S. Eisenbeiss & A. Vainikka. 1994. "The Seeds of Structure: A syntactic analysis of the acquisition of Case marking." *Language Acquisition Studies in Generative Grammar*, ed. by T. Hoekstra & B. D. Schwartz, 85–118. Amsterdam: John Benjamins.

Clark, E. 1985. "The Acquisition of Romance, with Special Reference to French." *The Crosslinguistic Study of Language Acquisition*. Vol. 1: *The Data*, ed. by D. I. Slobin, 687–782. Hillsdale, N.J.: Lawrence Erlbaum.

Epstein, S., S. Flynn & G. Martohardjono. In press. "The Strong Continuity Hypothesis in Adult L2 Acquisition of Functional Categories." *The Generative Study of Second Language Acquisition*, ed. by S. Flynn, G. Martohardjono and W. O'Neil. Hillsdale, N.J.: Lawrence Erlbaum.

Eubank, L. 1993/1994. "On the Transfer of Parametric Values in L2 Development." *Language Acquisition* 3.183–208.

Fukui, N. & M. Speas. 1986. "Specifiers and Projections." *MIT Working Papers in Linguistics* 8.128–172.

Grondin, N. 1992. "Functional Projections in Child Second Language Acquisition of French." Diss., McGill University.

Grondin, N. & L. White. 1995. "Functional Categories in Child L2 Acquisition of French." *Language Acquisition* 4.4.

Hamann, C., L. Rizzi & U. Frauenfelder. This volume. "On the Acquisition of the Pronominal System in French."

Harley, B. & M. Swain. 1984. "The Interlanguage of Immersion Students and its Implications for Second Language Teaching." *Interlanguage*, ed. by A. Davies, C. Criper & A. Howatt, 291–311. Edinburgh: Edinburgh University Press.

Kaiser, G. 1994. "More about INFL-ection and Agreement: The acquisition of clitic pronouns in French." *Bilingual First Language Acquisition: French and German grammatical development*, ed. by J. Meisel, 131–159. Amsterdam: John Benjamins.

Kaplan, T. 1993. "The Second Language Acquisition of Functional Categories: Complementizer phrases in English and Japanese. Diss., Cornell University.

Kayne, R. S. 1975. *French Syntax: The transformational cycle*. Cambridge, Mass.: MIT Press.

Keyser, S. J. & T. Roeper. 1992. "Re: The abstract clitic hypothesis." *Linguistic Inquiry* 23.89–125.

Lakshmanan, U. 1993/1994. " 'The boy for the cookie' - Some evidence for the nonviolation of the Case filter in child second language acquisition." *Language Acquisition* 3.55–91.

Lakshmanan, U. & L. Selinker. 1994. "The Status of CP and the Tensed Complementizer *that* in the Developing L2 Grammars of English." *Second Language Research* 10.25–48.

Lightbown, P. M. 1977. "Consistency and Variation in the Acquisition of French." Diss., Columbia.

Meisel, J. 1994. "Getting FAT: Finiteness, agreement and tense in early grammars." *Bilingual first language acquisition: French and German grammatical development*, ed. by J. Meisel, 89–129. Amsterdam: John Benjamins.

Müller, N., B. Crysmann & G. Kaiser. 1994. "Interactions between the Acquisition of French Object Drop and the Development of the C-system." Ms., University of Hamburg.

Pierce, A. 1992. *Language Acquisition and Syntactic Theory: A comparative analysis of French and English child grammars*. Dordrecht: Kluwer.

Pollock, J-Y. 1989. "Verb Movement, Universal Grammar, and the Structure of IP." *Linguistic Inquiry* 20.365–424.

Rivas, A. 1977. "A Theory of Clitics." Diss., Massachusetts Institute of Technology, Cambridge.

Rizzi, L. 1986. "On the Status of Subject Clitics in Romance." *Studies in Romance linguistics*, ed. by O. Jaeggli & C. Silva-Corvalán, 391–419. Dordrecht: Foris.

———. 1993/1994. "Some Notes on Linguistic Theory and Language Development: The case of root infinitives." *Language Acquisition* 3.371–393.

———. 1994a. "Early Null Subjects and Root Null Subjects." *Language Acquisition Studies in Generative Grammar*, ed by T. Hoekstra & B. D. Schwartz, 151–176. Amsterdam: John Benjamins.

———. 1994b. "Root Infinitives as Truncated Structures in Early Grammar." Paper presented at the Boston University Conference on Language Development, Boston, January.

Roberge, Y. 1990. *The Syntactic Recoverability of Null Arguments*. Kingston & Montreal: McGill-Queen's University Press.

Roberge, Y. & M.-T. Vinet. 1989. *La variation dialectale en grammaire universelle*. Montreal: Les Presses de l'Université de Montréal.

Schwartz, B. In press. "On Two Hypotheses of 'Transfer' in L2A: Minimal trees and absolute influence." *The Generative Study of Second Language Acquisition*, ed. by S. Flynn, G. Martohardjono & W. O'Neil. Hillsdale, N.J.: Lawrence Erlbaum.

Schwartz, B. D. & R. Sprouse. 1994. "Word Order and Nominative Case in Nonnative Language Acquisition: A longitudinal study of (L1 Turkish) German interlanguage." *Language Acquisition Studies in Generative Grammar*, ed. by T. Hoekstra & B. D. Schwartz, 317–368). Amsterdam: John Benjamins.

Sportiche, D. 1992. "Clitic Constructions." Ms., University of California at Los Angeles.

———. 1993. "Subject Clitics in French and Romance: Complex inversion and clitic doubling." Ms., University of California at Los Angeles.

Strozer, J. 1976. "Clitics in Spanish." Diss., University of California at Los Angeles.

Tarone, E., U. Frauenfelder & L. Selinker. 1976. "Systematicity/Variability and Stability/ Instability in Interlanguage Systems." *Language Learning* 4.93–134.

Vainikka, A. & M. Young-Scholten. 1994. "Direct Access to X'-theory: Evidence from Korean and Turkish adults learning German." *Language Acquisition Studies in Generative Grammar*, ed. by T. Hoekstra & B. D. Schwartz, 265–316. Amsterdam: John Benjamins.

Wexler, K. 1994. "Optional Infinitives, Head Movement and the Economy of Derivation in Child Grammar." *Verb Movement*, ed. by D. Lightfoot & N. Hornstein, 305–350. Cambridge: Cambridge University Press.

White, L. 1985. "The *Pro*-drop Parameter in Adult Second Language Acquisition." *Language Learning* 35.47–62.

———. 1989. "The Principle of Adjacency in Second Language Acquisition: Do L2 learners observe the subset principle?" *Linguistic Perspectives on Second Language Acquisition*, ed. by S. Gass & J. Schachter, 134–158. Cambridge: Cambridge University Press.

———. 1991. "Adverb Placement in Second Language Acquisition: Some effects of positive and negative evidence in the classroom." *Second Language Research* 7.133–161.

———. In press. "Universal Grammar and Second Language Acquisition: Current trends and new directions." *Handbook of language acquisition*, ed. by W. Ritchie & T. Bhatia. New York: Academic Press.

The Initial Hypothesis of Syntax
A Minimalist Perspective on
Language Acquisition and Attrition

Christer Platzack
Lund University

1. Introduction

The MINIMALIST program of Chomsky (1993, 1995) offers a new meaning to the concept MARKEDNESS: taking overt syntactic operations to be more costly than invisible operations, a markedness distinction is introduced in the very heart of the theory, saying that the mechanisms forcing overt operations in a language will be the marked ones. In this paper I will explore the psycholinguistic consequences of this markedness conception, demonstrating that the minimalist approach interpreted in this way offers great perspectives for our understanding of language acquisition (see Wu 1993 for a similar attempt) and also for language attrition, a subject not often studied from a generative point of view.

In general the minimalist program predicts every word order differing from the universal one to be the result of a marked value of some FUNCTIONAL projection. I will claim that the mechanism guiding all language learning, both L1 and L2, is the INITIAL HYPOTHESIS OF SYNTAX, IHS, according to which there are no marked values, hence only invisible movement is required. The IHS is part of (or maybe deduced from) Universal Grammar (UG), the genetically determined language system that all human beings are born with. Given this perspective, language acquisition can be seen as a gradual adjustment of the IHS to the target language, the main difference between L1 and L2 acquisition being that the system acquired within the critical period of L1 acquisition is *engraved* in the brain of the young child, creating the language-particular knowledge system that we automatically apply as our mother tongue.[1] As I will demonstrate, this conception of L1 also explains why the native speaker does not forget the marked values of his mother tongue. Hence also certain types of language attrition can be accounted for in terms of the IHS. For early syntax, this account makes the same predictions as Radford's (1994) MINIMAL LEXICAL PROJECTION HYPOTHESIS, although it departs from his structure-building approach in assuming the presence of functional projections from the very beginning.

My paper is organized in the following way. Section 2 will contain an overview of the theoretical framework, and Section 3 a presentation of the IHS, the particular markedness hypothesis which can be deduced from this framework. Section 4 reviews some empirical studies of language attrition, second-language learning and first-language acquisition. In addition to giving support to the general belief that once acquired, a marked value cannot be lost unless there is a brain injury, this section demonstrates the usefulness of the IHS as an explanatory tool in psycholinguistic research. The main part of my paper is section five, which is a case study of the acquisition of Swedish from the point of view of the IHS.

2. The Minimalist Program

In this section I will give a short overview of the most important aspects of the minimalist program of Chomsky (1993) and the way I implement this program for the purpose of the present study. As in earlier versions of generative grammar, the focus of interest is the generative component of the language faculty, I-GRAMMAR, that mediates between form and meaning. I-grammar is an automatic system which generates structural descriptions from lexical inputs: given a particular selection of lexical elements it builds up two sets of structural descriptions, one of which, called PF, functions as a complex of instructions for the articulatory-perceptual systems of the human cognitive faculty, the other one, LF, as a complex of instructions for the conceptual-intentional systems. The general hypothesis is that I-grammar has little or no properties of its own, being more or less totally characterized by the properties of PF and LF.

Each word, taken from the lexicon with its inflectional morphology specified, is considered to be a sequence of the type illustrated in (1), where α is a morphological complex, R is a root, and $morph_1 - .. - morph_n$ visible inflectional features. $Infl_1, ..., Infl_n$ are abstract features representing the basic syntactic relations in which the word participates.

(1)   Word = $(\alpha, Infl_1, ..., Infl_n)$, where $\alpha = [R\text{-}morph_1 - .. \text{-}morph_n]$.

See Chomsky (1993:28). The PF-rules only see α. Hence, only if there is a one-to-one correspondence between the expressed morphemes and the abstract inflectional features present in (1) do we have a full morphological representation of the basic syntactic relations in which the lexical element is involved. Usually the set of expressed morphemes only partially reflects the set of abstract features, as in the following illustration:

(2) $V = (kissed,$ ϕ-features$_{obj}$, past$_{tns}$, ϕ-features$_{subj}$, finite)
        where $kissed = (kiss + ed_{past})$

The verb *kissed* is morphologically inflected for past tense, corresponding to Past$_{tns}$ among its set of abstract features. This set also includes a finiteness feature, and two sets of Φ-features, expressing the relation of the verb to the object and the subject, respectively. I take finiteness to express the anchoring of the clause in time and space, either directly as in main clauses, or indirectly through the finiteness feature of the matrix clause, as for embedded clauses. Hence, finiteness is to be distinguished from tense.

The abstract features associated with a lexical head determine the range of its extended projection in the sense of Grimshaw (1991), i.e., the set of functional projections within which the lexical projection is embedded. In the case of (2) there must be four functional projections on top of the lexical one, as shown in (3), where an intermediate step in the derivation of the clause *John kissed Mary* is represented; finiteness is associated with CP, subject Φ-features with AGR(S)P, object Φ-features with AGR(O)P, and tense with TP. With Kayne (1994) I also assume that phrase structure of natural languages is universally organized with the order specifier–head–complement.[2] According to Chomsky (1993:28) each functional head may contain both a head feature and a specifier feature (or V- and NP-features). These features, as well as the abstract features associated with the lexical categories (i.e., the INFL-features of (1)) have to be eliminated before the interface levels PF or LF; being invisible to the cognitive systems interpreting these interfaces, the presence of such features at these levels would cause a violation of the PRINCIPLE OF FULL INTERPRETATION, according to which PF and LF may contain only elements interpretable at these levels.

It follows that the feature system is wholly internal to the automatic system, with the sole purpose of guaranteeing that each syntactic relation is expressed as a local X'-relation.[3] The head feature of a particular functional head F^0 is checked when a head with the relevant lexical feature is adjoined to F^0, forming a local head–head relation. Consider the lexical head *kissed* in (3), which contains the feature Past$_{tns}$ according to (2). The functional head T^0 has a corresponding head feature Tns; to eliminate these features the verb *kissed* must

(3)

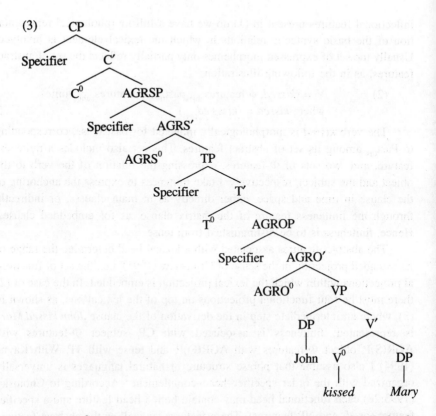

be adjoined to T^0, forming the necessary local head–head relation. Similarly, the specifier feature of a functional head F^0 is checked when a phrase XP with the relevant lexical feature is placed as the specifier of F^0, producing a local Spec–head relation. Assuming the subject *John* to contain Φ-features like third person and singular, corresponding to the specifier features of Agrs^0, *John* must move to Spec-AGR(S)P to eliminate these features. Note in particular that it follows that the actual functional categories present in a particular derivation are determined by the lexical elements: only those functional categories are present in a given convergent derivation that are needed for checking the abstract inflectional features of the lexical elements involved, since each feature has its particular checking configuration. If there is a mismatch of some kind, Full Interpretation will be violated and the derivation will crash.

Some features have the special property of being visible at PF: such features are called STRONG and must be eliminated prior to PF to avoid violation of Full Interpretation. Strong features contrast with WEAK features which are not visible at PF, and hence of no offence at this interface: to obtain Full Interpretation, it is enough if the weak features are eliminated before LF. It follows that the distinction weak/strong is of utmost importance to word order: knowing which features are strong, we know which features must be checked (eliminated) at PF, hence which positions in the tree must be filled at PF. Word order differences between languages can thus be expressed as differences with respect to the distribution of weak and strong features. With Wilder & Ćavar (1994) I will also assume that lexical categories contain only weak features, meaning that the strong/weak dichotomy responsible for word order differences is solely represented within functional heads.

Consider the PF representation (4) of the English clause *John kissed Mary* given below. Very few checkings have taken place in (4). Since the subject must be overtly realized in English, we conclude that the specifier feature of AGR(S)^0 is strong (see Platzack 1994, Chomsky 1995), hence the subject has moved to Spec-AGR(S)P prior to PF to check its Φ-features. On its way the subject must pass through Spec-TP, checking the Nominative Case feature of Spec-TP as well. Further checkings take place in covert syntax: here the verb raises to AGR(O)^0 to check its object Φ-features, to T^0 to check its tense feature, to AGR(S)^0 to check its subject Φ-features, and to C^0 to check its finiteness feature.[4] Subsequently, the object raises to Spec-AGR(O)P to check its Φ-features.[5] The resulting LF-structure is identical to the LF-structures of the corresponding sentences in other languages. Languages differ with respect to which features must be checked prior to PF, not with respect to LF. Hence to master the word order of a particular language, you must know where the strong features are.

In the following, I will discuss the implications for language acquisition and attrition of the theoretical framework outlined.

3.   The Early Stage

The system mediating form and meaning, i.e., the I-grammar of our mother tongue, is automatized during the first four to seven years of our lives.[6] This does not imply that children at seven are capable of using their native language like adults — on the contrary, there is still a lot to learn about the use of language for specific purposes, as well as new lexical items. With respect to the automatic system, though, there is no further development.

(4)

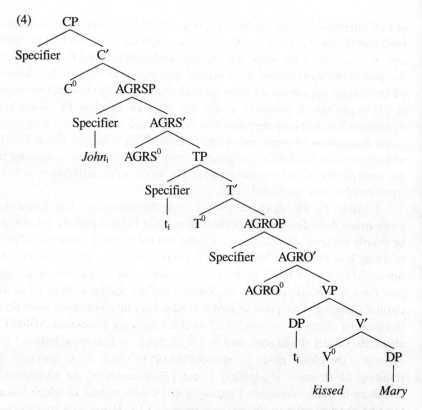

There are many different opinions regarding what is going on when the child is in the process of acquiring a first language. Whereas most researchers agree that the child combines inborn knowledge of the outer bounds of possible human languages with positive information extracted from the language surrounding it to set the parameters of its mother tongue, there is no consensus with respect to how this is happening, or to what extent the utterances produced by the child are representative of his/her degree of language knowledge. Virtually every possibility has found its proponent, including the opinion that the child has set all the language-particular parameters already prior to their first two-word utterances (e.g. Wexler 1994b) and the opinion that early grammar is very rudimentary compared to adult grammar, including only lexical categories (e.g., Radford 1986, 1994 and Platzack 1990, among others); the papers in Meisel (1992) are representative of the present confusion within the field in this respect.

To a particular degree, it seems to me that the confusion mentioned in the last paragraph is rooted in the grammatical theory underlying most of these works, i.e., the Principles and Parameters approach to syntax of Chomsky (1981, 1986a, b). This theory is not restrictive enough to indicate which ones of the different approaches are superior to the other. In this respect, the minimalist program seems to introduce a healthy amount of strictness to the field, at least given the implementation outlined in section two above.

The introduction of the concept PARAMETER in the pre-minimalistic theory, i.e., principles of language taking more than one value and hence the theoretical correlate to crosslinguistic variation, was an important step forward, since it enabled us to describe all human languages as different instances of the same basic object. However, the parameter concept itself was rather fuzzy, and most attempts to find constructions in different languages correlated by a particular value of a single parameter can be severely doubted.

In a minimalist grammar, on the other hand, there is no confusion regarding parameters. The range of possible differences between languages is laid down within the system as the dichotomy ⟨±PF-visible⟩, i.e., strong features versus weak features on functional categories. Future will tell if there are other theoretically unclear concepts undermining the validity of the minimalist program, but with respect to parameters, it is obviously a step forward. This has particular consequences for applied linguistics, as we will see below.

Given this background, I will return to a discussion of the early stage of language acquisition, showing how the confusion mentioned above may be eliminated. Consider e.g., the debate about functional categories, summarized as follows in the words of Jill de Villiers: does the child have "initially complete 'skeletons' of phrase structure, clothed in null elements," or is the early stage "characterized by the absence of all functional projections, with early grammars containing just thematic-lexical categories" (de Villiers 1992:423). Given a description where the position of an element at LF determines its syntactic relations to the other elements within the clause, it should be clear that children must have access to the relevant functional categories as soon as they understand what is expressed by these syntactic relations. How much the child understands of these matters is an empirical question. It must be kept in mind that much information is conveyed already by the semantic content of words. In practical work, it might be difficult to find out what role is played by the syntactic relations. In principle, however, the picture is clear: to understand an utterance in the same way as adult speakers, the child must have the same LF-representation of the clause as adults.

Considering language acquisition within the framework of the minimalist program, it seems obvious to me that the economy considerations of this program strongly imply that the initial syntactic hypothesis of the child must be that all syntactic features are weak. This would imply that the child expects to find the elements of the string in their base positions, and that the only movements involved are invisible movements of features. This hypothesis can be expressed as *Don't move!*, or more formally as in (5):

(5)   Initial Hypothesis of Syntax (IHS)
           All instances of feature checking take place after spell-out

In case a language does not postpone all feature-checking to LF, the child will recognize a particular tension between his expectations, deduced from the IHS, and the way speakers surrounding him express themselves. To understand what is said, the child must be prepared to deviate from the IHS. Since there are usually more than one position for a particular word to go to, (see the subject chain headed by *John* in (4)), it is not possible for the child to deduce the distribution of strong and weak positions just from the simple examples; as a matter of fact we must expect that for understanding, the child has to be able to process quite intricate structures before he has found out the strong/weak system of his mother tongue.

The presence of a stage in L1 acquisition during which the child produces both correct strings and incorrect ones is observed in almost every collection of child utterances: actually it is the presence of forms signalling a parameter set at the adult value already among the first sentence-like sequences which has inspired scholars to opt for an early setting of parameter values. Consider, e.g., the acquisition of Swedish verb second. The first examples of inversion signalling verb second may turn up more than a year before the child has automatized the construction. This is illustrated by the following excerpts from the recordings of Sara, who produces clear V2–cases already at 1;11, but does not consistently use V2 until as late as 2;10:

(6)   a.   *nu   får   pappa denna*   Sara(1;11)
             now get:PRES daddy this
       b1.   *INTE kan   han gå*   Sara(2;3)
             not   can:PRES he walk
       b2.   *DÄR han bor*   Sara(2;3)
             there he   live:PRES
       c1.   *vad gör   pappa här då?*   Sara(2;10)
             what do:PRES   daddy here then

c2. *stor han E*   Sara(2;10)[7]
     big he is

There is reason to believe that the child has access to the full range of functional categories already at the time of the first sentence-like utterances: to argue against this we have to prove that there are syntactic relations which the child does not understand.

So far I have not discussed the question how to interpret the fact that grammar is automatized roughly between four and seven years of age. Consider the picture outlined above. Equipped with UG and the IHS, as well as with a lexicon, the child knows that word orders not predicted by the IHS must be the result of a strong position somewhere among the functional phrases. Given enough input, it takes the child about two years to figure out where all the strong positions are to be found. The system is not automatized at this point, though, since the child must always be (although to a diminishing degree) ready to adjust its assumptions.

The general design of inborn UG, outlined as (1)–(3) above, must be laid down during the development of the brain, maybe as a kind of cortical map (see, e.g., Altman 1987 for an overview). A cortical map is a particular wiring of the brain, consisting of an intricate system of neurons (nerve cells) that make up the brain.

From physiological studies of the brain we know that memory is chemically coded in the synapses, the electrical connections between the neurons (Greenberg *et al.* 1987). Learning takes place when two neurons, each of which responds to a particular stimulus, are simultaneously activated, causing the synapse between them to be strengthened. The modified synapse links the two neurons into a circuit. Such circuits are the basis for automatization, which converts a series of smaller circuits into a subroutine (Evarts 1973) that is stored in the cortex and executed as a complex whole. The connections that are established by birth are not necessarily permanent but may be adjusted during development until growth is complete (Gaze *et al.* 1974). It is known that activity, competition and other interactive processes are responsible for this fine-tuning of the connections. We may now assume that the ENGRAVING in the brain of the particular system of strong and weak positions responsible for the automatic system of our mother tongue physiologically is the result of such a fine-tuning of the connections: this particular growth of the synapses may cease at the end of the critical period for language acquisition, i.e., around the 7th birthday. If this is correct, we could imagine that the completion of development of the synapses will close the open-mindedness of the child with respect to strong and weak features, permanently fixing the values as they are at this stage.[8]

The neurophysiological speculations outlined constitute a kind of biological background to the minimalist program adopted here, giving us a way to understand the commonly held belief that once set, a parameter cannot be reset. It is also in concordance with what we know about the resistance against oblivion of the automatic system, as well as with the fact that hardly anybody succeeds to develope a native speaker competence of a language he has not been exposed to in early childhood. I will return to a discussion of such matters below.

4.   The Use of the IHS in Language Acquisition and Attrition

4.1. Introduction

In this section I will present a survey of observations from the literature which generally support the assumption of section three that the IHS is playing a role for language acquisition and attrition, both with respect to L1 and L2. According to the discussion above, every human being is expected to assume from the outset that any unknown language s/he is exposed to, including the first language, has the word order subject–verb–complement: this is the order obtained if there is no strong features at all (see (3)). Language acquisition is seen as a gradual adjustment of this initial stage to the stage representative of the particular language, language attrition resulting from a brain injury is seen as a replacement of the particular language state with a state compatible to the IHS.

The general picture just outlined is obscured by conflicting tendencies. With respect to L2 acquisition, the fact that the learner already has acquired a human language is supposed to play a role — not the absolute role predicted by Schwartz & Sprouse (1994), but a mediating role, suggesting to the learner that all departures from the word order compatible to the IHS should be as in their first language. With respect to L1 acquisition, the fact that children learn to understand their mother tongue long before they begin to produce it gives us reason to expect that the first sentence-like utterances are not representative of the initial stage, but of a later stage; still we expect to find traces of the properties compatible to the IHS. Finally, with respect to language attrition resulting from a brain injury, the nature of the injury is naturally of importance for the degree of deviation in the direction of a grammar based on the IHS.

4.2. *L1 Acquisition Studies*

According to my account, we expect early child language to show traces of a stage where all syntactic properties were predictable from the IHS, i.e., a stage with no strong features. Deviances from adult grammar are thus predicted to be in the direction of a grammar determined by the IHS, but not in other directions. A survey of the literature gives general support for this prediction; a detailed study of L1 Swedish from the point of view of the assumptions presented here will follow in Section 5 below.

Consider first languages with a general word order which is not compatible with the order predicted by the IHS, i.e., subject–verb–complement (SVC): for such languages we expect to find instances of SVC in early child grammar. This has also been reported. According to Guilfoyle (1990:214 f.) there are many SVC-sequences in early Irish, in spite of the fact that adult Irish is a strict VSC-language. The same observation is made for Welsh, another VSC-language, in a study by Aldridge, Borsley and Clack referred to by Radford (1994). According to Radford (p. 48) there was not a single example of VSC-order in the early recordings (19–23 months of age) of the longitudinally studied subject Kevin. Similarly, both Backdash and Class, which are cited in Ouhalla (1991), observe that the predominant order in the early speech of children learning some Arabic dialects is SVC, despite the fact that the preferred order in the corresponding adult dialects is VSC. See § 5.4.3. below for a discussion of the order verb–complement.

Another property of early child language which can be related to the IHS is the abundant drop of subjects around the age of two, irrespective of whether or not the adult language is a null-subject language. As argued in Platzack (1994) (see also Chomsky 1995), null subjects indicate the presence of a weak specifier feature in AGR(S). The null subject option will therefore be predicted by the IHS, also for languages like English and French, which have obligatorily expressed subjects. Hence we predict earlier stages of these languages to have null subjects. This is also the case, as has been noticed in many studies. Hyams (1986) gives early English examples like *read bear book, throw it away, want more apple*, and Pierce (1992:109) early French examples like *est pas gros* 'is not big', *boit* 'drinks' and *veut lait* 'wants milk'. Similar examples can be found in early Swedish, despite the fact that adult Swedish, like English and French, does not allow the drop of subjects in finite clauses. See section 5.5.3 below.

4.3. *Second Language Acquisition*

Under the account presented above, it is expected that early INTERLANGUAGE will have properties compatible with the IHS. Since the IHS can be seen as a theoretically based markedness account, it is expected to work at least as well as earlier markedness accounts, consider e.g., the BACK-TO-UG proposal of Mazurkewich (1988). Given the IHS, the most straightforward hypothesis about L2 would be that we initially go back to the IHS when trying to come to grips with a second language. Certain well-known universal properties of interlanguage, like predominant SVC and the initial presence of null subjects, support such a view. Note e.g., that my account predicts the occurrence of sequences of SVO in the interlanguage of learners who have OV in their mother tongue, and who are targeting another OV-language, and the absence of OV-sequences in the interlanguage of learners coming from a VO-language and acquiring another VO-language. The occurrence of VO-sequences in the early interlanguage of Cevdet (a Turkish speaking person learning German), reported in Schwartz & Sprouse (1994:335), supports my account, although the fact that this word order is restricted to finite verbs also makes other interpretations plausible.

Another prediction of my account is that the interlanguage of speakers going from one verb second language to another will contain sequences that are not verb second: verb second is the result of a strong head feature in the beginning of the sentence (presumably in C^0), and is thus not assumed to exist in a grammar based solely on the IHS and UG. Such a case is reported in Håkansson (forthcoming), who found that many Swedes learning German make errors with respect to verb second, although German and Swedish are both verb second languages.[9] Further support for the role of the IHS for early interlanguage can be taken from studies of the L2 acquisition of negations in languages like English, German and Swedish (Hyltenstam 1977; Bolander 1988; Colliander 1993). These languages all have postverbal negation in main clauses, indicating verb raising to some strong head position and thus deviating from what is predicted by the IHS. Nevertheless, the relevant early interlanguages often display the order negation–verb, as predicted by my account.

I will claim that there are two basic differences between L1 and L2 acquisition: firstly, L2 acquisition is always performed against the background of a native language, and secondly, there is, presumably, no stage of automatization in L2 learning[10] — a good student may come increasingly close to perfect mastery of the new grammar, but it will never be engraved in the brain as the first language, meaning that it will be vulnerable in situations of stress, tiredness, intoxication and other situations where the speaker is not in full control.[11]

4.4. L1 Attrition Studies

The claim that automatized grammar indicates a particular brain structure has important implications for language attrition. In particular, a language property engraved in the brain is predicted to be resistent to oblivion, while other parts of the language should not be immune to forgetting. This theory tells us that a speaker would not forget where the strong features are to be found in his first language, even when he has been out of practice for a long time. In case of real brain damage, however, the situation is different: in such a case even knowledge of strong features may be lost. To see how the IHS may help us to understand language attrition, I will investigate two groups of speakers with partial loss of Swedish: aphasics, and bilingually raised expatriate Swedes, who have forgotten parts of their Swedish.

4.4.1. Aphasics

Since aphasia involves real brain damage, the particular brain structure corresponding to the strong value of some grammatical features might be influenced. This is how I would like to interpret agrammatism, one of the characterizing features of Broca's aphasics. At least some patients classified as Broca's type aphasics behave as if they have lost the knowledge of where the strong positions are,[12] as the following survey of two Swedish aphasics will show. With no strong positions, they are assumed to fall back on the IHS. If this is true, not only production but also comprehension should be damaged. Whereas I do not have any comprehension data for the two Swedish patients discussed below, this prediction is supported by the observation of Stuss & Benson (1986:169) that "the patient with agrammatism has (...) difficulty in comprehending (...) syntactical structures." See also Schwartz et al. (1980) and Saffran et al. (1980) for similar observations, and Caplan (1987) for a general overview.

In Swedish patients having lost the knowledge of the strong positions C^0 and Spec-AGR(S)P, we expect to find omissions of the subject and verb second errors. Such cases are indeed reported. The male patient presented in Ekerot (1988:265) has both types of errors, and the same types of errors are found in the speech of the female patient studied by Ahlsén & Dravins (1990). Some examples from the second study are given in (7), where (7a) is a main clause with V3, (7b) a clear case of null subject:

(7)   a.   *sen hon sa   att   jag ska   hem   sen*
             then she said that I   shall home then
                                         (Ahlsén & Dravins 1990:570)

       b.   *men han sover nu.   sen äter mat*
             but he   sleeps now then eats food
                                         (Ahlsén & Dravins 1990:575)

It is to be noted that other aspects of the grammar of these two patients were intact, including all properties compatible with the IHS. Thus, e.g., both patients placed the complement to the right of the verb. In general, the languages of these two aphasic patients conform closely to what we would expect, assuming that their brains have been injured in such a way that they have lost the knowledge of the strong features, falling back on the IHS.

4.4.2. *Expatriate Swedes*

A different type of error is found in the language of people that have not been exposed to their mother tongue for a considerable amount of time. In a recent paper, Håkansson (in press) has investigated the language of five bilingually raised expatriate Swedes, who have returned to Sweden at the age of about twenty years in order to study at a Swedish university, after having spent their school years abroad.[13] Much to their own surprise they failed the language test that is obligatory for all students who have not attented the Swedish "gymnasium" school. As a consequence of their failing the test, they were all attending a course in Swedish as a second language, together with other L2 learners of Swedish, at the time of the data collection. Data from the five informants include written and spoken material. Written material was also collected from the other students in the group, and was used as a comparison to the expatriate students. The results show that there are systematic differences between the two types of students. Whereas both groups made a lot of errors on agreement in NP and the correct use of finite forms, only the non-Swedish students made verb second errors. Among the expatriate Swedes, Håkansson reports only one single V2 error. There is no information about the use of null subjects among the two groups of students.

The results of Håkansson's study support the hypothesis that once set, a strong feature like the one responsible for verb second cannot be reset as weak. In the production of these expatriate students there was evidence that the verb second parameter had not deteriorated, although other areas of the grammar, and the lexicon, were impaired. Notice that both overt agreement and the use of finite and infinite verb forms are the result of a lexical choice, not necessarily corresponding to particular feature values, given the minimalist program. In particular, such aspects of grammar do not necessarily have a direct connection to the strong/weak dichotomy responsible for parametric differences. It is in accordance with the proposal of section three above that the areas affected by language forgetting involve such phenomena but not phenomena depending on the setting of a strong feature.

4.5. Children with Specific Language Impairment

IHS can also be used as part of an explanation for some aspects of the language of SLI-children, i.e., children with SPECIFIC LANGUAGE IMPAIRMENT. Hansson & Nettelbladt (1991) observed that some Swedish SLI-children omitted the subject to a higher degree than normal Swedish children, and they also report word order deviations, in particular errors with respect to verb second. Both these findings, which are illustrated in (8) below, indicate that these children, being between five and six years of age, have not automatized the Swedish system with a strong head feature in C^0 and a strong specifier feature in $AGR(S)^0$.

(8)	a.	*nu jag vill lyssna*	(Alfons)
		now I will listen	
	b.	*sen jag äta så många gånger*	(Beda)
		then I eat so many times	
	c.	*inte kan ha blommor i skorsten*	(Alfons)
		not can have flowers in chimney	
	d.	*vann med bilen*	(Alfons)
		won with car.the	

Håkansson & Nettelbladt (1993) compared the use of verb second in the speech of two SLI-children with the use of this construction in the speech of two normally developed Swedish children. Whereas the normal children practically never made any word order errors with respect to V2, there was a lot of errors in the speech of the SLI-children, as shown in Table 1.

We may ask why SLI-children have not internalized knowledge about the strong positions at the age of 5. One possibility is that these children are lacking some genetically coded component of the language faculty, preventing such an internalization.[14] Another possibility is that something in their general outfit prevents them from developing in the same manner as normal children. Support for the second assumption is found in Ors *et al.* (1994), who present data indicating that SLI children have a delayed P300-potential, i.e., they seem to process both pure tones and linguistic stimuli differently. Due to this deviance, SLI-children have maybe not been able to process the necessary amount of Swedish to find out where the strong positions are.

As is evident from the figures in Table 1, the SLI-children gradually succeed in adjusting their language to the Swedish norm, making no errors when recorded at the age of eight. Whether or not the null percentage of errors reported for these recordings show that Alfons and Beda have automatized their Swedish word order at this age cannot be determined: the absence of errors can also mean that Alfons and Beda are performing very well. One way to find out would be to investigate if their error frequency is influenced by external stress, etc.

Table 1. Relative Proportion (%) of Sentences without Verb Second in the Speech of Two Normal Swedish Children and Two Swedish SLI-Children*

L1				SLI			
Karin		Martin		Alfons		Beda	
age	% XSV	age	% XSV	age	% XSV	age	% XSV
1;11	0	2;08	0	5;11	26	5;07	35
2;07	0	2;11	1	7;01	20	6;07	13
3;01	0	3;01	0	8;03	0	8;04	0

* The data are taken from Håkansson & Nettelbladt (1993), tables 3 and 6.

4.6. *Summary*

In this section I have presented a number of observations supporting the assumption that a minimalist account of language structure, where the order Specifier-Head-Complement is universal, may help us to understand both language acquisition and language attrition. As we have seen, several aspects of language acquisition and language attrition can be traced back to the INITIAL HYPOTHESIS OF SYNTAX (5), saying that all instances of overt movement are marked: this is the assumption small children begin with (more about this in the next section), but this is also the starting point for us learning a second language. Furthermore, this is a stage we might fall back to when we have

experienced a brain injury, as shown by the aphasics data. Under this perspective, language acquisition, L1 as well as L2, is a gradual adjustment of the IHS
to the target grammar, i.e., we have to learn in which aspects the target grammar
deviates from the IHS. This insight is automatized if acquired within the critical
period, otherwise not.

When automatized, marked values can only be lost if there is a brain
damage, as indicated by the comparison of aphasics with repatriate Swedes.
There are interesting developmental data from SLI-children, indicating that the
reason these children acquire a deviant grammar from the point of view of adult
language might be a result of them being slower than normal children in
processing their perceptions: hence, these children may have been exposed to the
same amount of language as the normal ones, and they may have the same
language skill, but their performance problem might hinder them from getting
enough information of the target language prior to the end of the critical period.
As a result, they will continue to rely on the IHS to a higher degree than
children with normal perception.

Naturally much of what I have said here are speculations which have to be
rigorously tested before we know for sure that the IHS is playing the role I am
suggesting. In the next section I will present a more detailed study of one aspect
involved: the acquisition of the automatic system of the mother tongue. As I will
show, the assumption that the IHS is of importance for language acquisition is
corroborated by facts about L1 acquisition of Swedish.

5.   The Acquisition of Swedish and the Initial Hypothesis of Syntax

5.1. *Introduction*

In this section I will show how data from the acquisition of Swedish can be
interpreted as a gradual adjustment of a grammar based on UG and the IHS to
the adult system. As a background, consider my assumptions regarding the
universal outline of sentence structure, presented in (3) above, which according
to the theory is underlying the automatic system of all human languages,
including Swedish. I have not indicated the place of the negation in (3): in my
discussion of Swedish below, I assume that the negation is generated in Spec-
NEGP, where NEGP is taking VP as its complement.[15]

According to the IHS all checking takes place in covert syntax: adhearing
to this hypothesis the small child is supposed to produce only sequences that can

be generated within the lowest VP. However, as already mentioned in section four, the child acquiring Swedish must modify this picture in at least two ways: s/he has to be aware of the strong head position in C^0 responsible for the verb-second effect, and the strong-specifier feature of $AGR(S)^0$, forcing an overt subject in tensed clauses. Furthermore, the position in front of the finite verb in main clauses has particular properties: it is the basis for a division of the clause in two parts, one consisting of Spec-CP, the other one of the rest of the clause, expressing dichotomies like theme–rheme, topic–comment, focus–presupposition, or given–new. Whereas the interpretation of this division is determined by the context in each particular case, it is the division per se that is of importance from the point of view of grammar: whatever contextual reason we may find to front a phrase, grammar must provide us with the possibility to perform such a fronting. See Platzack (1995) for a relevant discussion.

Also a study of the weak positions will be of interest for the argumentation concerning the central role played by the IHS in early speech. Given the IHS, we predict that Swedish children will not produce errors with respect to the weak positions, i.e., we do not expect to find utterances in early Swedish which presuppose e.g., an analysis in terms of a strong specifier feature in AGR(O)P or a strong head feature in T^0, both positions being weak in adult Swedish. A strong specifier feature in AGR(O)P would lead to structures where the direct object is in front of the main verb without being topicalized, and a strong head feature of T^0 would lead to the raising of the tensed verb to a position in front of the negation and other sentence adverbials in embedded clauses, and a similar raising of the infinitive verb in control infinitives.

It deserves to be repeated (see Section 2 above) that I assume the functional projections to mirror the formal features of the lexical entries. This is particular-ly clear with respect to small clauses and other nonfinite sequences often used as full utterances in early child language (Radford 1986; Rizzi 1993; Wexler 1994a). These sequences, lacking a finite verb, are not supposed to have a CP-projection (see Rizzi 1993): this follows if C^0 is used for the checking of finiteness.[16]

The section is organized in the following way. After a short presentation of my material, I will discuss the abundant use of independent nonfinite sentences in early child language in Section 5.3., the purpose being to determine which functional projections are present in these constructions. In Section 5.4 I will discuss data regarding the weak positions, showing that the child practically never produces utterances that presuppose a strong interpretation of these positions. As I will demonstrate, this result has consequences for the analysis of utterances with auxiliaries. The discussion of the acquirement of the strong positions in Swedish grammar follows in § 5.5.

5.2. The Material

My data are taken from three different sources: the Stockholm Project, the Gothenburg Project, and the Lund Project. The Stockholm Child Language Syntax Project was carried out between 1970 and 1977 at Stockholm University, under the leadership of Ragnhild Söderbergh (see Söderbergh 1973). At fortnighly intervals over a period of eighteen months, six children were tape-recorded at home talking to adults. When recording began, the children were aged about 1;8, and at the end they were around 3;6. Efforts were made to get the spontaneous speech of the children in everyday situations. In my study I have used material from the recordings of Embla, Freja, and Tor.

The Gothenburg Project is led by Sven Strömqvist. The corpus of early Swedish assembled within this project includes recordings of four children; see Plunkett & Strömqvist (1992) and Strömqvist et al. (1993) for further details. Three series of recordings from the project are available on CHILDES; in my study I have used material from the Markus files, and occasionally from the Anton files.

The Lund Project, led by Gisela Håkansson and Ulrika Nettelbladt, is officially named 'Variation and deviation in language acquisition'. It is presented in Håkansson et al. (1991), and includes recordings of 18 children: six normal L1, six L1 with SLI, and six L2. I have used material from three of the normal L1 children, Joakim, Martin, and Sara.

5.3. Nonfinite Sentences

An important background for the study of weak and strong positions in early child grammar is an understanding of the structure of nonfinite sentences, which constitute a large amount of the independently used utterances in early child language. Consider the following examples from early Swedish:

(9) a. *bygga tåg*   Markus(1;10.14)
         build train

     b. *nu Embla bada*   Embla(2;1)
         now Embla bath

c.	*gubbe*	*vara där*	Markus(1;10.14)
	old.man	be there	
d.	*Embla inte ha*	*täcket*	Embla(1;11)
	Embla not	have quilt.the	

Nonfinite sentences are found in early stages of all languages I know of, although their relative frequency differ. For early Italian, Guasti (1993/1994) reports less than 5% independent infinitive sentences, whereas studies of the acquisition of other languages have revealed a considerable higher frequency. Pierce (1991) reports 76% nonfinite sentences in the speech of the French girl Natalie at the age 1;9–2:0; a couple of months later the frequency of nonfinite sentences has dropped to 24% (Natalie 2;2–2;3). For Dutch, Krämer (1993) reports 52% infinitival clauses in the speech of Maarten at the age of 1;11. As shown in Tables 2 and 3, early Swedish is more like French and Dutch than Italian. In these tables I give the distribution of nonfinite sentences in two Swedish corpora: Markus (the Gothenburg Project) between 1;10.14 and 2;0.9, and Embla (the Stockholm Project) between 1;8 and 2;1.

There is a drastic drop in the use of nonfinite sentences for both children around the age of two years. Markus 1;10.1–1;11.10 has a majority of nonfinite sentences, against a clear majority of finite sentences at age 2;0.9. The same overall picture holds for Embla, who has a majority of nonfinite sentences at 1;8–2;0, but 20% or less at 2;1.

As stated in § 5.1., I follow Rizzi (1993) in assuming that nonfinite sentences are truncated structures, having a node lower than CP as the top node. Note that I consider finiteness to express the anchoring of the clause in time and space (see Section 2 above), hence lacking finiteness, the nonfinite sentences are not supposed to be as closely bound to the speech act as the finite ones. Speculating about the deeper reasons for the abundant use of nonfinite sentences in early child language, and noticing that the option seems to fade away around the age of three,[17] it is tempting to relate it to the egocentric standard observed by Piaget, which is replaced by a contextsensitive standard at age four (see e.g., Piaget 1970).

I see no reason *a priori* to opt for a description where nonfinite sentences always have the same top node — this may differ as a result of the relations expressed in the utterance. As a matter of fact, this view is confirmed by the properties of Swedish nonfinite sentences, which the following survey will reveal.

As shown in (9), there are direct objects in nonfinite sentences, indicating that such sentences may contain AGR(O)P. The examples in (9) also show that

Table 2. *The Proportion of Finite and Non-Finite Sentences in the Speech of the Swedish Boy Markus*

age	1;10.14	1;10.25	1;11.0	1;11.10	2;0.9
MLU	1.6	1.7	2.75	3.0	3.8
FV/N	5/23	4/21	20/44	8/43	77/110
% FV	22	19	45	19	70
% IV	78	81	55	81	30

The MLU figures given are approximate caluculations, based on Figure 1 in Strömqvist et al. (1993). FV = fini sentences, IV = non-finite sentences, N = FV + IV.

Table 3. *The Proportion of Finite and Non-Finite Sentences in the First Ten Recordings of the Swedish Girl Embla*

age	1;8	1;9a	1;9	1;10a	1;10b	1;11a	1;11b	2;0	2;1a	2;1b
MLU	1.64	1.71	1.32	1.39	1.54	1.37	1.73	2.19	2.05	2.54
FV/N	0/8	12/39	1/9	2/8	7/26	2/12	17/40	26/93	40/50	63/75
% FV	0	31	11	25	27	17	43	28	80	84
% IV	100	69	89	75	73	83	57	72	20	16

For age and MLU, see Lange & Larsson (1973a,b). FV = finite sentences, IV = non-finite sentences, N = FV + IV.

nonfinite sentences in early Swedish may be negated: in Embla 1;8–2;1 there are 15 cases with negation among the 190 nonfinite sentences (8%), to be compared with 23 negated finite sentences out of a total of 170 finite sentences (14%).[18] If it is correct that negation is licensed at the TP level, as Zanuttini (1989) argues, the presence of a negation tells us that both NEGP and TP are potential structural elements of early Swedish nonfinite sentences.[19]

Nonfinite sentences may also contain overt subjects: as many as 56% of the nonfinite sentences in Embla 1;8–2;1 have an overt subject; for the same period there are 78% subjects in the finite sentences. Compared with Haegeman's (1994) figures for early Dutch, where only 14% of the root infinitives contained an overt subject, this is a remarkable number.[20]

The presence of a subject indicates that the structure of nonfinite sentences in Swedish must encompass the functional projections expressing the subject relation. For finite sentences I assume that the subject relation is compositional, expressed as a combination of Spec-TP and Spec-AGR(S)P, where Spec-TP is used for checking nominative Case, and Spec-AGR(S)P for checking Φ-features like person and number. Unless it can be shown that the subject-verb relation is different in nonfinite sentences than in finite ones, I see no reason to abstain from assuming the presence of both AGR(S)P and TP in nonfinite sentences with a subject.

There are three cases among the 190 nonfinite sentences in Embla 1;8–2;1 which are not accounted for by the description so far, all with a place adverbial in first position:

(10) a. *där trillat*   Embla(1;10)
        there fallen

    b. *där stå*   Embla(2;0)
        there stay

    c. *hemma kissa*   Embla(2;0)
        at.home pee

Although adverbials may occur in the middle field in adult Swedish, these adverbials are usually sentence adverbials or time adverbials (cf. (9b)), not adverbials of place. In the absence of a CP level, the structural position of these adverbials is unclear.[21]

5.4. Weak Positions

5.4.1. Introduction

The head features of AGR(S)^0, T^0, and AGR(O)^0, and the specifier features of T^0 and AGR(O)^0, are weak in adult Swedish, resulting in a grammar with surface VO-order and no verb raising except in V2-constructions. Due to V2, the weak head features are detectable only in embedded clauses, control infinitives, and the complements of auxiliaries and modals, where the verb remains to the right of the negation and other sentence adverbials. The absence of visible verb raising and object raising in adult Swedish is illustrated in (11):

(11) a. *att han inte kom*   (cf. *Han kom inte* 'he came not')
        that he not came

    b. *Han lovade   att inte komma.*
        he promised to not come

    c. *Han hade öppnat fönstret.*
        he had opened window.the

    d. **Han hade fönstret   öppnat.*
        he had window-the opened

The examples in (11a, b) may be compared to the corresponding Icelandic examples (11'a, b), where the relevant verbs are to the left of the negation, due to a strong head feature in T^0 in Icelandic. The examples in (11c, d) may be compared to the corresponding German examples (11'c, d), where the object precedes the main verb due to a strong specifier feature in $AGR(O)^0$; for a discussion of German and Dutch word order in this respect, see Koster (1993) and Zwart (1994), among others:

(11') a. *að hann kom ekki*   (Icelandic)
           that he   came not
       b. *Hann lofaði   að koma ekki*   (Icelandic)
           he   promised to come not
       c. *Er hatte das Fenster geöffnet.*   (German)
           he had   the windowopened
       d. **Er hatte geöffnet das Fenster.*
           he had   opened the window

According to the the IHS, the young child expects every functional position to be weak, hence initially s/he will expect cases like (11), not like (11'). Consequently, we predict the Swedish child to perform almost without errors in these respects, whereas the Icelandic child and the German child, respectively, are supposed to face some initial problems, since their target grammars provide evidence for strong features at these points.

The situation is complicated by the fact that Swedish also has examples where the weak features are checked overtly. This is the case in main clauses, where the verb on its way to C^0 must check the head features in $AGR(O)^0$, T^0, and $AGR(S)^0$, and cases with topicalized object and OBJECT SHIFT, where the object must be checked in Spec-AGR(O)P before proceeding. See (12):

(12) a. *Nu   sätter vi på TVn.*
          now turn   we on TV.the
      a'. $[_{CP}$ *Nu* $[_{C0}$ *sätter*$_v$ $[_{AGR(S)P}$ *vi*$_j$ t_v $[_{TP}...[_{T0}$ t_v $]$ $[_{VP}$ t_j t_v *på TVn*$]]]]]$
      b. *Dockan sätter jag där.*
          doll.the put   I   there
      b'. $[_{CP}$ *Dockan*$_i$ $[_{C0}$ *sätter*$_v$ $[_{AGR(S)P}$ *jag*$_j$ t_v $..[_{AGR(O)P}$ t_i t_v $[_{VP}$ t_j t_v t_i *där*$]]]]].$
      c. *Jag såg den inte.*[22]
          I   saw it   not
      c'. $[_{CP}$ *Jag*$_i$ $[_{C0}$ *såg*$_v$ $[_{AGR(S)P}$ t_i t_v $...den_j$ $[_{AGR(O)P}$ t_j t_v $[_{NEGP}$ *inte* t_v
          $[_{VP}$ t_i
              t_v t_j $]]]]]$

5.4.2. The Head Feature in T^0

Consider first the weak head feature in T^0. The IHS predicts the absence of verb raising to T^0 (visible as V + NEG) in early Swedish, both in embedded clauses and in nonfinite sentences. Since there are few embedded clauses in the earliest available recordings (but see §§ 5.4.4 and 5.5.2), we must concentrate on the word order in nonfinite sentences.

The prediction that young Swedes have the negation in front of the nonfinite verb is supported by available data: although there are few negated nonfinite sentences in early Swedish, as we saw in § 5.3, the ones that occur usually have the negation in front of the infinitive. In the recordings from Sara 1;11, for instance, the two negated examples both have the word order negation–infinitive. Similarly, the first negated utterances with an infinitive recorded from Markus (2;0.9) are of the same type; see the examples in (13):

(13) a.   *ja inget BADA*   Sara(1;11)
           I not   bathe
      b.   *inte HOPPA*   Sara(1;11)
           not jump
      c.   *de   inte röra*   Markus(2;0.9)
           they not touch
      d.   *inte röra den*   Markus(2;0.9)
           not touch it

A look at the material reveals the same general picture: there is only one example with the order infinitive–negation among the recorded utterances of Embla (1;8–2;1), Freja (1;10–2;3), and Tor (1;11–2;2),[23] whereas there is a total of 22 examples with the expected order negation–infinitive in these recordings. Furthermore, I found no example with a raised infinitive in the recordings of Anton (2;0.13–2;6.02), whereas there is a single one produced by Markus:

(14) *ja   kissemiss sitta inte där*   Markus(2;0.16)
      yes kitten   sit   not there

The occurrence of (14) does not prevent the general conclusion that only finite verbs are raised in early Swedish; note that (14) cannot be interpreted as an example of constituent negation.

5.4.3. The Specifier Feature of AGR(O)^0

Consider next the specifier feature of AGR(O)^0, which is weak in adult Swedish. Consequently, the verb usually precedes its complement. However, the position of the object may be hard to determine from simple clauses with just a main verb: in an example like *Jag har dockan* 'I have the doll', the verb is in C^0, and the object can be either in Spec-AGR(O)P or in the complement of V^0. To be sure that the object is outside of VP we must find examples like (15), where the object precedes an element which is outside of VP, like the finite verb in main clauses (15a) and the negation (15b).

(15) a. *Det tror   jag.*
     it   believe I
     I think so

   b. *Jag såg den inte.*
     I   saw it   not

According to the IHS, the child starts with the hypothesis that the object remains in the complement of V at PF. We may expect to find exceptions to this in the speech of the children only in cases that can be interpreted as instances of either topicalization (15a) or object shift (15b) (cf. the previous section). Since both these constructions presuppose that the main verb has moved out of VP, and since we know from the previous section that nonfinite verbs remain in VP, word orders deviating from the VO-order should mainly be found with tensed verbs. In all other cases, the IHS predicts the order verb–object. In the following survey I have therefore only considered the position of the object with respect to nonfinite verbs. I have counted all instances of nonfinite verb + object or object + nonfinite verb in the early recordings of seven children. Repetitions were excluded when the child uttered the same sequence more than once, without producing a different utterance in between. An overview is given in Table 4.

Table 4. The Frequency of Infinitive + Object and Object + Infinitive in Early Swedish

name	Embla	Freja	Tor	Joakim	Martin	Sara	Markus
age	1;8–2;1	1;8–2;0	1;11–2;2	–2;3	–2;2	1;11–2;3	1;10–2;3
V–Obj	46	36	29	14	3	7	60
Obj–V	1	0	6	0	0	0	1
% OV	2	0	17	0	0	0	2

Only cases where the object is adjacent to the verb are counted.

As expected, most of the children do not have a single example of the order object–infinitive. There is one example of the unpredicted order in the record-

ings of Markus, given in (16a), one in the recordings of Embla, presented in
(16b), and six in the recordings of Tor, some of which are presented in (16c–d)
(Tor uses the sequence in (16c) several times):

(16) a.   *eller sten   lägga där*   Markus(1;11.12)
           or   stone lay   there
      b.   *och vagnen   gömma*   Embla(2;0)
           and wagon.the hide
      c.   *penna ha*   Tor(1;11)
           pen   have
      d.   *pennan ha*   Tor(1;11)
           pen.the have

The figures in Table 4 are interesting to compare with the corresponding
figures for children learning an OV-language. Consider in this respect the data
in (17), taken from Penner *et al.* (1994), who have studied four Swiss-German
children and one German child with respect to the verb–complement order:

(17) *Swiss German*   *German*
      J.   6% VO, age 1;2–2;4 S. 1,6% VO, age 1;10.20–2;02.21
      S.   5,5% VO, –1;11
      M.   15% VO, –2;0
      A.&R. 11 % VO, –1;10

We see immediately that children targeting an OV-language make more
errors with respect to the adult norm than the Swedish children do. This is what
we should expect under the IHS, provided that the child learning an OV-
language very early becomes aware of the strong specifier feature of AGR(O)^0
and tries to adjust his/her grammar. On the other hand, these data are not
compatible with the hyposesis, put forward, e.g., by Penner *et al.*, that both OV
and VO are basic orders: if that were true, we would expect the same error
frequencies for both groups, since there should be no preference for one word
order over the other.[24]

According to Penner *et al.*, most cases of incorrect placement of the object
can be linked to some discourse function. In particular, they notice that the child
often uses infinitival VO-sequences on a par with regular imperatives, where the
verb is always fronted: hence a possible interpretation of an utterance like *hole
Boech* 'fetch book', which is used as a demand, would be that the child has
fronted the infinitive, despite the fact that there is no strong position for the
infinitive in front of AGR(O)P. In the same way, most errors in the Swedish
material can be explained away, in this case as raising of the object to Spec-

AGR(O)P in overt syntax, in spite of the fact that this position is weak. The following sequence from Tor illustrate this case:

(18)   M: *ja   var   är skeden?*
                      yes where is spoon-.he
           Tor: *där*
                      there
           M: *där   var skeden   ja*
                      there was spoon.the yes
           Tor: *sked också ha*
                      spoon also   have

In the last utterance of (18), Tor has raised the object to a position in front of the adverbial. Unless we are prepaired to say that there is a CP-level in root infinitives (see § 5.3. above), this position must be Spec-AGR(O)P. Nothing prevents me from analyzing all the examples with OV in early Swedish in the same way.

5.4.4. Auxiliaries

Being a verb-second language, Swedish has the finite verb in C^0 in main clauses. In embedded clauses, the finite verb remains in V^0: in this case the strong-head feature of C^0 is spelled out by the complementizer, and there are no strong positions between C^0 and V^0 for the verb to go to. Consequently the finite verb precedes the negation in main clauses but follows it in the corresponding embedded clauses: auxiliaries and main verbs behave the same in this respect.

(19) a1.   *Johan kan inte komma.*
            Johan can not come
      a2.   *Johan kommer inte.*
            Johan comes   not
      b1.   *Jag vet [att Johan inte kan komma].*
            I   know that Johan not can come
      b2.   *Jag vet [att Johan inte kommer]*
            I   know that Johan not comes

As we will see in Section 5.5.1 below, Swedish children raise the finite verb to C^0 already in their first finite clauses, i.e., prior to the age of two years. Negated embedded clauses appear much later: Håkansson & Dooley-Collberg (1994), who studied negated sequences consisting of at least a verb and a negation in the spontaneous speech of four of the children from the Stockholm

Project, found the first negated subordinate clause at the age of 2;6 (Embla). With one exception,[25] all subordinate clauses in their material with just a main verb had the correct word order negation–finite verb. This is what we should expect, since there are no strong positions for the verb to go to when C^0 is occupied by a complementizer.

Interestingly, Håkansson & Dooley-Collberg (1994) also found that among the earliest recorded negated embedded clauses with auxiliaries, several had the word order auxiliary–negation, a word order not expected if there is just one strong position (C^0) to fill in overt syntax. Later on this word order disappears, and the finite auxiliary is placed to the right of the negation. The two types of negated embedded clauses are illustrated in (20) and (21):

(20) Negated embedded clauses with finite main verb

   a. *tänk   om den lille   inte ramlar på pallen* Embla(2;9)
      imagine if the small(-one) not falls   on stool.the

   b. *jag håller   att det inte ramlar av*   Tor(3;0)
      I   hold (so) that it   not falls   off

   c. *så mamma inte kommer och tar   dom*   Freja(3;2)
      so mother not comes   and takes them

(21) Negated embedded clauses with finite auxiliary

   a. *smutsigt bröd som man kan inte äta*   Embla(2;9)
      dirty   bread that one can not eat

   b. *därför att hon har inte sett mitt rum*   Embla(2;10)
      because she has not seen my room

   c. *att domm får inte vara där*   Tor(3;1)
      that they may not be   there

Håkansson & Dooley-Collberg (1994) assume that the unexpected placement of finite auxiliaries in (21) indicates that these auxiliaries are generated in INFL (i.e., T^0 or AGR(S)^0 in the more elaborated structure in (3)), and that the children later on reanalyse these auxiliaries as Vs. Although this account is in accordance with the facts, it is not in accordance with the IHS: both T^0 and AGR(S)^0 are weak positions, and there should be no reason for the child to assume that any one of these positions must be filled in overt syntax.

The analysis of (21), suggested by Håkansson & Dooley-Collberg (1994), is not the only possible one, however. I will here suggest an alternative description, which does not force us to assume a weak position to be filled in overt syntax. In adult Swedish, auxiliaries are analyzed as verbs taking a minimally extended verb projection as their complement, at most headed by an AGR(O)P.

This analysis follows as a consequence of my interpretation of the minimalist framework: each (simple) syntactic relation in which a lexical head is involved should be expressed in the extended projection of that head. Hence we expect an AGR(O)P within the extended projection of the main verb, if this is transitive.[26] Consider (22b), illustrating the structure of (22a) prior to movement (functional projections above the auxiliary are excluded).

(22) a. *Han borde   köpa boken.*
          he   ought.to buy the.book

b.

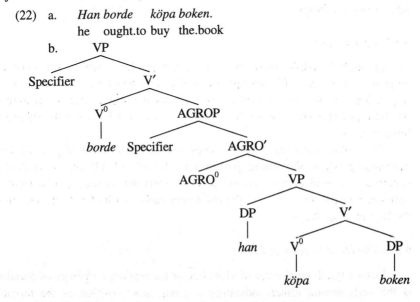

Although Swedish NEGP is placed between AGR(O)P and VP, we cannot insert a negation within the complement of the auxiliary: this follows from Zanuttini's (1989) demand that the negation must be licensed by tense. Hence although NEGP can be generated below the auxiliary, it cannot be licensed there. A negated clause with an auxiliary thus must have its NEGP on top of the VP within which the auxiliary is generated.

Consider now the unexpected examples in (21), which Håkansson & Dooley-Collberg (1994) interpreted as instances of an overtly filled INFL (T^0 or $AGR(S)^0$). Let us assume that it is not clear to the child at the beginning what the correct structure is of the complement of the auxiliary. A conceivable scenario is that the child at this early stage assumes auxiliaries to take extended verbal projections headed by TP: with this analysis it would be possible to generate NEGP within the complement of the auxiliary, since this complement contains licensing tense. Consequently, the tensed auxiliary may occur to the left of the negation. In addition to being compatible with the IHS, this analysis has the advantage over the analysis proposed by Håkansson & Dooley-Collberg (1994) in not forcing us to assume any kind of reanalysis of the syntactic status of lexical elements (auxiliaries): what the children must learn is that auxiliaries take a less elaborated complement than they first believed.

5.5. *Strong Positions*

5.5.1. *Introduction*

In adult Swedish, there are two strong positions within the extended projection of the verb, C^0 and Spec-AGR(S)P. The strong head feature in C^0 is responsible for the verb second effect, whereas the strong specifier feature in $AGR(S)^0$ is responsible for the fact that Swedish cannot leave out the subject in finite clauses.

The child acquiring Swedish does not seem to have any difficulties determining where the strong positions to the left of VP are situated. The occurrence of subject–verb inversion, cases with the tensed verb in front of sentence adverbs, etc., will tell the child very early that he has to deviate from the IHS in some ways.

5.5.2. *The Head Feature of C^0*

From a typological point of view, one of the marked properties of Swedish is the verb second effect, indicating a strong head position in the topmost functional projection. Being strong, this position must be filled in both main clauses and subordinate clauses. In main clauses, the tensed verb moves to C^0, checking the strong head feature. In embedded clauses, the strong head feature is checked by the insertion of a lexical complementizer, *att* 'that' in the unmarked case. Following Law (1991), I assume that complementizers are expletives, thus it is possible to adjoin the verb to the complementizer at LF. As a matter of fact, the verb must adjoin to the complementizer at LF, since the finite verb has to get rid of its weak finiteness feature before LF to avoid a violation of Full Interpretation. See also Groat (1995) for a slightly different implementation of this idea.

We have already seen that there is hardly any trace of verb raising in nonfinite sentences in early Swedish. With respect to finite ones, verb raising seems to occur almost always when it is called for in adult language. This observation was first made for early Swedish in Håkansson (1988), and has been repeatedly confirmed in subsequent studies. A quick scan of the material used for this article displays the same picture. Among the 170 finite sentences produced by Embla 1;8–2;1,[27] there are 23 with negation or other sentence adverbials, and all have the finite verb in front of the adverbial, i.e., the verb is raised out of VP. Some examples are given in (23):

(23) a.   *det är ju   mamma*   Embla(1;9)
           it   is ADV mother
      b.   *vill   inte tvätta nalle*   Embla(1;10)
           want not wash teddy
      c.   *älg säger inte mu*   Embla(1;11)
           elk says not moo

Cases like (23) indicate a raising of the tensed verb out of VP, but they do not reveal the landing site of the verb. More illuminating are examples with sentence initial non-subjects — in such cases the verb is almost always in second position, preceding the subject (if there is one). There are 24 examples of this kind in Embla 1;9–2;1, some of which are presented in (24):

(24) a.   *var   är dörr*   Embla(1;9)
           where is door
      b.   *där   är den*   Embla(1;9)
           there is it
      c.   *vad   är det*   Embla(1;11)
           what is it
      d.   *så trevligt sa   han*   Embla(2;1)
           so nice   said he
      e.   *så där gjorde han*   Embla(2;1)
           so there did   he
           'Like that he did.'
      f.   *skärp har hon*   Embla(2;1)
           belt has she

The examples in (24) display a variety of different constituents in first position: *wh*-adverbial (24a) and *wh*-object (24c), place adverbial (24b), manner adverbial (24e), and direct objects (24d, f). This variety is typical for Spec-CP in adult Swedish; furthermore the position of the verb in front of the subject in these cases clearly tell us that the tensed verb has raised to C^0. It deserves to be noticed that examples like (24a, b) indicate that Embla overtly realizes the CP projection already at 1;9.

Subject–verb inversion is also found in verb initial sentences. In adult language, sentences beginning with the finite verb followed by the subject are usually *yes/no* questions; in early child language there are also declarative clauses with this word order (see Håkansson 1994), as well as clauses which seem to be *wh*-questions without a *wh*-word (see Santelmann 1994). Some examples of these types from the Embla and Sara files are given in (25):

(25) a. *är det dörren*   *yes/no* question, Embla(1;11)
        is it   door.the

     b. *gjorde barnet*   *what-do* question, Embla(2;0)
        did   child.the

     c. *och åker   dom*   V1 declarative, Sara(2;6)
        and go:PRES they

There are 22 examples of this kind among the 146 finite sentences produced by Embla 1;11–2;1; all of them are questions, either *wh*-questions with a null *wh*-word, or *yes-no* questions.

Summarizing, it is obvious that Embla has access to the CP-layer as soon as she starts producing finite sentences. Already at this age (1;9) she has realized that the finite verb must be checked overtly in C^0 in Swedish, whereas the nonfinite verb is not allowed in this position. On the other hand, occasional errors indicate that the system is not automatized in the same way as in adult language. There is only one deviant example in the Embla files studied here, given in (26a). In (26b, c) another two examples, found in the early speech of Sara, are presented (cf. (6) above). Additional errors are reported by Santelmann (1994), who, studying a partly different corpus, gives the four examples (26d–g) with non-moved finite verb in early *wh*-questions:

(26) a. *julklapp   Embla har*   Embla(2;1)
        christmas.present Embla has

     b. *DÄR han bor*   Sara(2;3)
        there he   live:PRES

     c. *stor han E*   Sara(2;10)
        big he is

     d. *var   han bor*   Embla(2;1)
        where he   lives

     e. *vad det är*   Frank(2;1), Tor(2;5)
        what that is

     f. *vad för grejer du har med dig*   Lars(2;11)
        what for things you have with you

Whereas the occurrence of examples like (26) indicates that knowledge of a strong C^0 is not yet automatized at the age of three, the overwhelming majority of cases where the finite verb is in first or second position clearly shows that Swedish children know that there is a strong head feature in C^0 already when they start producing finite sentences. These findings contradict the conclusion I reached in Platzack (1990) that there are no functional categories in early Swedish. As Hyams (1992) has pointed out, that conclusion was the result partly of a biased interpretation of the frequency figures underlying my study, partly of my reluctance to keep finite and nonfinite structures apart.

Finally a short note about embedded clauses. The first subordinate clauses in Swedish appear around the age of two, see Lundin (1988). Since the Swedish children at this age are aware of the presence of a strong feature in C^0, as we have just seen, and the complementizer is realized in C^0 as mentioned above, we expect most subordinate clauses to be introduced by a complementizer in early Swedish. This prediction is confirmed by Lundin's study. Lundin (1988) has investigated the subordinate clauses in the recordings of five of the children in the Stockholm project (age 1;8–3;8). The first embedded clauses are relative clauses and comparative clauses; a couple of the earliest clauses of these types are given in (27):

(27) a. *sitta så som Ragnhild gör*   Nanna(1;11)
          sit   so as   Ragnhild does

      b. *precis som m/Berit har*   Embla(2;1)
          just as   Berit has

      c. *och det är babygrisen, den som heter   Ola*   Embla(2;2)
          and this is babypig.the it   that is.named Ola

      d. *han som är naken*   Embla(2;6)
          he that is naked

According to Lundin (1988:71), only 22 of 460 relative and comparative clauses, i.e., 5%, lack a complementizer. Hence, the awareness of the strong head feature in C^0 around the age of two years can be detected also from a study of embedded clauses.[28]

5.5.3. The Specifier Feature of AGR(S)[0]

Another marked property of adult Swedish is the absolute demand of a visible element in subject position. Taking the fact that most languages of the world can have empty subjects (see, e.g., the survey of Gilligan 1987) as my point of departue, the spirit of the minimalist program would lead us to expect that such a wide spread phenomenon should not be dependent on strong features of any kind, since strong features lead to costly operations in overt syntax. Rather, we would expect strong features to occur only in those cases where the subject cannot be left out; see Chomsky (1995). In Platzack (1994) I have outlined a way to describe visible and invisible subjects in terms of strong and weak specifier features in AGR(S)^0: it is not possible to recapitulate that argumentation here. It seems to be the case that Swedish children very early realize that overt subjects must be raised out of VP. This is shown by the fact that the subject almost always occurs in front of the negation or sentence adverbs. Disregarding the form of the verb, there are 12 examples in Embla 1;9–2;1 where a subject appears together with a negation or sentence adverb: in 10 of these cases the subject precedes the adverbial. The two exceptions are both found with infinitives, as illustrated in (28a, b);[29] in (28c–f) I present the general case:

(28) a. *inte mamma tvätta*   Embla(2;0)
          not mommy wash

      b. *inte mamma hjälpa Embla*   Embla(2;1)
          not mommy help   Embla

      c. *det är ju   mamma*   Embla(1;11)
          it is ADV mommy

      d. *jag vill inte*   Embla(1;11)
          I   want not

      e. *den inte sitta*   Embla(2;0)
          it   not sit

      f. *Embla inte ha   täcket*   Embla(2;0)
          Embla not have quilt.the

To understand what people are saying, it is important for the child to realize that the subject is outside of VP in adult Swedish. As with the position of finite verbs, Swedish children know that there is a subject position in front of VP already when they start producing finite sentences. Since the children use both subject first structures and inversion structures, it is furthermore clear that they do not equalize the subject position with Spec-CP. Although the examples do not reveal if the relevant position is Spec-AGR(S)P or Spec-TP, I will opt for the first alternative in the following discussion.

In adult Swedish, Spec-AGR(S)P is a strong position, i.e., there must be an overt subject in this position, unless the subject is topicalized. It has been observed for several languages (see e.g., Hyams 1986 for English; Pierce 1989 for French) that children around the age of two tend to drop the subject freely, irrespective of whether or not the target language is a null subject language. According to Hyams (1986) the Null Subject Parameter is initially set to the null subject value. Given the description mentioned above where the null subject value signals a weak specifier feature in $AGR(S)^0$, it follows from the IHS that children should start with a grammar where the subject can be dropped.

As in English and French, there is a lot of null-subject sentences in early Swedish, and a clear drop in frequency with increasing age. The distribution of finite sentences without an overt subject in the early recordings of Embla are given in Table 5: since there are few finite sentences prior to the age of two, these recordings are represented as a single totality.

Table 5. Finite Sentences with Null Subjects in the Recordings of Embla 1;9–2;1

age	1;9–1;11	2;0	2;1a	2;1b
no subject/ finite clauses	16/41	11/26	7/40	4/63
%	39	42	18	6

A closer look at the null-subject sentences reveals that in all the cases except two the subject is dropped from first position: typical examples are presented in (29a, b); in (29c, d) I give the only cases of null subject with overt topic in the studied files of Embla:

(29) a. *har gått sönder*   Embla(1;9)
          has gone broken

      b. *äter kött*   Embla(2;1)
          eats meat

      c. *där går*   Embla(1;10)
          there goes

      d. *där var*   Embla(2;1)
          there was

A similar observation has been made for early English: Valian (1991) and Rizzi (1994) report very few null subjects in clauses with a preposed non-subject *wh*-word. Cf. Rizzi (1994) for an interesting discussion. Since Swedish, like other Germanic V2-languages, has TOPIC DROP, i.e., may leave out the element in root Spec-CP when this element is contexually bound, it is difficult to tell if examples like (29a, b) are genuine null-subject cases or not. At least some of these cases can be analyzed as topic drop, consider the following passage from Markus(2;09):

(30)   F: *va va gjorde Michäla för nå-t*
                what did   Michäla for something
                'What did Michäla do?'
         M: *lekte   me   tåget*
                played with train.the

Only cases like (29c, d) are clear cases of null subjects, i.e., cases where Spec-AGR(S)P is empty at PF. There are occasional examples of the same kind in the speech of the other children:

(31) a. *dom   bilana   tänkte   inte på*   Markus(2;0.9)
          those cars.the thought not at
      b. *där   flyger*   Martin(2;2)
          there flies

Another context where we would expect to find true null subjects is in subordinate clauses. However, as Roeper & Weissenborn (1990) have noticed, there are no cases of null subjects in early English subordinate clauses. The same seems to hold for Swedish: Lundin (1988:174) found 1,815 (well-formed) embedded clauses in her study of early Swedish, to be compared with a total of 14 clauses which were considered to be defective in one way or another (lacking an obligatory phrase of some kind). According to Lundin, some of these 14 clauses do not have an overt subject, and she illustrates with the sequence *om är sönder* 'if is broken', without however telling us in which file this example is found. Nevertheless, it is obvious from Lundin's data that Swedish children, like English ones, very seldom leave out the subject in embedded clauses.

Concluding, it seems to be the case that Swedish children have learned that Spec-AGR(S)P is a strong position already before they start producing utterances with more than one word. Hence, we have a situation similar to the one that emerged for C^0. In both cases the great majority of utterances come out correct, from an adult language point of view. However, as I noticed in connection with verb second, the system is not yet automatized, hence occasionally the language of the children deviates from what we find among adults. There is a handful of V3–cases, as well as a handful of true null-subjects and cases where the subject has not moved to Spec-AGR(S)P. But these cases are so few that they are hardly detectable in everyday communication.

6. Conclusion

In this paper I have shown how a specific implementation of the minimalist program of Chomsky (1993) offers a grammatical correlate to the concept Markedness. The grammatical system underlying my study assumes a universally ordered phrase-structure, viz. Specifier-Head-Complement (Kayne 1994), it accepts the checking hypothesis of Chomsky (1993), and the assumption of Wilder & Ćavar (1994) that the strong features responsible for overt movement *x* are found only among the functional categories. On the basis of my implementation I set up the following principle:

(5)   Initial Hypothesis of Syntax (IHS)
          All instances of feature checking take place after spell-out

In my paper I provide support for the assumption that the IHS is responsible for several aspects of the acquisition and attrition of the automatic part of language. The role of the IHS with respect to L2 acquisition, the language of SLI-children, language oblivion, and the language of aphasic patients, is outlined in a survey-like section. The main part of my paper explores the role of the IHS for L1 acquisition of Swedish. In this part I discuss data concerning both weak and strong positions in the structure of adult Swedish, investigating the behavior of young Swedes with respect to these positions. Besides giving support to my assumption that language acquisition can be seen as a gradual adjustment of the IHS to the target language, my results support the view of Wexler (1994b) that children know the syntactic specificities of their first language at an early age, presumably before they produce sentence-like sequences. There is hardly any case in my material which indicates movement to a weak position, and very few *x* cases where the child does not move to a strong position.

To my mind, the mere fact that a psycholinguistic account based on the IHS and the minimalist assumption of a universal specifier–head–complement order has enabled me to account for observations about language behavior of different types, like L1 acquisition, L1 attrition, and L2 learning, indicates that the betrodden path deserves to be followed. In addition, the results support the general theoretical framework of the minimalist program, demonstrating the *x* psycholinguistic relevance of some of its basic assumptions.

Acknowledgements

Thanks to Gisela Håkansson for providing some of the material concerning language acquisition and language attrition that I make use of in this study, as well as for spending much time discussing different aspects of this paper with me. Thanks also to Lars-Olof Delsing, Cecila Falk, Gunlög Josefsson and Lynn Santelmann for valuable comments on an earlier draft, as well as to Marianne Ors for helping me with the neurological stuff. Furthermore, I have been greatly helped by the comments of three anonymous reviewers. The usual disclaimers apply, obviously. The paper was presented at the conference on the generative studies of the Acquisition of Case and Agreement at the University of Essex in March 1994, and at the higher seminar at the department of Scandinavian languages at Lund University, April 1994. I thank both audiences for their comments.

Notes

1. Chomsky has expressed this idea in several places. The following quote is from Chomsky (1991:31): "There is something about my brain — specifically, the state attained by its language faculty — that is different from that of monolingual speakers of Japanese, and is sufficiently similar to that of many others so that we can communicate, more or less."

2. In (3) I have provided each maximal projection with a specifier. Whether or not a specifier is necessary for convergence depends on the presence or absence of a specifier feature in the head of the projection.

3. This is a simplification. Chomsky (1995) distinguishes between features that are interpretable at LF, including categorial features and person and number features of nouns, and features not interpretable at LF, e.g., Case features and Φ-features of verbs and adjectives. For the purpose of this article, the distinction ⟨±Interpretable⟩ is not necessary to take into consideration.

4. This is a simplification. Presumably V raises to $AGR(O)^0$, the complex $[V^0-AGR(O)^0]$ to T^0, the complex $[[V^0-AGR(O)^0] T^0]$ raises to $AGR(S)^0$, and finally the complex $[[[V^0-AGR(O)^0] T^0] AGR(S)^0]$ to C^0.

5. Actually, LF-movement is restricted to movement of features. See Chomsky (1995) for details.

6. For the assumption that a critical period exists, that is an age after which it is impossible to attain native levels of proficiency, see for example Lenneberg (1967). Today there is a handful of studies supporting the existence of such a critical period. Newport

& Suppala (1987) studied the comprehension of various aspects of American Sign Language (ASL) of fifty-to-seventy-year old deaf people, and found that their error rates depended on when they had first learned ASL. Those who had been exposed to ASL from birth onward made very few errors. There was a little increase in the error rate for people who had acquired ASL between age four and seven, and a significant increase for those who had learned ASL as adolescents. Similar results have been reported for second language acquisition in a study by Johnson & Newport (1989) of native speakers of Korean or Chinese coming to the United States between age three and thirty-nine. In particular, people who had arrived before age seven performed as good as native-born speakers of English. See also de Geer (1992), who studied four children adopted by Swedish parents; her results show a clear difference in proficiency between the two children, who were adopted before the age of four, and the other two, who were adopted at the age of five.

7. In adult language an example like (6c2) would be interpreted as an elliptical embedded clause, used as an exclamation (*Va stor han är* 'how big he is'). If this is the correct analysis of (6c2), it is not an example of V3.

8. It must be stressed that I see the development of our mother tongue as the establishment of a particular subroutine within the neural network — in particular, we are not forced to enter this subroutine, but may always return to the inborn system. As we will see in the next section, this is what happens when learning a second language after the end of the critical period, or when the subroutine is damaged as a result of some brain injury.

9. About 30% of all learners were of this type, according to Håkansson (p.c.). See Sharwood Smith (1988) for a discussion of various initial strategies entertained by the L2 learner.

10. See, e.g., Krashen *et al.* (1979) and Long (1988).

11. There are in fact anecdotal observations supporting this conclusion, see Hansegård (1968) who reports about Lapps losing their more or less perfect mastery of Swedish after heavy drinking, which on the other hand did not seem to influence their Lappish mother tongue.

12. Consider also Ouhalla (1993), where agrammatism is described as the absence of functional projections.

13. The backgrounds of these subjects are somewhat different, see Håkansson (in press) for details.

14. Not all SLI-children become free of errors at the age of eight as Alfons and Beda.

15. I assume NEGP to be lower than AGR(O)P in Germanic languages (see Haegeman 1994 for a similar assumption for Dutch, and Zwart 1994 for Dutch and German). Judging from Belletti (1990), NEGP in Romance languages may be higher up in the structure, presumably between AGR(S)P and TP.

16. Wexler (1994a) suggests for mainland Scandinavian that C^0 hosts a tense-feature that is strong for finite tenses and weak for nonfinite tenses. This is an interesting alternative to the description I will propose.

17. The percentage of nonfinite sentences in the speech of three Swedish children between 2;6 and 2;10 is given in Lundin & Platzack (1988): Embla has 1% nonfinite sentences at age 2;6, Freja 5% at age 2;10, and Tor 7% at age 2;8.

18. Since the first negation in the recordings of Embla occurs at 1;10 (in a finite sentence), it is maybe more correct to determine the frequency of negated sentences beginning with this recording: if so, 11% of the nonfinite sentences in Embla 1;10–2;1 are negated, to be compared with 15% of the finite ones.

19. In her study of early Dutch, Haegeman (1994) concludes that root infinitives are truncated structures, beginning with AGR(O)P. Dutch acquisition data regarding the distribution of pronouns, demonstratives, and adverbs, as well as the absence of clitics and *wh*-phrases, clearly indicate that root infinitives in early Dutch lack CP and AGR(S)P; on the other hand scrambling data indicate the presence of AGR(O)P. It is less clear whether or not there is a TP in Dutch root infinitives. Basing her conclusion on the absence of auxiliaries, as well as on the reluctance of young Dutch children to negate their nonfinite sentences (as mentioned, the negation must be licensed by Tense, according to Zanuttini 1989), Haegeman takes Dutch root infinitives to lack TP.

20. Note that I have counted both infinitives and participial clauses, whereas Haegeman only counts infinitival clauses. However, since the number of participial clauses is low (5/190, i.e., 3% in the recordings of Embla 1;8–2;1), their inclusion should not prevent a comparison.

21. The weak adverbial *där* 'there', but not a strong adverbial like *hemma* 'at home' sometimes is scrambled into the middle field, as illustrated in (i), where the position in front of the negation indicates a kind of scrambling:

(i)   a.   *Han fanns där inte.*   b.   **Han fanns hemma inte.*

       he   was   there not   he   was   at.home not

Hence, there might be a middle field position for weak adverbials, at least.

22. The weak object pronoun is shifted to a position in front of the negation, where strong pronouns and full DPs cannot occur; compare (12c) with (i):

(i)   a.   **Jag såg DEN inte.*   cf.   *Jag såg inte DEN.*

             I   saw it   not   I   saw not it

       b.   **Jag såg dockan inte.*   cf.   *Jag såg inte dockan.*

             I   saw the.doll not   I   saw not the.doll

See Holmberg (1986, 1991), Johnson (1991) or Josefsson (1993) for relevant discussions of this construction.

23. This example is peculiar since it has both the infinitive and the object to the left of the negation:

(i)   *Gömma dockornainte*   Embla(2;0)

       hide   dolls.the not

It is not clear to me how to interpret this word order.

24. Due to the presence of a strong head position in C^0 (V2), German is not the ideal OV-language to use when looking for an early VO/OV-alternation, since there is always the possibility that verb fronting may have influenced the result. Similarly, although presumably to a lesser degree, OV-sequences in a V2–language like Swedish might be interpreted as cases of object topicalization.

25. According to Håkansson & Dooley-Collberg (1994), this example is presumably a performance error, since it is atypical also in several other ways.

26. The relation of the main verb to the subject is different: the subject relation is composed of several parts, forcing the subject generated in Spec-VP of the main verb to raise to Spec-VP of the auxiliary and further upwards within the extended projection of the auxiliary.

27. The first finite sentence is produced when Embla is 1;9.

28. It is interesting to note that adults leave out the complementizer in about 15% of the relative clauses, according to Jörgensen (1979:99 f.).

29. Naturally, since these examples are late (Embla is 2;0 and 2;1 when they are uttered), it is possible to analyze them as regular cases where the negation has been topicalized (placed in Spec-CP); since the verb is infinitive, it does not raise to C^0, but remains in VP. Under this analysis, the subject might be in Spec-AGR(S)P.

References

Ahlsén, E. & C. Dravins. 1990. "Agrammatism in Swedish: Two case studies." *Agrammatical Aphasia: A cross-Language narrative sourcebook*, ed. by L. Menn & L. Obler, 545–621. Amsterdam: John Benjamins.

Altman, J. 1987. "Cerebral Cortex: A quiet revolution in thinking." *Nature* 328.572–573.

Belletti, A. 1990. *Generalized Verb Movement*. Turin: Rosenberg and Sellier.

Bolander, M. 1988. "Is There any Order? On word order in Swedish learner language." *Journal of Multilingual and Multicultural Development* 9.97–113.

Caplan, D. 1987. *Neurolinguistics and Linguistics Aphasiology: An introduction*. Cambridge: Cambridge University Press.

Chomsky, N. 1981. *Lectures on Government and Binding*. Dordrecht: Foris.

———. 1986a. *Barriers*. Cambridge, Mass.: MIT Press.

———. 1986b. *Knowledge of Language: Its nature, origion, and use*. New York: Praeger.

———. 1991. "Linguistics and Cognitive Science: Problems and Mysteries." *The Chomskyan Turn*, ed. by A. Kasher, 26–53. Oxford: Basil Blackwell.

————. 1993. "A Minimalist Program for Linguistic Theory." *The View from Building 20: Essays in linguistics in honor of Sylvain Bromberger*, ed. by K. Hale & S. J. Keyser, 1–52. Cambridge, Mass.: MIT Press.

————. 1995. "Categories and Transformations." Chapter four of a book to appear at Cambridge, Mass.: MIT Press.

Colliander, G. 1993. "Profiling Second Language Development of Swedish: A method for assessing L2 proficiency." *Problem, Process, Product in Language Learning. Papers from the Stockholm–Åbo Conference, 21–22 October, 1992*, ed. by B. Hammarberg, 32–47. Stockholm: Department of Linguistics, University of Stockholm.

Ekerot, L.-J. 1988. *Så-konstruktionen i svenskan. Konstruktionstypen 'Om vädret tillåter, så genomföres övningen' i funktionellt grammatiskt perspektiv*. Lund: Lund University Press.

Evarts, E. V. 1973. "Motor Cortex Reflexes Associated with learned Movement." *Science* 179.501–503.

Friedemann, M.-A. 1992. "The Underlying Position of External Arguments in French: A study in Adult and Child Grammar." *Geneva Generative Papers* 0.123–144.

Gaze, R. M., M. J. Keating & S.-H. Chung. 1974. "The Evolution of the Retinotectal Map during Development in Xenopus." *Proceedings of the Royal Society, London [Biology]* 185.301–330.

Geer, B. de 1992. "Internationally Adopted Children in Communication: A developmental study." Lund University Department of Linguistics. *Working Papers* 39.

Gilligan, G. 1987. "A Crosslinguistic Approach to the *Pro*-drop Parameter." Diss., University of Southern California, Los Angeles.

Groat, E. 1995. "English Expletives: A minimalist approach." *Linguistic Inquiry* 26.354–365.

Greenberg, S. M., V. A. Castellucci, H. Bayley & J. H. Schwartz. 1987. "A Molecular Mechanism for Long-term Sensitization in Aplysia." *Nature* 329.62–65.

Grimshaw, J. 1991. "Extended Projections." Ms., Brandeis University.

Guasti, M.-T. 1993. "Causatives and Perception Verbs." Diss., University of Geneva. To appear at Turin: Rosenberg and Sellier.

————. 1993/1994. "Verb Syntax in Italian Child Grammar: Finite and nonfinite Verbs." *Language Acquisition* 3.1–40.

Guilfoyle, E. 1990. "Functional Categories and Phrase Structure Parameters." Diss., McGill University, Montreal.

Haegeman, L. 1994. "Root infinitives, Tense and Truncated Structures." *Geneva Generative Papers* 2.12–41.

Håkansson, G. 1988. " 'Hungry I am — breakfast I want.' On the acquisition of inverted word order in Swedish." Lund University, Department of Linguistics *Working Papers* 33.220–228.

————. 1994. "Verb-initial Sentences in the Development of Swedish." Lund University, Department of Linguistics, *Working Papers* 42.49–65.

————. Forthcoming. "Typological Markedness in Action in the Classroom: Some observations on the acquisition of German in Swedish schools." To appear in *Language Learning*.

————. In press. "Syntax and Morphology in Language Attrition: A study of five bilingual, expatriate Swedes." To appear in *International Journal of Applied Linguistics* 5.2.

Håkansson, G. & S. Dooley-Collberg 1994. "The Preference for Modal + Neg: An L2 perspective applied to Swedish L1 children." *Second Language Research* 10.95–124.

Håkansson, G. & U. Nettelbladt. 1993. "Developmental Sequences in L1 (Normal and Impaired) and L2 Acquisition of Swedish Syntax." *International Journal of Applied Linguistics* 3.3–29.

Håkansson, G., U. Nettelbladt & K. Hansson. 1991. "Variation and Deviation in Language Acquisition: Some hypotheses and preliminary observations." Lund University, Department of Linguistics, *Working Papers* 38.83–95.

Hansegård, N. 1968. *Tvåspråkighet eller halvspråkighet.* Stockholm: Aldus/Bonniers.

Hansson, K. & U. Nettelbladt 1991. "Swedish Children with Dysgrammatism: A Comparison with Normally Developed Children". *Lund University Working Papers in Logopedics and Phoniatrics* 7.11–48.

Holmberg, A. 1986. *Word Order and Syntactic Features in the Scandinavian Languages and English.* Stockholm: Department of General Linguistics, University of Stockholm.

————. 1991. "The Distribution of Scandinavian Weak Pronouns." *Clitics and their Hosts* (= *Eurotyp Working Papers,* 1), ed. by H. van Riemsdijk & L. Rizzi, 155–173.

Hyams, N. 1986. *Language Acquisition and the Theory of Parameters.* Dordrecht: Reidel.

————. 1992. "The Genesis of Clausal Structure." *The Acquisition of Verb Placement: Functional Categories and V2 Phonemena in Language Acquisition,* ed. by J. Meisel, 371–400. Dordrecht: Kluwer.

Hyltenstam, K. 1977. "Implicational Patterns in Interlanguage Syntax Variation". *Language Learning* 27.383–411.

Johnson, J.S. & E.L. Newport. 1989. "Critical Period Effects in Second Language Learning: The influence of maturational state on the acquisition of English as a second language." *Cognitive Psychology* 21.60–99.

Johnson, K. 1991. "Object Positions." *Natural Language and Linguistic Theory* 9.577–636.

Jörgensen, N. 1979. *Underordnade satser och fraser i talad svenska. Funktion och byggnad.* Lund: Walter Ekstrand.

Josefsson, G. 1993. "Scandinavian Pronouns and Object Shift." *Working Papers in Scandinavian Syntax* 52.1–28. Also published in *Clitics: Their origin, status and position* (= *Eurotyp Working Papers*, vol. 6), ed. by H. van Riemsdijk & L. Hellan, 91–120.

Kayne, R. 1994. *The Antisymmetry of Syntax.* Cambridge, Mass.: MIT Press.

Koster, J. 1993. "Predicate Incorporation and the Word Order of Dutch." Ms., Groningen University.

Krämer, I. 1993. "The Licensing of Subjects in Early Child Language." *MIT Working Papers in Linguistics* 19.197–212.

Krashen, S. D., M. H. Long & R. C. Scarcella. 1979. "Age, Rate, and Eventual Attainment in Second Language Acquisition." *TESOL Quarterly* 13.573–582.

Lange, S. & K. Larsson. 1973a. "Syntaxen i en 20–22 månader gammal flickas spontana tal." *Folkmålsstudier* 18.117–142.

————. 1973b. "Syntactic Development of a Swedish Girl Embla, between 20 and 42 Months of Age. Part I. Age 20–25 mo." *Project Child Language Syntax Report* 1, Stockholm.

Law, P. 1991. "Verb Movement, Expletive Replacement, and Head Government." *The Linguistic Review* 8.253–285.

Lenneberg, E. H. 1967. *Biological Foundations of Language.* New York: Wiley.

Long, M. H. 1988. "Maturational Constraints on Language Development." *Studies in Second Language Acquisition* 12.251–285.

Lundin, B. 1988. *Bisatser i små barns språk. En analys av fem barns första bisatser.* 2nd ed. Lund: Lund University Press.

Lundin, B. & C. Platzack 1988. "The Acquisition of Verb Inflection, Verb Second and subordinate Clauses in Swedish." *Working Papers in Scandinavian Syntax* 42.43–55.

Mazurkewich, I. 1988. "The Acquisition of Infinitive and Gerund Complements by Second Language Learners." *Linguistic Theory in Second Language Acquisition*, ed. by S. Flynn & W. O'Neil, 127–143. Dordrecht: Kluwer.

Meisel, J. (ed.). 1992. *The Acquisition of Verb Placement: Functional categories and V2 phenomena in language acquisition.* Dordrecht: Kluwer.

Newport, E. L. & T. Suppala. 1987. "A Critical Period Effect in the Acquisition of a Primary Language." Ms., University of Illinois.

Ors, M., G. Stenberg, I. Rosén, G. Blennow & B. Sahlén. 1994. "Delayed P300 in Children with Specific Language Impairment." Ms., Lund University, Department of Neurophysiology.

Ouhalla, J. 1991. "Functional Categories and the Head Parameter." Paper presented at the 14th GLOW Colloquium, Leiden.

————. 1993. "Functional Categories, Agrammatism and Language Acquisition." *Linguistische Berichte* 143.3–36.

Penner, Z., M. Schönenberger & J. Weissenborn. 1994. "The Acquisition of Object Placement: Object placement in early German and Swiss German." Paper presented at the Workshop on the L1–L2 Acquisition of Clause-Internal Rules: Scrambling and Cliticization, at the University of Berne.

Piaget, J. 1970. "Piaget's Theory." *Carmichael's Manual of Child Psychology*. 3rd ed., Vol. 1, ed. by P. H. Mussen. New York: Wiley.

Pierce, A. 1992. *Language Acquisition and Syntactic Theory: A comparative analysis of French and English child grammar*. Dordrecht: Kluwer.

Platzack, C. 1990. "A Grammar without Functional Categories." *Nordic Journal of Linguistics* 13.107–126.

————. 1994. "Small *Pro*, Weak Agr and Syntactic Differences in Scandinavian." *Working Papers in Scandinavian Syntax* 53.85–106.

————. 1995. "Topicalization, Weak Pronouns and the Symmetrical/Asymmetrical Verb Second Hypotheses." *Festvorträge anläßlich des 60. Geburtstags von Inger Rosengren* (= *Sprache und Pragmatik*, Special Issue), ed. by O. Önnerfors, 78–113. Germanistisches Institut der Universität, Lund.

Plunkett K. & S. Strömqvist. 1992. "The Acquisition of Scandinavian Languages." *The Crosslinguistic Study of Language Acquisition*. Vol. 3, ed. by D. I. Slobin, 457–556. Hillsdale, N.J.: Lawrence Erlbaum.

Radford, A. 1986. "Small Children's Small Clauses." *Bangor Research Papers in Linguistics* 1.1–33.

————. 1994. "Clausal Projections in Early Child Grammars." *Essex Research Reports in Linguistics* 3.32–72.

Rizzi, L. 1993. "Some Notes on Linguistic Theory and Language Development: The case of root infinitives." *Geneva Generative Papers* 1.16–25.

————. 1994. "Early Null Subjects and Root Null Subjects." *Language Acquisition Studies in Generative Grammar*, ed. by T. Hoekstra & B. D. Schwartz, 151–176. Amsterdam: John Benjamins.

Roeper, T. & J. Weissenborn. 1990. "How to make Parameters Work." *Language Processing and Language Acquisition*, ed. by L. Frazier & J. de Villiers, 147–162. Dordrecht: Kluwer.

Saffran, E., M. Schwartz & O. Marin. 1980. "The Word Order Problem in Agrammatism: Production." *Brain and Language* 10.263–280.

Santelmann, L. 1994. "Early *Wh*-Questions: Evidence for CP from child Swedish." Ms., University of Cornell.

Schwartz, M., E. Saffran & O. Marin. 1980. "The Word Order Problem in Agrammatism: Comprehension." *Brain and Language* 10.249–262.

Schwartz, B. & R. Sprouse. 1994. "Word Order and Nominal Case in Non-Native Language Acquisition: A longitudinal study of (L1 Turkish) German interlanguage." *Language Acquisition Studies in Generative Grammar*, ed. by T. Hoekstra & B. D. Schwartz, 317–368. Amsterdam: John Benjamins.

Sharwood Smith, M. 1988. "On the Role of Linguistic Theory in Explanations of Second Language Developmental Grammars." *Linguistic Theory in Second Language Acquisition*, ed. by S. Flynn & W. O'Neil, 173–198. Dordrecht: Kluwer.

Söderbergh, R. 1973. "Project Child Language Syntax and Project Early Reading: A theoretical investigation and its practical application." *Report* 2, Stockholm: Stockholms Universitet, Institutionen för nordiska språk.

Strömqvist, S., U. Richtoff & A.-B. Andersson. 1993. "Strömqvist's and Richtoff's Corpora: A guide to longitudinal data from four Swedish children." *Gothenburg Papers in Theoretical Linguistics* 66, University of Gothenburg: Department of Linguistics.

Stuss, D. T. & D. F. Benson. 1986. *The Frontal Lobes*. New York: Raven.

Valian, V. 1991. "Syntactic Subjects in the Early Speech of American and Italian Children." *Cognition* 40.21–81.

Villiers, J. de. 1992. "On the Acquisition of Functional Categories: A general commentary." *The Acquisition of Verb Placement: Functional categories and V2 phenomena in language acquisition*, ed. by J. Meisel, 423–443. Dordrecht: Kluwer.

Wexler, K. 1994a. "Optional Infinitives, Head Movement and the Economy of Derivation." *Verb Movement*, ed. by D. Lightfoot & N. Hornstein, 305–350. Cambridge: Cambridge University Press.

———. 1994b. "Extremely Early Knowledge of UG and Parameters: Evidence from the underspecification of tense in comparative acquisition studies." Paper presented at the conference on the Generative Studies of the Acquisition of Case and Agreement at the University of Essex, March.

Wilder, C. & D. Ćavar. 1994. "Word Order Variation, Verb Movement and Economy Principles." *Studia Linguistica* 48.46–86.

Wu, A. 1993. "The S-Parameter." *The GLOW Newsletter* 30.60–61.

Zanuttini, R. 1989. "The Structure of Negative Clauses in Romance." Paper presented at the 12th GLOW Colloquium, Utrecht.

Zwart, C. J.-W. 1994. "Dutch is head-initial." *The Linguistic Review* 11.377–406.

The Role of Merger Theory and Formal Features in Acquisition

Thomas Roeper

University of Massachusets, Amherst

1. Introduction

This essay, like the Minimalist Program (see Chomsky 1994, 1995) which inspired it, focuses on how abstract structures — without category labels — can capture neglected moments of acquisition. The core proposition is that nodes are direct reflections of lexical items. From this perspective we seek to evaluate several other propositions about Universal Grammar and acquisition.

We claim:

(1) a. there are LEXICALLY defined stages in acquisition;

   b. the child projects unique MAXIMAL PROJECTIONS, not (necessarily) found in the adult grammar;

   c. the child may project unique or restricted COMPLEMENTS (subcategorization);

   d. projection of FORMAL FEATURES, instead of category labels, defines and then revises each projection.

We discuss a number of details but our focus remains broad in scope and aims to pinpoint structure without a complete integration of these claims into Universal Grammar, which itself has been re-examined in a broad fashion recently (Chomsky 1994, 1995; Kayne 1994; de Zwart 1993). In general we argue that a child's grammar is a radical instance of ECONOMY OF REPRESENTATION,[1] but we leave untouched interesting questions about ECONOMY OF MOVEMENT. In the last section we sketch further acquisition principles.

In brief, Formal Features in words replace node labels but still entail the presence of Functional Categories; however lexical features can *further* restrict the content of those categories. This allows much narrower domains of generalization in adult grammar and predicts various stages of acquisition heretofore largely neglected. Consider one illustration. Both functional features, like +wh-, and lexical content features, like 'for what reason' are universally found in the word *why*, and define the CP-projection. Both features project to a higher maximal projection (= '*why*-CP'). Now we can represent the fact that only the word *why* appears (in numerous languages) with no AGR element as a complement to this unique MP: *why go downtown*. Another *wh*- word, *where*, disallows this complement: **where go downtown* (see below).

Are we advocating a less restrictive view of UG? A lexical approach to grammar appears to create the possibility of an infinite set of possible phrase markers, corresponding to possible words. Each *wh*-word, as with *why* above, could have a separately defined complement. However, we still expect the set of Formal Features to restrict the domain of possible words, and possible nodes and complements, in the familiar way, The exact restrictions on Formal Features are now the object of study. We do not simply assume NP, VP, AP, IP, DP, CP, but assume instead that this class of elements may be larger and may have significant internal interactions. Therefore we can eventually recapture the restrictiveness which we initially appear to lose. This is a familiar form of evolution in scientific theories.

1.1. *Notational Choices and the Role of Acquisition*

One of the most difficult questions to confront any science is the selection of notation at the right level of abstraction. The available systems of mathematical representation offer, quite often, abstractions which are too powerful and therefore overgenerate, producing (for linguistics) humanly impossible grammars. The idea of a transformation in linguistics had great power and therefore much effort was devoted to 'constraining' it. Constraints were first stated in terms of structural descriptions which defined terminal strings, and then the rule, MOVE-α, was reformulated as inherently free, but limited by the impact of other modules. The same evolution occurred for phrase-structure rules which were dissolved into a category-free notion of X' coupled with a variety of constraints on order (such as head-government) from other modules (Stowell 1981). A further step is the dissolution of the notion of syntactic category itself. Can it be a more complex form of lexical representation which includes both functional features that respect syntactic generalizations and lexical ones that reflect referential and verb-class features? Chomsky's Merger Theory moves in that direction.

1.2. *Biological Assumptions*

In most biological sciences, pre-eminence is given to genotypic information over phenotypic information, because mature organisms acquire properties that are difficult to analyze in terms of genetic contribution versus experiential effect. Linguistics has been unusual in giving priority to phenotypic information, namely, adult intuitional judgments, over developmental information, that is, very early grammatical behavior.

The justification for this preference was initially very plausible, namely that 'performance' factors could influence children's early utterances and make them opaque. For instance, it was assumed that their comprehension behavior was too easily overwhelmed by pragmatics and general inference for us to extract differences equal to the subtlety of adult judgments. Moreover, production behavior was supposedly limited by memory and articulation problems. But no performance theory of subtlety has emerged (although allusions to 'performance' remain commonplace). Broad claims about parsing or pragmatic differences are totally incapable of explaining subtle differences between children's two-word utterances, for instance why children say *you big* and never **big you,* or why uninflected verbs in German occur on the right and not the left. However, grammatical theory (e.g., small clauses) makes immediate predictions about these phenomena.

It is, furthermore, easily arguable that acquisition experiments provide better evidence about many subtle linguistic structures than intuition-based theories. For instance, young English children avoid the formation of superiority violations in the form of **what did who buy* while German children use the same sequence *(was hat wer gekauft)* readily.[2] This suggests that SUPERIORITY constraints are obeyed in English but not German. The intuitional evidence goes in the same direction, but speaker judgments remain quite mixed; the presence of a clear difference between four-year-old English and German children strongly suggests that the difference is real.

In the tradition of the biological sciences, therefore, it makes *a priori* sense to examine developmental data for direct representation of deeper mathematical representations. No guarantee exists that such an approach will be successful. However, the best test lies in the enterprise itself: does the data from acquisition reveal clear evidence in behalf of a given level of theoretical abstraction? Heretofore acquisition data has been given credibility in principle though often not in fact.[3]

2. Merger Theory

Chomsky (1994) has put forward an abstract theory of phrase structure, called bare phrase structure, in which he proposes a fundamental operation, MERGE, which is at once more abstract and more concrete than previous theories.[4] Once again, it is more abstract than previous theories insofar as it allows an unspecified set of combination of maximal projections, and more specific inasmuch as the maximal projections may be now lexically specific. It is theoretical operations of this kind — at a high level of abstraction — which we predict should receive direct representation in child grammar. Two important predictions for acquisition follow, which we shall illustrate in some depth:

A.   Unique Maximal Projections are generable.
     For instance, we might find a NEG-ADV-P as in Dutch children's use of
     kan-nie 'can-not'. Or there could be a NEG-P (no eat) whose scope is
     unique, and not found in the target grammar: NEGP-VP (without an
     intervening Tense P) a new phrase-structure sequence.
B.   Maximal projections could have lexically-specific subcategorizations.
     That is, if lexical features percolate to maximal projections, then the
     features could restrict the subcategorized MP to a single lexical item. For
     instance, a verb like wonder does not subcategorize CP, but only CP+wh
     (I wonder what/*I wonder that). A child might begin with an even heavier
     restriction: I wonder how and not *I wonder what.

We can also capture slightly more abstract subcategorization restrictions. The verb try allows only infinitives: try to/*try that. This is not captured by the notion CP, but calls for a node Inf-CP. The existence of lexical restrictions on subcategorization has always been known to be more tightly restricted than phrase-structure categories suggest, but it has not been reflected in the formal structure of phrase-structure itself.

Much of the work on 'underspecification' in child language fits such an approach,[5] but there has been no theory in which underspecification arose as a natural consequence of the formalism chosen. From this perspective, the proposal that there is 'underspecification' or the proposal that a fixed set of functional categories does not exist can be seen as different versions of the same theory.

2.1. *The Universal Base Hypothesis (UBH)*

In contrast to this system and these two predictions we find the traditional view of a UNIVERSAL BASE HYPOTHESIS (UBH) for functional categories. For instance, we find Rizzi (1994), Roeper (1992), Poeppel & Wexler (1993), among others, have assumed that children immediately have the full range of functional categories and their dominance relations.[6]

(2)   CP-AGR-NEG TP-AGR-ASP-VP-VP

This is a fairly full example of what must be assumed. The Merge operation by itself implies extensive deviation from the UBH. Chomsky (1994) suggests (see below) that the UBH may not hold. It remains possible that the choices in the lexicon (NUMERATION) re-introduce UBH as a property of the Formal Features chosen, but it is not inherent in the projection of tree structure by itself.[7] It is precisely in acquisition, where features of Numeration may not appear at once, that we may be able to separate the operation (Merge) from sequence and domination restrictions that are lexically dictated.

2.2. *Merger Definitions*

Let us now consider precisely the system that Chomsky has proposed:

One operation is necessary on conceptual grounds alone: an operation that forms larger units out of those already constructed, call it MERGE. Applied to two objects α and β, MERGE forms the new object T. What is T? T must be constituted somehow from the two items α and β; the only alternatives are that T is fixed for all α, β or that it is randomly selected, neither worth considering. The simplest object constructed from α and β is the set {α, β}, so we take T to be at least this set, where α and β are CONSTITUENTS of this T.

...The terms COMPLEMENT and SPECIFIER can be defined in the usual way, in terms of T.

...If constituents α, β of T have been formed in the course of computation, one of the two must project, say α. At the LF interface, T (if maximal) is interpreted as a phrase of the type α (e.g. as a nominal phrase if its head *k* is nominal), and it behaves in the same manner in the course of computation.

...The operation MERGE, then, is asymmetric, projecting one of the objects to which it applies, its head becoming the label of the complex formed ... we have only:

Chomsky then leaves open the possibility of substantial variation across languages, as well as the representation of uniformity (universality), in this framework. That is, the projected categories could be much more various than the current set of functional categories would indicate. For instance, the C-node that dominates *how* might be quite different from *how come* since they have quite different properties.[8] He observes, then, that the set of possible maximal projections that exists could have these origins:

> Suppose that the label for {α, β} happens to be determined *uniquely for α, β in language L* (my italics); we would then want to deduce the fact from properties of α, β, from L; or, if it is true for α, β in language generally, from properties of the language faculty. Similarly, if the label is uniquely determined for arbitrary α, β, L as may be the case.

The notion of 'arbitrary α, β as may be the case' implicitly allows any combination of elements. Our task then becomes one of constraining phrase structure in an insightful manner.

2.3. *Minimalist Program Background*

Although we focus on Merge, we sketch here the principles that govern its application. Merge applies as a result of selection of an array of elements from the lexicon, called NUMERATION, which creates heads and allows maximal projection projections. Numeration requires recognition of a feature, including both substantive features like ⟨nominal, verbal⟩ and Formal Features like Tense and Agreement. The Formal Feature will be strong or weak; Chomsky (1995) comments:

> Of the functional categories, only Tense, Complement, and Determiner remain.
> Strong features, which play a considerable role in language variation, are narrowly limited in distribution.

Strong features may be generated directly on functional nodes. The weak features, like -*s* (on verbs) in English, may be lexically generated on the verb but will be moved at LF to a TensePhrase, for instance, to be 'checked off'. Features which are purely formal must be 'checked off' and disappear before an interface is reached. Checking becomes therefore the motive for movement.

The lexicon has both Lexical and Functional categories (TenseP, DeterminerP, CompP), all of which undergo interpretation at some Interface.[9] Now the crucial question arises: what is the set of possible features? What feature allows a possible numeration which in turn can project into a maximal-projection node? This becomes a critical question for acquistion.

Once the numeration is set, the operation of Merge then combines the MP (maximal projection) as Spec-Head, or Head-Complement with other MP projections. In a word, any two elements are syntactically connected by assigning Head to one, and Spec or COMP to the other.

What is the minimal information needed in order to warrant the Merge operation? Does a word like *yes* generate a merged structure? There is no direct answer given to that question. We will now provide evidence for novel maximal projections in child grammar and return to minimalist implications for acquisition in a later section.

2.4. *Acquisition Perspectives on Merger Restrictions*

What restrictions does the acquisition evidence show? For instance, it would be natural for a two-verb utterance like *said ate* to exist, equal to *I said I ate*. But none has ever been recorded to my knowledge for children. The non-existence of **said ate* follows directly if no recursive rule equivalent to the form VP $\Rightarrow$ V (VP) exists for the child (excluding now the possibility that the second V originates as a CP). If each element has an identical formal feature in the Numeration ⟨+verb⟩, then no choice of Head is possible. No recursion could be stated as a first order restriction on a Merger Theory, although it might prove to be too strong an hypothesis.

In addition we must explain how CATEGORICAL INCOMPATIBILITY arises. It is ungrammatical to say **the this house* or **a your car* but precisely the latter is possible in Italian and occurs, according to Brown (1973), in child English we find *a your car, a my blue pencil* etc. (but never **your a car*). Here the child allows the MERGER of possessive with an article, with the POSS as specifier of N (presumably), until new features rule it out. The recognition of Case features (*'s*) which requires the presence of POSS in the DP, which then creates the incompatibility between Article and POSS. It is now dynamic features of the application of principles, not an inherent fixed sequence, which determines both the adult and the child grammar.

Merger Theory raises the question of how that incompatibility is stateable. We do not have a full answer to this question. In general, morphological features on inflections carry requirements that force functional categories into existence which in turn require CHECKING THEORY to be satisfied. The order of the elements presumably is in part a reflection of LF-requirements on interpretation, for instance scope, which follows from UG. In other words, the notion that AGR and Tense dominate V will have a UG basis that will prevent some inappropriate merger analyses.[10] This question is crucial for acquisition because we want to state what restrictions could possibly exist (and pre-exist in the initial state) for combinations of items. The challenge from the acquisition perspective lies then in determining how the children recognize those features of lexical items which will generate COMPLEMENTARY DISTRIBUTION.

If merged structures exist in acquistion, then a semantic question arises: how do merged structures receive an interpretation? We argue below that a general notion of 'adverbial' modification provides enough of the meaning to communicate (*mommy tired* = (roughly) *Mommy tiredly*).

From an historical perspective, Merger Theory produces a convergence between a tradition of work in acquisition theory and an abstract formulation of phrase structure within intuitional studies. Lebeaux (1988) formulated a notion of ADJOIN-α which captured a variety of non-adult phenomena in complex aspects of child language (see below). The concept of adjunction then acquired some specific constraints within UG which made it incompatible with the acquisition evidence (e.g. no adjunction to VP). Now a deeper generalization about Merger recaptures the convergence. Other sorts of underspecification can be captured within this system as well. (Platzack 1993; Hyams 1994 and Clahsen *et al.*, this volume). We now turn to acquisition evidence.

3.   Evidence for Lexical Maximal Projections: *are* and *auch* 'also'

Evidence for a lexical maximal projection comes from the sometimes brief appearance of a single item that subcategorizes a clause or a VP. Consider here one example that has been reported for several languages (drawn from Akmajian & Heny 1973, also Crain 1984):[11] A child may suddenly adjoin a question-word, either *are* or *is* to a sentence. The stage is short-lived.

(3)   *are you put this on me*
             are you get this down   *are you help me*
             are you know Lucy's name is   *are you want one*
             are you got some orange juice   *are this is broke*
             are you don't know Sharon's name is   *are you sneezed*

The examples suggest that modality (*are+don't*), tense (*are+got*) and agreement (*are+this*) information is not being carried by the word *are*, which seems to be a particle without a clear or correct syntactic category. It is noteworthy that the particle has SENTENCE-SCOPE although merged with an initial word (this is true for Latin as well). Kayne (1994) cites Bach (1971) to the effect that question particles are evident in an initial position in many languages, whether via movement or not, therefore it is not surprising that children would project *are* as a proto-functional category. We can represent it as:

(4)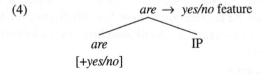

The hypothesis now is that the *yes/no* feature is the ingredient which becomes a functional category as a part of the word *are* and it is crucially located in the lexicon where, in Chomsky's terms, the selected NUMERATION constitutes the set of entities from which sentences will be formed (See Marantz 1994 for helpful exposition). No examples of sentence-final question adjunction in acquisition have been reported for acquisition (to my knowledge).

The crucial point here is that the representation of this form — which carries the illocutionary force linked to CP — is limited to a single lexical item. Penner (1991) argues that children have a QUESTION CLITIC for Bernese German, not found in the adult language, see Müller (1994) as well. He gives examples like:

(5)   *k'*   *het's hammer*
         Q PARTICLE has.it hammer
         'Where is the hammer?'

Though often short-lived, it is a very common phenomenon.[12]

3.1. *Lexical Maximal Projection: Spec and Complement*

In Merger Theory, as linked to Kayne's work (1994), every maximal projection has a Spec and a COMP in a binary structure. Under our hypothesis, a lexical item can instantly head just this structure. Tracy *et al.* (1993) discuss the phenomenon of *auch* 'also' which fits this model perfectly. They find that *auch* has two stages, first essentially as Head + COMP (*auch Nase* 'also nose'), and then as strictly second position, with now, Spec–*auch*-COMP structure:

(6)   Stage 1: X *auch*   *toto auch. ich auch, hauschen*
                                     auch
         Stage 2: subj *auch* DO   *stephanie AUCH Nase*
                  adv *auch* subj   *das auchn Rüssel*

subj *auch* adjective   *ich auch gross*
subj *auch* DO V$_{-infin}$ *ich auch Brot haben*
Stage 3:   X V-$_{fin}$ *auch* Y   *klebe das auch noch klebt*
macht des auch macht

In Stage 2, we have effectively a Spec-*auch*-COMP structure in which a VP with final infinitive is possible. At the same time, V-medial infinitives occur, but not with *auch*. Thus we have complementary distribution between the following sequences for a period of time:

(7) a.   Spec-*auch*-COMP
     b.   Spec-V-$_{finite}$-COMP

This could lead one to suppose that the *auch* is comprehended as a verb itself,[13] but it shows no signs of AGR or Tense. In addition, it is lexically specific. At a later point, the position will generalize to negation and other categories, presumably by the generation of an ADV + scope feature for *auch* whose complement is identical to the complement of NEG. The perspective advocated here is that the child simply has these two lexical representations initially.

Only at a later point will a further subcategorization of *auch* (or a ⟨+ADV⟩ feature) by V-finite occur,[14] based on exposure to sentences of this kind, producing:

(8)   *will   auch mal   die nete   haben*
      want also   once the duck have

Now the auxiliary directly subcategorizes for the adverb *auch* and they can co-occur.

3.2. *Dutch*

Another instance of a unique maximal projection lies in the projection of a node which has both auxiliary and adverb. Hoekstra & Jordens (1994) isolate a very early stage 1.10 in which a specific set of modal-like words are *adjoined* (*kannie* 'cannot', *magnie* 'like not' and *minne* 'want' are used exclusively in initial position at first:

(9)   a.   initial: *kannie zitten*
                    cannot sit[15]
                    minne die open
                    want   that open

It is particularly noteworthy that an expression like *kannie* is composed of two parts which have different categorical status: a verb and an adverbial negative. Frijn and de Haan (1991) seem to have isolated a stage in which there is lexical regularity with the similar expressions *(hoeft nie* 'need not', *kanwel)*.[16]

It is thus lexically specific representations of phrases which provide insight into the micro-steps of acquisition. It is our ability to represent these small steps which constitutes a new depth of precision in linguistic/acquisition representations.[17] Their rapidity suggests the mechanical process implied by a tight mathematical system.

4. Wh-questions, Unique Maximal Projections, and CP

Under Merger Theory it is predictable that the adult language will also exhibit lexically dominated Maximal Projections with unique complements. There are some straightforward examples which receive little attention. First we find that there are the following possibilities (10a, b) but not (10c, d, e), nor do absence of prepositions (**lunch*) or other prepositions work *(*when at lunch):*

(10) a.   *what about lunch*
      b.   *how about lunch*
      c.   **when about lunch*
      d.   **where about lunch*
      e.   **who about lunch.*

Expressions like *what about x* are learned early and not overgeneralized.

A more intricate example involves *why.* Here is a generic use of why-questions, no others, which involve the direction domination of a VP with no AGR, modals or TP-phrase available:

(11) a.   *why go downtown*
      b.   **why he go downtown*
      c.   **where go downtown*
      d.   **who go downtown*
      e.   **why went downtown*
      f.   **why can say he went down*

The *why-* is generated in an initial position which cannot be a Spec because it cannot have a long-distance origin (Collins 1991):

(12) **why say [he went downtown t]*

Therefore, as argued in Roeper & Rohrbacher (1994), we can project a lexically specific maximal projection with *why* as Head and an immediate VP complement:

(13)   *why* + subjunctive

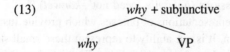

why   VP

If such lexical structures are immediately available to children, then we predict that they will be easy to acquire. In fact, by the age of four, Adam exhibits just this kind of *why* + subjunctive meaning, although with a larger array of VP-morphology suggesting that features of aspect are not fully commanded:

(14) a. *why put string on it?*   Adam(17)
      b. *why laughing at me?*   Adam(17)
      c. *why not # see it dat one?*   Adam(17)
      d. *why say oh oh?*   Adam(17)
      e. *why say # right now?*   Adam(17)
      f. *why not # take # take dose?*   Adam(17)

Before file 17, for reasons related to ⟨–AGR⟩-languages, all *wh*-expressions appear without subject or AGR 'where go', but after file 19, *all wh*-questions without overt subject belong to this type (cf. (44), therefore suggesting that the child has recognized a lexically specific *why* + subjunctive subcategorization. A few of these, but not all, appear to be essentially *why* + quotation, which is an interesting form of Merger in its own right, but each time taking just the VP, no AGR, and with the generic quality 'why take it apart':

(15) a. *why fall and hurt myself?*   Adam(20)
      b. *why finish waiting for my water?*   Adam(20)
      c. *why going to open it?*   Adam(22)
      d. *why always push this [= record button]*   Adam(28)
      e. *why take it apart?*   Adam(28)
      f. *why broken?*   Adam(28)
      g. *why have the yellow black thing [?]?*   Adam(33)
      h. *why go slowly?*

If these forms, which are relatively rare, were also highly marked syntactically, then we might expect them not to be acquired until perhaps college-age. If they reflect a basic lexical orientation of structure-building, then it is no surprise that they are acquired quickly. Other languages, like French, also exhibit non-inversion with *why (pourquoi)* suggesting that a feature of meaning is linked to - AGR in UG.

4.1. *Inversion and Subordination: Lexicon and Move-α*

If the initial analysis of each new feature is a lexical projection, then it should recur at various points in acquisition. De Villiers (1991) discovered an extremely robust phenomenon with respect to lexical *wh*-phrases and inversion. It is well known that children begin with non-inversion of many *wh*-expressions (from McNeill 1970):

(16)   *where small trailer he should pull*
        where the other Joe will drive
        why he don't know how to pretend
        why the kitty can't stand up
        how he can be a doctor
        how they can't talk
        what he can ride in
        what he can do

This could be a straightforward case of Merger between a *wh*-word and an IP. We must ask, however, if there is a CP involved and if there is a trace. Evidence for a trace for some *wh*-expressions comes from 16 long-distance sentences found by M. Takahashi from Adam:

(17)   *what chu think this taste like*
        'What do you think this tastes like *t*?'

If such a sentence entails a CP with a ⟨+*wh*⟩ feature, then we should expect all *wh*-words to suddenly exhibit movement and inversion simultaneously. However, de Villiers discovered that this is not true: inversion occurs with each *wh*-word independently over a two year period. Why should we find that three-year-olds fail to invert with both *what* and *why*, then learn to invert with *what* but only two-years later is *why* properly inverted? In between, *how where*, and *when* go from non-inversion to inversion. How is inversion separately triggered for each *wh*-word?

The inversion of each *wh*-word occurs systematically just after its appearance as an indirect question for certain verbs *(ask)*. Therefore de Villiers argues that the subordination triggers reanalysis of an IP-adjoined *wh*-word into a Spec-C *wh*-word, but it happens with each *wh*-word separately. That is, a

recognition of sentence-subordination for *ask,* hence CP as a complement, leads
to a CP representation for each *wh*-word in the matrix clause:

(18)   *what*-IP ⇒ *ask* [$_{COMP}$ *wh*- [$_{IP}$ ⇒ *wh* + inversion IP

Thus we have the following stages, where there is first adjunction then INDIRECT
QUESTIONS and INVERSION appear:

(19)   Stage 1:
    a.   NP object: *ask John*
    b.   No inversion: *what he can sing*
            Stage 2:
    a.   Indirect Q complement: *ask John what he wants*
    b.   Inversion: *what does he want*

This occurs for *how* around session 15, for *what* around session 20, and for *why*
in session 55 in Adam. This is roughly a year and a half later. The same holds
roughly for five other children.

This result is strong, with a large time factor, which does not fit any simple
theory of category acquisition. It is worth repeating the argument to see the
importance of the result. If children (a) have CP, and (b) have a full range of
lexical items for *wh*-, then why would they not insert this range of lexical items
into CP immediately? If we assume that they must be in CP, then we have no
explanation for the fact that inversion occurs with some, but not with other
wh-words.

If in contrast we assume that the child has another method for achieving the
meaning of a matrix question: Merger of *what* + *IP/why+IP*, etc., then nothing
forces a full simultaneous re-analysis of all *wh*-words as occupying a Spec-CP
position. Instead they are re-analyzed one by one in terms of subordination. This
view calls for a clarification of what happens under subordination by a higher
verb. Let us assume that functional categories are linked to illocutionary force
(Roeper 1992; Chomsky 1995) and therefore can be triggered by recognition of
a set of 'meanings': question, imperative, subordination are all linked to a
feature ⟨+CP⟩, which guarantees that they will not co-occur. Then it follows that
ask + complement must entail a CP-feature. Under Chomsky's definition of
Numeration the lexicon will be able to contain such a category feature. This
feature is representable on a given lexical item, and therefore can project to a
higher node as the item itself projects. Thus the child can have ⟨+CP⟩ linked to
each *wh*-word under *ask* individually.

The recognition then of question-force justifies the presence of a CP-feature
in matrix clauses, which in turn justifies the Spec–head configuration which

forces inversion. Why would the *wh*-words that Merge fail to project a CP-feature? The answer to this calls for a refinement of the notion of question. Here is a sketch of an approach. One feature of *wh*-words is that they function as variables. De Villiers and Roeper (1992) and Perez (1995) have proposed that initial *wh*-words do not function as variables, following suggestions of Rizzi (1993) and Lasnik & Stowell (1991), that a NULL CONSTANT is a possible form. Penner (p.c.) has obtained experimental evidence that children give a single, not a multiple answer, to questions at very early stages. Exhaustive answers are in principle required. If one asks *who was in the car during the robbery* one commits perjury if one mentions only one person and not all persons. If true questions require this feature, then pseudo-questions could make an equivalence between: *who is here* and *name a person that is here*. The latter is clearly different from an adult question. One possibility is that the *wh*-word unlinked to CP-inversion does not have variable force. This line of thinking, of course, requires further development.[18]

4.1.1. *Phases of* Wh-*Projection and Chain Links*

Thornton (1995) extends proposals about adjunction (Lebeaux 1988; de Villiers 1991) to include a node REFP above CP as in:

(20)   *which food that the spaceman didn't like*

This is a very sensible proposal because it captures the special features of *which*. The Merger Theory approach to acquisition advocated here provides the theoretical background her proposal implicitly anticipates.

It appears, however, that the proposal is insufficiently abstract because it (explicitly) excludes a large range of copying effects with infinitives that are evident in the adult language in examples like:

(21)   *how$_i$ did he say how$_i$ to sing* t$_i$

and have been shown to be present in children's judgments by Maxfield & McDaniel, and in extensive experimental work in Perez (1995), and de Villiers & Roeper (1994). It also excludes copying effects in her own data of the form: *which cat did he say which cat he saw*. See Perez (1995) for discussion.

The variety of subtle differences that Thornton exhibits are precisely what is expected under a lexically sensitive view of CP-links in phrase structure. However we also expect that the phrase-structure projections will undergo substantial revision as Formal Features are more abstractly identified. This will lead to the collapse of REFP and CP such that *which food that* becomes impossible for the child, perhaps via the introduction of dynamic agreement features in CP. Moreover, we expect that a single chain-link formal feature is discovered by the child which leads to a common analysis of all *wh*-chains, without excluding those connected to infinitives. It is only the initial lexical projection which allows the possibility that the chain-link feature could be different for every *wh*-word.

In conclusion, we have strong evidence in behalf of a lexically based operation of Merger. We turn now to the second question: unique maximal projection sequences.

4.2. *Maximal Projection Sequences*

The set of possible Mergers remains unstated, but in principle we may now admit a larger range of combinations from the lexicon than before. It is possible that there could be an acquisition stage in which two categories are merged, but then become impossible when new syntactic features are recognized. A strong hypothesis is this:

C.   Each new addition will first occur as Merger.

All of the lexical examples cited above are examples of one kind. But it is also possible that one could have more surprising syntactic combinations, such as NEG + VP/IP–NP, where (a) functional categories in the adult language appear to be skipped, or (b) combinations exist which are later replaced by other categories. Merger stages are then putatively a logical property of the system whether or not it occurs in a temporal (visible) fashion. Where might we find evidence for unique mergers?

Brennan (1991) points out that there is an interesting stage where adjunct PPs are just NPs, which then is a case of IP–NP, while argument PPs are present:

(22)   *we colored crayon*   (=with)
          Shirley get meat dinner   (=for)
          I cut it a knife   (=with)
          Richard bring snack Shirley   (=for)
          I went party   (=to)
          feed baby fork   (=with)
          Shirley cut fork   (=with)
          I sleep big bed   (=in)
          save some later   (=for)

She points out that where clear arguments are present the same children will use PPs:

(23)   *I played with Joan*
          Jim was at Cooperstown
          putting Daddy in wagon

There were 46 prepositions for arguments, and only three for adjuncts for three children. For "3 of 4 children studied, it was true that adjuncts never surfaced with PPs, while the distribution of PP's in argument position was haphazard". This is just what we predict if each new kind of verbal modification is initially Merged.[19] The preposition is not unknown or deleted, but rather it is identified first as a marker for verb arguments.[20]

How is meaning determined here? We assume that there is a kind of 'default' semantic modification roughly like an adverb (thanks to N. Chomsky for discussion of this point). This means that the semantics are not exactly equal to adult meanings, but rather:

(24)   *Shirley cut fork = cut forkly or forklike*

Brennan in fact argues that more abstract function/argument semantics should be used to account for these early utterances.

This provides a surprisingly clear example, after the onset of acquisition, of a novel syntactic sequence which is defineable under Merger Theory.

4.3. *Inversion as Merger*

Movement depends on what range of options exists in the arrayed numeration. The acquisition device will in principle face a choice for a new item:

(25)   Move or Merge

In principle Move will not arise until an element is already fixed in another position. This is particularly unlikely in the case of *what* which, outside of echo questions (which are learned early — see Maxfield 1991) only appears overtly in a moved position. Therefore we would predict Merge appears before Move. This would not necessarily hold for all instances of movement. We would expect that auxiliaries will appear in IP before they appear in CP. Nonetheless, there remains the possibility of homophones. Thus the child could analyze these sentences non-transformationally:

(26) a. *can I come*
     b. *I can come*

The existence of two *can*'s is no more surprising than the existence of two *there's*, one locative and the other expletive: *there is a house there*. And in fact there is a stage where we find both copies and separate elements (Menyuk 1969).

(27) a. *can I will go*
     b. *can I can go*

We do not have precise enough data for inversion, day by day, since the entire generalization sometimes occurs in a week (Felix, p.c.). We hypothesize a sequence of the form:

(28) I.   Numeration: CP selected = question force
     II.   Merge: *can I come*
     III. Formal Feature Fixation: INFL present in *can*
     IV.   Move substitutes for Merge

Roeper (1992) and Chomsky (1995) argue that CP is automatically present by virtue of the connection to illocutionary force.[21]

4.4. *V2 as Merger*

Consider now the case of German. There are several acquisition scenarios to consider. First assume the traditional view that the difference in the adult languages involves a final postverbal TP for German (S OV IP), and a preverbal TP for English (IP VO) which follows the head-parameter distinction.

If AGR is initially strong, then it could appear as an independent item, and it could occur in either initial or final position in UG. Let us assume that it is weak and is redefined as strong via additional Formal Features. Now it can be generated as part of a lexical item and appear in final position without our positing a final TP-element, just as Chomsky (1994) and Speas (1994) argue is the case for English. The verb can then move either in syntax or at LF, to be checked in TP, which could be either left or right, German or English. If it is on the right *Brot isst*, then movement is optional (Wexler 1994) and it is simply present as a lexical item. We now generate:

(29) a. *Brot essen*
     b. *isst Brot*
     c. *Brot isst*
     d. **essen Brot*

These are the classic facts as discussed by Pierce (1992); Meisel (1993); Clahsen & Penke (1992); Pierce & Depréz (1994). (d) is impossible because it would require movement not justified by the need to check any feature. Notably there are no verbal complexes at this stage: *Brot essen kannst / *kannst Brot essen.

Now we can argue that the strong affix triggers a final TP. The existence of an independent, hence strong affix is evident precisely in complex verb environments where the affix always appears on the last element. In fact, no errors of the following kind are reported to my knowledge: *Brot isst können where the inflection occurs on the non-final verb, which one might predict if the affix were just a part of the verb at this stage. In other words a child hears forms like:

(30) a.   kannst Brot essen
      b.   (dass du) Brot essen kannst

Recognition of this evidence, we hypothesize, causes a distinction between German and English and necessitates a V–TP order. It is at this point that the affix is analyzed as strong.[22] This would fit the evidence and argument assembled by Clahsen & Penke (1992) and Rohrbacher & Vainikka (1994).

Now let us consider the phenomenon from the perspective of the Universal Base Hypothesis as proposed by Kayne (1994). Here we assume that both English and German are S–IP–V–O structures:

(31)

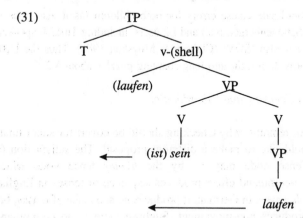

There is obligatory movement of laufen into the V-shell. Then there is optional movement of ist into the TP (Wexler 1994), depending upon whether a matrix clause or a subordinate clause is involved.[23] If a subordinate clause appears, then it is covert.

It is not clear why movement should be optional for children, nor why there is a difference between main (V2) and subordinate clauses (no V2) for adults. We combine acquisition and intuitional evidence in order to sketch a different approach. First there is a range of neglected facts that should be included. There is some local movement of inflection-bearing auxiliaries in subordinate clauses (32b), reflected in the red/green dialect split in Dutch.[24]

> (32) a. *dat hij gelopen heeft*
> that he run has
> b. *dat hij heeft gelopen*
> that he has run

The inversion is an arbitrary dialectal mystery, unless one assumes that it is a movement to a leftward TP as the SVO hypothesis proposes. The variation can be captured in familiar terms: is movement overt or covert? In general, the existence of a corner of grammar in which SVO-like behavior exists, constitutes evidence in behalf of the program associated with Kayne and the Universal Base Hypothesis (see Cinque 1995). A brief search undertaken by T. Hoekstra (p.c.) showed that children in the red/green-dialect split showed the variation at two years of age, producing both forms. We propose the following acquisition hypothesis, in a sketch of this interaction:

> (33) Maximize overt checking[25]

This will produce subordinate clause errors for both children (as it also does in Swiss German — M. Schönenberger, p.c.) and L2 users, including Turkish-speakers whose native language is also 'SOV' (Clahsen & Muysken 1986). Thus the UBH and checking theory provide insight into long-standing puzzles about V2.[26]

4.5. *A Speculation on Checking and Subordination*

The question then remains, why Checking should be covert for subordinate clauses. Here we would like to make a different proposal. The satisfaction (= checking) of the Tense node may be by the *higher* tense node which c-commands it. This c-command effect produces sequence of tenses in English *Did you say you had blue eyes*. In German, it produces no sequence of tenses, but perhaps instead, it produces non-movement. Suppose there is no c-command relation between main-clause VP and subordinate clauses initially for children. Since overt checking is the unmarked case, we predict that children will err in the direction of V2, if the clause is not properly c-commanded by the verb.

Merger Theory at a higher level may also explain the absence of verbal c-command. If CPs are merged (as under Generalized Transformations, see Lebeaux 1988, 1990 and Chomsky 1993), or if there is an IP–CP Merger, then subordinate clauses are not initially subcategorized by the verb, but linked to a higher projection (see Kayne 1994 for the structure given to conjunctions). The absence of verbal c-command (subcategorization) is precisely the analysis argued for by de Villiers & Roeper (1994) as an explanation for the appearance of partial movement effects among children. This is the kind of subtle evidence of a marginal phenomenon which provides direct insight into deeper formal operations. This analysis remains a speculation because the concept of 'satisfaction' under c-command as an alternative form of Checking constitutes a significant addition to the grammar which we cannot explore here.

4.6. Functional-Category growth under Merger

Now suppose a new node is created by Merger, distinct from the final IP, to which the verb moves, which will eventually house the CP. It is not necessary to assume that it is a full CP at once. One major fact that is evident in many languages is that children do not use complementizers initially, even if they are obligatory as they are in German and French.[27] Thus there is *prima facie* evidence that a full CP is not present (although again one can argue for its presence if meta-theoretical arguments from UG require it). The CP could be limited to tense features, which is what Clahsen & Penke (1992) have called the FP. The possibility of such a node with Formal Features, but not exactly the set of adult FF, is precisely the prediction that Merger Theory makes. It would be very natural under the SVO account of Zwart (1993) for Germanic languages to imagine that the child first projects an initial IP and then acquires leftward movement rules that create the SOV order. Once again, a variant of this approach is to state that the reason that the CP does not exhibit complementizers from the outset is that it is underspecified, as Hyams (1994) argues.

4.7. Adjunction as Merger

It is noteworthy that the possibility of Merger is logically independent of the question of whether there is a fixed array of functional categories, and whether the child has this fixed array in the initial state, although Merger Theory suggests that one need not make this assumption. Suppose we had the structure:

(34)

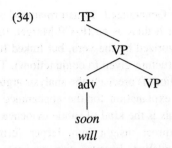

There remains the possibility that the modal is analyzed, briefly, as an adverbial, which is 'tucked in' to that hierarchy, as Lebeaux (p.c.) has suggested, to the existing lexical structure. The meaning is not far from existing adverbs as well: *I soon play* and *I will play* are roughly the same. This is possible under the approach which argues in behalf of iterative Specs as a landing site for movement (see Ura 1994 and Chomsky 1995).[28] Insertion of new nodes between those fixed by UG through meaning (like CP = illocutionary force) is then possible. For instance, under the more abstract theory of phrase structure, the initial operation of movement may not involve movement to a pre-existing CP which would require Spec–head agreement, but a simpler movement to adjoin to VP below CP.

4.8. *Negation as Merger*

Consider now the question of how negation should be represented. Déprez and Pierce (1992) and Haegeman (1994) proceed from the assumption that there is a NEGP which modifies the VP. If the negative modifies the verb, then it follows that the VP must be present. Drozd (1993) argues that the evidence is compatible with a sentence-external form of negation that is different from the typical anaphoric negation. He argues that these forms are equivalent to rejection:

(35)   *No (way) I am going to Chicago.*

Rizzi (1994) and Haegeman (1994) argue in behalf of the TRUNCATION HYPOTHESIS that the NEG appears above some portion of the IP, although Haegeman departs from the view that this is a universal phenomenon.

(36)   *no the sun is shining*   (Bellugi)
         no my play my puppet
         no lamb have it

no dog stay in the room
no Leila have a turn
no Mommy doing
no have it Mommy

And German cases:

(37)   *nein ich putt mache*   (*no I break*)
         nein Auto kaput   (*no car broke*)
         nein dieser Messer auaua   (*no this knife hurt*)
         nein Btasch hunger   (*no uncle hungry*)
         nein dick Baby   (*no fat baby*)

Roeper & Rohrbacher (1994) provide evidence that negation appears without the presence of an AGR-node:

(38)   *no do suitcase*
         no take suitcase
         no hurt head
         no drop boot
         no have one

There are virtually no examples of the form **no runs* where there is AGR but no subject. Roeper & Rohrbacher (1994), based on work by Speas (1993), argue that this is a selection of an option in UG found in Asian languages where AGR can be deleted. Hamann (1994) finds numerous cases in German as well where negation occurs together with infinitives (*nicht essen*).

There are in fact a large variety of locations and functions for negation: sentential negation, constituent negation, VP-negation, word-internal negation (*doubt*), and therefore it is not surprising that the child would not identify them all at once, nor be sure exactly which form a given sentence involves. The phenomenon of negative concord in child language is *prima facie* evidence that some aspect of scope may not be initially fixed, as in this sentence from Adam:

(39)   *no I am not a nothing boy*

How then should one represent early forms of this kind:

(40)   NEG-MP

One possibility is that Merger Theory allows an intermediate representation of precisely this form, linked to specific lexical items. There is a lexical link, since the children appear to use *no* exclusively in English, *nein* in German and *pas* in French. This projection then has the potential to cover an array of negation environments which, at a later point, will be represented by distinct projections.

5. Merger Interpretations

How is the meaning of such forms represented? We would argue again that a general notion of ADVERBIAL MODIFICATION will deliver a meaning that is not precisely equivalent to what an adult LF representation of negation would be, but communicatively adequate. This would be equivalent to:

(41)   *'not my play my trumpet'* = *I play my trumpet notlike*

Possibly we would want to express this as a cleft-type propositional denial:

(42)   *it is not the case that I play my trumpet*

Evidence that the adverbial representation is correct comes from the fact that some of these forms appear in three adverbial positions. After appearing in an initial subject position, where a syntactic feature associated with +adverb is triggered, a second stage shows clear adverbial analysis, where middle and final positions occur (drawn from Roeper 1992):

(43)   *that no fish school*
            I no taste them
            I no want envelope
            he no bite you

(44)   a.   *Peter, die <u>nee</u> (Peter, those no)*
       b.   *touch the snow <u>no</u>*
            book say <u>no</u>

It seems unclear here if *no* or *nein,* or *nee* is a NEG-head or an adverb, like *not* or like *never.*[29] We predict that adverbial negation could occur in medial and final position for the complex elements as well. This is reported for Dutch by Hoekstra & Jordens (1994):

(45)   a.   initial: *<u>kannie</u> zitten*   *(cannot sit)*[30]
       b.   middle: *Mijnie <u>kannie</u> optaan*   *(Mijnie cannot open)*
       c.   final: *opemake <u>kanniet</u>*   *(open make cannot)*

In sum, there is substantial evidence for adjunction prior to final fixation of features.

In general, the full system of negation involves intricate questions about how negative polarity items are learned and linked; there is the potential for many steps in acquisition. The claim here is simply that at the interpretive level a default interpretation may be available which is not fully equivalent to the meaning found in the target language, but still within the range of possibilities expressed by UG. The adverbial interpretation may apply to many of the acquisition Merger Structures.

5.1. *Further Issues in an Acquisition–Merger Theory*

Chomsky argues that Merge is a fundamental operation that reflects CONCEPTUAL NECESSITY. He says that the formation of syntax itself requires that we state a relation of dominance between any two elements interpreted together. From an acquisition perspective, many logically prior issues arise.

First the child must discriminate between word and phrase. There must be *a subword level form of merge* that allows the creation of compounds. We find that either compounds have a head of one kind (known very early to children Clark 1993) or we have unheaded compounds that are interpreted as separate lexical items, like *turncoat* (which means traitor) or *income* which means money. The notion of HEADED-COMPOUND will enable the child to represent a discontinuity: the expression *the truckdriver* entails that the DP-article *the* projected from the NP apply to *driver* but not to *truck*.

The child may not know immediately if word-level or syntax-level Merge is operative for a particular sequence. Suppose we assert:

(46)   WORD-LEVEL MERGE is assumed until evidence forces
          PHRASE-LEVEL MERGE.

Then *truckdriver* will be learned as a word with distinguishable parts without entailing projection of a Spec or COMP.[31] Likewise *I drive truck* could involve a word *drivetruck* (which may occur in polysynthetic languages). Then what ignites a syntactic analysis? Two possibilities exist, which may operate in concert:

(47) a.   Movement, or
      b.   recognition of Formal Features, such as AGR.

When the child recognizes past tense (*-ed* or vowel change), then movement allows *I drove the truck*. The NP and VP nodes would be separated by the necessity of movement.[32]

5.2. *Parentheticals*

Another challenge to the child comes from features of discourse or parentheticals. If a child hears *Yes I will* he must decide on the status of the word *yes* whose distribution is radically different from *no* and varies cross-linguistically. Thus we find that some languages, but not English, allow **I yes will go*.

Therefore the (possible) Formal Features of a word like *yes* must be scrutinized by the child. Does it have the properties of an adverb, a determiner, or a quantifier? These Formal Features are presumably identified from new inputs, if again, parentheticals are eliminated. That is, the sentence *I will — yes indeed — come on Monday.* These phenomena are, once analyzed, marginal for the adult, but they are core issues for a theory of acquisition and they become more powerful under a theory in which an abstract operation like Merge, that applies independent of categories, is called upon.

From this perspective the content of an acquisition device may be reducible to a single operation:

(48)   Fix Formal Feature (FFF).

Features of a Universal Base, Interface conditions, and the requirements of Checking theory would require no learning. The array of sentence-triggers needed to accomplish this task remains an opaque set, but one might expect that it will conform to a theory of triggers of the following kind.

5.3. *Interpretability*

Checking theory involves the features ⟨±Interpretable⟩. Those features which are ⟨+Interpretable⟩ do not require internal 'checking'. In effect, there is EXTERNAL CHECKING, at the interface, and INTERNAL CHECKING, via syntax. We can then make the natural proposal, giving substance to the concept of EPISTEMOLOGY PRIORITY, that elements requiring external checking, the interface itself, are triggered first.

We can advance the acquisition hypothesis:

(49)   Interpretable Features are recognized first ⇒.
            Prediction: substantive elements are interface-interpretable.

It follows that children will instantiate N and V before they instantiate certain AGR- or COMP-node features. We have argued elsewhere (Roeper 1992) that each functional category is itself associated with some interpretable features. That is, CP = illocutionary force, IP = Modality, VP = event, and DP = reference. The illocutionary force feature, which may be visible only through intonation, will entail the projection of a CP-form. Therefore it may be the special features associated with the word *that* which do not arise immediately. It should be noted that we are referring to *logical priority*. Temporal priority may or may not be involved. That is, several logical steps may occur instantenously.

5.4. DP-Acquisition

Let us look more closely at the instantiation of DP. It is a fact that articles appear either dependently or independently. It is possible in German to say: *ich mag den*. But it is impossible in English to say **I like the*. If the child performs FFF for the article, then why does it not allow him or her to say **I like the*. It is true that the child does not hear forms of this kind, but the child also does not hear *goed*, but still produces it. Therefore we must define the identification of articles in such a way that this generalization does not occur. That happens if one generates a higher DP in terms of the properties of a pre-existing NP. Assuming that not all NPs carry a higher DP, the DP must be independently triggered. DP could be automatically triggered by recognition of specificity (see de Villiers & Roeper 1995; Roeper 1995) from context, which is then linked to the NP, justifying a DP-projection.[34] Then the article can be acquired directly as a DP-clitic on an NP, which prevents the English use of **I ate the*. We conclude with the general observation that the domain of possible misanalysis in acquisition requires special scrutiny from a Merger perspective.

6. Conclusion

We have examined various snapshots of sometimes short-lived moments in acquisition. These, we argue, are quickly replicated many times (perhaps over a few days) in ways that our rather crude data-gathering abilities have not easily captured. The existence of a lexically-oriented Merger Theory allows us to represent (1) lexical stages in acquisition, (2) potentially unique maximal projections, (3) potentially unique subcategorizations, (4) the possibility of individual variation, (5) and the existence of 'underspecification' for functional categories. The acquisition data provides unusually sharp evidence for this deep claim about category-formation in Universal Grammar. Capturing such micro-steps in acquisition brings us a step closer to the articulation of a theory of UG that is biologically plausible.

Acknowledgements

Thanks especially to Noam Chomsky who suggested the application of Merger theory to these data. Also Jill de Villiers, Ken Drozd, John Frampton, Zvi

Penner, Ana Perez, Christer Platzack, Susan Powers, Bernhard Rohrbacher, Bonnie Schwartz, Peggy Speas, and Jürgen Weissenborn for various discussions, and to Andrew Radford and two anonymous reviewers for written comments, and finally to Teun Hoekstra and David Lebeaux for discussions at an earlier stage. Also audiences at Utrecht in the Dutch Graduate School, Essex, and UMass to whom these ideas were first presented and who helped sharpen various points.

Notes

1. See Roeper & Rohrbacher (1994) for a discussion in greater depth of economy of representation in acquisition.

2. See Weissenborn *et al.* (in prep.).

3. An exception is the work by Lebeaux (1988), who redeveloped a theory of generalized transformations on the basis of clear acquisition evidence, but much less clear intuitional evidence.

4. See Speas (1992) for discussion of how one might establish alternatives to X-bar theory. Chomsky (p.c.) points out that this approach resembles Categorial Grammar in many respects, but takes a stronger view of how much lexical information projects to a higher node. See Drozd (1993) for the development of categorial perspectives on the acquisition of negation.

5. Hyams (1994). See also Lebeaux (1988), Radford (1990), Penner (1992), Tracy *et al.* (1993), and Rizzi (1994) for pertinent discussion. See Platzack (1993) for a minimalist proposal on the dynamic use of underspecification. See Wijnen (1994) for particularly interesting evidence for lexically sensitive Merger.

6. In Roeper (1992) it is argued that dominance relations, but no head-parametric decision exists.

7. It does not follow that the maximal projections which occur for children are impossible in adult grammars just because they do not occur in any of the known grammars of the world. Were only Asian languages known, UG could easily be formulated to exclude any form of syntactic affixation. UG could easily contain possible unattested adult grammars which might appear in child language forms that diverge from the language being learned.

8. See Collins (1991) and Roeper & Rohrbacher (1994) for discussion.

9. See Chomsky (1995, March version), Chapt. 4, in which he assimilates AGRP to TenseP. This version has been further revised. Chomsky's approach is a further step beyond the approach of Speas (1994) who suggests that AGR is optional.

10. We use AGR for convenience. The analysis does not change under Chomsky (1995) where AGR is in Tense P as a feature in a Multiple-Spec analysis.

11. Davis (1987), Akmajian & Heny (1974), Fletcher (1979), Crain (1984), Otsu (p.c.). See Tracy's (1989) discussion of 'satellite projections' and the syntactic analysis of *oh* which obviously merges with typical syntactic sequences. See Kulikowski (1980) on syntax and 'possible words' analysis of the expression *uh-oh* and its syntactic position.

12. Similar results have been reported for Italian (Bottari *et al.* 1992).
Bottari *et al.* list what they call monosyllabic place-holders in a variety of contexts with hundreds of examples:

(i)   interrogative: *[an] vai ([an] go* = where you go)
[o] fai li ([o] you do there = what you do there)
[e] ta ([e] it stays = where does it stay)

   negative: *[e] centra ([e] there center* = it doesn't fit there)
[e] dico piu ([e] say no more)
[a] c'e ([a] there is (=not there -is = it isn't there)

   preposition: *[a] collo ([a] neck]*
   article: *[en] tata ([en] nanny])*
   clitic: *[e] pettini ([e] you]-comb)*

It is clear that some positions are identified, with obscure semantics, prior to a clear categorical decision.

13. A suggestion proposed in Tracy *et al.* (1993).

14. Chomsky (1994) specifically argues that the adverb positions will be determined by subcategorization and not by the possibility of raising, providing again lexically specific adverbial contrasts:

(i)   a.   *John always reads new books*
   b.   **John reads always new books*
   c.   **John everyday reads new books*
   d.   *John reads everyday new books*

15. Hoekstra & Jordens (1994) also observe that the child uses *kan* independently elsewhere, so the word *kannie* is not the equivalent of *kan*.

16. The notion that a specific syntactic position can be assigned to an element whose category is obscure is buttressed by the use of *well* by children at an early age. There are a number of instances in the first ten files of Adam, such as:

   well but they red

Acquisition of *well* in English (and similar forms like *yes, how, so*) are acquired very early and given a strict initial position, although their syntax remains quite undetermined. See Roeper (1992) for further discussion.

17. This approach should capture much of the variation in acquisition highlighted in the recent volume edited by Tracy & Lattey (1994).

18. See also Sano (1992) and Penner (1993).

19. The absence of a preposition raises the question of how Case is assigned. The answer is not clear, but there is evidence elsewhere in grammar for a default accusative Case. For instance, in answer to a question *who has a hat* we can say either *I do* or *me*. Children begin with *me*. See Abdul-Karem (1994)

20. Radford (1990) also reports the use of nominals without prepositions:
    Wayne go river
    Daddy go van
    gone school
    He considers this to be an instance of direct θ-role projection, as suggested by Lebeaux (1988), which belongs to the family of theories that allows children to project structures that are not pure instances of adult maximal projections.

21. This assumption deserves examination. General inference could lead to the same interpretation as a sentence (as in the game charades). It could be that inference is replaced by phrase structure only at a certain point in acquisition (See Roeper 1982) for discussion).

22. It is also possible that further Φ-features are associated with the affix and it becomes independent (See Rohrbacher 1994), possibly where the second person -*st* is acquired, as Clahsen has often argued.

23. We assume here that the CP contains complementizers and that the V2-effect is an operation on IP-extended IP-structures as Pesetsky (1991) has argued. This is also compatible with the Multiple Spec's analysis proposed by Ura (1994) and Chomsky (1995).

24. Of course, the construction *dass er hat kommen müssen* 'that he has come must' in German is suspiciously similar and suggests SVO-effects in German as well.

25. This implies that PROCRASTINATE may not apply. See Chomsky (1995) for other cases where Procrastinate is violated. See Weissenborn (1993) for discussion of similar constraints.

26. See Schwartz & Sprouse (1995) for other L2 analyses which are amenable to a Merger analysis.

27. Phinney (1981), Weissenborn *et al.* (1991), Penner (1994) and references therein.

28. See Frank (1992) and tag-grammars for extensive formalization and discussion.

29. See Hoekstra & Jordens (1994) for discussion.

30. Hoekstra & Jordens (1994) also note that the stress pattern is like that of adverbs.

31. See Kayne (1994) and Keyser & Roeper (1995) for treatment of some subwordlevel phenomena as involving Spec–Head–Comp. Although we definitely believe that syntactic structures enter the lexicon, the word/phrase distinction must be represented at some level. We will use the intuitive contrast for expository purposes.

32. This avoids complicating issues like the possibility of excorporation (see Rizzi & Roberts 1991). From an acquisition perspective, excorporation should be relegated to a LAST RESORT phenomenon.

33. This could moreover place constraints on how internal and external factors are represented in UG. The options are sufficiently extreme that they may seem not to be required. However it now follows that substantive features read at the Interface cannot be uniformly phonetically empty. That is, no language will have all subjects determined pragmatically by discourse, or as syntactically disjunct Topics. Or no language will lack all Tense reference. This essay is not the place to examine these hypotheses, but their content is fairly straightforward.

34. Language-specific decisions, such as the location of POSS in NP or in the Head of DP may complicate triggering. See Penner & Weissenborn (1995) for evidence of early DP triggering in Swiss German.

References

Abdul-Karem, L. 1994. "Case Acquisition in English and Arabic." Ms., University of Massachusetts, Amherst.

Akmajian, A. & F. Heny, 1973. *An Introduction to Transformational Grammar.* Cambridge, Mass.: MIT Press.

Bach, E. 1971. "Questions." *Linguistic Inquiry* 2.153–167.

Brennan, V. 1991. "Formal Semantics of Telegraphic Speech." *Issues in Psycholinguistics*, ed. by B. Plunkett. Amherst, Mass.: Graduate Linguistic Student Association.

Bottari, P., P. Cipriani & A.M. Chilosi. 1992. "Proto-syntactic Devices in the Acquisition of Italian free Morphology." To appear in *Language Acquisition*.

Brown, R. 1973. *A First Language.* Cambridge, Mass.: Harvard University Press.

Chomsky, N. 1992. "A Minimalist Program for Linguistic Theory." *MIT Occasional Papers in Linguistics* 1.

———. 1994. "Bare Phrase Structure." *MIT Occasional Papers in Linguistics* 5.

———. 1993. "A Minimalist Program for Linguistic Theory." *A View from Building 20*, ed. by S.J. Keyser & K. Hale. Cambridge, Mass.: MIT Press.

———. 1995. "Categories and Transformations." Ms., Massachusetts Institute of Technology, Cambridge.

Cinque, G. 1995. "Adverbs and the Universal Hierarchy of Functional Projections." GLOW Newsletter.

Clark, E. 1993. *The Lexicon in Acquisition.* Cambridge: Cambridge University Press.

Clahsen, H. 1990. "Constraints on Parameter Setting: A grammatical analysis of some stages in German child language." *Language Acquisition* 1. 361–391.

Clahsen, H., S. Eisenbeiss & A. Vainikka. 1994. "The Seeds of Structure: A syntactic analysis of the acquisition of Case-marking." *Language Acquisition Studies in Generative Grammar*, ed. by T. Hoekstra & B.D. Schwartz, 85–118. Amsterdam: John Benjamins.

Clahsen, H. & P. Muysken. 1986. "The Availability of Universal Grammar to Adult and Child Learners." *Second Language Research* 2.93–119.

Collins, C. 1991. "Why and How Come." Ms., Massachusetts Institute of Technology, Cambridge.

Crain, S. & M. Nakayama. 1987. "Structure Dependence in Grammar Formation." *Language* 63.522–543.

Davis, H. 1987. "The Acquisition of the English Auxiliary System and its Relation to Linguistic Theory." Diss., University British Columbia.

Drozd, K. 1993. "Negation in Child Language." Diss., University of Arizona.

Depréz, V. 1994. "Underspecification, functional Projections and Parameter-setting."

Depréz, V. & A. Pierce. 1992. "Negations and Functional Projections in Early Child English." *Linguistic Inquiry* 24.47–85.

Fletcher, P. 1979. "The Development of the Verb Phrase." *Language Acquisition*, ed. by P. Fletcher & M. Garman. Cambridge: Cambridge University Press.

Frank, R. 1992. "Formal Grammar and the Acquisition of Complex Sentences." Ms., University of Pennsylvania.

Frijn, J. & G. de Haan. 1991. "The Development of Movement and Inflection in Dutch." Ms., Utrecht University.

Hamann, C. 1994. "Negation, Infinitives and Heads." Ms., University of Geneva.

Haegeman, L. 1994. "Root Infinitives, Tense and Truncated Structures." Ms., University of Geneva.

Hoekstra, T. & P. Jordens. 1994. "From Adjunct to Head." *Language Acquisition Studies in Generative Grammar*, ed. by T. Hoekstra & B.D. Schwartz, 119–149. Amsterdam: John Benjamins.

Hyams, N. 1994. "V2, Null Arguments and COMP Projections." *Language Acquisition Studies in Generative Grammar*, ed. by T. Hoekstra & B.D. Schwartz, 21–55. Amsterdam: John Benjamins.

Jordens, P. 1990. "The Acquisition of Verb Placement in Dutch and German." *Linguistics*.

Kayne, R. 1994. *The Asymmetry of Syntax*. Cambridge, Mass.: MIT Press.

Keyser, S.J. & T. Roeper. 1995. "Asymmetric Morphology." Ms., University of Massasuchetts, Amherst.

Kulikowski, S. 1980. "A Descriptive Method for Child Language Disability." Diss., School of Education, University of Massachusetts at Amherst.

Lasnik, H. & T. Stowell. 1991. "Weakest Cross-over." *Linguistic Inquiry* 22.687–720.

Lebeaux, D. 1988. "Language Acquisition and the Form of the Grammar." Diss., University of Massachusetts at Amherst.

Maxfield, T. & D. McDaniel. 1992. "What do Children Know without Learning." *Papers in the Acquisition of Wh-*, ed. by T. Maxfield & B. Plunkett. University of Massachusetts Occasional Papers, Special Edition. Amherst, Mass.: Graduate Linguistic Student Association.

Marantz, A. 1994. "A Reader's Guide to 'A Minimalist Program for Linguistic Theory'." To appear in *The Principles and Parameters Approach to Linguistic Theory*, ed. by G. Webelhuth.

McNeill, D. 1970. *The Acquisition of Language*. McGraw-Hill.

Meisel, J. & N. Müller. 1992. "On the Position of Finiteness in Early Child Grammar: Evidence from the simultaneous acquisition of French and German bilinguals. *The Acquisition of Verb Placement: Functional categories and V2 phenomena*, ed. by J. Meisel. Kluwer.

Menyuk, P. 1969. *Sentences Children Use*. Cambridge, Mass.: MIT Press.

Müller, N. 1993. *Komplexe Sätze*. Tübingen: Gunter Narr.

Penner, Z. 1991. "Asking Questions without CPs: Parameters, operations, and syntactic bootstrapping in the acquisition of *wh*-questions in Bernese Swiss German, Standard German and English." Paper presented at GLOW 1991.

——. 1992. "The Ban on Parameter Setting, Default Mechanisms, and the Acquisition of V2 in Swiss German. *The Acquisition of Verb Placement: Functional categories and V2 phenomena*, ed. by J. Meisel. Kluwer.

Perez, A. 1995. "Resumptives in the Acquisition of Relative Clauses." *Language Acquisition* 4.105–139.

——. 1995. "Empty Categories and the Acquisition of *Wh*-Movement." Diss., University of Massachusetts, Amherst.

Pesetsky, D. 1991. "The Earliness Principle." Ms., Massachusetts Institute of Technology, Cambridge.

Phinney, M. 1981. "Syntactic Constraints and the Acquisition of Embedded Sentences." Diss., University of Massachusetts at Amherst.

Platzack, C. 1993. "Parameter Setting and Brain Structure: A minimalist perspective on language acquisition and Attrition From the point of view of Swedish." Ms., Lund University.

Poeppel, D. & K. Wexler. 1993. "The Full Competence Hypothesis of Clause Structure in Early German." *Language* 69.1–33.

Radford, A. 1990. *Syntactic Theory and the Acquisition of English Syntax: The nature of early child grammars of English*. Oxford: Basil Blackwell.

Rizzi, L. 1993. "Early Null Subjects and Root Null Subjects." *Geneva Generative Papers*.

——. 1994. "Some Notes on Linguistic Theory and Language Development: The case of root infinitives." Ms., University of Geneva.

Rizzi, L. & I. Roberts. 1991. "Excorporation." Ms., University of Geneva.

Roeper, T. 1982. "The Role of Universals in the Acquisition of Gerunds." *Language Acquisition: The state of the art*, ed. by E. Wanner & L. Gleitman. Cambridge: Cambridge Universtity Press.

————. 1992. "From the Initial State to V2." *The Acquisition of Verb Placement: Functional categories and V2 phenomena*, ed. by J. Meisel. Kluwer.

Roeper, T. & J. de Villiers. 1992. "The One Feature Hypothesis for Acquisition." Ms., University of Massachusetts at Amherst.

Roeper, T. & B. Rohrbacher. 1994. "Null Subjects in Early Child English and the Theory of Economy of Projection." Paper presented at Bern, Switzerland, January.

Schwartz, B. & R. Sprouse. 1995. "Cognitive States and the Full Transfer/Full Access Model." *Second Language Research* (in press).

Speas, M. 1990. *Phrase Structure in Natural Language*. Dordrecht: Kluwer.

————. 1994. "Null Arguments in a Theory of Economy of Projection." *Functional Projections*, ed. by E. Benedicto & J. Runner. *University of Massachusetts Occasional Papers* 17.

Stowell, T. 1981. "The Origins of Phrase Structure." Diss., Massachusetts Institute of Technology, Cambridge.

Thornton, R. 1995. "Referentiality and *Wh*-Movement in Child English: Juvenile D-linkuency." *Language Acquisition* 4.1/2.

Tracy, R. 1994. "Raising questions: Formal and Functional Aspects of the Acquisition of *Wh*-Questions in German." *How Tolerant is Grammar* ed. by R. Tracy & E. Lattey. Tübingen: Niemeyer.

Tracy, R., Z. Penner & J. Weissenborn. 1993. "On the Acquisition of *auch* 'also, too' in German and Bernese Swiss German and its Consequences for the Development of Grammar." Paper presented in Trieste.

Ura, H. 1994. "Varieties of Raising and the Feature-based Phrase-Structure Theory." *MIT Occasional Papers in Linguistics* 7.

Vainikka, A. 1994. "Case in the Development of English Syntax." *Language Acquisition*.

Villiers, J. de. 1991. "Why Questions." *Papers in The acquisition of Wh*, ed. by Maxfield & Plunkett.

Villiers, J. de & B. Plunkett. (submitted). Children show Superiority in asking *wh*-questions.

Villiers, J. de & T. Roeper. 1992. "The One Feature Hypothesis." Ms., University of Massachusetts at Amherst.

————. 1994. "Lexical Links in the *Wh*-Chain." *Binding, Dependencies and Learnability*, ed. by B. Lust, G. Hermon, & J. Kornfilt. Hilldale, N.J.: Lawrence Erlbaum.

Watanabe, A. 1992. "*Wh*-in-situ, Subjacency, and Chain Formation." Ms., Massachusetts Institute of Technology, Cambridge.

Wexler, K. 1994. "Optional Infinitives, Head Movement and the Economy of Derivations." *Verb Movement*, ed. by D. Lightfoot & N. Hornstein. Cambridge: Cambridge University Press 305–350.

Weissenborn, J. 1993. "Mommy's Sock Almost Fits: Constraints on Children's Grammars." Paper presented at ICSCL, Trieste.

Weissenborn, J. & Z. Penner. This volume. "Strong Continuity and the Acquisition of DP."

Weissenborn, J., T. Roeper & J. de Villiers. 1991. "The Acquisition of *Wh*-Movement in German and French." *Papers in the Acquisition of Wh*, ed. by T. Maxfield & B. Plunkett.

Weissenborn, J., J. de Villiers & T. Roeper. In prep. "The Acquisition of Superiority in English and German."

Wijnen, F. 1994. "Incremental Acquisition of Phrase Structure: A longitudinal analysis of verb placement in Dutch Child Language." Ms., University of Groningen.

Zwart, J. 1993. "Dutch Syntax: A minimalist approach." Diss., Groningen University.

Now, Hang on a Minute
Some reflections on emerging orthodoxies

Martin Atkinson
University of Essex

In this discussion, I want to focus on a small number of issues which seem to me to be pivotal in currently popular approaches to syntactic development. These all have something to do with the question of whether grammatical development is subject to a continuity condition and the related matter of the nature of DEVELOPMENTAL MECHANISMS. In flavor they embrace the conceptual and the methodological, while occasionally touching on the technical. I begin by offering some coarse-grained descriptions of the issues.

Among the most urgent problems exercising those working in first language acquisition at the moment is the status of developmental continuity and the linked notion of full competence. A survey of recent influential contributions to the field, including some appearing in this volume (e.g. those of Haegeman, Hyams, Harris & Wexler and Penner & Weissenborn), suggests that the proposal that the child embarks on grammatical development with a complete (in some sense) system of syntactic representation is widely supported. One consequence of this view is that development does not involve any theoretically significant discontinuity, and this is viewed by supporters of the position as an unashamedly good thing. Section 1 tries to get some perspective on what the continuity issues are and why people care about them so.

A bit more subversively, Sections 2–5, in different ways, seek to establish the possibility that, taking account of the evidence currently available, the popular continuity stance just might be wrong. In Section 2, I target the status of the *data* which have been particularly important in establishing the plausibility of full competence, whereas Section 3 focuses on temporal sequencing and the perils surrounding phrases like "the earliest stage of grammatical development." In Section 4, I bring together some of the evidence which is not easily accommodated in full competence accounts, and Section 5 assesses some of the developmental debts which the continuity position incurs.

It has recently become increasingly fashionable to back up claims about the distribution of this or that construction in a corpus of child speech by citing figures. Indeed, Radford (this volume) reports the opinion of a reviewer of his paper that deliberations and hypotheses not supported by figures are pretty much worthless. Radford's response to this is to note the potential importance of infrequently occurring constructions, an importance he sloganizes as: "every utterance counts." Well, I think this is wrong, and, of course, in his less confrontational moments Radford thinks that it is wrong too; he states it because he wants to oppose it to another slogan which he thinks is even more wrong: "count every utterance." Whether he's right to think that the latter is more wrong, I don't know. I'll settle for it being as wrong as the slogan he favors and Section 6 considers some of the issues surrounding the use and misuse of figures.

Finally, notions of minimalism and reliance on this or that minimalist framework are playing an increasingly important role in acquisition discussions. Instances can be found in a number of contributions to this volume and Harris and Wexler, Roeper, Radford, Haegeman, Platzack and Clahsen, Eisenbeiss and Penke all line up behind some minimalist concept or other during their presentations. There are obvious reasons for this emerging emphasis, residing in the parent linguistic theories from which acquisition scholars draw their inspiration, but there is also some attendant uncertainty. Most sharply, Harris and Wexler are strong supporters of full competence, but Radford, and in a somewhat different way, Clahsen, Eisenbeiss and Penke, favor a structure building approach.[1] If full competence and structure building are incompatible (and, surely, they ought to be, or what is all the fuss about?) and if *both* are consistent with minimalism, something requires clarification. In Section 7, I shall have a brief go at sorting out some of this uncertainty. We begin, then, with continuity and related matters.

1. Continuity, Full Competence and Developmental Mechanisms

To oppose the Full Competence Hypothesis for the purposes of this discussion, I shall rely on the structure building approach of Radford (1990, 1994, this volume). I am not concerned with the possibility that early grammars could be inconsistent with principles of Universal Grammar (Felix 1984), and I shall have nothing to say on the question of whether parameters are always correctly set at the first time of asking or can be re-set having been mis-set, an issue which Penner and Weissenborn (this volume) use to distinguish between what they refer to as Strong and Weak Continuity positions (cf. note 1 for a quite different sense of WEAK CONTINUITY). Nor am I going to rely on the details of Radford's, or anyone else's structure building story beyond utilizing the claim that there is a stage in syntactic development at which the child's grammar contains no functional category projections. Rather, I wish to use the general properties of structure building accounts to try to identify the perceived strengths (and ultimately, weaknesses) of full competence proposals. To get started on this, I need to say something about developmental mechanisms.

One of the propositions on which people find it easy to agree is that, if, contrary to the Full Competence Hypothesis, we suppose that certain aspects of grammatical representations are not around at day zero, then we have to account for how they show up when they do.[2] Accepting this responsibility is tantamount to taking seriously the DEVELOPMENTAL aspect of language acquisition study. But since nobody seems able to offer any sort of learning story for how aspects of grammatical representations might emerge, we're rapidly driven in the direction of suggesting that they mature.

Now, maturation, as a mechanism responsible for syntactic development, has had a mixed press recently, although, as we shall see, for it to work its mysteries outside formal syntax appears to be palatable enough for some (see Section 5). Given a role in the syntactic arena, it appears to grate on some scientific sensibility or other, and consequently a discontinuity position starts off in bad methodological odor. The steps from no discontinuity to continuity and thence to Full Competence are not giant ones. So, if our target is to air some uncertainties about Full Competence, we're going to have to confront these sensibilities. On the whole, it doesn't seem to me that methodological arguments can (or, indeed, should) get us very far, but as they have been invoked in support of the Full Competence Hypothesis, it would be imprudent not to have a quick look.

Here's how it goes in the abstract. We collect our data from two periods in the acquisition of grammar. If our two periods are sufficiently far apart, these sets of data will exhibit rather clear qualitative differences, and we construct grammars, G_1 and G_2, somehow reflecting the properties of our data sets. What would we wish to say about the general characteristics of G_1 and G_2?

One answer to this question which is unlikely to ruffle too many feathers holds that G_1 and G_2 are both possible grammars in that they are both constrained by the principles of UG.[3] Now, even at this early point we get to make a choice, but it's a choice which is not often advertised. One view of UG, the one that informs the consensus we are starting from, has it that any possible grammar instantiates the full set of functional categories which the theory makes available (in the relevant respects, $G_1 = G_2$). Accordingly, if the data informing the construction of G_1 do not contain *prima facie* evidence for the existence of functional category projections, the search is on for evidence which is perhaps not quite *prima facie*. As might be anticipated, quite a bit of what follows is about the pursuit of this strategy, and about the extent to which it has been successful.

But back to the choice. There are views around (for example, Fukui 1986, 1993) that UG allows some grammars to eschew some functional categories.[4] Specifically, from Fukui's perspective, any functional system which does not play an interpretive role at LF is a candidate for grammatical neglect, and he argues that Japanese is largely distinguished from English by virtue of lacking C and AGR. He goes on a bit about the difficulties of distinguishing the claim that these categories are not present from the view that they are present but somehow inert, but I don't see any good reasons for regarding this issue as anything other than a dead duck. So, if Fukui's views form our starting point, there is nothing pathological (from the perspective of UG) about an early child grammar lacking C and AGR. I guess this observation is not so much method-ological as ethical: let's not close our minds to alternative construals of UG simply because they don't originate in the right corridors.

Putting the choice behind us, here is a blatantly methodoiogical perspective on the same issue. Some (e.g. Crain 1991; Hyams 1994) are attracted by what we might refer to as the MINIMIZE DEGREES OF FREEDOM PRINCIPLE. Effectively, this says that embracing a maturational discontinuity should be a last resort, since the suggestion that two stages of development might not be identically constrained admits an additional degree of freedom into the accounts available to us — the very construction of our theories becomes too easy, one might suppose, since anything goes. Indeed, Hyams (*op. cit*) seems to sense a multi-plicity of routes for making life too easy, since she refers to the Continuity Hypothesis as having "*far fewer* degrees of freedom ..." (p. 22, my emphasis — MA). The general position she favors is boldly stated (pp. 21–22):

> While maturation of functional categories is in principle possible, it is not the optimal working hypothesis. A much stronger (sic) claim would be that children's grammars have the same basic form as adult grammars and are constrained by the same principles of grammar.

Now, it would be foolish not to join with the spirit of this manoeuvre, but in welcoming it, it is important to note that, like all methodological prescriptions, it carries as an adjunct a *ceteris paribus* clause. And just how equal everything else is might give us pause for thought.

Here's a straightforward way to illustrate what I'm on about. Another methodological principle we ought to find attractive is the Principle of Evidence: theoretical constructs should be supported by evidence. This is, of course, pretty venerable, one of its antecedents being the Principle of Parsimony formulated in the nineteenth century by the British biologist, Lloyd Morgan in response to the excesses resulting from the extension of the constructs of Wundtian psychology to animal consciousness (Mackenzie 1977). And it only gets into serious trouble when people start getting prescriptive about what is and is not evidence, the history of behaviorist psychology in the first half of this century offering a notorious lesson in this regard.[5] As I've already observed above, if data do not immediately provide evidence for certain aspects of a theory, ingenuity can be brought to bear and we can be persuaded that the relevant evidence exists. But it is easy to contemplate the failure of ingenuity, and in such circumstances, the Principle of Evidence may collide with the Minimize Degrees of Freedom Principle.[6]

In optimistic vein, we will suppose that conflicts such as that alluded to in the previous paragraph can be rationally resolved — the *ceteris paribus* clauses are there precisely so that they can be vigorously massaged when circumstances demand it. But, and this is the point, there is no particularly forceful methodological prohibition against maturational, discontinuous accounts of acquisition. More specifically, there is nothing in my manual which tells me I must massage the *ceteris paribus* clause associated with my Principle of Evidence before I contemplate messing about with that adjoined to my Minimize Degrees of Freedom Principle. Methodological shots are pretty cheap, which is one reason why I don't want to rely on them too much; but I don't think that others should be allowed to get away with much on the basis of them either.

Poeppel & Wexler (1993) offer some observations on maturation which can usefully be introduced at this point. They say (18):

> ... the Full Competence Hypothesis has no developmental question associated with it (except for the optional infinitive problem) whereas theories which assume less than full competence would have to explain how the missing or wrong properties were learned or matured.

Putting aside the optional infinitive problem to Section 5, this remark recasts
Hyams' worry in terms of explanatory load; a maturational account carries with
it an additional burden of explanation. Nor is this emphasis exclusive to the
work of Wexler and his colleagues. Clahsen, Penke & Parodi (1993), in a paper
which in other respects takes issue with some of the major claims of Poeppel &
Wexler, reiterate this specific theme when they say (400):

> The idea that the child's grammar generates a complete phrase structure tree ... in the
> earliest stage of syntactic development does not create any learnability problems ...,
> whereas under the other approaches, one has to *explain*, for example, how the CP-layer
> is acquired .... (my emphasis — MA)

It is important to get some sense of what is being called for here. Suppose, for
concreteness and counter to Full Continuity, that we are persuaded that some
aspect of grammatical representation, say the system of C-projections, is not
available to the child at some early stage of development. Our options for
dealing with this situation are rather limited.

Consider first a LEARNING account. This would maintain that the child's
primary linguistic data provide an adequate inductive basis for the testing of
hypotheses about the existence of C and its properties. Identifying the relevant
aspects of these data and articulating the process the child uses to engage them
would, in some sense, constitute an EXPLANATION of how C gets into the
grammar in the way it does. But there is also a sense in which this would *not*
constitute an explanation of the acquisition of C. Why is this? Because, as has
been eloquently argued on many occasions by Fodor (e.g. 1975), theories of
learning, when sufficiently explicit, require the learner to be able to formulate
hypotheses to test against data. For the case in hand, these hypotheses would
have to contain reference to C and its properties, and to this extent, learners
already have C in their representational systems. Furthermore, the classic
"triggering problem" (Hyams, this volume) immediately arises — if the child
has the ability to represent C and its properties, why is its consolidation in the
grammar protracted? In short, even within a learning account, it appears that we
are driven to seek alternative mechanisms to deal with protracted aspects of
acquisition.

Maturation is an alternative mechanism.[7] So now consider the proposal that
the reason for the child's early grammar not containing a C-system is that at that
stage, the child's representational capacities do not include C at all — these
capacities mature, and, only when they have matured, is the child able to figure
out the properties of C as instantiated in the local noise. The process of figuring

out the properties of C, once the latter is available, may of course yield to familiar notions of explanation, although in the context of well-known observations about rapidity and absence of logically possible errors, it seems likely that any LEARNING that goes on here will be within a tightly constrained set of options. But it is not at all clear what more can be legitimately called for as far as the very emergence of C itself is concerned. Arguably, it just is a feature of the structure of the human mind that at some biologically scheduled point, a novel representational capacity becomes available. Explanations of this process may be sought one (or more) levels down in biology, but the psychologist or linguist has no responsibility in this regard.

Putting things as I have above could well contribute to persuading critics that resorts to maturation are not only too easy but are also deeply dissatisfying; they do not stop at refusing to offer explanations but have the nerve to go on to seek *principled* grounds for this refusal. To close this section, I'll try to put a more optimistic construal on maturational accounts.

The position I am subscribing to above is, in some respects, not dissimilar from that arrived at by Fodor (1981:313) in his discussion of the acquisition of concepts, a process which "you can't [understand] by doing conceptual analysis .... *You have to go and look*" (italics in original). Now, going and looking is not a very lofty pursuit and I can already hear the howls that this is a retreat from theory, a reversion to an unambitious form of empirical enquiry and so on. I am not impressed, and here are a couple of reasons why.

First, it does not follow from the fact that we cannot deepen a maturational account to the point where it takes on some additional explanatory character that we cannot formulate predictions from it. For concreteness, suppose we have two representational capacities, X and Y, and our "going and looking" at the acquisition of L leads us to the conclusion that X becomes available before Y. Naturally, if this is a maturational sequence, it should survive transporting across linguistic boundaries, and we immediately predict the occurrence of the same developmental sequence universally. Intriguingly, of course, this will not always be a straightforward question to investigate, since X and Y will only be manifest via their properties, these properties may vary and figuring out these properties may be differentially difficult. Thus, there might be *prima facie* evidence for X not preceding Y in L' or, perish the thought, Y preceding X. But we have already noted that ingenuity can, and should, play its part too, and I see no reason why this should not lead to fun and interesting fun.

Secondly, investigation of the type envisaged will take place against the background of a linguistic theory. Now, I find the full competence stuff a bit slavish (in spirit if not in letter) here; what subscribers seem to be excited by is the prospect of producing an additional kind of support for the details of a theory developed on the basis of orthodox linguistic methodology. That's OK, of course, but, dare I suggest, a bit dull. As an alternative, suppose that we are persuaded by "going and looking" that two capacities, previously unrelated in the parent theory, become available simultaneously in a variety of acquisition contexts. The natural consequence would be to examine the appropriateness of regarding these capacities as distinct; thereby, we might in principle contribute to linguistic theory, a surefire antidote to rampant dissatisfaction (cf. note 3 for an example of where Borer and Wexler use *non*-simultaneity of emergence of A-chains and $\overline{A}$-chains to reinforce the view that there is a significant *theoretical* difference between these constructs). It is again tempting to let Fodor (1981: 315–316) speak for a perspective which, I am suggesting, may be of considerable interest in various ways: "Our ethology promises to be quite interesting even if our developmental psychology turns out to be a little dull."

One final observation on maturation. Everyone working on acquisition from a serious linguistic perspective seems to be persuaded by the Chomskian perspective on the nature of the linguistic enterprise. At some level of abstraction, we are all doing theoretical biology. Now, my biology is not up to much, but I have a sneaking feeling that most biologists would probably view maturation as the norm in the development of complex biological systems. We might, then, somewhat cheekily, invoke a further methodological principle specific to the problem domain of developmental biology. Let's call it the UNIFORMITY OF OBJECTS PRINCIPLE and give it content along the lines of: every complex biological system matures. Starting from this principle, the Full Continuity folk ought to be on the defensive and Ken Wexler should be writing an alternative version of this section.

In conclusion, methodological perspectives are a pretty mixed up lot and we aren't going to get a lot of clear prescription from them in the face of real problems. On anyone's scenario, evidence is going to matter an awful lot, so let's now turn our attention to this.

2.   The Evidence for Continuity — Optional Infinitives

One of the rocks on which the Full Competence Hypothesis is founded is the existence of the Optional Infinitive Stage (Wexler 1994) as the "earliest" stage of syntactic development. I shall have a bit to say about timing and the sense of "earliest" in the next section, but here I want to seek to justify some caution regarding the very existence of this stage. Addressing this question, Harris & Wexler (this volume: 2) suggest that "in many languages [it] is by now fairly uncontroversial" and this is echoed in a variety of sources (e.g. Krämer 1993; Rizzi 1994).

In a paper which is often seen as providing fundamental support for the existence of this stage, it is recruited to oppose a structure building approach (Poeppel & Wexler 1993: 21):

> It is now widely recognized by many that at least one functional projection is necessary to account for even the simplest facts of very early grammar.

It is noteworthy that the language employed in much discussion reeks of confidence; we do not here confront tentative suggestion nor are we beating the trail where some evidence has been carefully considered which is consistent with the conclusion that small children have the finite/non-finite distinction. No, to give one example, Poeppel & Wexler (1993) have "demonstrated" the representation of the distinction in young children's developing grammars (Krämer 1993: 197). Furthermore, the consequences for an approach which does not subscribe to the very early existence of functional category projections are dire — such an approach becomes untenable.

Overall, I think we should be persuaded of the existence of the Optional Infinitive Stage (but not of the demise of a structure building account, which will be the topic of the next two sections) and of the importance of understanding its nature. However, to be so persuaded is not to swallow all of the advertising. Particularly, I believe that the major contributions of Poeppel & Wexler (1993) and Wexler (1994) are not as compelling as some would suggest.

Let's start with French, which, along with German, is most frequently cited as providing convincing evidence for the Optional Infinitive Stage. The key observation from Pierce (1989) is that in the data she studied, children produced both finite and non-finite forms of lexical verbs in matrix clauses and these had systematically different distributions with respect to the negative morpheme *pas*; specifically, ⟨+finite⟩ verb forms appeared before *pas*, whereas ⟨–finite⟩ forms occurred after *pas*. These distributions are then taken to indicate that French-speaking children at this stage have control of the ⟨±finite⟩ distinction and know that ⟨+finite⟩ forms must raise so as to be within the domain of an appropriate functional projection above *pas*.

Pierce's generalization is based on quantitative evidence as summarized in the table in (1) (from Wexler 1994: 310):

(1)	⟨+finite⟩	⟨–finite⟩
pas verb	11	77
verb *pas*	185	2

In Wexler's discussion, this table is accompanied by illustrative examples, and what we might suppose is that these examples will have been chosen so as to most straightforwardly support the claims being made — why make life difficult for the sympathetic reader? What do we find?

For the infinitive examples, all contain *pas* followed by an *-er* infinitive. But, as is well known, the *-er* infinitive in French is homophonous with both the past participle form and the second person plural finite form, which is also used in imperatives.[8] Less ambivalent examples backing up the quantitative data might have included common French verbs such as *voir* 'see', *venir* 'come', *dormir* 'sleep', *prendre* 'take' and *faire* 'do'.

In the context of the above, it is of interest to note that Wexler (1994) found one example of *voir* in Pierce's data:

(2)   *voir   l'auto   papa*
       (to) see the car daddy

But there are two observations to make about this example. First, *voir* does not here co-occur with *pas*, so the example is irrelevant to the major point at issue; secondly, Wexler notes that Pierce does not discuss such verb types explicitly, so we do not know how many examples like this appeared in her data. In a study pioneering quantitative techniques this is not a trivial weakness.

A similar response is appropriate to Wexler's (*op. cit.*) discussion of *-ir* infinitives in Pierce's data. He cites eight of these, *none of which co-occurs with the negative marker*, thereby rendering their significance to the issue of whether the children had verb raising opaque.[9] And once again, he cannot quantify the occurrences of infinitives of this type in the original data sets.

On the basis of the above, I feel justified in being a bit cautious about the Optional Infinitive Stage in French. From the table in (1), we would appear to have 77 tokens which exemplify infinitive verb forms following *pas*. Yet, it seems that the infinitive status of the vast majority (possibly all) of these tokens only follows from discourse interpretations which were not formulated against the background of the hypothesis being considered. Furthermore, the near total non-appearance in the appropriate context of verb forms which would offer much less equivocal support for the generalization at issue is somewhat puzzling. Of course, this could be a mere sampling deficiency, but 77 is quite a large number, certainly large enough for me to wish to see a further detailed study of the relevant stage in the acquisition of French *with this specific hypothesis in mind*.

The case for German exhibiting an Optional Infinitive Stage, the structural consequences of which are that matrix finite verbs appear in second position whereas matrix infinitives are clause final is rather robust. However, the details of Poeppel & Wexler (1993) and Wexler (1994) still give me one or two itches which I want to scratch occasionally, so here goes.

The regularly cited contingency table from Poeppel & Wexler (1993: 7) appears as (3):[10]

(3)	⟨+finite⟩	⟨−finite⟩
V2	197	6
Vfinal	11	37

Again, this table is illustrated by a small number of examples, but what is of interest to me here is the criterion Poeppel & Wexler adopted for assigning a verb form to the ⟨±finite⟩ categories. They say (1993: 6):

> The criteria for classifying an utterance as finite or not were straightforward. If there was an *-en* ending in the verb stem (canonical infinitival morphology), the utterance counted as ⟨−finite⟩.... Otherwise the form counted as ⟨+finite⟩.

This is clear enough, and Poeppel & Wexler point out that the *-en* finite forms which signal first and third person plural agreement are not a confounding factor, as appropriate subjects for these forms were very rare in their data, always occurring with inappropriate singular agreement. There is, however, a residual worry which can be best illustrated in the light of an example cited in Wexler (1994, 314):

(4)	*Caesar tieg e nich*	'Caesar kriegt er nicht'
	Caesar gets he not	'He's not getting Caesar'

This is one of two examples chosen to illustrate the child's use of ⟨+finite⟩ verbs, and once again, it might be supposed that such examples would be as clear as possible. In (4), *tieg* obviously satisfies Poeppel & Wexler's criterion for being ⟨+finite⟩ — there is not an *-en* suffix in sight. But there is no other signal that it is ⟨+finite⟩ beyond the observation that it occurs in second position, and it is transparent that this cannot be invoked as a criterion in this context.

Now, I don't know what the facts are here — that's why I'm scratching my itch — but the *dangers* are pretty apparent. Suppose that we reverse the Poeppel & Wexler criterion and instead of focusing on the infinitival inflection, regard the appearance of non-infinitival inflections as criterial for finiteness, all other verb forms being assigned to the ⟨–finite⟩ category. We should first ask: what difference would this make to the contingency table? Clearly, (4) above would now contribute to a cell disconfirming Poeppel & Wexler's main hypothesis, but we do not know how many other utterances would shift. Suppose the significant differences hold up after we've shifted things around; then, my itch is appropriately scratched and my major worry about Poeppel & Wexler's argument disappears. Alternatively, suppose they don't; then, I'm left with the uncomfortable feeling that a non-overt criterion for finiteness in the Poeppel & Wexler discussion is POSITION.[11]

I conclude this section by looking briefly at the status of the arguments for an Optional Infinitive Stage in other languages, as these arguments have been presented by Wexler (1994).

The data from Dutch on which Wexler (1994) bases his claims are abstracted from Weverink (1989). Wexler cites four examples of both finite and non-finite verb forms, seeking to establish the same positional contingencies as are found in early German. A legitimate expectation might again be that these examples would be straightforward, but it is perhaps revealing that in the ⟨+finite⟩ set, one is a two-constituent utterance with the finite verb in final (as well as second) position (*baaby slaapt* 'baby sleeps') while another has it in initial position (*wou Tobiasje hebben,* 'wanted T. have'). Regarding the latter, Wexler refers to Weverink's argument that this is an example of topic drop, so the verb is actually in second position, and, while I am ready to suppose that this is a plausible argument, the fact remains that in a set of examples chosen to illustrate a major claim, two out of four of them require additional commentary in order to be seen as performing their intended function. Naturally, quantitative statements could easily allay my worries in this connection, but these statements are not available, and in these circumstances, Wexler's conclusion (1994: 317) that "The evidence seems quite strong that there is an optional infinitive stage in Dutch, as in French and German", is perhaps a little premature.

Consideration of the interaction of finiteness and negation in mainland Scandinavian languages forms a further focus of Wexler (1994). He cites Plunkett & Strömqvist (who are in turn citing Lange & Larsson), as providing three examples consistent with Swedish having an Optional Infinitive Stage: two of these examples exhibit the order V[+fin]–Neg, as predicted by a grammar containing the finite/non-finite distinction and obligatory raising of ⟨+finite⟩ verbs, and one has Neg—V[–fin]. Now, while these examples are suggestive, the numbers are far from compelling, and the same is true for another Swedish child described by Wexler but without illustrative examples.

For Danish and Norwegian too, Wexler (1994) relies on Plunkett & Strömqvist. He is able to cite small numbers of examples which are consistent with the children having verb raising for finite forms, but there are also numerous complications raised in footnotes. My own view is that the discussion of Mainland Scandinavian is useful and suggestive but that Wexler's own conclusion is hardly justified on the basis of the data he considers. He says (1994: 328):

> ... the data from six mainland Scandinavian children, two each from Swedish, Danish and Norwegian, *strongly confirm* the predictions of the optional infinitive stage.' (my emphasis — MA)

A problem with this way of putting things is that it might pre-empt further investigation of what, to my mind, remains an open question. I believe that we desperately need more hypothesis-led, intensive data collection from the appropriate periods of acquisition of a number of the languages referred to in this section. I shall not be surprised if this activity totally vindicates the Optional Infinitive Stage, but I do not feel that we should be too ready to accept the statement which Harris and Wexler make (this volume: 6):

> It has been shown by Wexler ... that children acquiring French, German, Dutch, Swedish, Norwegian and Danish all go through an optional infinitive stage.

Arguably, *some* of this has been shown; unarguably, not *all* of it has.

To close this section, it is perhaps worth noting that if we accept the view that non-inflected verb forms in English are just infinitives, thereby establishing that English-speaking children also go through a stage at which they use both ⟨+finite⟩ and ⟨–finite⟩ verbs in matrix clauses, I should also be jousting with the arguments of Harris & Wexler (this volume) that English-speaking children pass through an Optional Infinitive Stage. I want to do this, but for reasons which will, I hope, become clear, I want to put off doing it until Section 6.

3. On Difficulties in Knowing What We Are Talking about

At the beginning of the previous section, I introduced the Optional Infinitive Stage as the "earliest" stage of syntactic development. In this section, I shall worry about whether everyone is talking about the same thing, when they use "earliest" in this and similar contexts. First blush, indeed, any blush would suggest that this should not be an issue. But practice indicates that it almost certainly is, so something needs to be done about it.

It seems to me that there are a number of instances in the literature, where misunderstandings based on the usage of this and similar phrases are evident; and there are other examples where arguments to establish the existence of functional category systems are, shall we say, somewhat misleading in this respect. The flavor of this section, then, is not argument in any serious sense, but what might be regarded as the politics of exposition.

Let's start with a conflict which has already been aired. Poeppel & Wexler (1993) is a study of a corpus produced by Andreas, a German-speaking child, aged 2;1. The fundamental claim of the analysis, noted in the previous section, is that this corpus signals a highly significant correlation between verb placement and finiteness. Summarizing this, Poeppel & Wexler say (pp. 6–7):

> We infer from this analysis that the finiteness distinction is made correctly *at the very
> earliest stages of grammatical development* (my italics — MA).

Nor are Poeppel & Wexler alone in proposing this In-The-Beginning character for the Optional Infinitive Stage and all its consequences. Rizzi (1994: 373) is persuaded enough to say that children are exhibiting the appropriate Optional Infinitive characteristics "... from the beginning of their linguistic production ..." But what precisely is appropriately regarded as "the beginning of linguistic production"?

There are, of course, standard measures used in the literature for assigning children to stages (notably MLU somehow computed), and it is noteworthy that Poeppel & Wexler do not report an MLU for the Andreas corpus. It is possible to offer some sort of estimate on the basis of figures they cite, but this would be at best a crude guess, and it is perhaps more revealing to note that some of the examples they provide in support of Andreas not only having a finite/non-finite distinction signalled by movement of the finite verb to a functional projection, but also tokens of XP-movement into (Spec-CP) are, intuitively, at any rate, rather complex.[12] I have in mind such examples as (5) (Poeppel & Wexler 1993: 23):

(5)   *den tiegt a nich wieda*
         [glossed as 'he can't get that one again']

If there is evidence that such examples are not "routines", and in citing them at all, Poeppel & Wexler would appear to be committed to this, it seems to me that this is *prima facie* evidence that this child is *not* "at the very earliest stages of grammatical development."

Interestingly, this view is echoed by Clahsen, Penke & Parodi (1993). Commenting on Poeppel & Wexler's claim that the system of C-projections is available very early, they say (p. 401): "We think that the data from Poeppel & Wexler ... represent a later stage of syntactic development in German." Clahsen *et al.*, correctly in my view, believe that it is possible to identify an earlier phase of syntactic development than that studied by Poeppel & Wexler, and it is worth considering briefly how they proceed in this respect.

In their study, Clahsen *et al.* work from a number of corpora, for each of which they compute an MLU (in words). For them, any corpus with MLU ≤ 1.75 satisfies their criterion for representing the "earliest stage". This has the virtue of being clear, and Clahsen *et al.* are explicit in the status they assign to this stage (p. 403):

> We consider the period of development at which children produce word combinations (i.e. the two-word stage) to represent the earliest stage of syntactic development. In this study, we rely on a fairly standard criterion for determining the two-word stage: MLU should not exceed 1.75 ...

But note that even here, there is a cheerful naivety behind the notion that "the two-word stage" is a meaningful construct which needs independent operationalization via MLU measures and that "the two-word stage" can be identified with the earliest phases of grammatical development.

In fact, elementary arithmetic can rapidly embarrass Clahsen *et al.*'s position, particularly as they have earlier referred to the two-word stage as "the first stage exhibiting word combinations" (p. 397). It is clear that for children displaying an MLU of, say, 1.50, 50% of their utterances will be of 2 words (assuming that there are no three– or more-word utterances at this stage). Arguably, even this is inappropriately labeled the *earliest* stage of grammatical development, since typically a child will have utilized productive word combinations before reaching this MLU level. In short, it appears that there is a rather straightforward issue here, and that the main hurdle in addressing it may be practical — the intensity of data collection necessary to collect usable corpora from very young children is likely to be considerable with the obvious implications for expenditure of money and (sometimes unrewarding) effort. But if it is not done, talk of the earliest stage(s) of grammatical development is unlikely to generate anything other than unproductive dispute.[13]

The difficulties to which I have alluded above can be discerned in spades in part of the discussion appearing in Hyams (1994). In this paper, Hyams offers a range of evidence, including reference to the acquisition of the finite/non-finite distinction, suggesting that children acquiring a variety of languages *at a certain stage of development* have grammars containing the full set of functional categories. One of her arguments is specifically concerned with what she refers to as "the COMP system" and relies on citing data from Klima and Bellugi's

(1966) Stage C. The aim is to use the fact that English-speaking children's
wh–questions have "V-above-subject" at this stage indicating that their grammars
must contain a C position and its specifier. For the purposes of this discussion,
we can assume that the argument is sound.

The relevant observation here is that the mean age of the children instantiating Klima and Bellugi's Stage C was 3;0! Accordingly, there is no difficulty
whatsoever in accepting Hyams' conclusion that (28): "... the evidence from the
development of questions in English argues that children at this stage do have
a COMP system." But it is difficult to see that this conclusion is relevant to the
question of whether children's grammars contain functional systems at the
earliest stages of development. I believe that the conclusion is *totally irrelevant*
to this claim.

What it is tempting to conclude from examples such as this and others that
could be cited is that investigators appear fairly happy to plunder data from a
period which extends from before the second birthday to the third and to regard
these as germane to understanding the earliest stages of syntactic development.
Naturally, there is no *descriptive* reason why this period should not be characterized as the "earliest stage of grammatical development", but in circumstances
where there are massive overt changes through the period, it is not clear that it
is anything other than misleading to do so.

4. Concessions

Taking the observations of the previous two sections seriously, we confront
a situation where children acquiring a variety of languages pass through a stage
at which they use both finite and non-finite verb forms in matrix clauses
(although we would like to see some more convincing exemplification for some
languages), and that there is a good deal of uncertainty about the appropriateness
of regarding this stage as the "earliest" stage of syntactic development. In this
section, I shall bring together observations which collectively persuade me that
this stage is preceded by an earlier stage at which there is currently no evidence
for control of the finite/non-finite distinction. If supporters of the Full Competence Hypothesis are persuaded by these observations — and they are responsible for some of them — it will be necessary for them to identify new types of
evidence for the existence of functional category projections at the onset of
productive grammar (cf. note 6). The alternative will be to concede that

functional category projections are not present at this stage and face the developmental question of how they arise.

To begin, we might note that contributors to this volume who favor structure building accounts of development have no difficulties in accepting an Optional Infinitive Stage with its consequences for complete sets of functional category projections. Thus, we have already seen in the previous section that Clahsen in his earlier work, while taking issue with Poeppel & Wexler's treatment of Andreas as representing the "earliest" stage in the acquisition of German, does not suggest that the characterization they offer is inappropriate for Andreas *at that stage*. Equally, Radford (this volume: 77) can contemplate an Optional Infinitive Stage occurring *later* than the stage he is concerned with:

> Note also that I am assuming that the "Small Clause" stage described here precedes Wexler's (1994) optional infinitive stage and Rizzi's (1994) truncation stage.

It will be appropriate to structure this account around languages, and we may as well begin with English. The point is easily made: in his 1990 monograph, Radford maintained that the children he studied passed through a stage at which they had *no* verbal tense and agreement inflections, i.e. all their verb forms consisted of bare stems. In the framework of Wexler (1994), we might describe this as a stage at which the only verb forms were non-finite.

Turning to French, Pierce (1989) has provided the data on which most recent discussions have been based, and in Wexler (1994, 309) we find:

> Pierce discovered, first, that the children all produced non-finite (matrix) verbs *as well as* finite ones. (my italics — MA)

Here, the emphasis is on the existence of non-finite forms with the occurrence of finite forms at the relevant time being taken for granted. But more care is necessary. As Radford (this volume: 63) notes:

> ... if we read [Pierce's] work carefully, we uncover the observation that in the very first recording of Nathalie at age 1;9.3, ..., Nathalie uses *only* nonfinite verb forms, not finite verbs. (my italics — MA).

And he goes on to cite Pierce's own observation of a very early stage at which "inflected forms" are absent. Now, it is not entirely clear what uninflected forms Pierce has noted here, but it seems likely that at the very least she is identifying a stage in the acquisition of French at which there is no systematic finite/non-finite distinction.

The plausibility of the above is heightened by consideration of the way in which the ratio of non-finite to finite matrix verb forms in French shifts as children get older. As Wexler (1994: 312) notes, this ratio declines monotonically, and a likely, although not necessary, consequence of this is that the very first forms are exclusively non-finite.

A similar conclusion may be appropriate for the Germanic languages which have been subject to every sort of systematic scrutiny. For Dutch (and German), Wijnen & Bol (1993: 247) offer the following observation:

> ... there are indications that during the first phase of grammatical development, Dutch (and German) children only use nonfinite verbs. ... This implies that the optional infinitive phenomenon should be viewed not as the decline of nonfinite main clauses, but rather as the appearance and increasing use of finite verbs.

Finally, there is explicit acknowledgement of a pre-Optional Infinitive stage in Danish in the source which contains the fullest exposition of the Optional Infinitive phenomenon and its consequences. Wexler (1994: 326) summarizes Plunkett & Strömqvist's account of the early stages of the acquisition of Danish by two children, noting that both children passed through a stage at which their verb forms were exclusively infinitival.

As an excellent demonstration of the truth of the proposition that the best bits always appear in the footnotes, it is worth citing Wexler (1994: 347, note 28):

> The literature is somewhat unclear on the question of whether children in the languages under review always go through an early period in which only infinitives appear, though my impression is that this is generally true. The problem in determining whether this infinitives-only property holds at the earliest stage of all children is that often the children are not studied at a young enough age, and that even when they are there may not be sufficient utterances to make a safe generalization.

I would maintain that the observations I have briefly surveyed in this section are reasonably clear, particularly when contrasted with some of the tentative and inadequately quantified evidence cited in support of an Optional Infinitive Stage, some of which I drew attention to in Section 2 — see also Radford (this volume: 62).[14]

5.   The Costs of Continuity

In this section, I return to one of the themes of Section 1, by considering further developmental questions, specifically in connection with proposals which support continuity. To anticipate, I shall be suggesting that continuity positions inevitably incur a cost, since they need to somehow account for why the data sets produced by small children do change as development proceeds. A common strategy for dealing with this cost is to locate the locus of change outside the grammatical system and to offer some gestures as to what it might consist of. I suggest that the methodological cleanliness associated with such manoeuvres is largely chimerical, and that continuity theorists should be subject to the same strictures outside the grammatical system as they seek to impose on those who favor an account where there are systematic changes in the grammar. Balanced to the last, I shall also draw attention to what seem to me to be serious developmental problems in the proposals of structure builders too!

A good place to start is with Hyams (this volume). Hyams' paper exhibits considerable vision in seeking to bring together sets of phenomena which have previously been regarded as distinct, at least to some extent. Specifically, she tries to develop a unified account of optional infinitives and null subjects relying on the idea that the I constituent can remain "underspecified" in a wider range of contexts in early child grammars than in adult grammars. This enables her to maintain that early child GRAMMAR is identical in the relevant respects to the adult grammar — particularly, both contain an I constituent (or its equivalent within an articulated system), with the full range of indexical features available for I, enabling it to be co-indexed with a temporal operator, yielding present time interpretations, contra-indexed, yielding past time interpretations or "underspecified" in which case it bears a zero index — in this last case, the clause receives a default present time interpretation and this coincides with what Hyams takes to be the standard interpretation of root infinitives.[15] For the sake of this discussion, I shall suppose that the story Hyams tells about null subjects co-occurring with (apparently) finite verbs suffixed with -s and -ed can be maintained and focus on just two consequences of her analysis.

First, Hyams must say something about what changes, as the child ceases to use null subjects and as optional infinitives disappear. What she maintains is that there is a *pragmatic rule* which determines the range of indices compatible with I; once this principle is operative, it prevents I bearing the zero index when it appears in the domain of an indexed temporal operator, as the resulting interpretation would not be distinct for co-indexing I and the temporal operator. The obvious question to ask is: by what mechanism is the relevant pragmatic rule acquired?

The answer to the above question is alarmingly predictable (Hyams, this volume: 110):

> Once rule I [the pragmatic rule] appears (either through maturation of the rule itself ...,
> or of the mechanisms involved in the implementation of the rule) ..., the deictic
> assignment of temporal reference is blocked and I must be finitely specified, that is,
> indexed to the temporal operator.

So maturation re-emerges as a developmental mechanism of acceptable pedigree. However, it is not exercising its powers in the domain of grammar where we have relatively sophisticated understanding of representational capacities; rather it treads the somewhat murky domain of pragmatic rules or the positively foggy land of mechanisms involved in the implementation of such rules.

Of course, none of the above is intended to argue against the plausibility of Hyams' analysis (although in a different context, I would confess to not caring for it). It is supposed to show that she has no special claims to the methodological high ground, a conclusion which might be reinforced by the second observation I wish to make.

This point is sort of technical, but it illustrates a kind of difficulty that I believe acquisition theorists often get into when they start trying to squeeze their recalcitrant data into some version of contemporary syntax. Hyams claims that before the appearance of the pragmatic rule, the child can have structures like (6) (from Hyams, this volume: 106):

(6)   (TO$_i$) *Baby doll* [I$_0$] *cry*

In the adult grammar, (6) would be ruled out by the appropriate pragmatic rule on the grounds that it would be assigned the same interpretation (present time reference) as (7):

(7)   (TO$_i$) *Baby doll* [I$_i$] *cry*

Now, TO in these representations is supposed to be a tense operator, and it is a feature of operators that they BIND some item within their scope — in (7) this binding is indicated by co-indexation, whereas a past time interpretation will involve the binding of an index j on I by the condition that j precedes i in some temporal ordering or other. The consequence of this binding not being effected is that we will end up with a violation of something rather fundamental — the Principle of Full Interpretation (Chomsky 1991, 1993). Thus, focusing on (6), this does not simply violate some shady pragmatic principle; it is also inconsistent with one of the most basic principles of the linguistic theory of the last decade. Does this matter? Well, I think that it does, and that, to use a telling phrase from Donald Davidson, the "casual enrichment" of the system being adopted by the acquisition theorist should not go unchecked. In some cases, the consequences of such enrichment may be few and feeble; in others, they may be weighty, and I suggest that the example I have briefly examined here falls into this latter category.

Of course, Hyams is not alone in wishing to maintain a continuity stance, while ascribing a role to maturation in some poorly understood area. Rizzi (1994), in developing his truncation account of root infinitives and null subjects, adopts the view that in child grammars not all clauses project to CP. He formulates this idea in his well-known "axiom":

(8)   CP = root

If children do not have (8), the question immediately arises as to its origins, and Rizzi illustrates perfectly the sort of argumentation which informed much of Section 1:

> As for the question of why [8] is not operative initially, it does not seem plausible that such an abstract principle should (or would) be learned from experience. A maturational approach ... seems to be more promising.

Note that here we see not only the reliance on maturation, but the exclusiveness of learning and maturation; Rizzi, correctly in my view, can see no role for learning here, so maturation is *the* alternative. For him to say that there is "promise" here is perhaps also to betray a lingering desire for explanation, explanation which I have argued in Section 1, should not be the concern of the linguist or psychologist.

Unlike Hyams' pragmatic principle, (8) is not completely outside the grammar. Indeed, its status with respect to the grammar is somewhat unclear to me, and I therefore find myself uncertain whether Rizzi is a fully paid-up continuity theorist or not. To my knowledge, he does not declare himself explicitly on this, but Haegeman (this volume: 272), who largely follows his analysis, is quite adamant on his behalf:

> Rizzi ... accounts for the properties of child R[oot] I[nfinitive]s in terms of a full competence hypothesis ... with maturation of constraints.

According to Haegeman, then, it would appear that (8) is a CONSTRAINT, but it is clearly GRAMMATICAL in content, unlike the pragmatic rule of Hyams; nor can it readily be construed as an aspect of LINGUISTIC PERFORMANCE, the most natural way to see it as falling outside the child's linguistic competence. When Rizzi introduces (8) in his paper, he refers to it as being operative "in adult French" (375), and subsequent discussion in his 1994 paper is certainly consistent with it being part of the child's grammar. Of course, we can distinguish (8) from the full clausal structure including functional projections, which Rizzi assumes to be available at the Optional Infinitive Stage, but the proposal that the child's competence is exhausted by the latter is not an innocent remark, and at the very least raises the question of the status of (8).

Wexler (1994) contains another attempt to account for the Optional Infinitive Stage in terms of properties of Tense, and approval of this account appears in Harris & Wexler (this volume). The details of Wexler's proposals are complex, relying on aspects of Chomsky (1991) which have been superseded in more recent work, but they come down to the suggestion that either Tense or its values are not available in early grammars.[16] As Wexler notes (1994: 340), this gives rise to the now familiar question:

> Why does T take a while to develop? We have no particular answer to this; perhaps the values of T mature.... Perhaps certain categories (e.g. T) can be radically underspecified for the child.

This statement bothers me in a variety of ways. To mention three: (i) the life-easing maturation makes its predictable appearance in a domain which is poorly understood; (ii) it is not clear how a grammar lacking T or its values is consistent with Full Competence — the values of T (presumably $\langle \pm\text{PAST} \rangle$) are just features which make up structural positions, and for them to be missing is not logically distinguishable from there being missing functional projections (see Section 7 for relevant discussion); (iii) lest we be misled, the notion of "under-specification" mentioned here by Wexler is quite different from that of Hyams (see note 15 above) — for the latter, Tense takes on a default value; for Wexler, it appears that it simply lacks a value.

To close this section, I shall consider briefly one or two developmental questions which are posed by structure building accounts, first taking a peek at the Lexical Learning Hypothesis of Clahsen, Penke & Parodi (1993) and Clahsen, Eissenbeiss & Penke (this volume).

Over the last few years, Clahsen and his associates have developed a position according to which German-speaking children pass through a stage at which their grammars contain a functional head, F(inite). The domain of this head is a target for finite verbs, but, Clahsen argues, it cannot be identified with AgrS or C at this stage in the acquisition of German. Furthermore, Clahsen maintains that the transition from F to AgrS is effected by the child LEARNING the subject agreement paradigm of German — this is a token of LEXICAL LEARNING, a process also referred to by Clahsen *et al.* (this volume) as MORPHOLOGICAL BOOTSTRAPPING. Attempting to put some flesh onto this notion, they say (p. 133):

... functional categories such as IP, AgrP, etc. or syntactic features may come into the child's phrase structure representations *as a consequence* of the child's learning a regular inflectional paradigm. (my emphasis — MA)

And later in the paper (p. 143):

Our claim is that the acquisition of the regular subject-verb agreement paradigm *leads to the creation* of the functional projection AgrSP. (my emphasis — MA)

Of course, what Clahsen *et al.* try to do in their paper is present evidence to show that acquisition of the agreement paradigm (as revealed by overt morphological marking of verbs) precedes consistent placement of finite verbs, and for the sake of argument, let us suppose that the observations they make to this end are sound. What we have, at best, is then a case of *post hoc ergo propter hoc*, since the paper contains no attempt to specify a developmental *mechanism* which will take the child from the full agreement paradigm to a new head and its projections. The reference to "learning" concerns the acquisition of the agreement paradigm itself and Clahsen *et al.* do not suggest that learning is what mediates the step from this paradigm to projection of the appropriate phrase structure positions. Nor do they offer any other mechanism to underwrite this process.

Finally, what of Radford, the arch-structure builder? It is not uninteresting that he too (this volume) gets into difficulties when he occasionally confronts developmental issues. One such difficulty arises in connection with his discussion of *wh*-expressions, which, he argues, can be analyzed at his Small Clause Stage as VP-adjoined items; in this position, he regards them as quantifier-like. Of course, this raises the question of how they are reanalyzed as operators, and Radford (this volume: 59) suggests that "the range of quantifiers which function as operators varies parametrically, and ... has to be learned by the child." On the details of this learning process, however, he is silent.

More important for the theme of this paper, Radford feels that he must respond to the challenge posed by the absence of functional categories at the Small Clause Stage: how are they acquired? Note that the "how" in this question can be interpreted as requiring the specification of a manner (more specifically a temporal sequencing) or a mechanism, and it is revealing that it is the former interpretation which guides Radford's discussion. Interpretations of his earlier work (Radford 1990) by Déprez & Pierce (1993) fitted him up with the position that because the I- and C-systems mature, they should show up at the same time in the child's grammar, a possible but far from necessary interpretation of a maturational perspective. However, Radford himself (this volume) seems to

accept it, since he says (p. 66): "... I suggested that the capacity to form functional projections matures, so that different functional projections are acquired more
or less simultaneously ..." From here, he goes on to describe observations which
are consistent with a *gradual* acquisition of functional projections, thereby
addressing the sequencing interpretation of "how"; importantly, however, at no
point does he so much as raise the question of developmental mechanisms.[17]

For my own part, I have no difficulty in construing maturation as involving
a gradual unfolding of functional projection systems, but from a conceptual point
of view, I am equally comfortable with Radford's original claims — if the
mechanism concerned is maturation, it does not prescribe anything about order.
Everything depends on how the language-acquiring bit of the human mind is put
together. It is symptomatic of an unwillingness to think seriously about developmental mechanisms that Radford appears to be seduced by the quite fallacious
observation made by Déprez & Pierce.

6.   Tricks with Numbers

Sections 2–4 above have been loosely concerned with the "quality" of data
cited in support of specific positions. This section revisits this question, but pays
particular attention to the use of quantitative techniques in developmental
research. I should make it clear immediately that I have no reservations about
the desirability for presenting quantitative accounts of data sets, although it
would be useful if significance claims were consistently backed up by appropriate statistical tests. But I do think that it might be useful to reflect briefly on the
utterance counting exercise, then examine the numerical aspects of the proposal
developed in the first half of Harris & Wexler (this volume).

As far as utterance counting goes, we can get a sense of the issue that
concerns me from the classic verb-placement contingencies from French and
German already cited in (1) and (3). What are we to make of the cells containing small numbers in these tables? For concreteness, I shall focus on the German
case in (3), which has the advantage of being based on the data of a single
child. Wexler (p.c.) has asserted that he sees such contingency tables as effectively substituting for *grammatical intuitions*, and what he deduces from (3) is
that for Andreas, non-finite verbs in second position are ungrammatical, as are
finite verbs in final position. Accordingly, there is no alternative to regarding the
infrequently occurring constructions as instantiating some species of PERFOR-
MANCE ERROR. But it should be immediately clear that this conclusion is fraught

with danger: in the Andreas corpus, we have 11 examples of utterance TYPES containing finite verbs in final position, but, unless it is very unusual, the corpus will be based on only a small fraction of Andreas' speech output over the relevant period. Thus, the figure of 11 should be multiplied by whatever is needed to convert it to TOKENS and then by an appropriate factor to provide an estimate of the number of utterance final finite verbs Andreas produced.[18] I am led to suppose that this would probably be a very large number indeed, and I do not consider it sound to dismiss very large numbers as performance errors.[19]

Now, I turn to Harris & Wexler (this volume), and I should say at the outset that I do not intend what follows to be seen as seriously undermining the position they develop and defend — I am, however, concerned to assess whether the data they cite are as clearly supportive of this position as they maintain. The crucial contingency table is reproduced as (9):

(9)	affirmative	negative
−inflection	782	47
+inflection	594	5

Of this table, Harris & Wexler say (this volume: 16):

> ... about 43% of the affirmative sentences were inflected .... Compare this to the inflection rate for sentences negated by *no(t)* (e.g., *He not goes*), 9.6%. This comparison suggests that the addition of the inflectional marker is disrupted by the presence of negation.

Harris & Wexler are unusual in that they present the full set of negative utterances which contribute to the above table, and it is this set on which I wish to now focus attention. It contains a number of examples which are straightforwardly supportive of the Harris & Wexler position (e.g. *Saifi no knock on the door*). Additionally, however, it contains a number of null subject examples along with a smaller number of cases where aspects of the utterance are uninterpretable. Now, it seems to me that these examples are *not* straightforward and that, therefore, a more cautious count would not include them. Going through this exercise, reduces the 47:5 proportion in (9) to 20:4, still one might suppose significant, but certainly less so.

Consider, in the light of the previous paragraph, a further step in Harris & Wexler's argument. They note that the data in (9) come from a considerable age range (1;6–4;1). As they are seeking to confirm the credentials of an Optional Infinitive Stage in the acquisition of English from a very early stage, it is important for them to split the data into two sets, one covering the range 1;6–2;6 and the other the range 2;7–4;1. Of course, in the light of Section 3, we may harbor concerns about the year-long period embraced by the younger range, but this is not my point here. The contingency table Harris & Wexler present for the younger children is reproduced in (10):

(10)	affirmative	negative
+inflection	635	32
−inflection	320	3

But now we must ask what happens to the right hand column of this table if we remove from our counts examples which might involve complications. Unfortunately, it is not possible to do this on the basis of the Harris & Wexler appendix, since files are not linked to ages there. Thus, the possibility remains that the 20 or so examples which uncontroversially contain negation followed by an uninflected verb form might be distributed, say 6:14, between the younger and the older children. In these circumstances, the claim that the interaction between negation and inflection provides support for the hypothesis that English-speaking children pass through a *very early* Optional Infinitive Stage would not be strongly supported.

If the reasoning, briefly developed in connection with Harris & Wexler's treatment of their data is accepted, it is of course clear how to proceed. Once more, as suggested in Section 2, there is an obvious need for the collection of high intensity and high quality data *from the crucial period with the relevant hypotheses in mind*. In my view, most of the data on which existing theoretical claims are based are simply not robust enough to carry the weight of those claims.[20]

7. Minimalism

In this short section, I want to highlight two issues which can be construed as emerging from minimalist emphases. The first involves getting a preliminary grasp on how it is possible for both continuity theorists and structure builders to claim minimalist allegiance. Secondly, I shall start to set out how the minimalist framework of Chomsky (1995) can be linked to much of what has gone before in this paper and in the papers in this volume to which I have given most attention.

The first point is dealt with quickly. The notion of economy which has played a major role in much of Chomsky's recent writings can be interpreted in a number of ways. Chomsky's own emphasis has been on ECONOMY OF DERIVATION, and, taking this as pivotal, leaves the way open for the postulation of phrase structure representations which include the full set of functional projections. This is effectively the route followed in recent work by Wexler, amply illustrated in his paper with Harris (this volume), and is also the construal adopted by Platzack (this volume). This emphasis, however, can easily ignore ECONOMY OF REPRESENTATION as a distinct guiding principle, although Wexler, at least, would argue that some of the issues we have considered earlier in this paper indicate that rich assumptions about representations are appropriate for even the earliest stages. Supposing, however, that some of the skepticism about this position which has been developed earlier is justified, we are left with the earliest stages of acquisition not providing evidence for the full range of functional category projections. In these circumstances, economy principles drive us in the direction of the position initially developed by Grimshaw (1993) and adopted more or less directly by Clahsen *et al.* (this volume) and by Radford (this volume). In the former, we find a principle of STRUCTURAL economy (p. 131): "at any point in a derivation, a structural description for a natural language string employs as few nodes as grammatical principles and lexical selection require." As for Radford, he adopts what he calls the MINIMAL LEXICAL PROJECTION HYPOTHESIS, the view that (p. 44): "syntactic structures ... are the minimal syntactic projections of the lexical items they contain."

It should be clear from the above that any dispute between continuity and structure building with respect to their reliance on minimalism is probably more apparent than real. Minimalism in Chomsky's work has a number of independent aspects and economy of representation is only one of these. That two proposals can differ on the continuity question while both subscribing to minimalism ultimately comes down to the status of the evidence — there is nothing in the minimalist framework itself which requires the correctness (or incorrectness) of the continuity position.

To conclude, I want to briefly consider the account of Merger theory which appears in Chomsky (1995) and assess its significance for the topics of this paper. Roeper (this volume) tries to establish the attractiveness of Merger Theory in understanding the nature of sometimes short-lived, lexically restricted constructions. Obviously, the lexical specificity which Roeper seeks is available in the mechanisms of Merger Theory, although, as these restrictions have to be relaxed at later stages, it is not clear to me what developmental explanatory debt Roeper's account takes on.[21]

Here, I am more concerned to see Merger Theory as a rather straightforward way of conceptualizing some of the differences we have met earlier in this paper. Crucial to Merger Theory is the construct of a NUMERATION, which Chomsky introduces in the following terms (1995, 393):

> Let us take a *numeration* to be a set of pairs (l, n), where l is an item of the lexicon and n is its index, understood to be the number of times that l is selected.

Each item of the lexicon consists of a set of features, typed as phonological, semantic or formal, and the operation MERGE has access to these sets, associating with its output one of the input sets of features, this constraint reflecting the endocentricity of syntactic operations.

From my point of view, what is of interest in this characterization is what is missing from it. Specifically, there is no requirement that a convergent derivation should be associated with a designated category, i.e. there is nothing corresponding to the S of traditional rewrite systems nor to Rizzi's axiom, which was cited earlier. Equally, from a developmental perspective, there is no requirement that a derivation can only proceed on the basis of a complete set of features. Merge can operate on partial feature sets, just as it can on those sets which are complete from the perspective of the adult system; it follows, therefore, that it provides an ideal format for describing not only Roeper's quirky constructions but also capturing the sort of intermediate projection that Clahsen *et al.* regard as important in the acquisition of German.

A natural construal of structure building within this framework is in terms of the successive acquisition of features, and it may be salutary that Wexler and his colleagues have also talked about this process, but within a continuity perspective. A word of caution on which to close: if continuity thinking and structure-building can be brought together via Merger Theory, the developmental questions which have driven much of my discussion will of course re-emerge. Clahsen *et al.* still have to account for how the agreement FEATURES enter the child's grammar on the basis of the child having learned agreement paradigms; Radford still needs a story about how C and I (or their component features) get into the grammar, irrespective of whether they emerge simultaneously or in some determinate sequence; Wexler and his associates must have a view on how features of Tense emerge. If Merger Theory in the Minimalist Program can persuade us that the differences between continuity and structure building are not profound, this will be significant. However, the most searching questions which this paper has attempted to pose will remain outstanding.

Acknowledgements

I am grateful to Harald Clahsen and Andrew Radford for their comments on an earlier version of this paper. They are not, of course, responsible for any of the views expressed in the paper.

Notes

1. It is notable that Clahsen *et al.* (this volume) manage to combine a structure building approach with a notion of continuity. They define their concept of WEAK CONTINUITY as follows (p. 130): "all components of UG are available to the child from the outset of acquisition, but language particular grammatical knowledge increases over time." A survey of different senses of continuity, with or without a preceding "strong" or "weak" might be helpful in clarifying some issues, but unfortunately there is not the space to undertake this here. For some relevant discussion, see Hoekstra & Schwartz (1994).

2. The term "day zero" here should be taken with the proverbial pinch of salt. I don't know whether any operational sense can be attached to the notion of the onset of grammar, but it is this time that "day zero" in intended to denote. This issue is not without genuine content, and I shall roam around this area a bit in Section 3.

3. Obviously, this will rule out "wild" grammars but will permit grammars in which parameters are incorrectly set (perhaps at some unmarked value, so as not to run up against learnability questions); it will also be consistent with the position of UG-constrained Maturation supported by Borer & Wexler (1987, 1992). This latter position exhibits one particular obscurity which is relevant to one of the themes of this paper. As is well known, Borer and Wexler's views require a distinction between grammatical REPRESENTATIONS and grammatical CAPACITIES. The latter are exemplified by A-chains, and the major claim of Borer and Wexler (1987) is that A-chains MATURE. Now, if X^0-chains also exemplify grammatical capacities, parsimony would suggest that they too might mature. However, a consistent theme of Wexler's more recent work is that head movement (leading to the formation of X^0-chains) is present from day zero. It is not sufficient to conclude, as does Wexler (1994), that this developmental difference is consistent with the conjecture that different chain-types are subject to different grammatical principles — developmentally, chains of all types fall into the category of capacities and, *from this perspective,* they might be expected to exhibit relevant similarities. After all, the UG-constrained maturation position relies pretty heavily on the representation/capacities distinction. I suspect that careful reflection on these observations would lead to a collapse of this distinction and raise serious questions about the coherence of UG-constrained Maturation as presented by Borer & Wexler, but there is not space to pursue these questions here.

4. The position developed by Clahsen *et al.* (this volume) bears some similarities to that of Fukui. And in Clahsen, Penke & Parodi (1993:426) we find: "... the child's knowledge of X-bar theory does not specify that all functional heads are obligatorily instantiated in any language ..."

5. Indeed, it seems to me that contemporary, mainstream cognitive psychology continues to be unhealthily dogmatic on the nature of evidence. The postulation of elaborate theoretical constructs is welcomed, but the conducting of controlled experiments yielding quantitative measures of behavior remains a necessary condition on being taken seriously. I shall come back to some of my concerns about data and their quantitative aspects in Section 6.

6. To be more concrete, we can consider Wexler's (1994) arguments against the existence of a pre-functional stage based on the presence of optional infinitives in the relevant data sets. Whether this argument is sound is something to which I shall return, but it is a fine exemplification of the use of ingenuity in arguing that, contrary to initial impressions, evidence for a type of grammatical construct *does* exist. A problem for Full Competence can be raised in this context. Suppose we accept that from the appearance of the very earliest morphosyntactic combinations, there is evidence for functional category projections and thereby reassure ourselves that there are no serious developmental questions for these constructs. Now consider an immediately preceding stage at which there are no morphosyntactic combinations — for convenience, let us refer to it as the one-word stage. To my knowledge, no one has suggested that anything analogous to optional infinitives exists at this stage; indeed, no one has noted *any* evidence which suggests that the child already has functional category projections at this stage (although, Clahsen *et al.* (this volume) provocatively assert (p. 129): "... the early achievements seem to indicate that children know verb raising, properties of null arguments and agreement *even before they start producing sentences*" (my emphasis — MA). I do not see any justification for this remark in Clahsen *et al.*'s paper). Suppose ingenuity continues to fail in this context; then, the Principle of Evidence surely wins out over the Minimize Degrees of Freedom Principle and we conclude that there are no functional category projections in the child's system of mental representation at this stage. And the question the Full Competence Hypothesis has sought to finesse represents itself: how do we account for the development of these objects?

7. But, surely, there's also "triggering", I hear. This is not the time and the place, but while it retains a certain mystique in much of the discourse surrounding acquisition, I remain unconvinced that anyone has succeeded in making a coherent case for there being an *externally* driven process in grammatical development which is qualitatively distinct from learning (Atkinson 1990, 1992).

8. Wexler (1994: 310–311) does discuss in some detail the option of regarding these forms as participles and argues that it can be rejected on interpretive grounds, relying on Pierce's reliance on Lightbown's interpretation of the original data.

9. I should note that Déprez & Pierce (1993: 40) cite *pas la poupée dormir* 'not the doll (to) sleep' as produced by a French child of just over 21 months. It is the only cited example in this paper of an infinitive which is not an -*er* infinitive co-occurring with *pas*.

10. This table takes account of the Poeppel & Wexler manoeuvre which removes two-word utterances from consideration, the point being that in such utterances second and final positions are identical. In the light of Section 3 below, it is noteworthy that this manoeuvre removes only 31 of 282 utterances, i.e., at the stage examined, a large majority of the child's utterances including verbs contained three or more constituents.

11. The discussion in Clahsen, Penke & Parodi (1993: 408 ff.) is relevant to this matter. While they do not formulate explicit criteria for assigning verbs to the ⟨−finite⟩ categories, they go beyond Poeppel & Wexler in distinguishing finite forms which exhibit correct and incorrect agreement. Whereas the former show a strong tendency to occur in second position, the location of incorrectly agreeing forms is less predictable. It has been pointed out to me by Harald Clahsen that it could be appropriate to regard the verb in (4) as ⟨+finite⟩ because some uninflected stems (of modal verbs) are finite forms in German. This doesn't seem to me to constitute an *argument* in itself, although it is an observation to think about.

12. It is at this point that the observation in note 10 is relevant. If only 31 out of 282 multi-constituent utterances containing verbs were two-constituent utterances, this suggests that Andreas' MLU was some way in excess of 2.0.

13. It is noteworthy that, while Radford (1990) does not supply MLUs for his corpora, the vast majority of the examples he cites come from children younger than 2 years. The Stage I data in Clahsen *et al.*'s study (MLU ≤ 1.75) come from the age range 1;8 to 2;4, which as well as being protracted, extends well into the third year.

14. It is somewhat alarming in this respect to find Wexler retreating from the position he was embracing, albeit somewhat reluctantly in his 1994 paper in his contribution to this volume. Harris & Wexler (this volume: 36) say: "Of course it is possible that there is a stage with no functional categories before the OI stage.... It is difficult, however, to tell whether such a no functional category stage actually exists. The data supporting the nonfunctional category stage (e.g. Radford 1990) are given as examples of children's utterances, but no quantitative evidence is given, so we don't know, for example, whether the children studied produce only verbs without tense inflection, or whether they sometimes produce inflected verbs." This is a very puzzling statement in the light of Radford's clear assertion that at the stage in which he was interested, there were no examples of verbal inflections in his corpora — would his producing a table containing a cell containing a zero affect the content of this assertion? Of course, as I have already pleaded in connection with the Optional Infinitive stage itself, we need more concentrated, hypothesis-led collections of data from a variety of languages, but Radford's own analyses of his own corpora stand comparison, to my mind, to any of the (sometimes) quantitative, second- and sometimes third-hand analyses which have supported the Optional Infinitive Stage.

15. There are a number of further issues to note here. First, Hyams is also concerned to establish parallels between tense anchoring and reference anchoring in the DP-domain — I do not consider the latter at all in my discussion. Secondly, Harris & Wexler (this volume), following Wexler (1994), also locate the source of root infinitives in properties of the tense system. However, unlike Hyams, they do not regard infinitives as associated with a default "now" present time reference. For them, root infinitives pick up their temporal interpretations from the contexts in which they are used, and they suggest that 82% and 18% of matrix infinitives have respectively present and non-present interpretations. Something has to give here, but in circumstances where the authors of both papers are reconstructing their temporal interpretations from other people's data, it would be rash to vote one way or the other. Finally, the sense of "underspecified" used by Hyams is worthy of brief comment. Wexler (1994) and Clahsen et al. (this volume) also rely on a notion of underspecification (see later discussion in this section and in Section 7), but it seems to me that they are trying to capture a rather different concept to that developed by Hyams for I_0. To illustrate, for Clahsen et al., an underspecified position is one which employs only a subset of the features which would go to make up the category occupying that position in a comparable adult structure. For Hyams, I can bear the full range of features available in the adult system (arguably, we might regard this as I being specified for a three-valued indexical feature), but I_0, the default, can occur in more contexts than it can in the adult grammar. I would recommend not using "underspecified" for the notion Hyams is dealing with, as it is likely to engender confusion. Indeed, Hyams herself does some engendering to this end, as she suggests earlier in her paper that under-specification for I should be understood in terms of I containing *no* tense or agreement features. If this were the case, what could I possibly be in a framework in which categories are nothing more than bundles of features (Chomsky 1995)?

16. Before adopting this proposal, Wexler considers (inconclusively) the possibility that T may be optional at the Optional Infinitive Stage. Somewhat different considerations to those raised in the text would apply to this possibility.

17. It might be maintained that Radford's MLP (Minimal Lexical Projection) provides the mechanism whereby the child moves from lexical acquisitions to the projection of functional categories in syntax. This may be so, but it is important to be clear that the protracted nature of some lexical acquisitions then becomes the focus of developmental attention. If Radford wishes to maintain that the system of I-projections is acquired before the system of C-projections because inflectional lexemes are acquired before complementizers, he must then consider why this latter sequence exists in the form it does.

18. A further concern which is not strictly numerical is that performance errors are not expected to yield *types*. I would be mighty suspicious of a claim that a child has performed a type-identical performance error on a number of occasions — performance errors are just not like that!

19. There is, of course, an additional worry about reliance on numerical counts, which was already overt in Chomsky (1957). This is the emphasis which Radford is sensitive to when he proposes that "every utterance counts". The simple observation is that even such commonplace constructions as passives would run the risk of being relegated to performance errors if an adult corpus were approached in the way now commonly advocated for children. To my mind, there ought to be no prescriptions in this area — a sensitive approach to data in the light of significant theoretical proposals is the best we can hope for — hence "every utterance counts" is not a tenable proposition either. Sometimes this sensitivity will involve taking numerical differences very seriously and sometimes not.

20. It is of interest here to cite Poeppel & Wexler's (1993: 8) plea for a quantitative approach to acquisition work: "The 'example-based' approach in language-acquisition research leaves open the possibility that one is ignoring important effects or, alternatively, building theories based on the exceptions and outliers in the data rather than on the underlying grammar. Obviously, both example-based and quantitative approaches can be misused."

21. I must confess at this point that I find much of Roeper's detailed description difficult to follow. Specifically, the way he relies on the notion of NUMERATION suggests that he does not share my grasp of this concept. However, his general point that lexically specific features enable the expression of lexically restricted collocations via Merge is well taken.

References

Atkinson, M. 1990. "The Logical Problem of Language Acquisition: Representational and procedural issues." *Logical Issues in Language Acquisition*, ed. by I. Roca (ed.), 1–31. Dordrecht: Foris:

———. 1992. *Children's Syntax: An introduction to principles and parameters theory.* Oxford: Basil Blackwell.

Borer, H. & K. Wexler 1987. "The Maturation of Syntax." *Parameter Setting*, ed. by T. Roeper & E. Williams, 123–172. Dordrecht: Reidel.

———. 1992. "Biunique Relations and the Maturation of Grammatical Principles." *Natural Language and Linguistic Theory* 10.147–189.

Chomsky, N. 1957. *Syntactic Structures*. The Hague: Mouton.

———. 1991. "Some Notes on Economy of Derivation and Representation." *Principles and Parameters in Comparative Grammar,* ed. by R. Freidin. Cambridge, Mass.: MIT Press.

———. 1993. "A Minimalist Program for Linguistic Theory." *The View from Building 20: Essays in linguistics in honor of Sylvain Bromberger,* ed. by K. Hale and S. J. Keyser, 1–52. Cambridge, Mass.: MIT Press.

————. 1995. "Bare Phrase Structure. *Government and Binding Theory and the Minimalist Program*, ed. by G. Webelhuth, 383–439. Oxford: Basil Blackwell.

Clahsen, H., M. Penke & T. Parodi. 1993. "Functional Categories in Early Child German." *Language Acquisition* 3.395–429.

Crain, S. 1991. "Language Acquisition in the Absence of Experience." *Behavioral and Brain Sciences* 14.597–612.

Déprez, V. & A. Pierce. 1993. "Negation and Functional Projections in Early Grammar." *Linguistic Inquiry* 24.25–67.

Felix, S. 1984. "Maturational Aspects of Universal Grammar." *Interlanguage*, ed. by A. Davis, C. Criper and A. Howatt, 133–161. Edinburgh: Edinburgh University Press.

Fodor, J. 1975. *The Language of Thought*. New York: Crowell.

————. 1981. "The Present Status of the Innateness Controversy." *Representations*, ed. by J. Fodor, 257–316. Hassocks: Harvester.

Fukui, N. 1986. "A Theory of Category Projection and its Applications." Ph.D. dissertation, Massachusetts Institute of Technology, Cambridge.

————. 1993. "Parameters and Optionality in Grammar." *Linguistic Inquiry* 24.399–420.

Grimshaw, J. 1993. "Minimal Projection, Heads and Optimality." Ms. Rutgers University.

Hoekstra, T. & B.D. Schwartz. 1994. "Introduction: On the initial states of language acquisition." *Language Acquisition Studies in Generative Grammar*, ed. by T. Hoekstra & B.D. Schwartz (eds), 1–19. Amsterdam: John Benjamins.

Hyams, N. 1994. "VP, Null Arguments and COMP Projections." *Language Acquisition Studies in Generative Grammar*, ed. by T. Hoekstra & B.D. Schwartz (eds), 21–55. Amsterdam: John Benjamins.

Koopman, H. & D. Sportiche. 1991. "The Position of Subjects." *Lingua* 85.211–258.

Krämer, A. 1993. "The Licensing of Subjects in Early Child Language." *MIT Working Papers in Linguistics* 19.197–212.

Mackenzie, B.D. 1977. *Behaviourism and the Limits of Scientific Method*. London: Routledge & Kegan Paul.

Pierce, A. 1989. "On the Emergence of Syntax: A crosslinguistic study." Ph.d. dissertation, Massachusetts Institute of Technology, Cambridge.

Poeppel, D. & K. Wexler. 1993. "The Full Competence Hypothesis of Clause Structure in Early german. *Language* 69.1–33.

Pollock, J.-Y. 1989. "Verb Movement, Universal Grammar, and the Structure of IP." *Linguistic Inquiry* 20.365–424.

Radford, A. 1990. *Syntactic Theory and the Acquisition of English Syntax*. Oxford: Basil Blackwell.

————. 1994. "Tense and Agreement Variability in Child Grammars of English. *Syntactic Theory and First Language Acquisition: Crosslinguistic perspectives,* ed. by B. Lust, M. Suñer & J. Whitman, 135–157. Hillsdale, N.J.: Lawrence Erlbaum.

Rizzi, L. 1994. "Some Notes on Linguistic Theory and Language Development: The case of root infinitives. *Language Acquisition* 3.371–393.

Weverink, M. 1989. "The Subject in Relation to Inflection in Child Language." M.A. thesis, Utrecht University.

Wexler, K. 1994. "Optional Infinitives, Head Movement and the Economy of Derivations." *Verb Movement,* D. Lightfoot & N. Hornstein, 305–350. Cambridge: Cambridge University Press:

Wijnen, F. & G. Bol. 1993. "The Escape from the Optional Infinitive Stage." *Papers in Experimental Linguistics,* 239–248. University of Groningen.

Index of Names

Aldridge *et al.* [= M. Aldridge, R.D. Borsley & S. Clack] (1995) 64

Bloom *et al.* [= L. Bloom, K. Lifter & J. Hafitz] (1980) 103

Boser *et al.* [= K. Boser, B. Lust, L. Santelmann & J. Whitman] (1991) 8, 107, 193

Boser *et al.* [= K. Boser, B. Lust, L. Santelmann & J. Whitman] (1992) xxiii, 130, 272, 277, 285–287, 289, 292, 303

Bottari *et al.* [= P. Bottari, P. Cipriani & A.M. Chilosi] (1992) 167, 321, 328, 443

Cipriani *et al.* [= P. Cipriani, A.-M. Chilosi, P. Bottari & L. Pfanner] (1992) 263

Clahsen *et al.* [= H. Clahsen, M. Penke & T. Parodi] (1993) 80, 130, 134, 143, 465, 481

Clahsen *et al.* [= H. Clahsen, S. Eisenbeiss & A. Vainikka] (1994) 112, 129, 130, 133, 142, 148, 149, 196, 272, 294, 301, 302, 362

Clahsen *et al.* [= H. Clahsen, C. Kursawe & M. Penke] (1995) 135, 156

Clahsen *et al.* [= H. Clahsen, S. Eisenbeiss & M. Penke] (this volume) 107, 116, 120, 161, 162, 188, 190, 194, 195, 272, 301, 302, 422, 472, 473, 477–482

Epstein *et al.* [= S. Epstein, S. Flynn & G. Martohardjono] (in press) 335, 336

Gaze *et al.* [= R.M. Gaze, M.J. Keating & S.-H. Chung] (1974) 377

Greenberg *et al.* [= S.M. Greenberg, M., V.A. Castellucci, H. Bayley & J.H. Schwartz] (1987) 377

Guasti *et al.* [= M.T. Guasti, R. Thornton & K. Wexler] (1995) 241, 242, 244–246, 249, 261

Håkansson *et al.* [= G. Håkansson, U. Nettelbladt & K. Hansson] (1991) 387

Hamann *et al.* [= C. Hamann, L. Rizzi & U. Frauenfelder] (this volume) 276, 290, 297–299, 303, 354, 362, 363

Krashen *et al.* [= S.D. Krashen, D., M.H. Long & R.C. Scarcella] (1979) 407

Mayer *et al.* [= J.W. Mayer, A. Erreich & V. Valian] (1978) 72

Ors *et al.* [= M. Ors, G. Stenberg, I. Rosén, G. Blennow & B. Sahlén] (1994) 384

Penner *et al.* [= Z. Penner, R. Tracy & J. Weissenborn] (1993) 194

Penner *et al.* [= Z. Penner, M. Schönenberger & J. Weissenborn] (1994) 194, 195, 394

Roeper *et al.* [= T. Roeper, S. Akiyama, L. Mallis & M. Rooth] (1985) 78

Saffran *et al.* [= E. Saffran, M. Schwartz & O. Marin] (1980) 381

Schwartz *et al.* [= M. Schwartz, E. Saffran & O. Marin] (1980) 381
Strömqvist *et al.* [= S. Strömqvist, U. Richtoff & A.-B. Andersson.] (1993) 387, 389
Tarone *et al.* [= E. Tarone, U. Frauenfelder & L. Selinker] (1976) 356
Tracy *et al.* [= R. Tracy, Z. Penner & J. Weissenborn] (1993) 423, 442, 443
Weissenborn *et al.* [= J. Weissenborn, T. Roeper, & J. de Villiers] (1991) 444
Weissenborn *et al.* [= Weissenborn, J., J. de Villiers & T. Roeper] (in prep.) 442
Whitman *et al.* [= Whitman, J., K.-O. Lee & B. Lust] (1991) 193

Index of Subjects

In the series LANGUAGE ACQUISITION AND LANGUAGE DISORDERS (LALD) the following titles have been published thus far or are scheduled for publication:

1. WHITE, Lydia: *Universal Grammar Second Language Acquisition.* Amsterdam/ Philadelphia, 1989.
2. HUEBNER, Thom and Charles A. FERGUSON (eds): *Crosscurrents in Second Language Acquisition and Linguistic Theories.* Amsterdam/Philadelphia, 1991.
3. EUBANK, Lynn (ed.): *Point-Counter-Point. Universal Grammar and Second Language Acquisition.* Amsterdam/Philadelphia, 1991.
4. ECKMAN, Fred R. (ed.): *Confluence. Linguistics, L2 acquisition and speech pathology.* Amsterdam/Philadelphia, 1993.
5. GASS, Susan and Larry SELINKER (eds): *Language Transfer in Language Learning.* Amsterdam/Philadelphia, 1992.
6. THOMAS, Margaret: *Knowledge of Reflexives in a Second Language.* Amsterdam/ Philadelphia, 1993.
7. MEISEL, Jürgen M. (ed.): *Bilingual First Language Acquisition.* Amsterdam/Philadelphia, 1994.
8. HOEKSTRA, Teun and Bonnie D. SCHWARTZ (eds): *Language Acquisition Studies in Generative Grammar: Papers in honor of Kenneth Wexler from the 1991 GLOW workshops.* Amsterdam/Philadelphia, 1994.
9. ADONE, Dany: *The Acquisition of Mauritian Creole.* Amsterdam/Philadelphia, 1994.
10. LAKSHMANAN, Usha: *Universal Grammar in Child Second Language Acquisition: Null subjects and morphological uniformity.* Amsterdam/Philadelphia, 1994.
11. YIP, Virginia: *Interlanguage and Learnability. From Chinese to English.* Amsterdam/Philadelphia, 1995.
12. JUFFS, Alan: *Learnability and the Lexicon. Theories and second language acquisition research.* Amsterdam/Philadelphia, n.y.p.
13. ALLEN, Shanley: *Aspects of Argument Structure Acquisition in Inuktitut.* Amsterdam/Philadelphia, n.y.p.
14. CLAHSEN, Harald (ed.): *Generative Perspectives on Language Acquisition. Empirical findings, theoretical considerations and crosslinguistic comparisons.* Amsterdam/Philadelphia, 1996.